TRANSFORMATION
PRAYER MINISTRY

PRINCIPLES — PURPOSE — PROCESS

ED SMITH AND JOSHUA SMITH

SPECIAL CONSIDERATIONS

Some liberty has been taken in **boldfacing**, *italicizing*, and [bracketing] certain words and phrases in the biblical text for emphasis that may not have been included in the translator's copy.

Gender is not always specified in this book. The use of "his" and "her," "he" and "she" should not be assumed to mean only one gender or the other.

Whenever you see terms such as "the Spirit," "His Spirit," "God's Spirit," and "Spirit of truth" in this book, it is referring to the Holy Spirit unless otherwise specified. We believe that the Holy Spirit teaches, guides, comforts and intercedes for the believer and is the one who convinces our hearts of the truth. Even so, it is not uncommon for people to say that Jesus is the one who spoke to their hearts during a ministry session rather than attributing this to the Spirit. We believe that Jesus is presently seated at the right hand of the Father, and it is the Holy Spirit that illuminates our hearts of the truth. We also believe that the Father, Son and Holy Spirit are one, so we are not critical of differing perspectives concerning this.

This edition of the Transformation Prayer Ministry (TPM) training replaces <u>all other versions</u> of the training including the "Advanced Training" and "Difficult Cases" training. This edition is the <u>only</u> official training available as of its printing.

The expressed testimonies in this book are based upon true events but may be paraphrased accounts of several different people's similar experiences. The purpose of these personal anecdotes is to bring clarity or understanding of the points being made.

SPECIAL ACKNOWLEDGMENTS

Although my son and I were tasked with writing this book, we were hardly the *only* ones involved in its creation. We would first like to acknowledge the long sacrifice that our families have made. They surrendered thousands of hours to the cause of getting this book finished. Sharon and Kaitlyn, specifically, largely gave up their husbands for a sizable amount of time so that you could have this completed work.

To those around the world who generously supported us financially throughout this process, we say, "thank you!" Your contributions ensured we were able to stay focused on the task at hand. We would also like to thank those of you who helped by proofreading and offering feedback. Your involvement helped us craft a better version of what would have been.

Most importantly, we thank God. His guiding hand has been on us throughout this journey. We hope that He is well pleased with our work. We pray that He uses the words contained in this book to reach and bless those whom He has "predestined to be conformed to the image of His Son" (Romans 8:29 HCSB).

Contents

PREFACE

Part One

What is the purpose of this book?

If you are new to this ministry, welcome aboard! You may feel a little overwhelmed by what lies before you. Each person who is currently practicing this ministry started where you are today. We believe that if you invest the time and effort in learning what is in this book, it can change in part how you view and live the rest of your life.

Essentially, the intent of the ministry model is to provide both a practical understanding and systematic means to cooperate with what God is already doing in your life. He sent His Spirit to accomplish very specific goals in each of us. He wants to lead us into a deeper and fuller understanding of the truth (John 16:13). He wants us to know who He is and who we are in Him because of what He's done on our behalf. He was sent to persuade us to believe and trust in God's perspective. He desires that we not only know the truth in our heads but also believe it in our hearts.

You will learn in future chapters that what you believe in your "heart" has an incredible impact on nearly every aspect of your life. Your self-image, your understanding of God, your interpretation of the world around you, your perspective of past experiences, your interaction with other people, as well as your emotions, motivations, and behavior are all directly influenced by what you believe in your "heart." Because of this, it is vitally important that your heart's belief accurately reflects God's perspective.

Believe it or not, God carefully and lovingly works everything in your life together to accomplish this good purpose (Romans 8:28) to conform you into the image of His Son. He deeply desires for you to know the truth and walk in it. He is working to expose your need for His perspective so that you will humbly ask Him to grant it to you. He uses every situation, from mundane moments to tragic catastrophes, to move you in His direction. If you can recognize His involvement and learn how to appropriately respond, you can more intentionally cooperate with Him in this work.

This ministry approach provides a practical way for you to position yourself properly and humbly before God under His "mighty hand" (1 Peter 5:6) so that He may "shine in your "heart" to give the light of the knowledge of the glory of God..." (2 Corinthians 4:6, emphasis added). When the Holy Spirit persuades your "heart" of the truth and grants you His perspective, genuine transformation will always follow which will be made evident by you *effortlessly* experiencing the fruit of His Spirit.

You will effortlessly bear His fruit rather than continually struggle to perform the truth. Think about it: if it is <u>His</u> fruit, why would we need to struggle to bear it? Have you ever seen an apple tree straining to bear apples? As you will soon discover, if we are struggling to bear His fruit, something is wrong. It means we lack His perspective and need Him to convince us of the truth. For when you believe the truth in your heart, it will seem and feel true to you, and your emotions and behavior will reflect this change in perspective.

This may sound unobtainable or too good to be true, but it has been the experience of tens of thousands all around the world. God is good, and He is doing a good work in all of us "who love Him and are called according to His purpose" (Romans 8:28). When Jesus said, "Come unto me. . . and I will give you rest," (see Matthew 11:28) He really meant it. And to the degree that we understand His role and purposes, as well as our proper response to His involvement, we can intentionally cooperate with Him in His work. This is what you are learning to do by embarking on this journey.

Who is this book for?

This book was written with two primary audiences in mind. First, it was written for the person who is brand new to TPM, who heard about it from a friend or was sent here by their church leader, or someone who simply stumbled across TPM while searching online. If this is you, welcome! The main text was written to walk you through the general concepts and ideas in a simple-to-understand way with the goal of attaining a high level of comprehension as quickly as possible. We've also tried to organize the information so that it is easily searchable so that you can more readily find an answer to any specific question you may have in mind.

The second primary audience for this book includes those who are familiar with the basics of TPM but desire to learn the latest improvements and developments in this ministry. TPM has continually evolved and transformed since its inception in 1995, and this revision is evidence that we are continually moving forward. Many who have been following this ministry through the years have gone on to mentor others once they had a firm grasp of the *Purpose, Principles*, and *Process* of *TPM.* Because of this, they understand the importance of being capable, effective, and efficient when lending aid to others who would like to benefit from what is taught here. This only comes by way of commitment, study, and practice. This book was written and formatted to make it accessible, searchable, and usable for those who are mentoring others.

But, generally speaking, this book is for you! We do not believe that you found your way to this material by accident or chance. We are convinced that God has orchestrated your life and led you to this book. We also firmly believe that He plans to use this information to benefit you and, potentially, those in your circle of influence.

Is this the final update to the TPM training?

There have been multiple revisions to the TPM training since the first edition was released in 1996. You may wonder, *"Why another edition?"* In truth, our goal is to have the absolute best training possible, and we have learned and grown a great deal since this ministry's inception. It has been a journey of discovery, or most aptly put, a journey of *transformation*. The first edition was contained in a three-ring binder that our family hand-assembled. The initial iteration of the training spread by word of mouth and made its way around the world, touching countless lives. We were blessed and amazed at how God used such an imperfect tool to bring truth, freedom, and peace to so many people. This training has gone through several revisions through the years, and we expect that the refinements included in this update will have an even greater impact and further reach. Will this be the last revision? We hope so! But then again, we have hoped for that to be the case with every edition thus far.

In the early years, some people thought the training was disjointed, difficult to understand, and challenging to apply, and, for the most part, they were correct in their assessment. Each revision has improved the overall quality and clarity of the training, and we believe this revision will prove to be even easier to learn and put into practice. There are significant improvements in the structure and order of the foundational concepts and principles as well as helpful changes in the ministry process itself.

If you have worked through older versions of the TPM training, you will notice a shift in tone and target audience in this edition. Rather than teaching one person how to "minister" to another person, this edition of the training focuses on "you" and your personal journey with the Lord. This does not mean that you will not be involved in equipping others for their journey, for many of you will undoubtedly be called to this very task. But you will only be able to effectively mentor others in the concepts and practices that you have personally mastered. This can be compared to the safety instructions you always receive when flying on a commercial airliner: "In case of an emergency, secure your own oxygen mask before assisting others."

This edition is much more comprehensive, explainable, and systematic than any previous version. The focus and *Purpose of TPM* has been refined and expanded. The *Principles of TPM* are more organized and precisely defined for better comprehension. The *TPM Process* has been greatly clarified and simplified. God used the previous versions to accomplish a great deal in the Body of Christ, but we fully anticipate He will do incomparably more with the new!

Those who have journeyed with us for the last couple of decades are likely aware of the many significant improvements that came to the overall training around 2015 and thereafter. This was around the time when my son, Joshua, became a more active and involved part in the ministry's development. My wife and I raised all three of our children with the TPM principles, and each one of our children have made TPM an important part of their lives. But Joshua felt called by God to this work, and he has brought clarity, precision, and a greater depth of understanding to the TPM training material. I am grateful and blessed by what he has brought to this ministry. Even though I may be the founder of this ministry, I can say without any hesitation, he is being used by the Lord to take it to a new level, and I believe that you will see evidence of this throughout the training material.

Since the writing of this book was a collaborative effort, you will likely notice some variation in writing style and presentation throughout. But when you encounter the words "I", "me", or "mine" in the text, you can assume that it was written from my (Ed's) perspective unless otherwise specified.

ADDITIONAL INFORMATION (IMPORTANT)

Throughout this book you will find text that has been separated from the main text and highlighted like this. These highlighted sections offer additional insights and relevant discussions regarding the concepts that have been introduced. Although we believe these supplementary discussions are helpful and can strengthen your grasp on the principles and concepts that will be presented, they should not be considered "mandatory" reading. However, if your goal is to comprehend what is taught, rather than to simply read what has been written, we strongly encourage you to explore these additional offerings! For additional insight, watch for the "butterfly!"

How long is the TPM training?

Many will ask, *"How long will it take to complete the training?"* The answer to this question depends upon both your definition of the words "complete" and "training." If "complete" means how long it takes to read the book and watch all the videos, then it depends on how fast you can manage it. If by "complete" you mean "comprehend" or "master," then working through the material becomes a lifelong journey and a lifestyle.

To illustrate our perspective, apply this question to the culinary arts: at what point have you "completed" your training in the kitchen? Are you "trained" once you are able to reheat leftovers, or must you continue your training until you are recognized as a master chef? The answer all depends on what you hope to accomplish. You can go as far as you are willing to go. But just because you have spent an arbitrary amount of time in the kitchen does not mean that you have "mastered" cooking. Our goal is not to "train" you, but rather, to further equip you so that you might better cooperate with what God is doing in your life.

Similarly, we are confident that no one in the world has ever "completed" the TPM training. Some understand it better than others, but we know of no one who has fully mastered all that there is to know (we would not even put ourselves in this category). In fact, those who have the most experience in a particular field or skill are the least likely to claim to have "mastered" it. They undoubtedly know it better than their peers, but they are also more keenly aware of what they have yet to learn.

We might also compare this journey with studying the Bible. None of us would say we have "completed" the Bible. Who can know all that is there? When do we get our "certificate of completion" for our Bible training? If we read it cover to cover, have we completed it? Do we really know it? Of course, this training is not on the same level as the Scriptures, but the same learning principles apply.

With that said, there is no need to rush. If you view your training as a journey rather than a task to complete, a timeframe for the experience does not apply. You can obviously plan out your journey through the material and schedule training sessions in your calendar, but it is also important to be honest with ourselves when it comes to "completing" the training. When you can honestly say that you have genuinely mastered all of the material, then, we suppose, you have "completed" the training.

Until then, we encourage you to throw out the concept of "completing" the training and, instead, focus on becoming "equipped." So if your question is, "How long will it take me to become *equipped* in TPM?" then it all depends on how equipped you want to become! Thankfully, we believe this version of the TPM training will be the easiest to learn, apply, and evaluate.

Rather than approaching this "training" with the purpose of ministering to others, we encourage you to implement it as part of your journey with God. We hope that you will become equipped with the knowledge and perspective needed to intentionally position yourself to hear from the Spirit so that you can have your faith purified, your mind renewed, and your life transformed into the image of Christ. Focus your attention on living in the Spirit, and naturally experiencing the fruit of His Spirit, and walking in the "good works" that you were destined to walk. The Scriptures make this promise, "[you] are His workmanship, created in Christ Jesus for good works, which God prepared beforehand so that [you] would walk in them" (Ephesians 2:10).

This shift in focus may initially frustrate those who were hoping for a 12-week study guide to take their group through so that at the end of the "training" they could say, "Well Done! Here is your *Certificate of Completion.*" We realize that this is common practice in other areas of life, but can we honestly say that we are trained and equipped?

For instance, we go to college, graduate, and then claim to be educated, but if our comprehension of all that we were exposed to were to be tested, how would we honestly fare? How much would we be able to recall? Rather than claiming to have a college education, it may be more accurately stated that we were exposed to a vast amount of information but remember very little.

We hope that you approach TPM differently. Please form your study groups, but also help each member remember that our goal is not to become "trained," rather, it is to better cooperate with God in the transformational work He is doing in each of our lives. Also, instill in each member the importance of learning everything that we can in order to gain as much benefit as possible. The duration of your "training" is totally irrelevant. Comprehension, not "completion," is the goal! Take your time, work through the text in any fashion that best suits your context, and purpose to learn it well.

HOW MANY TIMES DO YOU READ THE SAME BOOK?

Why do we so often read a book, recognize that it contains concepts that are worth remembering, and then never read it again? We will only retain a small portion of what we read and quickly forget most of it unless we incorporate it into our daily lives. The truth is, even the most gifted student will only remember and comprehend about 15-20% of what he reads one time. If what you read in this book seems to have value, we encourage you to invest the time necessary to learn it well and make it part of your daily life.

If the thought of spending so much time working through the training stresses you out or seems daunting, then you are approaching it from the wrong perspective. There is no hurry or time limit for this journey. You are not running a race; rather, you are embarking on a journey. Enjoy the ride and stop at each point of interest. If you are traveling with a group, you can stay in step with them if you choose or you can run ahead at your own pace. No one will be left behind since we can return to the same place as a group and discuss and process particular points together.

Set your sights on becoming well-equipped, not on "checking off" the "completed" box. After you have applied TPM for a time, go back and revisit the material. We believe you will be surprised at how much more you will gain once you have some experience behind you. Keep learning and growing.

Part Two

What is the difference between a Mentor and a Mentee in TPM?

The early editions of the TPM training were focused on equipping people to minister to others like a doctor would his patients or a therapist would his clients. We mistakenly believed that one person facilitated the ministry session while the other person received ministry. However, we have since realized that the true dynamic of their relationship and responsibilities are very different! As such, the focus of the training has also shifted. Rather than attempting to train "Ministry Facilitators" to minister to "Recipients of ministry," we now focus on equipping every member of the Body of Christ to participate with God in the faith-refining, mind-renewing, and transformational work He is doing.

Today, we use the terms *"Mentor"* and *"Mentee"* to describe the roles of those involved in TPM. A TPM Mentor does not minister to the Mentee or facilitate the TPM session. Rather, the Mentor:

Serves in a supportive and instructive role,

Acts as a trainer who observes the Mentee's application of the TPM Process,

Ensures that proper protocol is being followed during a TPM session,

Reinforces the Mentee's understanding of the Principles and Purpose of TPM,

Helps the Mentee realize that TPM is a means of cooperating with God in His faith-refining work.

In reality, everyone is a Mentee, and some Mentees mentor others. There is no "them-and-us" mentality within this ministry. We are each on the same faith-refining and mind-renewing journey with God. The only potential difference between a Mentor and a Mentee is their familiarity with TPM and their experience in applying it. But there is nothing that the Mentor knows concerning the Principles, Purpose, or Process of TPM that the Mentee cannot know and apply for himself. This is an important concept worth reinforcing.

The Mentee is the person who applies the Process in every ministry session; he or she connects with emotion, recalls memories, identifies beliefs, checks for transformation, etc. He or she is the one actually applying the TPM Process (to the best of his or her ability and understanding). The Mentor, on the other hand, helps the Mentee learn how to accomplish each of these tasks, reminds him of the objective at hand by asking the prescribed questions, and offers orientation and instruction where needed.

Both roles are unique and important, and they each are focused on essentially the same thing: equipping the Mentee for his or her faith-refining journey with the Lord. The Mentee's understanding is paramount. As you will soon discover, most potential "issues" and "obstacles" are alleviated once the Mentee knows what they are doing. Because of this, every TPM Mentor first seeks to become a well-equipped Mentee and then applies what he has learned as he mentors others to do the same.

How is TPM *different from other ministries?*

The defined roles and responsibilities of TPM Mentors and Mentees makes TPM distinctly different from many other forms of ministry. The primary focus of TPM is to equip <u>you</u> (the Mentee) to better cooperate with God as He refines your faith (belief), renews your mind, and transforms your life. Again, this book was <u>not</u> designed to train the Mentor to apply the ministry on the Mentee, but rather, to equip everyone who reads it with the skills and understanding needed to intentionally cooperate with God as He ministers to them.

If you desire to be a Mentor, but you do not apply this information to your own life and only seek to help the "troubled people" who are "emotionally wounded," then you do not understand this ministry's true value or purpose. Also, if you are *not* finding freedom from your own lie-based beliefs and gaining God's perspective, the consequences of this will negatively impact your ability to mentor others. You will find yourself feeling anxious, frustrated, fearful and more during the ministry sessions when things do not go as you might desire.

Some of those who read this book will sense a call to mentor others in becoming equipped to apply this ministry. This is good and needed if this ministry is to be practiced by future generations of the church. Even so, becoming a Mentor is not a calling for everyone nor should it be anyone's primary goal. God has assigned each of us a role in the Body of Christ and mentoring others in TPM may not be what He has for you.

Another way in which TPM is fundamentally different from many other forms of ministry is that we attempt to honestly evaluate the results of what occurs in a TPM session. Rather than assuming that God performed a miraculous work in someone's life, we always test to see if it is so. As you will soon learn, we always check for verifiable evidence that the Holy Spirit was actually involved no matter how good, positive, productive, or even biblical something may initially appear to be. Rather than relying on subjective experience, intuition, or spiritual discernment, we look for undeniable proof. For when God does something, there is always verifiable evidence of His involvement that will hold up to any amount of scrutiny.

Simply put, we look for a change in belief. This is what the Holy Spirit was sent to accomplish, so it is also the metric that we use to evaluate what occurs in a TPM session. As we will discuss later, you may be able to distract yourself from your pain or think happier thoughts without having to involve Him. And you may be able to make better, more productive choices without first having the Holy Spirit "guide you into all the truth" (John 16:13). Just because you feel "better" or make "better" choices does not mean that the Spirit of Truth was responsible for this change. Because of this, neither emotion nor behavior, together or independently, are ever viewed as evidence of God's work. For if you still believe what you believed at the start, this form of "change" is not a fruit of the Spirit.

We have designated an entire chapter to discuss the differences between TPM and other forms of ministry that should prove helpful.

How do I find a Mentor?

We encourage you to equip yourself with at least a cursory understanding of this ministry even before attempting to involve someone else. And when searching for a Mentor, do not assume that a person is following protocol simply because they claim to be doing so. The TPM Process (what occurs in a ministry session) has a clear and precise protocol, and it should be easy to identify whether it is being applied properly or not. Therefore, it is important that you have a good understanding of this ministry so you will know what to look for in your search. Please take ownership of your own journey. No one in the world knows anything about TPM that you yourself cannot also know.

We are sometimes asked if we have a referral list of people doing TPM that might be available to provide mentorship. The truth is there are literally tens of thousands of people in the world who say that they have worked through the TPM training. But we do not know these people personally, nor do we know if their practices accurately reflect what is taught here. In the same way that we would refrain from recommending a restaurant or hotel that we have never visited, we reserve the right to withhold our recommendations regarding those who claim to be TPM Mentors.

Our encouragement to you is simple; educate and equip yourself with all that is taught so that you can rightly identify what others are doing. Rather than attempting to find a Mentor who you do not already personally know, we encourage you to form a training group with those around you whom you already know and trust. This way you have a team that can learn, practice, and pray with each other. Doing this will take a little time, but long-term fruit will be well worth the effort!

How do I introduce my church to TPM?

Some of you will desire to share this ministry with your local church. But we encourage you to move slowly when introducing your church to TPM if your fellow members are not already acquainted with it. Start with the lead shepherd of the flock. Humbly ask your pastor to evaluate the merit of the TPM training. You could send them the links to the introductory videos found on our website or give them a copy of this book (either digital or print). You could also refer your pastor to other pastors who are leading their flocks in this ministry. Your pastor can contact the TPM office and be placed in contact with other pastors who can provide testimony to this ministry's validity.

We also recommend introducing others to TPM by way of the *Principles* and *Purpose* rather than beginning the conversation talking about the *Process* (what happens during a ministry session). This usually piques their interest and curiosity and is less likely to offend or confuse them. They will benefit from understanding the *Purpose* and *Principles* even if they never choose to examine TPM further. Some may even ask you how to apply what you have shared, and then you can tell them all about the *Process*.

If you mistakenly introduce TPM by first discussing the *Process*, your audience typically misinterprets what you are saying as, "I think that you have emotional problems and are in need of this ministry." And, even if they are not offended by what they think you are saying, they will still likely assume that TPM is a ministry for emotionally "troubled" or "wounded" people.

Many churches using TPM have misunderstood its actual purpose and place in the church. More often than not, TPM is relegated to a "recovery" ministry or to the "counseling" side of things. It is often viewed as a ministry to those who are emotionally wounded and in need of special care. Even though TPM can be highly effective in these ministry contexts, this is not its actual purpose. When TPM is viewed as a helping ministry for those viewed as emotionally troubled, its potential effectiveness is dramatically diminished. What person in the Body of Christ does not need their faith refined, their mind renewed, and their life transformed into the image of Jesus? This is the end goal of TPM.

Rather, we hope that you come to rightly view this ministry model and its intended purpose. When it is properly understood and appropriately applied, TPM offers a systematic and consistent model to follow as you cooperate with God in His ministry to you. We hope God uses this book to bless and encourage you. He has used this ministry to radically transform many, many lives, and we are confident that He can do the same for you!

CHAPTER 1

THE BEGINNING
OF TRANSFORMATION
PRAYER MINISTRY

"Lord Jesus, what do you want her to know?"

Before the inception of TPM (1995), I offered pastoral counseling ministry to my small, rural community in central Kentucky, USA. A significant portion of those who came to me for help were women who survived childhood sexual abuse. I had come to understand that their emotional pain was NOT coming from their past or even their memory of it, but it was due to what they believed either about themselves or God. Their beliefs, not their memories or even the experiences themselves, accounted for their current feelings. What was most confusing for me was how they could intellectually know the truth about their abuse (they were safe now, it was not their fault, they were not dirty or shameful, etc.), and yet their emotional state revealed that they did not believe this truth in their hearts.

Even though they intellectually agreed with me concerning the truth, I could not convince them to believe it in their hearts. Their current emotional state revealed that their heart belief overrode what they intellectually agreed was true. No matter how many times I told them the truth that the abuse was not their fault, they were safe now, or that they were not dirty or shameful, I was unable to persuade them to believe me, and they still felt what their lie-based heart belief dictated: shame, fear, powerlessness and more.

Eventually I became disheartened because those I counseled year after year did not experience any real or permanent relief despite me telling them the truth repeatedly. Some improved in their ability to manage their pain as they "connected the dots" between their dysfunction and their abuse. Some functioned at a higher level after many sessions with me, but genuine and lasting transformation was not evident.

Anytime they recalled the memories of their abuse, the pain was still present. My "counseling" helped them to intellectually recognize the falsehood they held onto, but nothing I did reached the deception that was harbored in their hearts. Since I had told them the truth over and over again, I honestly didn't know what else to do. Little did I know that the Lord was about to dramatically change my ministry approach.

During one of my 'counseling' sessions, I asked the woman with whom I was meeting to think about one of her childhood memories of sexual abuse and tell me what she felt. She immediately began to cry and tremble as she described feeling emotions such as shame, fear, and guilt. I asked her why she felt that way. She then expressed several beliefs: "It was my fault." "I am dirty and shameful." "I feel trapped." "I can't make it stop."

I fully recognized that her beliefs did not reflect the truth, or at least they were not true for her at that present moment. Her words described her interpretation of what had happened to her. They represented her misunderstanding of herself and her "state of being." In other sessions I had repeatedly told her the truth, but even though she agreed with me intellectually, the truth did not *feel* true to her. She was aware of the truth, but she did not yet believe it with her heart. And no matter how hard I tried, I was incapable of convincing her to believe. I honestly didn't know what to do.

So on this occasion, I took a deep breath and prayed aloud something like, "Lord Jesus, what do you want her to know?" I honestly had no expectations about what might happen; I had simply run out of options. After a few moments, she stopped crying, sat up, and opened her eyes. With a bewildered but peaceful look she said to me, "It's gone." Puzzled, I asked, "What's gone?" She said, "the shame and guilt; I sensed it all lifted off of me!" I asked, "How is that?" She joyfully replied, "*He* said I am not there anymore, and what happened to me wasn't my fault." I responded, "I know. That is what I have been telling you." She said, "Yes, you have, but this time *HE* told me." I hesitantly asked her, "Who told you?" She said, "The Lord told me that it was not my fault! I am safe now. I am not there anymore!"

At that moment I believed that I had witnessed a miracle! I watched as the Holy Spirit transformed her beliefs right in front of me by simply revealing His truth and perspective *to her heart*. Of course, I had no idea that this was the beginning of a worldwide ministry that would touch hundreds of thousands of lives in the years that followed. I honestly thought it was a special encounter and working of God He had uniquely granted her.

What I witnessed in her life was the transformation that resulted from the Holy Spirit renewing her mind with the truth (we will discuss this concept in detail later). While thinking about her abuse, she had stated that she felt dirty, shameful, trapped, and guilt-ridden. She felt this way because she believed she was trapped, dirty and somehow responsible for what had happened to her as a child. But when the Spirit gently persuaded her of His perspective, she *"humbly received the implanted word"* (James 1:21, emphasis added) which brought forth a complete shift in her belief.

When she believed the truth with her heart, she immediately experienced the fruit of the Spirit, namely joy and peace. Before she believed the truth in her heart, her feelings matched the lies she believed; when she believed the truth, her emotions changed to match the truth. During the days that followed, I began doing the same thing with the others I was trying to help, and, to my amazement, the Lord showed up, and miracle after miracle occurred.

After having read this testimony, you might assume that TPM is a ministry for those who have experienced trauma. But in actuality, TPM offers the same hope for everyone no matter their life experiences. Again, this woman's problem was not that she had experienced trauma, but rather, her current suffering was due to her interpretation of what had happened to her. She had come to believe things about herself and God that were false. Her emotional state was caused by what she believed, not what she remembered. She needed God's perspective. She needed Him to renew her mind. This is true for all of us just as Paul described, *"be transformed by the renewing of your mind"* (Romans 12:2).

A Ministry of the Holy Spirit

I was amazed and blessed by what I witnessed in that first (unofficial) TPM session. However, I did not rush out and tell the world about what occurred. Instead, I intentionally waited for over a year practicing and applying what I was learning and continued to experience with many other people. Session after session, I witnessed the Lord free people from their lie-based beliefs by convincing them of His perspective. After a year of observing and learning, I developed a training seminar that I initially offered in my local church. After that first seminar people began telling others and within a few years TPM found its way into over a hundred different countries by word of mouth. We receive testimonies every day that glorify God for the good things He is doing all around the world.

I initially called this ministry model *Theophostic Counseling*. "Theophostic" is a word that I coined by combining two Greek New Testament words which essentially meant "God's Light." I initially called it "counseling" because I was a pastoral counselor and counseling was the only paradigm that I knew at the time. However, it did not take me long to realize that what was happening in a session was anything but counseling; rather, I was equipping people to prayerfully cooperate with the Holy Spirit's ministry in their lives. So, I eventually dropped the word "counseling" and replaced it with the words "Prayer Ministry."

The name *Theophostic Prayer Ministry* stayed in place until around 2015 when we transitioned to the name *Transformation Prayer Ministry.* For the most part, we dropped the Greek name Theophostic because we got tired of explaining its spelling and meaning and some people thought it had a "new age" feel to it. We chose the term "transformation" because this term best describes what we believe God is doing through this ministry. This also allowed us to keep the acronym "TPM" which was used by many to refer to this ministry.

What is the "Ministry" in Transformation Prayer Ministry?

The term "ministry" has different meanings depending on the context in which it is used. For example, in many governments around the world there is a ministry of finance, education, defense, etc. The most common understanding of the word, when used in the church, pertains to the individual believer's specific calling to Christian service. Ministry in that context is usually understood to be what the individual is doing to fulfill his or her role in the Body of Christ by "doing" ministry for, on, or with a recipient of ministry.

Some people have misapplied this meaning to TPM, but this understanding is not the intended meaning of the term. In TPM you will not find one person doing ministry with or for another person, but rather the ministry that occurs in a TPM session is that of the Holy Spirit. In TPM, God is ministering to us. Technically, the TPM Mentor is engaged in an equipping "ministry" with the Mentee, but any resulting transformation is solely attributable to the Holy Spirit.

We are all called to minister one unto the other through service and love and *"each of [us] should use whatever gift [we] have received to serve others, as faithful stewards of God's grace in its various forms"* (1 Peter 4:10 NIV). However, in TPM we understand that transformation is the result of the Spirit's work, not our own. Through "prayer" the Holy Spirit is "ministering" to us which results in "transformation," thus, the name, *"Transformation Prayer Ministry."* So then, when we use the term "ministry" to describe TPM, we are primarily referring to a specific aspect of ministry that the Holy Spirit is doing in the life of every believer. He is the "minister" in the context of TPM.

The Work of the Spirit

The Bible reveals that the Holy Spirit is at work within the Body of Christ in many diverse ways. For example, the Spirit leads the believer into all truth (John 14:26, 16:13; Ephesians 1:17-18), He gives gifts to every member in the Body (1 Corinthians 12: 4-7), He bears His fruit in the life of the believer as truth is illuminated within their heart (Galatians 5:22-23; Colossians 1:9-10), and He is the Father's sworn guarantee or seal given to assure the believer of his eternal destiny (Ephesians 1:13). These things and more describe the "ministries" of the Holy Spirit.

During a TPM session the Spirit ministers to us when He "opens the eyes of our hearts" (Ephesians 1:18) so that we might believe the truth with our hearts which then brings about the effortless transformation of our belief and consequential behavior (the fruit of the Spirit). This ministry of mind-renewal is what Paul was asking God to do when he said,

> We have not ceased to pray for you and to ask that you may be filled with the knowledge of His will in all spiritual wisdom and understanding, **so that** you will walk in a manner worthy of the Lord, to please Him in all respects, bearing fruit in every good work and increasing in the knowledge of God; strengthened with all power, according to His glorious might (Colossians 1:9-11, emphasis added).

This passage reveals what God desires to do in and for us *so that* we might live a life that reflects our transformation into the image of Christ. When you read this passage, did you notice the two little words "*so that?*" These words are positioned between what God is doing to renew our minds and the fruit of His Spirit that we bear as a result. People typically read verse ten without first reading verse nine and assume this passage is a call to action or a list of mandates that they are to follow. But unless God does what is stated in verse nine, verse ten cannot be realized. It is only because God grants us the "knowledge of His will in all spiritual wisdom and understanding" that we will experience the glorious expectations found in verse ten.

Then in verses eleven and twelve, Paul reveals where the power to walk out this knowledge and wisdom comes from when he says,

> ...strengthened with all power, <u>according to His glorious might</u>, for the attaining of all steadfastness and patience; joyously giving thanks to the Father, who has qualified us to share in the inheritance of the saints in light (Colossians 1:9-12, emphasis added).

The little phrase *"so that"* tells us that what follows thereafter is dependent upon what was stated first. It is because God has done "such and such" that we can experience "this and that" as a result. God must first fill us with the knowledge of His will in spiritual wisdom and understanding before we can live out a transformed life. Read this verse again and notice the seven beneficial outcomes of God filling us with knowledge, wisdom, and understanding.

<u>Because God has done what only He can do</u>, we are able to:

walk in a manner worthy of the Lord,

please Him in all respects,

bear fruit in every good work,

increase in the knowledge of God,

be strengthened with all power,

attain steadfastness and patience,

have joy.

Verse ten is not a "to-do" list of things for us to accomplish for God. On the contrary, each listed quality is what we can expect as the outcome of the transformational work He is doing within us. None of these things are attained through effort, willpower, or ongoing commitment or recommitment. All of this is the outcome of God filling us with *"...the knowledge of His will in all spiritual wisdom and understanding."* Or more plainly put, they are fruits of His Spirit.

This transforming work is accomplished by His Spirit as we *"submit [ourselves] under the mighty hand of God"* (1 Peter 5:6). As the eyes of our hearts are opened, and the Spirit persuades us of the truth, we discover more and more what God is really like and who we have been since we first believed (1 Corinthians 13:12). These passages describe what we hope to witness in every TPM session.

This training is designed for all those who desire to walk in the truth and effortlessly bear the fruit of God's Spirit. Some who take this training may also become mentors for others, but that is a secondary purpose of this ministry. The first priority is that you be equipped to effectively apply the *Purpose, Principles* and *Process of TPM* to your own life. This is our prayer for you as you make this ministry your lifestyle and daily walk with God.

CHAPTER 2

THE THREE ELEMENTS OF TPM
PRINCIPLES, PURPOSE, AND PROCESS

The Three Elements of TPM

The Three Elements of TPM consist of the *"Principles of TPM"*, the *"Purpose of TPM,"* and the *"Process of TPM."* These elements are the subject of this book and the focus of every TPM session, and your understanding of them will directly impact your ability to effectively apply what is taught. You can benefit from learning about any one of them, but to extract the most benefit from TPM, you <u>must</u> understand and apply <u>all three</u>.

In essence, the "Principles" explain how everything works, the "Purpose" discusses why those things are important, and the "Process" offers the practical steps you can take to apply what you have learned. The Principles, Purpose, and Process of TPM support and explain each other. And because these elements work together to form a cohesive system, any one of the elements is lacking if applied by itself.

For instance, if you only understand the *Principles*, you will be able to explain your perceptions, emotions, and actions, but be unaware of how to change any of them. If you only understand the *Purpose* of TPM, you will see the significance of what God is wanting to do in your life, but many of the opportunities for refinement that He offers will sneak by you because you won't know what to look for or how to properly respond to them. If you only understand the *Process*, you may be able to identify some lies and get some truth, but you will likely misuse this tool and only apply what you've learned when your emotional pain becomes unmanageable. And if you attempt to mentor others without understanding each of the *Three Elements of TPM*, you will inevitably create poorly equipped Mentees who are constantly dependent upon you and your involvement.

We encourage you to commit yourself to learning each of the *Three Elements of TPM* well. Again, understanding and applying them together offers exponentially more benefit than only handling one. With that said, let's take a moment to briefly introduce each *Element* before discussing them in detail in later chapters.

The Principles of TPM

The Principles of TPM provide explanations for everything that may occur within the context of TPM. They explain why we perceive the world the way we do, why we feel what we feel, why we do what we do, and why we believe what we believe. They also explain the roles of Mentee and Mentor in the context of TPM.

Familiarizing yourself with the principles will remove much of the mystery that initially may seem to envelop TPM. Understanding the principles enables you to more effectively apply what is taught and is vital if you hope to effectively mentor others in TPM.

The Principles also offer a versatile means of introducing new people to TPM. They allow you to discuss portions of the TPM training in smaller, applicable "chunks" rather than overwhelming a person with a torrent of information. This enables you to purposefully explain TPM by focusing on topics that are relatable and relevant to a person's current situation. They are also used by Mentors during TPM sessions as a form of orientation since they can effectively explain every aspect of the TPM Process.

The Purpose of TPM

The Purpose of TPM explains *why* we should learn and apply what is discussed in this book. It provides a frame of reference for viewing life's difficulties from a heavenly perspective. It explains why we should view our suffering, troubles, and misfortune as opportunities for God to transform us into the image of Christ rather than unwelcome difficulties we must somehow overcome or endure. What is typically viewed as meaningless misfortune is understood to be a refining fire managed by a loving and compassionate God who loves us and has an eternal plan for our good (Jeremiah 29:11).

By holding this perspective, we can intentionally choose to cooperate with God as He purifies our faith, renews our minds, and transforms our lives amidst our suffering. Our biblical basis for this viewpoint is based upon, but not limited to, passages such as,

> God causes all things to work together for good to those who love God, to those who are called according to His purpose. For those whom He foreknew, He also predestined to become conformed to the image of His Son (Romans 8:28-29),

> Beloved, do not be surprised at the fiery ordeal among you, which comes upon you for your testing, as though something strange were happening to you; but to the degree that you share the sufferings of Christ, keep on rejoicing, so that at the revelation of His glory you may also rejoice and be overjoyed (1 Peter 4:12-13).

We participate with Him in His faith-refining and mind-renewing work by positioning ourselves under His "mighty hand" so that after we "...have suffered for a little while, the God of all grace, who called [us] to His eternal glory in Christ, will Himself perfect, confirm, strengthen and establish [us]" so that we may effortlessly and naturally bear the fruit of His Spirit (see 1 Peter 5:6-10).

The Process of TPM

The TPM process is a series of actions that are taken, or objectives that you (the Mentee) accomplish, during a TPM session that offers you a systematic approach for humbly positioning yourself before God so that He will convince you to believe the truth. It consists of well-defined protocols that help you to acknowledge what you believe and position yourself to receive truth and perspective from the Holy Spirit. This Process can be applied by practically anyone, anywhere, at any time. Once you become familiar with the Process of TPM, you can easily incorporate it into your everyday life.

Initially, when you are accompanied by a Mentor, he or she will observe your application of the TPM Process and ask questions that are designed to remind you of your current objective and how you can accomplish it. But your Mentor is <u>not</u> the one who is applying the Process. He or she is there to further equip you with the knowledge and skills that are necessary to be able to apply the Process on your own. For this purpose, your Mentor will offer orientation regarding the Three Elements of TPM throughout your TPM sessions.

The TPM Process is distinctively different from counseling and other models of ministry. You go to a doctor to be treated and to a counselor to be counseled, but in TPM, you come to be *mentored*. This is <u>your</u> journey with God. Your Mentor is simply further equipping you to be more aware and intentionally involved in that journey.

"JUST TEACH ME HOW TO HELP PEOPLE!"

We understand that many who take this training will want to begin with the *Process* and start applying it as soon as possible. They want to quickly "complete" the training so that they can begin helping the "emotionally troubled" people in their circle and offer hope to those who struggle with troublesome behaviors. Though their intentions may be good, this perspective is very narrow and limited in scope.

By focusing primarily upon the ministry *Process* and failing to properly equip themselves with the *Principles* and *Purpose of TPM*, these would-be Mentors have essentially limited TPM's use to form of pain management. As consequence, they will likely forfeit much of the benefit they personally could have enjoyed. If the "troubled" people in their care only experiences the Process of TPM and do not understand the Principles and Purpose, they will likely misapply it. And once their pain reaches a tolerable and their behavior seems to be under their control, they will probably not seek to learn or apply TPM further. This is a completely avoidable tragedy.

As every TPM Mentor who has fully embraced each *Element of TPM* would agree, attempting to use the *Process of TPM* without also incorporating its Principles and Purpose is less than ideal. It could be compared to an experienced fisherman who attempts to feed his hungry neighbors by giving them his fresh catch but not teaching them how to catch fish themselves. This unintentional selfishness robs fisherman's neighbors of the freedom and blessing that comes from being able to feed themselves by going directly to the source of sustenance. In TPM, we want to equip people to "fish" for themselves. A good Mentor will make his or her involvement less and less necessary.

For that reason, we encourage you not to be in a hurry but to follow the training as it is presented. We have purposefully introduced concepts in the order we believe will make the most sense and will reinforce what you have learned in the past. That said, we would also suggest that you begin familiarizing yourself with the information included in the *TPM Map* and *Flowcharts* (found in the back of this book) as soon as possible. You will obviously not yet understand how to apply this information, but you will have a major head start when the time comes to learn the Process of TPM.

If it is not TPM, then it is not TPM.

Please understand the *Process of TPM* can be effectively applied even if you don't fully agree with the *TPM Principles* and *Purpose*. However, <u>if you do not follow protocol when applying it, then you are **not** actually applying the *Process of TPM* and should use a different name to describe what you are doing</u>. We feel no need to criticize anyone else's ministry, but it is important to clearly define what TPM is and what it is not. If someone has only sampled bits and pieces of TPM, or attempted to combine it with other practices, then they should not call what they are doing "TPM." Their ministry may be highly effective and blessed by God, but in order to preserve the integrity of both ministries, each should be uniquely identified.

Before seeking ministry from someone who claims to be practicing TPM, you should equip yourself with at least a cursory understanding of the Three Elements of TPM. This will better equip you to evaluate the mentoring you receive. You will only be able to determine if a mentor is following true TPM protocol if you know the material yourself.

Additionally, in the back of this book you will find an in-depth discussion regarding <u>what TPM is not</u>. There you will discover that the focus of TPM is not on counseling, spiritual warfare, the healing of memories, or helping "emotionally wounded people" find freedom from their pain. Granted, we fully expect a positive change in our thoughts, feelings, and behaviors as a result of the Holy Spirit's work in our lives, but this transformation is an outcome or benefit, not the actual goal or focus. Rather, TPM is a means by which all believers can intentionally cooperate with God as He purifies our faith, renews our minds, and transforms our lives. Our heart's desire is that you will approach this training for the purpose of becoming equipped for your lifelong journey with God as He works in your life.

CHAPTER 3

THE PRINCIPLES OF TPM

EXPLAINING THE PURPOSE AND PROCESS OF TPM

The Fundamental Principles of TPM

The *Principles of TPM* are the foundational concepts that support this ministry model. They explain the perspective we have of our life experiences, reveal why we feel what we feel at any given moment, describe what motivates and directs our behavior, and discuss the reason we believe what we believe.

There is a short list of fundamental principles that form the basis for all other principles that are applicable to this ministry model. These fundamental concepts are universal. They apply to everyone, everywhere, and have been true since Adam and Eve were in the Garden. Each examines a unique facet of our design and the way in which God uses it to accomplish His plan in our lives. We believe that God views these fundamental concepts as "good" (Genesis 1:31) and is using them as He works all things together "for the good of those who love Him, those who are called according to His purpose" (Romans 8:28).

We briefly introduce each principle below and offer a summary of the concepts that are involved, but know that each of them will be discussed in-depth in later chapters. Keep this in mind as you read. What follows is only meant to "whet your appetite," raise some questions in your mind, and get you thinking. They are <u>not</u> meant to teach or explain anything (although they can be used later as reminders to help you keep yourself sharp). They are only presented to spark your interest and get you thinking.

You may encounter concepts that cause you to initially react or want to recoil, but we encourage you to keep reading and embrace what you can while loosely holding onto the rest. Before rejecting one of these principles, read it again and consider what is presented (knowing that each concept will be discussed in detail in the coming chapters).

You can revisit this section to refresh your memory of what is discussed in the coming chapters after you have read them. As with every aspect of TPM, we encourage you to work towards *comprehension*, not mere *completion*. With that said, let's take a quick look at the fundamental principles of TPM.

The "Belief and Perception" Principle:
"We perceive what we believe."

Despite how it may seem, our perception is not reality. In fact, actual reality and our perception of it are often very different. You have likely heard it said that "seeing is believing," but this expression would be more aptly stated as "believing is seeing." What we believe to be true (even when it is not) will have great bearing on how we interpret life or what we see. The perceptions we have of ourselves, our surroundings, and of God are the result of our minds' interpretation of those things through what we have learned from previous experiences. Everything we experience in our lives, as well as our memory of it, is interpreted in this way. Our beliefs form our perception of reality. Because of this, our perceptions will feel or seem true to us, but our belief in something does not make that "something" true. God's Word is the standard by which all beliefs, perspectives, and opinions should be judged. Anything that is not perfectly aligned with His perspective is inaccurate, or at the very least, limited. God's perspective is truth and reality. If that which we believe to be true does not accurately reflect God's perspective, then we are walking in darkness and will suffer the consequences. Even when we intellectually know the truth, our lie-based heart belief will distort our perceptions and *seem* true to us. We will inevitably confront imaginary lie-based problems while missing God's solutions to our truth-based problems. However, if our perception genuinely reflects His, then we are seeing clearly and will effortlessly walk in the light of that truth. By God's design we perceive what we believe.

The "Belief and Emotion" Principle:
"We feel what we believe."

Although we typically blame our emotional pain and discomfort on the world around us, this approach imprisons those who employ it. Our emotions are neither random nor determined by the actions of others, the quality of our situation, or our conscious attempts at feeling a specific feeling. You can no more "choose" to feel joy than you can "choose" to feel unhappy. Our emotional state is an automatic and effortless result of the perception we have of ourselves, of our surroundings, and of God. Our feelings are a natural expression of what we believe in our hearts. If we believe the truth in our hearts, we will feel what the truth feels like. If we are deceived, we will feel emotional pain. We may choose to block out what we feel, but we cannot choose to feel something that does not already align with what we believe to be true. Our emotions simply indicate what we believe. This does not mean that we are doomed to continue feeling what we currently feel. If our beliefs change, so do our emotions. We will feel what God has promised (peaceful, joyful, compassionate, etc.) when our beliefs accurately reflect His perspective. By God's design we feel what we believe.

The "Belief and Choice" Principle:
"We do what we believe."

We all do things that we wish we wouldn't do. The obvious solution to this problem is to make better choices. Because of this we often attempt to adjust our behavior through commitment, determination, effort, and accountability. We applaud those who can push through the difficulty and choose to do the "right" thing. But if one of us fails to meet our unspoken behavioral standards, we are viewed as "*weak*," "*wayward*," or "*wounded*." Often those who perceive themselves to be at the bottom of this imaginary leaderboard believe that they "can't help themselves." But our behavior is not random or out of our control. Even though their chosen behaviors are different, *there is no meaningful difference between those who struggle to maintain the expected standard and those who seem to succeed in their outward performance.*

Everything we do is done deliberately and for a purpose, even if those purposes are not immediately apparent. Much of what we do is done in an attempt to solve the perceived problems that we *believe* we must address. We do what we choose to do because we believe it is the most appropriate and beneficial response to the perception we have of our current situation. At some level, we may even disagree with our own actions, but they are an automatic and effortless expression of what we believe to be true. When a behavior is in line with what we believe, we are motivated to do it; however, if a behavior contradicts what we believe to be true, we will face internal resistance and struggle while attempting to do it. Although this causes much of the struggle we face when attempting to obey the truths we read in Scripture, it is not a bad thing! For when we genuinely know these truths in our hearts, the struggle will cease, and we will effortlessly express the fruit of the Holy Spirit. He wants us to do what we believe, so long as our beliefs accurately reflect the truth. By God's design we do what we believe.

The "Belief and Persuasion" Principle:
"We believe what we are persuaded to believe."

Since our perceptions, emotions, and behaviors are the outcomes of what we believe, it is vital that our beliefs accurately reflect God's perspective. This is where many well-meaning believers hit a seemingly impassable obstacle. Many are of the opinion that we choose to believe what we believe, and faith is often equated to a conscious decision to trust someone or something. But this perspective is critically flawed! Did you choose to believe that two plus two equals four? Did you *decide* to believe that the sky is blue? Of course not! In the same way, we cannot begin believing that God loves us by simply *deciding* to believe this truth. The reality is that we are incapable of *choosing* to believe anything. We may genuinely want to believe something and commit ourselves to studying and memorizing it, but the fact that we have injected data into our minds does not mean that we also believe this information to be true. We may be able to recall and quote a concept, and even attempt to behave or act as though we believe it, but this does not mean that we are convinced that it is true. We believe what we believe because we have been persuaded to believe it. These beliefs will not change until we are persuaded to believe something else by someone or something that we <u>trust</u> and who seems to hold a greater level of <u>authority</u> on the subject than we do. This persuasion occurs automatically and effortlessly on our part and is the primary focus of the Holy Spirit's ministry to us. He was sent to guide us into all the truth (John 16:13). Because He is the truth and we *trust* Him, and because He holds the greatest measure of *authority*, we will automatically and effortlessly continue to believe what He persuades us of for all eternity! By God's design we believe what we are persuaded to believe.

Perception, Emotion, Choice, and Persuasion

We *"perceive," "feel,"* and *"do"* what we have been *"persuaded"* to believe is true. If properly understood, these seemingly simple concepts have the potential to completely change the way we live our lives. They serve as the connective tissue that joins each of the other TPM Principles together, they form the foundation that the TPM Process is built upon, and they help to explain the importance of TPM's Purpose.

Understanding these Principles will:

1. deepen your understanding of both the Process of TPM and its intended Purpose,
2. enable you to become more effective and intentional in your application of the Process,
3. determine the measure of benefit you will receive from your application of what is taught here,
4. better equip you to potentially mentor others.

Being Mentored in The Principles

Your TPM Mentor should talk with you about the *Purpose* and *Principles of TPM* each time the two of you meet for a TPM session. This does not need to be a lecture, but a spontaneous discussion based upon what is occurring in your life. They will offer help by calling your attention to various TPM Principles that apply to your current situation. Your Mentor serves an important role as you are learning all you need to know. There is no reason for you to solely depend upon your Mentor's involvement since everything that he knows about this ministry is freely available to you as well. The following dialogue illustrates what this might look like in a conversation between a Mentee and his Mentor in the context of a TPM session.

Mentor: *"So, Jim, how are things going?"*

Mentee: *"Not so good. As I was leaving the house this morning, my wife said to me, 'I hope you get fixed today. I am tired of your attitude!'"*

Mentor: *"How does that make you feel?"*

Mentee: *"How do you think it makes me feel? How would you feel if you had to live with some-one who constantly nags and patronizes you? If she would just back off and leave me alone, I wouldn't have an attitude! She's the one who needs to be fixed!"*

At this point the Mentor could continue by asking the next applicable question in the ministry process, but he could also take advantage of this opportunity to share some TPM principles. You see, the Mentee determines what should be discussed concerning the Principles, Purpose, and Process of TPM during each ministry session. His words and actions reveal his depth of understanding regarding the *Three Elements of TPM.*

The fact that the mentee has blamed his wife for his current attitude reveals that he does not understand some of the basic biblical concepts of TPM. Instead of attempting to proceed with the *Process*, the Mentor could devote a few minutes to discussing some applicable *Principles* that the Mentee clearly hasn't yet grasped.

Mentor: *"I understand why you would think this, however, there are a few important biblical principles in TPM you might want to consider. For example, if it were possible to effortlessly experience the peace of Christ rather than getting all worked up when your wife says those kinds of things, would you be interested in that?"*

Mentee: *"Of course, but I highly doubt that is possible!"*

Mentor: *"Actually, it is more than possible; it is a promise from God. The Bible says, 'May the Lord of peace Himself continually grant you peace in every circumstance' (2 Thessalonians 3:16). Can we take a few minutes and talk about this?"*

Mentee: *"Sure."*

Mentor: *"There are a few important principles that apply here..."*

In this scenario, the man believed that he felt what he was feeling because of the way he had been treated. If he receives some truth during his ministry session, he may be able to better tolerate his wife's behavior which has some value. But if he does not also understand the principle that *he feels whatever he believes*, he will *probably* continue to mistakenly assume that his wife's behavior causes him to feel what he feels. He will likely view the TPM Process as a means for managing his emotional pain, only applying it when the tension and discomfort seem to become unmanageable.

If the Mentor only discusses the *Process*, the Mentee will inevitably remain dependent upon the Mentor's involvement and forgo many of the opportunities he will be given to cooperate with God in His faith-refining work. This is tragic, but it is also easily avoidable if the Mentor mentors responsibly. The Mentee's understanding of the *Three Elements of TPM* is paramount! Because of this, it is important that you come to understand the *Purpose and Principles* of TPM and reap as much benefit as possible from this ministry model.

Again, simply stated, the four *Fundamental TPM Principles* (which we will discuss in detail in the next several chapters) are:

We perceive what we believe.

We feel what we believe.

We do what we believe.

We believe what we are persuaded to believe.

CHAPTER 4

THE "BELIEF AND PERCEPTION" PRINCIPLE

"WE PERCEIVE WHAT WE BELIEVE."

NOTICE: This chapter has been divided into five parts. The first part discusses the way in which we interpret life through our beliefs. The second part examines how we perceive ourselves and God. The third part primarily examines the concept of "truth-based perceived problems." The fourth part looks at "lie-based perceived problems." And the fifth part explains that God has solved (or promised to solve) all our problems.

Part One

We perceive what we believe.

Take a look at the image below. Do the horizontal lines seem as though they are bent, criss-crossed, or leaning diagonally? This is an illusion. If you cover-up all but one of the lines, the truth becomes apparent. In reality, they are actually perfectly parallel to one another, and they each intersect with the vertical lines at right angles. This is the truth, regardless of how it may *seem* or *appear* to you.

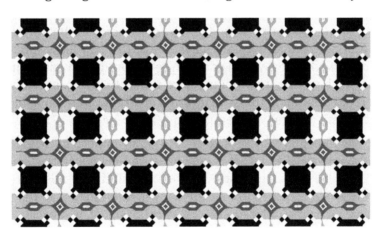

The image above is a desaturated version of Victoria Skye's Optical Illusion, "Skye Blue Café Wall." It is a remake of Richard Gregory's classic "Café Wall" illusion.

Although it should go without saying, the parallel path of each line remains true despite your flawed perception. Just because the lines *look* crooked doesn't mean they *are* crooked. And just because the lines *appear* to criss-cross does not mean that they actually do. The truth is the truth regardless of how it may *seem* to you.

The fact that you cannot change your mind's perception of the image does not mean that your perception is accurate. The image is clear and unchanging, but because your mind misinterprets what your eyes are seeing, you perceive what is not true. Your mind has simply been fooled into "seeing" something that is not real. The crooked and criss-crossed lines that you are seeing only exist in your flawed perception of what is really there.

No matter how hard you try to "see" the truth, the lines will *seem* and *appear* to be slanted as long as your mind continues to misinterpret the image. You can tell yourself the truth regarding the image and diligently try to perceive it correctly, but you will still "see" what your mind believes you are seeing. You are only able to perceive your mind's interpretation of what is actually there. Contrary to the popular expression, "seeing is believing," we often see what we believe.

Our minds are designed to gather input from our senses and interpret what it means. We then perceive the outcome of this interpretation as our experience. In a sense, we experience what we *believe* we are experiencing, and we perceive what we believe. The same interpretive process that informed you of what you were seeing in the image above interprets practically every aspect of your life.

For instance, if you are sitting at an airport and suddenly hear someone screaming in the distance, your experience of this will be determined by what you believe is happening. Is someone in danger or hurt? Was the person startled or scared of something? Or was the screamer simply overjoyed to be reunited with a loved one after a long journey? After scanning your surroundings for contextual clues, your mind will take the information you have gathered, compare it to what you have learned from past experiences, and create your perception of the scream.

The truth of the matter is one thing, but your perception and experience of it is something altogether different. For example, the scream may have been an expression of excitement, but if you believed it signaled trouble, your experience and response will not reflect the actual truth. But if the sound really was someone's warning of a potential threat, but you believed it to be innocent, you will not likely heed the warning.

Everything we perceive is an interpretation of what is actually happening around us. Much of our ongoing interpretation of what happens around us may seem accurate, but this is not always the case. In fact, many portions of our perspectives are flawed or, at the very least, limited. Typically, we are only aware of a portion of what is really going on and we are prone to misinterpreting the few details we actually notice. So much so that we often perceive things that are not really there or miss what is right in front of us (I am accused of this whenever I cannot find something in the refrigerator, and then my wife makes the item magically materialize in front of me).

As we explore this "Fundamental TPM Principle," it is vitally important that we understand the difference between *what we perceive* and *what is*. Just because the lines in that optical illusion (above) seem slanted and jagged doesn't mean that they are; our minds are misinterpreting what we are seeing. Just because the scream seemed to indicate danger, it doesn't mean that there was danger; it just means that we have interpreted the sound as a warning signal. Just because I can't seem to find the ketchup bottle in the refrigerator, it doesn't mean that it isn't right in front of me; I simply do not yet perceive what is already there.

Our minds interpret everything through what we believe to be true.

You can compare this function of your mind to the role of an interpreter. It deciphers the meaning behind the words and actions of others, your current situation, your past experiences, and other life events, and then translates them into a "language" you can understand. This interpretation shapes your understanding of absolutely everything! Therefore, it is vital that the interpretation be accurate.

As with all forms of interpretation or translation, the "interpreter" needs to have a solid grasp on the relevant languages and needs to pay close attention to the intended meaning which has to be translated. If the interpreter fails to see or hear important details of the message or has an incorrect understanding of the meaning behind certain words, the interpretation or translation will be faulty at best! The interpreter may accidentally omit important aspects of what is being translated, thereby changing the meaning entirely, or they might alter the conversation by mistakenly conveying something that was never said.

To quickly illustrate this point, consider the following scenario:

Let's assume that you are visiting a country where you need an interpreter in order to communicate with the locals. It is hot outside, so you and your interpreter walk into a nearby store hoping to find something to drink. They have a large selection of cool refreshments, none of which are familiar to you. But since your interpreter is on the other side of the store, you make your selection based upon the price and hope for the best.

As you approach the woman who is sitting behind the checkout counter, you say hello, but she does not seem to respond. Your interpreter greets the store employee in the local language, she smiles back, and begins ringing-up your items. When she reaches for the drink you selected, she pauses for a moment, looks up at you, and says something to your interpreter.

He seems a bit distracted but relays her message, "*She says that she doesn't like you.*" Shocked and slightly offended, you ask, "*Why not?*" He asks her, and she responds. "*She says it's because of the smell. It makes her nauseous.*" Feeling a bit self-conscious, you pay for your drink and walk out of the store. "*Do I really stink?*" you ask your interpreter as he exits the store. Confused, he responds, "*What? No. What are you talking about?*" "*You said that she doesn't like me because my smell makes her nauseous!*" He chuckles and says, "*Oh, no. I meant to say that she doesn't like your drink. Its smell grosses her out. Sorry, I was browsing their snack options while she was talking. I guess I was a little distracted.*"

If you've ever needed an interpreter or translator, you can probably relate to this story. In this instance, the interpreter was distracted, but imagine the consequences of using an interpreter who did not yet know the definition of important words (limited understanding) or, worse yet, misunderstood their meaning (flawed understanding) yet cobbled-together an interpretation despite this handicap. In this illustration, your perception of the world around you, your interaction with other people, and your ability to respond appropriately to what is happening are all dependent upon your interpreter. Because of this, it is vitally important that he or she is equipped for the task.

This concept also applies to our mind's role as our mental "interpreter." If it is either under-equipped (because it does not yet know the truth) or ill-informed (due to its misunderstanding of the truth), the messages we receive from the world around us will be incomplete, incorrect, or both. As a result, we will have no choice but to view our situation from a flawed and limited perspective. We will fail to notice important details of our situation and come to wrong conclusions. Worst of all, these faulty interpretations will *seem* true to us because they are the only interpretations we are offered.

In the illustration above, the poor interpretation resulted in you experiencing a verbal insult that didn't actually occur. Likewise, our poor mental translations have the potential to cause us to perceive ourselves, our situation, and the people in our lives from a perspective that is blindingly limited and critically flawed. But in either case, the source of the problem is our "interpreter." If our interpreter incorrectly interprets what is happening or fails to notice important details, our perception, experience, and initial reaction will also be misguided.

The quality of our mind's interpretation
depends upon what we believe to be true.

None of this is meant to suggest that our minds are deliberately misleading us, intentionally misinterpreting the people around us, or tricking us into "seeing" things that aren't there. Just like in the previous illustration, our mental interpreter is doing the best it can with the information that it has been given. But the information that it has at its disposal is limited and flawed, and so the interpretation that it offers is also problematic.

The accuracy of our perception is dependent upon the accuracy of our interpretation, and the accuracy of our interpretation is determined by the accuracy of our beliefs. As with the optical illusion at the beginning of this chapter, we can only "see" what our beliefs allow us to "see."

There are countless examples of this found in Scripture. For instance, those who were privileged to interact with Jesus during His time on Earth interpreted Him through what they believed. Their perception of His teaching and actions differed dramatically depending upon what they believed about Him. Those who realized He was the Son of the living God were captivated, overwhelmed, humbled, and full of gratitude; although even they had trouble correctly interpreting His words before He sent His Spirit to guide them into all the truth (John 16:13).

On the other hand, those who believed He was a disruptive heretic perceived Him as a noisy and distracting threat which needed to be eliminated. Those who were unaware of His words and miracles were likely confused or irritated by all the commotion. Each group only saw a portion of who Jesus really was and many of them misinterpreted what they heard and saw. They were only able to perceive that which they believed was true.

Our perspective is never complete or entirely accurate.

Like the people who followed Jesus and listened to His teachings, our perceptions are never a perfect representation of what is actually happening. For instance, let's say that you found out someone was talking about you behind your back. If you were able to rightly understand what the person said about you, why they said it, when they said it, who they said it to, where they were when they said it, what they hoped to accomplish in saying it, what their motives were, and even what they were thinking and feeling as they said it, you would not begin to scratch the surface of the fuller context of the situation.

Even if you clearly perceive each of these details in their entirety, you are perceiving less than 0.0001% of God's perspective when He assesses your situation. He is the only one who rightly and completely "sees" what is happening. His perspective is all-encompassing and always accurate; ours is not.

This is not meant to belittle your ability to interpret what has happened to you. Rather, we simply want to encourage you to be open to the possibility that you are not seeing the whole picture and that some of what currently seems clear and obvious may actually be untrue (much like the optical illusion at the beginning of this chapter).

This becomes even more complicated when you realize that your response to this rude person will be interpreted by their mind, and they will perceive your reaction through the lens of their beliefs. Regardless of your intentions, word selection, and demeanor, your message is interpreted by the other person's mental "interpreter," and their response to you is then interpreted by your "interpreter."

You misinterpret them, they misinterpret you, round and round we go. What a mess! Does this sound familiar? This likely describes at least a few of your interactions with others, even with the people that you genuinely care about and with whom you truly want to communicate. But, again, this issue is related to our mental "interpreters," not our surroundings or the people involved.

We need to address the reasons why our "interpreters" sometimes do such a terrible job. We need to address the beliefs that our limited and flawed perspectives are built upon. When we rightly perceive our situation from a more complete and accurate perspective, many of the problems we typically wrestle with go away on their own. The truth really does set us free (John 8:32).

Part Two

We perceive ourselves the way we do because of what we believe to be true.

Before I head into town, I typically glance at myself in the mirror to make sure I am somewhat presentable. Just because I *believe* I look acceptable doesn't mean that this assessment is correct! I am notorious for leaving my house donning mismatched socks, a backwards shirt, or uncombed hair (hopefully, not all at once!). Thankfully, my family is faithful to lovingly suggest that I address such issues before sending me on my way.

Likewise, when we figuratively look into a "mirror" for self-evaluation, our perception of who we are, what we are worth, why we are here, and so on, is an expression of what we believe about ourselves. If you *believe* that you have great value, then it will *seem* as though you do. However, if you *believe* that you are worthless, that assessment will also *seem* true. You are not "seeing" yourself; you are perceiving who you *believe* yourself to be. But, like the self-evaluation of my appearance, the perception you have of yourself is often both limited and flawed.

The Apostle Paul explained this concept in this way, "For now we see in a mirror dimly, but then face to face; now I know in part, but then I will know fully, just as I also have been fully known" (1 Corinthians 13:12). Paul uses the imagery of a dimly lit and imperfect mirror to describe the way in which we see ourselves. The mirror is meant to show us what we look like, but it cannot provide a perfect perception. The more polished and clean the mirror is, the more accurate its reflection will be.

A first-century mirror would have been crude by modern standards, likely either a bowl of water or a polished metal surface. Even if it were clean, it would still likely be warped or pitted. Because of its inherent imperfections, the mirror would display a distorted version of your true reflection. It is also important to note that Paul's mirror would likely have been lit by candlelight. This soft, flickering flame would only produce enough light to illuminate part of the reflected image, while the rest remained unseen.

With these two realities (the limited light and the skewed reflection) it would be nearly impossible to have a complete and accurate perspective of what you really look like. We face these same limitations when we evaluate ourselves. When our self-perception is based upon a flawed and limited perspective, we will only be able to see a dimly lit distortion of who we really are.

Our true self is who we are in Christ, but the mirror of our belief often reflects a very different image. If our belief is accurate, then the mirror will reflect this. But if our belief is impure, we will mistake these distortions for negative personal qualities. The perception we have of ourselves (our "self-identity") is simply an outcome of what we believe to be true. We are only able to see ourselves in the flawed and limited reflection that our beliefs reveal. We are unable to see all that is really there, and the little that we do see often misrepresents who we really are. We only "know in part" (1 Corinthians 13:12) what God sees accurately and fully.

Thankfully, when we are "face-to-face" with Christ, we will rightly know who we are, which, according to Scripture, is who we have always been. We will view ourselves as we "have been fully known" by Him. When the Apostle wrote the words, *I will know fully just as I also have been fully known*" (1 Corinthians 13:12) he is saying, *"I will finally see myself the way that God has seen me all along!"*

God desires to correct our inaccurate self-understanding so that we see ourselves the way He sees us. He wants us to have an accurate understanding of who we really are. And when the glory of His finished work in us is revealed, we will "rejoice and be overjoyed" (1 Peter 4:13)! As our "mirror" is cleaned and polished, it will more accurately reflect what has been true since we first believed.

We perceive God the way we do because of what we believe to be true.

This same dynamic applies to our perception of God. We are unable to see all of who He is, and our interpretation of what we do see may not be entirely accurate. We are only able to see that which our "mirror" allows us to see. If the light emitted is too dim, or the impurities too obstructive, then we will be unable to see the truth of who He really is. For instance, if God ever seems cold, absent, or uninterested, then your perception of Him is a skewed and incomplete reflection of His true identity and nature. For He truly is loving, close, involved, and invested!

God has expressed His heart and intentions, but because of our flawed and limited perspective, our ability to enjoy Him and rest in His finished work is diminished. We may know the truth in our heads, but until we also believe it in our hearts, we will continue to misinterpret His words and actions. He loves us, cares for us, and is with us wherever we go, but due to our beliefs and misinterpretation, our experience often does not reflect this reality. We perceive what we believe.

Here again, God wants us to know the truth. He wants us to know who He really is and what He's really like. When we see Him rightly and realize His intimate involvement in our daily lives, we will experientially know that He knows all, sees all, and is in complete control. Until we are convinced of this reality, it will not *seem* true from our perspective.

The image in our "mirror" will not improve without addressing the lack of light and the imperfect reflective surface. We cannot see ourselves or God clearly without first addressing our limited and flawed perspectives. We are only able to "see" what we believe.

The truth is the truth regardless of what we believe.

It is not good that we have been deceived into believing things that are untrue, but, thankfully, our belief in something does not make that "something" true. You may genuinely believe that you have won the lottery, but if your ticket doesn't match the winning numbers, you will not receive the prize in spite of your fervent conviction. The truth is the truth regardless of what we believe.

We have all had moments in which we were utterly convinced of a "fact" only to find out later that we were wrong. Our beliefs do not determine reality, but they do produce what we perceive. Believing that God is distant or unloving does not push Him away or change His affection for us. He is who He says He is (Exodus 3:14), and what He says is the truth (Psalm 119:160). Likewise, if you believe you have no value, you are not seeing clearly. And if you believe that you are alone, you fail to see the truth of God's presence. If you have been "saved through faith" (Ephesians 2:8), but feel shameful when you think about past sins, this does not mean that God has not completely forgiven you and "taken your sins away" (see 1 John 3:5). It simply means that you do not yet believe the truth.

There are billions of opinions, but only God's perspective is both complete and accurate. The way God sees things is the way things are. Some of what we believe may *reflect* the truth, but none of us are able to perceive the whole truth, and a sizable portion of what we are able to see is either a misinterpretation or entirely inaccurate.

If our perspectives align with God's, then we have interpreted our situation rightly. If our opinion differs from God's, then our opinion is wrong. God's perspective is not subjective; it is the absolute, authoritative, objective truth. And His truth is THE truth regardless of what you believe.

Surely every believer would agree that God's description of Himself is more accurate than our perceptions of Him. No matter how clear or complete our perceptions may *seem*, if we "see" God differently than He claims to be, then our perceptions are wrong. Likewise, if we do not "see" ourselves the way God sees us, then the perception we have of ourselves is limited and flawed. As depicted by the optical illusion at the beginning of this chapter, we misinterpret reality and perceive what is not true.

Our perspectives "feel" and "seem" true to us.

Our perspectives will feel and seem true even when they are not. For instance, after checking-out at my local hardware store, I walked across the parking lot, opened the driver's side door of my vehicle, and sat down in my seat. Suddenly, a mocking voice behind me made it clear that my perception was flawed. "Hey man, what are you doing? This ain't your car!" I turned around to see the confused faces of two young boys who were waiting for their parents. This was obviously not my car! Thankfully, it was clear to everyone involved that this was not a case of attempted theft and kidnapping. We all laughed as I exited their vehicle and tried to remember where I had parked.

The *fact* that it wasn't my car had no impact on my experience until I *knew* that it wasn't my car. The consequences of my belief in a lie were much the same as if the lie was true. It *seemed* as though the car was mine, and I acted as though it was mine. My perception seemed true to me until it was corrected by two startled boys.

If we believe something is true, it will seem true to us, even if it is not. You may intellectually know that Jesus said He would be with you "even to the end of the age," but if you believe in your heart that you are alone, this inaccurate perception will *feel* and *seem* true. If God seems to be unloving, then your perception is flawed even though it *feels* true. If your situation appears to be out of control, then you are misinterpreting it even though it *seems* as though you are seeing clearly.

The accuracy of our perspective has no impact whatsoever on how true it seems to us. Likewise, our belief and perception have no impact on whether or not something is actually true. Our perception of ourselves, others, God, and our situation will feel or seem true to us regardless of how "right" or "wrong" we are. The truth will remain true regardless of what feels or seems true to us.

For instance, before the advent of GPS navigation and smartphones, there were several occasions in which I would be driving somewhere, fully convinced I was heading the right direction, only to find out several minutes (or, dare I say, hours) later that I was moving further and further away from my intended destination. I recall one time in particular when my wife and I set out on a trip to Indiana. We were newlyweds and lived in central Kentucky, sandwiched in between Tennessee and Indiana. Once we made it to the interstate, we expected to drive northbound for about an hour to the Kentucky/Indiana border. But when we arrived at the state line, I was confused by a very large billboard that read, "WELCOME TO TENNESSEE." I immediately exclaimed, "This makes no sense! Why would they put this sign here?" I pulled over at the next exit to ask for help. I asked one of the locals, "Can you tell me where I am?" He replied, "Like the sign said, "Welcome to Tennessee." Truth is truth no matter what you feel or think about it. We were in Tennessee even though I was fully convinced that we were somewhere else. Up until that sobering discovery, it seemed as though I was driving in the right direction, and I felt confident in my progress, but the truth was the truth regardless.

Your perception will *feel* or *seem* true regardless of whether it is based upon a lie or God's perspective. If you are believing a lie, the actual truth will <u>not</u> *feel* or *seem* true because it is not in line with your belief. You perceive what you believe.

Part Three

"Truth-based problems" seem to be unsolved because our perspectives are limited.

When interpreting our circumstances, we often miss important details and fail to see the "big picture." What we see may be true, but it is not the whole truth. Because we lack a fuller understanding of our situation, our limited perception often seems problematic. In other words, our situation *seems* troubling because we lack a greater perspective.

A simple example of this would be any of the times one of my children would run up to me and describe their sibling's errant behavior. *"She just hit me!" "He's not sharing!" "They won't let me play!"* Each of these reports may be partially true, but they likely do not represent the whole story. Almost without exception, there are important details that are strategically omitted from their complaint.

For instance, if little Joshua complained to me about his sisters and their refusal to play with him, it might initially *seem* as though he is a victim of their selfish behavior. But if I investigate the matter further by asking *"Girls, what is going on? Joshua says you two aren't playing nicely."* they might respond by saying, *"Yeah, well, it's because he keeps throwing our dolls against the wall!"* This important bit of context brings clarification to the original complaint. If my perception of the situation is based solely upon *"they won't let me play,"* then I am unknowingly operating from a limited perspective. However, with the expanded perspective provided by my daughters, my viewpoint is expanded, and I am able to more appropriately respond to the situation.

Without the necessary details and context, it is impossible to correctly view our circumstances. We may accurately perceive the facts of what happens to us, but if we view them from a temporal, limited perspective, we will be unable to rightly interpret our situation. We may accurately see what is in front of us, but we will fail to appreciate the bigger picture.

To illustrate this concept further, consider the conflict between David and Goliath. For the most part, each combatant (as well as the onlooking troops) viewed the encounter accurately. It was obvious to everyone involved that an unarmored teenager was about to challenge a war-hardened soldier who was several times David's size. It was true that the giant was well-armed and experienced. It was also true that David was a mere shepherd boy. But these facts alone do not tell the whole story!

David was able to see a greater truth that offered the appropriate perspective by which to view the situation. He first acknowledged the obvious, "You come to me with a sword, a spear, and a saber," but David also attempted to expand everyone's perspective to include a greater truth, "I come to you in the name of the LORD of armies, the God of the armies of Israel, whom you have defied. This day <u>the LORD will hand you over to me</u>, and I will strike you and remove your head from you. Then I will give the dead bodies of the army of the Philistines this day to the birds of the sky and the wild animals of the earth, so that all the earth may know that there is a God in Israel, and that this entire assembly may know that the LORD does not save by sword or by spear; for <u>the battle is the LORD'S</u>, and <u>He will hand you over to us</u>" (1 Samuel 17:45-47, emphasis added).

The Israelites failed to realize this greater truth. They were unable to see God's solution to their problem. They viewed the giant rightly but misinterpreted their situation due to their lack of perspective. They weren't necessarily deceived, but they lacked important truths regarding God's involvement. Similarly, Goliath's perspective wasn't wrong or inaccurate. He was bigger, stronger, better equipped, and more experienced than David. The boy was no match for Goliath. But the towering Philistine doubted God's involvement, and his limited perspective had dire consequences!

David trusted God and rightly discerned the greater context of the conflict. It was not a battle between a young Israelite and a giant. In fact, it was not a battle at all! The God who created the universe was about to make an example of an ignorant Philistine. The Almighty had planned to place a defeated giant into the hands of a small sheep herder "so that all the earth may know that there is a God in Israel" (1 Samuel 17:46). Goliath didn't stand a chance!

In the same way, when we fail to see God's involvement in our lives, we inevitably misinterpret our situation through this limited perspective. It may be true that you were mistreated by someone, that you have unpaid debt on your credit card, that you lost your job, or that your spouse wants to divorce you, but that is only a partial description of the truth. This limited view of reality, however, will *appear* to be the whole truth (remember my tattling children) and will result in our perceiving seemingly unsolved problems (like the blasphemous giant).

If you find out that you have terminal cancer, this truth-based problem is not a figment of your imagination or the outcome of your being deceived. It really exists and has real consequences. But, just as with Goliath, if you view this problem through a limited and temporal perspective, you will not see God's involvement, intention, or plan. Without the greater context provided by an eternal perspective, your situation will seem problematic. The "giant" will seem to go unchallenged, and the problem will appear to be unsolved.

We are confronted by such truth-based problems when we face job loss, injuries, war, disease, physical maladies, poor choices, sinful behavior, injustices, the death of loved ones, and more. Due to our limited, temporal perspectives of these difficult realities, we often don't see God's involvement or His response to them, and these perceived problems seem to be unsolved and will remain problematic for us.

Just because we don't initially see God's involvement or the solutions that He offers, it does not mean that He is not involved or that His solutions are not available (just ask Goliath!). The truth is still the truth regardless of what we believe. We simply need to realize this greater perspective.

When we experience difficulty, we should seek God's perspective.

According to Jesus, we are to expect problems. He said, "In this world you will have trouble. . ." (John 16:33b NIV). He wants us to be aware of the fallen, sinful, troublesome world around us. But He doesn't want us to stop there. He also wants us to realize the "greater" or "additional" truth that He has solved these problems on our behalf. His complete statement was this, "I have told you these things, so that in me you may have peace. In this world you will have trouble. But take heart! I have overcome the world" (John 16:33 NIV, emphasis added). When we know in our hearts that He has "overcome the world," we will have "peace" in spite of our "troubles." One truth sheds light on a problem, and the other reveals the solution. If we are only aware of the "tribulation," we will be without the hope and peace that comes with knowing Christ's victory over it.

Perhaps an innocuous, real-world illustration might help to further explain this concept. On many occasions I have *blindly* searched for my eyeglasses while unknowingly wearing them on the top of my head. I had a genuine and legitimate truth-based problem in that I was practically blind! This was the truth and it had very real consequences. The longer I went without my glasses, the more I realized my need for them. But my problem remained only because I could not see the solution to it (literally!). I had a real problem and there was a real solution available, but due to my limited perception, my "blindness" remained.

If someone were to notice my predicament and draw my attention to the glasses on my head, I would immediately reach up and procure the solution to my problem. My glasses were freely available to me the entire time, but my limited perspective kept me from perceiving this reality and my blindness was prolonged. Much like the cowering Israelites, my limited perspective kept me from appropriating the solution that I already possessed, and my truth-based problem remained problematic.

WE NEED TO APPROPRIATE WHAT GOD HAS GIVEN TO US.

What we have described here is the concept of appropriation - the bringing into effect that which we already possess. I was in constant possession of my glasses but was walking around blindly. The moment that I realized what was resting on my head, I slid them down onto my face and could see clearly. As soon as I fully realized what I already had, I appropriated it. Even though I had a hard time seeing, I did not need glasses: I needed perspective.

According to Peter, God has "granted to us everything pertaining to life and godliness, through the true knowledge of Him who called us by His own glory and excellence" (2 Peter 1:2-3). Miles Stanford, the author of the great little book "Green Letters" said it this way, "Appropriation does not necessarily mean to gain something new but to set aside for our practical possession something that already belongs to us."

God has already given us everything we need for living our life in Christ; however, we need to appropriate what we have. Peter reveals to us how we are to do this by saying, "through the true knowledge of Him. . ." "True knowledge" is not something that we can choose or accomplish for ourselves. Like salvation, it is a free gift from God. We will discuss this in greater detail in a later chapter.

God wants us to know of His involvement and trust in His solutions.

This same dynamic applies to each of our "truth-based problems." The most consequential example of this is our sinful, unrighteous, depraved state-of-being and need for a Savior. This is a truth-based problem (if not THE greatest truth-based problem), and it has eternal consequences! According to God's word, you have violated His laws, dishonored His authority, and deserve punishment, death, and destruction (Matthew 25:46, James 2:10, Romans 3:23, 6:23, 2 Thessalonians 1:9, Jude 1:7, Revelation 14:11). This is the grave reality of your natural-born identity and sinful state of being.

This truth-based problem has only two satisfactory solutions. Either you can accept your just punishment or you can take advantage of "God's solution" to your problem. You can attempt to solve it yourself or allow God to solve it for you. Just as with every other genuine truth-based problem, God has made a solution freely available to us (Romans 5:15, 6:23). Much like when I was searching for my glasses, all we need to do is look up!

Since the Garden of Eden, God's people have faced one problem after another. But God has always been involved, providing His solutions to them. For example, consider the Israelites' journey out of Egypt. They were unable to escape their captivity and enslavement, but God had a miraculous plan to get them out (Exodus 7-12). Then, when they were seemingly trapped between the Red Sea and the advancing Egyptian army, God offered a solution that no one could have expected (Exodus 14). When they were out of supplies and in need of food and water, God provided (Exodus 16-17; Numbers 11:19-35, 20:10-13). God's people were entirely unable to meet these genuine needs on their own; they needed God's solutions to their truth-based problems. We are often in this same predicament!

Having read their history and knowing how God solved their problems, we might want to travel back in time and shout, "*Silly Israelites, do you not realize that God is able to pull you out of Egypt, part the Red Sea, bring down manna from Heaven, send enough quail to feed millions of people, and even pour water out of a stone? Where is your faith?*" Yet, with their current heavenly perspective, they might ask us the same questions!

God is involved in every aspect of our lives and can meet any challenge that we face, even when it doesn't seem that way from our perspective. But if we are not yet convinced of this reality in our hearts, it will not *seem* true to us. We will be unable to see and accept His solutions to our truth-based problems. The "giants" we face will continue to *seem* unchallenged until we are able to view them through the correct "eyeglasses."

He desires to expand our limited perspectives so that we will see, appreciate, and ultimately appropriate what He offers. He wants us to experience His love, feel His closeness, and see His involvement in our lives. When we are able to see the big picture from His eternal perspective, we will appropriate what was ours all along and finally find rest in His finished work.

If nothing else, we need to realize that even our biggest, most troublesome problems are being worked together for our good (Romans 8:28). No matter how difficult, overwhelming, or devastating our circumstances appear to be, they rest securely in the hand of a loving God. When we are fully convinced of this reality, like David, we will view our "Goliaths" as nothing more than opportunities for God to glorify Himself and showcase His character.

Part Four

We perceive "lie-based problems" because our perspectives are flawed.

The problems we perceive are usually not the result of our lack of truth, but rather, they are the consequence of our belief in a lie. We come to wrong conclusions about ourselves, our situation, or even God Himself, which cause us to view ourselves as being worthless or helpless, God as being distant or cruel, or our situation as being out of control or hopeless. Though these flawed perspectives are not true, they will *feel* and *seem* true to those who believe them to be true.

In other words, because of our flawed perspectives, we perceive that which does not even exist: a false "reality" that contradicts and opposes the true reality that God created. We will perceive and experience a world of our own making. By definition, this flawed "reality" is imaginary, but it will *feel* or *seem* true to us, and we will be forced to face the problems it creates. The consequences of this are very real indeed!

To illustrate this concept, think of a little girl who genuinely believes a monster lives under her bed. Because of this lie-based belief, the child will perceive her room as unsafe, and she will likely have trouble falling asleep, or even staying in bed for that matter! The fact that no monster actually resides in her room has little-to-no impact on her whatsoever. There may as well be one lurking around because, from her perspective, many of the consequences would be the same.

Her inaccurate belief and flawed perspective create problems for her. She must contend with these problems until she comes to believe the truth. While she remains deceived, she may form behaviors or perform rituals that seem necessary for her safety. She may pile dozens of stuffed animals onto her bed to keep her company and beg for her parents to keep the lights on throughout the night. These desperate acts are completely unnecessary and unfounded since they "solve" a nonexistent problem. She simply needs to know the truth; she is safe; there is no monster under her bed.

The same is true for each of us! No matter how realistic and threatening our lie-based problems seem, they are not real. For example, perceived problems such as "I have no value" are not true. This is proven by God's words that were spoken by His Son when Jesus said, "Are not two sparrows sold for a penny? Yet not one of them will fall to the ground outside your Father's care. And even the very hairs of your head are all numbered. So don't be afraid; you are worth more than many sparrows" (Matthew 10:29-31 NIV). In spite of this, if you have been deceived into believing that you have no value, this skewed version of reality will *seem* true to you, and you will have to face the consequences of believing in this "monster."

These lie-based problems stem from our hearts being deceived into believing things that are untrue and then misinterpreting our situation through these lie-based beliefs. When we believe lies about ourselves, God, or our situation, we will inevitably perceive some sort of lie-based problem. Beliefs such as "I am defective," "I am unlovable," or "I am stupid," create problems related to your _self-identity_, whereas beliefs like, "I am trapped," "I am alone," and "my situation is out of control," describe problems that you perceive regarding your _state of being_ and God's involvement in your life. (We *will elaborate on these two forms of lie-based heart beliefs later*.)

These lie-based beliefs are reflected in our flawed perspectives. For instance, if you believe that you are alone, then it will seem as though you are alone; even though the Lord is with you always (see Matthew 28:20). If you believe that you are defective, then it will seem as though you are defective even though you were "awesomely and wonderfully made" (Psalm 139:14). If you believe that your situation is out of control, this skewed perspective of reality will seem true even though it is not (Romans 8:28, Jeremiah 29:11, Proverbs 16:4). These perceived problems will seem true as long as we continue believing the lies that produce them.

Just as the scared child from the illustration formed tactics to address her imaginary monster, we too devise solutions to the problems that our beliefs create. The little girl's behavior resulted from believing that she would be safe if she buried herself deep enough in a pile of toys. Likewise, we respond to our lie-based problems in ways that we *believe* will help, and we continue those behaviors when they *seem* to work. Just like the scared little girl, all we need is the truth.

If we knew the truth regarding who we are and who God is, as well as His intimate involvement in our lives, most of the problems we currently face would seem to disappear. They are no more than figments of our imagination. This is not to say that we are purposefully creating these problems (for we are not!); they are simply the result of our flawed perspectives. Like the imagined monster living under the bed, our lie-based perceived problems only seem real because we believe that they are real. If we knew the truth, these lies would have no impact on us.

The consequences of our lie-based problems are very real.

It is important to restate that if you believe lies, the consequences will be pretty much the same as if they were true. Your beliefs not only impact your perceptions, they also directly influence what you feel and choose to do. If you believe a lie such as "I am unwanted," "I can't do anything right," or "I am a disappointment," it will impact your life just as much as if it were true. Your perception of yourself, your situation, and God will all reflect this lie-based belief.

If you believe that you are unlovable, it will seem as though you are unlovable, you will feel as though you are unlovable, and this perspective will also obviously interfere with your relationships.

These negative effects are just a few of the very real consequences of believing something that is not true. Your being unlovable is a lie-based perceived problem that is not true, real, or legitimate, but the problematic consequences it creates are very real indeed!

WHAT IF JESUS DIDN'T KNOW WHO HE WAS?

To illustrate a few key points in this discussion, we would like to encourage you to answer a few questions and then consider a hypothetical scenario. Read the following questions and consider your answers carefully. According to what we find in Scripture:

1. Was Jesus the Son of God? [ ] Yes [ ] No
2. Was Jesus loved by His Heavenly Father? [ ] Yes [ ] No
3. Did Jesus have uninhibited fellowship with God? [ ] Yes [ ] No
4. Did Jesus possess the Spirit of God? [ ] Yes [ ] No
5. Did Jesus' heart reflect God's character? [ ] Yes [ ] No
6. Was Jesus as holy as God is holy? [ ] Yes [ ] No
7. Did Jesus have a special purpose? [ ] Yes [ ] No

Hopefully, your answer to each of these questions was, "Yes, of course!" But take a moment to consider the following **heretical hypotheticals**:

1. What if Jesus <u>didn't know</u> that all of these things were true?
2. What if Jesus was aware of these claims but <u>didn't fully believe</u> them to be true?
3. What if He <u>believed lies</u> that were contrary to these truths?

We know we are stepping into some seemingly murky waters, but it is for the purpose of making an important point. Obviously, Jesus knows the truth, He is the truth (John 14:6), and He cannot be deceived. Nevertheless, would any of these impossible scenarios change Jesus' true identity, value, or purpose? Would they cause His Heavenly Father to love Him less? Would they provoke the Holy Spirit to leave Him? Would they result in Jesus becoming less-than-holy? No, on all counts!

But think of the dramatic impact that any of these hypothetical scenarios would have on Jesus' perception of Himself, His Father, and the world around Him. His ministry would suffer, His relationships would be strained, and His prayer life would likely feel empty and fruitless. The truth would still be the truth, it just wouldn't *feel* or *seem* true to Him.

Although these scenarios may seem uncomfortable to imagine, we propose that they paint a vivid picture of the average believer. For each of the truths that were listed above and attributed to Jesus are also true for each of those who believe in Him and possess His Spirit. Clearly, none of us are God's "one and only Son" as Jesus is (John 3:16), but if you are born of God's Holy Spirit, then, like Jesus, you are a holy (*hagiois*) child of God deeply loved by your Heavenly Father and living in uninhibited fellowship with Him (John 1:12, Romans 1:7, 8:14, Galatians 3:26, Hebrews 4:16, 1 John 3:1).

If any of these truths fail to *feel* or *seem* true, this doesn't make them untrue, it simply means that you do not yet *fully* believe them. If you were fully convinced of your identity in Christ, it would *seem* true to you. If you completely believed that you are loved and accepted by Him, this reality would *feel* true. You do not yet fully *perceive* the truth because you do not yet fully *believe* the truth. God wants you to see yourself, Him, and the world around you from His perspective. For when you are able to view your life from His vantage point, you will know fully, just as you have been fully known (1 Corinthians 13:12).

A lie that "feels" true indicates our need for God's perspective.

There are obvious and genuine consequences to our lie-based problems, but these perceived problems are not the actual problem we face. In fact, our problem is not even the fact that we have been deceived. Our real problem is that we lack God's perspective. We need the truth. If we knew the truth and had His perspective, we would realize that the lie-based problems we perceive are nothing but figments of our imagination.

Regardless of what you believe, you are not worthless. You have great value! But if you believe that you are worthless, it will *seem* or *feel* as though you are worthless. The "reality" of your worthlessness is not your real problem (because the truth is you have great value), but neither is the fact that you have been deceived into believing that you are worthless. For even if someone could magically erase that belief from your heart and mind, would you then know your great value? No! You would still lack God's perspective. This is our real problem: we lack God's perspective.

Remember, whatever you believe will *feel* or *seem* true to you. Because of this, if a lie such as, "I am abandoned," "I am dirty and shameful," or "my situation is hopeless," *feels* true, then this indicates that you believe it in your heart to be true. And the fact that you believe a lie indicates your need for God's perspective. Thus, if a lie-based belief or untrue thought *seems* or *feels* true, this indicates your need for God's perspective. Likewise, if a truth (such as the reality of your value, God's love for you, or the security you have in His finished work) does not *seem* or *feel* true, then you do not yet fully believe it in your heart and have likely been deceived into believing something contrary to it. This too indicates your need for God's perspective.

Part Five

God wants to solve our perceived problems.

God desires to correct our inaccurate, flawed perspectives. He wants us to know the truth. When we know the truth, the problems that were created by the lies we believed dissolve, and we can rightly view them as imaginary, unfounded, and unsubstantiated (just as they always have been). And we will find rest and peace, knowing that the "monsters" under our beds were never real.

The thought, "I am worthless" has no impact on you if you know the truth in your heart. If you know how to gain God's perspective (which we will discuss in detail later), then it is a good thing to be made aware of this need! So, we encourage you to view the moment you realize that you have been deceived as a good thing. We are not saying that *believing lies* is good but *realizing* that you believe them is. Moments such as these represent opportunities for you to gain God's perspective!

The consequences of our flawed and limited perceptions are worked together for our good. They show us something very important; we need God's perspective! If it wasn't for the negative effects of believing a lie or missing a truth, we would never know that we need His help. They are designed to point you in His direction.

Remember, just because it feels like you are dirty, worthless, or defective, doesn't mean that you are any of these things. It just means that you don't yet see yourself the way He sees you. If your situation seems out of control or hopeless, it doesn't mean that this assessment is true. These perceptions are simply reflective of what you believe. When you have His perspective, the truth will *seem* and *feel* true to you, and you will effortlessly walk in it. Your perceptions will finally reflect reality and you will see yourself the way He sees you and appreciate Him for who He really is.

God has solved (or promised to solve) all of our problems.

We face problems that need to be solved every day, but not all our perceived problems are real. Many are simply a consequence of our flawed perspectives. We have been led to believe that we have problems that do not even exist. We believe that we are worthless even though we have value, we think we are alone even though He is with us, and we've been led to believe that God is angry with us even though those who have been justified by His Son's blood have also been saved from His wrath (Romans 5:8-9). God has promised to "solve" these problems by convincing us of the truth (John 16:13).

We are often misguided in our responses to truth-based problems as well, for many of them are not ours to solve. Trivial problems such as removing a stain from a shirt, needing to cut the grass, figuring out what to cook for dinner, cleaning up after the dog got into the trash, or even having to deal with a troublesome coworker are essentially ours to address (although they would be rather difficult for us if God did not first give us breath!). But many of the important and pressing issues we face are actually God's responsibility.

Thankfully, God either *has* solved or *will* solve all of our real problems. He typically allows us to solve our "shirt" and "dinner" problems ourselves, but He has promised to take care of most other issues. However, even if we clearly see and understand these problems, if we fail to realize God's solution to them, it will seem as though we are without hope, and we will likely search for ways to "solve" them ourselves.

In these instances, we do not need God to solve our problems; we need to realize that He already has! Our truth-based problems only seem problematic because we have yet to fully be convinced of God's involvement and purposes. When we see both our problem and His solution from His perspective, our hopelessness turns to confidence and gratitude.

To illustrate this concept further, consider the fact that every one of us has sinned (broken God's laws and failed to meet His standard of perfection) and is entirely incapable of fixing this problem (Romans 3:23). This is the truth, and this truth is a problem. It is incredibly important for you to discover this truth as quickly as possible! For if you are unaware of your sin problem or disagree with

God in this matter, you are destined for eternal destruction since "the truth is not in you" (1 John 1:8). Even if you are aware of your sin problem, if you do not yet know God's gracious and satisfactory solution to this problem, you are no better off.

God has freely offered His Son, Jesus, to be sacrificed on our behalf and to become "the propitiation (atoning sacrifice) for your sins; and not for yours only, but also for the sins of the whole world" (1 John 2:2, emphasis added). Christ's death is a sufficient sacrifice for every sin that was, is, or will ever be committed by every person who has ever lived or will live on this planet (John 3:16, 2 Corinthians 5:19).

Jesus has already done everything necessary for us to be saved, but most people still do not believe Him. They either simply have not heard this or have been deceived into believing lies about Him and their sinful state. God wants everyone to have a change of mind (Biblical Greek: "*metanoia*") that leads to eternal life (2 Peter 3:9), but only those who believe Him in their heart will be saved (John 3:15, Mark 16:16). Those who do not believe will be condemned even though Christ died for them (Romans 5:8, 2 Corinthians 5:14-15).

Christ died for those who were to become the first century church while they were still sinners (Romans 5:8), and He died for you thousands of years before you were born. Because of this, you do not need Him to solve your sin problem, you need to realize that He already has. What you now need is to believe what He has said about your sin problem and His solution to it is true. Simply put, we must agree with God that we had a problem and that He has solved it. To do anything else is to remain in deception and refuse this life-giving gift. When we believe in our hearts that He has done for us what He said He did, we are forgiven and are born again as new creations in Christ.

Listen again to what Jesus said regarding your sin problem, "the one who hears My word, and believes Him who sent Me, has eternal life, and does not come into judgment, but has passed out of death into life" (John 5:24). In this instance, if you believe the truth (i.e., agree with God's perspective) regarding your desperate need for Jesus' perfect sacrifice, then you have eternal life and will not face judgment; but if you do not believe the truth (or believe something other than what God has said is true), then you do not have eternal life and will face judgment.

We also see this emphasis on belief in the life of Abraham. He trusted that God would do what He said since he was "fully assured that what God had promised, He was also able to perform" (Romans 4:21). God's faithfulness and promises were true regardless of Abraham's beliefs, but since he was "fully assured" of these truths, it was "credited to him as righteousness" (Romans 4:21-22).

Just like Abraham, we are "saved through faith" (Romans 4:3, Ephesians 2:8). Because of this, unbelievers will face God's judgment not because they lacked a Savior but because they lacked "faith" in their Savior. A person's sin problem remains problematic only if he disagrees with God about it. But if this person comes into agreement with God (Biblical Greek: "*homologeo*") regarding his sin problem as well as his God-given Savior, he will be saved (Romans 10:9-11). Understanding this concept also brings hope and clarity when applied to our other perceived problems.

For instance, if you are faced with a problem that seems to be unsolved, it is not because you "lack a Savior," but simply means you lack perspective. You do not yet rightly see His involvement. For instance (and hear us out), you do not need Jesus to die for your sins (since He has already done so); rather, you need to "believe in your heart that God has raised Him from the dead" (Romans 10:9).

Now, take this concept and apply it to the following examples:

You don't need God to bless you (for He already does); rather, you need to *realize* that He already has "blessed us with every spiritual blessing" (Ephesians 1:3).

You don't need Him to provide for your needs (for He already does); rather, you need to *realize* the fact that "God shall supply all your needs according to His riches in glory in Christ Jesus" (Philippians 4:19).

You don't need Him to guide your steps (for He already does); rather, you need to *realize* the reality that He establishes every step you take (Proverbs 16:9).

You don't need Him to be with you (for He already is); rather, you need to *realize* that He has promised to be "with you always, to the end of the age" (Matthew 28:20).

You don't need Him to rescue you from darkness (for He already has); you need to *realize* that He has already transferred you into the kingdom of His beloved Son (Colossians 1:13-14).

You don't need Him to sanctify you (for He already has); rather, you need to *realize* that you have been "sanctified through the offering of the body of Jesus Christ once for all time" (Hebrews 10:10).

You don't need Him to make you holy (for He already has); rather, you need to *realize* that you share your Heavenly Father's nature and possess His Spirit (John 1:12-13, 3:5-6, 1 Peter 1:23, 2:9, Revelation 22:11).

Hopefully, you are beginning to see a pattern here...

Despite how it may seem, you do not have unfulfilled needs or unsolved problems. If it *seems* as though you do, this is because you have a flawed perspective or simply fail to see His promised involvement (2 Peter 1:3-4). In either case, your real problem is a *belief* problem; you lack God's perspective. God wants you to know the truth about your problems (example: 1 John 1:10), but He also wants you to have His perspective so that you can see His solutions to them (example: 1 John 1:9). Knowing the truth (agreeing with God) brings freedom (John 8:32). This book is meant to equip you to cooperate with God for this very purpose!

CHAPTER 5

THE "BELIEF AND EMOTION" PRINCIPLE

"WE FEEL WHAT WE BELIEVE."

Part One

We feel what we believe.

Imagine that you are asleep in your bed when you are abruptly woken up by the sound of broken glass hitting the floor in the room next to you. No one in your household is typically up this late at night. You believe that someone has broken into your home! As soon as this thought crosses your mind, what do you feel? Scared? Nervous? Worried? Helpless? Vulnerable? You push through what you feel and muster up the nerve to investigate the sound. As you peer around the corner, you notice a shadowy figure moving in the center of the room. The unidentified looter is rustling through something on the floor. You turn on the lights to identify the culprit and make a discouraging but welcome discovery. There is no burglar! The sound you heard came from your clumsy dog rummaging through the kitchen trash. The glass of a broken bottle lay on the floor. Although you now must deal with the dog and the mess that it made, you know you are safe. Upon making this discovery, what do you feel? Relieved? Safe? Thankful? Angry at the dog? The vulnerable emotions that were present just moments ago now seem to evaporate and are replaced with feelings of relief. You felt one way when you were woken up by the sound but felt something completely different when you saw your dog. Why did this shift in emotion take place? You did not decide to feel afraid, nor did you decide to feel relieved, you simply felt the emotional consequences of your belief. We refer to this important concept as the "Belief and Emotion" Principle.

As we previously discussed, our minds act as interpreters that examine our surroundings, refer to what we've learned from past experiences, and offer us explanations for what seems to be happening. Our minds also use our beliefs to determine how we will emotionally respond to this interpretation. In the previous illustration your emotionally charged reaction was not to the sound itself; you were reacting to what you *believed* that sound potentially meant.

Your mind assessed the situation ("*I heard something.*"), used what you have learned from past experiences to interpret and explain what might be happening ("*It sounded just like glass hitting the floor. It might be from a broken door or window. Someone might be breaking into my home!*"), and determined how you will respond emotionally ("*I might be in danger and I am afraid.*"). You felt what you felt as a result of your interpretation of what you heard. This mental process of association and interpretation is what created your perception and produced your emotional response.

When you saw your dog digging through the opened trash bag, your interpretation and perception of the situation changed (the sound I heard was probably that bottle breaking, and it broke because of what my dog is doing). Since you believed you were safe (your dog, not a burglar, was responsible for the noise you heard), you no longer felt afraid, but rather secure, relieved, and, perhaps, a bit frustrated. Throughout the scenario your emotions reflected what you believed. This is why we say, "We feel whatever we believe."

Our emotions are the result of our mind's interpretation which is based upon what we believe to be true. We are not emotionally reacting to what is *actually happening*, we feel what we feel because of what we *believe is happening* and what we believe that *means*.

For instance, in the previous illustration, your initial belief may have caused you to feel nervous and on alert, but it did not indicate the truth. Was your home *actually* being broken into? Maybe, maybe not. You *believed* that it was, so you reacted accordingly. Likewise, when you discovered your dog rummaging through the trash, your emotions shifted to reflect what you *believed this discovery meant*. Was your dog *actually* responsible for the noise you heard? Probably. But it is also possible that a criminal was hiding in the shadows of the adjacent room as you cleaned up the mess! In either case, your emotions are simply an expression of your *belief* regarding who woke you from your sleep.

This distinction may seem minor, but it has far-reaching implications. Many people assume that they feel what they feel because of what is happening to them at that moment. They blame their emotional reactions on what others do or say or on their plight in life. They say things like, "she makes me happy," "he makes me so mad," "my work stresses me out," "that really scared me," or "I am having a really bad day." They mistakenly assume that their emotional status is determined by others or their situation, as though someone or something can "make" you feel something.

Even though you have an emotional reaction immediately after someone does or says something to you, it is not a result of what that person did or said; you are reacting to your *interpretation* of what you *believe* just happened. This is why it is possible for a group of people to have different emotional reactions to the same situation. Think about it; why does flying in an airplane seem enjoyable for some but terrifying for others? Why does the thought of a family reunion evoke positive emotions in some but feelings of panic, anxiety, and anger in others? It all boils down to belief and interpretation!

Imagine that two people board a roller coaster together and sit next to each other. As their safety harnesses lock into place, they both hear an audible "click." One of them believes the sound indicates that the locking mechanism is now engaged while the other believes it was the sound of something breaking. As they ascend the first of many drops, one of them is excited while the other begins to panic. Even though they are on the same ride and heard the same sound, their emotional reactions are drastically different! Their emotional state is determined by what they believed to be true when they heard the "click."

The reality is they are either safe, or they are in danger. In either case, one of them is right, and the other one is wrong. But each person's current perspective will *feel* and *seem* true to them regardless of what the truth actually is. If the ride truly was perfectly safe, this truth will have no impact on the panicked rider who continues to *believe* that he is in danger. On the other hand, if their safety harnesses genuinely were faulty, and they were risking serious injury or even death, this would not dampen the enjoyment of the rider who fully *believes* that he is safe. Ignorance is bliss after all! But, if the rider who currently has the flawed perspective comes to believe the truth of the situation, then his emotions will change to reflect this shift in belief.

Since they each feel what they feel as a result of their interpretation of the sound they both heard, it would be a mistake for either of them to blame their emotions on the roller coaster. Neither the ride nor the sounds it makes is causing them to feel anything. If the sound *didn't mean* anything to them, they wouldn't feel anything in response. But because it *did mean* something (from their perspectives), they had an emotional reaction to it.

In the same way, our emotions are not the result of what happens to us, they are the result of what we believe those things *mean*. When we encounter something that *means* something "bad" (from our perspective), we have a negative emotional response to it. If it seems to *mean* something "good" (again, from our perspective), we will feel some measure of positive emotion in response. We will feel whatever we believe.

All of this takes me back to the abuse victims I tried to help before the development of TPM. Their emotional pain was not a result of their abuse nor was it caused by their memory of the genuine hardship that they had to endure. Their emotional pain was coming from what they believed. Their present perception of themselves and their perceived state of being was the source of their pain. They felt trapped, out of control, dirty, and worthless because they believed in their hearts this was true. When the Holy Spirit convinced their hearts of the truth, their emotions immediately changed to reflect the truth.

WE DO NOT FEEL WHAT WE REMEMBER.

Some have suggested that our "troubled past" or "painful memories" are the reason for why we feel what we feel. They claim that our emotions flow from what we remember or are stored in our memories themselves. But these theories are based on a misunderstanding of the relationship between what we feel and what we remember.

For a moment, imagine that you are flipping through an old family photo album. It contains page after page of pictures that memorialize your life up to this point. Some of the images seem to make you smile while others leave you feeling embarrassed and uncomfortable. Why is that? The photo album obviously does not *make you feel* what you feel. Your mind is associating what you are seeing with past experiences and interpreting it through what you learned from those experiences. Your feelings are a result of this interpretation; you feel what you *believe*.

In the same way that these photographs do not make us feel anything when we look at them, our memories of life experiences are not to blame for the pain we currently feel. We do not have "painful" memories anymore than we have "painful" photo albums. We may feel pain while flipping through the album, just as we might feel badly when we remember past experiences, but neither "makes us feel" anything. Rather, we interpret what we remember from our past through what we believe in the present. This belief-based interpretation is the source of what we feel.

The photographs are not to blame for the emotion you feel when you look at them. In the same way, your memories are not the source of your emotional pain. Like a photo album, your memories are simply the mental documentation of your journey so far. You feel what you feel as a result of how you are interpreting what you remember. *We do not feel what we remember; we feel what we believe.*

This principle not only applies to the perception you have of your past and present, but it also applies to your thoughts on the future. For instance, do you feel anxious or worried while thinking about your uncertain future? If so, this emotional response is not determined by what might happen; rather, it reflects what you *believe* about what might happen. Your perception of your potential future is the outcome of what you believe to be true. And your emotional status corresponds with those beliefs.

We do not feel what we feel because of what has happened to us in the past, what is happening to us in the present, or what might happen to us in the future. We interpret all three through what we currently believe and respond emotionally based upon this interpretation.

No one makes us feel anything.

As we have discussed, many people make the mistake of blaming their emotions on their circumstances, the people around them, their difficult past, the devil, or even God, but making this assumption inevitably leaves you in a troublesome predicament. If this misconception was actually true, then your emotional state is entirely at the mercy of your situation and the people around you. From this flawed perspective, agreeable circumstances would seem to allow you to feel positive emotions, but if even one aspect of your situation fails to cooperate, it will "rob" you of your joy and disrupt your peace.

By blaming those around us for causing us to feel what we feel, we unknowingly put ourselves in an emotional prison. If it were true that the actions of others were the actual source of our emotional pain, then we would be doomed to continue feeling what we feel until everything around us changes. This perspective forces us to live in a world in which there is no hope for positive change without the cooperation of everyone and everything in it. In this alternate reality, we must beg or force others to act in accordance to what we believe will make us happy. It is probably safe to assume that each of us knows someone who has attempted to accomplish this impossible task!

This dynamic is on full display in the lives of small children. We do not have to teach little ones to blame one another for why they are upset. They all do it. It is natural and expected, but it is also based upon a lie. If a little boy walked up to his little sister and grabbed a toy from her hand, the little girl would likely become upset, and if you were to ask her why she is distraught, she would probably point her angry little finger at her brother and say, "Because he took my toy!"

Little Suzie is not upset *because* Johnny took her toy. She is upset as a result of how that event was interpreted through her flawed and limited perspective. She may believe that she is powerless, helpless, and neglected, and it may seem to her that Johnny is getting by with what he did. As a result, Suzie is upset.

Now, just because Johnny's behavior is *not* to blame for Suzie's outburst, it doesn't mean that what he did was innocent. Johnny's actions may have been wrong, hateful, and inexcusable. If so, he is responsible for his poor choices, and he deserves to be disciplined and corrected. But his bad behavior is not the source of little Suzie's emotional pain. She feels what she believes.

This is another instance where we intuitively understand a portion of the truth. It is highly unlikely that any of us would feel what Suzie feels if Johnny were to take a toy from us. Why is this? We react differently because, in this specific example, we have a different perspective than that of a child. We would perceive his actions through a different lens. We are better equipped to rightly interpret the situation because we have a better handle on the truth.

And yet, how many times have we fallen into the trap of blaming those around us for the pain that we feel? We attempt to cast blame on our spouse, our job, our family history, our economic standing, or even God Himself. Doing so is no different than blaming a roller coaster for making you afraid or accusing little Johnny of making you cry.

If you continue to blame others or your situation for what you feel, you are doomed to an irresolvable cycle of defeat and disappointment. Worse yet, you will *likely* attempt to resolve the problem yourself by running from what you believe to be the source of your pain, self-medicating by distracting yourself from what you feel, or simply giving up altogether. You may run but you will discover that when you get to your new location, your same lie-based beliefs will be there when you arrive, and you will eventually feel the same. Again, if others or your situation are truly the reason you feel what you feel, you are helpless to feel differently unless others or your situation changes. There is no hope of freedom while operating from this flawed perspective.

Peace and freedom do not come as a result of blame-shifting and accusations. If we want lasting relief from our stress, anxiety, worry, and fear, we must first accurately determine why the negative emotions are present. You do not feel worried because of your uncertain future, you do not feel out of control because of your kids, you do not feel alone because of your spouse, you do not feel stressed because of your finances, and you do not feel angry because of your parents. Regardless of your circumstances or the people involved, you only ever feel what you believe. When properly understood, this principle offers hope, encouragement, and freedom. The fact that you feel what you believe means that no person or circumstance can *make you feel* anything! You feel what you believe.

Part Two

We feel what we believe in our "hearts."

We feel what we believe, but not all that we believe produces emotion. In fact, most of it does not. For instance, how does believing that "two plus two equals four" make you feel? Probably nothing. The data, facts, figures, and the general understanding that we each use throughout our lives do not cause us to feel anything. But this is not solely due to the subject matter; rather, these beliefs fail to cause us to feel anything due to *how* they are believed. Or, to put it another way, it is due to *where* they are believed.

In Scripture, the Biblical Greek word "nous" is often used to describe our minds. We use our "nous" to think, perceive, understand, and reason. In more current terms, that which we believe with our "nous" is believed in our "heads." Although the information stored in our "heads" may be useful and even reflect the truth, it is not the only place where we believe things, nor is it the source for what we feel. Our emotions appear to come from somewhere else. We feel what we feel because of what we believe in our "hearts."

A simple example of this concept can be found in the final chapter of Luke's gospel. Shortly after Jesus' resurrection, two of His disciples were discussing the disappointing fate of their Redeemer as they left Jerusalem and were traveling to the village known as "Emmaus" (Luke 24:13-35). As they are talking, Jesus shows up and begins walking with them, but He prevents them from recognizing His true identity. He then asks them what they are talking about (as though He didn't already know). The two of them are initially shocked at the stranger's apparent ignorance regarding what has just happened in Jerusalem, but they go on to describe the details of Jesus' identity, purpose, unjust conviction, and eventual death. And as they are offering a report of how some of the women visited the now empty tomb, Jesus abruptly responds, "How unwise and <u>slow you are to believe in your hearts</u> all that the prophets have spoken! Didn't the Messiah have to suffer these things and enter into His glory?" (Luke 24:22-26 HCSB, emphasis added).

It was clear that these disciples had a solid understanding of the "facts," as they were able to recite them to their fellow traveler. They saw the indications that Jesus was the Redeemer of Israel and understood that He was to rise from the dead on the third day (Luke 24:21). They had even heard that His tomb was verifiably empty (24:22-24). They knew the truth in their "heads," but it was obvious to Jesus that they did not yet believe the truth in their "hearts" (Luke 24:25).

Jesus pointed out their problem; they were slow to believe in their hearts. Then He exposed the fact that their intellectual understanding of Scripture was not enough when He asked the rhetorical question, "Didn't the Messiah have to suffer these things and enter into His glory?" They already knew what the prophets had said regarding the Messiah, and Jesus knew that they knew. He was essentially asking them, "Why is it taking so long for your hearts to believe what you already know in your heads?"

Although they believed the truth in their "heads," they felt disappointed and discouraged in response to His death. They felt what they felt because of what they believed in their "hearts." But as Jesus explained the Scriptures to them, their "hearts" began to burn within them (Luke 24:32). In response to His words, they began to believe the truth in a new and deeper way. They began believing with both their heads and their hearts. This change in "heart belief" led to a change in their emotional status. They were no longer disappointed but joyous and motivated (Luke 24:41).

A change in heart belief also dramatically impacts a person's behavior. After their encounter with Jesus, the two disciples did not continue walking towards Emmaus, but rather quickly returned to Jerusalem and shared the good news (Luke 24:33-35). This transformation in both emotion and behavior occurred when they finally believed the truth in their "hearts."

In Scripture, the word "heart" is derived from the Greek word *"kardia"* which means "the fountain and seat of the thoughts, passions, desires, appetites, affections, purposes, endeavors...the heart, inner man, etc." (Strong's Concordance - 2588). Our feelings and motivations flow from our "kardia," our "hearts." More specifically, we feel what we feel because of what we _believe_ in our "hearts."

Although we believe all kinds of things in our "heads," the two forms of belief that are planted in our "hearts" are those which pertain to _who we are_ and _who God is_. These "heart beliefs" either describe our *"self-identity"* (who and what we believe we are) or our *"state of being"* (our understanding of God and His involvement in our lives). These beliefs might be such things as, "I am worthless, a reject, don't matter, not loved, etc. (self-identity)" or "I am alone, helpless, powerless, trapped, out of control, etc. (state of being—our perception of God's involvement in our lives)". Putting all of this together, we find that our feelings reflect what we believe in our *hearts* about ourselves, God, and His involvement in our lives.

When the disciples had not yet believed in their hearts that Jesus had been raised from the dead, they *felt* fearful, discouraged and disappointed. But when they came to believe the truth of His resurrection in their hearts, they were filled with joy. Likewise, until you believe in your heart that God loves you, you will not *feel* loved by Him (John 3:16, Romans 8:35). Until you know in your heart that He is your protection, you will not *feel* safe (1 John 5:18). Until you know in your heart that you are His beloved child, you will not *feel* accepted by Him (John 1:12). Until you know that the Lord is your helper, you will continue to be afraid (Hebrews 13:6). You may already know these truths in your "head," but until you believe them _in your heart_, they will not *feel* true. We feel what we believe in our hearts.

When our "hearts" disagree with our "heads," we are "double-minded."

Like the disciples traveling on the road to Emmaus (Luke 24:13), we can believe the truth in our "heads" while believing something else in our "hearts." In fact, it is quite common for there to be a disagreement between what we believe in our "heads" and what we believe in our "hearts." According to the apostle James, when we believe two opposing things in this way, we are "double-minded" and will experience the inner turmoil of being "driven and tossed by the wind" (James 1:6).

The Greek New Testament word translated *double-minded* is *"dipsuchos."* It means to possess two "souls" or "minds." We are double-minded when we know the truth in our heads but believe something contrary to it in our hearts. Because of this, the lie will *feel* or *seem* true even though we logically know that it is not. We may fully agree with the truth in our heads, but it will *not feel* or *seem* true until we also believe it in our hearts. As a result we are pulled in two different directions (i.e. as James says, "driven and tossed by the wind").

If you believe in your heart that you are a sinful wretch, this perspective will *seem* and *feel* true even if, in your head, you know that you are born of His Spirit (John 3:6). In this instance, you believe the truth in your "head" but not yet in your "heart." In fact, what you believe in your "heart" contradicts what you believe in your "head."

You may have read and even memorized the fact that you are one of "God's chosen ones, holy and beloved..." (Colossians 3:12 ESV), but you will only *feel* chosen, holy, and beloved if this is what you believe in your heart. You may genuinely believe the truth in your "head," but if it does not feel or seem true to you, then you have been deceived into believing something else in your "heart." When this is so, you are double-minded.

In other words, if you feel as though you are worthless, defective, or unlovable (even if you intellectually know otherwise), then this indicates what you really believe in your heart. You may genuinely believe the truth in your head, but your emotions indicate what you believe at a heart level. Our emotions may not accurately reflect the truth, but they truthfully reflect what we believe in our hearts!

This dynamic is on full display in every TPM session. I (Ed) recall my first TPM session in which I sat across from that dear woman who had been sexually molested as a child. She could clearly articulate truths such as *"I am safe now," "It was not my fault," "I am not dirty or shameful," "I am not out of control," "I am not going to die."* And yet, when she would recall her childhood abuse, her "heart belief" was expressed in her emotions. She felt unsafe, guilty, dirty, shameful, out of control, and as though she was going to die. She knew the truth in her head, but she did not yet believe the truth in her heart. She was double-minded.

She was unable to resolve her double-mindedness by trying harder to believe, denying what felt true, choosing to obey the truth, or even acquiring additional Bible knowledge. Like the disciples on the road to Emmaus, she needed the Lord to lead her into the truth. She needed Him to convince her heart to believe what she already knew in her head. When He finally did, she experienced a glorious transformation!

But, as we will discuss in future chapters, it is not a bad thing to experience painful emotions that contradict the truths we believe in our heads. In fact, painful emotions are quite helpful when we understand their purpose and rightly respond to them. They serve an important role in our mind-renewing journey with the Lord. But, for now, just know that we feel what we feel at any given moment because of what we believe in our hearts. Our emotions are accurate indicators of what we believe in our hearts.

Part Three

It is possible to have peace in every circumstance.

The Bible says, "Let the peace of Christ rule in your heart" (Colossians 3:15 NKJV) and "may the Lord of peace Himself continually grant you peace in every circumstance" (2 Thessalonians 3:16). God desires for His peace to rule (or govern) our hearts. He wants us to "continually" experience His peace in "every circumstance." So, unless Paul was mistaken, our lack of peace is not due to our circumstances.

Statements such as: "You make me so mad," or "If you would just stop doing that, I wouldn't feel this way," or "I always feel nervous and anxious whenever she is around," or "I feel trapped and helpless when I am with him," indicate a lack of understanding regarding this important principle: *we feel what we believe.* We interpret life through what we believe to be true, and our emotions automatically change to match our interpretation (remember the dog/burglar illustration from the beginning of this chapter). Our circumstances simply expose what we believe in our hearts. If we ever lack His peace, this indicates our lack of His perspective.

This principle can be initially difficult to embrace due to its ramifications. If our feelings are produced by our own belief, then we must take responsibility for what we feel. It often seems easier or more natural to blame others, our situation, the devil, or even God for what we feel. Being a victim sometimes seems easier than taking personal responsibility, but these two paths lead us in entirely different directions. One is the way of truth and life, while the other encourages us to assume the role of victim and keeps us in a perpetual cycle of defeat and frustration.

Again, this does not minimize unjust behavior. If someone acted inappropriately, then this is the truth. But our emotional response to this injustice is based upon how we are interpreting it through what we believe. People can commit terrible and unjust acts, but when we have God's perspective, we will respond like He would. Here again we recall the words of Jesus who said to love our enemies, do good to those who hurt us and bless those who curse us (Matthew 5:44, Luke 6:27-28). We cannot respond in this fashion apart from gaining God's perspective and believing the truth in our hearts.

This principle also does not minimize the severity or difficulty of our circumstances, for truth-based problems, as well as the effects of lie-based problems, are very real. However, it does show that the Lord desires for us to know His peace in the midst of our difficult circumstances. Rather than focusing on changing our circumstance, our primary goal should be to have God's perspective of our perceived problems and His solutions to them. For when we believe the truth in our hearts, the truth will set us free (John 8:32), and we will have peace in every circumstance (2 Thessalonians 3:16)!

The prophet Isaiah describes Jesus using the imagery of a lamb on its way to be slaughtered (see Isaiah 53:7). Sheep can be led to the slaughterhouse and killed without any outward display of stress or fear. Granted, they do not know what is about to happen to them or their reactions might be different! Jesus, on the other hand, knew fully what was going to happen to Him, but He journeyed through the experience just as a calm and trusting lamb. How was Jesus able to do this? He knew the truth and was operating in the will of His Father.

The same can be said about Stephen on the day he was stoned to death. When the eyes of Stephen's heart were opened, and he saw Jesus standing next to the heavenly Father, he expressed genuine joy and compassion even though he was being stoned to death. Like Jesus, Stephen's emotional reaction was a result of the truth that he knew in his heart, not the outcome of his difficult situation. The same is true with us! Our circumstances do not determine how we feel; we feel what we believe.

Jesus feels what He believes.

Some have argued that our negative emotions are justified because Jesus felt and expressed negative emotions as well. While it is true that Jesus experienced "negative" emotions, this argument needs to be more carefully examined. One notable detail that tends to be overlooked is the fact that the Gospel narratives never show Jesus expressing emotions such as worry, fear, anxiety, powerlessness, helplessness, depression, or hopelessness. Even on the day He was crucified, Jesus expressed a calm assurance, patience, empathy, and compassion for those who mistreated Him. Not once did He feel afraid, panicked, or helpless (all of which many of us would feel if we were in His situation).

In the few places where Jesus does express negative emotions, He either felt angry, grieved, or both (See Mark 3:5 for an example of this). Some people suggest that Jesus felt immense stress and anxiety in the Garden of Gethsemane the night before His crucifixion; this is not so. Jesus told His disciples, "My soul is <u>deeply grieved</u>, to the point of death; remain here and keep watch with Me" (Matthew 26:38, emphasis added). He felt tremendous grief that caused blood to excrete out of His pores on His skin, but He was not anxious or stressed. Anxiety and stress have to do with uncertainty and unfounded expectations. Jesus was neither uncertain or second-guessing the Father's intention; He knew exactly what was about to happen and what His Father was asking of Him. Jesus perceived the full weight of His Father's request, and this grieved Him. This was an example of *truth-based pain.*

Have you ever wondered why Jesus prayed three times in the Garden asking His Father if the "cup could pass by Him?" Something must have happened after His third and final inquiry because He then went to His sleepy disciples and said, "Arise... the hour has come" (See Matthew 26:38-47). I personally believe this is an example of Jesus seeking His Heavenly Father's greater perspective.

Jesus often went off by Himself to pray. Why? Most would say in order to receive the Father's direction. In the fifth chapter of John's Gospel, Jesus gives a lengthy discourse declaring His equality with God and then says, "I can do nothing on My own. As I hear, I judge; and My judgment is righteous, because I do not seek My own will but the will of Him who sent Me." (John 5:30). Jesus was continually dependent upon what His Father revealed to Him.

The question to ask is, "How much did Jesus know?" Was He omniscient (all-knowing) like His Father in Heaven? If so, why did He need to ask the Father anything? Why would He ask that the "cup" be passed from Him if He already knew the Father's will? We suggest that the great grief Jesus felt in the Garden that caused Him to sweat drops of blood was based upon the truth of the suffering that lay before Him. We also believe that it was not until He had asked three times that the Father apparently revealed the greater perspective that caused Jesus's grief to turn to joy. For as the Hebrew writer says, "[because of the] joy set before Him endured the cross" (Hebrews 12:2).

Jesus continually had proper perspective because He sought out the Father's will in every situation. As He explained, "Truly, truly, I say to you, the Son can do nothing of Himself, unless it is something He sees the Father doing; for whatever the Father does, these things the Son also does in the same way" (John 5:19). He always interpreted His situation correctly, He knew who He was, He knew His Heavenly Father, and He could see His Father's involvement in His life. He knew the truth, perceived the truth, and walked in the truth. The truth of God's perspective always seemed and felt true to Him. In fact, He was and is the truth (John 14:6). Because of this, He always emotionally responded appropriately to His situation.

Jesus passed through His suffering, trials, and tribulations with peace, assurance, and even joy. Although Jesus experienced unimaginable grief in the garden, again, it was He who "...for the joy set before Him endured the cross..." (Hebrews 12:2, emphasis added). Even as He endured great physical pain, Jesus maintained a right perspective. He was deeply grieved, but He was not stressed, anxious, fearful, worried, or discouraged. The same could not be said of His disciples or of us.

The stark contrast between Jesus' emotional responses and those of His disciples was due to the fact that He had God's perspective, and they often did not. The disciples responded differently because they believed differently. Jesus always operated in the truth; His disciples did not.

We also see this where Jesus was asleep in the boat during the storm while His disciples panicked (Matthew 8:24). The disciples had a flawed and limited perspective of their situation; Jesus perceived the truth. And when Jesus was being arrested in the Garden, He was not afraid or anxious. His disciples, on the other hand, scattered in fear (Mark 14:50). Jesus' emotions indicated what He believed, the disciples' emotions indicated what they believed, and our emotions indicate what we believe.

Jesus provides the standard for "normality."

Merriam Webster defines "normal" as, "conforming to a type, standard, or regular pattern; characterized by that which is considered usual, typical, or routine." With that in mind, if you found out that your credit card was used to make purchases at a store you have never visited, or learned that your connecting flight back home was canceled due to weather, or discovered that a coworker was saying nasty things about you, what would be the "normal" emotional response to have? Is it "normal" to be offended, irritated, stressed, or upset?

Many would argue, "Of course! Everybody would respond in that way. Those are perfectly normal responses to troubling situations." Without question, such responses are what most people *normally* feel in these types of circumstances, but does this mean that it is "normal" to respond in this way? Do such feelings reflect God's normal response? Is His normal our normal? If not, how many of our *"normals"* are actually *abnormal*?

God's normal reaction to any life event is one that is rooted in truth and reality. In order for our response to be divinely normal, it must be the logical and expected outcome of rightly understanding our situation from God's perspective. Jesus always responded in this way. He always knew the truth, had a clear view of reality, and operated from this perspective. As a result, He always responded normally to whatever happened around Him. We suggest that Jesus' response is the standard for normality for those who are in Christ. Everything else falls short and is *abnormal.*

For example, Jesus' reaction to the Roman guard who came to arrest Him in the garden was based upon an accurate understanding of the situation and was "normal." His disciples, on the other hand, did what most of us would normally do; they reacted abnormally and fled for their lives in fear (Mark 14:50).

Jesus also had a "normal" response to the storm (Matthew 8:24). The disciples, however, lacked this perspective and were filled with fear which led them to respond *abnormally*. They were just as safe as Jesus was, but because of their flawed and limited perspectives, they perceived the situation very differently. Jesus' beliefs led Him to respond *normally* while the disciples' beliefs resulted in their fear and panic. When we use this standard to evaluate our own lives, we find that a large portion of our responses are "abnormal."

When we fully believe the truth and view our situation from a heavenly perspective, our responses will be normal. But if we lack God's perspective, we will respond abnormally. Our response may be "normal" according to how most people would react, but that doesn't mean it is normal according to the truth.

To respond to our life situations with emotions such as fear, anxiety, stress, and worry is to respond *abnormally*. This is not how Jesus (or anyone else operating from His perspective) would respond. Responding in fear, anxiety, or worry shows our lack of perspective. We either do not yet understand the whole truth of our situation, or we have been deceived into believing lies. Either way, we need God's perspective.

All this begs the question, "What should our normal response to life's difficulties look like?" There are many passages in Scripture to help us with this question. For example, we are to "*consider it all joy* . . . [when 'bad' things happen]" (see James 1:2), and "Rejoice in [your] sufferings" (see Romans 5:3 ESV). We are also instructed to "rejoice in the Lord always [both in good times and bad times]" (Philippians 4:4). Biblically speaking, joy is the *normal* response to everything that comes our way. Troubles in this life are inevitable (See John 16:33), and when they arise, we often feel emotional pain. Even so, these bad feelings are not caused by the troubles themselves. We feel what we believe. The only way for us to genuinely "rejoice in the Lord always" is to have God's perspective. When we view ourselves, God, and our situation from an eternal perspective, we will rejoice!

Without question, there are evil people doing evil things, but for us who believe, God has promised to work all things together for our good (Romans 8:28). So even if a situation is genuinely "bad" for the believer, it brings about that which is genuinely "good." For a clear example of this, you need only to look to the cross. The day that Jesus died was undoubtedly a "bad" day. But, for the believer, it was a very good day! This does not make the "bad" actions of "bad" people good, but it does bring great hope and peace to those who understand and live in this truth. As Paul declared, "If God is for us, who can be against us?" (Romans 8:31, Psalm 56:9, 118:6).

Part Four

Pain was purposefully designed by God.

None of us likes feeling the effects of our flawed and limited perspectives. So why did God create our capacity to feel emotional pain in the first place? To find the answer to this question, consider the following illustration. Let's say you are walking outside on a warm summer's day. You take your shoes off to enjoy the soft, cool grass with your bare feet when, suddenly, you step on a thorn, and it lodges itself into the bottom of your foot. When this happens, do you want your foot to hurt? Now, you may be thinking to yourself, "*No! Of course not! Why would I want my foot to hurt?*" But we encourage you to revisit the question again. You are not being asked, "Do you *like* when your foot hurts?" but rather, "Do you *want* your foot to hurt if you step on a thorn?" For a moment, consider the implications if your foot didn't hurt in this scenario. If it wasn't for the discomfort caused by the thorn, you would likely continue on your way, unaware of the injury, and cause further damage to your foot while risking infection. This is definitely NOT what you *want*!

Pain is a God-designed mechanism that alerts us to the fact that something is wrong. Without this painful alert system, we would accidentally cut our feet, burn our hands, bite our tongues, and unknowingly inflict all kinds of self-harm on a daily basis. Pain is important, and it serves a purpose. It does not feel good, but it certainly has its benefits!

Viewing our emotional pain as *the problem*, rather than *a symptom* of our problem, might be compared to a man who goes to the dentist because of terrible pain in his jaw. After the dentist takes a few X-rays, he concludes, "You are in pain because you have a rotten tooth." The man replies, "I did not come here because of my tooth. I can live with that. I just want the pain to go away!" The dentist responds, "But Sir, the tooth is causing your pain. It is rotten, and I need to pull it out." "Oh, no!" the man exclaims, "That will only hurt me more! Just give me something for the pain so that I can be on my way!" This is obviously meant to be a silly example, but it is no more illogical than attempting to distract yourself from feeling what you don't want to feel.

Emotional pain serves many of the same purposes as physical pain. None of us enjoy feeling emotional pain, but it was designed by God, and it serves an important purpose. The sooner we come to understand this, the sooner we can start responding to it appropriately and benefiting from its inevitable role in our lives.

Our emotional pain is helpful because it points out that which needs our attention: our need for God's perspective. Painful emotions are like trusted friends who honestly tell us what we *need* to hear rather than simply sharing what we *want* to hear. They are not always fun to be around, but they are "good" friends!

Emotional pain indicates our need for God's perspective.

You may not like the way it feels, but you need emotional pain. The anxiety you feel when you believe a lie is just as purposeful and beneficial as the pain in your foot when you step on a thorn. Both types of pain tell us when something is not as it should be and alerts us to that which needs our attention. Emotional pain indicates that our current perspective is limited, flawed, or both. It was designed to make us aware of our need for God's perspective and motivate us to seek Him out.

Without physical pain we would be unaware of when we have injured ourselves, and without emotional pain we would likely fail to notice when we need God's perspective. In this sense, both physical and emotional pain are gifts from God that were designed for specific purposes. Neither are enjoyable, but both are vitally important. None of us would truly want to live without the capacity to feel physical pain because we understand its purpose. It is good that our injuries produce pain. And in the same way, although we don't like the way our negative emotions feel, it is good that we feel bad when we believe lies. When we realize the purpose that our emotional pain serves, we can embrace pain as an honest "friend" rather than an enemy or something to overcome.

You are not hearing us say that being fearful, anxious or depressed is a good thing. For God has told us many times to "fear not." In fact, the phrase "fear not" is one of the most frequent directives mentioned in the Scriptures. But when God directs us to be unafraid, He typically includes an explanation as to why we do not need to fear, He shares the truth that we are lacking. For instance, "Do not fear, I will help you" (Isaiah 41:14), "Do not fear them, for the LORD your God is the One fighting for you" (Deuteronomy 3:22, 2 Chronicles 20:15-17), "Do not be terrified nor dismayed, for the LORD your God is with you wherever you go" (Joshua 1:9), "Do not be afraid; for behold, I bring you good news of great joy" (Luke 2:10). Jesus told us not to be afraid and said, "take courage; I have overcome the world" (John 16:33).

The recipients of these "fear not" messages were initially afraid because they lacked the truth. They did not yet fully believe that they would be helped, defended, protected, accompanied, or saved. In the same way, when we respond to our situations with fear, anxiety, worry, stress, etc., our emotional responses indicate that we do not yet fully believe the truth either. For when we know the truth, we will "fear not."

Instead of viewing emotional pain as a bad thing, a defect, a curse, or some sort of burden we must bear, we need to begin viewing it as a function of the created order that God put in place for our good. In fact, God wants you to feel bad if you lack the truth and need His perspective (*You may want to read that last sentence again*). It is by God's purposeful design that we feel what we believe.

So, if you believe that you are worthless and unloved, God wants you to _feel_ worthless and unloved. God doesn't like that you feel this way, but He likes even less your belief in a lie. He doesn't want you to continually live in emotional pain, but His primary focus is upon the reason why you feel it. He wants you to know the truth of your value and His love.

He designed emotional pain to alert you to this problem and to motivate you to address it. It lets you know that you need God's perspective. He designed pain to make you aware of when your current perspective is either flawed, limited, or both, and He hopes that you will respond responsibly to it. He desires for you to see yourself, your situation, and Him through His eyes.

"Positive thinking" can have negative consequences.

Sadly, most people do not view their negative emotions as gifts from God or opportunities to gain His perspective. Instead, they view pain as the enemy and actively attempt to eradicate it from their lives. Some take it a step further by focusing their attention away from their pain by mustering up positive emotions and thinking "happy" thoughts or engaging in some form of behavior that distracts them from what they are feeling. They may argue, "Whenever I feel stressed, nervous, or overwhelmed, I look for the positive in the situation. I choose not to focus on the bad and shift my attention to that which is good, hopeful, and true. I choose to focus on Heavenly things. When I do this, I feel better! The negative emotions fade into the background, and I move forward feeling better!" Typically, people support this strategy with Bible verses such as Colossians 3:2 that says, "*Set your minds on the things that are above, not on the things that are on earth.*"

On the surface this seems perfectly reasonable, effective, and even biblical, but it is a misapplication of this passage. Without question, we should set our minds on heavenly things rather than the things of this earth, but for what purpose are we to do this? Why did Paul direct us to, "set your mind on the things above?" In its context the passage reads,

> If you have been raised with Christ, keep seeking the things *that are* above, where Christ is, seated at the right hand of God. Set your minds on the things *that are* above, not on the things that are on earth. <u>For you have died, and your life is hidden with Christ in God</u>. When Christ, who is our life, is revealed, then you also will be revealed with Him in glory (Colossians 3:1-4, emphasis added).

We are to set our minds on the things above because (according to Scripture) that is where we are! Our lives are hidden with Christ in God, and we are presently seated with Him in the heavenly places (see Ephesians 2:6). We need to continually look upward so we might discover the truth of our new life and position in Christ. Paul is encouraging us to discover who we are in Christ.

In telling us to set our minds on the things above, Paul is saying, "Look up! See where you are seated! Realize who you are and who is seated next to you! See what God has done!" We are to focus on the things above for the purpose of realizing the truth of our life and identity which is hidden with Christ. We believe that the eyes of our hearts are opened a little each time that the Holy Spirit persuades us of the truth. When this happens, we see a little more of the heavenly reality of our hidden life in Christ.

Paul's direction to focus on heavenly things is not some form of denial or distraction. For if we focus our attention towards "Heaven" for the purpose of distracting ourselves from emotional pain, doing so is counterproductive, and we are both misapplying Paul's instructions and misunderstanding the purpose of pain. In fact, anything that we do to distract us from what we feel runs contrary to the system that God designed to alert us to our need for His perspective. Regardless of how spiritual our distractions may appear to be, they are counterproductive.

Nevertheless, someone might say, "I just choose not to feel bad. I choose to dwell on the positive and choose to rejoice instead!" This sounds good and noble, but it is not really possible. We don't *choose* to feel any of what we feel (whether positive or negative). For instance, do we choose to feel depressed, scared, or anxious? No. We automatically feel these emotions in response to our interpretation of our situation. Likewise, we do not feel love, joy, or peace by *choosing* to feel them. Emotions are automatic: *we simply feel what we believe.*

If our perspectives are flawed or limited, we will automatically feel painful emotions as a result. But if we believe the truth in our hearts, we will, just as easily, feel at peace and be filled with joy. Our beliefs produce our emotions, and our emotions indicate our beliefs. There is no "choosing" involved in this automatic, God-designed process. Those who say that they "choose not to feel bad" are actually simply choosing to distract themselves from their pain. This is merely a form of suppression and runs contrary to God's purposes.

We may succeed in altering our emotional state by diverting our attention elsewhere, but this is not the same as "choosing" to feel something. If anything, it is the act of "choosing" <u>not</u> to feel something! It is the conscious decision to ignore the effects of our flawed and limited perspective for the purpose of momentarily feeling "better." This tactic is simply a well-intended form of mental distraction to suppress that which we don't want to feel, but it has no impact on what we believe. Focusing on the "good" does not make the "bad" go away. We still believe what we believe even while ignoring the signs and consequences of it. In fact, the only pain we *can* ignore is that which we *already feel*, and we only feel it because of what we *believe*. If we didn't believe what we believe, we wouldn't feel what we feel. The fact that there is pain to be ignored means that our belief problem remains.

To illustrate the points being made, consider the following (admittedly crude) illustration:

> As soon as you walk into your living room, you realize that your dog has dropped a warm, wet "present" for you on the floor. The overwhelming odor has permeated the entire house. It would not surprise you if your neighbors could smell what your dog has done, but rather than addressing the source of the aroma, you choose to "focus on the positive and the good." While holding your nose to reduce the unpleasant sensation there, you begin scanning the room for "positives." You begin by thanking God for your supply of scented candles and light a few of them to help cover the smell. You then pause to enjoy the beautiful flowers that a friend gave you which are displayed on your table. As you walk across the room to admire the various family photographs that hang on the wall, you are filled with nostalgia and gratitude. You get cozy underneath the soft, warm quilt that your mother made and begin sipping a cup of hot chocolate. You genuinely enjoy and are comforted by each of these activities, but the pile on the floor remains intact and pungent fumes continue to fill the room. You may temporarily succeed in avoiding the smell or masking the stench; you may even get used to the unconventional atmosphere as the new "normal." But the fact remains, there is dog poop on your floor!

In reality, no one would address this smelly problem by engaging in such behaviors. As much as we would dislike the activity, each of us would view the removal of the "pile" as our top priority. This is because we understand that the smell is not the real problem (as terrible as it is!), and any attempt to alleviate the unpleasant aroma is futile unless the mess is also addressed.

Because we rightly understand the real problem, we can clearly see that attempting to ignore or mask the odor is unproductive and only prolongs the pungent pile's presence. Even if you were able to suppress the smell and live as though the dog droppings didn't exist, your dinner parties would undoubtedly be a disaster, for none of your guests would be impressed with your positive attitude or your ability to function uninhibitedly with dog poop on your floor.

This same dynamic applies when we rightly understand the relationship between what we feel and what we believe. We may succeed in feeling "better" by diverting our attention to more "positive" aspects of our situation and ignoring it, but there is little hope of finding real, lasting resolution without attending to the actual reason for the "smell." Ignoring our pain and "focusing on the good" may make us feel better, but if the steaming pile that produces those painful emotions remains intact, have we really solved the problem?

The "stench" of the dog's mess makes its presence on the floor apparent. It also helps us locate its source and motivates us to do something about it. We propose that our emotional pain does the same thing! Even the most trivial examples of emotional pain stem from our lack of God's perspective. Either we are experiencing the emotional consequences of believing a lie or have thus far been unable to recognize God's involvement and His solutions to our problems. In either case, by focusing only on what feels good and ignoring that which feels bad, we are purposefully blocking the alarm system that God specifically designed to notify us of when we need His perspective. As a result, we inadvertently cut ourselves off from the benefit that we could otherwise gain. We are unintentionally blocking ourselves from receiving His truth and having His perspective. Most people do this unknowingly and with good intentions. But that doesn't change the reality of the situation. The truth is the truth regardless of what we believe.

Freedom comes through honesty, not denial.

Essentially, what we are proposing is honesty. We encourage you to own what you feel and honestly assess *why* you feel it rather than simply trying to feel "better." Rather than ignoring our negative emotions and undermining the purpose for which God gave them to us, we need to honestly acknowledge them and explore why they are there. If what you are reading here is correct, then our emotional discomfort indicates our lack of perspective. We need the truth. All of us do! God is patiently waiting for us to acknowledge the "smell" and its source so that He can graciously clean it up for us.

All that said, there is good news! Like with everything God does, He goes far above and beyond our highest expectation (see Ephesians 3:20). If we invite him to clean up the mess in our smelly living room, He not only cleans up our mess, He graciously bestows an abundance of additional blessings upon us! Immediately after carefully removing that which should not be there, the Lord lovingly gives us a portion of the most valuable thing in existence: a personal and experiential knowledge of Him. There is nothing more precious or important than to know God. We must come to realize that each of the stinking piles in our lives represents an opportunity to come into a deeper understanding of who we are and who He is. They are opportunities for us to humbly acknowledge our need for Him, invite Him to grant us His perspective, and receive that which is more precious than gold - a purified faith (1 Peter 1:7).

We encourage you to view your emotion as a trustworthy friend that is pointing out your need for God's perspective. Negative emotions do not feel good, but they are part of the "all things" that God is working together for our good (Romans 8:28). The emotional pain is not our problem, our problem is that we do not yet have His perspective.

When faced with the emotional consequences of our flawed and limited perspectives, we must realize the fundamentals. We do not feel what we feel because of what is happening around us. We feel what we believe. The pain we feel is not a bad thing. It is there to let us know that we need God's perspective and to motivate us to move in His direction. Rather than attempting to escape from or eliminate the pain we feel (remember the dentist illustration), we need to gain God's perspective. When we believe the truth in our hearts, the truth will set us free (John 8:32), and we will effortlessly experience His peace in every circumstance (2 Thessalonians 3:16). We should focus on the "things above" where we are "hidden with Christ in God," not for the purpose of distraction but for the purpose of discovery. If you have this perspective of your emotional pain and know what to do in response to it, you can more intentionally and consistently move towards truth, peace, and lasting freedom!

Part Five

We feel "truth-based pain"
when we perceive "truth-based problems."

All emotional pain is the outcome of what we believe, but not all of these beliefs are untrue. Sometimes the truth produces its own pain. As we discussed in the previous chapter, this world is full of truths and realities that are genuinely problematic and painful. Jesus spoke the truth when He said, "You will have suffering in this world" (John 16:33 HCSB). Solomon, the wisest man who has ever lived, concluded that our suffering increases as we discover more and more truth. He wrote, "In much wisdom there is much grief, and increasing knowledge results in increasing pain" (Ecclesiastes 1:18). Pain and suffering are unavoidable realities in this world. And when we face difficult and painful challenges, we feel some measure of "truth-based pain" in response.

Truth-based pain does not include emotions such as worry, fear, anxiety, abandonment, helplessness, powerlessness, etc. We can never righteously feel worried, anxious or afraid (Matthew 6:25, Philippians 4:6), but there are times where we may rightly feel anger, grief, disappointment or regret.

What follows are a few examples of truth-based problems:

Scenario One:

Pulling into his driveway, Dan notices two policemen waiting at the front door of his house. They are talking to his wife. She is covering her mouth with one hand while gripping the door frame with the other. "Is there a problem officers?" Dan hesitantly inquires. "She's gone Dan!" his wife cries, "Our baby is gone!" Shocked and confused, Dan slowly mutters, "What are you talking about? What is going on?" One of the officers slowly approaches him, "Sir, your daughter was injured in a car accident this afternoon. She was rushed to the hospital, but the paramedics were unable to stabilize her. She was pronounced dead on arrival in the Emergency Room." The officer clears his throat, "I'm sorry for your loss." Dan's stomach turns, his knees weaken, and tears begin to steam down his face. He rushes past the police officers and embraces his wife. They have just been made aware of a truth-based problem and are feeling immense truth-based pain in response.

Scenario Two:

Taylor avoids the baby sections in her favorite stores. She feels uncomfortable and ashamed when walking past the tiny shoes, little pajamas, and soft, pink blankets. Regret gnaws at her when she thinks about her visit to the abortion center. Memories of cold medical tools and rushed decisions whirl in her head. It makes her nauseated. She failed to fully comprehend what she was doing and wishes that she could undo what she did. But she knows that she can't, and that fact eats at her. Looking back, she realizes that she was misled into believing that she had no other recourse, and she never wants to be put in such a vulnerable position again. Although her church family has genuinely tried to comfort her, she knows that she disappointed them. But more than anything, she feels deeply disappointed in herself. Taylor has confessed her "choice" over and over again and genuinely believes that she has God's forgiveness, but she still seems to carry the burden of her truth-based pain.

Scenario Three:

Alison loved her job. She was a passionate elementary school teacher who yearned to invest in the next generation. But her heart broke when she discovered scrapes and bruises on one of her students' face and arms. The little one cautiously looked up at her and said, "He didn't mean to do it. He was just tired. Please don't tell anyone!" Alison's heart sank. She had suspicions that all was not well in the child's home, but this seemed to be undeniable proof. After contacting the school nurse, Alison's principal informed her that the child's father was just arrested. She felt sickened for the poor student but was furious at the child's father. She felt truth-based pain in response to this truth-based problem.

Sometimes the truth hurts. The deep pain we feel in response to our truth-based problems is often appropriate. God feels this way too. However, He is capable of carrying the weight of such emotional burdens; we are not. If we attempt to carry them, we will inevitably buckle under their weight at some point.

Thankfully, He is bearing all of our burdens (Isaiah 53:4), and when we genuinely believe this truth with our hearts, we will experience freedom and relief from the pain they cause. We must learn to follow Peter's instruction to "Cast all your anxiety [care, worry] on Him, because He cares about you" (1 Peter 5:7, emphasis added). Some people who experience tragic life events continue to carry their truth-based pain throughout life and never realize that God is carrying the burden and they are not required or even expected to carry it themselves. This is unfortunate and is not God's will for his children.

When we initially experience life tragedies, we have no choice but to feel what we feel in response to our truth-based problems. This is not a bad thing. It is expected and understandable. For as Solomon wisely wrote, "To everything there is a season, a time for every purpose under heaven...a time to weep and a time to laugh; A time to mourn and a time to dance" (Ecclesiastes 3:1, 3:4 NKJV). Weeping and mourning are just as natural and expected as laughing and dancing.

Likewise, God expects us to get angry when we witness acts of injustice and unrighteousness as the Scriptures make it clear that we are to "be angry, just don't sin." (Ephesians 4:26a) Even Jesus was angry on several occasions (Matthew 21:12-17, Mark 3:5, John 2:13-22). The question is, when we feel such emotion, how long will we carry it (Ephesians 4:26b), and what should we do with it when it rises up within us?

The problem is not that we initially react with anger, grief, disappointment or regret, but it is what we do thereafter that God is most concerned with. Truth-based pain serves a purpose just as any other form of emotional or physical pain. It can help motivate us to look to God for additional perspective. And when He changes our mindset to reflect a more *complete* perspective, we find freedom in this greater truth.

God wants us to know the truth and feel the emotions that are produced by it, whether good or bad. Just as we discussed earlier, God wants us to feel the pain associated with the lies we believe so that we are motivated to turn to Him for truth, and He also wants us to know the painful truths of reality so that we will seek His solutions to them and come to view them from an eternal perspective. If we are only able to see part of the truth, it will seem as though we have no option but to continue carrying our truth-based pain and continually look for ways to manage it.

God designed us to feel what we believe, but He also intended for us to know the truth, the whole truth, not just some limited aspects of it. When we only have a portion of the truth, we may rightly feel the pain that is associated with that part, but we will be unable to see the greater truth that releases us from the pain. However, when we see the total picture from His vantage point, we may discover that He is carrying "all our grief and sorrow" and can finally find rest in Him.

If we only have that portion of the truth that is causing us to feel its pain and lack God's fuller perspective, we will continually feel grief, sorrow, disappointment, and regret. However, when we genuinely believe that God is carrying our burdens and has an eternal solution for all our troubles, we will "exult in our tribulations" (Romans 5:3), "Consider it all joy, my brothers and sisters, when we encounter various trials…" (James 1:2) and "Rejoice in the Lord always. . ." (Phillipians 4:4). But responding to our difficulties in this manner is impossible apart from true, biblical "metanoia" (a change of thought/belief).

He wants us to be fully convinced of His intimate involvement in our lives. He doesn't want us to continually live in pain, but if our temporary emotional pain motivates us to look to Him for perspective, then our suffering was used for our good. For we know that "our momentary, light affliction is producing for us an eternal weight of glory far beyond all comparison" (2 Corinthians 4:17). We conclude this discussion by reading again what Paul said concerning godly sorrow (truth-based emotion) that produces "repentance" (Biblical Greek word meaning "a change in belief or perspective"). He said, "the sorrow that is according to the will of God [based upon the truth] produces repentance [a change in our belief and perspective] without regret, leading to salvation" (2 Corinthians 7:10, emphasis added).

TRUTH-BASED PAIN IS THE RESULT OF OUR PERCEPTION.

For clarification, it may be helpful to restate the fact that we do not feel truth-based pain because of what happens to us, but rather, we feel what we feel because of what we believe in our hearts. Our *perception* of reality, not reality itself, is the reason for our grief, disappointment, regrets, and anger. If your house burned down, but you were unaware of this tragedy, you would not feel emotional pain. Only after you are made aware of the house fire would you perceive this truth-based problem and feel a measure of truth-based pain. And if someone convinced you that your house had burned down when it actually hadn't, you would still feel a measure of pain in response to this *perceived* problem. If you believe you are perceiving the truth, then it will feel and seem true. We *perceive* and *feel* what we *believe*.

Part Six

We will be burdened by our "truth-based pain" until we believe in our "hearts" that God is carrying it for us.

Unless we realize the reality that God is bearing the weight of our emotional burdens, we will continue trying to carry them ourselves. Consider the following:

> A traveling merchant was driving his horse-drawn cart to a neighboring town. On his way he encountered a man who was walking on the side of the road. The man was obviously struggling due to the large bag on his back. It seemed as though every step was a challenge for him. The merchant pulled the reins to slow his horse and stopped the cart next to the weary traveler. *"It looks like you could use some help."* the merchant exclaimed. *"Yes, indeed. I'm not sure how much further I can walk before I'll need to take another rest!"* the man desperately replied. Feeling compassion for the man, the merchant asked, *"Why don't you climb into the back of my cart? My horse is strong and can easily handle the extra weight."* The man gratefully accepted the offer and climbed onto the cart. *"Thank you, sir, I am on my way home after attending my uncle's funeral. Before I left, my widowed aunt gave me the wood-working tools that my uncle used in his shop. And although I genuinely appreciated her thoughtfulness, my uncle's tools are quite heavy. Since the gift was unexpected, I was not prepared to travel with such a load. It is almost more than I can bear."* Just then, the merchant noticed that the man had not yet removed the pack from his back and replied, *"Thankfully though, you can now rest! Feel free to place your pack anywhere."* *"Oh, no!"* the man replied, *"I am genuinely grateful for your offer to let me ride in your cart. I wouldn't dare ask for you to bear my burden as well!"*

Much like this weary traveler, if we fail to realize that our "burdens" are already being carried, we will continue attempting to carry them ourselves. The weight of our truth-based problems, as well as the problems themselves, are already in God's possession. He is presently addressing the problems and bearing their full weight! But if we fail to realize this reality or have been convinced that we must bear them ourselves, it will *seem* as though we have no option but to contend with our sadness, grief, regret, disappointment, and anger.

We may rightly perceive our situation, but if we fail to see God's involvement, our truth-based problems will appear to go unsolved, and we will feel some measure of truth-based pain. And we will continue to carry these burdens until our perspectives are expanded, enabling us to see the "big picture." There is undoubtedly a time for *"weeping with those who weep"* (Romans 12:15), but until we see that Jesus bears our burdens (Isaiah 53:4), it will seem as though we have no choice but to struggle under their weight.

We are not somehow suggesting that our grief and sorrows are unwarranted or inappropriate; for the exact opposite is true! We *should* feel grieved when we lose a loved one. We *should* feel sad when tragedy strikes. We *should* feel angry at the sight of genuine injustice. However, we are also suggesting that these emotions only persist due to our lack of an eternal perspective.

Again, we draw your attention back to the cross. The ridicule, torture, and murder of our Saviour was grievous indeed! In fact, our imagined picture of His torment likely comes nowhere close to the graphic and heart-wrenching nature of the truth! He suffered greatly and died a gruesome death. This was true then and will remain true for all eternity, and the appropriate response to discovering this truth is to feel truth-based pain.

How do we find relief from our grief? How did the disciples find relief from theirs? For they too were grieved at Christ's crucifixion. Their burdens were not lifted from their shoulders because a certain amount of time had passed. Nor did they find freedom because they somehow processed through their grief or gave their sadness to God. They did not need to *do* or *give-up* something; they needed to *receive* and *perceive* something. They needed God to give them an eternal perspective of the truth that God the Father was in control, that He had a plan for redemption, and Christ's death was its foundation. Only when they perceived these greater truths did they find relief from their truth-based pain.

It was (and is) still true that Jesus died, and His death was truly cruel and unjust, but this is only part of the story. In the same way, when we are made aware of truly tragic situations, we only perceive a portion of the truth. We need His greater perspective. We need to be convinced of His involvement, purpose, and plan. We must come to realize that our Heavenly Father can handle our problems, no matter how big or painful they are. When we can view the loss, disappointment, or injustice from His eternal perspective, we will find relief from the truth-based pain that they cause knowing that He is bearing our burdens. Because the weight is on His shoulders, it doesn't also need to be on ours.

We need to trust in God's solutions to our "truth-based problems."

When you become aware of a painful truth, you will bear the burden of truth-based pain until you are made aware of a greater or additional truth which is God's fuller and complete perspective. For example, there was a swing in our backyard that our grandchildren loved. On one of their birthdays, I wanted to surprise them with something special. I built a small zipline for them and was planning on using their beloved swing as the seat they would ride on. But when my oldest granddaughter (who was 6 years old at the time) witnessed me taking down the swing, she panicked! "*Stop!*" she shouted, "*We love that swing!*" I could see the confusion and horror in her eyes. "*Just trust me, Ruby.*" I reassured her. "*No, stop! Put it back up! Please, Papa!*" She saw what I was doing but didn't understand why it was happening. She lacked perspective. Yes, I was taking down their swing. If that was all that was happening, I suppose she had a right to feel offended and robbed. However, this was not the whole story. She only saw a small portion of the truth.

I tried to encourage her by explaining that a zipline would be even more fun than a swing. This only upset her more as she protested, "But Papa, we don't have a zipline! And now we don't even have a swing!" She begrudgingly followed me to the cable that I had hung between two large trees. And as soon as I attached the swing to the zipline, she realized the value of her new ride, and her grumbles and tears turned to shouts of joy. She realized *why* I had taken down their swing. She was able to see the big picture. The reality of the swing being removed was painful when that was all she could perceive. But when that truth was coupled with the greater truth of the zipline, the burden was lifted off her shoulders.

Likewise, when we are able to rightly see God's plan and involvement in relation to our truth-based problems, we will rejoice in our suffering. As Paul said, "*We also celebrate in our tribulations, knowing that tribulation brings about perseverance; and perseverance, proven character; and proven character, hope; and hope does not disappoint, because the love of God has been poured out within our hearts through the Holy Spirit who was given to us*" (Romans 5:3-5). Paul knew that he could celebrate in his suffering because he viewed it from a heavenly perspective. He knew that the tribulations, no matter how painful, had a purpose and were being used by God to accomplish His plan. And he encourages us to have the same perspective so that we will join him in celebration!

When our hearts are convinced that God has a plan to solve our truth-based problems, we will rejoice and celebrate too. We can continue to weep until we enter into eternity, where we will have our tears wiped away (see Revelation 21:4), or we can look to God and become convinced of His perspective, so that we can begin celebrating now!

The reason so many people wait until heaven to have their tears wiped away is because they lack a heavenly perspective. They hold the portion of truth which is grievous, sorrowful, disappointing, and regretful, but they lack the rest of the truth that would cause them to rejoice. They realize the truth that their "swing set" has been dismantled, but they lack the greater truth that it was taken apart in order to construct a heavenly "zipline!" The moment they are convinced of this reality, their tears will dry up and their joy will be made full.

When we enter Heaven, all our tears will be wiped away. However, we do not have to wait until then to gain a Heavenly perspective. Our tears flow today because we do not yet see through His eyes. If the Holy Spirit gives us His perspective now, we can begin rejoicing on this side of glory.

Our truth-based pain is resolved when we realize greater or additional truths.

On multiple occasions, Jesus offered additional or greater truths to those who were struggling with truth-based pain (just as I attempted to comfort my granddaughter regarding her swing). He provided an eternal context and expressed God's motivation behind what was happening. He did this with Peter as He was being arrested in the Garden of Gethsemane when He said, "Put your sword back into its place; for all those who take up the sword will perish by the sword. Or do you think that I cannot appeal to My Father, and He will at once put at My disposal more than twelve legions of angels? How then would the Scriptures be fulfilled, which say that it must happen this way?" (Matthew 26:52-54). Peter was reacting to his limited perspective of the situation. He missed the big picture. He failed to put the immediate moment in its proper eternal context. Jesus attempted to expand Peter's perception so that he might see His Heavenly Father's involvement.

Another simple example of this was when his disciples were troubled by the fact that Jesus would be physically leaving them, and He further explained the necessity for His absence (John 16: 5-15), described His purpose in leaving (John 14:2-3), and promised His eventual return (John 14:18-20, 28). Each of these additional truths, if believed in the heart, offered comfort and confidence to the otherwise sorrowful truth of Jesus' physical departure.

If it wasn't for the eternal context and explanations that these additional truths provided, the reality of Jesus leaving would have been nothing but sorrowful. Jesus realized as much when He said, "*But because I have said these things to you, sorrow has filled your heart*" (John 16:6). His disciples needed to know that Jesus was leaving, but they also needed to know the rest of the story. They needed to see the big picture. When we only perceive part of the truth, we are left with painful truth-based problems. And freedom only comes when we are convinced of a greater truth in our hearts.

To take it a step further, consider the disciples' perspectives as they helplessly witnessed Jesus' crucifixion. They personally saw the truth of Christ's death. They knew in their hearts that He had been killed. This was the truth, and it was utterly devastating! Thankfully, as we all now know, this single truth does not tell the whole story. It is a singular thread in a great tapestry that is being woven by a loving and omniscient Creator. But because of their limited perspective, Jesus' disciples could not yet perceive the big picture, and they were left with truth-based pain and desperate questions.

We find ourselves in a similar state when we are confronted with truth-based problems but are unable to clearly see God's involvement. But just as the disciples' grief and bewilderment turned into joy at the recognition of their risen Savior (Luke 24:52-53), our truth-based pain is resolved when we realize greater or additional truths regarding our perceived problem. The reality of Christ's death remains true, but the greater truth of His resurrected life offers the eternal context from which we can rightly interpret His sacrifice. Likewise, when we are able to see God's purpose, plan, and involvement in our lives, we will more rightly perceive our situation.

Truth-based problems such as "tribulation, or distress, or persecution, or famine, or nakedness, or peril, or sword," (Romans 8:35) may still be present in our lives, but the fact that "all these things we overwhelmingly conquer through Him who loved us" (Romans 8:37) brings undeniable comfort, security, and purpose to our situation. You may still be *persecuted*, *naked*, and *hungry*, but if you are able to see the bigger picture and know that nothing can *"separate us from the love of God"* (Romans 8:39), then you can still rejoice in your suffering (Romans 5:3). Truth-based emotions are produced by the truth but continue due to our lack of perspective. Once we see the bigger picture, that truth will set us free from our truth-based pain.

All of this should also further encourage you to begin viewing your emotional pain as an honest friend, rather than a cruel enemy. It indicates what you believe in your heart. Even when your perspective is accurate, it is also often limited. When this is the case, your emotional reaction is not reflective of the whole truth of your identity, your situation, and God's involvement in your life. You are in need of a "greater" or "additional" truth to expand your perspective. The truth-based pain we feel is an indication that we are operating from a limited perspective. But if you know what to do in response, you can come into a deeper understanding of the truth and gain eternal benefit (Hebrews 12:11). Here again, this is by God's design and is good.

God's perspective provides peace and relief.

When confronted with truth-based problems, we need to see that God is in control and realize that nothing can thwart His plan. Like the disciples who were huddled together in bewildered confusion after Jesus was crucified, we must come to understand that Our Heavenly Father is accomplishing a good work in our lives no matter how tragic or futile our current situation seems. When we are able to view our situation from His perspective, we will realize that He "causes all things to work together for good to those who love God, to those who are called according to His purpose" (Romans 8:28).

Knowing a greater truth may not get you your job back, or allow you to travel back in time to correct past mistakes, or bring a loved one back to life, but it does offer the eternal context that is needed to rightly understand what has happened. Just as Christ's resurrection provides context, comfort, and purpose to His tragic death, knowing the greater truth regarding our truth-based problems allows us to see the whole truth of what is happening. When we are able to perceive and accept God's solutions to our problems, we are able to genuinely have "peace in every circumstance" (2 Thessalonians 3:16).

Recognizing God's motive and involvement provides the relief, assurance, and rest that we all desperately need. Someday soon, we will finally be able to see the big picture in all its magnificence from an eternal perspective, every tear will be wiped away, and "there will be no more death or mourning or crying or pain..." (Revelation 21:4). Come quickly, Lord Jesus!

THE DEATH OF MY CHILD WAS A "TRUTH-BASED PROBLEM."

One of the most burdensome examples of truth-based problems that my wife and I have experienced was the loss of our little girl. Sarah Michelle was a few days shy of her first birthday when she died suddenly from a brain aneurysm. We were devastated and experienced what seemed to be unbearable grief. Some well-meaning supporters warned that we would never fully "get over" the loss of a child. Thankfully, this was not true.

Over the course of several ministry sessions, my wife and I were each convinced of several important truths that resolved the pain of our loss. Now, when we think about Sarah, we only feel His joy and peace. The grief we felt was real, crippling, and appropriate for a time, but we are no longer carrying it. The fact that our daughter died was and is sad, but today we are no longer bearing that burden. When we were able to see her death from God's perspective, we were completely released of this heavy load. We will not see Sarah again until eternity, but the grief, sorrow, and loss are no longer on our shoulders.

When faced with a truth-based problem (such as being fired from your job, being falsely accused, getting betrayed by a friend, losing a loved one, etc.), we will feel some measure of truth-based pain. This pain is the result of our perspective of the situation, but our perspective is limited. We cannot rightly see all that is going on. The greater truth is that God is involved in more ways than we can possibly imagine.

Part Seven

We feel "lie-based pain" when we perceive "lie-based problems."

Our limited, temporal perspectives can make it difficult to see God's involvement in our lives and leave us feeling some measure of grief, sorrow, regret, disappointment, or anger. If we feel these emotions for righteous reasons (as Jesus did), then the Scriptures grant permission for feeling them, though not without specified time limitations (See Ephesians 4:26, Ecclesiastes 3:4, Romans 12:15). But as you will recall from the previous chapter, our perspectives are not only limited; they are also usually flawed.

Because of our flawed perspectives, we perceive problems that leave us feeling anxious even though we were clearly directed to "be anxious for <u>nothing</u>" (Philippians 4:6, emphasis added). We feel afraid despite the fact God has repeatedly told His people to *"fear not"* (Genesis 15:1, Isaiah 41:10, Daniel 10:12, Haggai 2:5, Matthew 10:31, Luke 12:32, Revelation 1:17, just to name a few) and explained that "perfect love expels <u>all fear</u>" (1 John 4:18 NLT, emphasis added). We worry about the future even though Jesus explicitly said, "<u>do not worry</u> about tomorrow" (Matthew 6:34). Why can't we seem to follow such simple instructions?

The issue is not with these commandments or the reality in which we live. It is not due to the devil's involvement or the desires of our old nature. Our disobedience stems from what we believe in our heart. Our heart belief contains lie-based impurities. Our emotional reactions are simply the result of how we have interpreted what is happening around us. When these interpretations are based upon inaccurate information, they are flawed, and our reactions are unfounded. This is why our feelings so often contradict the truths that are presented in Scripture. Nothing *we* can do will alter the fact that we will feel whatever we believe.

I have flown all around the world. Most of my flights have been uneventful and smooth. However, there were a few flights that tested the purity of my faith. One flight in particular exposed my lack of truth concerning God's care for and protection of me. The flight became very bumpy due to the turbulence, and at one point, the plane violently lost altitude. I immediately thought I was going to die! Panic and fear stirred up in me. My fellow passengers screamed, and some began to cry. I gripped the arm rests of my seat and started talking to myself out loud, "You are okay. It is just a little turbulence. The pilot has everything under control. Breathe! Focus! The Lord is my Shepherd. . ." Nothing I told myself seemed to help.

Obviously, I didn't die that day; I wasn't even harmed for that matter. The plane eventually leveled off, and we arrived safely at our destination. My perception did not reflect this reality. I didn't believe that I was safe. I believed I was going to die. My belief in this inaccurate prediction caused me to be afraid. The panic and fear were produced by my beliefs, not the plane's erratic movement. I felt what

I believed. I wonder what Jesus would have done in that moment when the plane lost altitude? More than likely, He would have been asleep.

When we misinterpret life through the lies we believe, we will perceive lie-based problems and feel lie-based pain as a result. We will feel emotions such as worry, stress, anxiety, fear, powerlessness, hopelessness, and abandonment when we view life from our skewed perspective. Much like the physical pain caused by a thorn in your foot, lie-based pain is the natural and automatic outcome of believing a lie in your heart. When you believe a lie in your heart, you will feel painful emotions as a result.

Quick Note: What follows are various scenarios which are meant to further illustrate the relationship between lie-based problems and lie-based pain. They are intended to be an investigation into misinterpretations of life events through the lies we believe. Rather than examining the context of the situation or the legitimacy of the person's reaction, simply notice that when they view their situation through a flawed perspective, they are presented with a lie-based problem and feel lie-based pain.

Scenario One:

Marcus had to unexpectedly work overtime again. The situation at his job did not allow him to call his wife to inform her of the change in plans. When he was finally able to make a phone call, she released upon him a flurry of questions and accusations. "Where were you? I told you that I couldn't pick up the kids from school today! They sat there for two hours waiting for you! I ended up leaving work early to get them. What am I supposed to say to my boss?" Marcus' mind immediately interprets his wife's words through the beliefs, "I am a failure," "There is something wrong with me," and "I'm not good enough." Because of this, her words seem to sting. He feels immense shame and guilt. But his emotional reaction is not caused by his wife's complaints; it stems from his lie-based misunderstanding of his identity. Her words simply exposed what Marcus believes about himself.

Scenario Two:

Elizabeth volunteered at her local crisis pregnancy center, was head of the planning committee at her church, served every weekend as one of the main greeters during Sunday worship, and had built up a reputation of being dependable, hardworking, and selfless. If someone needed help with something, they asked Elizabeth. But during the quiet moments in between her many responsibilities, Elizabeth felt uneasy and unsettled. Much of her behavior was driven by this emotional pain. In spite of the truth that she knew in her head, she felt rejected, overlooked, and unloved. And when she looked into the mirror, she didn't see what everyone else saw. It seemed to her that she didn't matter. This, too, was a consequence of her lie-based heart belief. She may genuinely be overworked and spread too thin, but her ongoing negative emotion was due to her flawed perspective, not her many responsibilities. If Elizabeth knew the truth in her heart, she would feel seen and treasured and would be able to devote her time responsibly rather than feeling compelled to do all that she was asked to do.

Scenario Three:

Aaron reluctantly opened another credit card bill. He lived paycheck to paycheck and was barely able to pay the interest on his accrued debt. He could not see a way out. Aaron regularly reminded himself of the truth described in Philippians 4:19 but never quite felt like God was supplying for his needs. He felt helpless, and this lie-based pain continually distracted him from following sound financial advice. His situation seemed overwhelming and hopeless. But his feelings of helplessness, discouragement and worry were merely exposing his beliefs, not his financial situation. If he knew the truth in his heart, he could reassess his monetary problems with peace and assurance.

Scenario Four:

Elaine was at her wit's end. It seemed as though most of her day was spent cleaning up after her four children, barking orders at them, and convincing them to obey. She read books and blog posts on parenting. She followed all the experts on social media. She desperately wanted to find help and direction in how to manage her daily routine. But she always felt like she was barely able to keep her head above water. Every task took longer than it should, and the children seemed to become less attentive and more disrespectful with each passing year. She felt discouraged and powerless. There were many times in which she wanted to escape the whole debacle. Her situation felt like it was out of control. But her discouragement and powerlessness was a consequence of her flawed perspective, not her disorderly household. If she could view her situation from God's perspective and see His involvement in it, she could tackle these challenges with peace, love, patience, and compassion and would be able to make right decisions with a clear mind.

Scenario Five:

Allie was convinced that she was being oppressed by the Devil. She felt a constant heaviness and depression looming overhead. She couldn't find the motivation to read her Bible or attend her weekly small group meeting. She would have impure thoughts and feel tempted to sin. She felt dirty and shameful. She genuinely wanted to reach out for help, but she felt as though something was pulling her back. From her perspective, she was oppressed, and she felt trapped because of it. But Satan was not holding her captive, nor was he causing her emotional pain, for he is incapable of doing either of these things (as we will discuss later). Allie was feeling the effects of what she believed in her heart. Blaming the Devil does not make it his fault. Her flawed perception of the situation seemed true, not because it was true, but because she believed it to be true. She was deceived. If she believed the truth in her heart regarding who she is in Christ and what He accomplished on her behalf, she would realize her freedom and not feel oppressed or trapped.

In each of these simple examples, the person's emotional status was an outcome of what they believed in their hearts. They interpreted their situation through what they believed to be true and felt the emotional consequences. Their lie-based heart beliefs produced lie-based pain. They were convinced that lies such as "*I am not good enough,*" "*I don't matter,*" "*I am trapped,*" "*I am helpless*", and "*I am going to die*" were actually true and felt the negative emotional consequences of this. They each may have known the truth in their heads, but their lie-based pain exposed their flawed perspectives. They each perceived lie-based problems and felt lie-based pain in response.

We feel what we believe, but the truth is still the truth.

By combining several of the principles we have discussed, we find that we perceive and feel what we believe in our hearts, but the truth is still the truth regardless. This concept offers hope to those who grasp it! Because of this reality, we can have confidence that when our situation seems dire, hopeless, or out of control, it simply means that we lack God's perspective. We are not seeing and experiencing the truth, but we are simply perceiving what we believe.

Likewise, our emotions are only an expression of what is believed in our hearts, not an expression of what is true! For example, if we are in Christ but feel as though we are defective, worthless, "dirty," or unforgiven, we are not viewing ourselves rightly. This is a symptom of our flawed perspectives. Our heart belief is on full display; we believe that we're something we're not.

If you are in Christ, then you <u>are</u> a "new creation" and "the old <u>has</u> passed away" (2 Corinthians 5:17, emphasis added). So, if you feel sinful, broken, or corrupted this simply means you do not yet believe the truth in your heart. When we know the truth of our identity in Christ at a heart level, it will feel true to us and will produce feelings of confidence, peace, and gratitude (Hebrews 4:16, Romans 5:1, Colossians 3:15). The problem is not with who we are but rather with what we believe. We only "know in part" what we really look like (1 Corinthians 13:12). This is an issue of heart belief and perception, not identity!

When you feel as though God has abandoned you or that your situation is out of control, this is only descriptive of your *belief*, *perception*, and *emotions*, but it does <u>not</u> describe *reality*. God has not abandoned you, but if you believe that He has, it will *seem* and *feel* as though He is absent. God is with us even when we don't see Him, and He is at work even if we don't notice it. He is who He says He is regardless of what we believe and how He appears. We are only able to see a dimly lit reflection of ourselves and of God (1 Corinthians 13:12). The issue is with our mirror and lack of light, not with reality.

Our flawed perceptions do not accurately reflect reality. They are nothing more than deceptive fabrications. Nevertheless, the consequences of our flawed perspectives and the lie-based pain they produce is very real indeed! If you believe that you are worthless, it will seem as though you are, and you will feel lie-based pain in response.

If we rightly understand their intended purpose, these lie-based emotions can be helpful and productive. They are designed to draw our attention to something. They show us our need for God's perspective. If we humbly position ourselves at the Lord's feet and have Him correct our flawed perspectives, the lie-based pain will have accomplished its purpose and evaporate. When the "thorn" is removed from our "foot," the pain ceases.

BEING "TRIGGERED" INDICATES OUR NEED FOR GOD'S PERSPECTIVE.

In TPM, we borrowed a term from the psychological community that describes being emotionally "set off" or "sparked" because of someone's words or action, an event or situation, or even by a fleeting thought one might have. This borrowed term is the word "triggered." The word first emerged following World War I to describe the emotional reaction some soldiers experienced from "battle fatigue" (now referred to as "Post Traumatic Stress Disorder").

In TPM we understand that the state of being triggered is an outcome of the natural God-created mental process of association. When something happens to us and we interpret it through one or more of our heart beliefs, we will immediately *feel whatever we believe*. This emotional surge is the outcome of our heart beliefs being accessed or "triggered."

After becoming familiar with this concept, most people are initially surprised at how often they seem to get triggered. It is safe to say we all get triggered on a regular basis. Some people, unfortunately, live in a constant state of being triggered as they continually feel some measure of anxiety, stress, worry, fear, are easily angered, impatient or frustrated.

These "knee-jerk" emotional reactions to life situations feel bad in the moment, but they also represent invaluable opportunities. They are part of God's warning system that alerts us to the fact that we need His perspective. If we respond appropriately, we can greatly benefit. When we embrace and apply this principle, we will view the actions and behaviors of others as less of a threat and realize that they are simply 'tools' in the hand of God.

We typically deny what we feel, make excuses for it, blame those around us, or distract ourselves through some form of "self-medication." It often seems easier to make excuses such as, "I'm just having a difficult day" (blaming our circumstance), "He makes me so mad!" (blaming others), or "I'm just not myself today" (deflecting personal responsibility). We need to realize that any measure of emotional pain indicates that we are operating from a flawed and/or limited perspective.

When our emotions get stirred up, we must slow things down and attempt to honestly answer the question, "Why am I feeling what I feel?" If we rightly understand what God is trying to accomplish while we are "triggered," we will be able to "rejoice always, pray without ceasing, [and] in everything give thanks" (1 Thessalonians 5:16-18)

CHAPTER 6

THE "BELIEF AND CHOICE" PRINCIPLE

"WE DO WHAT WE BELIEVE."

NOTICE: This chapter has been divided into seven parts. The first part explores the concept that we do what we believe. The second part examines the relationship between our emotions and our behavior. The third part generally discusses the way in which we employ solution behaviors to "solve" our perceived problems. The fourth part explains the specific reasons why we engage in solution behaviors. The fifth part addresses the importance of the motives behind our actions. The sixth part explains that even our "good" behavior can be done with impure motives. And the seventh part revisits the idea that there is no meaningful difference between those who perform well and those who struggle.

Part One

We do what we believe.

Why did you brush your teeth today, or wear what you are currently wearing, or begin reading this book? Why do you go to work, or study the Bible, or watch television? Why do you do any of the things you do? Simply put, you do what you choose to do. Your behavior is the result of choice.

This simple explanation begs several important questions: "Why do you make these choices?" "What are your decisions based upon?" "And if you wanted to choose differently, could you do so?" To explore the potential answers to these questions, consider the following illustration.

Imagine that you are a participant on a TV game show. You are randomly selected to play a game in which your only task is to choose whether to open "door number one" or "door number two." You are then awarded the prize that is hidden behind the door you select. At first glance, this choice seems completely arbitrary. However, after explaining the rules of the game, the host comments, "*Just so you know, there is $10,000 dollars in cash hidden behind door number one.*" Given this information, which door would you choose? But if you then heard him say, "*...and 1,000,000 hidden behind door number two,*" would your decision change? But if the host followed this remark with, "*...yes, you heard that right, there are 1,000,000 tiny ants hidden behind door number two,*" this clarification would obviously impact your decision!

As you gain more information, your perspective and preferences change. Your decision is entirely dependent upon the information you have. Or, more specifically, it depends on what you believe to be true. But notice the important fact that you did not consciously *choose* to prefer one door over the other. This happened automatically as you gained more information and as your perspective changed.

You will select the door that you *believe* leads to the most valuable and beneficial prize. You have specific reasons for opening "door number one," as well as reasons for keeping "door number two" closed. Would you knowingly choose to forfeit the money and accept the tiny creatures as your prize? Probably not! You would likely only select "door number two" if you either hadn't heard what was behind it or had mistakenly believed it was hiding a greater, more valuable prize. In either case, your limited and flawed perspective would have resulted in your choosing the wrong door and forfeiting the better prize.

Not to belabor the point, but it is important to emphasize the fact that your decision would be based upon what you *believe* to be true, not necessarily what is *actually* true. Do you know for certain that the host is telling you the truth? There is obviously the potential that he is lying or misinformed. It is just as possible that you misheard him. Regardless, if you *believe* what you heard, this belief will impact your final decision.

You will choose to do what *seems* best from your current perspective (Proverbs 21:2). But just because something *seems* like the "best" option doesn't mean that it is the "best." It only *seems* to be the best option because it is in line with what you believe is best. Your decision will reflect your belief. This is why we say, "*we do what we believe.*"

We commonly refer to this concept as the "Belief and Choice Principle." And this relationship between what we believe and what we choose to do forms the basis of many important discussions throughout this book. We make the choices we make and engage in the behaviors we do because of what we believe to be true. Again, we do what we believe.

We "obey" what we believe.

Another way to think about this concept is to replace the word "do" with the word "obey." We *obey* what we *believe*. Here again, you may still have a choice in the matter, but your decision in who or what to "obey" is highly influenced by what you believe to be true. For instance, if the game show host from the previous example asked you to select "door number one," you would likely "obey" his request without hesitation because His suggestion is in line with what you believe is best.

However, it would be quite difficult for you to "obey" him, if he asked you to choose the door that you believed was less than ideal. It would be hard to "trust and obey" him if you believed that you were forgoing $10,000 to become an ant farmer! But in either scenario, the ease or difficulty in your obedience has little to do with the inherent difficulty of the task at hand. Rather, the difficulty you experience when choosing to obey is directly related to what you believe to be true.

This concept makes me think of the countless times I've asked my children to do something only to be met with grumbling and complaining. My children would experience difficulty in obeying because the thought of cleaning their rooms failed to follow what they believed was "best." However, if I issued a command that reflected what they believed to be good, right, and profitable, such as, "Kids, put your shoes on, and get in the car because we are going to get ice cream!" then their obedience would be immediate and effortless. They would not struggle to obey; in fact, they would obey with enthusiasm and joy!

The actual task of picking up dirty clothes off the floor and putting them in the hamper is hardly more difficult than putting on shoes and walking to the car, but obeying the former command clearly *seemed* more difficult for my children, and they would experience real struggle when attempting to obey this simple directive. Their reaction to my requests indicated what they each believed. It was obvious when my instructions were in line with what seemed "best" to them, but it was just as obvious when my words conflicted with their beliefs!

They would mutter their objections and try bargaining with me in hopes that I would change my mind or issue different commands. They had reasons for disobeying, and because of this, obedience seemed difficult for them. But the difficulty they experienced while attempting to obey stemmed from their belief, not from my instructions or even the task itself.

If they would have been able to rightly perceive my motive, the reasoning behind my requests, and the extent to which they would personally benefit, they would have automatically and instantaneously obeyed my requests without difficulty. The effort involved in the activity would remain, but the mental barrier between them and their obedience would be removed. Instead, they leaned on their own understanding (Proverbs 3:5), and their limited and flawed perspectives of me and my instructions made it quite difficult for them to obey their father!

Obedience is effortless when we agree with the command.

Our choices and actions reflect what we believe to be true. This concept helps to explain much of our behavior. It sheds light on why some of us struggle to drive under the posted speed limit or wash our hands *every time* we use the restroom or come to an agreement on what to watch for movie night. But it can also help us understand why we struggle with more important decisions.

For instance, why do we struggle to obey what God asks us to do? For the most part, we struggle to obey God for the same reasons my children struggled to obey me. At some level and to varying degrees, His words conflict with our current beliefs. Our flawed and limited perspectives make it impossible for us to rightly perceive and understand what He has said and why He has said it. We may genuinely intellectually know that His ways are "good," but they do not seem "best" according to other beliefs that we also hold.

In reality, His plans are for our good (Jeremiah 29:11), and those who obey His words are blessed (Luke 11:28). King David clearly laid out the facts when he wrote,

> The instruction of the Lord is perfect, renewing one's life;
> The testimony of the Lord is trustworthy, making the inexperienced wise.
> The precepts of the Lord are right, making the heart glad;
> The command of the Lord is radiant, making the eyes light up.
> The fear of the Lord is pure, enduring forever;
> The ordinances of the Lord are reliable and altogether righteous.
> They are more desirable than gold - than an abundance of pure gold;
> And sweeter than honey, which comes from the honeycomb.
> In addition, Your servant is warned by them; there is great reward in keeping them.

(Psalm 19:7-11 HCSB)

Every word of this passage is entirely true. But if we don't fully believe them in our hearts, they will not *feel* or *seem* true to us. At some level, we will be resistant and hesitant to follow His commands, even though they are pure, enlightening, righteous, and more desirable than gold. This is especially true when we have been deceived into believing that some ungodly behavior is more desirable than what God has prescribed!

You may agree with God in your head, but if your heart's belief is contrary to the truth, His ways will not *feel* or *seem* "right" and "perfect." Consequently, it will *feel* and *seem* as though obeying God is a less than "perfect" option. Or, worse yet, another strategy will appear to offer a better prize than the "great reward" that David describes. When this is the case, much like the hypothetical TV game show, you will feel compelled and motivated to open a different "door" than the one God offers.

Our disobedience is no one's fault but our own.

Like my *occasionally* disobedient children, you will experience some measure of difficulty when attempting to obey a "commandment" that you do not completely agree with. On the other hand, if what you are asked to do reflects what you believe to be true, you will automatically and effortlessly obey without hesitation. Either way, you choose to do what you do because of what you believe to be true.

Some may protest and claim that their actions are the result of their circumstances, family history, upbringing, the injustices in their lives, or some other external influence. Although we do respond to each of these factors, none of them are the reason we do what we do. None of us plan to stand before God and defend our behavior by claiming, "the devil made me do it!" And yet, blaming anyone else for our lackluster performance is just as baseless and illogical. Blaming others for our behavior is an empty and weak defense.

Blame-shifting is akin to the childish arguments that we discussed in the previous chapter. If I *hypothetically* discovered two of my grandchildren bickering and asked, *"What is going on?"*, my granddaughter might explain, *"he just pulled my hair!"* Shocked, I might ask my grandson, *"Elijah, why did you pull your sister's hair?"* *"Because she kicked me!"* *"Penelope, why did you kick your brother?"* *"Because he threw dirt at me!"* *"Why did you throw dirt at your sister?"* *"Because she won't stop following me."* At some point, enough blame was passed around for everyone to receive a punishment, and I'm left wondering where their parents are!

Humanity has been doing this since the Garden of Eden. Just as Adam blamed his wife and Eve blamed the serpent, we blame those around us to defend our poor behavior (Genesis 3:12-13). "I wouldn't have done this if she hadn't done that!" we claim. This "eye for an eye" mentality never results in godly behavior, and it keeps us from recognizing the real problem.

Obviously, none of this discussion takes anything away from the fact that people are capable of cruelty, malice, and evil, and their behavior is inexcusable. But no matter how unjustly we have been treated, our choices and behavior are our responsibility. The sooner we can take ownership of what we do and why we do it the sooner we can expect to find freedom and release.

There is a difference between our "will" and our "desire."

We may genuinely *want* and *desire* to follow God's promptings, but our *"will"* is expressed in what we do. Our "desire" is what we *want* to do, but our "will" is what we *choose to do*. We *want* to quit cursing but are *willing* to let a few words slip if the context seems to merit it. We *want* to stop searching for graphic images online but are *willing* to look "just one more time." We *want* to forgive those who have wronged us but are not *willing* to release the debt. We *want* to spend more time in prayer but are not *willing* to invest the precious moments that it would require. We *want* to speak the truth but are not *willing* to publicly admit that certain sins are sins. We *want* to walk in truth and freedom, but we are not *willing* to accept responsibility for the emotions we feel or the choices we make.

We want what God wants for us, yet even a cursory examination of our behavior makes it clear that we are often unwilling to do such things. Unless we view our situation through His eyes, we will be drawn aside and compelled to engage in behaviors that contradict what we genuinely desire. The difficulty we experience when attempting to obey God's instructions has little to do with the actual tasks. Rather, our struggle indicates that we have a belief problem! What we are choosing to do at any moment is reflective of what we believe.

You can observe this dynamic in practically every TPM session. Our default behaviors frequently contradict what we genuinely *want* and *desire* to do. When this happens to people who do not yet understand this principle, they often feel "stuck." Even if they try their best to do what they know they should do, they still feel inhibited. This is because they are unknowingly attempting to act in opposition to what they believe. The reality is that they deliberately choose to do what aligns with their current beliefs and perspectives.

Our struggle to obey God indicates our need for His perspective.

Hopefully you now see the importance of having God's perspective as it relates to obeying His commands. If our beliefs mirror His instructions, we will effortlessly obey with the same enthusiasm that my children had when told that they were getting ice cream. When we rightly and fully perceive His motive and purpose, as well as the nature of His instructions, we will delight in His commandments.

We see this relationship between our understanding of God's instruction and our obedience to it in Scripture where it says,

> Teach me, Lord, the meaning of Your statutes, and I will always keep them.
> Help me understand Your instruction, and I will obey it and follow it with all my heart.
> Help me stay on the path of Your commands, for I take pleasure in it.
> Turn my heart to Your decrees and not to material gain.
> Turn my eyes from looking at what is worthless; give me life in Your ways.
> Confirm what You said to Your servant, for it produces reverence for You.
> Turn away the disgrace I dread; indeed, Your judgments are good.
> How I long for Your precepts! Give me life through Your righteousness.
> (Psalm 119:33-40 HCSB)

Like the Psalmist, when we understand God's instruction, we will obey and follow it with all our hearts and take pleasure in it (Psalm 119:34-35). Because of this, we can logically infer the inverse of this truth; if we do not follow God's instruction with all our hearts and take pleasure in it, then we lack understanding. In this instance, we have a belief problem, not an obedience problem!

It is not so much that we need God to help us obey as it is that we need Him to help us perceive and understand the truth. We need Him to turn our hearts and eyes from that which is material and worthless to that which is righteous and life-giving. When this happens, we will obey.

By learning to view our struggle and disobedience as indicators of our need for God's perspective, we are taking steps in the direction of true obedience. But before we can gain His perspective, we must first honestly realize our need for it. When we acknowledge our need and position ourselves to receive, He will gladly grant us His truth, and once we have it, we will express our love for Him by obeying His commands (John 14:15).

Part Two

Our emotions motivate our behavior.

You are never more driven to "do something" than when you are in a heightened emotional state. For instance, if someone gave you a brand new car, wouldn't you feel the urge to express gratitude? If one of your friends was diagnosed with terminal cancer, would you not feel compelled to offer comfort and help? How many times have you felt the need to bring "correction" to those you feel angry towards? When we feel something, we are compelled to do something. Our emotions drive us forward and push us to act. As surprising as it may sound, this is not a bad thing. The relationship between what we feel and what we do was designed and created by God.

God created us to be motivated by our emotions just as He is motivated by His. He gave His one and only Son because of the love He feels for us (John 3:16), Jesus obeyed His Heavenly Father and willingly suffered and died because of the joy that filled His heart as He anticipated what was being accomplished (Hebrews 12:2), and the Lord's wrath, which is provoked by humanity's sin (Romans 1:18), requires Him to bring about justice (Ecclesiastes 3:17).

Like God, we are motivated by what we feel; but unlike God, our beliefs do not always reflect the truth. His actions are often an expression of the love, joy, peace, sadness, and anger that He feels because He knows (and is) the truth. Our behavior, on the other hand, is often an expression of our lie-based pain. We sulk in depression, act erratically with anxiety, and cower in fear. When these painful emotions are stirred, we instantaneously feel the need to express what we feel. When we feel something, we do something.

Here again, a comparison to physical pain may be helpful. Over the course of my life, I have owned many kinds of farm animals, some requiring the use of electric fencing. And when my children were younger, my wife, Sharon, and I had to constantly remind them of the invisible danger living in that thin metal wire. Granted, the "danger" was superficial and temporary, but it was still quite unpleasant. Despite our fervent efforts, someone always got zapped!

I recall the day that Joshua, who was eight or nine years old at the time, learned to respect the fence through first-hand experience. I had just run a new strand of fencing across the backside of our property. Joshua was meeting with one of the neighborhood kids while each stayed on their respective sides of the barrier. My son was shirtless due to the warm Kentucky weather when his bare belly bumped into that electrified line...*ZAP!* He jumped back, let out a high-pitched squeal, and his not-so-compassionate friend laughed at my son's expense.

As much as Joshua disliked the pain, it was designed to help him. The moment he touched the wire, the jolt made him aware of the fact that he had a problem. He instinctively responded to it by jumping back to escape the perceived threat. The discomfort he felt motivated him to respond to the problem.

If it hadn't hurt, he would not have moved. But because it did, he stepped back. He felt something, so he did something.

Just as Joshua jumped away from the electric fence, we instinctively "jump back" from what *seems* to be causing the stress, anxiety, or fear that we feel. Our automatic, knee-jerk reaction is driven by the emotions that are produced by our *heart belief*. In other words, our beliefs create the perceptions we have and the emotions we feel, and in response, we make an emotionally charged decision to do something.

We see this dynamic in action just before Jesus shocks his disciples by calming the stormy sea (Matthew 8:23-27, Luke 8:22-25). Jesus was with His disciples, aboard a boat, when He fell asleep. While He was sleeping, a great storm came down on the lake and began rocking their boat and filling it with water. The disciples were terrified! They woke Jesus saying, "Save us, we are perishing!" Jesus pointed out their "little faith" (Matthew 8:26), rebuked the winds, calmed the storm, and again asked, "where is your faith?" (Luke 8:25).

He was riding-out the same storm, in the same boat as His friends, but they had an entirely different reaction to what was happening. Because they lacked the truth regarding who was in their boat, they *believed* they were in mortal danger. From their limited perspective, the wind and waters *seemed* out of control. Because of this, they were filled with fear and their panic drove them to wake their sleeping Savior. They woke Him up because they were afraid, but they were afraid because they lacked God's perspective!

If these men had genuinely known in their hearts that the Son of the Living God was riding in the boat with them, would their situation still have seemed out of control? Would they have been filled with the same fear and panic? Would they have still felt compelled to wake Jesus from his nap? The answers to these questions should be obvious. Their perception of the storm, the terror they felt, and their compulsive behavior all indicated what they believed to be true. We see this same principle at play in Jesus' reaction.

Jesus did not respond to being woken up by thanking his disciples or applauding their quick decision-making. They might have expected Him to say something like, "It's a good thing you guys woke me up. That was a close one!" But He recognized that their current emotional state and compulsive behavior was an expression of their flawed and limited perspectives. He pointed this out when He asked them, "*Where is your faith?*" Essentially, He was asking, "*Are you still not convinced of who I am?*" Because, if they were convinced, they wouldn't have behaved in the way that they did.

Jesus viewed their reaction to the situation as *abnormal* because that is exactly what it was! They were acting as though the situation was out of control when it wasn't. They were fearful because they believed that they were going to die even though this wasn't true (Matthew 8:25). They were not seeing clearly. They misinterpreted the storm because they did not yet fully know Who was in their boat. They lacked perspective. From the disciples' point of view, Jesus *appeared* to take control of the situation when, in reality, it was never out of His control!

Each passenger's perception, emotional reaction, and behavior was the outcome of what they believed to be true. Jesus' emotional response and subsequent behavior were drastically different from that of His friends because He had a proper perspective of their stormy circumstance. They lacked God's perspective and suffered the consequences. Jesus, on the other hand, saw the situation from His Father's point of view and enjoyed the peace and self-control that comes with it.

Our Heavenly Father's involvement and authority have not diminished since that stormy day. But if you believe something contrary to this fact, then your situation will *seem* and *feel* as though it is out of control, and your emotions will compel you to respond to this perceived problem. You are feeling the emotional consequences of believing a lie, and this pain will inevitably impact your subsequent behavior.

You may try to escape the pain by avoiding an awkward situation, securing a new job, finding a new spouse, or immersing yourself in a novel. You might attempt to protect yourself from future "shocks" by vowing never to let it happen again, altering your outward appearance, or becoming angry at the one who hurt you. You might attempt to escape the "storm" by trying harder, regretting past sins, recommitting to doing the "right" thing. But whatever you choose to do will be motivated by the pain that you feel because you lack God's perspective.

Would Joshua have jumped away from the fence if he didn't feel the jolt? Would the disciples have still disturbed Jesus's nap if they didn't feel afraid? Would the lies we believe have the same impact on our behavior if they didn't cause us to feel emotional pain? Probably not! Our emotions motivate our behavior. We will go as far as to say that when your *heart beliefs* begin producing noticeable emotional pain, you <u>will</u> do something in response.

Now, someone will argue, "I don't allow my emotions to control me! I simply ignore them. I don't let my feelings impact the choices I make!" However, it is only possible to ignore that which is presently there. The fact that you are now choosing to ignore your emotional pain is a direct result of its impact on you. You wouldn't have to ignore it if you were genuinely unaware of it. Your attempt at controlling your emotions is the way you have chosen to "jump back" from them. Rather than "waking Jesus up," you have simply decided to ignore what you feel. Your decision to ignore your pain is actually a clear example of how it is governing you.

Little Joshua could have decided to ignore the electrical shock and refrain from stepping away from the live wire, the disciples could have tried to suppress their fear and willfully chosen to let Jesus sleep, and you can choose to ignore the pain you feel and attempt to keep it from impacting your behavior. Hopefully, you see the illogical and self-destructive nature of these strategies. The better option is to address the problem head-on. Like we discussed in the last chapter, freedom comes through honesty, not denial. We must acknowledge what we feel and humbly admit that we too are "men of little faith" (Matthew 8:26). Rather than attempting to ignore, suppress, or escape our emotional pain, we must investigate the reason for why it is there in the first place. When we know in our hearts that Jesus is in the boat with us, we will have no need for these short-sighted solutions, for we will not be afraid!

Behaviors that are motivated by emotional pain indicate our need for God's perspective.

Rather than attempting to ignore the effects of what we feel, we need to recognize them for what they are and learn how to responsibly attend to them. When we are anxious, worried, scared, or stressed, we will feel compelled to do something about it. But rather than viewing these emotions and our compulsion to act as problematic, we need to view them as additional components of the God-designed warning system that makes us aware of when we are in need of His perspective.

When you feel angry and are compelled to tell someone off, you need the Lord's perspective. When you feel anxious and want to hide from social interaction, you need the Lord's perspective. When you are worried and feel driven to prepare for every potential future possibility, you need the Lord's perspective. When you are scared and feel the need to maintain your defenses, you need the Lord's perspective.

If you only believed the truth in your heart, you would not perceive lie-based problems or feel lie-based pain, nor would you feel the need to engage in certain behaviors in response. So, the fact that you do perceive such problems, and feel emotional pain, and are compelled to act in response, indicates that you are believing lies. As such, you need God's perspective.

Your compulsion to act in response to what you feel has potential consequences, but it also represents a valuable opportunity to gain God's perspective. When you understand this facet of your design as a part of God's divine warning system that alerts you to your need for His perspective, even these unwanted compulsions and drives can be used for your good (Romans 8:28).

We must escape the oppressive and mistaken perspective that our emotional pain and poor behavior somehow thwart God's plan. No matter what you think, feel, or do, God will use every aspect of every facet of every moment of your life to finish what He started (Romans 8:28, Philippians 1:6). The thoughts that you have, the pain that you feel, the choices you make, and the situations in which you find yourself are all being used for your good!

This does not mean that they *themselves* are good. On the contrary, much of what we think, feel, and do is quite bad, and the motives of those around us are often impure or worse! However, all of it exists within God's hands (Job 12:10, Psalm 31:15). Even when we face gale-force winds and surging waves, God is in complete control (Hebrews 2:8, Psalm 8:6, Luke 8:22-25). When we recognize this reality and trust His intentions, we will find rest alongside Jesus, no matter the weather (Hebrews 4:10)!

TPM MENTORS ALSO NEED GOD'S PERSPECTIVE.

People commonly approach the TPM training with the intention of using this ministry model to help others. Although this is a noble cause, helping others on their journey is nowhere near as important as submitting to God's refining work in your own life. Our desire to offer "help" is sometimes contaminated by our own emotional pain. Each Mentor must make a conscious effort to model what they are helping others to learn. It is often easy to detect when someone else is triggered, but noticing our own opportunities for refinement can sometimes elude us.

This can be especially problematic when attempting to mentor someone else in a TPM session. Whenever a Mentor's impure faith is exposed during a session, he or she will likely be motivated by their emotional pain to do something that shouldn't be done. For instance, a triggered Mentor may find him or herself wanting to guide, direct, make something happen, engage in some form of "spiritual warfare," or share personal opinion and "spiritual" insight. Such behaviors violate TPM protocol and will distract or hinder what needs to happen in the session. Beyond that, they are also *likely* motivated by emotional pain and deception.

This does not mean that we cannot offer ministry until we have fully grasped His perspective and are no longer "triggered." For if we wait until this is so, we will never minister. But when Mentors are triggered in a ministry session, they should attend to what has been exposed as soon as possible (before attempting to mentor anyone else in another session). If they fail to do so, God will inevitably use another TPM session to further expose what He wants to address.

To illustrate this, consider the following common experience that those who fly on an airline have witnessed. Before taking off, the flight attendant will provide basic instructions such as, "In the case of an emergency, secure your own oxygen mask before assisting others." There is a reason for this. If you pass out from a lack of oxygen, then those around you who need aid will also likely perish. The same is true for the Mentor in a TPM session.

Without exception, every Mentor will experience sessions where he or she becomes triggered by what is happening. The anxiety, stress, fear, panic, or frustration that stirs up will impact what the Mentor does next. In these moments Mentors need to acknowledge their need for "oxygen" (truth) and secure their own "masks" before assisting others.

If we choose to respond inappropriately when we find ourselves "triggered" or simply choose not to address what has been exposed in us, we will fail to benefit from the faith-refinement and mind-renewal that God desires for us. We will have forfeited an opportunity to be persuaded of the truth within our hearts. We inadvertently deprive ourselves of "oxygen" while attempting to help others breathe. This is unnecessary and counterproductive. Instead, we should recognize that being triggered is part of the warning system that God has designed to alert us to our need for His perspective. If we respond appropriately, we benefit from gaining truth, and those around us are given a model to follow.

Part Three

When faced with problems, we look for solutions.

If you notice that your bicycle tires are running low on air, you will likely fill them up. If you spill your drink, you will probably grab a rag or towel to clean up the mess. If you cut your finger while chopping vegetables, you will put on a bandage to protect the injury. When we are confronted with a *problem*, we will look for a *solution*. This is perfectly natural and exactly what God intends for us to do. However, when we search for solutions, we typically look in the wrong direction.

When confronted with difficulty, we look for a way to ease it. When we feel pain, we try to make it go away. When we receive unjust treatment, we attempt to take justice into our own hands. When we are victimized, we erect and maintain extreme boundaries to protect ourselves from further harm. When our emotional pain stirs, we attempt to soothe it by putting food in our mouths. When we feel out of control or vulnerable, we seek out "safe" contexts that enable us to live relatively untriggered. We engage in such "*solution behaviors*" to "solve" the problems we believe we face.

As we have discussed, some of the problems we perceive are based upon the truth and fully legitimate; this is so much so that they even have God's attention. For instance, if your dream house burns down, or you become paralyzed due to a freak accident, or someone you love takes his own life, these are all very real problems that have very real consequences. But when we are unable to recognize the "greater" truth of God's plan and involvement, we tend to react inappropriately.

We are like Peter on the night Jesus was arrested (Matthew 26:47-56, Mark 14:43-49, Luke 22:47-53, John 18:1-11). When he saw the armed mob and realized their intentions, Peter interpreted the situation as dire and looked for a way to solve the problem. He reached for his sword and attempted to fend off those who would lay hands on Jesus. Peter had succeeded in cutting off the ear of one of those who came to arrest Jesus, but, sadly, his efforts were unhelpful, misguided, and entirely unnecessary.

Jesus responded by first exposing the futility of Peter's actions by saying, "Put your sword back into its place; for all those who take up the sword shall perish by the sword. Or do you think that I cannot appeal to My Father, and He will at once put at My disposal more than twelve legions of angels?"(Matthew 26:53). He then offered the proper perspective by asking a couple of rhetorical questions, "Am I not to drink the cup the Father has given Me?" (John 18:11 HCSB); "How then shall the Scriptures be fulfilled, that it must happen this way?" (Matthew 26:54); and clarifying, "But all this has taken place that the Scriptures of the prophets may be fulfilled" (Matthew 26:56).

Peter drew his sword because he lacked perspective. He couldn't see the eternal context of his immediate situation or God's solution to the problem, so he devised one himself. If he could have viewed the ordeal from Jesus' perspective, he would have acted very differently.

Like Peter, we "draw our swords" when our situation seems dire. Although our solutions may address the temporal problem in front of us, they also expose our ignorance of the big picture. We do not see where God is, what He is doing, or the purpose He has in mind. Because of this, we stay angry at injustices in an attempt to bring punishment and correction, or hold onto our grief to prove our love for those we have lost, and use past regrets and disappointments to motivate us to do better in the future. All the while, God desires for us to realize the greater context so that we will trust in Him and put our "swords" away (Matthew 26:52).

What's worse is that much of the time the problems we attempt to "solve" are not even real. They are the outcomes of our lie-based heart belief. We are deceived into believing that we are worthless, broken, or unlovable and are then left to solve these problems on our own. Just as Peter misinterpreted his situation, we wrongly view ours as hopeless, threatening, and out of control. Although this perspective is flawed, it *feels* and *seems* true, and our behavior is driven by the emotional pain it produces. We will feel just as compelled to "solve" these lie-based problems as we do their truth-based counterparts.

We try to attain our worth and value by securing a high paying job. We seek out love and meaningful connection from those who cannot provide them. We attempt to gain control over our lives through the use of strict regiments, calendars, and checklists. We pour ourselves into hobbies, sports, political parties, and even church services to find purpose and identity. But each of these behaviors represent a faulty solution to a nonexistent problem. If the problems we are attempting to solve are based upon lies, then any solution we come up with will also be based upon lies.

Our solutions create more problems.

The issue is further compounded by the fact that our chosen solutions tend to complicate things, make matters worse, or create new problems altogether! Our angry desire for vengeance and justice eats away at us with little to no impact on the offender. Our attempts to block out painful emotions keep us from enjoying the positive ones. Our desperate striving for satisfaction and acceptance leads us down dark roads of addiction and regret. Our fervent efforts to follow in Christ's footsteps and conform ourselves to His image results in our becoming self-righteous and judgmental. We do the best that we can to solve our own problems, but this inevitably leaves us without hope or, worse yet, confident in our own efforts.

Peter reached for his sword because he thought it would help, but it only complicated the situation. Jesus had to then stop what He was doing and reattach the recently removed appendage. Jesus was following His Father's plan by subjecting Himself to false accusations, abuse, and eventual crucifixion.

Despite Peter's assessment of the situation, everything was moving along according to God's plan. Jesus was not in need of Peter's help. God had a perfect plan that He was executing right on schedule. However, He does occasionally stop to reattach some of the "severed ears" that result from our "helpful" involvement.

Imagine how different that night would have been if Peter would have simply admitted that he was afraid and asked Jesus for perspective and direction. Jesus may have assured Peter by saying something like, "Peter, this is not about you. It is going to be okay. I don't need you to do anything. Just trust me and go home. I will see you in a few days!"

Peter was doing what he thought was "best." Since he lacked the greater perspective of the Lord's purpose, power, and position, he acted inappropriately. His intentions may have seemed noble, but they were based on a flawed and limited perspective. Granted, this is obviously not a slight against Peter's reaction to the situation, for had I been there, I would have been leading the hasty retreat out of the garden! Our point is that Peter's solution did more harm than good (both literally and figuratively).

Our use of "*solutions*" might be compared to my grandchild who discovered that she had grape jelly all over her hands. As soon as she realized the mess on her fingers, she looked for a solution to her sticky problem. She tried every trick she thought would work. She wiped it on her shirt, flung it on the floor, attempted to lick it off (while inadvertently spreading it to her face), and then, worst of all, wiped her messy hands on her Paw Paw's pant leg. But the harder she tried to clean herself, the messier she (and I) became.

In the same way, when we attempt to solve our problems ourselves, we typically end up making a messy situation worse. Yet we often continue using our chosen solutions even when we experience their inevitable consequences.

We binge on a television show knowing that our workload is piling up, we scurry around looking for loose change so we can buy one more lottery ticket even though the previous 32 scratch-offs failed to produce the big prize, we spout off aggravated remarks even though we know they make a tense situation worse, we search online for explicit content when we know the crushing effects it has on our mental state and relationships, we lie about our behavior though we know dishonesty only traps us, and we bottle-up our feelings, put on a fake smile, and pretend that everything is fine, even though we know that these behaviors never lead to resolution or freedom.

At some level we see the effects of our choices and disagree with our own behavior. So much so that we are often able to warn others not to do what we do because we intimately know the cost involved. But we fail to follow our own advice. We smoke cigarettes to calm our nerves even though we know the health risks. We eat more food than we actually need because it distracts us from what we feel, but we are reminded of the consequences every time we look in the mirror. We spend countless hours at the gym each week chasing a sense of achievement and control at the expense of our family and household responsibilities. We feel the urge to buy something that promises to satisfy us even though our bank account is depleted and our credit cards are nearly maxed out. We feverishly work at an unsustainable pace to avoid feeling useless or left behind.

We don't *want* to do such things, but we do them anyway. We would like to change our behavior, but we feel compelled to continue doing what we do. It often *feels* or *seems* as though we are at war with ourselves, pulled in two different directions. The Apostle Paul described a similar struggle when he wrote, "I do not understand what I am doing; for I am not practicing what I want to do, but I do the very thing I hate" (Romans 7:15). Like Paul, we often feel unable to do what we truly desire. So why do we continue doing things that we don't really want to do? The answer is simpler than you may realize!

Part Four

We engage in solution behaviors because we believe lies about them.

The fact that we engage in solution behaviors shows that we believe the problems we face are solvable and that we believe our efforts will help. If we genuinely believed that our problems were unsolvable, we wouldn't look for a solution. And if we thought we were incapable of doing anything that might help, we wouldn't attempt to solve them ourselves. But we *do* believe our problems can be solved, and we *do* believe we are able to solve them, so we engage in solution behaviors. Our belief is displayed in what we do.

We pay our electric bills because we *believe* doing so ensures that the lights stay on, and we lock our doors at night because we *believe* it keeps us safe. Many of us have been led to *believe* that holding onto our anger ensures that those who have wronged us will be held accountable, and we choose not to think about certain events in our past because we *believe* doing so keeps us from being overwhelmed. We pay our bills and lock our doors because we *believe* those behaviors will help us, and we hold onto our anger and block certain memories because we *believe* these "solutions" will work as well. The important detail to notice here is that we *believe* our solutions will help. This obviously does not mean that they *will* help, it simply means that we have been led to *believe* that they will.

The consequences of the lies we believe are much the same as if they were true. Solution behaviors are another perfect example of this concept! For instance, think of all the superstitious behaviors that sports fans engage in before a big game. They wear specific jerseys each time their team plays. They feel the need to eat certain foods or sit in their special spot while they cheer from the couch. Why do they do this? Do these behaviors have any actual impact on the outcome of the game? Of course not! But because these diehard fans *believe* their actions are necessary, they are compelled to do what they do.

Like these superstitious sports fans, we attempt to solve our perceived problems by engaging in behaviors that seem to be helpful, productive, or effective. We avoid discussing certain topics because we believe it protects our relationships. We erect social barriers because we believe they will keep us safe. We suppress our emotions because we believe it will keep us from becoming overwhelmed. We repeatedly recite certain songs and prayers because we believe it impacts our spiritual reality. We punish ourselves because we believe doing so will improve our behavior. Even those who attempt to end their own lives do what they do because they believe it will "solve" their problem.

We do what we do because we believe it will help. None of us would implement a "solution" that we knew, beyond a shadow of a doubt, would <u>not</u> work. The very fact that we are engaging in a particular behavior shows that we believe (at some level) it just might work.

We perceive "problems" because our perspectives are limited and flawed, and we engage in "solutions" because we have been deceived into believing that they will help. This deceptive strategy of the enemy has been in play since the very beginning. In fact, as we will discuss later, one of Satan's primary schemes is to offer us short-sighted *solutions* to our perceived problems.

The Serpent led Eve into *believing* that she had a problem that would only be solved by exploring options other than the one God had offered. He tricked Eve into doubting God's honesty and authority (Genesis 3:4-5) making it seem as though she needed to lean on her own understanding to decipher what to do (Proverbs 3:5-7). Satan helped Eve craft humanity's first solution behavior. His deceptive schemes were effective then, and they remain effective today! We can learn a great deal about our current behavior by examining our first attempt at self-sufficiency in the Garden of Eden.

OUR NEED FOR "REPENTANCE" CONCERNING OUR SINFUL BEHAVIOR

Hopefully repentance follows our sinful behavior, but this does not mean what many believe it to mean! Paul wrote in his letter to the church in Corinth about how godly sorrow brings about a "repentance without regret." If we try to apply the misleading "turn from sin" definition here, it becomes awkward and confusing. He wrote;

> Now I rejoice, not that you were made sorrowful, but that you were made sorrowful to the point of <u>repentance</u>; for you were made sorrowful according to the will of God, so that you might not suffer loss in anything through us. For the sorrow that is according to the will of God produces a repentance without regret, leading to salvation, but the sorrow of the world produces death (2 Corinthians 7:9-10, emphasis added).

Again, the word that is translated as "repentance" in this verse is the Greek word *metanoia*. For a moment push out of your mind the idea of *turning from sin*, and replace it with *God granting a change in belief* and then reread this passage with this understanding in mind. I think that you will see that it takes on a clearer and fuller meaning.

Paul writes a peculiar sounding phrase when he says, "the sorrow that is according to the will of God produces a repentance without regret." This is where a proper understanding of "metanoia" (repentance - change of belief) becomes very important. For why would we ever regret *turning from sin*? (misunderstanding metanoia). Paul was explaining that this "sorrow" was designed by God to move them toward the truth. The "repentance" (transformation of their belief) would not disappoint them or ever cause them to regret the change.

Again, *metanoia* does not mean to "turn from" anything, but rather it is a change in perspective or belief. When our belief changes, we will turn from our sin without ever looking back or feeling regret! When we are persuaded of the truth regarding our sin, turning from it becomes natural and effortless. There is no regret because going back to it will make no sense in light of the truth. Every sin we ever commit is motivated and accomplished in the context of deception.

However, I have known of people who "turned from their sin and turned to God '' and then later regretted doing so. How could this be? There was never a change of belief (*metanoia*). The reason for their regret is that true "repentance" never occurred. Choosing not to sin and trying to follow Jesus will not take you very far. At some point you may regret the decision like the Isralites longing to return to their Egyptian captivity (Exodus 16:3). Without a change in belief, regret and disappointment will eventually find their way into your life. Your turning from sin may go a full 360°, and you find you have turned all the way around and are back where you started.

To illustrate this concept further, consider the following. Many of my grandchildren love playing with frogs. They inspect every rock and shrub until they have found enough small, slimy creatures for each member of the search team. The kids kindly handle the amphibians while building (what they believe to be) perfect houses and habitats for their newly found friends. This outdoor activity consumes many hours of playtime, to the delight of child and parent alike!

Thankfully, we don't have to worry about many dangerous varieties of frogs where we live! If we were located in the Amazon, however, this would not be the case! Take the Golden Poison Frog for example. Although these tiny creatures are small in comparison to our local frogs, they are brightly colored and beautiful to behold. My grandchildren would be drawn to pick them up and play with them, but to do so could prove deadly! There is enough poison in its skin to kill multiple people. You could die by simply touching it! Even though my grandchildren might initially feel tempted to play with this adorable creature, the revelation of its poisonous potential would rightly kill their enthusiasm. This change of thinking (metanoia - "repentance") would have an immediate effect on their desire to engage in this "sin" that leads to death!

In the same way, until we are convinced of the dangers, risks, and costs associated with our solution behaviors (or at least their ineffectiveness), we will *likely* feel drawn to engage in them. It may genuinely *seem* desirable to do what we are tempted to do, but this is only because we are unaware of their drawbacks and dangers or have been deceived into believing that they are worth the risks. When we have His perspective of our short-sighted solutions, they lose their appeal!

We always think before we act even if not at a conscious level.

Remember, we do what we do because of what we believe to be true. This means that even our poor behavior is an outcome of our belief. In spite of how it seems, our choices and behaviors are calculated, measured, and reasoned. In fact, the worst decision ever made by a human being was contemplated first.

Eve concluded that the fruit from the tree of the knowledge of good and evil (which was not to be eaten, see Genesis 2:9, 17) was "good for food," a "delight to the eyes," and "desirable to make one wise" (Genesis 3:6). Because of these beliefs, she ate. Her actions were the result of her choice, and her choice was the result of her beliefs. Her problem wasn't that she didn't think about it first. Her problem was that her reasoning was blindingly limited and horribly flawed!

Eve could have responded to the problem that Satan described in any number of ways. First and foremost, she could have asked God about it. She could have honestly and openly talked with Him regarding her interaction with the serpent. Who knows, God might have straightened her out (Proverbs 3:6)! But she could have also simply discussed the matter with her husband, or resisted Satan and told him to leave (James 4:7), or tried convincing the serpent to sample the fruit first. Of all the options available to her, why did she choose to do what she did? The fact that she decided to eat from the tree indicates that, at some level, she believed doing so was her best option.

We also eat "forbidden fruit" when we believe there are legitimate reasons for doing so. At some level we may know that the behavior is illogical, unhelpful, misguided, or even destructive, but it will still *feel* or *seem* as though we should do it. We feel compelled to act in accordance with what we believe. Because of this, when our beliefs "miss the mark" and contradict God's standards, so does our behavior (Romans 14:23). We do what we believe, no matter where those beliefs point us. We always have reasons for doing what we do.

A behavior is a "solution" if it is done to solve a perceived problem.

Eve ate the fruit because she thought it would accomplish something. She believed it would solve a problem. Because of this, the act of eating the forbidden fruit was Eve's "*solution behavior*." The motive behind her behavior, not the behavior itself, is what makes this distinction. Even if a solution behavior has the outward appearance of innocence or insignificance, the beliefs and motivation behind it may be rotten.

Eve's act of disobedience may have seemed unthreatening on the surface (*she only took a bite of fruit, for goodness' sake!),* but the lie-based belief lurking behind it led her to solve her own perceived problems and resulted in condemnation and death. Many of our own behaviors are done for similar reasons. For instance, someone who abuses medication for the purpose of escaping angst and depression is obviously engaged in a solution behavior, but what about the man who donates to charities for the purpose of gaining recognition, or the woman who serves on the worship team at church so that she feels important and included, or the couple who refrains from talking about certain subjects because the conversation always leads to a fight? Is supporting local charities or volunteering at church wrong? No. Aren't we supposed to be careful with the words that we use? Of course!

But let's go back to Eve for a moment. She took a bite of fruit. So what? We've all done that. In reality, her behavior wasn't the main problem. The true offense is found in the reasoning behind her behavior. The issue is in what her choice represented. Her actions indicated that she trusted her own perception and reasoning instead of relying upon what God had said. Although it likely seemed harmless at the time, her illegal snack was a defiant protest against God's authority. Again, it may not have *felt* or *seemed* like a big deal, but the truth was still the truth regardless of what she believed. In the same way, when we attempt to resolve the problems that stem from our limited and flawed perspectives, we are inadvertently copying Eve's poor behavior.

When we attempt to meet our own needs and solve our own problems, we mistakenly attempt to assume God's role in our lives. We attempt to keep ourselves safe even though He is our Protector (Psalms 5:12, 18:2, 32:7, 121:1-8, 2 Thessalonians 3:3). We try to provide for our own needs even though He has promised to do so (Philippians 4:19, Psalm 54:4, Matthew 6:31-33). We try to make ourselves clean and live rightly through our own efforts even though He is the only source of righteousness (Romans 3:22, Jeremiah 23:6, Genesis 22:14). We seek out justice in our own lives even though He is the One who will bring it about (Ecclesiastes 3:17, Hebrews 10:30, Psalm 37:8-9, 50:6). We attempt to bear the weight of our grief and sorrow even though He has taken it upon Himself and promised to bear our burdens (Isaiah 53:4, Matthew 8:17). We do everything we can to control our behavior even though He guides our path (Psalm 32:8, 119:105, Proverbs 3:5-6, 16:9, Romans 8:14). But regardless of what we believe, the truth remains: God is who He said He is, and He will do what He said He will do.

No matter how helpful, productive, or moral our behavior seems to be, if we are attempting to do God's job for Him by acting as a "problem solver," we are engaged in a "solution." But again, this is a belief issue, not a behavior issue! Until we have His perspective, our efforts will seem to be needed. But when we rightly perceive His involvement in our lives, we realize that much of what we do is, at best, unnecessary.

Solution behaviors indicate our need for God's perspective.

If Adam and Eve genuinely understood the true ramifications of eating from the forbidden tree, do you honestly think they would have taken a bite? Knowing what you know now, if you were to trade places with them, would you eat of that tree? The fact that they disobeyed God and ate of the fruit clearly indicated their lack of perspective. They failed to comprehend what they were forfeiting by disobeying God. They didn't fully understand what they were doing.

Jesus obviously had this sympathetic perspective of those who were with Him on Calvary. As He compassionately watched those in attendance, He asked His Heavenly Father to "forgive them; for they do not know what they are doing" (Luke 23:34). If the onlooking mob knew the truth of what was taking place that day, their behavior would have been dramatically different. But we can't sit in judgment, for it seems that we are just as ignorant of the gravity of our behavior as those who cheered for the execution of our Savior. They didn't know what they were doing, but then, is our behavior any less short-sighted and foolish?

We would stop doing much of what we do if we perceived ourselves and our situation from God's perspective. Since we have been deceived by "empty words" and arguments, we behave improperly, in a manner that is unsuitable for "children of light" (Ephesians 5:3-10). These lie-based beliefs have led us to do things we would not otherwise do. Like Adam and Eve, we step out of line because we've been tricked!

We are drawn to engage in improper behavior because we have been led to believe that it will be worth it. This concept is not too different from the marketing strategies that the food industry employs. They create delicious looking "foods" for their commercials that are designed to draw our attention and make us drool. In reality, these succulent-looking dishes are almost never what they appear to be. They are typically made of unappetizing or inedible materials. They are hand-crafted to look like real food, but they are fake. The milk in those cereal bowls is actually glue, the grill marks on those perfectly grilled "steaks" are made using shoe polish, and the warm maple "syrup" dripping down those steaming stacks of pancakes is nothing more than motor oil. If you truly knew what you were looking at, you wouldn't feel nearly as hungry after viewing these misleading advertisements. They are meant to represent something scrumptious and delightful, but they are often inedible or toxic.

In the same way, our solutions only seem "appetizing" to us because of what we believe about them. More than anything else, our solution behaviors indicate that we have been deceived. We have been led to believe that there are legitimate reasons for doing what we do. Because of these *solution beliefs,*" our misguided ways seem right in our own eyes (Proverbs 21:2), and we are compelled to act out our deception.

God desires for us to rely upon His involvement and trust in His solutions, and He knows that we will when the eyes of our hearts are opened (Ephesians 1:18). He is working to expand and correct our limited and flawed perspectives. But He also wants us to realize the futility of our "solutions" and the sufficiency of His.

We need to learn what Peter discovered in the Garden of Gethsemane through panic and embarrassment; we are not equipped to solve our own problems. They require more than a reckless reaction with a fisherman's blade. Our best attempts to take control of the situation will only make things worse. But before we can put our "swords" away, we must admit our reasons for drawing them in the first place and acknowledge the mess that we have made while attempting to solve our own problems.

Like my granddaughter with jelly on her hands, we are doing the best that we can (given our immature perspectives). But if we will stop to admit that we have been trusting in earthly solutions and humbly ask our Heavenly Father for help, He will lovingly and carefully clean our hands and purify our hearts.

Part Five

To rightly understand our behavior we must examine both our motives and context.

Imagine that someone kicked-in your front door, entered your home, grabbed one of your loved ones, and ran back outside. What would you feel? What would you want to do in response? What would you think of this person's actions? Although this scenario might initially seem tragic, to rightly interpret the situation, you must take into account the person's motives and the greater context of what happened. For instance, if the home invader was a concerned neighbor who "broke in" because your house was on fire, would this not dramatically alter your response to his actions?

Now, you may be thinking, "That's not really fair! Your initial description was misleading. If I would have known about the fire and the neighbor's reason for rushing into my house, I wouldn't have reacted the way that I did." But this is precisely the point! Your limited perspective resulted in a misinterpretation of the situation and a misattributed motive behind the person's behavior. We each do this every day! We fail to see the "big picture" from an eternal perspective and come to wrong conclusions regarding what is happening in our lives. (This point will become clearer when we apply it to God, and His involvement in our lives, in our discussion of TPM's Purpose.)

The person's behavior must be interpreted through a proper understanding of why he is doing it and the context of the situation. Without these elements, it is impossible to rightly judge his actions. For this same reason, Jesus' words and behavior constantly confused those around him. For the most part, the observing crowds failed to fully fathom who was speaking, why He was sent, and the eternal context of His time on earth. Because of this, they watched, listened, and wrongly concluded that He was John the Baptist, Elijah, or one of the prophets (Matthew 16:14). Others assumed He was simply a "good teacher" (Luke 18:18). Much of the religious leadership viewed Him as a law-breaking heretic. Ironically, many of those who had the most accurate understanding of Jesus were the demons He encountered during His ministry, but even they were confused by His presence and purpose (Mark 1:34, Mark 5:6-7, Luke 4:34, 4:41, Luke 8:28).

The events leading up to Jesus' death were misinterpreted by practically everybody because no one fully understood His motive or the greater context of what was transpiring. Our Savior's actions seemed foolish, confusing, unnecessary, and hopeless, but the exact opposite was true!

Here again, we see that just because something *seems bad*, doesn't mean that it *is bad*. Granted, those who falsely accused God's Son were driven by self-seeking motives, those who mocked Him were expressing their sinful desires, and those who hurt Him were obviously driven by hate. If we view these events through a limited or flawed perspective, we will fail to see God's purpose and involvement. Each of these immoral acts were used to accomplish an eternal goal of unfathomable glory (Romans 8:28, 2 Corinthians 4:17). Christ's crucifixion seemed terrible, but when it is understood in its eternal context, it is clearly very, very good!

The inverse of this concept is also true. Just because something *appears to be good*, does not mean that it *is good*. For instance, if someone gave you a $500 gift card to your favorite store, this might seem like a welcome blessing and an example of that person's generosity. But if you later discovered that the card was stolen from the store by the one who gave it to you, this revelation would likely spoil the gift. Here again, the person's motive and the context of their actions make all the difference.

Even if someone does the "right" things for seemingly the "right" reasons, if they are done in the wrong context, their actions are often not needed, unhelpful, and ineffective. Jesus attempted to make this very point when He berated the scribes and Pharisees (Matthew 23:13-36). He repeatedly pointed out the fact that they were in desperate need of a savior despite their efforts to uphold the Law of Moses, clean themselves through rituals, and convince others to do the same. He shed light on the fact that their best efforts were nowhere near good enough. Their tactics were so ineffective that Jesus said to them, "you travel around on sea and land to make one proselyte; and when he becomes one, you make him twice as much a son of hell as yourselves" (Matthew 23:15). Jesus was unimpressed with their short-sighted strategies. Even if some of their motives were pure, the scribes and Pharisees would never be able to enter the kingdom of heaven by the merits of their outward performance!

To properly judge people's behavior, their motive and context must be examined. Otherwise, it is impossible to perceive the whole truth of what they are doing. We must also recognize that a surface level evaluation is rarely sufficient. We must take a close and honest look to see what is really there. The home invader may be there to save your life, the surprisingly generous gift may be the result of a crime, and the religious leaders' prescribed path may be nothing more than performance-based spirituality.

<u>Note</u>: Although it might seem like we are belaboring the point, this concept will prove to be vitally important when attempting to rightly interpret and evaluate the actions of others, God's involvement in our lives, and (especially) our own behavior.

God evaluates our motive, not just our behavior.

Our Heavenly Father cares deeply about the reasoning and motivation behind our behavior. He said, "I the Lord search the heart and examine the mind, to reward each person according to their conduct, according to what their deeds deserve" (Jeremiah 17:10 NIV). Notice that it does not say that He searches *and* rewards; He searches *to* reward. Our behavior is rewarded based upon what God finds in our hearts and minds. He evaluates why we do what we do. He checks our motives. We can donate millions to feed the hungry, but our eternal reward will be based upon *why* we gave what we gave. He sees the difference between the person who gives generously out of love and compassion and someone who publicly gives to those in need for the purpose of receiving recognition and status.

The Apostle Paul echoes this truth in one of his letters to the church in Corinth when he wrote that God will "disclose the motives of human hearts; and then praise will come to each person from God" (1 Corinthians 4:5). God doesn't simply want us to do the "right" thing; He wants us to do it for the "right" reasons. As Paul continued, "*Let all that you do be done in love*" (1 Corinthians 16:14). God sees past our outward behavior and examines our innermost thoughts. He looks at that which motivates our actions.

Even when Jesus was physically on Earth, He looked into the hearts of men and perceived their thoughts and motives. Consider the following passage:

> Some men were carrying a man on a stretcher who was paralyzed; and they were trying to bring him in and to set him down in front of Him. But when they did not find any way to bring him in because of the crowd, they went up on the roof and let him down through the tiles with his stretcher, into the middle of the crowd, in front of Jesus. And <u>seeing their faith (the beliefs that motivated their actions)</u>, He said, "Friend, your sins are forgiven you." The scribes and the Pharisees began thinking of the implications, saying, "<u>Who is this man who speaks blasphemies? Who can forgive sins, except God alone</u>?" But Jesus, <u>aware of their thoughts</u>, responded and said to them, "<u>Why are you thinking this way in your hearts</u>? Which is easier, to say: 'Your sins are forgiven you,' or to say, 'Get up and walk'? But so that you may know that the Son of Man has authority on earth to forgive sins," He said to the man who was paralyzed, "I say to you, get up, and pick up your stretcher, and go home." And immediately he got up before them, and picked up what he had been lying on, and went home glorifying God (Luke 5:18-25, emphasis added).

Notice where Jesus' attention was focused; He saw their "faith" and was "aware of their thoughts." He was not distracted by anyone's outward actions. He was concerned with what was most important: *why* they were doing what they were doing.

Jesus saw the faith that motivated the paralytic and his friends and was blessed by it. He responded positively to those whose actions were motivated by faith (truth believed in the heart), but He confronted those who were blindly walking in ignorance and darkness. The scribes and Pharisees thought to themselves, "*Who is this man?*" as they doubted what they saw. But the paralytic man and his party knew in their hearts who Jesus was and what He could do. Their faith was on full display.

Theoretically, a few of these Pharisees could have decided to help lower the man down to Jesus. But they would have likely done so for ulterior motives, such as gaining the trust of Jesus' followers or simply to get a better view of the action. Nevertheless, Jesus would have perceived this as well. They might have chosen to behave as though they had faith, but their actions would not have hidden their true motives from Jesus' eyes. He would have still perceived the motivation of their hearts.

The wise King Solomon recognized the relationship between that which we believe in our hearts and the choices we make when he wrote, "*Above all else, guard your heart, for everything you do flows from it*" (Proverbs 4:23 NIV). Our hearts' beliefs lead us to perceive problems and motivate us to act in response (primarily by producing emotional pain). But, as we learned from our discussion of "solution behaviors," our actions are also highly influenced by what we believe in our heads. We are drawn to engage in certain behaviors because we have been led to believe that they will help us solve the problems we face.

When our behavior is motivated and directed by our limited and flawed perspectives, it is impossible to walk rightly even if we choose to do the "right" thing. Our impure motives detract from our "good" behavior. Again, God is evaluating our motive, not just our behavior.

Our Heavenly Father sees through the veneer of our outward performance and peers deeply into our hearts (1 Samuel 16:7). He knows what we think and why we act. Our words and actions may convince those around us, they may even distract us from our true motives, but they cannot fool God. He knows the truth of why we do what we do, and He is patiently waiting for us to come out of denial and admit our motives to Him and to ourselves.

God is not spitefully overlooking your behavior, waiting for you to admit your wrongdoing. He wants you to admit the reasoning behind your behavior so that He can correct it. Yes, God wants you to do the right thing, but more than that, He wants you to do the right thing for the right reasons. He wants your obedience to be an expression of love and truth, not fear or duty (See Proverbs 12:22, John 4:24, 13:34, 14:15, 15:12, 1 John 4:18). He examines your motives because He wants to be sure that your actions are "rooted and grounded in love" (Ephesians 3:17) and motivated by "the hope of His calling" (Ephesians 1:18) and "the boundless riches of His grace" (Ephesians 2). For as we will soon discover, God is not impressed by outward obedience and good behavior when they are driven by flawed and limited perspectives.

Part Six

"Good things" done with impure motives are not "good things."

If I were to ask any of my grandchildren enough times to help me with a simple project like checking the mailbox, pulling weeds from the garden, or putting books away after story time, they would eventually agree. But let's assume that one of them eagerly volunteers to help, and, after we finish the job, she looks up at me and asks, *"Papa, did I do a good job?"* I happily respond by saying, *"Yes, Skylar. You did an excellent job! Thank you for helping me!"* She continues, *"Is there something else I can do for you?"* Impressed with her initiative I say, *"Wow, I am proud of your good attitude and work ethic! But no, you helped me finish all I was hoping to accomplish. Thank you very much. You can go play now."* Disappointed, she looks up at me and asks, *"Are you sure? I really want to help you!"* I curiously inquire, *"Don't you want to play outside with your sister?"* *"No!"* She exclaims, *"I want to help you so that you will love me like you love my cousins!"* Discovering her hidden motive for helping me immediately turns my joy and gratitude into heartbreak and confusion. Her sweet gift of service was actually an attempt to meet a need she thought she had. And the importance of correcting her misconception of my love towards her far outweighs the value of her helpful service. She did all the "right" things, but her reasoning for doing them is what determined if those things were actually "good."

Just because our outward behavior seems good, moral, and godly, it does not mean that we are doing it for the "right" reasons. We sometimes engage in productive, helpful, and even life-saving work with impure motives. When this is the case, the "good things" that we do fail to be "good things."

This is not to say that God cannot use our actions to accomplish good, for He obviously causes "all things" to work together for that purpose (Romans 8:28). But "good things" that are done with impure motives are not themselves "good things," they are simply part of the "all things" that God works together for the "good."

Paul spoke of this dilemma in his letter to the church in Philippi:

> Some, to be sure, are <u>preaching Christ even from envy and strife</u>, but some also <u>from good will</u>; the latter do it <u>out of love</u>, knowing that I am appointed for the defense of the gospel; the former proclaim Christ <u>out of selfish ambition, rather than from pure motives</u>, thinking to cause me distress in my imprisonment. What then? Only that in every way, whether in <u>pretense</u> or in <u>truth</u>, Christ is proclaimed; and in this I rejoice (Philippians 1:15-18, emphasis added).

Paul was thankful that Christ was proclaimed by so many, but he also acknowledged that this was happening for many different reasons. Some wished to share the life-changing freedom they found in Christ, while others desired to hijack the message for personal gain. Both groups were engaged in roughly the same behavior, but they did what they did for vastly different reasons. Again, just because someone does the "right" thing does not mean that it is done for the "right" reasons.

We encourage you to revisit Paul's first letter to the church in Corinth. In the thirteenth chapter he describes many positive and productive behaviors that we often applaud (including many of our spiritual gifts), but directs our attention to the motive behind the behavior by repeatedly using an important qualifying phrase:

> If I speak with the tongues of mankind and of angels, <u>but do not have love</u>, I have become a noisy gong or a clanging cymbal. If I have the gift of prophecy and know all mysteries and all knowledge, and if I have all faith so as to remove mountains, <u>but do not have love</u>, I am nothing. And if I give away all my possessions to charity, and if I surrender my body so that I may glory, <u>but do not have love</u>, it does me no good (1 Corinthians 13:1-3, emphasis added).

Even the use of our spiritual gifts can be tarnished by impure motives. No matter how helpful or godly our outward behavior seems, if it is done for ungodly motives, it amounts to nothing but "noise." Paul goes on to describe what should motivate our behavior: love (a fruit of the Spirit that we effortlessly bear when we know the truth in our hearts). Paul continues:

> Love is patient, love is kind, it is not jealous; love does not brag, it is not arrogant. It does not act disgracefully, it does not seek its own benefit; it is not provoked, does not keep an account of a wrong suffered, it does not rejoice in unrighteousness, but rejoices with the truth; it keeps every confidence, it believes all things, hopes all things, endures all things (1 Corinthians 13:4-7).

We are fully capable of doing "good" things for impatient, unkind, or jealous motives. We give generously but then brag about it (even if only to ourselves). We speak the truth to our spiritual brothers and sisters out of arrogance (we want them to know that we are right). We keep an account of the wrongs that we've suffered (and hold onto our anger in response). And how much of what we do is done seeking our own benefit (to alleviate our own perceived problems). All *solution behaviors* fall into this *"but do not have love"* category; no matter how productive, helpful, acceptable, or godly they outwardly appear.

Even our "best behaviors" have the potential of being nothing more than "solution behaviors."

Sometimes our "good" behaviors are motivated by the truth we believe in our hearts. It is also very possible for us to engage in "good" behaviors in response to our own emotional pain. We sometimes even confuse our spiritual gifts (outlined in Romans 12) with behavior that is actually motivated by deception.

When we do "good" things to meet a need that we believe we have, to escape the pain that we don't want to feel, or to otherwise "solve" a perceived problem, we are simply engaging in a solution behavior regardless of how moral, productive, or "healthy" it may seem. In fact, some of the "solution behaviors" we employ can even seem spiritual in nature.

For practical examples of this concept, consider the following illustrations:

Scenario One:

> Martha faithfully serves at her local church. She works in the nursery, feeds the hungry at the shelter, volunteers on cleanup day, sings in the choir, and more. People say she has the gift of service. Maybe she does. But then, she may simply have difficulty saying "No" when

asked to do something. She may be stuck in a major double bind. The thought of saying "No" makes her feel bad, but when she says "Yes," she feels conflicted and mad. If she does have the spiritual gift of service, it is being hampered by her lie-based pain.

Scenario Two:

Pastor Joseph's ministry is highly organized. He follows a rigid schedule, his staff are closely monitored, and everything always seems to be in order. He even has three years of sermons already planned and scripted. Some say he has the gift of administration or leadership. Maybe he does. But his organized behaviors could also simply be his way of managing the anxiety he feels when things seem out of order. In this case, his productivity and organization, though helpful, stem from his efforts to "solve" his lie-based problems.

Scenario Three:

Brian is a generous giver. He regularly tithes to his church, supports several international ministries, donates to local Christian charities, and even offers one of his houses as a location for church small groups to meet. It would seem he has the gift of giving. Maybe he does. But Paul says, "Each of you should give what you have decided in your heart to give, not reluctantly or under compulsion, for God loves a cheerful giver" (2 Corinthians 9:7 NIV). So, if Brian were to honestly assess his emotional state when he is asked to give, he might be surprised at what he discovers. Does he feel cheerful and joyous, or does he feel compelled and pressured? He might realize that he has been handing out money in order to get recognition, appreciation, attention, or status in the community. Maybe he gives because he feels guilty for having so much when others have so little, or he might be fearful of others' responses if he refuses to help. If he feels compelled to give any amount by such motives, then his behavior indicates his need for God's perspective.

Scenario Four:

Kathy is a prayer minister in her church who works with "emotionally wounded" people. She meets with those who have suffered abuse in one form or another. She claims that the ministry time with them is emotionally draining because of the compassion she feels for the "wounded." She believes that she "feels their pain." Their tragic stories revisit her mind and leave her feeling emotionally fatigued. She sometimes feels overwhelmed by a deep sadness. Some say she has the gift of mercy. Maybe she does. But her "compassionate" response to those "wounded" people and their stories may simply be her own lie-based pain that gets triggered by the work she is doing. In reality, she never feels the pain of others; she only feels what she believes. Any measure of emotional pain she feels is entirely her own. She may be feeling sad while someone else feels sad, but each person is only feeling the emotional consequences of their own beliefs. And if they each feel emotional pain, they each need God's perspective.

Scenario Five:

Trent claims to have the gift of prophecy. He has a "spiritual word" for nearly every person who crosses his path. And those who receive his words feel blessed and encouraged. He is often asked to share in his small group. His pastor invites him to the front of the room to close each Sunday service in prayer. His spiritual maturity and closeness to God inspires those around him, almost to the point of being intimidating. Does Trent have the gift of prophecy? Maybe. But even if he does, it is still important to check his motive. What drives his behavior? Is he honestly using his gift "in proportion to [his] faith" (Romans 12:6, emphasis added), or does he simply share every time an opportunity seems to arise? Has he mistakenly found his identity in his spiritual gift? What does he feel when he thinks about not sharing? What does he feel when someone won't listen, rejects his words, or criticizes his insight? Does he share a word from God hoping to get something in return, such as gratitude, affirmation, or respect? If so, Trent needs to hear from God before attempting to speak on His behalf.

None of these examples are meant to irritate or offend anyone. And we are not at all suggesting that genuine spiritual gifts are somehow expressions of our lie-based pain. Rather, we are simply suggesting that each of us should be honest with ourselves, with each other, and with God. We encourage you to take inventory of the motivations behind your actions.

Surely we can each admit that it is *possible* for at least a portion of the "good" things we do to be motivated by intentions that are less than pure. If we are in Christ, then we *do* have spiritual gifts. But even our giftedness may need tempering and maturing, and it is just as possible that our use of spiritual gifts, Christian service, and "good" behavior are tangled in some measure of deception.

We are not casting blame or pointing fingers at anyone. We simply want what God wants: for our outward behavior to reflect the inner work that God has done in our lives and for our actions to be motivated by the truth we believe in our hearts. This truly is possible! But it requires us to first closely examine our motives and evaluate why we do what we do.

So much of what we do (more than we care to admit) is a futile attempt at solving our perceived lie-based problems. Many of our solution behaviors tend to look good on the outside, but they are driven by impure motives. Our actions may bring about genuinely good outcomes, but if they are motivated by emotional pain and directed by lie-based beliefs, this is obvious to God. We must learn to slow things down and honestly attempt to answer the question, *"Why am I doing what I am doing?"* God wants us to know the truth in our hearts so that we are motivated and directed by our faith in His perspective (see Hebrews 11:6).

COMPASSION OR CONFLICTION?

It is not uncommon for people to mistake their own lie-based pain for feelings of compassion or empathy. While there is clearly a time and place for true compassion, if we feel emotional pain in response to hearing other people's stories, then what we feel is probably not true compassion. People who seek to minister with those who are emotionally troubled may find themselves conflicted by what they feel. Witnessing someone express deep emotional turmoil might stir up pain within them. This pain is often identified as compassion because one person is thought to be "feeling" the pain of the other. It is more likely that the sight of someone else's emotional pain has simply triggered their own. We encourage those who become stirred emotionally while mentoring others in TPM sessions to consider the possibility that what they feel is not compassion, but rather their own lie-based pain.

We must learn to take the important, but sometimes difficult, step of honestly acknowledging our own feelings and motives. We may genuinely feel empathy and compassion for others, but if our desire to come alongside them is motivated by our own emotional pain, then it is important to recognize this. Rather than assuming our motives are always pure, we should investigate even what compels us to engage in "good" behaviors. If it is of God, then it will hold up to any amount of scrutiny. But if our motives are impure, then they need to be exposed and addressed.

Part Seven

We do what seems "best" from our current perspective.

Each of us is motivated by what we believe in our hearts and guided by what we believe in our heads. We do what seems "best" according to our current perspectives, and our perspectives are the result of what we believe to be true. When our beliefs inaccurately or incompletely reflect the truth, they cause us to see unsolved problems that seem to need our attention and feel compelled to do something about it or, at the very least, do something in response to it.

If you believe that focusing on the truths in Scripture and reciting them to yourself will be effective, that is *probably* what you will do. But if you believe that committing yourself to self-improvement strategies and reading all the "self-help" books you can find will somehow work better, then you will *likely* attempt this strategy first. If you believe that ignoring your emotional pain will help you stay focused on addressing the problem of your supposed defectiveness, it is safe to assume that you will do just that.

Whatever behavior *appears to be* most helpful, productive, or effective will seem more enticing to you than the other options that are available. This does not mean that it *actually is* more helpful, productive, or effective; it only *seems* that way because of what you currently believe. The drivenness you feel to engage in that particular behavior is a direct result (and indication of) what you currently believe to be true.

THE WAY OF DEATH

We feel compelled to do what we believe is "best." Solomon understood this when he wrote, "there is a way *which seems* right to a person, but its end is the way of death" (Proverbs 14:12, 16:25). The way *seemed* right, but it obviously was *not* right, considering it was the "way of death." Even so, "every person's way is right in his own eyes" (Proverbs 21:2), otherwise we would pick a different "way." Again, we do what *seems* best from our current perspective.

This concept should bring hope and comfort to those struggling with unwanted behaviors. The fact that you are drawn to take a "way of death" indicates that you have been deceived. For that "way" would only seem attractive if you either doubted that it leads to "death" or you believed that the benefits outweigh the potential cost. In either case, you are not thinking straight! The "way of death" only seems like a valid option because you lack God's perspective of it. If you saw that "way" from His perspective, you would look for a different option.

We need to realize that our poor behavior stems from the fact that we've been deceived into believing that the "way of death" is what we want. This is not a behavioral issue; it is a belief issue. Again, if you knew the truth, had God's perspective, and were able to see the "way of death" for what it is, you would not select that path!

Because of this, if you believe (at some level) that alcohol will "solve" your problems, this isn't an alcohol problem, it is a belief problem. If you believe that holding onto a perceived debt will "solve" your problem, this isn't a forgiveness problem, it is a belief problem. If you believe that lying will "solve" your problem, this too is a belief problem, not an issue of dishonesty. Again, before we can hope to effectively address the issue, we must first accurately identify it, otherwise we run the risk of wasting time and energy treating symptoms rather than focusing on the actual source of the problem.

Both the "struggler" and "performer" solve their problems by doing what seems "best" from their current perspectives.

Since our behavior reflects what we believe is "best," we must evaluate the rationale and thinking behind our behavior rather than focusing primarily on the behavior itself. This is especially true for solution behaviors that do not seem especially threatening or immoral.

For instance, let's say I feel compelled to play praise music whenever I feel anxious. Is the behavior of listening to worship music wrong? Of course not! Is it a better option than getting drunk or gorging on ice cream? Obviously! But why do I choose to do it? What is my motive? If I am listening to music for the purpose of reducing my anxiety, I am engaged in a solution behavior and forfeiting God's superior option. He wants me to know the truth. When I know the truth in my heart, I won't feel anxious. If I still want to play some praise music, then I can worship in spirit and in truth (John 4:24)!

In the same way, someone may choose to go for a run to "relieve" stress, avoid elevators to keep from feeling claustrophobic, or start a blog in order to feel valued and seen. Obviously, there is nothing inherently wrong with exercising, taking the stairs, or posting your opinions online, but if any of these behaviors are done to "solve" perceived problems, then they are just as misguided as my misuse of music.

This is no different than a believer who struggles with the compulsion to steal. Instead of blasting music to ease his pain, he takes what does not belong to him. He knows that doing so is wrong, but it *seems* like it is the "best" way to meet his perceived needs, and it is hard for him to resist the urge to commit this type of crime. But why? Why is he drawn aside and enticed to grab items from store shelves and sneak them into his pockets? He is compelled to do what *seems* best from his current perspective, and he struggles when attempting to do the right thing because doing so requires him to act in opposition to what he believes to be true.

Although his stealing has consequences, the behavior itself is NOT the real issue! His fundamental problem is the fact that he lacks God's perspective. The believer doesn't really want to steal, he has been tricked into thinking that stealing will help "solve" a perceived problem. If he knew the truth, he would not do what he currently does.

God designed you to act out your beliefs by doing what seems "best." But He also wants you to know the truth so that the options that *are* best will *seem* best to you. Until then you will feel compelled to engage in shortsighted solutions which deceivingly lead you by the "way of death" (Proverbs 14:12). Some of these behaviors are obviously bad ideas to most of us while other solutions are more common and socially acceptable. But is my misuse of worship music morally superior to someone else's struggle with stealing? The consequences of each option are dramatically different, but our motives are very much the same! Because of this, I shouldn't view my musical compulsion as more spiritual than his obviously problematic behavior.

In fact, a person who struggles with inappropriate behavior may have some form of advantage over those who seem to have their acts together. For, unlike those who perform well, the "strugglers" at least realize that their current strategies are not working, and they are looking for a better way. Many of us, on the other hand, have been reassured that our behavior is acceptable and "right" simply because it is productive or biblical. So, let's not think more highly of ourselves than we ought to (Romans 12:3).

It may seem to some that we are dwelling too long on a trivial topic, but we believe that the implications of this concept are far reaching and apply to every reader. It can offer hope to those who feel lost in the chaotic cycle of poor behavior and regret. But it also potentially encourages those who feel confident in their own "good" behavior to take a closer, more honest look at why they do what they do. (It is also a concept that plays an important role in the TPM Process.)

God is not looking for more "Marthas" who will work hard on His behalf, pouring themselves into misguided productivity. He desires for us to sit next to Mary at His feet and receive the "good part" that He has for us (Luke 10:38-42). He wants to work *in us* more than He wants us to work *for Him*. He desires for us to know the truth of who He is, what He's done, and who we are in Him. This is what is necessary (Luke 10:42).

If we were able to believe the truth, the whole truth, and nothing but the truth both in our heads and in our hearts, our thoughts and behavior would always reflect God's heart and mind. When this is not the case, we have room for growth and still need God's perspective. We do not yet fully know God and are unable to see ourselves the way God sees us (1 Corinthians 13:12).

Anyone who honestly believes they have "*taken hold of it*," we say, "*Congratulations! You have surpassed the Apostle Paul*" (Philippians 3:13). But we would also lovingly challenge you to take a closer look at your motives. We lie more to ourselves than we do to anyone else. It may seem difficult to honestly assess why you do what you do. You may not yet know how. So, keep reading; we'll get to that soon enough!

The rest of us should be reminded to "not become discouraged in doing good, for in due time we will reap, if we do not become weary" (Galatians 6:9), because "after you have suffered for a little while, the God of all grace, who has called you to His eternal glory in Christ, will Himself restore you, secure you, strengthen you, and establish you" (1 Peter 5:10 BSB, emphasis added).

PERSONALITY AS PROTECTIVE GEAR

We each have unique, God-given temperaments, quirks, and personalities, but some of what we project outwardly is nothing more than a mask. In fact, the English word "personality" is derived from the Latin word "persona" which refers to the mask or disguise that actors would wear over their faces when playing different roles in a stage performance. It allowed the performers to act as though they were someone other than their true identity. In similar fashion, we construct "masks" to hide who we think we are.

Most people assume that our unique perspectives, personal preferences, predictable responses, and patterns of behavior somehow indicate our identity or temperament. But couldn't each of these just as easily be the outcome of our beliefs? For instance, consider the following examples:

Is Siena simply a shy person? Why does Mary always choose to sit near the door at the back of the room? Why does Paul have difficulty looking into the eyes of the person he is talking to? Why does Bill need his socks and shirts to be organized by color in his closet? Why does Julie feel compelled to serve on every church committee? Why does Shannon never feel loved by her husband even when he is acting lovingly toward her? Why does Karen always need to be the center of attention? Could it be that these behaviors are, at least in part, simply solution behaviors?

We are who we are, but we might not be who we think we are. It is possible that at least a portion of our outward presentation (as well as our inward self-perception) is nothing more than our attempt at hiding what we don't want others to see. We might simply have been deceived into thinking that acting a certain way will "solve" the problems associated with being who and what we believe we are.

The "introverted person" may withdraw socially because he fears being hurt, mistreated, or rejected and believes that retreating ensures security, whereas an "extrovert" may be overcompensating for his hidden feelings of worthlessness. A driven, "type A" personality may be trying hard to measure up, whereas a "type B" personality may have just given up trying. In either case, they are not acting like themselves, they are doing what they believe.

CHAPTER 7

THE "BELIEF AND PERSUASION" PRINCIPLE

"WE BELIEVE WHAT WE ARE PERSUADED TO BELIEVE."

NOTICE: This chapter has been divided into five parts. The first part summarizes the relationship between what we perceive, feel, do, and believe and discusses our need for God's perspective. The second part explores our failed attempts at changing our own beliefs. The third part explains the concept of persuasion. The fourth part introduces the "Trust and Authority Principle." And the fifth part explains that only the Holy Spirit is able to persuade us of God's perspective.

Part One

We perceive, feel, and do what we believe to be true.

So far, we have discussed why we perceive what we perceive, why we feel what we feel, and why we do what we do. Our perceptions of God, ourselves, the world around us, as well as our emotional responses and subsequent behavior, all stem from what we currently believe. In other words, we perceive, feel, and do what we believe to be true.

We interpret absolutely everything through that which we believe. If what we *believe* to be true is actually true, then we will be more able to *rightly* interpret our surroundings and have an accurate perspective of what is happening. But since we have been deceived into believing things that are untrue and are prone to missing the greater truth and eternal context of our situation, our perspectives are typically flawed or limited at best. We need our flawed perspectives corrected so that we can see clearly, or our limited perspectives expanded so we can see the "big picture."

Until our perspectives align with His, we will also continue to have abnormal emotional reactions to what we *believe* is happening around us. Our flawed perspectives will keep us concerned about the imaginary monsters that seem to be lurking under our beds. And we will struggle under the burden of our truth-based pain because we do not see the "big picture" from God's perspective.

While we are unable to rightly perceive God's plan and promises, we will attempt to enact counterfeit justice. We will cling to the debts that we are owed, dispense punishment through the use of our anger, and carry the guilt of our own disappointing decisions. Although we may disagree, at some level, with our own choices and genuinely desire to change our behavior, we will continue employing such solution behaviors until our beliefs change. For if we have been deceived into believing that certain inappropriate behaviors will help us "solve" our perceived problems, we will feel drawn to engage in such acts. Even the most illogical and immoral behaviors will *seem* enticing and worthwhile if we believe they will help us address the problems we seem to be facing.

Our perceptions, emotions, and behaviors are not the real problem.

We perceive what we believe, we feel what we believe, and we do what we believe. If we knew the truth both in our heads and in our hearts, then, like Jesus, we would "see" clearly, have normal emotional responses to what happens around us, be motivated to act for the right reasons, and make good choices in response, all automatically and without effort on our part. All of this "fruit" is the expressed evidence that we are walking in the truth. Since our perspectives do not yet always accurately reflect God's perspective, we misinterpret what happens to us throughout our daily life, spontaneously feel a measure of emotional pain in response, and are drawn aside and enticed to engage in behaviors that do not accurately reflect who we are in Him.

Rather than having a negative view of our flawed and limited perspectives, the emotional pain they produce, and the troublesome behaviors they lead us to engage in, we encourage you to view them as part of the "all things" that God is working together for your good (Romans 8:28). Although they are unpleasant and crippling, they each point out a greater, more important issue: your need for His perspective.

But, here again, realizing this need is not a bad thing; it is a good thing. In fact, it is vital! This realization is your first step towards acquiring what you need. If we genuinely desire to know the truth, we must first be able to recognize and humbly admit when we need it. This may initially seem difficult, but until you realize and acknowledge your need for His perspective, you are unlikely to focus on the real problem.

The fact that you misinterpret your situation, fail to see the full truth of who God is, and have a flawed understanding of who you are in Him has far-reaching consequences, but none of these things is the primary issue. The emotional pain you carry and express is unpleasant and may even seem crippling, but it is not the actual problem. Although your unhealthy, immoral behavior is wrong and should be avoided, it should also be viewed as a symptom of the problem rather than addressed as the problem itself. Your perspective, emotions, and behavior are symptomatic of your underlying belief problem. They are simply pointing out the fact that you lack God's perspective.

THE TRUTH IS STILL THE TRUTH REGARDLESS OF WHAT YOU BELIEVE.

It is important to remember that your perceptions, emotions, and behaviors <u>can not</u> be trusted to accurately or reliably describe that which is *actually* true (at all, ever). The truth is the truth regardless of what you believe, which also means that the truth is the truth regardless of your perspective, your feelings, or the choices you make. Just because something seems true, feels true, appears to be true, and is motivating your behavior, <u>does not</u> mean that it is true; it just means that you believe it to be true. The truth is one thing, but your beliefs, perceptions, emotions, and behaviors are something else entirely. Your belief may occasionally reflect reality, but the two are entirely independent of each other.

For example, God loves you so much that He sent His Son to take the brutal punishment that you deserved (John 3:16, Romans 6:23). This fact is true regardless of what you think, perceive, feel, or do. The truth is the truth. If the reality of Christ's selfless sacrifice doesn't *seem*, *feel*, or *appear* to be true in your life, this indicates that you do not yet fully believe it to be true. Your beliefs do not affect the truth, but they have an enormous impact on your experience of it. The truth will not fully *feel* or *seem* true to you until you fully believe that it is.

In response to this, some may feel compelled to try focusing on the truth by ignoring their perceptions, emotions, or behaviors. But those who employ this strategy unknowingly undermine

God's design and intention. Rather than ignoring what we perceive, feel, and do, we should pay close attention to them, understanding that they often indicate what we believe more accurately than we care to admit. Again, they cannot be trusted to accurately depict the truth, but they can absolutely be trusted to express what you believe. Because of this, rather than ignoring or vilifying the outcomes of what we believe, we should honestly assess them to determine whether we are walking in truth or need God's perspective.

Our real problem is the fact that we lack God's perspective.

Regardless of what you perceive, feel, or do, your real need is truth. You need your limited perspective to be expanded and your flawed perspective corrected. You need to see yourself, your situation, and God through His eyes.

To illustrate this further, consider the following:

If I were to accidentally put on a pair of eyeglasses that were the wrong prescription, my ability to see would be further impaired, my head would begin to ache, and many simple but essential tasks would become much more difficult for me to perform. These crippling and painful consequences of wearing the wrong glasses are very real, but none of them is the real problem. It would be a mistake for me to focus my attention on alleviating these symptoms by trying harder to get my eyes to focus, taking medicine to reduce the pain in my throbbing head, and attempting to perform tasks like cooking, mowing the grass, or driving a car while being unable to see clearly. But it would also be a mistake to view the fact that I am wearing the wrong glasses as the problem. For if I were to take them off, I still wouldn't be able to see properly! The real problem is my need for the correct glasses. As soon as I exchange the problematic glasses for my real ones, my vision will return, the pain will subside, and I will be able to do what I need to do uninhibitedly. Each of these crippling consequences is automatically resolved when I wear the proper lenses. Because of this, rather than attempting to alleviate the negative effects of wearing the wrong glasses, I need to view them as symptoms of my real problem: my need for the correct glasses.

In the same way, if we hope to address our real problem, we must first accurately identify it. Although our inability to rightly perceive the truth, the painful emotions we are forced to endure, and our unwanted draw toward illogical and immoral behavior are undoubtedly *problematic*, they are, more importantly, also *symptomatic*. They are the symptoms of our need for God's perspective and were designed to motivate us to look in His direction.

Obviously, none of this diminishes the consequences of these symptoms, for the practical impact of our limited and flawed perspectives, our emotional pain, and our troublesome behavior cannot be overstated. The pain we feel is very real, and its effect on our lives is undeniable. Our behavior has both immediate and lasting consequences. But, again, these are symptoms of our belief problem.

If our only goal is to *feel* and *do* "better," then we are missing the point and robbing ourselves of what we really need while doing the best we can with what we currently have. But this is no more logical or productive than attempting to improve our quality of life while wearing the wrong glasses.

By rightly understanding the relationship between what we perceive, feel, do, and believe, we can focus on the source of the problem rather than burning ourselves out while attempting to treat symptoms. Instead of trying to act as though we believe the truth by attempting to alleviate painful emotions and correct less-than-ideal behavior, let's focus on the underlying problem that these symptoms are designed to point out.

Your limited and flawed perspective of yourself, God, and the world around you is not the real problem, nor are the painful emotions you feel or your compulsion to engage in poor behavior. Each of these simply indicate your need for God's perspective. We believe that viewing life through this lens offers clarity, purpose, compassion, and hope to otherwise seemingly confusing, chaotic, and bleak situations.

Again, if the truths you read in the Scriptures do not feel or seem true, then you need God's perspective. If you feel any measure of anxiety, stress, worry, or fear, then you need His perspective. If you struggle (at all) with letting go of sadness, grief, disappointment, regret, or anger, then you need His perspective. If you have difficulty doing what you know you should do, then you need His perspective. If you feel compelled or drawn to do things that you know you should not do, then you need His perspective. And if none of these scenarios seem to apply to you, then you *definitely* need His perspective!

Part Two

We each need God's perspective, but we may not know how to get it.

Honestly acknowledging this need often seems challenging and even counterintuitive (especially if we already know the truth in our heads), but it is only the first step in this journey. As you will recall, when we are confronted with a seemingly unsolved problem, we look for a solution to it, and if we are unable to see God's intended solution, we typically attempt to solve the problem ourselves. This dynamic applies to our current discussion as well. When we realize our need for God's perspective, we will do whatever we *believe* is most likely to meet this need. Here again, we need to honestly assess our chosen strategy to determine if it is really working.

For instance, what do you do when you realize that a Bible verse does not *feel* or *seem* true? What do you typically do in response to a flareup of painful emotion? How do you handle situations that leave you feeling angry, sad, or disappointed? What do you do when you feel compelled to act inappropriately? How do you address the resistance or hesitancy you feel at the thought of sharing your faith with a stranger? What do you do when obeying God's word seems difficult and challenging? How have you handled those areas in your life where you could use more peace, joy, love, or patience?

Each of these situations indicate your greater need for God's perspective. How have you typically addressed this need? Has your chosen method consistently worked thus far? Has it resulted in a lasting change in your belief, perspective, emotions, and behavior? If so, does this change require you to do something in order to maintain it? If you were to disengage your chosen method, would the painful emotion come back, would the negative thoughts return, would the struggle and compulsion intensify? If so, we would like to suggest that this means your chosen method is not actually changing what you believe to be true. You may have succeeded in altering your mood or changing your behavior, but the beliefs behind them both seem to be unchanged which means you still need God's perspective.

I ran into this problem time and time again during my years of counseling before the formation of TPM. Those with whom I met would come to understand that the pain they felt was caused by the lies they believed, and they would quickly recognize their need for truth. But this is where our progress slowed dramatically.

In those early years I basically understood that their problem was their belief in a lie, and the solution was to correct their faulty thinking with the truth. But I operated from the flawed assumption (as many do) that it was my responsibility to somehow change their belief. I would tell them the truth, show it to them using Scripture, equip them with practical strategies, and encourage them to "choose" to deny their feelings and believe what the Bible said.

To help them understand this process I used a borrowed analogy that went something like this; "FACT, FAITH, FEELING." I would encourage them to start by focusing on the FACTS found in Scripture. Then I would have them *choose to believe* the truth by FAITH. And finally, we would expect their FEELINGS to eventually reflect this "change." But, as we will discuss shortly, there was a major flaw in this strategy.

At that point in my journey, I did not yet understand why this strategy was not consistently working with those I was trying to help. The fact that most of them already knew the truth in their heads only confused me further. For they intellectually knew that a small child is never responsible for the abuse they receive, that neither their traumatic experience nor their memory of it would actually kill them (considering they obviously survived), and that the Lord would, in fact, bring justice. They were able to say things like, "I'm not dirty," "I'm not there anymore," "I'm not alone," "The Lord was with me," "I do have value," "It was not my fault," but when they focused back on the memories of their abuse, it was as though they had somehow "forgotten" the truth. (It was at this point that I would bring out the "FACT, FAITH, FEELING" tool and hope for the best.)

They genuinely wanted to believe what they were saying. They memorized it, quoted it to themselves and to each other, and practiced living as though they believed these truths (hoping that it would one day "click" for them). But no matter how many times they heard the truth, they still only believed it in their heads. They would read it, reread it, memorize it, quote it, act it out, and try their best, but nothing they did had a lasting impact on what they believed in their hearts. The pain was still present, their perspectives had not changed, and the lies still felt true.

It wasn't until later that I realized why they were struggling. We were unknowingly attempting to act outside of God's created order. He did not design us to believe what we "choose" or "try" to believe. We cannot change our beliefs through fervent effort or willful choice. By God's design, we believe whatever we are <u>persuaded</u> to believe. And nothing I could say to these people would persuade their hearts to believe what I was saying. I could only offer words, while their beliefs were rooted in their own first-hand experiences. They needed to hear the truth from someone more convincing than myself. They needed to be persuaded by an experiential encounter with the Spirit of truth (John 16:13).

We do not choose to have God's perspective, we receive it.

When attempting to address their lack of God's perspective, many people attempt to "choose to believe" the truth. Proponents of this method suggest that the issue is with us. They claim that we simply need to make better belief choices; we need to ignore what *feels* or *seems* true to us and "choose" to believe the truth, "choose" to trust God, and "choose" to rely on His word. Initially, these suggestions seem straightforward and logical, but they each suffer from the same critical flaw: they are impossible tasks.

To illustrate the impossibility of choosing to believe something, we encourage you to attempt it. Right now, as you are reading this, take a moment to *choose to believe* that two plus two equals five. Go ahead, we'll wait... If it doesn't seem work, try again. Deliberately choose to believe that two plus two equals five. Write it down, memorize it, and maybe use this catchy song sung to the tune of "Jesus Loves Me!"

> *"Two plus two is five not four,*
> *What used to be now is no more,*
> *I choose to change the way I think,*
> *Say 'Up is down and blue is pink."*

If singing this song has not helped, you might ask a few friends to hold you accountable to believing this new mathematical "truth." Do you believe it yet? Really? You can obviously act or pretend that you believe it, but do you really believe it? Does it genuinely *seem* or *appear* true to you? Probably not.

You may be thinking, "*Of course I can't choose to believe that two plus two equals five; I already know that two plus two equals four. Why would I choose to believe what I know is untrue?*" We partially agree with this sentiment. None of us are able to choose to believe something that contradicts what we currently believe to be true; but this is precisely our point! Part of the reason for why "choosing to believe" doesn't work is that you are already convinced that something else is true. Since you know this simple mathematical truth, you cannot choose to believe something that contradicts it.

On the other hand, you also can't choose to **stop** believing that two plus two equals four. It is just as impossible to choose not to believe something as it is to choose to start believing something. You didn't choose to believe that two plus two equals four and you are not choosing to continue in this belief. This is not how God designed our minds to work. We do not believe anything as a result of choice.

Just as you cannot choose to change your belief regarding even a simple mathematical equation, it is impossible for you to "choose to believe" the truths found in Scripture. No matter how badly you may want to believe the truth, and regardless of how hard you try, your struggle, effort, and determination will not result in you coming to believe the truth in your heart. Although your motives are noble and your desire is genuine, you must be honest about the results of your efforts.

WE DON'T "CHOOSE TO BELIEVE" LIES, AND WE CAN'T "CHOOSE TO BELIEVE" THE TRUTH.

To illustrate this concept further, consider your own beliefs. If it ever *seems* or *feels* as though your situation is out of control, this indicates what you believe in your heart. But, in these moments, are you *choosing to believe* that your situation is out of control? No. Was there a time in your life at which you *decided* to believe that your situation was out of control? Probably not. If you attempted to *choose to stop believing* that your situation is out of control, should we expect a change in your perception? Unlikely! You did not *choose* to start believing this lie, you are not *choosing* to continue believing it, and you cannot simply *choose* to stop believing it.

You started believing this lie the moment that you were persuaded that it was true, and you continue to believe it because you remain persuaded. Choice and effort played <u>no</u> part in the matter. If anything, you may be *trying* to convince yourself of the truth that you already know in your head. You remind yourself that God's plans always prevail (Proverbs 19:21), that He holds all things together (Colossians 1:17), and then uses them for your good (Romans 8:28). Nevertheless, if your situation still *feels* and *seems* like it is out of control, then your heart belief remains unchanged. You still do not have His perspective.

We need to honestly evaluate the outcomes of our efforts.

Again, revisit the God-designed indicators of belief. What *feels* true? What *seems* true? What *appears* to be true? What *emotions* are you feeling? What are you *motivated* to do? What do you feel *resistant* or *hesitant* to do? Your honest answers to these questions offer a reliable description of what you believe. If these indicators are unchanged after attempting to convince yourself of the truth, then what you are doing is not working.

You cannot gain God's perspective by simply *choosing* to have it. He must grant it to you as a gift. This is revealed in Paul's prayer in his letter to the Ephesians. After he declares fifteen verses of glorious truths related to who they are in Christ, he recognizes their need for God's Spirit to open the eyes of their hearts and give them a spirit of wisdom and revelation so that they will believe. He writes,

> [I] do not cease giving thanks for you, while making mention of you in my prayers; that the God of our Lord Jesus Christ, the Father of glory, may give you a spirit of wisdom and of revelation in the knowledge of Him. I pray that the eyes of your heart may be enlightened, so that you will know what is the hope of His calling, what are the riches of the glory of His inheritance in the saints, and what is the boundless greatness of His power toward us who believe (Ephesians 1:16-19).

We need to honestly assess the fruit of our labor and humbly acknowledge our need for a better solution. We cannot *choose* to have God's perspective and until we genuinely grasp this concept, we will continue our failed tradition of attempting to change what we believe through effort, determination, willpower, and choice either until the Lord returns or until we realize the futility of our actions.

We hope that you hear our hearts in this matter. For this is genuinely not a criticism of anyone's motives. Every believer has an innate desire to know the truth at both a head and heart level. We were spiritually born for it! We each do the best that we can to come into His truth and perspective, but we must honestly evaluate our chosen tactics to see if they are actually working. If our current methods do not lead to genuine and lasting transformation in what we believe in our hearts, then we need to look for another strategy. Thankfully, as you will soon discover, God sent His Spirit to provide a better way!

Part Three

We are persuaded by our experiences to believe what we believe.

Picture yourself on a camping trip with a friend. While you are setting up your tent, you are startled by the sound of his screaming. Your friend runs up to you and frantically explains that he just saw a large hairy creature that he believes was "Bigfoot." Panting, he says, "It was huge! It was walking on two feet and had big claws and an ape-like face." Although you have no reason to believe he is being anything but honest with you, you didn't see the creature in question and assume that he must have been mistaken. After comforting your frantic friend, you continue constructing your campsite.

Later that night, as you look for a private place to answer nature's call, you are startled by an unfamiliar animal noise. You quickly cast the light from your flashlight to the path in front of you and are shocked at what you discover! A nine-foot tall, dark colored, hairy creature standing on its back legs, waving its claws in the air. It lets out a blood-chilling roar and exposes its impressive set of teeth. Paralyzed by fear, you only manage to quietly slip the word "Bigfoot" out of your mouth before the great creature turns from you and runs deep into the forest. Your doubt is gone. You have been thoroughly convinced that Bigfoot is real!

Up until your close encounter in the woods, your life experience had convinced you that "Bigfoot" was nothing but a figment of people's imagination. But when you were confronted with this great beast, your beliefs changed. This experience persuaded you to believe. You did not choose to believe, try to believe, or even think about believing; you were immediately *persuaded* to believe due to your experience.

Everything you currently believe is supported by some form of experience. But not all experiences carry the same weight. The experience of hearing your friend's panicked report was not enough to cause you to doubt what you had learned up to that point. Your friend told you about his encounter with "Bigfoot," but you were not persuaded to believe what you were hearing. You were made aware of the creature's *potential* existence, but you were not yet convinced that it was real. It wasn't until your close encounter in the woods that you truly believed!

In this sense, everything that you now believe to be true is based upon past experiences. At some point in your life, you heard, saw, felt, smelled, tasted, or otherwise experienced something that led you to believe everything you currently believe. In the same way that you believe "two plus two equals four" because of your experience at school, you know how to tie your shoes, brush your teeth, and wash your hands because of past experiences. You know how to perform tasks at your job because of what you experienced in your training. You know the sound of fingernails on a chalkboard, the smell of freshly baked bread, and the feel of a wool blanket because of your experience with these items.

This is not to say that you can only know something if you have had a "hands on," personal encounter with it. You do not need to have personally visited the Grand Canyon or the Eiffel Tower or the Moon, for that matter, to know about these locations. For you can obviously learn a great deal from simply reading a book, but it is your *experience* with that book that persuades you to believe what you have read. Unless your eyes encountered the printed letters on its pages (or your ears heard them read), the book could not convince you of anything.

Likewise, your belief and perception regarding weightier matters such as your worth, purpose, and identity, as well as your understanding of God and His involvement in your life, are rooted in what you have experienced. There is an experience (or many experiences) that support and explain every belief that you currently possess, both in your head and in your heart. These experiences convinced you of what you now believe to be true and continue to serve as the evidence that supports your current perspective.

But our experience leads us to believe things that are both true and untrue. We have been deceived into believing lies because of what we have experienced, and we will only know the truth when we are able to experience it. We believe what we believe because of what we have experienced.

This concept is more intuitive than it may initially appear. Consider the following examples:

Rhonda believes that she has an amazing singing voice.
Why? Because she was always praised for it when she was growing up.

Charles believes that he has the right to do whatever he wants.
Why? Because his parents spoiled him and failed to enforce rules.

Shelby believes that sushi is gross.
Why? Because she got food poisoning after the first and only taste of it.

Kevin believes he can't do anything right.
Why? Because his father always seemed critical of his work.

Rachael believes she has to be skinny in order to be accepted.
Why? Because of the harsh words of her childhood bullies.

Tyler believes that God is distant and unjust.
Why? Because his older brother was killed by a drunk driver.

Joe believes that he is worthless.
Why? Because his father left the family when Joe was a child.

We have reason to believe all that we believe. We each have specific experiences that explain why we believe what we believe. In a sense, our experiences testify to the validity of our current perspective. They serve as the evidence that supports what we currently believe to be true. They serve as the source of our current perspective.

To illustrate this concept further, think about how you would respond to a question like, "*Why do you believe that God exists?*" Your answer will likely be a combination of various personal experiences as well as the lessons you learned from them. Your experience, life events, and memories form the basis of the evidence you provide to prove God's existence. Even statements such as, "the Bible says so," represent some form of experience. For how would you know what the Bible says without reading it (or hearing it read) first? Your experience with God's written word supports your belief in what it says. Beyond that, the Bible itself is, in a sense, a preserved record of personal experiences that people have had with God.

Your current perspective is the culmination of your past experiences. If you believe in your heart that you are loved by God, this belief is based upon something that you experienced in the past. Likewise, if you believe that you are worthless, this too is supported by what you have experienced. If God seems to be distant or uninvolved in your life, this limited and flawed perspective is based upon your personal experience.

We cannot choose to believe anything; we must be persuaded. We must see, hear, or otherwise experience something that leads us to believe. Without some form of experience, we will not be persuaded nor will we believe. As Scripture clearly states, "How then are they to call on Him in whom they have not believed? How are they to believe in Him whom they have not heard? And how are they to hear without a preacher?" (Romans 10:14). We cannot believe without first "hearing." Obviously, hearing does not *cause* someone to believe; otherwise everyone who hears would also believe which we know is not true (just ask your local pastor!). But the experience of "hearing" is a prerequisite for belief.

This concept further illuminates the primary issue sitting in front of us. We have misinterpreted what we have "tasted" and "seen," and it has led us to believe that God is not good (see Psalm 34:8). Our life experience has only allowed us to "see in part" our dimly lit reflections, making it impossible for us to fully know who we are (see 1 Corinthians 13:12). Our beliefs reflect what we have experienced, but they do not yet reflect the truth.

If we believe what we believe because of what we have experienced, how do we go about changing what we believe? We can't go back and change the past or alter the experiences our current beliefs are built upon. Our experience is what it is. What we need now is a new experience. We need to experience the truth in such a way that it convinces us to believe it.

WE ARE NOT ALWAYS PERSUADED ON PURPOSE.

Although we are persuaded to believe by what we experience, this is not always the intended result. Many times we learn lessons from our experiences that were not intentionally being taught. For instance, if I overheard someone claiming to have gotten a bad case of food poisoning from their recent visit to a local steakhouse, I may feel hesitant about visiting the restaurant in question. This person was not trying to convince me of anything, for they were not even talking to me. I simply happened to be standing close enough to overhear their conversation. Nevertheless, I was persuaded by what I heard.

Another example of this would be if a small child observed her mother's terrified response to a spider crawling across their kitchen table. "Sienna, watch out! Get back! Don't let it crawl on you!" The little girl may be persuaded to believe that spiders should be feared even though this was not her mother's intention. In reality, the mother's intentions are irrelevant, for they are not what determines whether or not the child will be persuaded of anything. The little girl will be persuaded by what she experiences.

Sometimes those who persuade us do so on purpose (such as teachers, preachers, or politicians). But we are also often convinced of things by unintentional "persuaders." Just because someone tries to convince us of something does not mean that they will be successful. On the other hand, it is very possible for us to be persuaded by those who have no intention of persuading us of anything. In any case, we are not persuaded by what is said to us but are persuaded by what we *hear* (our interpretation of those words). We are not persuaded by a person's intentions, we are persuaded by our interpretation of their actions (what we believe they mean). We are not always persuaded by what is most true, we are persuaded by what *seems* most true from our perspective.

Part Four

We are persuaded by that which seems most trustworthy and authoritative.

We are persuaded to believe what we believe through experience. Thankfully though, we are not persuaded by *everything* we experience; if we were, our beliefs would shift and change every time we came across a new idea or perspective. But even the most gullible among us are only persuaded to believe certain things, at certain times, by certain people. In a very simple sense, we are persuaded by that which seems most persuasive.

For the most part, we intuitively recognize this reality. For instance, would you heed the advice of someone who seemed to have no grasp of what they were talking about? Of course not. And even if they *seemed* experienced and *could* provide reliable advice, if they also *seemed* to be lying, you will still not believe what they said. You must trust that they were being honest and believe that they have adequate authority in the matter before being persuaded of anything. Their opinion will only be persuasive if it seems to be both trustworthy and based upon relevant experience and expertise. We commonly refer to this principle as the *"Trust and Authority" Principle*.

To illustrate this principle, imagine that you are a judge in a bench trial who is tasked with hearing testimonies, considering evidence, and passing judgment. Essentially, you must evaluate what you see and hear to determine which side has presented the most compelling case and then rule in favor of whoever constructed the strongest argument and offered the most convincing evidence.

To properly fulfill your role, you must weigh the strength and credibility of the information that is provided. If the evidence and testimonies seem truthful, relevant, and authoritative, then you will likely be convinced that what they propose is true. But if the evidence seems unrelated or deceptive and the witnesses appear to be uninformed or lying, this casts doubt on the believability of their arguments. You would only be persuaded by that which seems both trustworthy and authoritative.

No matter how illogical, unlikely, or impossible something may seem to be, if the provided evidence seems reliable and conclusive while suggesting that it really happened, then you will be compelled to believe that it did happen. For example, we have all heard the stories of misguided criminals who get themselves into humorously improbable predicaments. They run out of gas shortly after stealing a car, get caught pawning stolen jewelry to a store managed by the person who was robbed, inadvertently lock themselves in a bank vault while attempting to steal from it, or unknowingly drop their ID at the scene of a crime. If such impossible stories are supported by convincing evidence, you will believe these tall tales.

Even things that you don't want to believe will seem believable if supported by sufficient evidence. While presiding as judge, you may recoil at the gruesome brutality detailed in the prosecution's case against the defendant, but if the evidence is convincing, then you will be convinced. You may wish to believe that no one would commit such abhorrent crimes, but if you are provided with enough compelling evidence, you will be persuaded to believe that they did. No matter how terrible or discouraging the accusations are, if they are supported by seemingly trustworthy and authoritative evidence, you will be compelled to rule in their favor.

We cannot stress enough the fact that you will be persuaded by the body of evidence that "*seems*" to hold authority and "*appears*" to be trustworthy; whether it actually "*has authority*" and "*is trustworthy*" is an entirely different matter. Even if the provided evidence was incomplete and only told part of the story or if the witness was simply a convincing liar, the legal consequences would tragically be the same as if that information was true. Your ruling is based upon the *provided evidence,* not the *actual truth* of what happened! If you *believe* the source of information "*has authority*" and if you know of no reason to distrust it, you will be persuaded to believe what you hear.

In the same way, our beliefs are based upon the most compelling "evidence" that has been presented to us thus far. Our experiences are like eyewitnesses in a courtroom who offer subjective accounts of what seems to be true. Their accounts might be thorough and accurate, but more often than not, they are limited and flawed. In either case, we will be persuaded to believe the most convincing explanation of what seemed to have happened and what that experience means.

If our most compelling experiences seem to indicate that we have value, then we will believe that we do. But if our experience seems to show our worthlessness, then our inner "judge" will be persuaded to believe that we have no worth. This is because our experiences serve as the basis for what we believe even when they fail to tell the whole story and offer perspectives that are flawed and untrue.

We may not want to believe everything we believe, but we will continue to believe it if the "evidence" suggests that it is true. You can't choose to stop believing that you are worthless anymore than you can stop believing that two plus two equals four. Once you are persuaded of something, you will continue believing it until you are presented with stronger "evidence" that shows something else to be true.

This concept helps to explain the dynamic of "double-mindedness" as described in James' epistle (see James 1:8, 4:8). When our intellectual understanding conflicts with the lessons we've learned through personal experience, we are double-minded. We may intellectually know what the Bible says, but if our experience testifies against what we have read and memorized, our first-hand eyewitness account will *seem* to hold more weight than even the words we find on the pages of Scripture.

You may be able to recite John 3:16, but if your experience thus far suggests that you are not loved by God, then this dissenting opinion will seem more persuasive, and the truth will not feel or seem true to you. You may genuinely want to believe that you are loved, but this desire has little-to-no impact on the evidence that has been presented in the courtroom of your heart. You obviously do not want to believe that you are unlovable, but if your experience testifies that you are, then this distorted self-perception will appear to be true.

We are perfectly capable of believing the truth with our heads while believing something contrary to it in our hearts. You may be able to quote 1 John 3:2 and intellectually believe that you are a "child of God" but still not feel as though you are part of God's beloved family. You may be able to recite Jesus' words, "I am with you always, to the end of the age" (Matthew 28:20), but be unable to sense His closeness and even feel abandoned by Him. The Bible verse "There is no condemnation for those who are in Christ" (Romans 8:1) may be your favorite verse in all of Scripture, but you will still feel condemned and rejected until you believe this truth in your heart.

In other words, just because you *know of* the truth does not mean that you also *believe in* the truth. You may genuinely want to believe it, you may even mistakenly *try to believe* the truth, but you will not believe it until you are persuaded that it is true.

This is not a bad thing; it simply means that you need stronger evidence. You need someone you can trust to offer you the truth and support it with evidence that holds a greater measure of authority than you currently possess. You need to experience something that is more convincing than that which convinced you of your current belief.

This concept was on full display in my very first TPM session. After exhausting all other options, I finally asked the Lord if He wanted to share something with the person sitting across from me. I fondly recall the woman sitting up, opening her eyes, excitedly announcing that the pain was gone, and exclaiming, *"The Lord told me it wasn't my fault! I am not there anymore!"* I had told her these same truths countless times, and she already knew them in her head, but only the Lord, through His Holy Spirit, was able to persuade her heart to believe. The shift in her thinking was the result of the Lord's divine persuasion.

God is working to accomplish this same work in each of our lives <u>every day</u>. He wants to convince our hearts of His perspective, and He desires for us to know the truth because we have experienced it. He wants our knowledge of Him to be based upon our experiences with Him. He doesn't just want us to know <u>about</u> Him through reading and study. He wants us to know Him personally, deeply, and experientially. Intellectual knowledge is vitally important, and we should diligently study the Scriptures to grow in our understanding of His word but, as with Job, God wants us to move from simply "hearing" about Him to "seeing" Him (Job 42:5). This shift in belief results only from a personal encounter with Him. Only He can persuade our hearts of His perspective.

WE WILL CONTINUE TO BELIEVE WHAT WE CURRENTLY BELIEVE UNTIL WE HAVE BEEN PERSUADED TO BELIEVE SOMETHING ELSE.

This concept of persuasion explains why we believe what we currently believe, but it also defines the parameters that must be met in order for our beliefs to be changed. Once you have been persuaded of something, your beliefs do not change until you are presented with a differing opinion that is supported by stronger evidence; one that seems to be more trustworthy and holds more authority than your own. In other words, your perspective will not change until you are persuaded that someone else's perspective is more accurate than your current understanding.

For an example of this, consider the following scenarios:

Scenario One:

Lindsay was shopping for a new fish bowl for her beloved pet, Gill. She had narrowed her search down to two options, a round one and a square one. They seemed to be nearly equivalent both in quality and in price. She scrolled through the reviews of each item to help her determine which one to select. The reviews of the round fish bowl seemed mostly positive, and she didn't notice any unwanted surprises. But when she saw that the square bowl had nearly twice as many five-star reviews, the choice seemed obvious. However, upon further investigation, she realized that nearly all of the square bowl's high ratings came from people who were paid to review the product or are themselves employed by the company that produces it. Realizing this potential conflict of interest, Lindsay decided to buy the round fish bowl for Gill.

Scenario Two:

Pete's video conference call was suddenly interrupted by the screaming sound of some kind of siren. "What's that noise?" asked the others on the call. "A smoke alarm is going off in the room across the hall. It's fine though, I was told by management that they were going to be testing the new fire suppression equipment at some point today," Pete responded. "Oh, ok. Then can we get back to business?" inquired a voice from the computer. "Of course," he replied. But then Pete noticed the smell of smoke and could see an orange glow in the hallway. He stood up from his chair, "Um, actually, I think I'm going to have to call you back!"

Scenario Three:

Debbie received an unsolicited email from someone named Reverend Zimbolo who claimed to be a "pastor" in a third world country. He described the perilous times he and his church were facing under the hands of ruthless persecutors. He sounded genuine and sprinkled Bible verses throughout his message. Towards the end of his email, Reverend Zimbolo asked Debbie to pray for his church and consider helping her suffering spiritual siblings by giving a meager financial donation. He was not asking for much but gave specific instructions to send her support in the form of gift cards from a short list of retail stores. Debbie was initially surprised to hear that these particular "high end" stores were located in the country in which he lived, but she dismissed this concern and mailed him the cards as quickly as she could. She felt good about being able to help her brothers and sisters from across the globe. A week later, however, her suspicions were raised when the beloved pastor sent her another email asking for additional funds. This time his tone seemed even more urgent and strained. Debbie felt uneasy about the whole ordeal. After a bit of research, she discovered an online forum of people who had been tricked by the same "pastor" into giving their money away just as she had done. Their testimonies convinced her that she had been duped by his deceptive scheme.

In each of these scenarios, the person went from believing one thing to being convinced of something else. They were initially convinced that something was true, but when they discovered that their source of information was either ill-informed or outright deceptive, they came to believe something else. They were automatically and instantaneously convinced of whatever "perspective" seemed most trustworthy and authoritative.

Lindsay almost ordered the item with the most reviews before realizing that the rating was likely biased and inauthentic. Pete's belief that the alarm was part of a drill was based upon the trusted words of his bosses, but when his own senses seemed to contradict what he was told, he felt inclined to exit the building. Until Debbie was convinced by the online testimonies of others who had similar experiences, she believed that she was helping a fellow believer in need.

None of these individuals chose to change their beliefs. Their beliefs were automatically changed when they were presented with a more persuasive source of information. As soon as both requirements of the "Trust and Authority Principle" were met, their beliefs changed.

We will remain convinced of what we currently believe to be true until we are persuaded of a different opinion. But we will only be persuaded if this new perspective seems to be supported by stronger evidence than we currently possess. If it does, we will not have to "choose" or "try" to believe differently, we will automatically and effortlessly be persuaded.

This is both good news and bad news. The bad news is that no matter how hard we try, our beliefs will not change until we are convinced of a new perspective. The good news is that if we are persuaded of the truth by someone who is more trustworthy and holds more authority than anyone else, it is impossible for us to be deceived out of believing this truth, considering that we have been persuaded by the strongest "evidence" that is available. As we will discuss shortly, this is exactly what the Holy Spirit was sent to accomplish!

Part Five

The Holy Spirit is trustworthy and has authority.

Our beliefs will not change until we are persuaded of a new perspective by a source we trust and who seems better informed than we are. I recall encountering this problem in my years of counseling (primarily with survivors of childhood sexual abuse) before the development of TPM. I would explain the truth and support it with Scripture and logic, but nothing I said or did seemed to fully convince those who were seeking help. They understood the truth intellectually, to the point that they could explain it to others in the group. But whenever they would focus back on what they felt and remembered, the truth seemed distant and ineffectual. They were still not convinced.

I failed to persuade them to believe the truth because I lacked the necessary credentials. Even if they genuinely trusted me and believed that I was speaking honestly, I could not meet the second requirement of the "Trust and Authority Principle." I could not offer a stronger case or more convincing evidence than that which they already processed. It was my second-hand opinion against their first-hand experience.

I couldn't convince them, and they couldn't convince themselves. They needed to hear from someone else; someone with higher credentials than either of us possessed. They needed to hear from someone who has a better, more accurate, and complete perspective than they already owned. I couldn't provide what they needed. I wasn't there when they were abused; I didn't see what happened; I didn't know what they felt; I couldn't perceive the eternal context of what happened. But God did!

He was there, He heard, He saw, He was present, and He can offer perspective that comes from a greater, more accurate and complete vantage point. He can make sense of what happened. His words of comfort are rooted in truth and backed by experience. He knows what we were thinking, feeling, and experiencing. During what seemed like your darkest moments, He was there. He knows.

Just as the comfort and advice offered by someone who genuinely knows what you have been through holds more weight and is more impactful than the caring comments from those who "can only imagine," God's words carry weight and have meaningful impact. He knows what we have been through because He went through it with us. He is acutely aware of the important details that we missed, such as His involvement and purpose. He wants to expand our limited perspective and correct our misinterpretations. And, most importantly, His loving words are trustworthy, authoritative, and true.

He meets all the requirements and holds all the credentials necessary to persuade us of His perspective. He has authority (1 John 3:20, Romans 11:33-36). He sees all and knows all. He is present and involved in every aspect of our lives (Psalm 139:7-12, Ephesians 4:6). He is faithful and trustworthy (Deuteronomy 32:4, Joshua 21:45, Psalm 33:4). He is the truth (John 14:6, 17:17). He wants to fully convince us of His perspective and holds the necessary credentials to do it!

COLLEGE STUDENTS DON'T "LOSE THEIR FAITH."

The whole concept of *persuasion* explains how a "believing" college student can be seemingly swayed out of their "faith" by a liberal professor. As you know, there is a huge difference between understanding the gospel message with our heads and believing it with our hearts. If a student only believes the truth of the gospel in his head, nearly any motivated secular professor can challenge his theological position or even talk him out of his "firm belief" in Jesus. This is because the unbelieving professor is probably able to meet the requirements of the "Trust and Authority" Principle. The professor will likely appear to speak honestly and seem as though they have the necessary authority to disprove the student's beliefs.

However, if a student believes in his heart that "Jesus is Lord" and that "God raised Him from the dead" (Romans 10:9 NIV), then his belief is the result of God's divine persuasion. Only the Holy Spirit is able to convince a person to believe these truths in his or her heart. Because of this, no matter how hard an intellectually compelling professor tries to discredit the student's faith, the gospel message will stay firmly rooted. The student's belief will be based upon more trust and stronger authority than the professor is able to conjure.

Remember, we do not *choose to believe* anything; we are persuaded to believe what we believe. So if a student can actually be talked out of his belief in God by the cunning linguistics of a college professor, then it wasn't God who initially persuaded him to believe. The truth was likely only believed intellectually.

So, when a student seems to "lose" his faith at school, this is simply not the case. Either his "faith" was never actually believed at a heart level, or he has been deceived into denying what he really believes in his heart. But in either case, the problem remains the same; he needs God's perspective. For if the student was convinced by the Spirit of Truth, he believes! So join the Apostle Paul in praying that "the eyes of [the student's] heart may be enlightened, so that [he or she] will know what is the hope of His calling..." (Ephesians 1:18, emphasis added).

God sent His Spirit to personally persuade you of the truth.

God loves you so much that He gave His only Son to take the punishment that you deserved and offer you new life in Him (John 3:16, 10:10). This was necessary because we could not solve our sin problem ourselves; we needed Him to do it for us. We accept this free gift by acknowledging our desperate need and asking Him to graciously meet it. But even after the sin issue has been taken care of, we still have a crippling problem that is in need of a God-sized solution; we do not yet fully believe the truth of this finished work. Thankfully, God has a solution for that problem too!

You see, God is highly invested in your coming to know the truth of who He is, what He has done, and who you are in Him. He wants you to know these truths both in your head and in your heart. He wants the eyes of your heart to be open so that you will not only rightly perceive the truth but also walk in it (Ephesians 1:18, Psalm 86:11).

God doesn't simply want you to know *about Him*; He wants you to *know Him*. He wants more than for you to intellectually grasp the truth of His love; He wants it to *feel* true to you and motivate your actions (1 Corinthians 16:14). He wants you to be fully convinced of your new spiritual identity so that you will have confidence in His finished work (John 1:12, 1 Corinthians 6:17, Romans 8:1, Hebrews 4:16). He wants you to know the truth, all of it, and has taken it upon Himself to convince you of it (John 16:13).

During His time on Earth, Jesus spoke of the importance of this task. Before He submitted Himself to be crucified and knowing that He would be physically leaving His disciples soon, He explained, "it is to your advantage that I am leaving; for if I do not leave, the Helper will not come to you; but if I go, I will send Him to you. And He, when He comes, will convict the world regarding sin, righteousness, and judgment...I have many more things to say to you, but you cannot bear them now. But when He, the Spirit of truth, comes, He will guide you into all the truth" (John 16:7-8, 12-13).

Upon hearing this, the disciples should have been filled with hope, joy, and gratitude. But because they did not yet fully comprehend His words, they were simply left with more questions (John 16:17-18). Perceiving their inner turmoil, Jesus offered further encouragement and explanations, "Truly, truly, I say to you, that you will weep and lament, but the world will rejoice; you will grieve, but your grief will be turned into joy. Whenever a woman is in labor, she has pain, because her hour has come; but when she gives birth to the child, she no longer remembers the anguish because of the joy that a child has been born into the world" (John 16:20-21).

Jesus compares their agony and struggle to the labor pain of childbirth. His disciples were struggling with the confusing reality of Jesus' words and coming departure because they did not yet fully realize His purpose or the freedom and forgiveness that would result from His sacrifice. They were fearful because they misunderstood what was happening, and they grieved because they only perceived part of the truth. They were operating from limited and flawed perspectives. They needed to pass through this painful stage and enter into the freedom and release that comes with the next one. They desperately needed what Jesus already possessed: God's perspective!

Jesus knew why He was sent, what He was accomplishing, and could perceive the fruit that would be produced by His redemptive work. Because of this, as with labor pain, He still felt grieved by the coming physical torment, but He also joyously anticipated welcoming those who would be born of the Spirit into His kingdom (Romans 12:2, John 3:6, Ephesians 2). He also knew that His disciples would share in His joy once they were convinced that what He said was true. They needed to have His perspective.

Notice how Jesus planned to accomplish this monumental task. He didn't challenge His disciples to study harder or pray more. He didn't ask them to *choose to believe* or even *try to believe* what He was saying. In fact, He didn't ask them to believe at all. He recognized that they were incapable of believing the truth through their own effort or willful choice. They needed help. Specifically, they needed the "Helper" (John 14:16).

How was the Helper going to help the disciples? Did God send His Spirit to *empower* them to believe? Was He sent to *encourage* them to *choose* the truth? Was the Spirit of truth sent to *motivate* them to *try harder* to believe? No, no, and no.

Jesus said that God was sending His Spirit to "teach" them all things, "remind" them of what He had said, "convict" them regarding sin, righteousness, and judgment, and "lead" them into all the truth (John 14:26, 16:8-13). The Spirit's role was active while their role was passive. They were to simply take a receptive posture and be *taught, reminded, convicted,* and *led.*

These men were given more first-hand experience and evidence of Jesus' true identity and plan than anyone else, but, according to Him, they were still unable to "bear" it (John 16:12). They could recite His teachings, repeat His many parables, and describe the miracles He performed to anyone who would listen. They knew a great portion of the truth in their heads, but much of it had still not made it into their hearts (Matthew 16:16, 26:69-75).

The reality of Jesus' identity and purpose did not yet *seem* or *feel* completely true, was not yet reflected in their emotions (Mark 4:40-41), and did not yet direct their behavior (Mark 14:50). They had an intense desire to believe His words in their hearts, but try as they may, they could not convince themselves to fully believe the truth that was staring them in the face. Then again, neither can we!

It wasn't until the Spirit of Truth was sent to convince their hearts to believe that their perceptions, emotions, and behaviors finally and definitively reflected the truth. Before Simon Peter's heart was persuaded of the truth of the gospel, he was afraid to even speak of his relationship to Jesus (Luke 22:60-62). But after the Holy Spirit convinced him of the truth, Peter spoke boldly (see Acts 2) and led the first century church. This transformation resulted from the promised Helper's involvement in Peter's life (John 14:16).

We need God's Spirit to persuade us of the truth.

Paul recognized the importance of the Holy Spirit's role in leading believers into the truth. Like the other apostles, he had experienced the transformation that comes from receiving perspective directly and personally from God's Spirit (Galatians 1:11-12). He knew that if believers were to be effective witnesses, they must be fully convinced of the truth at a heart level. He recognized that this depth of belief was only possible through the inner work of the Spirit.

In his letter to the Ephesians, he explained that he had not ceased giving thanks for them and praying "that the God of our Lord Jesus Christ, the Father of glory, may give [them] a spirit of wisdom and of revelation in the knowledge of Him," and that "the eyes of [their] heart[s] may be enlightened, so that [they] will know what is the hope of His calling, what are the riches of the glory of His inheritance in the saints, and what is the boundless greatness of His power towards us who believe" (Ephesians 1:15-19, emphasis added).

Here again, notice who Paul attributes as the *giver* of "wisdom" and "revelation," and who will "enlighten" the eyes of their hearts? He did not ask the readers to *choose to believe* the truth; nor did he encourage them to *open their hearts* to it. He fully recognized that they were unable to do so. He knew that "the God of our Lord Jesus Christ, the Father of glory" is the one who could "give" them what they needed (Ephesians 1:17).

Paul revisits this idea in his letter to the church in Colossae by asking God to personally fill them with "the knowledge of His will in all spiritual wisdom and understanding" (Colossians 1:9). He knew if they were to "walk in a manner worthy of the Lord," God must first fill them with the knowledge of His will (Colossians 1:9-12). As James later describes in his epistle, they needed to "humbly receive the implanted word" (James 1:21 HCSB). This reality is just as true for us today!

Like these first-century believers, we need God's help. We need the "Spirit of Truth" to *convince* us of God's perspective and *persuade* us to believe it (John 14:17). We need Him to enlighten the eyes of our hearts so that we can rightly see His glory and power (Ephesians 1:18-19). We can't accomplish this task any more than the disciples could; we need the Counselor to guide us into all the truth (John 16:13).

The unavoidable reality is that no one has ever come to believe anything through choice, willpower, or conscious decision. And yet, this misguided notion is prevalent in the Body of Christ and is currently holding many of our spiritual brothers and sisters hostage. Through no fault of their own, they try their best to believe the truth and wear themselves out acting as though they do. But unless the Holy Spirit intervenes and convinces them of His perspective, they inevitably either give up the charade and search for another solution behavior or, worse yet, become confident in their own performance.

God has a better option. He wants us to realize the fruitlessness of our feeble attempts at doing His job so that we might look to Him for help. He is patiently waiting for us to look up at Him so that He can lovingly share His perspective with us.

When my children were young, if I wanted them to know something important, if I really wanted them to hear me, I would bend down to their level, hold their hands in mine, look them in the eyes, and speak directly to them. In similar fashion, God desires to graciously and personally persuade you of His perspective. He wants to look us in the eyes and say, "You are mine," "I am with you," "I love you," "You are safe now," "I am in control." He wants to persuade your heart to trust in Him. He wants to personally prove to you that He is loving, kind, gracious, just, present, and enough.

We pray that the eyes of your heart will be opened so that you can experientially know each of these life-giving truths. We also hope that more and more people will realize the impossibility of "choosing to believe" the truth and come to recognize their need for the One who was sent to persuade us of the truth (John 16:13). Rather than wasting our effort and misplacing our discipline by trying to convince ourselves of the truth, we need to focus our discipline on making ourselves available to the Holy Spirit to do what only He can do.

We need Him to personally fill us with "the knowledge of His will in all spiritual wisdom and understanding, so that [we] will walk in a manner worthy of the Lord" (Colossians 1:9-10). Rather than attempting to convince ourselves of the truth and trying our hardest to act as though we believe it, we need to learn from our spiritual brothers and sisters to humbly take a receptive posture and be *taught*, *reminded*, *convicted*, and *led* by the Spirit of Truth.

CHAPTER 8

THE PURPOSE OF TPM

GAINING GOD'S PERSPECTIVE
THROUGH HIS DIVINE PERSUASION

The Intended Purpose of TPM

Our discussion of the *Fundamental Principles of TPM* lays the foundation of this ministry's intended purpose. The *Principles* explain why we perceive the world, ourselves, and God the way that we do; they show the relationship between our beliefs and emotions; they shed light on that which drives and directs our behavior; and they expose both our inability to change what we believe and God's capacity to persuade us of the truth.

But what are we to do with this information? What do we hope to accomplish by learning these concepts? This is where TPM's purpose comes into play. *The Purpose of TPM* explains the reasons for why we seek to learn the *Principles* and apply the *Process*. Your understanding of TPM's purpose will serve as the metric that you use to measure your progress and success.

For instance, if you mistakenly believe that TPM is meant to be used to "help the hurting," then this goal will motivate your efforts. You will be driven to use what you've learned to bring comfort and hope to those who suffer from emotional pain. If those with whom you minister consistently report freedom from pain and the presence of peace, then you will feel as though you have accomplished your purpose.

Although the alleviation of pain seems like a worthwhile goal, applying TPM for this purpose greatly diminishes its overall use and distracts us from what God is seeking to accomplish. As you will recall from our discussion of the "Belief and Emotion" Principle, our emotional pain serves several important purposes and is used by God to accomplish good in our lives. The pain itself is not the problem, and its elimination should not be our goal. Additionally, if someone believes that TPM is meant to be used to quell surging emotional pain, they will only see the need to apply it when their pain becomes unmanageable. Much like a fire extinguisher, TPM would remain untouched until an out-of-control, emotional "fire" began burning through their daily lives.

Likewise, if you believe that TPM is a helpful tool for addressing troublesome behavior, then this too will determine when and why you use it. Whenever you (or someone in your circle) admits to struggling with some unwanted behavior, you will see this as an opportunity to apply what you've learned. And, if after applying TPM better choices are made, this will be viewed as a success. But just like in the earlier example, this mentality limits TPM's use to those rare times in which we honestly admit to making poor choices. If the consequences of your actions are relatively acceptable, the thought of applying TPM will likely not cross your mind. But as we discussed in the "Belief and Choice" chapter, our behavior has consequences, but the behavior itself is not the main problem, and even positive and productive behavior can be motivated by impure motives and emotional pain.

Genuine peace is obviously preferred over emotional pain, and good decisions are always better than bad ones, but neither our emotions nor our behavior are the focus of TPM's Purpose. So if TPM is meant for more than finding freedom from emotional pain and overcoming unwanted behaviors, what is its true purpose? The Purpose of TPM is to equip you to cooperate with God as He exposes your need for His perspective, persuades you of the truth, and transforms your life through the inner work of His Spirit. Essentially, our purpose is to have God accomplish His purpose. He wants us to know the truth of who He is and who we are in Him. He desires to refine our faith, renew our minds, and transform our lives.

Each distinct element of TPM's purpose (the refining of our faith, the renewing of our minds, and the transformation of our lives) is accomplished by God, but we are still responsible for our involvement. We seek to intentionally and purposefully position ourselves "under His mighty hand" (see 1 Peter 5:6) and invite His Spirit to do what He was sent to do (John 16:13).

Our goal is to recognize when He has exposed the impurities in our faith, giving us the opportunity to have Him renew our minds by persuading us of His perspective. As a result of His refining work in our faith (belief), we can expect to experience a genuine and lasting transformation in our perspective, emotions, and behavior. (Remember, we perceive, feel, and do what we believe to be true.) This transformation allows us to view life from His eternal perspective (Colossians 3:1-2, 23-24, 1 Corinthians 9:24-27). And having a purified faith (without doubting) we can look to Him for the wisdom that is needed to live out this transformation (James 1:5, Proverbs 2:6-7). When we know the truth both in our heads and in our hearts, not only will we have a proper perspective of God and ourselves, but we will also know what God wants us to do and be motivated to do it for the right reasons.

TPM is meant to help you cooperate with God as He transforms your life by exposing the impurities in your faith and persuading you of His perspective. This purpose should be your motivation and the measure of your success. This is why we learn the *Principles* and apply the *Process*. We want to intentionally and consistently cooperate with God as He transforms us by renewing our minds (see Romans 12:2).

Three Components of TPM's Purpose

The Purpose of TPM consists of three primary components: the <u>refinement of our faith/belief</u>, the <u>renewing of our minds</u>, and the <u>transformation of our lives</u>. Each of these components could quickly be summarized as follows:

Faith-refinement

We learn to recognize the Holy Spirit's involvement in our daily lives as He exposes our need for His perspective amid our trials, tribulations, and life difficulties. Like with the refinement of precious metal, the fire exposes the impurities making it possible to identify and remove them. When the "refiner's fire" comes, whatever we believe will be made evident through our perspective, emotional response, and behavior. When the impurities in our faith are exposed amid the "fiery ordeal" (see 1 Peter 4:12), we can humble ourselves and purposefully invite the Holy Spirit to persuade us of His perspective and renew our minds with the truth, rather than settling for an intellectual agreement with the truth.

Mind-renewal

Mind-renewal is the change in belief that results from God's divine persuasion. When He convinces us to believe the truth, we experience mind-renewal. Intellectual agreement with the Scriptures is beneficial, but knowledge alone is no guarantee of transformation. When the Spirit renews our minds, there is always verifiable proof: a change in our belief. The lie we believed will no longer *feel* true, and the truth will resonate in our hearts. This noticeable shift in belief is the evidence that the Holy Spirit has persuaded us of the truth.

Transformation

Genuine transformation is the outcome of having the Holy Spirit renew our minds with truth. This transformation is not accomplished through self-effort, willpower, or outward obedience to the truth, but rather is the result of our submission to God's Spirit as He works in us. The proof of this transformation is made manifest through our effortless expression of the fruit of

His Spirit. When this transformation occurs, we will be loving, joyful, peaceful, patient, kind, gentle, good, faithful, and self-controlled (see Galatians 5:22). This fruit is His fruit and not behaviors that we are attempting to perform. It is an effortless outcome of having been persuaded of the truth within our hearts. When the truth is implanted by His Spirit, fruit will follow.

Put succinctly, God orchestrates our lives to expose the impurities in our faith so that He can persuade us of His perspective (*faith-refinement*). When He convinces us to believe the truth, there is a shift in our thinking (*mind-renewal*). In response to this shift, we can expect an automatic and effortless change in our perspective, emotions, and behavior (*Transformation*).

TPM IS NOT ENTIRELY UNIQUE.

Some might say that the purpose that is described here is nothing new and we would obviously agree! This purpose is, and should be, shared by all those who are in Christ. It is correct to say that neither the *TPM Principles* nor the *TPM Purpose* are new or unique (though we do believe there is some unique insight found in them). The most unique aspect of this ministry model is, arguably, the *TPM Process*. It offers a systematic way of cooperating with God as He refines our faith, renews our minds, and transforms our lives. And even though these steps have been loosely followed and applied in other contexts throughout church history, as far as we know, they have not been organized or presented in this format. Learning the TPM Process and how to apply is important, and we'll get to it later. But before that, it is crucial that you first understand the *principles* that it is based upon and the *purpose* for which it is applied.

We need the Spirit of Truth even if we already know the truth in our heads.

Most of us have a good working knowledge of God's Word, at least at an intellectual level as we have filled our minds with Scripture. We know what the Bible says about many things. But how much of this information is also fully believed with our hearts? Someone might quickly say, "*I believe all of it with my heart!*" Maybe so. However, there is a simple test; whatever we believe in our hearts will *feel* and *seem* true to us and our emotions and behavior will be an expression of this belief.

For example, do we believe in our hearts that God is our provider if we are stressed and worried over our finances (Matthew 6:25-34, Philippians 4:6)? Do we genuinely believe in our hearts that we are holy members of His royal priesthood (1 Peter 2:9) if we feel dirty, shameful, worthless, or less than holy? Do we fully believe in our hearts that Jesus is with us if we sometimes feel abandoned and alone (Matthew 28:20, Hebrews 13:5)? The truth is, it would be impossible to feel any of these negative emotions if we genuinely and fully believed the corresponding truth in our hearts. Where there is the absence of His peace, something is wrong, since the "Lord of peace Himself [desires to] continually grant you peace in every circumstance" (2 Thessalonians 3:16).

We may be able to quote Bible verses that proclaim His faithful provision and our priestly status, but the fact that we are anxious and guilt-ridden reveals what we truly believe in our hearts. If we feel emotions such as fear, worry, stress, anxiety, abandonment, etc. then we lack His perspective. Again, we feel whatever we believe.

But this plight is shared by all! We are each in need of God's perspective. The signs are obvious: we perceive we have problems that do not really exist, fail to see the extent to which God is involved in our lives, have irrational emotional responses to what happens to us, are compelled to do things that we wish we wouldn't do, and feel inhibited when we attempt to do the things we believe that God desires of us to do (Romans 7:15–18).

In response to this pressing need for God's perspective, we attempt to attain it ourselves by studying and memorizing Scripture, meditating on it, and filling our heads with truth, but no matter how hard we try, no matter how many times we "choose" to, we cannot convince our hearts to believe the truth. Each of these disciplines may increase our intellectual knowledge of the Scriptures, but they will not convince our hearts to believe; that is solely the work of God's Spirit.

God desires that we fully know who He is (Jeremiah 29:12–13) and who we are in Him. He is committed to fulfilling this purpose and does this by refining our faith, renewing our minds, and transforming our lives. He is at work in us (Philippians 2:13) and He will finish what He started (Philippians 1:6). We can fill our minds with truth (and we should), but it is His job to convince our hearts that it is true.

This concept is not a new revelation, for most of us have experienced moments in which the Holy Spirit persuades us to believe what we are actively trying to believe. For instance, while rereading a familiar passage, the words suddenly seem to leap off the page. The truth seems to explode with meaning. It impacts your heart and stirs a positive emotional reaction. For the first time, that truth actually *feels* and *seems* true to you. You believe it!

These experiences may occur at "mountaintop" moments when we feel particularly close to God (such as during mission trips, summer camps, retreats, worship events, etc.). But, more commonly, we encounter God in a transformative way when we have seemingly exhausted all other options. Like the "prodigal son" (Luke 15:11-31), when we finally hit rock bottom, with our face in the mud, feeling as though we have nowhere else to turn, we "come to our senses" and humbly beg our Father to help us.

In these seemingly dark moments of despair and hopelessness, we are forced into a position of humility and submission, and the Holy Spirit is able to accomplish the work He seeks to accomplish (John 14:26, 15:26). This is the appropriate response we should have to our troubles and if we learn to deliberately respond in this way, we can more consistently cooperate with what God is doing in our lives.

Thankfully, we don't have to wait for a "mountain top" or "rock bottom" moment before asking for help. Our Heavenly Father is ready and waiting on us. Hopefully, you have heard our heart-felt plea for you to allow the Holy Spirit to do what He was sent to do. He is here to persuade you of the truth (John 16:13). Rather than attempting to do His job for Him, or even helping Him do it, we must humbly submit to His mighty hand and allow Him to work (1 Peter 5:6). *This is, essentially, the Purpose of TPM: to gain God's perspective through His Spirit's persuasion.*

TPM provides a frame of reference for viewing your daily life events as opportunities for the Holy Spirit to refine your faith, renew your mind and transform your life. It provides a systematic protocol that enables you to intentionally and purposefully cooperate with God as He performs this work in your life. There is no reason to wait until you are on the mountain or walk through the "shadow of death" to have your heart persuaded of the truth. He is at work at all times and has invited you to join Him in His work.

In response to this, you may be wondering, "What does this look like, practically, in my day-to-day life? What does His ministry of persuasion entail? How can I more readily recognize His involvement? And how do I respond appropriately?" Our ability to answer these questions directly impacts our ability to consistently and deliberately cooperate with Him. We will more closely examine such topics as we examine TPM's intended purpose. Rightly understanding the purpose of TPM will help you to be more intentional and productive in this refining journey.

We want you to benefit as much as possible from this ministry method. For that purpose, we encourage you to learn its supporting principles and its intended purpose well. Too often this ministry is relegated to the context of a recovery ministry or used as a strategy for managing emotional pain or dealing with a present crisis. The purpose of TPM is far greater than any of these applications. God's desire is that we come into the full knowledge of who He is, who we are in Christ, and how loved we are by Him. This occurs as He refines our faith, renews our minds and transforms our lives.

With the Apostle Paul, we pray,

> "[may God] grant you, according to the riches of His glory, to be strengthened with power through His Spirit in the inner self, so that Christ may dwell in your hearts through faith; *and* that you, being rooted and grounded in love, may be able to comprehend with all the saints what is the width and length and height and depth, and to know the love of Christ which surpasses knowledge, that you may be filled to all the fullness of God" (Ephesians 3:16-19).

CHAPTER 9

COMPONENT ONE

"THE REFINEMENT OF OUR FAITH"

NOTICE: This chapter has been divided into four parts. The first part discusses faith and defines the Refiner's "fire." The second part explains that suffering is to be expected and discusses the pain we feel in the midst of the Refiner's fire. The third part explores what is accomplished through His use of this refining fire. And the fourth part summarizes the discussion and more clearly defines what is being refined in God's refining process.

Part One

Understanding Faith

When we consider the meaning of "faith," we usually think of it as something positive and good. But we need a fuller, more detailed understanding of this word since not all "faith" is the same. Peter alluded to the fact that there are different "kinds" of faith when beginning one of his letters with the words, *"To those who have received a faith of the same kind as ours, by the righteousness of our God and Savior, Jesus Christ..."* (2 Peter 1:1).

In much of the New Testament, the word most often translated as "faith" is a derivative of the Biblical Greek word *"pistis."* An example of this understanding is found in Romans 10:17 where it says, "So faith (pistis) comes from hearing, and hearing by the word of God." And the verb form of *pistis* (*pisteuó*) can often be interchangeably translated as *believe*, as when Jesus said, "For God so loved the world, that He gave His only Son, so that everyone who believes (*pisteuó*) in Him will not perish, but have eternal life" (John 3:16, emphasis added).

Pistis comes from the root word *"peitho,"* which simply means "to persuade" or to "be persuaded." So, a pure faith/belief (*pistis*) is the result of God's divine persuasion (*peitho*). It is the truth that God persuades us to believe in our hearts. Faith stirs our emotions and motivates our actions. It is the kind of belief in which we have complete assurance and confidence. The writer of Hebrews described faith as "the assurance of things hoped for and the conviction of things not seen" (Hebrews 11:1).

But, again, some of what we believe at a heart level is untrue and fails to reflect God's perspective. In other words, some of our faith is inaccurate and impure. Someone other than God has convinced us to believe things that are untrue. Because of this, we have "assurance" and "conviction" in things that oppose or contradict God's perspective. This is the portion of our faith that is impure.

Think of it this way: imagine you are mixing a bowl of brownie batter, and just before pouring the mixture into a pan, you decide to add an extra helping of chocolate chips to the bowl. But after sprinkling a generous amount into your batter, you realize that you've made a terrible mistake: those weren't chocolate chips, they were raisins! Although these tiny, dried fruits are now part of your batter, they are unwelcome! So, it is with our faith. Most of it may be positive and good, but it also contains unwanted impurities.

This is why, according to the Scriptures, our faith needs to be refined (James 1:2–8, 1 Peter 4:12-13, 1 Timothy 1:5, 1 Peter 1:7). James, Peter, and Paul tell us that our faith needs to be tested, refined, and proven, which suggests that at least a portion of our faith contains impurities. We need God to remove the raisins and add more chocolate chips!

God has granted a measure of faith to every believer (See Romans 12:3), and we can safely assume that this aspect of faith is pure since it originates from God. But, yet again, the fact that our faith needs to be refined reveals that our faith contains impurities, beliefs that originated from someone or something other than God.

These impurities cause major problems for us. For it is by faith/belief that we live our lives. From our pure faith we trust, follow, depend upon, commit ourselves to, and obey God. Since our faith is not entirely accurate or pure (our brownies contain raisins), we also trust in things we shouldn't, follow people who mislead us, commit to causes that are not of God, and obey the lusts of the flesh (1 John 2:16).

There are times when we live by a faith that is "of the same kind" as Peter's (see 2 Peter 1:1); unfortunately, there are also times when we live by a different faith that is less than pure. When our faith does not accurately reflect the truth, we will stumble along. The writer of Hebrews instructs us to make our paths straight and free of obstructions where he said, "*make straight paths for your feet, so that the limb, which is impaired may not be dislocated, but rather be healed*" (Hebrews 12:13). Our "walking" is not the problem, but how and where we walk may need to be addressed. If our limb is already impaired (impure faith) and our pathway is crooked and filled with potholes (the direction we are currently going), then a twisted ankle or dislocated joint can be expected.

We all walk by faith, but not all faith is pure.

We were created to walk by faith and that is exactly what we do. Each of us lives our lives based upon what we believe in our hearts to be true (whether or not it is *actually* true). If our faith is pure, good works will follow. Because a portion of what we believe in our hearts is untrue, our impure faith often results in our engaging in the "deeds of the flesh" (Galatians 5:19-21). In either case, we are genuinely walking by faith, but problems arise when we walk by a faith that is impure. A purified faith is from God and reflects the truth; the other faith is impure and contradicts God's perspective.

Unbelievers live by faith, as well. They obviously don't only believe lies; portions of their faith may accurately reflect the truth. But they are not "saved" until they have faith in the Gospel of Jesus. They must believe in their hearts and agree with God (confession) that Jesus is Lord (See Romans 10:10). Until they are persuaded of this specific truth, their *faith* may partially reflect the truth, but their souls are still in peril (for an example of this, revisit the "rich young ruler" in Mark 10:17-27).

Everyone lives by faith, but portions of our faith are impure. There are raisins in our brownie batter! God desires to remove these impurities by persuading us of the truth. Before this can happen, these impurities need to be exposed. Thankfully, God works all things together for this great purpose.

Reframing Crisis as a Benefit

To rightly understand God's faith-refining process we must reframe our life troubles, difficulties, and crises. Rather than seeing them as something to get through or overcome, we must come to view them from a heavenly perspective. Our daily difficulties, trials, and tribulations are not obstacles to overcome or some drudgery to be endured; rather, they represent God-allocated opportunities for our faith to be refined.

Before a precious metal, like gold, can be refined, it must be heated to its melting point. Doing so will cause the gold to settle to the bottom, forcing any impurities that are present to rise to the surface. Once the impurities have been separated from the gold, they can effectively be removed. A similar refining process is applied to our faith (1 Peter 4:12-13, James 1:2). God's refining fire exposes the purity of our faith (that which we believe to be true at a heart level). If we believe the truth, we will "celebrate in our tribulations, knowing that tribulation brings about perseverance; and perseverance, proven character; and proven character, hope; and hope does not disappoint, because the love of God has been poured out within our hearts through the Holy Spirit who was given to us" (Romans 5:3-5).

If our faith is impure, the lie-based impurities will rise to the surface and be expressed in our perspective, emotional state, and behavior. But as we come to genuinely recognize God's handiwork amid our crises, difficulties, and trials, the "Refiner's fire" ceases to be a threat and takes on a whole different meaning. When we have a heavenly perspective of our life difficulties, we will, "Consider it all joy . . . when you encounter various trials, knowing that the testing of your faith produces endurance. And let endurance have *its* perfect result, so that you may be perfect and complete, lacking in nothing" (James 1:2-4).

Did you hear what James just said? You can be perfect, complete, lacking in nothing. This is the Word of God for you. This may not *feel* true now, but it is true nonetheless. James says that there are conditions to be met. First, we must *know* (believe in our hearts) that the *testing* (refining) of our *faith* (that which we believe in our hearts) will bring about an outcome James describes as "endurance." Second, we must allow *endurance* to complete the work it is doing in us. This raises the question, "What is endurance and how is it used to accomplish this work?"

Understanding "Endurance" And Its Work In Us

For most of my Christian life, I assumed the opening of James' epistle was meant to encourage us to *endure* by staying focused, pressing on, standing strong, and persevering through our life difficulties. I was not alone in my thinking. Recall the prayer requests that are often shared at your church meetings from those who are having difficulties. Don't they typically ask for God to help them endure, get through, or escape the hardship?

A closer look at these verses can shed light on what James is trying to explain. The Greek New Testament word translated "endurance" is *hypomonḗ*. It is derived from the root words *hypó* ("under") and *ménō* ("to remain"). This combination of Greek words means "to remain or be placed under." It also can mean to "wait from behind" or be "held back." So, the idea is not that we are to endure our trial and testing, but rather, the trial and testing are there to produce the state of *hypomonḗ*, the state of endurance, in which we are held back, placed under, and constrained.

At first, this might seem confusing or unnecessarily complicated, but think about how your life difficulties impact your life. Were you slowed, held back, pushed down, and held under? James is not telling us *to* "bear down" and "endure" the suffering, but rather, *hypomonḗ* is the *expected outcome of* the suffering. Endurance is what is happening, not what we are choosing to do. James is not telling us to endure our testing, but rather that our testing is "holding us under," exposing our weakness, and rightly positioning us so we might receive God's perspective. When we are "held back or placed under," we are in the state of "endurance."

Hypomoné is not what we do in our trials, it is what our trials do to us. This is why James says, "the testing of your faith *produces* endurance." In other words, endurance is not what you need in order to *go through the trial*, but rather it is part of what you experience *because of the trial*, and it is meant to accomplish something important. For while we are in this "pushed down, held under" state, God is working. He wants to use the difficulty to refine and mature our faith.

So many have assumed that we need endurance in order to make it through our trials. In reality, everyone gets through their trials no matter what. Regardless of how bad, painful, or difficult your suffering is, you will pass through it. And no matter how long it lasts, it is temporary; you will get through it. Whether you pray, sing, meditate, eat, drink, smoke, or binge watch TV, you will get through your trials! It is not a question of whether or not you will "endure" your trials, but rather, whether you will *benefit* from enduring your trials.

Paul also had this perspective of endurance as he wrote,

> "We also celebrate in our tribulations [suffering, trials], knowing that tribulation brings about perseverance ["hypomonēn" - endurance]; and perseverance, proven character; and proven character, hope; and hope does not disappoint, because the love of God has been poured out within our hearts through the Holy Spirit who was given to us" (Romans 5:3-5, emphasis added).

It seems that both Paul and James are saying that moments of suffering and tribulation offer us the opportunity to develop a genuine hope that is based upon the unshakable proof of God's love and care for us. Without suffering, the basis of our hope would go untested, and the outcome of our hope would be unsure. But once the purity of our faith has been proven, our hope is made sure, and we grow in spiritual maturity. This is why you can (and should) "consider it all joy...when you encounter various trials" (James 1:2).

Suffering forces us into a humbled position in which the purity of our faith and the foundation of our hope are exposed. If there are impurities in our faith, suffering will expose them and give us the opportunity to have our minds renewed by the Spirit of Truth. On the other hand, if our faith is already pure, the "various trials" we encounter will verify its purity. Once the purity of our faith has been proven, we can rest assured that the hope we have in Christ will not disappoint us.

We are not saying that our times of testing are all joyful because they can be extremely painful. The writer of Hebrews alludes to this where he says, "all discipline seems not to be pleasant, but painful (Hebrews 12:11a, emphasis added). But even though we may not enjoy it, we need the suffering that comes from these "various trials" (James 1:2). And if we can be trained by them, they will yield "the peaceful fruit of righteousness" (Hebrews 12:11b).

That said, if we face these trials with bitterness, frustration, resentment, confusion, anxiety, fear, or any other negative emotion, it is likely due to a combination of two things: our misunderstanding of the trial's purpose and our need for God's perspective. This is not to say that all negative emotion is lie-based pain, for as we discussed in an earlier chapter, we also occasionally feel emotional pain due to truth! Until we gain a greater, more complete perspective from God, we will continue to carry this *truth-based pain*. But whether our pain is the result of our belief in a lie or our lack of a heavenly perspective, it still indicates our need for the Spirit of Truth's divine persuasion. Once we have His perspective of our trials, we will be able to "consider it all joy" (James 1:2).

It is also important to notice that James <u>did not</u> say, "IF you encounter various trials..." He said, "WHEN you encounter various trials..." We have no choice about whether difficulties will come or not, but what we do amid them is about choice. We can either "<u>let</u> endurance have its perfect result. . ." (verse 4) or choose to do something else. Some take the victim role, blame others, distract themselves from the pain by pleasuring their flesh, while others just bear down and hope to "get through it."

Getting through the trial is a given; no matter what you do, you <u>will</u> get through it! Take a moment to think through the various trials that you have "gotten through" so far. Which one did you <u>not</u> get through? But God wants us to benefit from the suffering and endurance.

So then, what are we to do in this unpleasant place of *hypomoné*? Peter says it clearly, you are to

> Humble yourselves <u>under</u> the mighty hand of God, so that He may exalt you at the proper time...[and] after you have suffered for a little while, the God of all grace, who called you to His eternal glory in Christ, will Himself perfect, confirm, strengthen, and establish you (1 Peter 5:6,10, emphasis added).

> You are to first "humble yourselves <u>under</u> the mighty hand of God," and <u>wait</u> for Him to "exalt you at the proper time." This is not the act of enduring, but rather the act of "letting endurance have its perfect work." We are choosing to submit to what God is doing. In this state we are *under (hypó)* and *waiting (ménō)* for God to lift us up. This verse clearly describes both our role and God's role in this refining process. Our role is to let endurance have its perfect work in us as we humble ourselves under God's hand, and wait for Him to do what only He can do. Too often we try to "humble ourselves" and endure while attempting to change our situation or control our behavior. This is not what this passage instructs.

While we are waiting under God's mighty hand, the Holy Spirit can persuade us of the truth we need to know. Then "after you have suffered for a little while, the God of all grace, who called you to His eternal glory in Christ, will Himself perfect, confirm, strengthen, and establish you" (1 Peter 5:10). While we are in this place of endurance, God can bring about the transformation that our hearts desire.

As we submit to this state of endurance and allow it to accomplish what it is designed to do (its perfect work), we can expect to be "perfect, complete and lacking in nothing" (see James 1:4). God is refining our faith and is using every life difficulty to help bring it about. Our role is to submit ourselves under "his mighty hand" and expect that He will "exalt us in due season."

Part Two

There is nothing strange about suffering.

When troubles arise and crises come, many conclude that something strange or unexplainable is going on. Without a biblical understanding, we are prone to cry out, "*God! Why is this happening to me?*" When we are unaware of the purpose of trials, our suffering becomes the enemy, and we see ourselves as victims of our circumstance. Peter dispels this perspective when he says: "...do not be surprised at the fiery ordeal among you, which comes upon you <u>for your testing</u> [refinement], as though some strange thing were happening to you" (1 Peter 4:12, emphasis added).

When viewed properly, there is nothing strange about suffering. God does His finest work in the life of a believer through His use of it. The Bible is clear that even though suffering is often perpetrated through the acts of evil people, nothing anyone might do to us (no matter how horrific or unjust it may be), can supersede the work that God is doing through it. He will bring about an eternal good for "those who are called according to His purpose" (Romans 8:28), even when the most horrendous evil comes against us.

Someone might protest and say, "My trial is way too terrible. How can there be any good in what I am going through?" Without question, some people suffer in unimaginable ways. Ungodly atrocities and injustices are incomprehensible. Even so, the truth is still the truth. God has said He will work "all things" for our good. We might use the suffering of Jesus' crucifixion as a baseline for our own suffering. As you will remember from our discussion of the TPM Principles, the crucifixion of Christ was a terrible, confusing, and hopeless experience for the loving onlookers who were present, but did God not also cause the suffering and death of Jesus to work for good? He accomplished more good than we could have possibly imagined! So much so that we now boast in the cross (Galatians 6:14)! Since this is the case, is it not also possible that God is working in each and every one of our trials? Of course He is! If this reality does not *seem* or *feel* true, then you simply do not yet believe it in your heart.

THE IMPORTANCE OF KNOWING THE "PRINCIPLES"

This discussion of suffering is a perfect example of why it is so important to understand the TPM Principles. For example, when we understand that we perceive, feel, and do what we are persuaded to believe is true, our difficulties take on a new meaning. These principles explain why (and how) we can "*rejoice in the Lord always*," "*count it all joy*" and "*exalt in our tribulations*" (Philippians 4:4, James 1:2, Romans 5:3). If we mistakenly assume that our circumstances are bad because they *seem* and *feel* bad while blaming those around us or the devil for our emotional pain and attempting to "solve" or escape our difficult situations, we will unknowingly forfeit much of the "good" that God is working together moment-by-moment. Before we can intentionally benefit from our suffering, we must understand its intended purpose and our role in God's faith-refining process.

Viewing Our Affliction from God's Perspective

We need to have an eternal perspective of our temporal suffering. Paul shed light on this when he wrote, "our momentary, light affliction is producing for us an eternal weight of glory far beyond all comparison" (2 Corinthians 4:17). Someone may point out that Paul refers to his suffering as a "light affliction," and therefore assume that the more severe cases of suffering might not apply here. It is important to rightly interpret biblical passages in their proper context. Paul details his "light afflictions" in the verses that precede verse seventeen where he writes,

> We are afflicted in every way, but not crushed; perplexed, but not despairing; persecuted, but not abandoned; struck down, but not destroyed; always carrying around in the body the dying of Jesus, so that the life of Jesus may also be revealed in our body. For we who live are constantly being handed over to death because of Jesus, so that the life of Jesus may also be revealed in our mortal flesh (2 Corinthians 4:8-11).

Paul's description of the momentary and light affliction includes a wide spectrum of possible difficulties when he says, "We are afflicted in *every* way. . ." And the purpose of this suffering is clearly displayed; "so that the life of Jesus may also be revealed in our mortal flesh." He describes his earthly suffering (a portion of which is summarized in 2 Corinthians 11:23-28) as "light" and "temporary" in view of the "eternal weight of glory" that awaits him in heaven.

Most people are okay with applying the Bible verse that says, *"All things work together for the good..."* to the relatively small inconveniences of life (such as getting a flat tire or catching the flu), but when a hurricane destroys their home, or their child dies from cancer, or their spouse commits adultery, then they cry out *"Why God?"* But His explanation as to "why" remains consistent regardless of the immediate cause or magnitude of the suffering itself. Those who fail to see God's loving hand working in and through suffering will view these difficulties and hardships as purposeless, threatening, or evil. But suffering has the potential of bringing about an eternal transformation in the life of those who "are trained by it" (see Hebrews 12:11).

Without question, the immensity of losing a child far exceeds the inconvenience of having a flat tire, but does God's involvement change anywhere on the spectrum? God obviously remains constantly attentive and faithful in every circumstance. (For a fuller understanding of this reality, we can ask Job, Paul, or any of the saints who have suffered and have gone before us when we get to Heaven!)

God works all things together for "the good" (Romans 8:28), but what is the *"good"* that God is bringing about? Some argue that we will only know the answer to this question when we arrive in Heaven. But Paul defines it in the very next verse, "For those whom He foreknew, He also predestined to become conformed to the image of His Son..." (Romans 8:29). God knew us before He formed us in the womb (Jeremiah 1:5, Psalm 139:13). We were predestined to bear good fruit—the fruit of the Holy Spirit. God uses "all things" to conform us into the image of Christ, making it possible for us to effortlessly bear His fruit, just as Jesus did while upon this earth. We do not have to wait until heaven to experience this transformation. God is working to transform us into the image of Christ moment by moment!

In light of this, we should not view ourselves as victims of circumstance; rather, we should realize that we are recipients of refinement. God is carefully at work in the life of every believer, and He uses *"all things"* to conform each of us into the image of Christ. The Psalmist declared, "Test me, Lord, and try me; examine my heart and mind. For Your faithful love is before my eyes, and I live by Your truth" (Psalm 26:2-3 HCSB). The Hebrew word translated as "test" in this verse is a term that is used to describe the process of refining precious metals through the use of intense heat (as we discussed earlier). In similar fashion, God refines our faith through the intense heat of our challenges and suffering. Our difficulties expose the impurities in our faith by bringing them to the surface where we can see them.

Recognizing God's Refining Fire

The Refiner's fire can be intense and at times seemingly unbearable. But it can also be as subtle as someone getting your parking place, a harsh word from your spouse, or when you are not acknowledged at the workplace. No matter how difficult or seemingly insignificant your situation may seem, God is using it as part of the Refiner's fire to expose the impurities in your faith.

Is your current difficulty somehow exempt from the category of "all things" that God is causing to work for your good? (This question is obviously rhetorical.) It should go without saying that every situation, challenge, hardship, and moment is part of the "all things" that Paul mentions. Our Heavenly Father uses every moment of everyday life to conform us to the image of His Son (Romans 8:28-30). So, no matter how terrible or severe your life difficulty may be, God's involvement remains the same.

The "fire" reveals the authenticity of our purified faith.

Finally, is the authenticity of your faith being proven by the "fire" that you are currently enduring? When purifying gold, the heat that is applied proves the authenticity of the precious metal, but it does not change the gold itself. If the gold is pure before it is melted, it remains pure in its liquid state. Impurities will only rise to the surface if they are present in the gold before heat is applied. Peter recognized that suffering not only purifies one's faith, but it also verifies its purity where he said,

> For a little while you may have had to suffer grief in all kinds of trials. These have come so that the proven genuineness of your faith—of greater worth than gold, which perishes even though refined by fire—may result in praise, glory and honor when Jesus Christ is revealed (1 Peter 1:6-8 NIV).

Peter says that when the life of Jesus is revealed in us, the outcome will be praise, glory, and honor. Some suggest that we must wait until the return of Christ before this benefit will be realized. But we believe that the "revealing" Peter is referring to here is not of the Lord's second coming, but rather of our inner transformation into His image occurring day by day.

When the image of Jesus is revealed in us, there will be "praise, honor, and glory." His image is progressively revealed as we come into the truth of who we presently are in Christ. Paul says, "we all, with unveiled faces, looking as in a mirror at the glory of the Lord, are being transformed into the same image from glory to glory, just as from the Lord, the Spirit" (2 Corinthians 3:18).

So then, the short answer to whether your situation falls under the heading of God's refining fire, is "yes," as do "all things." There is never a moment in your life in which the Spirit is not actively at work conforming you to the image of Jesus. This is God's purpose in our suffering. When we resist suffering, blaming others or our circumstances for what we feel, and fail to take ownership for what has been exposed in us, we are resisting God and the refining work He is attempting to accomplish. So, the real question is, are we cooperating with God or denying His involvement?

The 'Refiner's Fire' can be hot, but it is not the source of what we feel.

When we find ourselves amid the Refiner's fire, any emotional pain that surfaces is only present because of what we believe. The fire exposes what we believe (1 Peter 4:12-13), but it does not produce what we feel. As we learned in our discussion of the TPM Principles, our emotional response to any given situation is not due to what happens to us, but rather, it is a reflection of how we interpret what has occurred. We feel what we believe.

The pain we feel is the result of having the impurities in our faith exposed. The flame that is used to expose these unwanted beliefs does not cause us to feel anything. Gold is unharmed by the refiner's flame. Only that which is not gold is impacted. These impurities rise to the top where they can be removed. Once everything that is not gold is removed, and all that is left is purified metal, the heat may continue, but the gold is not negatively affected by it.

A similar dynamic is also present whenever my granddaughters are getting their hair brushed. They initially wiggle and whine as the brush passes through their knotted hair, but as they've been told countless times, the brush is not causing their discomfort. Since they only feel the unpleasant tug when the hairbrush is involved, they conclude that it must be the source of their pain. But this is not the case. For once the tangles have been eliminated, the brushing can comfortably continue.

Their uncomfortable tugs simply indicate when a tangle has been found and is being addressed. This is not a bad thing; it is the intended purpose of the tool. The hairbrush dislodges tangles. The refiner's fire exposes the impurities in the gold. And the "fiery ordeal...comes upon you for your testing" (1 Peter 4:12). Each of these tools are designed to expose that which needs to be exposed, but they are not to blame for the unpleasantness of the exposure. Once the unwanted elements have been removed, the tool that was used to expose them can continue to be used without discomfort.

Similarly, when our faith has been purified, the "fire" will have no negative impact on us, and it will prove the purity of our faith. Peter used this same analogy to describe the authenticity of our faith where he said,

> Even though now for a little while, if necessary, you have been distressed by various trials, so that the proof of your faith, *being* more precious than gold which is perishable, even though tested by fire, may be found to result in praise and glory and honor at the revelation of Jesus Christ (1 Peter 1:6-7, emphasis added).

This also explains how it is possible to "rejoice in the Lord always" (Philippians 4:4), and "exult in our tribulations" (Romans 5:3) because we will believe the truth that, "tribulation brings about perseverance; and perseverance, proven character; and proven character, hope; and hope does not disappoint, because the love of God has been poured out within our hearts through the Holy Spirit who was given to us" (Romans 5:3-5).

Such passages are commonly misunderstood to be mandates that we are to attempt to accomplish. Some people take the perceived challenge and choose to "exult" in their tribulation and "make a joyful noise" even though what they are feeling is completely contrary. The key ingredient again in all of these passages is belief. Whatever we believe in our hearts will dictate what we feel. When we are persuaded to believe in our hearts that tribulation and troubles are bringing about an "eternal weight of glory," we will feel joy in the midst of the fire.

Obviously, these truths do not detract from the physical pain we might feel if we were to be tortured or physically mistreated. But, as you will recall, any *emotional* pain we may experience is due to what we believe. Because of this, it is very possible to endure extreme physical pain without experiencing negative emotions such as fear, worry, anxiety, or despair. However, as with Paul and his "thorn," we may become aware of our weakness, inadequacies and dependence upon God, but all of this is based upon the truth. When this is so, we need additional truth to join with Paul in saying, "I will rather boast about my weaknesses, so that the power of Christ may dwell in me" (2 Corinthians 12:9b).

This same phenomenon is reported in the biblical account of Stephen's death by stoning. While being pelted with stones, Stephen observed a heavenly vision of Jesus standing next to the throne of God. Seeing this, Stephen declared, "Behold, I see the heavens opened up and the Son of Man standing at the right hand of God" (Acts 7:56). This vision brought much joy and peace to Stephen and the Bible says,

> He called on the Lord and said, 'Lord Jesus, receive my spirit!' Then falling on his knees, he cried out with a loud voice, 'Lord, do not hold this sin against them!' Having said this, he fell asleep (Acts 7:59-60).

How Stephen died was physically traumatic but not emotionally traumatic. He simply fell asleep, a Biblical euphemism meaning: "he died." In like manner the Lord's death was brutal and traumatic and yet peaceful and controlled. After Jesus had accomplished all He had come to do He said, "It is finished!" And He bowed His head, and gave up His spirit" (John 19:30).

People can hurt our physical bodies and even kill us, but they do not touch *us* in doing so. Remember, our bodies are merely our temporary dwellings in which we live our earthly lives, but they are not who we are. The flame will consume the dross, but it has no impact on the gold.

We see God's careful use of a literal fire to accomplish His faith-refining purposes in the lives of Hananiah, Mishael, and Azariah (commonly known by their Babylonian names: Shadrach, Meshach, and Abed-nego). These men had their faith tested and proven true by the evil king's fiery furnace (Daniel 3:19-30). The purity of their faith was on full display in their perspectives, emotions, words, and actions. Before they were ushered into the flames, their faith *seemed* genuine and pure, but God used what was meant for evil to prove the genuineness of the faith He had given them.

God also used this fire to purify king Nebuchadnezzar's faith. The king angrily defied and attacked these men and their God until the heat was applied. He ordered ropes to be tied around the rebels and commanded valiant warriors to lead them to the flames (Daniel 3:20). This too exposed his lack of God's perspective. The king believed that he was in control, but God used the fire that was built to punish these faithful men to prove the very opposite.

Not until this fiery ordeal did the king realize the futility of his "power" or the true identity of these rebellious Jews as "servants of the Most High God" (Daniel 3:26). Without God's use of fire, the king would have remained deceived and the faith of these brave men would have continued to be questioned.

The refining fire that we face today is like the fire God used thousands of years ago. It exposes the imperfections of impure faith and proves the quality of purified faith. It does not burn us; it is used to burn up what keeps us bound and to showcase the "eternal weight of glory" that God has given to us (2 Corinthians 4:17).

PHYSICAL PAIN IN THE REFINER'S FIRE

During times of difficulty we may experience both physical and emotional pain, which are present for the same basic reasons. Physical and emotional pain are designed to alert us that something is wrong and needs our attention. If we feel a sharp pain in our foot, we will take off our shoe and shake out the stone. If we feel anxious, stressed or fearful, we should ask ourselves what we believe that is causing us to feel that which is contrary to the truth. However, just because you have some reason for feeling physical pain, it does not mean that you should also feel emotional pain as well.

If you are given thirty lashes for being a Christian, you will feel each of them in your body, but any panic, terror, or sense of hopelessness and abandonment that you experience while being beaten is the result of what you believe in your *heart*. If you are hit, expect to feel it. But if you feel afraid of the coming blows, you lack God's perspective (Matthew 10:28, Romans 8:31). The strikes you receive will hurt no matter how you interpret them, but your emotional response will reflect your current perspective. The good news is that God has promised us "peace in every circumstance" (2 Thessalonians 3:16). When we believe the truth in our hearts and have His perspective, His peace will flow continually regardless of what physical pain we may have to endure.

To further illustrate this concept, consider a fighter in a boxing ring. The extent of physical suffering that occurs during the boxing match may be brutal. Even so, the level of emotional "trauma" that a fighter experiences is directly related to how he has interpreted his experience. In the ring he feels hopeful and driven because he believes this is his chance to prove he is the better fighter. If he loses the match, he may feel negative emotion, but this would be due to his interpretation of what that loss means, not the physical punishment that he was forced to endure.

But let's say that this same boxer is accosted by a gang of muggers in a parking lot the following night. The beating he receives may be very similar to the one he endured in the ring, but this time he ends up with post-traumatic stress disorder (PTSD). What is the difference? It all has to do with what he believes. He may feel disappointed in losing the boxing match but looks forward to the next fight. But since he believed that he was going to die in the parking lot, he is plagued by a lingering cloud of despair and anxiety. His belief and interpretation is what determined his experience of each physical beating.

Our perspective of the physical pain we endure has an enormous impact on our emotional experience of it. Another aspect to consider is the purpose behind the physical pain. For instance, back in 2021, I was diagnosed with kidney cancer. My doctor was able to remove the cancerous portion of that organ, and I am grateful for his skill and God's involvement. But in order for the doctor to accomplish this life-saving task, he had to hurt me. He knocked me out, cut me open, removed a part of my body, and sewed me back up. This was obviously an extremely painful ordeal. But the purpose behind his actions is what makes the pain "worth it." I would never allow someone to do what my doctor did just for fun. If someone performed this same task with ill motives, they should be imprisoned. But because he did what he did for the purpose of saving my life, his actions were welcomed (or, at least, as welcomed as they could be!).

In the same way, when we rightly understand God's purposes, we are able to "rejoice in our afflictions" (Romans 5:3 HCSB). This doesn't mean that our "afflictions" won't hurt; it simply means that we will be able to rightly interpret what is happening to us. Since we know that God is in control and is working all things together for our good (Romans 8:28), we can rejoice. Just as

Jesus who "for the joy set before Him endured the cross" (Hebrews 12:2), we can rejoice "knowing that tribulation brings about perseverance; and perseverance, proven character; and proven character, hope; and hope does not disappoint, because the love of God has been poured out within our hearts through the Holy Spirit who was given to us" (Romans 5:3-5).

Part Three

Rejoicing in the Fire

Even if we rightly understand the eternal purpose and benefit of our trials and tribulations, none of us enjoy them when they come upon us. We can fully believe that God works all things together for our good (see Romans 8:28-29) but still experience a great deal of physical and emotional pain. As we said before, if you receive thirty-nine lashes, you will feel each one! And if you lack God's perspective of your beating, then you will undoubtedly misinterpret it and feel the emotional consequences. Nevertheless, your hardship is being used to conform you to the image of His Son.

The writer of Hebrews uses an analogy of a father disciplining a son he loves where he says, "For the moment, all discipline seems not to be pleasant, but painful; yet to those who have been trained by it, afterward it yields the peaceful fruit of righteousness" (Hebrews 12:11, emphasis added). The fire is hot, and what it exposes in us will not be "pleasant, but painful." However, for those who have submitted to God's training, the outcome of His "discipline" is the purification of their faith. This purification will be expressed by the "peaceful fruit of righteousness."

Sometimes we attempt to run from the fire, distract ourselves from it, or, like Paul, ask God to remove the difficulties from our lives. Paul wanted his "thorn in the flesh" (2 Corinthians 12:7) removed. God revealed the necessity of Paul's suffering to him and showed him how it was through weakness that the power of God was made evident in his life. We too can ask God to remove the fire in our lives, but we shouldn't expect to receive a different answer from the Lord than the apostle received.

God's response to Paul was a good description of the refining work He desires to bring about in our suffering. He said, "My grace is sufficient for you, for My strength is made perfect in weakness" (2 Corinthians 12:9 NKJV). Paul discovered that in order for him to experience Jesus living His life in and through him, he had to become weak and actually die (See Galatians 2:20). It was in his helpless, weakened position that the strength of Christ was made perfect or complete. He declared "*it is no longer I who live…*" (Galatians 2:20).

When we understand the purpose of our difficulties and view them as a necessary part of our journey into truth and believe this truth in our hearts, we will rejoice in what God is doing and "*count it all joy*" (James 1:2 NKJV). This rejoicing is not a choice we make in spite of our circumstances (as many believe). We cannot "choose" to feel joy any more than we can "choose" to feel love, patience, or peace.

Trying to rejoice when you are not already rejoicing is like trying to make yourself laugh when you are not already laughing. It is a natural expression of our current belief and perspective, not the result of a willful decision. Paul did not "choose" to rejoice in spite of the "thorn," he rejoiced when the Lord convinced him of its purpose.

The suffering Paul described as a "thorn" was the means by which *endurance (hypomoné)* was having its "perfect work." His thorn was holding him "back and under" exposing his weakness so that the Lord's strength could be perfected in him. *He was not enduring the thorn, rather the "thorn" was producing endurance in him.*

Peter partially revealed the joy that is available to us in our times of suffering when he wrote,

> Beloved, do not be surprised at the fiery ordeal among you, which comes upon you for your testing, as though something strange were happening to you; but to the degree that you share the sufferings of Christ, keep on rejoicing, so that at the revelation of His glory you may also rejoice and be overjoyed (1 Peter 4:12-13).

After Peter declares that our suffering is not strange or unexpected, he continues by saying, "to the degree that you share the sufferings of Christ, keep on rejoicing, so that also at the revelation of His glory [in you] you may rejoice with exultation" (1 Peter 4:13, emphasis added). There are two stages of rejoicing mentioned in this passage. The first rejoicing he mentions is one of *expectation*. We are to "keep on rejoicing" during the "fiery ordeal," expecting that God will bring about a glorious work within us. The second manner of rejoicing he mentions is one of *exultation* that flows from the realization of the work that God has completed in us.

Our joy will break forth when we behold His glorious reflection revealed in our transformation. This is the genuine transformation being expressed through and made evident by the presence of the fruit of His Spirit. The "fire" is used to reveal the evidence of our eternal inner change. This is the expected and effortless transformation that follows having our faith refined and our minds renewed (Romans 12:2).

I used to think that the phrase, "at the revelation of His glory," was referring to the return of Jesus. But this understanding does not fit the context of the passage. The analogy Peter uses here describes the 'testing' or purification of a precious metal. The "revelation" must have to do with the refining process. In other places the Scripture reveals that our sharing in His suffering brings about a 'testing' that comes with a promise of sharing in His glory. Paul said, "We share in his sufferings in order that we may also share in his glory" (Romans 8:17 NIV). His glory is made manifest in us as we are transformed into His likeness.

Like the reflective surface of purified gold, we will reflect the image of the Refiner. When His glory is revealed in us (that is, in our faith), we will rejoice with exultation! Again we read where Paul declared, "we all, with unveiled faces, <u>looking as in a mirror at the glory of the Lord, are being transformed into the same image</u> from glory to glory, just as from the Lord, the Spirit" (2 Corinthians 3:18, emphasis added).

Also, keep in mind that rejoicing is not something that we somehow choose to muster up and produce at will. Authentic rejoicing requires the presence of joy, and joy is a fruit of the Spirit. The fruit of joy is only present as an outcome of having been persuaded of the truth by the Spirit within our hearts. Before we can rejoice in expectation of what God is doing during our suffering, we must believe that the purification of our faith is coming. Our belief in what God is doing creates this expectation and produces the fruit of joy. When His glory is revealed in us, we will rejoice with an uncontainable joy.

Without realizing that God has a purpose for our difficulties (the refinement of our faith and renewing of our minds), we will be prone to view our troubles and triggers as something we must endure, bear under, and somehow get through. If this is our perspective, we will forfeit the greater benefit that He has intended us to reap. The goal of every trial is the same. It is not just to get to the other side; for that is a given. Rather, the goal is for us to benefit. The benefit is our transformation.

This sheds light on the life of Paul who suffered so much for the cause of Christ, and even while in prison his emotional response was that of joy. How was this possible? Because he knew in his heart the truth that "the Lord is near!"

> Rejoice in the Lord always. I will say it again: Rejoice! Let your gentleness be apparent to all. The Lord is near. Be anxious for nothing, but in everything, by prayer and petition, with thanksgiving, present your requests to God. And the peace of God, which surpasses all understanding, will guard your hearts and your minds in Christ Jesus (Philippians 4:4-7 BSB).

Again we read what Paul says in his letter to the church in Rome,

> We also exult in our tribulations, knowing that tribulation brings about perseverance; and perseverance, proven character; and proven character, hope; and hope does not disappoint, because the love of God has been poured out within our hearts through the Holy Spirit who was given to us (Romans 5:3-5).

Peter the Apostle said this concerning our suffering:

> Those who suffer <u>according to God's will</u>, should commit themselves to their faithful Creator and continue to do good (1 Peter 4:19 NIV, emphasis added).

And Jesus said this concerning the benefit gained through suffering,

> Blessed are you when people insult you and persecute you, and falsely say all kinds of evil against you because of Me. Rejoice and be glad, for <u>your reward in heaven is great</u>; for in the same way, they persecuted the prophets who were before you (Matthew 5:11-12, emphasis added).

Without question some people have suffered great difficulties far beyond what most of us will ever know. But no matter how horrible the suffering may be, we must again return to the truth of the Scriptures that declare that our, "momentary, light affliction is producing for us an eternal weight of glory far beyond all comparison" (2 Corinthians 4:17). This was also true for Jesus. The day He was crucified He suffered unimaginable physical pain, and yet He rejoiced in it because He knew the truth. It was because of "the joy set before Him [that He] endured the cross" (Hebrews 12:2, emphasis added). Jesus looked beyond His immediate suffering and looked forward to the glory that was set before Him.

This same truth that Peter wrote about, applies to each of us who are in Christ. Yes indeed, the suffering is not pleasant but rather "sorrowful" (Hebrews 12:11). But it is all "momentary" and "light" in comparison to the eternal weight of glory that is ours! When we believe this in our hearts we will rejoice. These promises provide the foundational truths that define the *Purpose of TPM*.

Again, it is not the magnitude of the trouble that should determine when you humble yourself or not, since "it is God who is at work in you, both to desire and to work for His good pleasure" (Philippians 2:13). Only as we choose to "humble [ourselves] under the mighty hand of God" (1 Peter 5:6) during our difficulty will we experience the benefit from having God work in and through all of our troubles.

Some of us live under the crushing and seemingly unanswered question, *"Why God?"* But God's Word is clear; suffering is not strange and should be expected (John 16:33). We live in a fallen world, and bad things happen, but God is still at work in bringing about an eternal good for those who love Him and "those who are called according to His purpose" (Romans 8:28). Until we recognize God's purpose in life's difficulties and know how to practically cooperate with Him as he accomplishes it, we will likely continue to forfeit the opportunities that He has provided to have our faith refined, our minds renewed, and our lives transformed.

I remember trying to process this idea and apply it to my life years ago during the loss of my little girl. I remember thinking, "I am willing to forfeit any good if I could just have my daughter back." That was a long time ago. After many years of watching God do a mighty work in my heart and life, I no longer feel this way. God has accomplished many good works through the loss of my child; TPM itself is counted among them!

When you understand this first element of the Purpose of TPM, you will view your daily difficulties as a *benefit* rather than a trial to endure and suffer through. Life's difficulties are understood to be *instruments* in the hand of a loving God, transforming us into the image of His Son (Romans 8:28-29). When we discover that our life's difficulties are the primary means through which God does His finest work in refining our faith, renewing our minds, and transforming us, we will "consider it all joy..." (James 1:2), "exult in our tribulations..." (Romans 5:3), and "rejoice in the Lord always..." (Philippians 4:4).

Part Four

Faith-refinement In Summary

To summarize this concept, let's revisit the gold analogy we used earlier. The gold that is contained in raw ore form is still pure gold even though contaminated with impurities. The impurities are not a part of the gold itself; they are merely present with it in the melting pot. The fire heats the gold to its melting point and, because of the gold's density, it sinks to the bottom, forcing any impurities to rise to the surface (further distinguishing them from the precious metal). The fire first exposes what should not be there and then, once all that is not gold is removed by the refiner, it reveals the purity of the gold. When only gold remains in the melting pot, its purity is made evident even if intense heat is continually applied!

Likewise, the truth of who God is and who we are in Him is like the gold in the refiner's melting pots. The impurities in our faith do not take away from this reality. They do, however, inhibit our ability to enjoy and rest in His finished work. When the "heat" of tribulation and suffering is applied, these impurities float up and make it nearly impossible for us to see the glorious reality that is just beneath the surface. The truth of who we are and who He is remains but cannot be seen through the thick sludge of deception.

When the Refiner removes these lie-based impurities, the reflective surface of the molten gold is revealed and, as He peers into the melting pot of our lives, He sees the reflection of Himself in us (1 Peter 1:7-8). The gold had been there from the beginning of this refining process. The only thing left to do was to put it on full display.

Throughout this refining process, we are not becoming more like Jesus. Rather, the impurities in our faith are being removed so that our true selves (the new creations) may be revealed. We are like the "pure gold" that contains impurities, but the impurities are not a part of who we are. Paul affirms this where he declares that the Church (of whom you are a part if you are in Christ) is the fullness of Jesus. He said, "[God] put all things in subjection under His feet, and made Him head over all things to the church, which is His body, the <u>fullness of Him</u> who fills all in all" (Ephesians 1:22-23).

As the fullness of Christ, we are the true reflection of Him. We simply do not yet realize who we are and have been deceived into believing that we are something we are not. John said it this way, "Beloved, <u>now</u> we are children of God, and it has not appeared as yet what we will be. We know that when He appears, we will be like Him, because we will see Him just as He is" (1 John 3:2, emphasis added). We are now children of God (who and what we presently are), and God did not bear defective children. He is not fixing or changing the baby itself, He is merely wiping off anything that is not a part of the child.

There is a two-fold purpose of the "Refiner's fire." First, the fire is used to expose the impurities in our faith so that they might be removed. But if we are required to remain in the fire, or if the fire comes back later, it serves an additional purpose as it affirms or "proves" the purity of our faith. Here is where the fire manifests the fruit of God's Spirit in us. For when the heat is applied after our faith has been refined, our purified faith (pure gold) is put on display for all to see.

If you are in Christ and His Spirit is in you, then the transformation of who and what you were has already happened. We are presently new creations and have put on the new self that has been created in the image of God in His righteousness and the truth (see Ephesians 4:24). The problem is, we do not yet fully believe this truth in our hearts. God sent His Spirit to make this reality evident in your life by exposing your lack of perspective and then persuading you of the truth (John 16:5-16). Any of our beliefs that do not accurately depict God's nature and character also fail to accurately describe our newly created selves. We are His workmanship (Ephesians 2:10), created in His image (Genesis 1:27, Ephesians 4:24), born of His Spirit (John 3:6) and of imperishable seed (1 Peter 1:23). But if you have been deceived into believing that you are something else, then your self-image will be distorted.

Your inaccurate perception of God is based upon that which you have been convinced is true, so it will feel true even though it is not. Just because it is believed to be true does not make it so. It will, however, impede your ability to see, feel, and experience the truth, just as the impurities cover-up the gold.

Again, this skewed perspective, as well as the lie-based beliefs that produce it, impact us, but they are not us. We possess what we believe, use what we believe, and suffer the consequences of what we believe, but our beliefs are not who we are. Paul made this distinction when he said, "if I do the very thing I do not want, I am no longer the one doing it, but sin that dwells in me" (Romans 7:20). The sin which dwelled in Paul's flesh was not Paul, and the same is true for every believer! We are not our fleshly bodies or the beliefs we hold, since we have "put on the new self, which in the likeness of God has been created in righteousness and holiness of the truth" (Ephesians 4:24). This is who we are. If this reality doesn't *seem* or *feel* true, then the impurities in your faith are impairing your ability to see who you really are in Him!

Submitting To God's Refining Work

In the context of a suffering church, Peter revealed the work that God is accomplishing in us when he says, "After you have suffered for a little while [in the Refiner's fire], the God of all grace, who called you to His eternal glory in Christ, will Himself perfect, confirm, strengthen, and establish you" (1 Peter 5:10, emphasis added). Notice who brings about the finished work. It is God himself who will "perfect, confirm, strengthen, and establish you."

Our response to the troubles that come upon us indicates whether or not we are walking in this truth. If we honestly, automatically respond with peace, kindness, joy, love, and behaviors that accurately reflect God's character, this indicates that we are operating from His perspective. If not, this represents an opportunity to submit to His "mighty hand" and have our faith refined and our minds renewed.

Again, God uses suffering to expose what needs to be exposed. If our faith is impure, suffering will make this obvious, giving us the opportunity to have The Great Refiner perform His masterful work. If our faith has been purified already, suffering will make this clear for all to see as we effortlessly bear His fruit. Our Heavenly Father's careful and loving use of suffering enables us to more accurately see Him and ourselves through His eyes (by refining our faith) and displays His heart and character to the world (though our fruit bearing). Although the experience can be difficult and painful, "we also celebrate in our tribulations" (see Romans 5:3) knowing that "God causes all things to work together for good" (see Romans 8:28).

WHAT EXACTLY IS BEING REFINED?

It is important to note that the refinement of our faith purifies our faith (heart belief), and therefore, it affects our perspectives, emotions, and behaviors, but it has no impact on who or what we are in Christ. The moment that we believed the Gospel in our hearts, we became new creations. Keeping with the gold refining analogy, the *truth* of our new self, which was created in the likeness of God in righteousness and holiness of the truth (see Ephesians 4:24), is pure gold. However, not all that we *believe* about who we are is pure. This should sound very reminiscent of our discussion of the Fundamental Principle, "*we perceive what we believe.*" God desires that our heart belief be brought into alignment with the reality of our new created selves. He wants us to see ourselves the way He sees us (i.e. accurately, from an eternal perspective).

The "refiner" does not change or alter the gold throughout the refining process. Rather, he carefully separates the gold from that which is *not* gold by exposing it to intense heat and then removes the distracting impurities that make it difficult to rightly see and appreciate the precious metal hidden beneath the surface. In like fashion, as God performs His refining work, we are not becoming more like Jesus, but rather, the impurities in our faith (which do not accurately reflect God or our new identity) are being removed so that our Christlikeness might be made more evident. When these distracting impurities are removed from our faith, His glorious finished work in us is put on full display.

Throughout this process the "gold" is not becoming more *golden*. For at the moment of our salvation, we were "born of God" (1 John 5:1). We are not *becoming* like Jesus; we are *already* like Him because we were born of God, and again I say, "God does not give birth to defective children." We are born as *infants* who need "milk" rather than "solid food" (Hebrews 5:12), but nevertheless, we are still His children and are as much like Him as we'll ever be. We are like our Heavenly Father, but much of what we believe is inconsistent with the reality of our new birth. Because of this, our limited and flawed perspectives hinder our ability to see who we really are.

I used to believe that I was on a long, progressive journey of becoming more and more like Jesus. And I expended much effort in attempting to conform my behavior to what I believed was Christlike. Although it was true that God desired to transform me into His image (Romans 8:29), He did not call me to transform myself. He was calling me to submit to His faith-refining process.

God declared this through His prophet, "I will give them one heart, and put a new spirit within them. And I will remove the heart of stone from their flesh and give them a heart of flesh" (Ezekiel 11:19, 36:26). Since He has given me a new heart and spirit, the remaining transformation that needs to occur is also His work as He renews my mind. My problem is that I cannot yet rightly "see" what God has already done.

The prophet Ezekiel was obviously not referring to our physical hearts but our inner, spiritual ones. He also made it clear that we only possess one spiritual heart and not two. There is a singularity expressed here where God says, "I will give them one heart..." and "I will remove the heart of stone from their flesh and give them a heart of flesh." The old heart has been both *removed* and *replaced*. We only have one heart, and it is good since the "the love of God has been poured out within our hearts through the Holy Spirit who was given to us" (Romans 5:5).

Someone may protest and say, "But Jesus said, 'Out of the heart come evil thoughts—murder, adultery, sexual immorality, theft, false testimony, slander' (Matthew 15:19 NIV). So how can we trust our hearts to do right?" Yes, it is obviously true that evil things come out of evil hearts. But in this passage, Jesus was making a comparison between a good heart and an evil one. He confirmed this where He also said, *The good person out of the good treasure of his heart brings forth what is good; and the evil person out of the evil treasure brings forth what is evil; for his mouth speaks from that which fills his heart"* (Luke 6:45).

The question is, "what kind of heart do we have?" Paul said it clearly, "Examine yourselves, to see whether you are in the faith" (2 Corinthians 13:5 ESV) and Peter echoed this by saying, "be all the more diligent to confirm your calling and election" (2 Peter 1:10 ESV). We must determine whether we have an evil heart of stone or a new heart of flesh (see Ezekiel 36:26). We cannot have both at the same time for God took one out and put the other in.

Evil is expected to flow from hearts that are "evil" but not out of the new hearts that have been placed within each of His children. The moment I was born of His Spirit, I was transformed completely within my inner man. My new heart is part of the new creation that I became as a result of my having died with Jesus and being raised with Him. My new heart and new self, "which in the likeness of God [have] been created in righteousness and holiness of the truth" (Ephesians 4:24, emphasis added) is who I am, whereas, my beliefs, perceptions, emotions, and behaviors are not. I am not what I think, feel, or do; I am who He says that I am. Thankfully, these things (perceptions, emotions, and behaviors) are being transformed so that they will reflect who I truly am in Christ.

Not only has God given us a new heart, He has also placed a new spirit within us. There is reasonable evidence that the new heart and new spirit spoken of by Ezekiel are synonymous and his use of *synonymous parallelism*. Synonymous parallelism is a form of speech found often in the Psalms and in Proverbs. It is used where the same idea is stated in succession in order to emphasize a point or to say the same thing in a different way. I am comfortable with either understanding, knowing that whatever I used to have was replaced with the new.

I believe that the "new spirit" is another way of describing the "new self" that replaced our old self when we died with Christ and were raised up with Him (see Galatians 2:20, Colossians 2:12, Ephesians 4:24). We are new creations with new hearts! Our old self —who we were before Christ— was crucified with Jesus and we have "put on the new self, which in the likeness of God has been created in righteousness and holiness of the truth" (Ephesians 4:24). Note: This verse from Ephesians is repeatedly quoted here because we want you to memorize it. It describes who you really are. You are a new self that God has created in His likeness founded in righteousness and truth!

Since you have a new heart and have put on a new self, you are not becoming like Jesus in your inner man. Rather, you are on a journey of discovery of who you already are in Christ. Your true self is presently "hidden in Christ with God" (Colossians 3:3) so you must "set your mind on the things that are above, not on the things that are on earth. [Why?] For you have died, and your life is hidden with Christ in God" (Colossians 3:2-3, emphasis added). As your mind is renewed with truth you will become more fully aware of the inner change in your heart that occurred when you initially came to Christ. You were born again as a new creature, as a child of God!

The reason we need to focus our attention *upwards* is because that is where our new self is "hidden in Christ with God." He wants us to discover the reality of our new selves. All those who are in Christ are presently like Him because they are born of God and created in righteousness and holiness of the truth. This truth is still true before you "look upwards," but you will be unable to fully realize and appreciate it until your attention is turned to the heavenly "things that are above."

If you are in Christ, then you are presently as much like Jesus in your inner person as you will ever be! Peter reveals this when he says, "*His divine power has granted to us everything pertaining to life and godliness, through the true knowledge of Him who called us by His own glory and excellence*" (2 Peter 1:3, emphasis added). God has divinely given us everything; we possess it all! Paul, too, affirms this reality when he declares, "*[God has] blessed us with every spiritual blessing in the heavenly places in Christ*" (Ephesians 1:3, emphasis added).

Did you also notice the means by which God grants us everything? It is "through the true knowledge of the one who called us. . ." We will experience the reality of this truth to the degree that we come into the knowledge of Him or as we come to know Him. This was the cry of Paul's heart. He cried out, "I want to know Christ. . ." (Philippians 3:10 NIV).

As our faith is refined and our minds are renewed, our beliefs, perspectives, emotions, and behavior will come into alignment with the reality of our new inner selves and this will be made evident by the effortless expression of the fruit of the Spirit. Again, we are not "becoming like Jesus," the truth of who we already are in Him is being made more evident.

CHAPTER 10

COMPONENT TWO
"THE RENEWING OF OUR MINDS"

Renewed in the Spirit of Your Mind

In the last chapter we explored the first element in the Purpose of TPM (the refinement of our faith). We discovered that God uses "all things" to expose the impurities in our faith. This exposure is made evident through what we feel and how we respond. This exposes our need for His perspective. We need Him to renew the *spirit of our minds* (see Ephesians 4:23) by persuading us of the truth. When this happens, the lie we once believed no longer *feels* or *seems* true, and the truth *feels* or *seems* true from our new perspective. We refer to this change in belief as "mind-renewal."

Mind-renewal (a transformation of belief) is the expected outcome of the refining work that God is doing in our lives. For as Paul explained, you must "be transformed by the renewing of your mind" (Romans 12:2). He also asked God to grant us "a spirit of wisdom and of revelation in the knowledge of Him" and he further prayed "that the eyes of [our] hearts may be enlightened, so that [we] will know what is the hope of His calling" (Ephesians 1:17-18, emphasis added). This only happens as a result of the Holy Spirit's work in us. Paul did not instruct us to enlighten the eyes of our own hearts; rather, he prayed that God Himself would enlighten them. Mind-renewal is not something that we can accomplish ourselves, but we can humbly cooperate with God as He brings it about.

As we have stated, there is immense value in the accumulation of Biblical knowledge, but becoming "Bible smart" is not the same as genuine mind-renewal. Intellectual understanding of the truth is the "front door" to the heart, but it does not guarantee a change in what we believe at a heart level. True mind-renewal always results in some measure of transformation. Bible knowledge can lead to mind-renewal, but it itself is not mind-renewal.

Acquiring Biblical knowledge increases our reservoir of intellectual truth (which is a good thing), but true spiritual change only takes place when the Spirit of Truth persuades our hearts of His perspective. Simply knowing the facts of the Scriptures will not transform us, but growing in knowledge of the One who is the Truth will. Again, Paul said that he wants to know Christ—yes, "that I may know Him and the power of His resurrection and the fellowship of His sufferings, being conformed to His death" (Philippians 3:10). Paul did not say, "I want to know more about Jesus," but rather, he wanted to *know* Him. This verse does not describe an intellectual agreement concerning the truth about Jesus, but rather it is a statement describing a dynamic relationship.

Some have cited Ephesians 1:17 and suggested that God has already given us "a spirit of wisdom and revelation in the knowledge of Him" in the form of His written Word and that all we need to do is read and apply it. The Scriptures are obviously the full and complete revelation of truth that God has given to His church. Even so, this passage clearly explains that Paul is praying for God to grant a spirit of wisdom and revelation that will result in the believer coming into the knowledge of Christ. If Paul was merely praying that his reader would read the Bible more, then he would have said so (besides, at the time this letter was written to the church in Ephesus, they did not yet have the completed Scriptures). In this passage, Paul was not asking God for new or additional revelation that would add to or supersede Scripture. He wanted the eyes of their hearts to be opened so that they could see the truth that was already available.

Paul also writes, "until we all attain to the unity of the faith, and of the knowledge of the Son of God, to a mature man, to the measure of the stature which belongs to the fullness of Christ" (Ephesians 4:13). These passages reveal that there is a deeper level of knowing Christ that supersedes our intellectual pursuit of the truth. This spiritual knowing is relational, experiential, and life-changing, and it is brought about solely by the Spirit's work. Our self-attained intellectual knowledge cannot accomplish this. God desires that you "<u>know</u> the love of Christ which <u>surpasses</u> knowledge, that you may be filled to all the fullness of God" (Ephesians 3:19, emphasis added).

An unbeliever is perfectly capable of memorizing Bible verses, but only the Spirit can persuade him to believe those truths in his heart. Growing in knowledge of the Scriptures will increase our intellectual reservoir of truth, but if there is not a notable and effortless change (transformation) in our emotions and behavior, then we cannot say that mind-renewal has occurred. Transformation expectedly follows genuine mind-renewal (again see Romans 12:2-3). We need God to persuade our hearts of the truth, and He has promised to do just that! God is the one who initiated our faith, and He has promised to finish what He started (see Philippians 1:6).

This does not diminish the importance of studying the Word of God, since the Spirit persuades our hearts to believe the truths that have already been stored in our heads. The intellect is how we learn what the Bible says and brings us a step toward believing the truth in the heart, but mere intellectual agreement with the truth will not transform us. Believing with the heart is brought about by the Spirit, not our struggle to believe through commitment, willpower, and controlled behavior. We only believe the truth with the heart when the Spirit opens the eyes of our hearts and illuminates His truth within us.

As we learned from our discussion of the TPM Principles, we can believe with our intellect what the Bible says about God's endless love for us and yet not feel loved by Him. We may quote the passage that says, "For God so loved the world, that He gave His only Son, so that everyone who believes in Him will not perish, but have eternal life" (John 3:16) and yet not believe it in our hearts. Unless this truth is believed in the heart, salvation will not occur. For it is "...with the heart a person believes, resulting in righteousness..." (Romans 10:10). Unless the Spirit convinces us of the truth of the Gospel we will not believe.

Regarding salvation, we read, "How then will they call on Him in whom they have not believed? How will they believe in Him whom they have not heard? And how will they hear without a preacher?" (Romans 10:14). This passage reveals that we must "hear" the truth of the Gospel (processed with the intellect) before we can "believe" it with our hearts. This deeper level of belief is only possible when it is brought about through the illumination and persuasion of the Holy Spirit. Again, "hearing" the truth is a precursor to faith, but it provides no guarantee of salvation and transformation apart from God's divine persuasion.

The Persuasion of Faith

As you will recall, the writer of Hebrews described faith as "the assurance of things hoped for, the conviction of things not seen" (Hebrews 11:1). It is not hoping for something to be true, it is the absolute assurance that it is true (even when it cannot be seen). The Greek word most often translated "faith" in the New Testament is *pistis*. Again, depending on the context in which it is used, this word may also mean "trusting in," "relying upon," or "putting confidence in someone or something." In TPM we don't view these actions or behaviors as faith, but rather, we see them as the result or outcome of faith. Faith is not something that we do; it is something that we possess. We trust, rely upon, place confidence in, obey, and follow because of our faith. Simply put, we do what we do because of the faith we possess (which should sound very reminiscent of one of the Foundational Principles of TPM).

Just like Abraham, who believed God, and it was credited to him as righteousness (Romans 4:3), you too were saved because of your faith. It is *because* you first *believed* that you then *trusted* in Him, *chose* to follow Him, and *committed* your life to Him. None of these actions saved you. Rather, you *trusted*, *chose* and *followed* as the outcome of your faith and salvation.

It might be helpful to revisit the original meaning and root of the Greek word *pistis* to understand this perspective. Although *pistis* has many different interpretations depending on the context, its root, *peitho*, has one basic meaning: "<u>*persuasion*</u>" - *to persuade or to be persuaded*. In the biblical context this word describes the result of God's divine persuasion.

When the Holy Spirit persuades or convinces us of the truth within our hearts, we become assured that it is true, and as a result, we believe. It is because we are persuaded by the Spirit in our hearts that we have the "assurance of things hoped for, the conviction of things not seen" (Hebrews 11:1). When we are persuaded of the truth in this way, we will believe it with absolute certainty. Much of TPM is built upon this understanding.

Paul expressed this perspective of faith when he said, "I know whom I have <u>believed</u> and <u>am persuaded</u> that He is able to keep what I have committed to Him until that Day" (2 Timothy 1:12 NKJV, emphasis added). The two words translated as "believed", and "persuaded" in this verse are derived from the same root word *peitho* (persuasion). Paul is saying, "I am *persuaded* because I know the One who *persuaded me*." Peitho brings about the faith that transforms our lives so that they more accurately reflect the image of Christ. But notice who did the persuading! Paul did not persuade himself to believe the truth. This was the work of God that was accomplished by His Spirit.

Persuasion is not self-achieved.

This form of persuasion is never more obvious or important than when a person believes the Gospel with his or her heart resulting in salvation. We did not enter this grace by merely *deciding* to believe and trust in Christ, rather our trust in Christ resulted from His persuasion. He calls us to Himself (see John 6:44). God shines His light into our hearts, persuading us of the truth of the Gospel, and as a response, we trust Him, resulting in our salvation. "For God, who said, 'Let light shine out of darkness,' made his light shine in our hearts to give us the light of the knowledge of God's glory displayed in the face of Christ" (2 Corinthians 4:6 NIV). And since we believe, we also confess Him, since "with the heart a person believes, resulting in righteousness, and with the mouth he confesses, resulting in salvation" (Romans 10:10).

The Spirit must first persuade us of our need for a Savior. For until we are convinced that we are sinful and agree with God in this matter (*homologeo*: "confess"), forgiveness of our sin is not possible. This is the essence of John's message where he says,

> If we say that we have no sin, we are deceiving ourselves and the truth is not in us. If we confess [agree with God about] our sins, He is faithful and righteous, so that He will forgive us our sins and cleanse us from all unrighteousness. If we say that we have not sinned, we make Him a liar and His word is not in us (1 John 1:8-10, emphasis added).

But once God convinced us of our sinfulness and the need for a Savior, we were positioned to be persuaded of the truths of His mercy and grace. When this occurred, we believed, resulting in our righteousness. We did not initiate the process that resulted in our salvation. For as Jesus clearly states, "No one can come to Me unless the Father who sent Me draws them" (John 6:44 NIV). John also affirms that "we love, because He first loved us" (1 John 4:19). Both our salvation and transformation are initiated and accomplished by God. We simply submit, are persuaded, and then receive.

There is an old praise and worship song titled "I Have Decided to Follow Jesus." I am sure that you have sung it many times yourself. It is true that we make the decision to follow Jesus, but deciding to do so is not faith. Deciding to follow Him is an expression or outcome of the faith He has given to us. It is because I have faith that I follow, trust, obey, etc. If we struggle to do these things, it is a faith issue; we need His perspective. When we believe the truth in our hearts, our behavior will reflect this.

CHAPTER 11

COMPONENT THREE

"THE TRANSFORMATION OF OUR LIVES"

NOTICE: This chapter has been divided into two parts. The first part defines transformation and discusses what is being transformed. The second part explores our role in this process of transformation.

Part One

Transformed by the Renewing of Our Minds

Paul assured us that no matter our circumstance, God is at work causing "all things" to work together to conform us into the image of Christ (see Romans 8:28-29). He brings this about in similar fashion to a refiner of precious metal, exposing the impurities in our faith: our lie-based heart beliefs. The outcome of His refining work is the renewal of our minds: the persuasion of the truth in our hearts. As a result of this mind-renewal, our lives are transformed. As we learned in our discussion of the TPM Principles, we perceive, feel, and do what we believe. So, when our beliefs change, our perceptions, emotions, and behaviors are also impacted. This change is the result of the Holy Spirit's work in us and occurs automatically and effortlessly on our part.

The Greek word "*metamorphoō*," which is often translated as "transform" in the New Testament, is used to denote a change from one thing to another. This change results from forces beyond one's own effort or power. We are being transformed, but we are not transforming ourselves. To illustrate, if you strike a wooden matchstick, the flame will transform the wood into carbon. The wood is not transforming itself, but merely submitting to the flame. And after the flame has finished its transforming work, the wood effortlessly maintains its transformed state; it can never be wood again. We also experience transformation through "fire" as we submit to the Refiner and His flame.

Paul expressed this in his letter to the Romans when he said, "Do not be conformed to this world, but be transformed by the renewing of your mind" (Romans 12:2). According to this passage, transformation is the expected outcome of having our minds renewed with the truth. As important as it is to grow in knowledge of the Scriptures, if our intellectual agreement with the Scriptures does not consistently bring about transformation, then it does not constitute the Biblical definition of mind-renewal. We can achieve various levels of cognitive restructuring and diligent attempts in behavior modification, but mind-renewal is a divine work accomplished by God's Spirit. And the resulting transformation is expressed when we effortlessly bear the fruit of the Holy Spirit (see Galatians 5:22-23).

Transforming Versus Conforming

As we learned from our discussion of faith-refinement, our problem is not that we fail to "walk by faith," but rather that the faith we "walk by" is impure. These lie-based impurities cause us to feel negative emotions and lead us in sinful directions. Typically, people attempt to combat the effects of this deception by denying their feelings and trying to do the right thing. Although their intentions are noble, this strategy is entirely dependent upon their commitment to the cause and the effort they pour into it. If we are honest, it inevitably results in spiritual fatigue, frustration, and eventual failure (or, worse yet, a sense of accomplishment and confidence in our own efforts).

God is not impressed with our ability to study, memorize, and perform as we attempt to conform our behavior to the truth. He is not interested in seeing how well we can perform as we struggle to "walk rightly," and obey the truth. He has a much greater goal in mind: transformation — good works that are an effortless expression of fruit-bearing.

When God persuades our hearts of the truth of Who He is and who we are in Him, we will stop trying to "perform the fruit," and will begin to "bear the fruit." Rather than trying to **act** loving, joyful, peaceful, patient and kind, we will **be** loving, joyful, peaceful, patient and kind. God wants us to effortlessly bear and express these characteristics as an outcome of His work within us. Genuine transformation is only achieved through God and is sustained by God. The fruit we bear is His, not ours. Performing the "fruit" is not the same as *bearing* it. Even an unbeliever can choose to *act* like Jesus, but only the Spirit can cause us to *be* like Jesus.

This is not meant to minimize the value of our efforts, but rather, we are only suggesting that there is a vast difference between what He does in us and what we can do on our own. It does take effort and personal discipline to humble ourselves under His mighty hand (1 Peter 5:6) and position ourselves to receive from the Spirit, but the transformation that follows is the result of His work alone. Our struggle to live out the truth that we intellectually believe exposes our need to have the Holy Spirit persuade our hearts to believe it. When we believe the truth in our hearts, struggling to obey will cease and no longer be burdensome (1 John 5:3).

Conformity to the truth is what we often attempt to do, whereas transformation is what only God can do. Conformity requires constant effort, but transformation naturally results in godly character and behavior (the fruit). Conformity requires our constant attention and maintenance, whereas transformation is spontaneous, effortless, and eternal. To the degree that the Spirit has persuaded us of the truth in our hearts, we will be transformed by it, and Christ will live His life in and through us.

What Is Being Transformed?

We have established the fact that we experience the transformation that God brings into our lives, but what specifically is being transformed as a result of His refining process? Contrary to what many believe, the transformation we are discussing is not in who or what you are. As we discovered in the last chapter, if you are a born-again believer who possesses the indwelling Spirit of God, then you are a "new creation" (2 Corinthians 5:17) who has put on a new self that was created "in the likeness of God . . . in righteousness and holiness of the truth" (Ephesians 4:24). You have been "born again" (1 Peter 1:23) into God's eternal family and your "inner man" has been completely transformed into the likeness of Christ.

Paul clearly stated that "if anyone is in Christ, this person is a new creation; the old things passed away; behold, new things have come." (2 Corinthians 5:17). If you are a new creation, no aspect of who you are needs to be transformed! Your inner man - your actual, newly formed, God-given identity - is a finished work. You are God's child, born of His Spirit. Now, just as a physical newborn, you need to grow and mature, but nonetheless, you are as much a child of God as you will ever be. John said it plainly, "We are NOW children of God. . ." (1 John 3:2, emphasis added)

Again, I declare that God's Spirit does not give birth to defective children! If you are born of God, you are as holy, acceptable, and pleasing as you will ever be! You *may* have a limited and flawed perspective, feel unfounded emotional pain, and make misguided choices, but you remain a child of light who does not belong in darkness (1 Thessalonians 5:5). Sin, deception, and darkness are incongruent with who you truly are. You are His and you share His spiritual DNA. When your thoughts, perspectives, feelings, and behaviors oppose God, they also oppose your true identity.

According to Paul, the "law of sin" is *"waging war against the law of [our] minds, and making [us] a prisoner of the law of sin, the law which is in [our] body's parts"* (Romans 7:23, emphasis added). Even though we are new creations, we temporarily dwell in fallen earthly bodies which possess the old "law" of sin (Biblical Greek word "nomos" - law, custom, a system of religious thinking) that was present before our salvation. This "law" is reflected in the unrenewed mindset that we brought into our new life in Christ. It needs to be replaced with His truth so that our beliefs are consistent with the "new creations" that we are. Until we are able to see ourselves (and God) from His perspective, we will continue to think, feel, and act as though we are something that we are not. Our unrenewed minds will remain in constant "war" with the inner person of our new hearts (our true selves). Paul described this predicament where he said,

> I joyfully agree with the law of God in the inner person, but I see a different law in the parts of my body waging war against the law of my mind, and making me a prisoner of the law of sin, the law which is in my body's parts (Romans 7:22-23).

This flawed thinking must be laid aside (Ephesians 4:22) so that we can operate from God's perspective and offer up the members of our earthly *"bodies as living sacrifices, holy and pleasing to God"* (Romans 12:1 BSB) and as *"instruments of righteousness for God"* (Romans 6:13). In a sense, our unrenewed mindsets and lie-based beliefs belong to us and continually influence us, but they are not us, nor do they reflect who we really are (if we are born of God). To the degree that God persuades us of His perspective, our beliefs will align with our true identities.

Now, some may protest, "I sure don't *feel* as holy or accepted as these passages claim that I am, and I still *struggle* with sin on a daily basis. When I take an honest look at my life, it definitely *seems* like I am sinful, dirty, unworthy, held captive, etc." But these sentiments represent the exact type of thinking that needs to be replaced with His truth. Your current perspective may rightly describe your old self (the one that was crucified and buried with Christ, see Galatians 2:20 and Romans 6:1-11), but it does not accurately depict your newly created self "which in the likeness of God has been created in righteousness and holiness of the truth" (Ephesians 4:24). This simply means that you do not yet fully believe these truths in your heart.

As we have discussed in earlier chapters, just because something seems or feels true doesn't mean that it is true; it simply means you believe it to be true. You perceive what you believe. And if God's assessment of you doesn't seem or feel true, then you do not yet fully believe Him. The truth is still the truth, but it will not seem or feel true until He persuades you of it.

You see, much of what we believed before the cross remained intact even after our spiritual death and resurrection with Jesus. For example, if you believed that you were stupid before trusting in Jesus' finished work, you probably continued to believe that you are stupid even after being born of the Spirit. The cross radically changed many things, but it had little impact on our former way of thinking.

Someone may react to this idea by saying, "Not so fast! 2 Corinthians 5:17 says that if we are in Christ, the old things have passed away and new things have come." Although this is obviously true, we must ask, "<u>what has passed away</u>, and <u>what has become new</u>, and <u>when did each of these things take place</u>?"

Every old thing that pertained to who we were before Christ has passed away. Paul summed this up by saying, "I have been crucified with Christ…" (see Galatians 2:20). The New Living Translation (NLT) precisely says it as, "My old self has been crucified with Christ. It is no longer I who live, but Christ lives in me." And then, everything pertaining to who we are in Christ —that is, the inner person of the heart, is brand new, raised up from the dead with Christ and has been created in "righteousness and truth." But our old way of thinking was only slightly impacted, and most of the lies and misconceptions we believed followed us into our new life with Christ.

So we are indeed new creatures created in righteousness and holiness of the truth, but we continue to believe most of what we *believed* in our former manner of life. And until we believe the truth about who we are as new creations, we will continue to walk according to our former manner of belief. Nevertheless, we are still who we are in Christ even though we do not yet fully believe or comprehend it.

This is why God sent His Spirit: to persuade us of the truth so that we will see, feel, and walk in it (see John 14:26). He is renewing your new self to a "<u>true knowledge</u> according to the image of the One who created it" (Colossians 3:10, emphasis added). This clearly indicates that your new self, which was born of God (John 1:12-13) and created in righteousness and holiness of the truth (Ephesians 4:24), is still in need of something; you need to be renewed in the spirit of your mind (Ephesians 4:23) so that you can come to a "true knowledge" of who God is and who you are in Him (Colossians 3:10).

So, in light of all this, what specifically needs to be transformed? Simply put, it is <u>our beliefs</u>. The old thinking and unrenewed mindset is still presently in our possession and is wreaking havoc in our lives. We need God to convince us of who we really are. We need Him to persuade us of His perspective. Thankfully, He desires to replace all of our lie-based beliefs that we brought with us from our former manner of life with the truth. We need God to update our thinking and beliefs so that they accurately depict the truth of who He is and who we now are in Him.

As you are persuaded of the truth regarding your new creation, your perceptions, emotions, and behavior will automatically begin to change to reflect this reality. In other words, you will bear His fruit when you are convinced of His perspective.

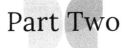

Part Two

Our Role in This Transformation

Genuine transformation is a work of God, solely accomplished by Him and Him alone. There is much we can do to support and cooperate with the work that He is doing, but nothing we do will bring about transformation. Our best attempts at overcoming sin, acting like Jesus, or keeping the commandments will contribute nothing to the transformation that God is bringing about. The transformation itself requires no effort on our part.

In TPM we sometimes refer to what God is doing as an *effortless transformation*. This is because we do not expend any effort in the transformation itself. We do expend effort as we choose to move into position to receive, but the transformation itself is not of our doing. We would all agree that our salvation was effortless on our part as it was a gift from God (see Ephesians 2:8-9). Even so, once we are saved, there is often a temptation to go to work, trying to maintain our holy standing with God. This is an absurdity since we did not bring our holiness about, nor can we sustain it. Paul confronted the Galatian church over this very issue when he asked, *"Are you so foolish? After beginning with the Spirit, are you now going to be made complete by the flesh?"* (Galatians 3:3 HCSB). The answer to this rhetorical question is, *"We are already complete; we simply do not realize the full extent of our salvation!"*

We are called to cease our struggle with performance, and make every effort to enter into His rest (See Hebrews 4:11). This may seem foreign or impractical at first, but it is the truth. Our struggle, striving, and labor shows our need for God's perspective. We simply have not yet been convinced of the truth in our hearts. When the Spirit persuades us of the truth, the struggle and striving will cease.

Someone may protest by saying, "My striving against sin is an expression of my desire to be obedient to the truth and act like Jesus!" This sounds good, but any effort invested in overcoming sin (which Jesus took away at the cross) or in controlling our behavior (which is not a fruit of the Spirit) is the outcome of our failure to recognize the finished work of Christ and our misunderstanding of how we are to appropriate the victory we have been given in Christ.

We have victory because of what He has accomplished. If we are in Him and He is in us, then His victory is our victory (1 Corinthians 15:57)! But until we are convinced that we have been raised in "incorruption," "glory," and "power," we will not fully enjoy this victory (1 Corinthians 15:42-44 HCSB). In fact, it will likely seem as though we are still corrupt, dishonorable, and weak. Consider the following question: who would be more prone to struggle with sin in an effort to maintain victory: a believer who is fully convinced of who he is and what Christ accomplished on his behalf, or, one who still believes he is sinful, broken, and in bondage? One is standing in the truth and reality of his victory while the other is unnecessarily trying to bring it about.

If we are striving to overcome sin, even though the Scriptures declare that we are "dead to sin", therefore free of it (Romans 6:11), "more than conquerors" (Romans 8:37 NIV), and have the promise that God *"always leads us in triumph in Christ"* (2 Corinthians 2:14), then our struggle indicates we do not yet believe the truth and, therefore, we need the Holy Spirit to persuade us of it.

Victory is not achieved by our choosing not to sin and choosing to live rightly. Victory is what we have already been given. We do not lack victory; we lack the faith necessary to realize and enjoy the victory we already possess. Again, the Lord's victory and our victory are the same victory. We rejoice with Paul by saying, *"thanks be to God, who gives us the victory through our Lord Jesus Christ"* (1 Corinthians 15:57).

The Scriptures are clear that we have been given a new heart (Ezekiel 36:26), and we are risen with Christ as new selves (Romans 6:1-4). As new creations, we are children of God, holy and beloved, who happen to temporarily dwell in fallen flesh (2 Corinthians 5:1), with minds that need to be renewed in the knowledge of the truth (Ephesians 4:23-24). With this understanding, we declare that transformation is the expected outcome of having the Holy Spirit convince our hearts of the truth, and this transformation is manifested through our behavior as the fruit of the Spirit. Rather than attempting to simply control our behavior, we need to focus our attention on having our minds renewed through the Spirit's persuasion (Biblical Greek - *peitho*).

What About Self-Discipline?

Someone may ask, "What about self-discipline? Are we not to discipline ourselves to act rightly?" Self-discipline has its place in many areas of our lives, but no measure of effort or controlled behavior will purify our faith, renew our minds, or transform our lives. We can discipline ourselves in choosing to submit to God as He accomplishes His work in us, but faith-refinement and mind-renewal are solely a work of the Holy Spirit where we lay aside our old garments and deeds of the body "by the Spirit" (See Romans 8:13). We can do this because we have put on Christ (Galatians 3:27). Our lie-based beliefs are only discarded as the Spirit shines His light of truth into our hearts (2 Corinthians 4:6). He will gladly do so when we humbly position ourselves before Him (1 Peter 5:6). Someone might protest and say that, according to Paul, we are to put to death the deeds of the body which would suggest some manner of self discipline and effort. The actual Bible passage says,

> So then, brothers and sisters, we are under obligation, not to the flesh, to live according to the flesh— for if you are living in accord with the flesh, you are going to die; but if <u>by the Spirit</u> you are putting to death the deeds of the body, you will live. For all who are being led <u>by the Spirit of God</u>, these are sons and daughters of God (Romans 8:12-14, emphasis added)

The key phrase Paul uses in this passage provides the proper understanding we are looking for. Paul says all these things are accomplished "by the Spirit." We are clearly mandated to put to death the deeds of our fallen bodies, but how we do this is crucial. If your strategy is willpower, self-effort, commitment, and determination, the best you can hope for is a temporary state of controlled behavior.

Rather than focusing our attention on managing our emotional pain or poor behavior, we should ask ourselves, "Where is God focused, and what is He trying to accomplish?" As we have already discussed, God has replaced our old heart with a new one, we are new creations, and He is now working to refine our faith, renew our minds, and transform our lives. We should focus on cooperating with Him in His refining work. We may better position ourselves to receive what God desires to give us through personal discipline, but nothing we do will bring about transformation.

In a similar fashion, practicing the process of TPM as a lifestyle requires a measure of discipline on our part. We submit to God by cooperating with Him as He accomplishes His work within us. This requires discipline. Sadly, much of what we do is contrary to His work. When we blame others, our situation, the devil, or even God for what we feel, we move in the wrong direction. It requires discipline to take responsibility for our thoughts, feelings, and behavior, and then position ourselves so we might receive His perspective.

If we hope to cooperate with God, we must first choose to stop looking for ways to manage our pain and instead choose to humble ourselves under "His mighty hand" (1 Peter 5:6) during His refining fire. As we do this, we can reap the benefit of the pure faith and effortless transformation He has available for us.

There is immense value in daily Bible study, prayer, and fasting, but these things will not transform us. The primary benefit in such spiritual disciplines is that it helps to position us so that God can bring about His transformation within us. Growing intellectually in the knowledge of the Scriptures can prepare and better position us so that the Spirit might persuade us of the truth in our hearts, but our intellectual understanding of the Bible will not bring forth transformation of its own. Fasting may help us to focus on that which is important, and center us, but it will not transform us. Even prayer will not transform us unless we hear from the Spirit, and He shines His light of truth into our hearts. Too often our prayers are directed toward God with the hope that He will hear us and fulfill our requests when our focus should be on hearing from Him. If we invest our energy into taking a humble, honest, and receptive posture at Jesus' feet, rather than trying to copy His behavior through willpower and determination, our efforts will prove much more fruitful.

"JUST DO IT" EFFORTLESSLY

Too often, we approach our spiritual walk with a "Just Do It" mentality, rather than addressing what keeps us from being able to effortlessly bear His fruit. We attempt to push through our struggles and do what we know we have to do regardless of the internal conflict. Although this strategy may be employed with good intentions and appear to be better than giving-up the fight all together, it is rooted in our own grit and determination which typically contradicts what God is trying to accomplish in the moment.

We may desire to do the right thing and perform the best we can, but we inevitably hit the same wall - a wall of contrary belief. Our futile attempts at pushing through this wall have led to an epidemic of burnout in the life of many believers. We are worn-out from attempting to obey the truth that we know in our heads while being drawn aside and discouraged by what we believe in our hearts. Jesus exposed this struggle when He called to the worn-out "law keepers" saying, "Come to Me, all who are weary and burdened, and I will give you rest. Take My yoke upon you and learn from Me, for I am gentle and humble in heart, and you will find rest for your souls" (Matthew 11:28-29).

This "just do it" attitude neglects some of the most basic concepts regarding the fruit of the Spirit. Being loving, joyful, peaceful, patient, kind, good, gentle, faithful and self-controlled is God's fruit (Galatians 5:22-23), not our own. If we stop and think about what we are doing, we will see the illogical position we hold. We probably all agree that the fruit of the Spirit is His fruit and that we are not expected to *produce* it ourselves but rather *bear* it, and yet we talk about working on being more patient, kind, good, and self-controlled. Do you see the contradiction here?

We encourage those who have embraced the slogan, "Just Do It" as their motto for living their Christian life, to take a serious look at why they are struggling to do what they are doing. We need His perspective. We need Him to convince us of the truth so that we will "Just Do It" but without the struggle.

Rather than attempting to change our behavior through willpower, determination, and commitment, we should look closely at why we are doing what we are doing and seek His perspective. When we are convinced of the truth in our hearts, our emotions and behavior will also transform.

If you are "attempting to obey" Him who is the Truth, then you are not "obeying" the truth. "Attempting" indicates that you are struggling or putting effort into it (which also suggests that you are not, in fact, obeying). You are doing something else. True obedience is effortless on our part because "[His] yoke is easy and [His] burden is light" (Matthew 11:30, emphasis added).

Bearing Fruit Is Effortless.

When our heart's belief (faith) is made pure, we will walk effortlessly in the truth since it requires no more effort to walk in the truth when we believe it in our hearts than it does to walk in lies when we believe them. If we believe that we have been abandoned by God, it requires no effort for us to feel alone and to act accordingly. When we believe the truth in our hearts, we will, just as easily, bear His fruit. Bearing His fruit is the natural outflow of Christ living His life in and through us (Galatians 2:20). The listing of the fruit in Galatians 5:22-23 is not a list of behaviors that God demands for us to perform but the expected outcome of His work in our life.

Someone might wonder how our behavior could be the work of the Spirit if we are the ones doing the behaving? This is where we must differentiate between *controlled behavior* and the fruit *of self-control.* Controlled behavior is what all people do in some measure every day. This is a human trait that all people possess. Self-control is a fruit of the Spirit that is brought about by the Spirit and not through self-effort. An unbeliever can choose to act like Jesus (in some measure) by simply controlling his behavior, but this is not transformation. Most of us can control our behavior and *act* loving, joyful, peaceful, patient, kind, good, gentle and self-controlled at least for a time. This is not fruit.

Fruit is a natural and effortless expression of the truth that is made evident when we believe it in our hearts. The difference between the fruit of the Spirit and controlled behavior is made obvious by whether or not we are expending effort. If I have to "try" to be loving, joyful, peaceful, patient, kind, gentle, good, faithful, and self-controlled, then this "fruit" is simply my own controlled behavior. God desires to grant us His fruit of *self-control*, which is the outcome of His work. Controlled behavior is a human trait that is ineffectual and contingent upon our ability to maintain it. Self-control is the Spirit's fruit solely accomplished by Him.

Summary

The purpose of TPM is to provide a heavenly frame of reference for viewing what God is doing amid our life's difficulties as He refines our faith, renews our minds, and transforms our lives. These three tasks are solely the work of God accomplished apart from any effort or work on our part. In fact, He often accomplishes this work while we are actively fighting Him or attempting to do His job for Him. Nevertheless, we do not accomplish or maintain them ourselves. The best we can do is submit to His "mighty hand" as He performs His refining work.

The *Purpose of TPM* explains why we do this ministry. It took us a while, but we eventually realized that this purpose was *not* limited to those we assumed were "emotionally wounded," but rather, TPM provides each of us a way to willingly participate in what God is doing in each of our lives. If you are a counselor, pastor, or lay minister seeking to help others, then the first person in line for ministry should be yourself. Once you are in line, you never need to get out. Faith-refinement and mind-renewal are life-long journeys. If you are taking this training solely to help others and are not making TPM a daily practice to cooperate with God as He refines your own faith, you do not yet understand the intended Purpose of TPM.

A person once said to me, "I have been using TPM in my counseling practice for many years and have seen remarkable results." I asked her, "How many personal sessions would you say that you do with yourself each week?" She looked at me as though I was speaking a foreign language; she did not respond. This showed that she did not rightly understand the purpose of TPM.

CHAPTER 12

THE PROCESS OF TPM
APPLYING THE "PRINCIPLES" TO ACCOMPLISH THE "PURPOSE"

NOTICE: This chapter has been divided into four parts. The first part introduces the Process of TPM and explains many important terms. The second part describes the various training resources that relate to the TPM Process. The third part discusses the people involved in a TPM session, their roles and responsibilities, as well as their relationship with each other. The fourth part illustrates what a TPM session might look like.

Part One

What is The Process of TPM?

I still vividly remember my first TPM session (although I didn't know that's what it was at the time). I was greatly surprised, excited, and grateful to see the Lord lovingly share His truth with the dear woman who sat across from me. In an instant she went from pain to peace as the eyes of her heart were opened to the truth. I had no idea that I was witnessing the birth of a worldwide ministry that would impact hundreds of thousands of people in the years to come. The method and protocols have been greatly refined since those early years, but God is still performing the same miraculous work!

The *Process of TPM* (the third *Element of TPM*, which is also sometimes referred to as the *TPM Process*) is the result of decades of refinement. It is a systematic means of accomplishing the *Purpose of TPM* (which, as you have already learned, is to participate with God as He brings about our faith-refinement, mind-renewal and genuine, lasting transformation in our lives). TPM is by no means the only method for accomplishing this task, but it does offer a systematic process for doing so. It is designed to help each of us identify and take ownership of what we believe and intentionally position ourselves to receive the truth and perspective from the Holy Spirit.

We sometimes refer to the TPM Process as "*positioning prayer*" because it is a way we can prayerfully position ourselves in a receptive posture and invite the Holy Spirit to persuade us of the truth. The TPM Process consists of well-defined protocols and clearly defined objectives that are accomplished as we acknowledge what we believe and position ourselves to receive truth and perspective from the Holy Spirit.

Once you become familiar with the objectives and protocols involved in the *Process*, as well as the *Principles* that it is based upon and the *Purpose* for which it should be applied, you can incorporate TPM into your everyday lifestyle. Doing so allows you to gain as much benefit as possible from what will be presented here.

We recognize that God is not limited to any particular ministry model to bring about the transformation He desires for each of us. We rejoice in the good things that are happening in the lives of God's children all around the world outside of the TPM model. Even so, should any portion of the TPM Process be changed, replaced, omitted, or expanded, then it should no longer be considered or called

TPM, but rather be given a different name. Though we feel no need to dictate what people may do in their personal ministry, we do not want people to be misinformed about what TPM is or is not.

I have personally found this ministry process to be a tried-and-true approach that has reportedly had positive and consistent results since its inception in the mid-nineties. Since that time, it has been updated and revised where needed, but the fundamentals have stayed the same. The TPM Process is a systematic tool we can use to intentionally cooperate with God as He refines our faith, renews our minds, and transforms our lives.

As stated before, the TPM Process is part of a whole. The Three Elements of TPM work in conjunction with one another. If you only focus on learning and applying the Process while neglecting the Principles and Purpose of TPM (explained in earlier chapters), you will dramatically reduce the benefits and gains that would otherwise be available to you. It would be akin to a doctor learning to properly wield a scalpel without first studying human anatomy. He may be able to make clean cuts, but if he does not understand when and why to make these incisions, much of his hard-earned skill will go to waste and the outcome might prove less than desirable.

This is especially true when it comes to mentoring others. If a Mentor fails to equip the Mentee with the Principles and Purpose of TPM and only focuses on applying the Process, those being mentored would have no explanation for why they are learning this ministry method, what its purpose is, when they should apply it, with whom they should apply it, or why the protocols are what they are. So, again, we encourage you to learn all three of the elements of TPM well.

What is a TPM Session?

A *TPM session* is essentially an allotted time devoted to a person's application of the TPM Process. The context for this may vary from case to case. For example, a TPM session may take place in a professional's office, where a Mentor meets with a Mentee for a scheduled ministry appointment. But it is just as likely for a TPM session to take place at a friend's house, where a small group meets to practice applying the TPM Process. A couple may spontaneously have a TPM session after discovering that one (or both) of them is triggered during their normal, day-to-day routine. A TPM session can also occur as a child applies the TPM Process under the caring supervision of his or her parent. A TPM session can even take place when you are by yourself sitting on the couch, riding to work on the subway, mowing the lawn, or taking a shower. A TPM session can take place anywhere, anytime, with anyone.

What a TPM session actually looks like is largely dependent upon the circumstances and the people involved. Although they are applying the same process, a person who is just beginning to learn about TPM will have a session that looks different from one involving a person who has years of experience. The new person will also likely receive greater benefit from having someone act as a Mentor in his or her session. The more familiar a person is with TPM, the easier it will be for him or her to apply the TPM Process independently. But no matter how many people are in the room, and regardless of whether it takes place in a professional or private setting, whenever and wherever someone decides to set aside time to apply the TPM Process, it is referred to as a TPM session.

What are the primary goals of a TPM Session?

During every TPM session there are three distinct goals to be accomplished: 1) To have an encounter with the Holy Spirit that results in your being persuaded to believe the truth, 2) to gain a better understanding of the Principles and Purpose of TPM, and 3) to grow more proficient in applying the Process of TPM.

Accomplishing each of these goals is your responsibility, but doing so can be aided with the involvement of a knowledgeable Mentor (especially when you are just starting out). Ideally, you will become familiar enough with the Process of TPM to be able to apply it and accomplish both goals without involving anyone else (except the Holy Spirit, of course). But even so, having a friend in the room is always welcome since "we are all members of one body" (Ephesians 4:25 NIV).

The first goal in the ministry session is accomplished as you connect with what you feel, take an account of what you remember, acknowledge what you believe, and position yourself to receive perspective from the Holy Spirit. Again, this is why we sometimes refer to TPM as a form of "Positioning Prayer." God is faithful to speak to us when we position ourselves to receive from Him. As you choose to "draw near to God" [He will] "draw near to you" (James 4:8). This was illustrated in the Bible narrative with Mary and Martha (See Luke 10:38-42).

Martha was aggravated with her sister Mary who was not helping in the kitchen. Jesus was their house guest on this particular day and Martha wanted her sister's help in the kitchen. But Mary had positioned herself at Jesus' feet so that she could soak in every word that He spoke. After a time, Martha had had enough (and was very triggered) and complained to Jesus concerning the situation. Jesus' response to Martha's complaint revealed a vitally important principle. Jesus said, "only one thing is necessary, for Mary has chosen the good part, which shall not be taken away from her" (Luke 10:42).

It appears that the good thing Mary had chosen was to do nothing but position herself at the feet of Jesus and receive. Jesus did not say that Martha's service wasn't appreciated, but it was not necessary. Mary's receptive position was deemed more "necessary" than Martha's service. Martha was performing well and serving others, but according to Jesus it was not *necessary*. The "good part" is not found by doing something for God (like Martha) but in receiving something from Him (like Mary). If we will receive the truth from Him, we will be transformed by it and then bear the fruit of His Spirit.

Too often, we spend our time and energy trying to mimic the life of Jesus by committing ourselves to the task, managing our negative emotions, and controlling our behavior. But God desires that we be like Jesus, not just act like Him. We must be transformed into His image if we are to be like Him. Only God can bring this about as we position ourselves at His feet.

TPM is a form of *positioning prayer* that helps us to intentionally position ourselves at Jesus' feet so that He might convince us of the truth and persuade us of His perspective. When we come to believe the truth, we will be transformed by it. When applying the TPM Process (the protocols that are followed in a ministry session), we humble ourselves before God, acknowledge our imperfect faith, and invite Him to reveal His truth to us. *This fulfills the first goal of the ministry session.*

The second and third goals (becoming familiar with the Principles and Purpose and gaining proficiency in applying the TPM Process) are accomplished primarily through ongoing study and practice. This can obviously be greatly enhanced by the involvement of an experienced Mentor. Every single TPM session should result in your becoming more skilled in applying the Process and more familiar with the TPM's Principles and Purpose. As you gain experience and understanding, your sessions typically become smoother and even more productive.

Part Two

What is the TPM Map?

The TPM Process may initially seem complicated or confusing, but once you become familiar with what is involved and how it all works, it is straightforward and consistent. There are numerous resources available to aid you on your learning journey (many of which can be found at the back of this book). A primary training resource is the *TPM Map.* It is an illustrated training tool that was designed to help you visualize the protocols that you are about to learn. The various versions of the *TPM Map* portray each of the seven "*Boxes,*" the questions contained in each box, the specific objectives that are to be accomplished and, generally speaking, how you typically transition from one box to another.

The Mentee's version of the TPM "*Questions*" Map can be found below as an example.

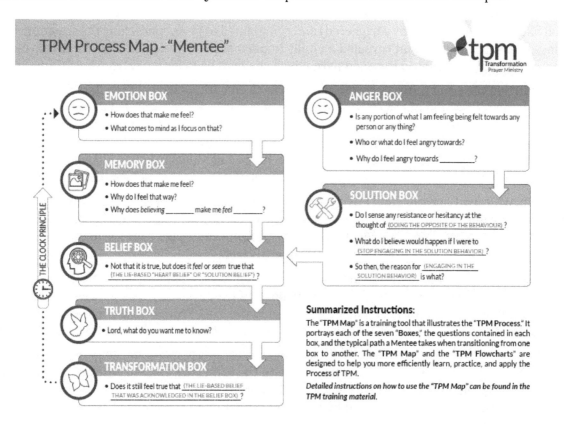

As you can see, the primary stages, or *Boxes*, include the *EMOTION Box*, the *MEMORY Box*, the *BELIEF Box*, the *TRUTH Box*, the *TRANSFORMATION Box*, the *ANGER Box*, and the *SOLUTION Box*.

IMPORTANT CONSIDERATION:

We highly recommend that you begin memorizing the title of each Box, their position on the Map, and the questions assigned to each box as soon as possible. Doing so will lay the foundation that we will build upon in future chapters. Having this information in your head will prove invaluable when you are applying the TPM Process. Otherwise, you will be dependent upon having the MAP in view during a TPM session. You might take a blank sheet of paper, draw seven boxes and then write the names of each box and the included questions from memory. Copies of each version of the TPM Map are available in the back of this book and online at the TPM website.

The Map is designed to help you learn the TPM Process, but it does not offer any explanation or instruction on how to perform the tasks that are involved. It serves as an overview of each of the potential stages of the TPM Process but does not specifically illustrate what to do in each stage. The Map alone <u>does not</u> equip you to apply the process. It is designed to serve as a reminder of what you (as the Mentee) are expected to do at each stage in the Process.

The Mentor's "*Questions*" version of the TPM Map can be found below. Notice the additional Box in the bottom-right corner labeled *LOST/UNSURE*. This Box includes a question that is only used in rare and specific circumstances (and will be discussed in a future chapter).

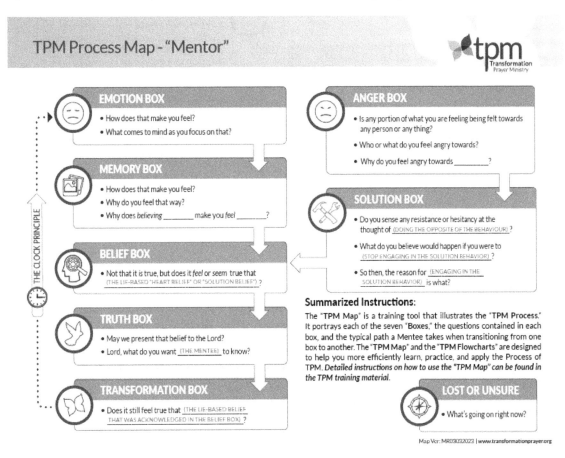

There are several different versions of the TPM MAP, and depending upon which version you are looking at, you will see either questions or objectives included in each *Box*. The "*Objectives*" version of the Map illustrates your objectives in each phase of the Process, while the *"Questions"* version displays each of the questions that are asked while in each corresponding *Box*. You will notice that each included question is related to a particular objective. This shouldn't come as a surprise as the questions are designed (in part) to remind you of your objectives as you work through the TPM process.

The *"Objectives"* version of the TPM Map can be found below:

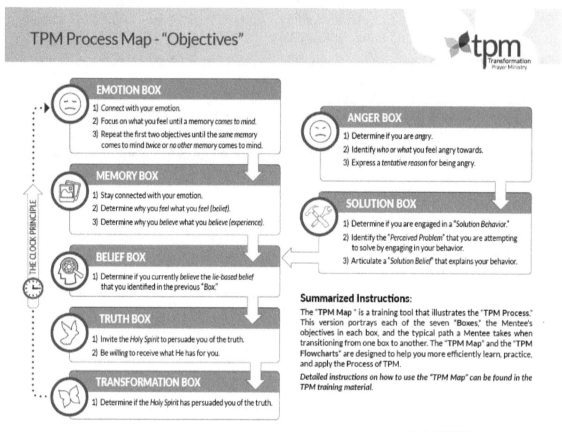

TPM Process Map - "Objectives"

EMOTION BOX
1) Connect with your emotion.
2) Focus on what you feel until a memory comes to mind.
3) Repeat the first two objectives until the *same memory* comes to mind *twice* or *no other memory* comes to mind.

MEMORY BOX
1) Stay connected with your emotion.
2) Determine *why you feel what you feel (belief).*
3) Determine *why you believe what you believe (experience).*

BELIEF BOX
1) Determine if you currently believe *the lie-based belief that you identified in the previous "Box."*

TRUTH BOX
1) Invite the *Holy Spirit* to persuade you of the truth.
2) Be willing to receive what He has for you.

TRANSFORMATION BOX
1) Determine if the *Holy Spirit* has persuaded you of the truth.

ANGER BOX
1) Determine if you are *angry.*
2) Identify who or what you feel angry towards.
3) Express a *tentative reason* for being angry.

SOLUTION BOX
1) Determine if you are engaged in a *"Solution Behavior."*
2) Identify the *"Perceived Problem"* that you are attempting to solve by engaging in your behavior.
3) Articulate a *"Solution Belief"* that explains your behavior.

THE CLOCK PRINCIPLE

Summarized Instructions:

The "TPM Map " is a training tool that illustrates the "TPM Process." This version portrays each of the seven "Boxes," the Mentee's objectives in each box, and the typical path a Mentee takes when transitioning from one box to another. The "TPM Map" and the "TPM Flowcharts" are designed to help you more efficiently learn, practice, and apply the Process of TPM.

Detailed instructions on how to use the "TPM Map" can be found in the TPM training material.

Map Ver: MO03032023 | www.transformationprayer.org

The *"Questions"* version of the Map is available in both a first-person perspective (your perspective) and a third-person perspective (your Mentor's perspective). For example, the version labeled, *"The 'Questions' Map - Mentor's Perspective"* includes each of the TPM questions which are worded as they would be asked by a Mentor. Whereas the version titled, *"The 'Questions' Map - Mentee's Perspective"* presents the questions as you would ask them of yourself.

In its most basic form, the *TPM Map* consists of seven individually labeled *Boxes*. However, each of the objectives and questions are also a part of the overall Map concept. When we use the general term *TPM Map*, we are typically referring to the visual aid in its entirety.

THE TROPICAL ISLAND OF TPM

You might compare the TPM Map to a tropical island. You may find yourself anywhere on the island, but departure from the island is impossible. You are always in one of the seven potential locations that are illustrated on the TPM Map. Each of us is <u>always</u> somewhere on this "island" every moment of our lives. During a ministry session we are merely choosing to focus and attend to this reality.

What are the TPM Flowcharts?

Another helpful training aid is the group of *Flowcharts* that are available in this book and at our website. The *TPM Flowcharts* offer an expanded or "zoomed-in" view of the corresponding *Boxes*. They include the objectives that are to be accomplished, the questions that can be asked, and the context that determines where you are in that Box. They can help you answer the question, "What do you do if this or that happens in a TPM session?" They suggest the next step to take based upon what is happening in any given moment. Essentially, they offer detailed illustrations of the protocols found in the *Process*. They show the logical flow and requirements that must be met before asking the assigned questions in each "*Box*." They also offer helpful tips that relate to their specific Box.

Unlike the TPM Map that contains the questions to be asked during a ministry session, you are not expected to memorize all that is contained in the Flowcharts. Like the TPM Map, the Flowcharts serve as visual aids that can help you become more familiar with what you read in this book. You are encouraged to familiarize yourself with each chart and be able to navigate through each one. They will help you learn the Process, the order in which the *objectives* are to be accomplished, and what to do at virtually any point in a TPM session.

There are *Flowcharts* for the EMOTION Box, the MEMORY Box, the ANGER Box, and the SOLUTION Box. And each of these Flowcharts is also available from both a Mentee and Mentor's perspective. These Flowcharts will be helpful when we discuss the protocols for each of these *Boxes*. A copy of each Flowchart is available in the back of this book. You will not find flowcharts for the BELIEF, TRUTH or TRANSFORMATION Boxes since the objectives in each of these boxes are straightforward and typically do not need further explanation.

<u>NOTE</u>: Before you explore what these Flowcharts have to offer, be aware that if you do not understand their purpose, you may initially become overwhelmed by them. Some people react and assume that it is more information than they can possibly assimilate. First, you are <u>not</u> expected to sit down and memorize the entire contents of these flowcharts before you can use them or attempt to apply the TPM Process (although you should progressively become more familiar with them). The TPM Map and Flowcharts are training aids that are designed to help you learn what you need to know as quickly as possible. We encourage you to not view them as obstacles in your way but as resources that will help you get to where you want to go.

For now, keep them close by and refer to them as needed. If you are in a ministry session and come to a place where you are not sure what to do, take out the appropriate flowchart to quickly identify where you are in the process and determine your next move. These flowcharts will prove invaluable in time, but for now, let's just get acquainted with them.

The Mentee's version of the *EMOTION Box Flowchart* is shown below as an example:

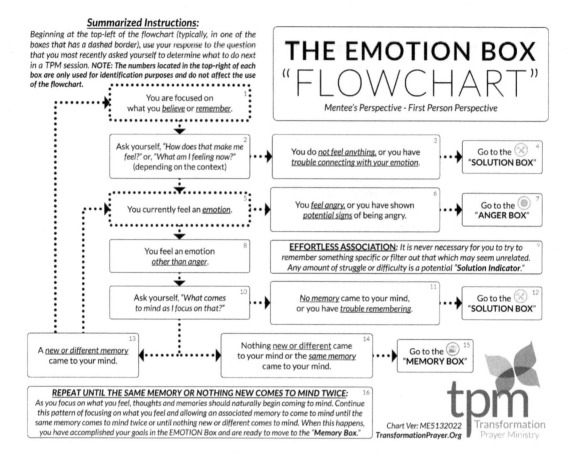

Now someone might ask, "*Why do we need so many different versions of the TPM Map and Flowcharts? Why not just put it all on one page so that we can see it all at once?*" Although we love the idea of being able to see the completed illustration all at once, putting all the questions, objectives, and protocols onto a single page would be overwhelming and difficult to navigate (not to mention incredibly hard-to-read due to the necessity of a tiny font). Rather than displaying all of this on one sheet, we have taken the basic form of the Map with its seven box locations and created a two-page presentation: one page dedicated to the objectives and another page that includes the questions. Likewise, each single-page *Flowchart* only pertains to a single *Box* in order to simplify its use and navigation.

How are the Map and Flowcharts to be used?

The purpose of *The Map* and *Flowcharts* is essentially the same. They are training aids that are designed to help you visualize and understand the TPM Process. They can obviously be used as you study this book, but they can also be of great value in an actual TPM session. For example, those who are new to TPM can use these resources as a guide while attempting to apply the TPM Process by themselves. A Mentor can use the Flowcharts to more efficiently determine where the Mentee is in the Process and to identify which question to ask next. The Mentor could also use them to explain specific aspects of the TPM Process to a Mentee or answer the Mentee's questions about the TPM

Process. They can even be used as a guide when practicing the TPM Process through role-playing with others. We believe you will find them invaluable in your journey with TPM.

Again, we encourage you to begin familiarizing yourself with these training aids, as you will eventually need to have the questions and objectives memorized. Have them physically available to you as you practice, but as quickly as possible, store them in your brain.

FOLLOW ALONG USING THE TPM FLOWCHARTS.

Throughout our discussion of the TPM Process, you will find many examples and samples of ministry sessions. Within these role-played demonstrations we will indicate your "location" on each corresponding *Flowchart*. We will do this by utilizing a simple numbering system. The EMOTION Box is indicated by an (E), the MEMORY Box with an (M), the ANGER Box with an (A) and the SOLUTION Box with an (S). For example, "(E1)" represents the first box shown on the EMOTION Box Flowchart and "(E8)" represents the 8th box on the EMOTION Box flow chart. This numbering system lets you identify where you are on the corresponding Flowchart.

An example of this numbering system can be found below:

Mentee: *"My wife is driving me crazy! She goes on and on about how we need to visit her family, but we just don't have the money to put towards a trip like that!" (E1)*

Mentor: *"How does that make you feel?" (E2)*

Mentee: *"I feel out of control. I can't make her stop pestering me about it!" (E5) > (E8)*

Mentor: *"What comes to your mind as you focus on that?" (E10)*

<u>NOTE</u>: The full color versions of the Flowcharts (available on our website) do not include this numbering system.

Part Three

Who applies the Process during a TPM Session?

In the early years of TPM, we mistakenly believed that the Mentor (who we used to refer to as the "*ministry facilitator*") was the one who applied the process *on* the Mentee (who we called the "*ministry recipient*"). Because of this misunderstanding, the older training was focused almost entirely upon the Mentor and his role in a *TPM session*. We now realize that this flawed understanding was unintentionally misleading.

Although the Mentor obviously has an important role, he is not the one who applies the Process during a TPM session. The Process consists of the specific steps and objectives that the Mentee accomplishes during a TPM session for the purpose of positioning himself so the Holy Spirit will persuade his heart of the truth. The Mentee applies the *Process of TPM* under the supervision of a Mentor who can offer orientation and explain the Process along the way, but nothing the Mentor does is part of the Process itself. Put simply, the Mentor is there to mentor while the Mentee applies the Process.

If you are familiar with any of the older versions of the TPM training, this shift might seem odd or unnecessary. But consider the following question: "Is it possible for a Mentee to apply the Process of TPM without the involvement of a Mentor?" The answer is obviously, "*Yes.*" Now, the Mentee's ability to do this is obviously limited to his or her understanding of the Process, but it is still clearly possible.

The TPM Process can be applied with or without the involvement of a Mentor. This reality impacts both Mentees and Mentors alike. Everyone involved in a TPM session should clearly understand who is doing what. The Mentor is not there to apply the TPM process on, with, or to the Mentee. Rather, the Mentor's role is to ensure that the Mentee understands what must be done, how to do it, and why it is important.

What you just read in the last few paragraphs is very important. This is especially true if you have been practicing TPM based upon a former edition of the training prior to 2010. Our goal is to equip people with the knowledge of how they can personally and intentionally cooperate with what God is doing to refine their faith (heart belief), renew their minds, and transform their lives. TPM is not designed to equip ministry facilitators to do ministry on emotionally troubled people or those who struggle with unwanted behaviors; rather, we seek to equip every person with the knowledge and skill to participate with God. This is a very important shift in this ministry model that is vital in fulfilling its designed purpose.

"THE QUESTIONS DON'T WORK!"

<u>Notice</u>: Some of the concepts referenced here will be discussed later in this book. If something seems new or unexplained, it probably is. As with every other part of the training, we encourage you to revisit this section after you have read through everything. Remember, comprehension (not "completion") is the goal!

Novice mentors sometimes complain that the questions "don't work!" But this statement indicates that the Mentor does not yet understand the purpose of the questions that he or she is asking. Usually, this person believes that the questions are asked to help guide the Mentee through the TPM Process. When a Mentee failed to move forward in a TPM session, many concluded that the questions were somehow at fault, and some even attempted to reword them to get things moving.

This, however, was nothing more than an attempt to solve a misunderstood problem. Faulty questions were not the issue. The problem was the Mentee (and possibly the Mentor) did not understand the objective or task the question was reminding them to do. Yes, the questions help to remind the Mentee of where he is in the ministry session and what objective is to be accomplished next, but a Mentor asks these questions for a slightly different purpose.

A Mentor's primary role is to ensure that those he mentors know what they are doing. In order to effectively accomplish this task, he must first discover the Mentee's current understanding of the *Three Elements of TPM*. One of the ways he determines a person's level of comprehension is through the use of the TPM questions. A Mentor asks these questions throughout a session for the purpose of exposing the Mentee's current understanding of the TPM Process.

Generally speaking, your response to each of the TPM questions indicates (to some degree) what you currently know about the TPM Process. Your response may indicate that you know what you are doing or, at the very least, that you are inadvertently applying the TPM Process in response to the questions that are asked. But your responses could also indicate that you either do not yet understand what to do or that you are potentially engaged in a solution behavior (purposefully choosing not to move forward in the session).

For example, if you were to answer any of the TPM questions by saying, "Ok, I'll try..." this indicates that you do not yet understand that effort, struggle, and conscious choice are not the way forward. You should never have to "try" to do something while applying the TPM Process. This sentiment also indicates that you do not yet understand that the presence of struggle indicates that you are attempting to push through some measure of resistance and hesitancy (which indicates that you have a lie-based reason for not moving in that direction). In other words, by saying, "I'll try," you are also saying, "I don't realize that I shouldn't have to apply effort in order to move forward, and I might also be engaged in a solution behavior right now."

If you knew what you were supposed to do (and how to do it), you would do it regardless of what your Mentor might ask. So, if you are still dependent upon a Mentor's involvement, it simply means that you are not yet fully equipped. This is perfectly fine! It is a journey. As you grow in your understanding and experience of applying TPM, the Process will become more and more intuitive. And when you know what to do while applying the TPM Process, the questions essentially become unnecessary.

Since the beginning of this ministry, the fundamental problem during a TPM session has always been the same; the <u>Mentee</u> does not yet know what he or she is doing. The Mentor may ask all the right questions at all the right times, but if the Mentee fails to understand what he or she is to do and how to do it, the results will inevitably be underwhelming. Essentially, even in the best case scenario, the Mentee would simply inadvertently apply the TPM Process in response to the Mentor's questions, completely unaware of what he or she was doing. (This is why it is so important for a Mentor to actually mentor.)

A Mentor who believes that they are leading others through the Process by asking questions will become discouraged when a Mentee doesn't do what he or she is "supposed to do" in response to the questions that are asked. However, the questions will serve their true purpose no matter how the Mentee responds to them. If the Mentee moves forward, the question has either passively helped them learn the TPM Process or it has reminded them of what they have already learned. And if the Mentee fails to move forward, the question has helped to reveal their need for more orientation or exposed a potential solution behavior.

Those who are only familiar with the early versions of the TPM training may find this shift to be awkward or even confusing. Unfortunately, as previously stated, we misunderstood the Process of TPM and unintentionally misled some of you. We mistakenly believed that the "*Ministry Facilitator*" was the one who applied the TPM Process by asking questions while the "*Ministry Recipient*" was having TPM "done" to them as they passively answered the questions that were asked. Where this was the case, the questions played a much more important role.

Today, the questions serve a different purpose. They are reminders of the task at hand. When the Mentee understands the objective to be achieved, the questions simply serve as reminders of that objective. Until then, they help to expose what the Mentee does and doesn't know regarding the Process of TPM.

For example, if the Mentor asks the second question in the SOLUTION Box, "What do you believe would happen if you were to let your anger go?"(where anger is the solution behavior being addressed) and the Mentee responds, "That would be wonderful! I would be in a much better place than I am now," this clearly reveals that the Mentee does not understand his or her current objective. The Mentee's statement indicates what he knows (or doesn't know) regarding both this stage in the TPM Process as well as any applicable TPM Principles. This will obviously make more sense after we fully explain the TPM Process.

When the Mentor is faithful to equip the Mentee in what his responsibility is within the ministry session, all issues simply go away. For example, if you were to apply TPM with me (Ed) in a ministry session, the questions would work perfectly because I know what I am supposed to be doing at every step along the way. In fact, I don't even need you to ask me the questions since I have memorized them and know the objectives they are designed to remind me of. To the degree that the Mentee knows what is expected of him during the ministry session, all problems, concerns, and issues, simply go away.

If a Mentee's answer to a question shows that he or she does not understand the objective at hand, this should alert the Mentor that orientation is needed. So then, rather than the Mentor trying to explain the question or worse yet, attempting to reword the question, he should explain the objective at hand as well as any applicable TPM Principles. When the Mentee knows what he needs to do at any given point during the ministry session, the questions themselves become secondary to the objective. When the Mentee understands his or her role, as well as the protocols and objectives involved in the TPM Process, then he or she can effectively and consistently apply the *Process* regardless of what a Mentor may or may not do in the *Session*. In fact, even if a Mentor were to ask the wrong question at the wrong time, it would have little to no impact on a well-equipped Mentee. <u>The Mentee's understanding of TPM is paramount!</u>

The Value of a Mentor and the Questions

Someone might ask, "If you can apply the Process of TPM without the use of the questions or the involvement of a Mentor, what role do these elements play in a TPM session?" Obviously, you can apply the process yourself and learn these things on your own, but it is undoubtedly helpful to have someone with you who has spent time studying and applying TPM. Your Mentor's primary role is to support you in this endeavor by explaining the Principles, Purpose, and Process of TPM. He or she will 1) use the Map to follow your application of the TPM Process, 2) ask the prescribed questions associated with your current objective, and 3) continually equip you by expanding your understanding of the Three Elements of TPM. Your Mentor should be aware that your responses to the questions reveal what you do and do not understand regarding TPM. And he should be ready and able to offer orientation when it is necessary. It is wonderful when all things go smoothly and you receive the Lord's perspective, but learning the three elements is crucial for the long haul.

Mentors are helpful, but Mentees can equip themselves.

Even though it is the role of the Mentor to help equip you for this journey, becoming equipped is your responsibility. This is your journey of faith-refinement and mind-renewal with God. Your Mentor is here to help along the way, but you must take full responsibility for growing in the knowledge that is freely available to you. There is no reason that you should not be applying yourself to learn all that is here. There is nothing that your Mentor knows about TPM that is not available to you. Come prepared for each ministry session by studying the principles and purpose of TPM. Memorize the questions on either the Mentee's or Mentor's version of the *TPM Map,* and familiarize yourself with the objectives on the *Objectives Map.*

Your Mentor is to evaluate your current understanding of TPM by observing your application of the *Process* as well as your responses to the TPM questions. When you are first starting out, your Mentor's role will be much more involved as he or she provides explanations and orientation and asks the questions on the TPM Map. But even during your very first session, you (the Mentee) are applying the *Process* even if you are unaware that this is so.

During a TPM session, you are the one who is connecting to your emotions and focusing on what you are feeling (EMOTION Box), allowing your mind to associate to a related memory and identifying the belief that is causing you to feel what you are feeling (MEMORY Box), confirming that the identified belief feels true to you (BELIEF Box), asking the Lord for truth and perspective (TRUTH Box), and verifying that the Spirit has transformed your thinking (TRANSFORMATION Box). If you are ever feeling angry during the session, then it is your responsibility to acknowledge this and to identify when you feel any resistance or hesitancy to move forward (the ANGER and SOLUTION Boxes). And as you grow in your understanding of TPM and gain experience applying the TPM process, your Mentor's involvement should become less and less necessary.

Likewise, the questions can help you stay on track by reminding you of where you are in the *Process* and what objective you are currently working on. But as you become more familiar with the objectives in the TPM Process, the questions related to those objectives will seem less and less necessary (considering you already know what to do). In fact, as you become more familiar with the TPM Process, you will likely begin accomplishing your goals before the relevant questions are even asked.

Another illustration may be helpful here. I remember feeling somewhat nervous sitting in the passenger's seat next to Joshua the first day he was learning how to drive. I explained exactly what to do the entire time because he did not yet know how to operate the vehicle. At first, the experience was a bit challenging, a little bumpy, and it provided me with an opportunity for a few personal ministry sessions of my own.

Throughout the learning process I was in the car with him, instructing him step-by-step on what to do, but at no point was I driving the car. Even though I obviously had more experience, from the moment we strapped on our seatbelts, he was the driver, and I was the passenger. He was doing every aspect of the driving process; I was merely his mentor. Once he understood what he was supposed to do and practiced applying what he learned, I became less and less necessary to the point where he was ready for me to get out of the car.

This same dynamic is found in TPM. When you understand the *Three Elements of TPM*, your Mentor will become less needed or not needed at all. You can fulfill the objectives of the *Process* and "drive the car" whether or not the Mentor is present or the questions are even asked.

Does this mean that we can just throw out the questions? Yes and No. If you fully understand what to do at each stage in the *Process* then the answer is, *"yes."* However, if you do not yet understand what each question is reminding you to do, then you will likely still benefit from using the questions. Joshua needed me in the car when we started, but when he mastered the driving process, I was no longer needed.

When you know where you are on the Map, which objective you are to focus on, as well as how to accomplish that objective, then you can intentionally and effectively apply that aspect of the *Process*, with or without the involvement of your Mentor. As you learn to do this in each location on the Map, you will be that much more effective and consistent in applying the TPM process.

TPM *as Discipleship*

The relationship that you share with your Mentor is based upon a biblical model of discipleship. It is this model that Jesus used with His twelve disciples when He poured Himself into their lives. As a result, they followed His example, and this model has continued to this day. We are followers of Christ today because of the success of His mentorship of them. In TPM some act as Mentors who "disciple" and encourage their brothers and sisters in Christ, equipping them, and building them up (Ephesians 4:12). Others act as Mentees who are seeking to position themselves under the "mighty hand of God" (1 Peter 5:6) so that their hearts may be convinced of the truth.

The only real difference between a TPM Mentor and a Mentee is the role they are playing. The Mentor is helping to equip the Mentee for his journey in faith-refinement and mind-renewal by growing in knowledge of the *Three Elements of TPM* (the *Principles, Purpose* and *Process)*. Technically, both individuals are Mentees learning and growing in this knowledge, the only difference being their familiarity with the three elements and their experience in applying what they have learned. Not all are called to be Mentors, but (as we are all Mentees) we are each on the same faith-refining and mind-renewing journey with God.

Mentoring others in this ministry is a calling just as all other forms of ministry found within the church. Not everyone is a *"hand or a foot"* (see 1 Corinthians 12:20), but all play an important role in the Body of Christ. Even so, we are all Mentees on a life journey with God. All of us need our faith refined, our minds renewed, and our lives transformed to more accurately reflect the new creations that we became when we first believed.

HOW MANY SESSIONS DO I NEED?

We are sometimes asked how many ministry sessions a person needs before they are in a better place and no longer in need of TPM. Those who ask this question do not yet understand the *Principles* and *Purpose* of TPM. TPM is not a ministry to just help people feel better, to get past some crisis in their lives, or overcome some undesirable behavior. Rather, the goal of TPM is to equip each of us to participate with God as He refines our faith, renews our minds, and transforms our lives to reflect the inner newness of our divinely created selves.

This is not accomplished in a few sessions, but rather is a lifelong journey with God. It is our goal to equip as many as possible with the skills and understanding needed to intentionally cooperate with God's Spirit as He leads us into all truth (John 16:13). We want you to be really good at intentionally inviting the Holy Spirit to perform His refining work in your life. When you know what it looks like to have Him expose your need for His perspective, and understand what you should do in response, you will be better equipped to cooperate with Him as he ministers to you.

How long does this "equipping" take? We don't know. We've never met anyone (ourselves included) who has completely mastered this task. However, we know countless individuals who would testify to having more purposeful and fruitful journeys with the Lord because they have learned and applied what you are reading in this book. One day we will no longer have a use for TPM, for we will "see His face" (Revelation 22:4) and see ourselves the way we "have been fully known" (1 Corinthians 13:12). But for now, set your sights on becoming better equipped.

Part Four

What might a TPM Session look like?

As stated before, what a TPM session involves will vary depending upon your familiarity and experience with TPM. But your goals and the protocols that are to be followed, are the same each time the TPM Process is applied. In a moment you will see what it might look like for someone to apply the TPM Process, but a couple of caveats need to be made before we begin.

First, it is important to note that it is very common to spend some time in the SOLUTION Box or ANGER Box when applying the TPM Process. However, for the sake of simplicity, we will omit them from the following example.

Second, know that <u>what follows is only an example of what it *might* look like to apply the TPM Process; it is not a detailed example of what to do</u> in a TPM session. Many important details have been intentionally omitted but will be discussed later. The main thing we want you to see are the tasks or objectives that are accomplished during a TPM session. It might be helpful for you to place a copy of the *Questions Map* and the *Objectives Map* beside you as you read through this section. With that in mind, consider the following example:

Your session typically begins in the EMOTION Box. The first objective here is to ensure that you are currently connected with your emotion. This is often accomplished by recalling a recent time in which you were "*triggered*" (such as an argument with a family member, the loss of a loved-one, a stressful situation at work, or when your football team lost the big game). This will likely cause you to experience a stirring of negative emotions. Typically, however, when meeting with a Mentor for prayer ministry, you have something going on in your current life situation that has already triggered you and emotionally stirred you up. Because this is so, your next task is to focus on this emotion, and through the God-created process of *association*, memories of past experiences should come to your mind. You will not be searching for or trying to find some particular memory but allowing association to work naturally as God designed it to do.

After the same memory comes to mind a couple of times, or when nothing new comes to mind, you then move to the MEMORY Box. While recalling the experience, you maintain your connection to your emotions and identify a belief that seems to produce what you are feeling.

When this is accomplished, you then move to the BELIEF Box and determine if the identified belief feels or seems true. This establishes a point of comparison, or a "base-line," that will be used in a moment. You then continue to the TRUTH Box and invite the Holy Spirit to convince you of the truth.

After a few moments have passed, whether or not you notice anything happening, you move to the TRANSFORMATION Box and check for a shift or change in your thinking. If the Holy Spirit has convinced you of the truth, there will be a noticeable change in what you believe. The lie that felt true just moments before while in the BELIEF Box will no longer feel or seem true. This transformation in belief should also result in future changes in your emotion and behavior. At this point, if you have time, you can return to the EMOTION Box and apply the TPM Process again, looking for another opportunity to be convinced by the Spirit of a truth that you do not yet believe in your heart.

As we said before sharing this example, we deliberately did not include going to the SOLUTION or ANGER Box. However, in most sessions you can expect to spend time in either or both. We will look at the specific protocol for these boxes soon. This example also did not reflect the amount of time you might spend in each box. For example, it is not uncommon to spend a significant amount of time in the EMOTION Box, the MEMORY Box, or even the SOLUTION Box.

Throughout your application of the TPM Process, you could ask yourself the questions that are found on the *TPM Map* to help keep yourself on track. You could also be accompanied by a Mentor who would observe, ask the TPM questions, and offer orientation where needed. But in either case, you (the Mentee) are the one applying the *Process*.

NOTICE: It bears repeating that what you just read **DID NOT** equip you to apply the TPM Process. An immense amount of valuable information was intentionally left out. We were only offering a brief synopsis of what a TPM session *might* look like. We strongly encourage you to keep reading and learning!

WHAT ABOUT FOLLOWING THE HOLY SPIRIT?

In response to the example above, some may begin to wonder, *"What about following the leading of the Holy Spirit? Have you taken the Spirit out of the TPM Process?"* And in response to that we say, *"Of course not!"* The Holy Spirit has a vital role to play in the TPM Process. He is the One who grants us the truth once we are positioned to receive it. If this component of the TPM Process was somehow removed, then all we could hope to accomplish would be to come to a better intellectual understanding of our need for His truth and perspective, with no hope of fixing it. His involvement is the most important part of TPM.

Apart from the Spirit granting us His truth, there is nothing that occurs (or needs to occur) in the ministry session that we do not accomplish ourselves. The Spirit grants us His perspective when we choose to position ourselves to receive it. Contrary to what many believe, we don't need the Holy Spirit to take us to our memories, reveal things that are hidden, expose memory content, tear down walls, open doors, drive the devil away, or even offer us direction during the course of a *TPM session*. He also does not need anyone to speak for Him concerning the truth He wants to grant us. We will hear His voice when we are ready to listen. His "sheep" hear his voice (John 10:27) when they are in the right position to hear.

As strange as it may initially seem, there are no locked doors, walls, or barriers standing between you and the truth and freedom that God has for you. You do not need the Holy Spirit, or anyone else for that matter, to open doors, tear down walls, or destroy anything. You do not need someone to rescue you from darkness, fight the devil off, or speak on God's behalf. Apart from your own belief and choice, nothing can keep you from receiving the truth that God has for you. (We will revisit this concept in the SOLUTION Box chapter.)

Aside from the Holy Spirit's role of persuading you to believe the truth, every aspect of the TPM Process can be accomplished without additional involvement by the Holy Spirit. It really does come down to your own understanding of what to do and your willful decision to do it. This is not to say that the Holy Spirit is not fully involved in every aspect of the ministry session, for indeed He is. Even so, you are the one who is choosing to feel emotion, recall memories, identify beliefs, and look to God for truth and perspective.

This reality should be encouraging to you. There is nothing standing between you and the truth, peace, freedom, and transformation that He offers. Freedom is within your reach. The Holy Spirit is patiently waiting for us to position ourselves to receive what He has for us. As soon as we are in position, He graciously pours out what we need. And this book was written to help you learn how to intentionally and consistently do just that!

An Important Note on Future Chapters

In the next several chapters, we will discuss each of the *Boxes* in detail. The goals and objectives of each Box will be explained, each question will be introduced, and examples of what it might look like to apply that specific part of the TPM Process will be given. But it is important to note that even though *solution behaviors* can appear at nearly every stage in the Process, we will postpone our discussion of *solutions* until we reach the SOLUTION Box chapter. This will allow us to lay a foundation and framework to build upon later. This should also make it easier to follow along as we work through the TPM Process.

Our primary focus will be upon learning the concepts and protocols that make up the TPM Process. Saving our discussion of *anger* and *solutions* until the end seems to be the most efficient way to accomplish this goal. So, for now, we will discuss the TPM Process, one Box at a time, and pretend that in every TPM session everyone always knows what they are doing, and everything runs as smoothly as possible! After thoroughly discussing these five *Boxes (left side of the TPM Map)*, we will return to reality and learn all about the ANGER and SOLUTION Boxes.

Lastly, the first few paragraphs of each chapter offer a summary of the protocol that will be discussed. If these paragraphs seem confusing or rushed, keep reading. By the end of the chapter, these summarizing paragraphs should make more sense.

Again, make your goal *comprehension*, not simply "*completion.*" It is better to understand what is discussed here than it is to have simply read it. Ask yourself, "*Why am I reading this?*" Are you simply trying to complete the reading? Or is your goal to fully equip yourself so you can benefit from what is here? If this is the case, do not rely on your Mentor to "spoon feed" you when you have an open buffet at your disposal. We encourage you to study prior to every session. Take responsibility and equip yourself for this lifelong journey of cooperating with God as He refines your faith, renews your mind, and transforms your life!

WHAT ABOUT CONFIDENTIALITY?

It is important to briefly mention that any information that you share with your Mentor during a TPM session should never be disclosed to anyone else without your permission. The only potential exception would be that which is required by law to be disclosed (such as the suspicion of abuse of children, the disabled or the elderly, the threat of suicide, etc.). We recommend that all parties involved become aware of what the law requires from each of you.

CHAPTER 13

THE EMOTION BOX

The Mentee's Objectives While in the EMOTION Box:

1. Connect with your emotion.
2. Focus on what you feel until a memory comes to mind.
3. Repeat the first two objectives until the same memory repeatedly comes to mind or no other memory comes to mind.

The EMOTION Box Questions:

"How does that make you feel?"

"What comes to your mind when you focus on what you are feeling?"

NOTICE: This chapter has been divided into three parts. The first part discusses the objectives that are to be accomplished in the EMOTION Box. The second part explains the importance of repeating the EMOTION Box objectives until the same memory repeatedly comes to mind. The third part describes what it looks like to apply this portion of the TPM Process.

Part One

A Preview of The EMOTION Box

A *TPM session* usually begins in the EMOTION Box. The first step or objective is for you to connect with your emotion. Typically, this is not a problem since you may be feeling something even before the session begins. While in the EMOTION Box, you connect with and focus on your emotion, prompting the natural process of *association* to work. You never need to start looking for a memory, but only focus on what you are feeling. If association is not hindered, you should quickly have some memory come to mind.

Continue this pattern of focusing on what you feel and allowing something to come to your mind until the same memory repeatedly comes to mind or until nothing new or different comes to mind. When this happens, you have accomplished your objectives in the EMOTION Box. If you feel angry or have trouble connecting with any emotion while in the EMOTION Box, you will follow a slightly different protocol, which will be explained later.

Connecting to Emotion

It is important to note that your first objective is simply to connect with emotion. Or, more specifically stated, your objective is to determine whether or not you *are* currently connected to some measure of emotion. Since most people apply the TPM Process only after they notice some measure of negative emotion, this first objective (connecting with emotion) is often already accomplished at the start of a TPM session.

For example, you may feel anxious as you search for a snack even though you are not hungry, feel overwhelmed when your boss shortens the deadline for the big project, or feel nervous as you walk towards the mailbox, expecting a credit card bill to be there. Perhaps you are grieving the loss of a loved one, feeling helpless as you watch the news, or struggling with a recent cancer diagnosis. Whatever the case, as soon as you realize you are feeling scared, anxious, worried, stressed, overwhelmed, out-of-control, helpless, hopeless, alone, rejected, etc., you have accomplished your first objective in the EMOTION Box and are ready to work on your next objective.

The only exception to this is if the emotion you are feeling is anger. If you feel mad, frustrated, irritated, ticked-off, aggravated, etc., then you move to the ANGER Box (which we will discuss in a later chapter). So, again, if you currently feel an emotion (other than anger), you have accomplished your first objective.

Occasionally you may find that you are not feeling anything at the start of a TPM session. This is especially common when your TPM session takes place in a pre-scheduled context such as in a ministry center or counseling office, rather than as a natural response to life as it happens. Thankfully, your lack of emotion at the start of a TPM session is often easily remedied by simply thinking or talking about a recent time in which you did feel something. By doing this you can "*trigger*" yourself and begin feeling something immediately. For example, as you discuss or even think about last week's family get-together, you will likely begin to feel as stressed and anxious as you did during the actual event.

If it *seems* as though you are unable to connect with any negative emotion, it is either because you no longer believe the lies you believed during the earlier experience or, *more likely*, because you believe there is a reason for choosing not to connect with your emotion (which will be covered when we discuss *solutions* in a later chapter).

Following the Smoke

It is important to note that your first objective is to *connect* with your emotion, not to *intensify*, *stir-up*, *isolate*, *name,* or even *identify* the emotion. You are to connect with what you feel, not simply remember what you felt. You must *currently feel* your emotion in order to accomplish your objectives in this "Box." In a general sense, if you are not feeling, then you are not moving.

To illustrate this point, consider the following:

Imagine that you walk out of your house and immediately notice a sweet, smoky aroma in the air. The savory scent signals to you that somewhere nearby is a barbeque. Smelling the smoke is enough to make you aware of this reality. You don't need to see the grill, hear the meat sizzling, or feel the warmth radiating off the coals. You know someone is grilling simply by smelling the smoke, and you would be able to find the barbeque easily by simply following your nose.

Your emotions act in much the same way. They can help guide you to their source just as the smoke can guide you to the grill. This is one of the reasons why we view emotional pain as useful and beneficial rather than a problem. If you understand the TPM Principle, "we feel whatever we believe" and also know what to do when negative emotions flare-up, you can take advantage of the situation and benefit from the pain.

Taking this simple illustration further, how much smoke would be needed for you to be able to follow it? Obviously, smoke wouldn't need to billow into your yard, causing you to choke or make your eyes water. You only need enough to smell its scent. If it is noticeable, then there is enough to follow it. The same is true with your emotions. In a TPM session, it is unnecessary to intensify or stir-up what you feel because feeling *anything* is enough. It is not *how much* you feel but only that you feel something.

If you wanted to follow the scent, would you need to determine first if what you are smelling is beef, chicken, pork, lamb, or fish? Of course not! Regardless of what's on the grill, the fact that you smell it is enough. You only need enough to notice. This is true in a TPM session as well. You do not need to accurately label or identify what you feel in order to move forward. (This is true for all emotions except anger, which will be discussed later.) The fact that you are feeling something is what matters. Again, if you are currently feeling something, then that is enough. So while in the EMOTION Box, one of the objectives is to connect to and feel what you are feeling, but "naming" or correctly labeling the emotion is not needed or necessary to proceed with the process.

Associating Emotion with Memory

Your next objective is to focus on the emotion you feel. Doing this should automatically and effortlessly bring some sort of memory to mind via the natural, God-designed process of association. God designed our minds to associate one thing with another. We use this function every day, all day, to interpret the current moment as we naturally and automatically access memories, beliefs, and impressions of earlier life experiences. Observing someone talking on their cell phone might remind you to call your mother and wish her a happy birthday. This association happens effortlessly and automatically.

The mental process of association might be compared to using a word search on the Internet. If you do an internet search using the word "fireworks," you will be supplied with page after page of information that relates to "fireworks." In similar fashion, if you think of the word "fireworks," your mind will immediately associate this word with life experiences. It may even trigger you and stir up some emotion. Have you ever noticed how your emotions are stirred when some old song is played on the radio? When this occurs, your mind is associating the song with some aspect of your life. In such moments your mind links the song with a related life experience and established belief, causing you to feel the emotions related to that belief. This is how God designed your mind to work.

As you focus on what you feel and allow association to work, memories of other times when you had similar feelings should come to mind automatically and instantaneously. The reason for this is simple. Emotion flows from heart belief, every heart belief was learned in a life experience, and life experiences are recorded as memories. As a result, when we focus on what we are feeling, we are linked to beliefs that are linked to memory. If it ever seems as though it would require effort or struggle for this to take place, then there is a specific reason for this (which will be discussed when we get to the SOLUTION Box chapter).

Your TPM Mentor has no need to interfere or attempt to do something to make it work. Should a misguided Mentor ever ask questions that suggest anything about your past experiences or that direct you to do something outside of the specific protocols that are outlined in this book, gently remind them to adhere to what is taught.

Some well-meaning ministers approach a person's reluctance to remember something by having them first focus on something positive, go to some "happy place" in their mind, think about a time where they encountered the Lord before, sense for Jesus's presence in their mind, attempt to build something up or tear something down, or pray against the devil or demonic manifestations. Their reasoning is that if you can feel *good* before you feel *bad,* doing so can be empowering. They believe the person sometimes lacks the emotional capacity or ability to allow themselves to remember their painful past. But as you will learn later, none of these solutions is necessary once you understand how association works.

Although these practices may seem helpful, they fail to address the actual problem. They typically result in you temporarily feeling better, safer, more in control, less vulnerable, less anxious, etc. What is actually occurring in these moments is a form of *solution behavior.* Here again, our discussion of *solutions* will clarify this phenomenon.

You never need to go on a "memory hunt" or intentionally search for anything specific. In fact, if you are having to expend energy trying to remember, then something is wrong. Association is effortless and continually working moment-by-moment. You also should not attempt to filter-out or prioritize any of what may come to your mind or try to determine if what comes to mind is important or relevant. All you need to do is feel and associate. Association is a God-designed, natural, effortless, and passive task, so simply focus on what you are feeling and see what comes to your mind. Don't go looking for "it;" let "it" come to you.

The fact that you are feeling something means that the associative process is already working. Your mind has already referred to what you remember and believe so that it can "rightly" interpret what is happening around you. So, in a sense, if you are feeling, then you are remembering, albeit not consciously. You simply need to pay attention to what you feel so that you can discover which memories and beliefs your mind has used to interpret your current situation.

The process of association is not a bad thing. It describes the way God designed our minds to use what we've learned in the past to interpret our present. Although God designed association to assist us as we navigate through life, God intended association to operate in truth so that we might interpret life correctly. When we interpret current events through lie-based beliefs, we will view them from a flawed perspective. God wants to correct our flawed perspectives by correcting our flawed beliefs.

"DON'T YOU CARE HOW I FEEL?"

Some people may wonder why their TPM Mentors do not ask them for more details regarding their current situation, their family history, their background, etc., or attempt to comfort them in their pain. This is because their Mentors understand the purpose of pain and its true source. They are focused on equipping Mentees for their faith-refining journey with the Lord. They may genuinely feel compassion and empathy, but they also know that the way forward begins with connecting to the pain, not running away from it or blaming it on others. If you are in pain because you believe lies, you need God's perspective, not a Mentor's consolation.

Although your current situation may seem painful, chaotic, or genuinely unjust, it is not the source of what you feel. Remember: we feel whatever we believe. Specifically, we feel what we feel today because of what we believe today, and we felt this same way in the past because we believed the same things then. This is how God designed our minds to work. Although we do not like how it feels, emotional pain serves a vital role in our journey towards the truth and freedom that He has for us. We do not need to be comforted out of our pain; we need God's perspective regarding why we feel it.

Part Two

Repeating Until the Same Memory Repeatedly Comes to Mind

While in the EMOTION Box, you continue this pattern of focusing on what is felt and seeing what comes to mind until nothing new or different comes to mind or until the same memory repeatedly comes to mind. To illustrate this pattern, let's revisit the online search engine illustration. While in the EMOTION Box, you first input your currently felt emotion into your mental "search engine," and wait for the results to automatically appear. When this happens, take the first result (whatever comes to your mind), verify that you are still feeling something (other than anger), and then perform another "search" using whatever came to your mind most recently.

For instance, imagine that while you are focusing on your anxiety, you immediately begin thinking about the stressful situation going on at your place of work. Now, recheck your emotional status. If you still feel something (other than anger), focus on it and see if anything else comes to your mind. If nothing but the workplace memory comes to your mind, then you move to the MEMORY Box. If a different memory comes to your mind, stay in the EMOTION Box. Focus again on your emotional response to this memory, and wait for the next set of "search results" to appear in your mind. Continue this process until nothing new or different comes to your mind or until the same memory remains.

This protocol is a slight shift in process from what was taught in years past. In earlier versions of the training, we misunderstood the purpose that memory serves in this Process, and we believed that a memory of an earlier life experience was preferred over that of a later one. Because of this, we gave less attention to memories of experiences that occurred later in a person's life.

Today, we recommend that you focus on what you are feeling and allow association to occur. When the same memory repeatedly comes to mind, whether early childhood or not, move to the MEMORY Box and begin working on your objectives there. Your age at the time of the remembered event <u>does not</u> determine whether or not you are ready to move to the MEMORY Box.

The two questions in the EMOTION Box remind you to follow this prescribed pattern. First, you ask, "How does 'this' make me feel?" followed by, "What comes to my mind as I focus on what I am feeling?" This part of the Process may initially seem redundant or repetitive, but there are several significant reasons why it is important to do this. One of the primary reasons for doing this is to protect your role and responsibility as Mentee. It allows you to determine when it is time to move to the MEMORY Box as opposed to your Mentor attempting to make this decision.

You alone are the one who determines when to move to the next *Box*. By repeating your first two objectives in the EMOTION Box —connecting with what you feel and focusing on it— until no new memory has come to your mind, or the same memory has repeatedly surfaced, you allow the natural process of association to indicate when *you* should move to the MEMORY Box. Your Mentor does not know with any certainty when to move to the MEMORY Box. He is dependent upon you and your responses to his questions. When the same memory repeatedly comes to mind you will know that it is time to proceed.

It is important to realize that you are <u>not</u> searching for the source of the pain, rather, you are only focusing on what you feel and allowing your mind to freely associate and recall any related memories. When no other memories come to mind or the same memory repeatedly comes to mind while focusing on what is felt, the EMOTION Box objectives have been accomplished, and you are ready to move to the MEMORY Box.

Once properly understood, this portion of the TPM Process becomes simple and intuitive. Until you clearly understand your objectives and how to accomplish them, you might become confused or even frustrated by your Mentor incessantly asking the same two questions over and over. When you understand what to do and how to do it, you will become more intentional in your application of the *TPM Process* and less dependent upon your Mentor's involvement.

God doesn't "take us" to our memories.

The "Holy Spirit" is obviously the most important person in the room during the ministry session, and His involvement is absolutely vital. But He has given us the freedom to do certain things without needing any further involvement from Him. For instance, you probably don't ask God to help you breathe. It is very unlikely that you start your day by praying that He will give you the strength and courage necessary to continually inhale and exhale. Does this mean that He is not involved in your every breath? Of course not, for He gives breath to all of us whether we ask for it or not (Isaiah 42:5). God created your mind to associate just as He designed your lungs to breathe. Both actions are natural and automatic.

But just as you can choose to hold your breath, you can purposefully choose not to remember by ignoring these automatic mental associations (as we will learn in our discussion of *solutions*). This is why we do not attempt to "dig up" a memory or ask God to "help" us to remember. As bizarre as it may sound right now, if you are struggling to remember what you *need* to remember, this should not be viewed as a problem. Rather, your "inability" to recall a memory indicates that you are attempting to *solve* a perceived problem by choosing not to remember.

Hearing this may initially shock or confuse some readers because we have not always held this position. In those early years of TPM, we mistakenly prayed asking Jesus to help us to remember. We would even pray something like, "Lord Jesus, will you take John to the source and origin of where he learned to feel this way?" And when a person remembered what they needed to remember after this prayer had been prayed, it *appeared* as though God was granting us our requests, and this *seemed* to further prove the validity of the prayer, but we were also puzzled by the times in which the Lord seemed to be uncooperative. We now understand that Jesus *never* took any of us to memories; we simply chose to remember.

Just because "something happened" after we asked for the Lord to do something, it does not mean that He actually did anything. To illustrate this point, take a moment to pray, asking Jesus to take you to a childhood memory related to Christmas. Did it work? Did a memory relating to "Christmas" come to your mind? Should we then conclude that the Lord answered your prayer? Probably not. This may seem silly, but it illustrates an important point. Jesus did not take you to the memory; your mind effortlessly and automatically surfaced a memory just as God designed it to do.

God neither forces us nor helps us to remember, feel, or choose anywhere along the way. He does not need to since we were created to do these things naturally. He also respects our free will and waits for us to make the decision to move in His direction. James said it this way, "Draw near to God and He will draw near to you" (James 4:8 NKJV). It cannot be said that if God draws near to us that we will necessarily draw near to Him. Too often we despair while waiting for God to do something, when in fact, He is waiting on us to move in His direction. He will not take us to any memory that we do not choose to remember, but He will grant us His perspective if we draw near to Him and listen.

Today, we realize that asking God to "take" you to a memory is totally unnecessary and even contrary to what actually happens in a TPM session. Despite all appearances, no one needs help remembering anything during a ministry session. In fact, you never even need to ask God to help you to remember! If it ever *seems* as though you need His help to recall a specific memory, this indicates that you are actually hindering the natural process of association from occurring (again, we will discuss this later).

For those of you reading this who were trained in TPM prior to about 2015, this may be a difficult paradigm shift. But it is crucial that you spend the time necessary to learn and comprehend the concept of "*solutions*." None of us need "help" in moving forward in a TPM session. We simply need to learn what to do and identify any lie-based reasons for choosing not to move forward (this will make more sense after reading the SOLUTION Box chapter).

Part Three

Working Through The EMOTION Box in a TPM Session

If you are applying the TPM Process without a Mentor, you can use *The EMOTION Box Flowchart* to help keep yourself on track while accomplishing the objectives of the EMOTION Box. If you are in a TPM session with a Mentor, he or she will ask the EMOTION Box questions to remind you of where you are in the TPM Process and of your objectives while in this Box. If you are ever unsure about your current objective, pull out your copy of the *TPM 'Objectives' Map* for a quick reference. Your Mentor should also be prepared to explain each objective when necessary.

The first question in the EMOTION Box should remind you of the first objective (connect to emotion), and the second question should remind you of the second objective (focus on what you are feeling to associate emotion with memory). These questions are visible on both the *TPM Map* and *The EMOTION Box Flowchart* (found in the back of this book).

"How Does that Make You Feel?"

The first question in the EMOTION Box is, *"How does that make you feel?"* This is asked as you think about or discuss what has "triggered" you. For example, a person might say, *"I have really been struggling at work this week. They just hired a new guy, and he can't seem to mind his own business. I swear he spends more time in my office than he does in his!"* In response, the Mentor asks, *"How does that make you feel?"* or even, *"How does that make you feel right now?"* (to remind the Mentee of the importance of being connected to the emotion, not just remembering what was felt during an earlier experience).

This first objective can seem more complicated than it is. Again, your only goal is to determine if you are currently feeling emotion. You are not trying to accurately label or identify what you are feeling. You are not attempting to "stir it up" or intensify it. You are not seeking to narrow down or limit what you are feeling to one specific emotion. All you should be focused on is whether or not you are currently feeling something. If you are feeling something (anything), then you have accomplished your first objective in the EMOTION Box.

No matter how much or how many emotions are present, if you are feeling something, you are ready to move to your next objective. The only exception to this rule is if the emotion you feel is anger. If you are angry, you need to move to the ANGER Box (*but we will discuss that in detail in a later chapter*).

"What comes to your mind as you focus on that?"

The purpose of the first question in the EMOTION Box is to determine if you are presently feeling the emotion that you are describing. The "that" found in the first question is referring to whatever triggered your emotional response. However, the "that" stated in this second question is referring to the emotion that you currently feel.

After expressing what you feel or that you <u>are</u> simply feeling something (assuming it is anything but anger), the Mentor will ask, "*What comes to mind as you focus on <u>that</u>? (the emotion you are feeling),*" or "*Does a memory come to mind as you focus on what you are feeling?*" (to remind you of what should naturally result from your mental association). These questions are essentially asking, "*Does <u>anything</u> come to your mind as you focus on what you feel?*" or "*Does <u>anything else</u> come to mind as you focus on that?*" If anything comes to your mind, then the Mentor will ask how you feel in response to what has come to mind. This pattern continues until nothing new comes to mind or until the same thing repeatedly comes to your mind.

DON'T RUSH OR SKIP AHEAD.

The second question in the EMOTION Box is designed to remind you to focus on your feelings and allow association to engage. But novice Mentors sometimes get ahead of themselves while in the EMOTION Box and mistakenly ask the MEMORY Box question, "Why do you feel that way?" This question should only be asked when you are actually in the MEMORY Box. It is important to remember that *you are never attempting to determine "why" an emotion is felt while in the EMOTION Box.* You simply need to connect with your emotion and allow association to work.

Another common misstep new Mentors sometimes make is rushing to the BELIEF Box too soon. There is never any reason to move from the EMOTION box to the BELIEF Box. Even if you begin a TPM session by saying something like, "I am a filthy worthless piece of trash, a reject, despised, and surely hated by God." Even though what you have confessed is clearly a lie, you are still in the EMOTION Box. <u>You can only get to the BELIEF Box by way of the MEMORY Box or the SOLUTION Box.</u>

Example Scenarios of the EMOTION Box

Let's look at a couple of examples of what this protocol might look like in a TPM session. As you read through the following scenarios you will notice numbers following each statement (E1, E2, E3, etc). These numbers are provided to guide you through the EMOTION Box by using the *Flowchart* (found at the back of the book) as a visual aid. The numbers help to identify where you are on the *Flowchart*. In no way do these numbers represent the order of "steps" in the process (i.e. Step 1, Step 2, Step 3, etc.); they only identify where you are on the Flowchart.

The EMOTION Box Flowchart offers a visual illustration of the protocol that has been described in this chapter. We have only covered a portion of the protocol that is illustrated on the Flowchart. All remaining portions of the Flowchart will be discussed in later chapters.

EMOTION Box Example One:

Mentee: *"My wife is driving me crazy! She goes on and on about how we need to visit her family, but we just don't have the money to put towards a trip like that!" (E1)*

Mentor: *"How does that make you feel?" (E2)*

Mentee: *"I feel out of control. I can't make her stop pestering me about it!" (E5) > (E8)*

Mentor: *"What comes to your mind as you focus on that?" (E10)*

Mentee: *"I am reminded of other times that she has approached me about the trip. She just goes on and on and on..." (E13) > (E1)*

Mentor: *"How does that make you feel?" (E2)*

Mentee: *"Like I said, it makes me feel out of control." (E5) > (E8)*

Mentor: *"What comes to your mind as you focus on that?" (E10)*

Mentee: *"Well, I don't see how this is related, but what comes to mind is my first car. It was a piece of junk. Every time I inserted the key into the ignition, I would pray for it to start. It was all rusted out and leaked fluids. I had to add water to the radiator almost everyday. I had to keep jugs of water in the back seat just in case!" (E13) > (E1)*

Mentor: *"How does that make you feel right now?" (E2)*

Mentee: *"...out of control and nervous." (E5) > (E8)*

Mentor: *"Ok, what comes to mind as you focus on that?" (E10)*

Mentee: *"That's kind of weird, I remember a time in 3rd grade when a bully kept chasing me during recess, threatening to beat me up. It was all I could do to get away from him!" (E13) > (E1)*

Mentor: *"How does that make you feel?" (E2)*

Mentee: *"It makes me feel nervous and scared." (E5) > (E8)*

Mentor: *"What comes to mind as you focus on that?" (E10)*

Mentee: *"...I keep thinking about that kid on the playground. He just wouldn't stop. No matter how far I ran, he was right behind me! I couldn't escape him!" (E14) > (E15)*

At this point in the example, the Mentee has focused on his emotion and the same memory has repeatedly come to the Mentee's mind. He has accomplished the objectives in the EMOTION Box and is ready to move to the next part of the TPM Process. Before we explore the MEMORY Box, let's look at another example of what it might look like when a Mentee is in the EMOTION Box.

EMOTION Box Example Two:

Mentee: *"It has been super stressful at work lately. They had to lay-off another person last week, and my workload has almost doubled. I don't know how I am going to get everything done on time!" (E1)*

Mentor: *"How does that make you feel right now?" (E2)*

Mentee: *"I feel overwhelmed!" (E5) > (E8)*

Mentor: *"What comes to your mind as you focus on that?" (E10)*

Mentee: *"I think about all the projects that I have to get done for work, but in the back of my mind I also see the list of other things I need to get done. I think about all the stuff that needs to happen before we sell our house. I know that I need to go to the grocery store. I have to pick up my daughter's medication from the pharmacy. There is a pile of laundry on my living room floor that still needs to be folded and put away. There is always so much going on that I can't ever get ahead." (E13) > (E1)*

Mentor: *"How does that make you feel?" (E2)*

Mentee: *"I just feel overwhelmed. It seems like I always have too much going on. I'm never prepared for what I have to do." (E5) > (E8)*

Mentor: *"What comes to your mind as you focus on that?" (E10)*

Mentee: *"It seems like I'm always in this situation. I even remember feeling anxious when I was younger. Like, for example, I always felt this way in school." (E13) > (E5) > (E8)*

Mentor: *"What comes to your mind as you focus on that?" (E10)*

Mentee: *"I remember worrying about one test in particular. It was going to count for most of my grade in the class. I studied and studied, but I never felt prepared. I was so nervous walking into the classroom that day. (E13) > (E1)*

Mentor: *"How does that make you feel?" (E2)*

Mentee: *"I can still feel that anxious, panicky feeling that I felt right before the tests were handed out." (E5) > (E8)*

Mentor: *"What comes to your mind as you focus on that?" (E10)*

Mentee: *"I see my teacher handing-out the tests, and I remember feeling completely unprepared." (E14) > (E15)*

Here again, the Mentee has accomplished the objectives in the EMOTION Box and is ready to move to the MEMORY Box. Although the Mentee did not use the same exact wording to describe the memory in the two previous statements, it could be inferred that they were of the same life event. Notice that the same protocol was followed in each of these example scenarios. The path that was taken in each example was slightly different, but both paths exist within the outlined *Process*. Every TPM session is different, but the objectives, questions, and the protocols that are to be followed are the same. Therefore, it is important to understand each of the *Three Elements of TPM* so that you know what to do, how to do it, when to do it, and why to do it.

EMOTION Box Example Three:

This last example illustrates what it might look like to work through the EMOTION Box on your own.

Your Thought: *"I can't believe he forgot our anniversary again!" (E1)*

Ask Yourself: *"How does that make me feel?" (E2)*

Your Response: *"It feels as though it's not important to him...like I am not important to him." (E1)*

Ask Yourself: *"How does it make me feel to think that I am not important to him?" (E2)*

Your Response: *"That feels really bad."* (E5) > (E8)

Ask Yourself: *"What comes to mind as I focus on that?"* (E10)

Your Response: *"...This is just like what Dad always did. He was never there for the important things."* (E13) > (E1)

Ask Yourself: *"How does that make me feel?"* (E2)

Your Response: *"I feel like I am forgotten and unimportant. That hurts!"* (E5) > (E8)

Ask Yourself: *"Ok, what comes to mind as I focus on that one?"* (E10)

Your Response: *"I remember my last game in 7th grade. Dad had promised to be there."* (E13) > (E1)

Ask Yourself: *"How does that make me feel?"* (E2)

Your Response: *"Anxious. I remember looking for him in the crowd but not being able to find him. That was devastating!"* (E5) > (E8)

Ask Yourself: *"What comes to mind as I focus on that?"* (E10)

Your Response: *"I knew he wasn't going to show up that night. He never showed up to any of the other games. Why would he come to that one?"* (E14) > (E15)

The TPM Process is the same whether you are applying it on your own or are accompanied by a Mentor. This is because in every case you are the one who is applying the Process, not your Mentor. Your Mentor's role is to ensure you are following protocol and to further equip you for your faith-refining journey with the Lord. This is your journey. The better equipped you are, the more consistent and intentional your journey will be.

The EMOTION Box in Review

Typically, you begin a TPM session in the EMOTION Box. Your first objective is to simply connect with your emotion —to feel what you are feeling. As you focus on what you feel, thoughts and memories should naturally come to mind. Continue this pattern until no new memory comes to mind or until the same memory repeatedly comes to mind. When this happens, move to the Memory Box.

The EMOTION Box in Reality

Some TPM sessions may go as smoothly as the previous examples, but many will not. It is not uncommon to have trouble connecting with your emotions or have nothing come to mind as you focus on what you are feeling. You may even feel angry while in the EMOTION Box. There are specific reasons why this might happen and protocols in place for when it does. Each of these scenarios will be addressed later in this book. For now, let's assume you are able to effortlessly accomplish the objectives in the EMOTION Box and you move on to the MEMORY Box.

CHAPTER 14

THE MEMORY BOX

The Mentee's Objectives While in the MEMORY Box

1) Stay connected with your emotion.

2) Determine why you feel what you feel (belief).

3) Determine why you believe what you believe (experience).

The MEMORY Box Questions:

"How does that make you feel?

"Why do you feel that way?"

"Why does believing that make you feel that way?"

NOTICE: This chapter has been divided into five parts. The first part covers the protocols that are involved before answering the "looping" question. The second part explains the "looping" question. The third part discusses what to do after the "looping" question has been asked. The fourth part describes the protocol that is to be followed before moving to the BELIEF Box. And the fifth part explains what to do when a "truth-based problem" is identified in the MEMORY Box.

Part One

A Preview of The MEMORY Box

After the same memory repeatedly comes to mind while focusing on what you feel in the EMOTION Box, you move to the MEMORY Box. This is the only path to the MEMORY Box. When you were in the EMOTION Box, you paid attention to what you felt and allowed the mental process of association to work as God intended. Your objectives in the MEMORY Box will share some similarity to the EMOTION Box in that you will continue to focus on what you feel, but you will also be looking for _why_ you feel what you feel.

Since you feel whatever you believe, it is important to maintain your connection with what you are feeling while attempting to determine _why_ you feel it. Paying close attention to your emotions will help you to identify the beliefs that are producing them. These beliefs will either fit the description of "_heart beliefs_" or describe a "_truth-based problem._"

While in the MEMORY Box, you will also uncover another important facet of what you believe: an explanation for _why_ you believe what you believe. Recalling our discussion of the TPM Principles, you believe what you are persuaded to believe, and you are persuaded by something that you experienced. So, in the MEMORY Box, you attempt to identify both (1) the belief that is causing you to feel what you feel and (2) the experiential evidence that supports what you currently believe to be true. Both of these objectives can be accomplished by examining what you remember.

For example, Janice remembered an experience in her childhood when her father refused to believe her when she told him what her uncle had done to her. Rather than coming to her aid, her father became angry and called her a "dirty little liar." In that moment she was persuaded to believe that she was not loved or protected. By examining what she remembered, Janice not only identified the beliefs that are causing her to feel what she feels, but also the context that led her to believe what she believes.

Once you have identified a heart *belief* that seems to explain why you feel what you feel and determined the general context that led you to believe what you believe, you have accomplished your objectives while in the MEMORY Box.

REMINDER: WE PERCEIVE AND FEEL WHAT WE BELIEVE IN OUR HEARTS TO BE TRUE.

As we have previously discussed, we both "perceive" and "feel" what we believe in our hearts. Because of this, the things that you believe in your heart to be true will feel true to you. They will appear or seem to be true, even if you intellectually know that they are not. You may intellectually know that you have value and be able to quote Jesus' words when He said that we have more value than many sparrows (Matthew 10:31), but if you *feel* worthless, it is because, at some level, you *believe* that you are worthless. This type of belief goes beyond mere intellect, it is your heart belief. It is the essence of your faith and plays a pivotal role in all aspects of your life.

Each of us intellectually believes certain things to be true even though they do not *feel* or *seem* true to us. If we are honest, much of what we learn from Scripture may fall into this category. We can intellectually agree with what we read in the Bible but not yet be fully convinced of it in our hearts. When this is the case, the biblical truth will not *feel* or *seem* true to us. Likewise, there are many things that *feel* or *seem* true to us even though we intellectually know they are not. But, as you will recall, if you have been convinced of something in your heart, it will *feel* or *seem* true. These untrue, lie-based beliefs that *feel* or *seem* true represent the part of your faith that needs to be refined. Becoming aware, acknowledging and taking ownership of what we really believe is a vitally important step in this process of refinement. When we honestly assess our limited and flawed understanding and acknowledge our need for His perspective, we position ourselves to receive what we need from Him.

"How does this make me feel, and why do I feel this way?"

While in the MEMORY Box you are attempting to acknowledge and admit what you truly believe. You accomplish this by focusing your attention on what *feels* or *seems* true as you work through the memory that repeatedly came to your mind in the EMOTION Box. Identifying what you believe and how you came to believe it is made possible as you think about what you remember, take notice of what you feel and attempt to identify *why* you feel that way. You are looking for the belief that is producing what you currently feel.

The three questions in the MEMORY Box will help you to do this. One of the questions used to remind you of your objectives here is the same as one of the EMOTION Box questions and serves the same purpose. The question is simply, "*How does this make me feel?*" This should remind you to stay connected with what you are feeling and have it in focus during your search.

For example, if a memory from your childhood repeatedly comes to mind, how does this make you feel? Are you still connected to your emotions? If so, why do you feel what you are feeling? Ask yourself, "*Why do I feel this way?*"

When attempting to answer this question, it is important to remember that you are looking for what *feels* or *seems* true, not necessarily what *is* or *was* true. Your objective is to identify what you *believe* to be true, not what is *actually true*. Because of this, do not be surprised if your honest response to this question initially seems illogical or *obviously* untrue, as this is often the case.

For instance, as an adult, you may logically know that if a child's parents get divorced, it is not the child's fault. However, as you remember hearing your mother explain that your father was moving away, it *feels* or *seems* true that you somehow played a role in his leaving. You intellectually know that it was not your fault, but as you remember your father leaving, it *feels* or *seems* as though you are to blame. This is because, at a heart level, you *believe* that it is your fault. You might believe that your father is leaving the family because there is something wrong with you. After you have identified a *tentative* reason for why you feel what you feel, double-check to make sure that you are still connected with your emotion by asking, "*How does this make me feel?*" Then, ask yourself again, "*Why do I feel this way?*"

It is important to note that these two questions are <u>not</u> asked in any particular order. They are not necessarily asked one after the other. Instead, the question, "How does that make you feel?" is asked after a statement of belief or memory content has been reported. And the question, "Why do you feel that way?" is asked in response to a stated emotion.

This part of the TPM Process is not as complicated as it may initially sound. You are searching for the belief that is responsible for what you currently feel while also examining the experience that convinced you that this belief is true. In other words, feel what you feel, remember what you've experienced, and acknowledge what you believe.

Continue this pattern of connecting with your emotion and attempting to determine why you feel that way until your description of what you believe or remember becomes repetitive. We refer to this repetition as "looping." (*Understanding the concept of "looping" is important as it will determine when to move to the next step in the Process.*) You will likely answer these two questions over and over long before your responses to them become repetitive and consistent.

In a ministry session where you are being mentored, this might look something like the following example. We will assume that the same memory has repeatedly come to your mind, and you are presently in the MEMORY Box. As was noted in the EMOTION Box, the number system in this example corresponds with the MEMORY Box Flowchart, which can be found at the back of the book. (As a reminder, "E" refers to the EMOTION Box and "M" refers to the MEMORY Box.)

In this particular example, we have underlined the various belief statements to make it easier to recognize when the Mentee begins to "loop" or repeat one of them.

Mentee: *"Again, that same memory of my ninth birthday came to mind. <u>My mom and dad were fighting right in front of me and my friends.</u>"* (M4)>(M6)

Mentor: *"How does that make you feel?"* (M3)

Mentee: *"I feel scared."* (M1)

Mentor: *"Why do you feel that way?"* (M2)

Mentee: *"Because <u>my mom was really furious with my dad.</u>"* (M4) > (M6)

Mentor: *"How does that make you feel?"* (M3)

Mentee: *"Nervous and afraid."* (M1)

Mentor: *"Why do you feel nervous and afraid?"* (M2)

Mentee: *"<u>Because of the way she was acting. I remember her yelling and screaming at him. I couldn't figure out why she was so angry. It came out of nowhere</u>!"* (M4) > (M6)

Mentor: *"How does that make you feel?"* (M3)

Mentee: *"I feel really uneasy and nervous and a little embarrassed. I felt so helpless."* (M1)

Mentor: *"Why do you feel that way?"* (M2)

Mentee: *"<u>Because I don't know what she is going to do next.</u>"* (M4) > (M6)

Mentor: *"How does that make you feel?"* (M3)

Mentee: *"I feel really helpless."* (M1)

Mentor: *"Why do you feel helpless?"* (M2)

Mentee: *"<u>Because I am powerless to do anything to make her stop</u>"."* (M4) > (M6)

Mentor: *"How does that make you feel?"* (M3)

Mentee: *"Like I said, I feel helpless <u>because I'm completely powerless. I can't make her stop.</u>"* (M4) > (M5)

In this example, the Mentee stayed connected with emotion and worked through a memory searching for *why* he felt what he felt (the person's belief). The Mentor helped the Mentee accomplish this by asking the appropriate questions at the appropriate times. Towards the end of the example, the Mentee repeatedly expressed that he believed he was "powerless." This repetitive statement of belief is exactly what we are looking for. While in the MEMORY Box, you will continually refocus on what you feel and examine why you feel that way until you have repeatedly expressed what you <u>believe</u>.

Until this repetition occurs, your Mentor will continue to ask either "How does that make you feel?" or "Why do you feel this way?" depending on your most recent response. If your most recent response was a description of what you believe or remember, then your Mentor will ask, "How does that make you feel?" And if you most recently described what you feel, then he or she will ask, "Why do you feel that way?" Again, continue to focus on what you feel and articulate reasons for why you feel that way until your <u>belief</u> statement begins to "loop" or repeat.

Repeatedly Answering the Same Question Without "Looping"

It is common to answer the same question over and over again while in the MEMORY Box. But just because you have repeatedly answered the same question <u>does not</u> mean that you are looping. This is important to understand because if you are asked the question, "How does that make you feel?" multiple times in a row, it may initially seem as though your Mentor is not paying attention or does not know what he is doing. But this is not the case (hopefully)! Rather, he is simply asking whichever question is most appropriate based upon your most recent response. He will continue to do this until you have offered the same repetitive explanation of <u>why</u> you feel what you feel.

Below is an example of what it might look like to answer the same question over and over again without "looping." Here again, we have emphasized the belief statements (by underlining them) to show that the Mentee is not yet "looping" despite the fact that the Mentor asks the same question again and again.

Mentee: *"<u>I remember how he used to look at me during family get-togethers.</u>" (M4) > (M6)*

Mentor: *"How does that make you feel?" (M3)*

Mentee: *"Very uncomfortable. <u>It was as though he wanted me to know that he saw me.</u>" (M4) > (M6)*

Mentor: *"How does that make you feel?" (M3)*

Mentee: *"I feel exposed. <u>I couldn't escape the situation.</u>" (M4) > (M6)*

Mentor: *"How does that make you feel?" (M3)*

Mentee: *"It seems like <u>I'm trapped.</u>" (M4) > (M6)*

Mentor: *"How does that make you feel?" (M3)*

Mentee: *"<u>Out of control. I couldn't make him stop doing that.</u>" (M4) > (M6)*

Mentor: *"How does that make you feel?" (M3)*

Mentee: *"I feel like <u>I wasn't protected. My parents were there, and they didn't help me.</u>" (M4) > (M6)*

Mentor: *"How does that make you feel? (M3)*

In this scenario, the Mentor asked, *"How does that make you feel?"* six times in a row, but the Mentee had still not begun to "loop." Again, you are not "looping" until your description of *why* you feel what you feel begins to repeat. This typically occurs in response to the question, "Why do you feel that way?" but regardless of which question is asked, you are only "looping" if your <u>description of belief</u> (*your explanation for why you feel what you feel*) becomes repetitive.

Repeatedly Describing the Same Emotion Without "Looping"

It is also possible for you to feel the same specific emotion during your entire time in the MEMORY Box. This is perfectly fine. Remember, your first objective is to simply remain connected to what you feel (whatever that may be). Properly identifying <u>what</u> you feel is nowhere near as important as determining <u>why</u> you feel it. You are looking for the belief that is producing what you feel. So, even if your description of *what you feel* sounds repetitive, it does not mean that you are "looping." Consider the following example of what this might look like in a TPM session. (*Again, pay close attention to the Mentee's belief statements.*)

Mentee: "*I remember walking around the grocery store with my family as a child. I got distracted by all the cereal boxes and then suddenly realized that my family had left. I ran up and down the aisles of the store looking for my parents.*" (M4)>(M6)

Mentor: "*How does that make you feel?*" (M3)

Mentee: "*I feel scared...panicked.*" (M1)

Mentor: "*Why do you feel that way?*" (M2)

Mentee: "*Because I wasn't sure if I was going to be able to find them. I was lost and all by myself!*" (M4)>(M6)

Mentor: "*How does that make you feel?*" (M3)

Mentee: "*I feel really afraid.*" (M1)

Mentor: "*Why do you feel that way?*" (M2)

Mentee: "*Because I thought that they might have left me at the store. I really felt like I was all alone.*" (M4) > (M6)

Mentor: "*How does that make you feel?*" (M3)

Mentee: "*Like I said, I feel really afraid.*" (M1)

Mentor: "*Why do you feel afraid?*" (M2)

Mentee: "*Because I didn't know what to do.*" (M4) > (M5)

Mentor: "*How does that make you feel?*" (M3)

Mentee: "*I feel scared...very afraid.*" (M1)

In this example, the Mentee reported feeling "scared" and "afraid" multiple times in a row, but his explanation for <u>why</u> he felt scared and afraid was different each time. Because of this, the Mentee is not yet "looping." This is very common, especially when you are new to applying the Process of TPM. But again, just because you offer the same repetitive explanation of <u>what</u> you feel does not mean that you are "looping."

In summary, you may repeatedly answer the same question and describe what you feel or believe over and over again, but if the explanation for <u>why</u> you feel what you feel is not repetitive, you are not yet "looping." When the description of what you <u>believe and/or remember</u> begins to "loop" or repeat, you are ready for the next step in the MEMORY Box: the *"looping"* question.

RECOGNIZING BELIEF STATEMENTS

Most of the time, your description of what you believe will be obvious. Statements such as, "I wasn't as smart as the other kids," "My sister always got all the attention," "I thought I was going to die in that crash," or "It didn't seem like God cared that I was hurting," all clearly describe what you remember and believe. But occasionally, you may find that you describe what you believe by starting your sentence with words that tend to explain how you feel. For instance, you may say something like, "I feel like I am all alone," "It felt like the whole situation was out of control," "I feel like nobody cares about me." Although they begin with words like "feel" and "felt," each of these statements describe what you believe, not what you feel.

This may initially seem confusing when you are first becoming familiar with the TPM Process. But as you practice and gain experience, recognizing these more subtle belief statements will become more intuitive. If you offer this type of response while in the MEMORY Box with the support of a knowledgeable Mentor, he or she will likely ask, "How does that make you feel?" For example, "How does believing that you are all alone make you feel?" or "How does it make you feel to believe that nobody cares about you?"

Though this is not a hard and fast rule, there is a clue that may help you to discern whether a statement describes a belief rather than an emotion. For example, statements such as, "*I feel like no one loves me,*" "*I feel as though no one cares about me,*" or "*I feel like I am trapped,*" are more descriptive of belief than emotion even though they include the word "feel." Whenever you (or someone else) describe something that "feels like _____" or "feels as though _____," it is likely a statement of belief rather than an emotion.

Part Two

The "Looping" Question

"Why does believing that make you feel what you feel?"

The *"looping" question* is the last question in the MEMORY Box. It essentially asks, *"Why does believing what you believe cause you to feel what you feel?"* It invites you to re-examine the explanation you gave for why you feel what you feel. It is typically asked when your description of what you <u>believe or remember</u> begins to "loop" or repeat. (Again, the "looping" has to do with belief and memory content, not statements of emotion or the questions that are asked.)

An example of "looping" while in the MEMORY Box:

Mentee: *"She grabbed my arm, looked me right in the eyes, and said, 'Wow! I can't wrap my fingers all the way around your wrist. That means you are really fat!' I didn't know what to do or say in response. I just stood there as she giggled and then ran off."* (M4)>(M6)

Mentor: *"How does that make you feel?"* (M3)

Mentee: *"I feel terrible...ashamed and embarrassed."* (M1)

Mentor: *"Why do you feel that way?"* (M2)

Mentee: *"Because I thought she was my friend. But that was a really hurtful thing to say!"* (M4) > (M6)

Mentor: *"How does that make you feel?"* (M3)

Mentee: *"The same...ashamed and embarrassed."* (M1)

Mentor: *"Why do you feel ashamed and embarrassed?"* (M2)

Mentee: *"Because my supposed friend just called me fat in front of the other 5th grade girls."* (M4) > (M6)

Mentor: *"How does that make you feel?"* (M3)

Mentee: *"Like I said...ashamed and embarrassed."* (M1)

Mentor: *"Why do you feel that way?"* (M2)

Mentee: *"Because she called me fat in front of all my friends."* (M4) > (M5) *(The underlined statement of belief/memory content has begun to repeat. This "looping" indicates that the "looping" question should be asked next.)*

Mentor: *"Why does that make you feel ashamed and embarrassed?"* (M8) *(Notice the simplified wording of the question. This is done to better fit the context of what the Mentee has said while retaining the original meaning and intent of the question.)*

In the previous scenario, the Mentee repeatedly expressed that she felt ashamed and embarrassed because of what her 5th-grade friend had said to her. The exact words were not used every single time, but she was clearly describing the same thing over and over again. Even though her emotions remained constant throughout, she was not "looping" until her explanation for *why* she felt what she was feeling became repetitive.

Also, notice that her explanation was not a description of heart belief (self-identity or state of being), but rather, it was an example of memory content (what she believes she has experienced). Nevertheless, it was a tentative explanation for why she feels what she feels that was expressed several times in a row. This would be considered "looping." Statements such as "she called me fat in front of all my friends" is not a description of _what_ she is feeling, it is her attempt at describing _why_ she feels what she is feeling. It is a statement of belief.

While in the MEMORY Box, you continue your search until you begin to "loop" with any form of belief. Again, when your explanation for _why_ you feel what you feel becomes repetitive, it is time to ask the *"looping"* question.

The *"looping"* question essentially invites you to dig a bit deeper while you search for a belief that explains why you feel what you feel. Ask yourself, *"Why does believing _____ make me feel _____?"* For example, *"Why does believing that I'm trapped and can't get away make me feel anxious and scared?"* In response, you may think, *"Because I'm trapped. Duh!"* But you could have just as easily replied with a different response like, *"If I can't get away, I will die."* or, *"Because I am going to get caught. They are going to find me."* or even, *"Because I am all alone and by myself."* However you respond to it, the *"looping"* question helps you to either move in the right direction or verify that you are doing so already.

Answering Both Questions at Once

Occasionally, you may find that you respond to either of the first two MEMORY Box questions by answering both of them at the same time. For example, responses like, "I feel scared because I thought I was going to die," or "I felt all alone because they left me in the car by myself" expresses what you feel as well as what you believe and remember. This is another appropriate time at which the *"looping" question* is asked.

Below is an example of this:

Mentee: "I remember seeing my dad enter the room. He seemed so angry!" (M4) > (M6)

Mentor: *"How does that make you feel?" (M3)*

Mentee: *"Scared! He began hitting my mother. I thought he was going to kill her. I feel terrified even thinking about it!" (M4) + (M1) (This response describes both how the person feels, "scared, terrified", and what they believe or remember.)*

Mentor: *"Why does believing that your dad was going to kill her make you feel terrified?" (M8)*

Another example of the *"looping" question* being asked in response to the Mentee answering both of the other MEMORY Box questions at once:

Your Thought: *"I can still remember the hateful smirk on her face after she said that to me!" (M4) > (M6)*

Ask Yourself: *"How does that make me feel?" (M3)*

Your Response: *"Belittled. Unimportant." (M4) > (M6)*

Ask Yourself: *"How does believing that I am belittled and unimportant make me feel?" (M3)*

Your Response: *"I feel miserable...sad...unwanted...like I am nothing...like I don't matter to anyone." (M4) + (M1) (The person has described both emotion and belief.)*

Ask Yourself: *"Why does believing that make me feel sad and miserable?" (M8) (Notice how the question included the word "that" in place of the beliefs that were identified. This is often helpful when the description of belief is lengthy or complicated. This can also be done with the emotions that are described. For example, "Why does believing that I am unwanted make me feel this way?")*

Why You Believe What You Believe

The third objective of the MEMORY Box is to determine why you believe what you believe. And although it is a crucially important step, it is typically accomplished automatically during your search for what you believe as you work through your memory. You are essentially looking for the circumstance that explains how you came to believe what you currently believe. It may seem overly complicated at first, but it really is as simple as this: you feel what you feel because of what you believe, and you believe what you believe because of what you have experienced.

To illustrate this concept, consider the following examples:

Mark feels panicked at work because he interprets the situation through his beliefs, "I am powerless and helpless." And he believes that he is powerless and helpless because, when he was nine years old, he accidentally let his dog escape their fenced-in yard, and it chased an elderly lady back into her house, and he had no way to stop it.

Sasha feels uncomfortable and nervous whenever her husband approaches her intimately because she interprets these moments through her beliefs, "I am dirty and shameful." And she believes that she is dirty and shameful because of what her uncle did to her when she was eleven.

Trent feels anxious as he walks on stage for his band's performance because he interprets the experience through his belief, "I am not good enough." And he believes that he is not good enough because his childhood piano teacher would strictly scold him for the mistakes he would make during practice.

Hannah feels empty and depressed when thinking about living alone because she interprets her circumstance through the belief, "I am unlovable." And she believes that she was unlovable because she was passed around in the foster care system throughout her childhood.

In each of these cases, the person's experience explains why they believe what they believe. These experiences are what persuaded each person to believe what he or she believes. This explanation would be naturally expressed as they worked through the MEMORY Box. Because of this, your third objective in the MEMORY Box is almost always accomplished as you are determining *what* you believe.

MEMORY'S PURPOSE IN THE TPM PROCESS

As a reminder, the purpose of remembering past events in the context of a TPM session is not to determine the validity, authenticity, or accuracy of what may have happened in the past. We are focused on very specific tasks throughout the Process of TPM, but it is never our goal to determine what happened to us, why it happened, who was involved, what their motives were, when it occurred, how often it occurred, etc. This type of information may be helpful in other contexts, but it is never the focus or priority in a TPM session.

When applying the TPM Process, you are essentially focused on acknowledging what you believe and inviting the Holy Spirit to persuade you of the truth. While in the MEMORY Box, you are simply trying to determine *what* you believe and *why* you believe it. That's it! You can accomplish these basic tasks regardless of the "accuracy" or "thoroughness" of your memory. Again, you are focused on identifying what you believe, not on determining the "facts" regarding what may or may not have happened. Because of this, it is never necessary or appropriate to try to determine the "truth" of what may or may not have happened in the past while in a TPM session. You are free to do what you want in other contexts, but while applying the Process of TPM, follow protocol.

Part Three

After Answering the "Looping" Question

As you will recall, the "looping" question is asked when you become repetitive in your description of what you believe while in the MEMORY Box. This obviously includes your description of what you believe about yourself, your situation, and God, but it also includes all other forms of belief, such as your assumptions regarding other people's motives, the conclusions you drew from previous experiences, and your memory content itself (since it represents what you *believe* you have experienced). If your description of belief-related content becomes repetitive, *the "looping" question* should be asked.

Sometimes your response to the *"looping" question* may be <u>different</u> from your repetitive responses to the previous MEMORY Box questions (Flowchart - M9). No matter how you respond, if your response to the "looping" question is different from the repetitive responses you gave moments before, go back to using the other MEMORY Box questions while you search for belief and stay connected to your emotion. Continue this pattern until your response to the *"looping" question* is the same as your repetitive responses to the other MEMORY Box questions (Flowchart - M12).

To illustrate this, consider the following example:

Mentee: *"I remember waiting for my turn to read. I was shaking." (M4) > (M6)*

Mentor: *"How does that make you feel? (M3)*

Mentee: *"Scared and stressed-out." (M1)*

Mentor: *"Why do you feel scared and stressed-out?" (M2)*

Mentee: *"Because all the other kids were able to read without pausing and correcting themselves all the time. I always messed it up." (M4) > (M6)*

Mentor: *"How does that make you feel?" (M3)*

Mentee: *"I feel like there is something wrong with me." (M4) > (M6)*

Mentor: *"How does that make you feel?" (M3)*

Mentee: *"I feel embarrassed. It's like there is something wrong with me." (M4) > (M5)*

Because the Mentee's responses to the questions have become repetitive ("there is something wrong with me"), the Mentor asks the "looping" question.

Mentor: *"Why does believing that there is something wrong with you make you feel that way?" (M8)*

Mentee: *"Because I can't do this simple task. I feel like I'll never be able to do it." (M9) > (M10) > (M4)*

Notice that the Mentee's response to the "looping" question is different from the repetitive "there is something wrong with me" response. Because of this, the Mentee's search continues, and the Mentor helps by asking the other MEMORY Box questions.

Mentor: *"How does it make you feel to believe that you will never be able to do it?" (M3)*

Mentee: *"I feel ashamed." (M1)*

Mentor: *"Why do you feel ashamed?" (M2)*

Mentee: *"Because, apparently, I'm stupid." (M4) > (M6)*

Mentor: *"How does that make you feel?" (M3)*

Mentee: *"Embarrassed and ashamed." (M1)*

Mentor*: "Why do you feel embarrassed and ashamed?" (M2)*

Mentee: *"Because I am stupid." (M4) > (M5)*

At this point, the Mentee's responses have become repetitive again, which means that it is time for the "looping" question to be asked.

Mentor: *"Why does believing that you are stupid make you feel embarrassed and ashamed?" (M8)*

Mentee: *"Because that is what I am; I am stupid." (M12)*

In this instance, the Mentee responded to the *"looping" question* with the <u>same</u> belief statement that was repeated before this question was asked (M5) > (M8) > (M12). Because of this confirmed repetition, the next step is to determine whether or not the Mentee's response fits the definition of *lie-based heart belief.*

Defining "heart belief"

As a reminder, *heart belief* consists of everything we believe in our hearts. It is the essence of our faith. As we learned in an earlier chapter, each example of *heart belief* either reflects the perception we have of ourselves (*Self-Identity*) or of God and His involvement in our lives (*State of Being*). Basically, the two categories of lie-based heart belief answer the questions, "Who am I?" and "Who is God?"

When we have been convinced at a heart level of who we are in Christ and how intimately involved God is in our lives, we will rest in His finished work and enjoy bearing His fruit. However, not all that we have been persuaded to believe in our hearts is true. Some of our heart beliefs are lie-based; this is the part of our faith that needs to be refined. But before these impurities can be removed, they must first be exposed and acknowledged.

Again, examples of a lie-based *"Self-Identity" heart belief* may include: *"I am worthless," "I am stupid," "I am defective," "I am unlovable,"* or *"There is something wrong with me."* This type of *heart belief* defines who and what we believe we are. It pertains to our identity, purpose, value, character, and so on. The Lord desires to convince our hearts of the truth regarding each of these attributes.

The other category of *heart belief* is referred to as a *"State of Being" heart belief.* It describes our perceived surroundings, condition, environment, and status. Our perception of what is happening in our life reveals our view and understanding of God's involvement. When we lack God's perspective of our situation or fail to see His involvement in our lives, we tend to misunderstand our condition.

For example, if I have been deceived into believing that *I am alone*, this indicates that I have not yet been fully convinced that the Lord is omnipresent and with me *"even to the end of the age..."* (Matthew 28:20). How could I simultaneously be convinced in my heart that *God is with me* and that *I am alone*? If God is always with me, then I can never be alone. What if I believed that *my situation was out of control*? Then I do not yet fully believe that God is in control and causing *"all things to work together for the good..."* (Rom. 8:28). Our understanding of God and His involvement shapes our perception of the world in which we live. As such, it is vital for this type of *heart belief* to accurately reflect the truth.

Repetitive Non-Heart Belief Responses

As you work through the MEMORY Box, you will likely report belief statements that do not fit the definition of *lie-based heart belief*. For instance, your belief statement may reflect the definition of a *truth-based problem* (which we will discuss momentarily). But you may also simply describe what you remember or divulge your own assumptions and conclusions such as, "My dad was never happy with me," "Nothing I ever did was good enough for them," "She never believed anything that I ever said," "None of the other kids wanted to be with me," "They never wanted me on their team," "They hated me," or "My mother did not protect me from what he was doing to me." None of these kinds of statements fit the definition of *lie-based heart belief* for a few different reasons.

First, as terrible as it may sound, each of them is *potentially* true. You may have genuinely been unwanted by your parents; they may have truly been disappointed in you, and the other kids at school may have hated you. Nevertheless, none of these beliefs (whether true or untrue) are the reason why you feel what you feel. You could still have peace in each of these scenarios and react to them with compassion and kindness if you were able to interpret them through the truth of who you are and who God is; this brings us to the second reason for why these beliefs are not *"heart beliefs."*

Second, none of the beliefs that are listed above describe your *self-identity* (who you are) or your *state of being* (a reflection of who God is and how He is involved in your life). They describe what seemed to have happened, offer context for what occurred, or potentially explain the motive of those involved, but they are not indicative of your heart belief. For if you fully believed in your heart the truth of who you are (self-identity) and who God is and how He is lovingly involved in your life (state of being), you would respond to each of these hypothetical scenarios by effortlessly exhibiting the fruit of His Spirit. Because emotions flow from our heart beliefs, it is safe to assume that these beliefs are not causing you to feel what you feel, and thus, are not the beliefs you are looking for.

That said, if you respond to the "looping" question with these kinds of statements, you will stay in the MEMORY Box and continue attempting to accomplish your objectives. Use the other MEMORY Box questions to help you focus on your feelings and identify your beliefs.

It should be noted that if you begin "looping" with these kinds of statements and then answer the "looping" question with these same repetitive responses, it probably means you don't yet fully know what you are doing. But hopefully, you are working with a Mentor who can explain this portion of the Process. Now, this is not a criticism of anyone, it is simply an observation. For if you truly knew what you were doing in the MEMORY Box, you would never answer the "looping" question with this type of response; that is, unless you had a lie-based reason to respond in this way. But we will discuss that concept in the SOLUTION Box chapter.

Part Four

When to Move from the MEMORY Box to the BELIEF Box

You might be tempted to run to the BELIEF box as soon as you discover a potential lie-based heart belief, and, without question, there are times when doing this *could* eventually result in the Spirit revealing His truth. But there will also be times where prematurely moving to the next Box causes unnecessary difficulty! The proper protocol to follow while in the MEMORY Box was designed to eliminate as much wasted time as possible and to put the full responsibility of the Process on you (the Mentee).

Once you have begun repeating yourself while describing what you believe, AND you answer the "looping" question with this same repetitive response, you then (and only then) examine the belief statement to figure out what kind of belief it is.

The <u>only</u> time you are ever concerned with whether or not a belief fits the definition of lie-based "heart belief" is when you respond to the "looping" question with the same repetitive response that you gave to the other "MEMORY Box" questions. Read the previous sentence again as it contains vital information concerning the TPM protocol. You should also carefully examine the MEMORY Box Flowchart (found at the end of this book) as it illustrates this part of the Process.

Even if you are convinced that the stated belief is a lie-based heart belief such as "I am worthless," or "I am trapped and going to die," you need to follow protocol until your stated belief starts "looping". When this occurs, you proceed by answering the "looping" question. If this belief statement continues to loop in response to the "looping" question, you are ready to determine if it meets the definition of a heart belief.

<u>If a lie-based belief that appears to fit the definition of "heart belief" comes to mind at ANY other point in a "TPM session," this fact has no impact on what you are to do at that moment.</u> For example, you might be in the EMOTION Box and claim that you are a "worthless piece of trash who is hated by God." Although this belief statement fits the definition of "heart belief," it should be treated like any other belief statement while in the EMOTION Box. Even though this belief clearly meets the definition of a heart belief, you are not yet ready to address it as such. You lack important information that is obtained by working through the MEMORY Box.

Even if you were able to determine *what* you believe, you cannot truly understand how you came to believe what you currently believe apart from examining what you remember from past experiences. So, even though you have voiced what seems to be a heart belief, you should remain in the EMOTION Box and follow the protocol for that box.

We realize this sounds (and is) repetitive, but even if you have identified a lie-based belief that seems to fit the definition of "heart belief," this alone <u>does not</u> mean that you are ready to move to the BELIEF Box. You have not yet begun to "loop" or repeat. <u>The **only** time you should be concerned about</u>

identifying heart belief is in the MEMORY Box and only after answering the *"looping" question* with a repetitive response. Again, the MEMORY Box Flowchart may help to make this part of the Process more clear. The protocols that are currently being discussed can be found on boxes (M4) > (M5) > (M8) > (M12) > (M13) > (M14).

IMPORTANT NOTE: When determining if a "looping" belief fits the definition of a lie-based *heart be-lief*, your goal is not to decipher whether it is specifically a statement of *Self-Identity* rather than *State of Being*, or vice versa. You are simply checking to see if it fits the more general definition of *heart belief*. *If it does,* you are ready to move from the MEMORY Box to the BELIEF Box.

WHY ALL THE "LOOPING?"

Some have asked, "Why is it so important to "loop" before moving to the BELIEF Box?" One of the primary reasons for this is that it ensures that you, the Mentee, are the one who determines when to move from one *Box* to another *Box*. The timing of this transition is not determined by your conscious choice or the direction of a Mentor (*which should never happen*). Rather, it is determined by the God-designed process of association. You do not move to the BELIEF Box until the same belief comes to mind several times (at least *twice* before answering the "looping" question and *once* in response to it).

This is similar to how you only move to the MEMORY Box after the same memory has come to your mind a couple times while in the EMOTION Box. Here again, this movement is based upon what your mind is automatically doing rather than your best guess or your Mentor's ill-informed "discernment." Your Mentor never knows what you need to focus on or remember, and it is very likely that you do not either (consciously, at least).

As we have previously discussed, throughout the TPM Process you are essentially slowing things down and deliberately taking notice of what your mind is naturally doing. It has already accessed what you have learned from previous experiences (recorded as memories) and used those beliefs to interpret your current situation. It has also produced what you currently feel and is guiding your current behavior. As you move through the Process, you are simply following this interpretive path in reverse. You are honestly acknowledging and taking responsibility for what you perceive, feel, and do for the purpose of identifying the beliefs that precede them. This is a passive process. You are merely taking notice of what is already happening.

That said, another important reason for "looping" is that it ensures a higher probability that you will not move to the BELIEF Box prematurely. For instance, if you mistakenly move to the BE-LIEF Box as soon as a potential *heart belief* shows up, it is very unlikely that this initial instance of belief is as refined and exact as it would be if you were to dig a little deeper. Because of this, you may unintentionally be moving forward with a belief that you don't actually believe. Or, at the very least, you will eventually be asking the Lord for truth without first fully acknowledging the actual lies you currently believe. This tends to have less than ideal results, whereby no truth is received and no transformation is evident.

As we will discuss later, you never really know if you have correctly identified a lie-based belief that you actually believe until you've asked for God's perspective and checked for evidence of a shift in your thinking. That said, you can move to the BELIEF Box with a bit more confidence if you spend adequate time in the previous Box and allow *association* to inform your decision to move forward. At its initial discovery, a lie-based heart belief may seem like it *might* be what you are looking for; but if you allow enough time for it to repeatedly come to your mind, it is much more probable that it *is* what you are looking for.

Moving to the BELIEF Box prematurely is especially problematic when it initially seems as though you feel what you feel because of a *truth-based problem*. For, as we will soon discuss, not all *perceived problems* that seem to be based upon the truth are actually *truth-based problems*. But it is only after taking a closer, more honest look at our heart beliefs that we discover the true source of our emotional pain.

Before moving to the BELIEF Box, you should identify what you believe (as accurately as possible) and honestly admit the experience that led you to believe it. Each of these objectives can sometimes seem as though they require a bit of digging, but it is worth spending a few extra moments in the MEMORY Box to avoid wasting time by moving to the BELIEF Box prematurely.

Examples Of Identifying heart belief In The MEMORY Box

Again, you leave the MEMORY Box to go to the BELIEF Box only after responding to the *"looping" question* with the same lie-based *heart belief* that you repeatedly stated before the *"looping" question* was asked. (*Referring to the Flowcharts can help you visualize these protocols.*)

The following are examples of a Mentee accomplishing the objectives of the MEMORY Box and a Mentor asking each of the MEMORY Box questions. We have emphasized the moments where a belief statement begins to "loop" or repeat by underlining them.

Mentee: *"I keep thinking about that time when my dad told me to watch over my little brother, but I got distracted, and he crawled all the way across the yard and into the street." (M4) > (M6)*

Mentor: *"How does that make you feel?" (M3)*

Mentee: *"I feel really bad about it." (M1)*

Mentor: *"Why do you feel that way?" (M2)*

Mentee: *"Because it was an important job, and I messed up. It could have ended really badly." (M4) > (M6)*

Mentor: *"How does that make you feel?" (M3)*

Mentee: *"I feel as though I am worthless...like I can't even be trusted with a simple task." (M4) > (M6)*

Mentor: *"How does that make you feel?" (M3)*

Mentee: *"It makes me feel really bad. Terrible even." (M1)*

Mentor: *"Why do you feel that way?" (M2)*

Mentee: *"Because <u>I am worthless</u>." (M4) > (M5) (The belief statement is "looping.")*

Mentor: *"Why does believing that you are worthless make you feel that way?" (M8)*

Mentee: *"Because that is what I am. <u>I am worthless</u>." (M12) > (M13) > (M14)*

The Mentee's belief statement began repeating and was reported again in response to the "looping" question. Since his belief statement fits the definition of "heart belief," he has accomplished the objectives in the MEMORY Box and is ready to move to the BELIEF Box.

Another example of someone in the MEMORY Box:

Mentee: *"I tried to push the door open, but it was locked. I couldn't get out of there. I was trapped in the basement!" (M4) > (M6)*

Mentor: *"How does that make you feel?" (M3)*

Mentee: *"I feel scared." (M1)*

Mentor: *"Why do you feel scared?" (M2)*

Mentee: *"Because I was alone down there. It was such a creepy place when we were kids." (M4) > (M6)*

Mentor: *"How does that make you feel?" (M3)*

Mentee: *"I feel nervous and scared." (M1)*

Mentor: *"Why do you feel that way?" (M2)*

Mentee: *"Because I don't think anyone can hear me banging on the door." (M4) > (M6)*

Mentor: *"And how does it make you feel to think that no one hears you?" (M3)*

Mentee: *"Scared. Terrified." (M1)*

Mentor: *"Why do you feel that way?" (M2)*

Mentee: *"Because <u>no one hears me</u>." (M4) > (M5) (This belief statement has begun to "loop.")*

Mentor: *"Why does believing that no one hears you make you feel scared?" (M8)*

Mentee: *"Because that means that <u>I am alone</u> down there." (M9) > (M10) > (M4) (different/ new)*

Mentor: *"How does that make you feel?" (M3)*

Mentee: *"Scared." (M1)*

Mentor: *"Why do you feel scared?" (M2)*

Mentee: *"Because <u>I am alone</u>." (M4) > (M5) (Now this belief statement is "looping.")*

Mentor: *"Why does believing that you are alone make you feel scared?" (M8)*

Mentee: *"I don't want to be alone down there, but I am. <u>I am alone</u>." (M12) > (M13) > (M14)*

Again, the Mentee has accomplished the MEMORY Box objectives and is now ready to move to the BELIEF Box.

QUESTIONS YOUR MENTOR SHOULD NEVER ASK

Remember, when working with a Mentor, you are the one who is applying the TPM Process. Your Mentor only needs a relatively small amount of information from you to be able to do their job. For instance, in the MEMORY Box, they need to know whether you are currently focused on what you are feeling or recalling what you have experienced. This will determine which questions they ask next.

However, a Mentor does not need to know information such as specific details of what happened, how old you were at the time of the experience, or the names and relationships of those involved. Because of this, they will only ask the questions that are outlined in the TPM protocol and never ask for this kind of information. For example, they should not ask questions such as "Do you think that...?" "What happened next?" "Who was there?" "Is it possible that...?" "Why do you think that happened?" "Was there an earlier time in which this happened?" etc.

Additionally, your Mentor should NEVER suggest or insinuate that you might have suffered abuse, experienced trauma, or survived some hardship of which you are unaware. Nor should they ever attempt to have you look for a "hidden" memory or search for something specific. It is never your Mentor's role, responsibility, or right to lead, direct, suggest, or "discern" anything in relation to what you may or may not have experienced.

Again, you are the one who is applying the TPM Process. This is your faith-refining journey with the Lord. Your Mentor is only there to help you learn the Three Elements of TPM and ensure that you are following protocol when applying the Process. Anything else falls outside of their role as a TPM "Mentor."

Part Five

Truth-based problems in the MEMORY Box

Sometimes your response to the "looping" question is the same repetitive response that you gave to the other MEMORY Box questions, but it does not fit the definition of *heart belief*. Rather than describing a lie that you believe about yourself, your situation, or God, the belief statement might describe a potential *truth-based problem*.

An example of this might include the following:

Mentee: *"I can still see the look on his face when he passed away." (M4) > (M6)*

Mentor: *"How does that make you feel?" (M3)*

Mentee: *"Deeply saddened..." (M1)*

Mentor: *"Why do you feel sad?" (M2)*

Mentee: *"Because I am sure that he did not yet know the Lord!" (M4) > (M6)*

Mentor: *"How does that make you feel?" (M3)*

Mentee: *"It makes me very sad." (M1)*

Mentor: *"And why do you feel that way?" (M2)*

Mentee: *"Because he died without knowing the Lord..." (M4) > (M5)*

Mentor: *"Why does believing that he died without knowing the Lord make you feel sad?" (M8)*

Mentee: *"Because that is sad! It makes his passing that much more difficult to know that he died without knowing Jesus!" (M12) > (M15) >(M16) > (M17)*

As you learned from our discussion of the "Belief and Emotion Principle," when we face *truth-based problems*, such as the reality of being victimized, the consequences of poor decisions, or the death of a loved one, we will feel some measure of *truth-based pain* in response. This is natural and expected. God feels badly about the truly bad things that happen, and we should too, but not forever.

Again, the presence of *truth-based pain* also indicates our need for God's perspective. We need Him to expand our limited perspective and convince us of His involvement and purpose in the midst of our difficult circumstances. We need Him to *open the eyes of our hearts,* so that we can see His eternal plan and intimate involvement in our lives. Until we are able to see and trust in His solutions to our *truth-based problems*, we will continue to feel *truth-based pain* in response. And we will be encumbered by the weight of this burden until we believe in our "hearts" that God is carrying it for us.

Another example of someone identifying a *truth-based problem* can be found below:

Mentee: *"I feel like I've forgiven my mom. She did the best that she could. But I still feel a heaviness when I think about all the years I spent in foster care because of her decisions." (M4) > (M6)*

Mentor: *"How does that make you feel?" (M3)*

Mentee: *"I feel like I had my childhood taken from me. At no fault of my own, I was taken from my family and moved from one bad situation to the next." (M4) > (M6)*

Mentor: *"How does it make you feel to think that you had your childhood taken from you?" (M3)*

Mentee: *"It makes me feel sad and disappointed...almost as though I am grieving the loss of the childhood that I never had." (M4) + (M1) (This response describes both how the person feels and what they believe or remember.)*

Mentor: *"Why does believing that you are grieving the loss of your childhood make you feel sad and disappointed?" (M8)*

Mentee: *"Because it is sad that I was robbed of my childhood!" (M12) > (M15) >(M16) > (M17)*

In this example, the Mentee identified a potentially truth-based *perceived problem*. This person needs the Holy Spirit to persuade his heart to believe the greater truth of His involvement, but first, he needs to be sure that he is not attempting to "solve" it himself. More often than not, after we become aware of painful truths, many days, weeks, or even years pass before we gain God's perspective of our situation. In the interim, we almost always become convinced that we should hold onto these truth-based burdens.

We become deceived into believing that we can *solve* or alleviate some *perceived problem* by holding onto our *truth-based pain*. For instance, we may continue to grieve because we have been deceived into believing that doing so maintains our connection with those we've lost; we might hold onto our disappointments to motivate us to do better next time; we may even believe that continually bearing sadness ensures that we receive attention, affirmation, and comfort.

If your repetitive statement of belief (following the "looping" question) appears to describe a *truth-based problem*, your next move IS NOT to the BELIEF Box, but rather, to the SOLUTION Box. You do this to determine if your ongoing *truth-based pain* is present because you are engaged in a *solution behavior*. You might be surprised to discover how often our *truth-based pain* is only present because we believe a lie about it. This is not always the case, but it is always a likely possibility!

As we will discuss later, if you are holding onto truth-based pain because you believe doing so will help you "solve" a problem, you need God's perspective regarding this decision. Until you see the reasoning behind your behavior through His eyes, you are *unlikely* to change what you are doing, and you will continue to feel the weight of your painful burden.

Do not be discouraged if this feels a little confusing! We will elaborate more on the topic of *truth-based problems* in the context of a TPM session when we discuss the SOLUTION Box. Until then, we strongly encourage you to review the chapters where we discuss the *Fundamental Principles of TPM* and revisit the concepts of *truth-based problems*, *truth-based pain,* and *solutions*.

WHEN TRUTH-BASED PAIN IS NOT TRUTH-BASED PAIN

Just because you feel an emotion that is typically associated with *truth-based problems* (such as sadness, grief, disappointment, regret, anger, etc.) it doesn't mean it is actually truth-based pain. For instance, it may seem as though you feel disappointed because your friend was late to your scheduled lunch get-together, when in reality, their tardiness has simply exposed the fact that you believe in your heart that you are not important. In this case, your emotional reaction is based upon a *lie-based heart belief*. What initially seemed like *truth-based pain* was actually *lie-based pain*.

Let's look at an example of this in the context of a TPM session (the scenario will begin with the Mentee in the MEMORY Box).

Mentee: *"I keep recalling the night my parents died. I was too young at the time to fully understand what had happened. But I vividly remember my aunt sobbing the whole way home from the hospital." (M4) > (M6)*

Mentor: *"How does that make you feel?" (M3)*

Mentee: *"I feel really sad." (M1)*

Now, at this point, you may be thinking, *"She feels sad in response to this terrible truth-based problem, so this must be truth-based pain."* But, as we discussed earlier, it is important to continue working through the MEMORY Box until your statement of belief begins to "loop" or repeat and then answer the "looping" question. This scenario will hopefully shed more light on why that is...

Mentor: *"Why do you feel sad?" (M2)*

Mentee: *"It upset me to see her crying like that. She kept saying that we were all going to be ok, but I knew that something was really wrong! Something bad had happened." (M4) > (M6)*

Mentor: *"How does that make you feel?" (M3)*

Mentee: *"It makes me feel really sad and uneasy." (M1)*

Mentor: *"And why do you feel that way?" (M2)*

Mentee: *"Because I could tell by the way my aunt was acting that something really bad had happened. I had never seen her so shaken before that night."* (M4) > (M5)

Mentor: *"Why does believing that something bad happened make you feel sad and uneasy?"* (M8) (The "looping" question)

Mentee: *"Because I wasn't sure that my little brother and I were going to be ok. I wanted to know that we were safe. But, based upon my grieving aunt's outbursts, I thought that we might be in some kind of danger."* (M9) > (M10) > (M4) > (M6)

Mentor: *"How does that make you feel?"* (M3)

Mentee: *"I feel vulnerable."* (M1)

Mentor: *"Why do you feel vulnerable?"* (M2)

Mentee: *"Because I believed that my brother and I were in danger."* (M4) > (M5)

Mentor: *"Why does believing that you and your brother were in danger make you feel vulnerable?"* (M8)

Mentee: *"Because we were in danger! Or, at least, I thought that we were."* (M12) > (M13) >(M14)

Notice how the Mentee moved from claiming to feel sad in response to her parents' death and her aunt's emotional reaction to reporting that she felt vulnerable because she believed that she and her brother were in danger. What initially seemed as though it could have been *truth-based pain* turned out to be the emotional consequence of believing a lie (the *lie-based state of being heart belief*: "we are in danger").

Remember, the feeling itself is never what qualifies an emotion as *truth-based pain*. Rather, the belief that is producing what is felt is the deciding factor. Since her emotion was an outcome of a *lie-based heart belief*, it is not considered to be *truth-based pain*. But she would not have known this if she decided not to follow protocol while in the MEMORY Box.

The MEMORY Box in Review

After the same memory has repeatedly come to your mind while focusing on what you feel in the EMOTION Box, you go to the MEMORY Box. There you maintain your connection to what you feel as you search for what you believe. You look for what *feels* or *seems* true as you work through the memory that came to your mind. When the same belief begins to repeatedly come to mind, ask yourself the "looping" question, *"Why does believing this make me feel what I feel?"* If you respond to this "looping" question with something new or different, stay in the MEMORY Box and continue processing. If, however, you respond to the "looping" question with the same repetitive belief, and it fits the definition of a lie-based *heart belief*, you are ready to move to the BELIEF Box.

The MEMORY Box in Reality

In a real TPM session, you may be able to seamlessly accomplish your objectives while in the MEMORY Box, but this is not always the case. As we will discuss in a later chapter, *"solutions"* can pop up at any time while working through the MEMORY Box. You may notice that you have trouble staying connected with your emotion or staying focused on what you remember. You may discover that you feel angry in response to the experiences that you have recalled. You may respond to the *"looping" question* with a statement that does not fit the definition of a lie-based *"heart belief."* Or you may even discover that the emotion you feel is potentially *"truth-based pain"* that relates to some *"truth-based problems."*

There are numerous scenarios that could take place. If you find yourself in any of these situations, your next step is likely <u>not</u> to go to the BELIEF Box. These scenarios will be addressed in later chapters, but for now, to keep things simple, let's assume that you stayed connected to your emotion, identified a lie-based *heart belief,* and determined why you believe it so that we can discuss the *BELIEF Box.*

CHAPTER 15

THE BELIEF BOX

The Mentee's Objective While in the BELIEF Box

1) Determine if you currently believe the lie-based belief that you identified in the previous "Box."

The BELIEF Box Question:

"Not that it is true, but does it feel or seem true that…?"

A Preview of The BELIEF Box

Your only task while in the BELIEF Box is to determine if you currently believe the lie-based belief that you identified in the previous "*Box*." This establishes a point of comparison that you will use in the TRANSFORMATION Box to determine if the Holy Spirit has convinced you of the truth. If you confirm that you believe the lie that you've identified, then you are ready to move to the TRUTH Box. If, however, you determine that you do not truly believe it, then you return to the EMOTION Box.

"Determining If the Lie Feels True"

In order to accomplish your objective in the BELIEF Box, you will need to take an honest look at the lie-based belief that you identified in the previous "Box" (*either the MEMORY Box or the SOLUTION Box, depending on the context*). As you will recall, if you are convinced in your heart that something is true, it will *seem* or *feel* true to you even when you intellectually know that it is not. Because of this, if the belief *feels* or *seems* true, then you believe it to be true. If it doesn't, then you don't believe it. It really is that simple.

So, you are not attempting to determine if the lie *is* true or *was* true, but rather if it currently *feels* or *seems* true. You are not determining if the belief reflects what you may logically know to be true, what the "correct answer" is, or even what Scripture says. You are only concerned with whether or not the belief *feels*, *seems,* or *appears* to be true to you at this moment.

This task is more akin to *feeling* or *sensing* for something than it is to deciphering something or figuring something out. You are simply taking a careful look to see if the lie-based belief that you identified is reflected in what you feel and experience.

For this reason, the BELIEF Box question is worded, "*Not that it is true, but does it feel or seem true that* ____?" It is meant to remind you of what you <u>are</u> and <u>are not</u> looking for in the BELIEF Box. You are attempting to determine whether or not you actually believe the lie that you have identified. If it *feels* or *seems* true, then the answer is "*yes!*" which indicates that you currently *believe* it to be true.

Some examples of how you might ask yourself this question could be:

"*Not that it is true, but does it feel or seem true that I am worthless?*"

"*Not that it is true, but does it feel or seem true that I am abandoned and alone?*"

Or, if you are in a TPM session with a Mentor:

"*Not that it is true, but does it feel or seem true that you are a defect?*"

"*Not that it is true, but does it feel or seem true that you are going to die?*"

Establishing a Baseline

While in the BELIEF Box your objective is to determine if you actually believe the lie-based belief you have identified in the previous box (either the MEMORY Box or the SOLUTION Box). You will probably rationally know that it is not true. Your task is not to determine what *is* true, but rather, what *feels* or *seems* true. Confirming that you do believe this lie-based belief will give you a point of comparison or baseline to use later in the TRANSFORMATION Box.

Establishing this baseline for comparison is the fundamental purpose of the BELIEF Box. Because of this, it is important to accurately document it. Doing so will provide an accurate record and reference; otherwise, you have no reliable way of testing for genuine transformation. For example, if you confirmed that you believe the lie, "*I am worthless,*" but after inviting the Lord to reveal His perspective, you compared the belief with something slightly different such as, "*I have no value,*" this may result in an unreliable test. Although these thoughts may seem similar, their meanings may or may not be identical. Because of this, if you are applying the Process of TPM by yourself (especially if you are just starting out), you are encouraged to write down the belief before moving to the TRUTH Box.

If you are working with a Mentor, he or she should write down the belief exactly as you describe it to ensure that the test applied for transformation is reliable. If the coming test is to be reliable, you obviously have to check the same belief that you are currently focused on. Any variation in its wording could influence the test's results. The question asked in the TRANSFORMATION Box is the only test you have for determining if you received truth from the Spirit or not. (*We will discuss this in greater detail when we get to the TRANSFORMATION Box chapter.*)

"But I know the Bible says..."

Don't be surprised if it seems counterintuitive or feels a little strange the first few times you try to accomplish the objective of the BELIEF Box. Attempting to identify what *feels* or *seems* true to you can initially seem counterproductive, especially if you have been taught to deny such things, and focus your attention on the truth. You will likely know the truth intellectually and recognize that the belief you have identified is not true. But again, you are not looking for what IS true but what FEELS true. This is why the BELIEF Box question is worded, "*Not that it is true, but does it feel or seem true that. . .?*"

Many of us have been misled to believe that it does not matter what feels or seems true to us and that outward obedience is of utmost importance. As the old hymn proclaims, we are expected to "Trust and obey! For there's no other way. . ." We may intellectually know that our current perspective and emotional state are not based upon the truth, but this does not change the impact that our heart belief has on us. Unless our beliefs are addressed, we will continue to suffer the consequences of our deception.

In spite of this, when asked the BELIEF Box question, some people will quote Bible verses that they have memorized or recite what is obviously or logically true in an attempt to disprove a lie that they believe. And although these behaviors may be acceptable and beneficial in other contexts, this is not needed or helpful in a TPM session. They are attempts at solving the very problem that God is patiently waiting to address.

Rather than attempting to convince yourself of the truth, own and acknowledge what you do believe and then invite the Holy Spirit to do the convincing. This is essentially what we are seeking to accomplish in a *TPM session*. Again, if you could honestly convince yourself to believe the truth, wouldn't you have done so already? (*Revisit our discussion of the "Belief and Persuasion" Principle for more on this topic.*)

In a sense, being in the BELIEF Box is like visiting a confessional booth. The New Testament word often translated "to confess" is *"homologéō"* which simply means "to agree with and openly acknowledge something," or even more literally it means to come into alignment with another and share the same perspective. When we openly declare and agree with God regarding what He has exposed (the lies we believe), we position ourselves to receive His perspective. We are basically saying, "God, I agree with you that I am deceived and lack an eternal perspective. Please bring my belief into alignment with your truth."

The BELIEF Box in Review

After you identify a lie-based belief in either the MEMORY Box or the SOLUTION Box, you will go to the BELIEF Box. Your only objective here is to establish a "baseline" by determining if the identified belief is actually believed. If the belief *feels* or *seems* to be true, go to the TRUTH Box. If it doesn't *feel* or *seem* true, go back to the EMOTION Box.

The BELIEF Box in Reality

When you understand what you are trying to accomplish in the BELIEF Box, it becomes one of the simplest parts of the TPM Process. You will likely find that it only takes a few moments to determine if the identified lie-based belief feels or seems true. However, there may be times when the lie-based belief that was identified in the previous Box does not initially *feel* or *seem* true to you. This is especially common when you are new to applying the *TPM Process*. It may seem difficult or counterintuitive to own and admit that you believe things that you intellectually know to be untrue. When this is the case, take a moment to reassess the belief. Even if it only feels a little true, that means you still partially believe it. And if you only partially believe a lie, you are still deceived. Remember, your objective is to determine if you believe the lie you have identified. If it feels or seems true at all, then, at some level, you believe that it is true.

However, if after double-checking the belief, the lie does <u>not</u> appear to *feel* or *seem* true, do <u>not</u> go to the TRUTH Box; instead, go back to the EMOTION Box (examples of this will be included in a later chapter). This scenario may potentially occur if you somehow went to the BELIEF Box prematurely or simply failed to rightly identify a lie that you do believe. This can be the result of a *solution behavior* (which will be addressed in a later chapter). For now, let's assume that you have verified that the lie-based belief does *feel* or *seem* true and move on to the TRUTH Box.

CHAPTER 16

THE TRUTH BOX

The Mentee's Objectives While in the TRUTH Box

1) Invite the Holy Spirit to persuade you of the truth.
2) Be willing to receive what the Spirit has for you.

The TRUTH Box Questions:

"May we present that belief to the Lord?

"Lord, what do you want _(the Mentee)_ to know?"

A Preview of The TRUTH Box

After working through the BELIEF Box, the next step in the TPM Process is to ask the Lord to share His perspective. The Holy Spirit is the only One who can persuade us to believe the truth. He is the "Helper" and "Counselor" who will lead us into the knowledge of the truth (John 16:13). In the TRUTH Box your objectives are to be willing to hear from God, and then petition the Lord, asking Him to persuade (Biblical Greek - *peitho*) you of the truth.

"Lord, what do you want me to know?"

If you have been following protocol and made it to the TRUTH Box, it means that you have identified a lie-based belief that *feels* or *seems* true and are ready to invite the Holy Spirit to accomplish His work by convincing you of His perspective. Your Mentor may even ask, "*May we present that belief to the Lord?*" as a way of reminding you of your next step.

Up to this point in a TPM session, any questions that have been asked were directed at you, the one who is applying the *TPM Process*. In the TRUTH Box, however, you are asking God a question, "*Lord, what do you want me to know?*" By doing so, you are inviting Him to reveal His perspective regarding the lie that you have admitted to believing and the truth that you need to know. It is an act of submission and an acknowledgment of His role as "*Truth-giver*." He is the one who "*leads us into all truth;*" we cannot do this ourselves (John 16:13).

Assuming that you are ready and willing to receive from the Holy Spirit, you can accomplish your next objective by simply asking, "*Lord, what do you want me to know?*" This question is essentially a short prayer. It does not need to be any more complicated, lengthy, or "spiritual" than that. You are simply inviting the Lord to speak to you.

Some people balk at the idea that the Spirit will readily communicate to our hearts. I have had many people say to me after their first session, "This is the first time that I know with certainty that God spoke to me." Although most Christians claim to believe that God communicates with His children and that His "sheep hear His voice" (see John 10:27), many are still surprised when He does. But we fully expect the Spirit to "speak" to us and persuade us of the truth when we are in the right position to receive from Him.

An example of working through the TRUTH Box:

Ask Yourself: *"Not that it is true, but does it feel or seem true that there is something wrong with me?"* (BELIEF Box)

Your Response: *"...Yes, that feels true."*

Ask God: *"Lord, what do you want me to know?"* (TRUTH Box)

Or, if someone was applying the TPM Process under the supervision of a Mentor:

Mentor: *"Not that it is true, but does it feel or seem true that you are inadequate?"* (BELIEF Box)

Mentee: *"Yes."*

Mentor: *"May we present this belief to the Lord?"* (TRUTH Box)

Mentee: *"Yes, of course."*

Mentor: *"Lord, what do you want (Mentee's Name) to know?"* (TRUTH Box)

The moment you identify what you believe and are ready and willing to receive what the Spirit has for you, invite the Holy Spirit to share His perspective. When you are rightly positioned before Him, He will perform His work. God is not withholding what you need until you ask a certain number of times or wait long enough; He is waiting patiently for you to position yourself to receive what He offers. He is ready the moment that you are!

The objectives in the TRUTH Box are automatically accomplished unless you have a lie-based reason for not accepting what He offers. If it seems as though you are unwilling to receive His perspective, or, at the very least, you are resistant or hesitant at hearing what He has to say, this is likely because you are engaged in a *solution behavior* (which we will discuss when we learn about the SOLUTION Box). For now, let's assume that you are willing and able to hear what the Lord has to say.

"Hearing" from the Lord

After you have asked for the Holy Spirit to grant you His perspective, you receptively wait for a few moments. He may use words, visuals, sensations, or any other form of communication to persuade you of the truth. You may hear the words, *"I was with you," "I chose you," "You do have value," "You are safe now,"* or, *"I am in control."* Or an image of Jesus with a smile and outreached hands may come to mind. You may sense His presence or feel as though a weight has been lifted off your shoulders. The pain that you felt earlier may seem to evaporate and a deep sense of peace may envelop you, or you could simply sense a realization of the truth in a way you hadn't before.

You could also simply sit in silence and not notice anything happening at all. This is perfectly fine. Never assume that the Spirit hasn't done anything simply because you didn't notice anything happen. The Holy Spirit is perfectly capable of working in your life without you initially being aware of His involvement.

That said, just because it seems as though God did something doesn't mean that He actually did. If the Holy Spirit persuades you to believe the truth, there will be undeniable proof of this change. We always check for reliable indicators of His involvement and transformative work, but we do not perform this "test" for transformation in the TRUTH Box.

Because your Mentor understands this concept, he or she will never ask you questions like, *"Did you hear or sense anything?" "Do you see Jesus?" "What is Jesus doing in your memory?" "What did God say* to you?" "*Do you feel as though you heard from the Lord?*" Each of these questions are misleading and, in a sense, are a form of guided imagery. If your Mentor asks questions such as these, he is (knowingly or unknowingly) planting ideas and suggesting imagery in your mind that did not originate with you. If this ever occurs, then your Mentor is **not** following the protocols outlined in the TPM training!

Your Mentor will also refrain from encouraging you to "soak-in" the message you just "received," to continue enjoying your moment in the LORD's presence, or to ask the Lord for additional truths after "hearing" from Him. Although these practices may *seem* helpful or good, they are based upon the mistaken assumption that your conscious experience after asking for truth is an indicator of whether or not the Holy Spirit did something. But this is simply not the case, and we never want to make this potentially misleading assumption.

For example, after asking the Lord for truth, if you consciously hear the words, "I am with you," does that mean that you have heard from God? Possibly. But it could have, just as easily, been your own thoughts in an attempt to tell yourself the truth. What if you suddenly feel the anxiety and fear dissipate? Was that due to the Holy Spirit's involvement? Potentially. But it might actually be the result of your unconscious decision to suppress your emotion. If a comforting Bible verse comes to your mind, is this the work of the "Comforter" (John 14:26, KJV)? It might be, but it also might simply be the result of your diligent study of Scripture and unconscious attempts to solve your belief problem.

Conversely, if you do not sense anything happening, or if what you do notice seems bad, ineffective, or unhelpful, do not assume that God has not done anything. As strange as it may seem, what you may or may not experience immediately after asking for the Lord's perspective is no definitive indication of anything whatsoever. No matter what you see, hear, sense, feel, or otherwise experience after asking the Lord for truth, you should never make an assumption that something has or has not happened (for you will confirm whether or not something has happened in the next *Box*).

This is also why your Mentor will refrain from asking questions such as, "*What else did He say?*" "*Lord, is there something else you want ____ to know?*" or "*God, what else do you have for ____?*" etc. Again, these types of questions are based upon the assumption that the Holy Spirit just persuaded you of the truth (even though this may not be the case). Asking these types of questions also assumes that the Holy Spirit will wait to be asked before sharing more or offering all that you need. This, of course, is also untrue. The Mentor must be careful to avoid all of these practices as they are misleading and, of course, not a part of TPM protocol.

Again, this is not to say that what you may experience after asking the Lord for truth is unimportant or irrelevant, for it may very well describe your personal encounter with the Lord. But when the Holy Spirit does something, there is always fruit, or evidence, that will hold up to scrutiny. His work cannot be undone (Isaiah 43:13). This does not discount anything that you might experience, but it is a reason to hold loosely whatever you experience in the TRUTH Box until you have tested for transformation in the TRANSFORMATION Box.

If He is responsible for what you saw, heard, felt, or experienced, then it should result in a lasting and effortless transformation in what you believe that may also lead to further transformation in your perspective, emotions, and behavior. No matter what seems to happen in the TRUTH Box, the next step is always to move to the TRANSFORMATION Box where you will "*test for transformation.*"

That said, if you sit silently for a few moments after asking for God's perspective, your mentor may ask something like, "What's going on?" to determine if it would be appropriate to move to the TRANS-FORMATION Box. Again, this question is not meant to gather information regarding what the Holy

Spirit may or may not have said or done, but rather, it is only asked to help your mentor know when you are ready to test for transformation. (Note: this question is shown on the Mentor's Question Map in the LOST/UNSURE Box.)

THE WORD OF GOD AS THE STANDARD

The written word of God represents the standard of what is and is not true. If anything or anyone stands in opposition to what God has said is true, they are in error and need correction. Because of this, many have proposed using the Scriptures to verify whether or not that which occurs in the TRUTH Box is valid and of God. In fact, this strategy was part of the very early editions of the TPM training. But we have since discovered that this method of verification is not as simple or reliable as it may initially appear. I quickly learned that not everyone agreed with my personal interpretation of the Scriptures.

You do not have to dig too deeply into the church's history to discover that we have supported all manner of activities with our limited understanding of Scripture. Without getting into the details, let's just say that not all of the so-called "Bible-backed" behavior we have engaged in turned out to be godly (see 2 Peter 1:20).

We can, and should, attempt to hold each other to the standard of truth that has been laid out in Scripture, but we must also humbly admit that just because something *seems* or *appears* to be biblically true from our perspective, it does not mean that it accurately reflects what is actually true. The truths of Scripture are true, but our understanding of them is not always accurate.

Each of us have examples of "truths" that we fervently believed but have since learned were oversimplifications or misunderstandings. There is only One who fully knows what is meant by the words contained in the Bible, and He is at work in each of us as He refines our faith and leads us "into all the truth" (John 16:13), though none of us have completed this journey (See Philippians 3:12).

Thankfully, as we will discuss in the next chapter, we do not need to lean on our own understanding of the Bible to verify the Holy Spirit's work. When He persuades someone of the truth, there is always evidence of His involvement; you simply need to know what to look for. Paul says that "the Lord is the Spirit, and where the Spirit of the Lord is, there is freedom" (2 Corinthians 3:17). When the Holy Spirit persuades our hearts of the truth, freedom will follow, and this freedom will be effortlessly expressed through the fruit of the Spirit. The lies we believed that are replaced with His truth will no longer feel or seem true to us, and the truth will resonate within our hearts. This is how we know that a person has encountered the presence of Christ. A change of thought (metanoia) and a subsequent transformation will always follow.

We may not all agree about what the truth is (that is, in how we interpret the Scriptures), but we probably agree more closely when it comes to lies. Most believers would agree that God does not hate us, He hasn't forsaken us, He does not view us as dirty or shameful, we are not worthless but hold great value with Him. So then, while applying the TPM Process, we are primarily looking for lies. When the Spirit seems to shine His light of truth in someone's heart, we are not overly concerned about making sure that what is reported fully aligns with our personal theology, but rather, we look for evidence of transformation. Has there been a shift in what is believed? We judge what happens based upon evidence rather than our subjective view of Scripture.

Again, you are not hearing us say that the Word of God is not true or reliable, for it absolutely is! We are only suggesting that using your current understanding and interpretation of God's word to evaluate a person's experience may not be the best course of action to take (especially in the context of a TPM session).

Communicating with Your Mentor

You should never feel pressured to share anything with your Mentor. This is true at every stage of the TPM Process. That being said, it is helpful to clue him or her in as to where you are in the process as you apply it. For example, even though what you experience after asking the Lord for truth is no indication of anything, it is still helpful to let your Mentor know when you are ready to move to the TRANSFORMATION Box.

Whether it seems like something may have happened or it seems like nothing is happening at all, you can let your Mentor know by saying something like, "Ok," or "I think I'm ready to check the belief." Or, better still, check it yourself and let your Mentor know what you find (which will be discussed in the next chapter).

The TRUTH Box in Review

After establishing a "baseline" in the BELIEF Box, you move to the TRUTH Box and invite the Holy Spirit to persuade you of the truth. After a moment of receptive waiting, or if it seems as though something has potentially happened, continue to the TRANSFORMATION Box to see if there has been a change in your belief.

The TRUTH Box in Reality

The objectives in the TRUTH Box are simple and do not take long to accomplish once you understand them. You simply invite the Lord to convince you of His perspective and receive whatever He has for you. There are times when we are not ready to hear from Him about the lie-based belief we have identified. Just because you desire to hear from God does not mean that you are willing to listen or accept what He offers. When you have reason to reject God's perspective, you will likely do so even if you genuinely want to hear from Him and have asked Him for truth. Another common reason for not hearing from God is that we are angry at Him. We will explore the reasons why we might resist hearing from God when we discuss the SOLUTION Box.

There is no "normal" experience to be expected after acknowledging a lie you believe and asking the Lord to persuade you of the truth. You may also find it difficult to refrain from assuming the Holy Spirit has or has not done something. This is especially true when what you experienced seemed like a glorious, spiritual encounter with Jesus, or when you seemed to experience nothing at all! But remember, no matter what you see, hear, feel, or experience, make no assumptions one way or the other. No matter what happens after you have asked the Holy Spirit for truth and perspective, your next step is always the TRANSFORMATION Box.

SIMPLE TRUTHS

An interesting aspect of what typically occurs in the TRUTH Box is how simple the truths people report actually are. Rarely do they report some deep theological tenet of the faith, but rather a simple assurance such as, "I love you," "You are special to me," "You are safe now," "I am with you," "I am in control," "You are mine," or "You are valuable to me." The truth is, much of the deep theological truths that the Scriptures declare are based upon such simplicity. When the Creator of the universe persuades our hearts of His love by simply saying, "I love you," this is huge! God does not need to speak many words to accomplish great things. Remember what happened when He simply said, "Let there be light!" Paul's prayer reveals the enormity of knowing how we are loved by God when he prayed,

"May [you] be able to comprehend with all the saints what is the width and length and height and depth, and to know the love of Christ which *surpasses* knowledge, <u>that you may be filled to all the fullness of God</u>" (Ephesians 3:18-19, emphasis added).

CHAPTER 17

THE TRANSFORMATION BOX

The Mentee's Objective While in the TRANSFORMATION Box

1) Determine if the Holy Spirit has persuaded you of the truth.

The TRANSFORMATION Box Question:

"Does it still feel true that _____ (the belief confirmed in the BELIEF Box)?"

NOTICE: This chapter has been divided into two parts. The first part describes the protocols involved in the TRANSFORMATION Box. The second part discusses what to do after you have checked for transformation.

Part One

A Preview of The TRANSFORMATION Box

After confirming what you believe in the BELIEF Box and inviting the Holy Spirit to persuade you of the truth in the TRUTH Box, your next objective is to test for transformation in the TRANS-FORMATION Box. As we discussed in the previous chapter, when the Holy Spirit accomplishes His refining work in us, there is always lasting and verifiable proof. While in the TRANSFORMATION Box, you are checking for something that only God could have accomplished: a change in what you believe.

"Does the lie still feel true?"

In order to determine if there has been a shift in your thinking, you will use the baseline that was established in the BELIEF Box. The lie-based belief that you identified, just moments ago, *felt* or *seemed* true to you. Your goal while in the TRANSFORMATION Box is to check to see if that lie still *feels* or *seems* true. You are checking for a shift or change in what you believe. When in the TRANSFORMATION Box, simply ask yourself one question, "Does it still feel or seem true that ____?"

For example, if you were applying the TPM Process on your own, you would ask yourself:

"Does it still feel or seem true that I am worthless?"

Or, *"Does it still feel or seem true that I am dirty and shameful?"*

Or, if you were applying the TPM Process under the supervision of a Mentor, he or she would ask:

"Does it still feel or seem true that you are out of control?"

Or, *"Does it still feel or seem true that you are vulnerable and defenseless?"*

Notice that you are checking the lie, not the truth. Does the lie still feel or seem true? If it does, then you still believe it to be true. If not, then your belief has changed. This shift in your thinking is the result of the Holy Spirit's work. This change in belief is evidence that He has persuaded you to believe the truth. If the lie no longer feels true, then there has been a shift in your belief. Only the Holy Spirit can bring about this transformation.

Until you check to see if the lie still feels true, you have no clear or reliable means of determining if God has done something. This is true even if it seems as though you have just had a vivid encounter with the Lord. But no matter how glorious your experience in the TRUTH Box might seem to have been, it alone is no guarantee that anything spiritual or lasting has occurred. As you learned in the previous chapter, what you may or may not experience immediately after asking for the Lord's perspective is no certain indication of His involvement.

After asking the Lord for truth, a Bible verse might come to your mind, you may hear a comforting message of truth in your mind, see an encouraging mental image, and even feel noticeably better after inviting God to share His perspective. But none of these things, on their own, are any indication of transformation. You may seem to have a "glorious" experience while in the TRUTH Box, believe that you hear choirs of angels singing, envision the Lord standing nearby, and feel your pain subside, but if the lie still *feels* true, then this only indicates that you have a good imagination.

If what you see, sense, hear, or otherwise experience after the TRUTH Box is accompanied by a shift in your thinking, indicated by the fact that the lie-based belief no longer feels or seems true, then the Holy Spirit has accomplished this work, because only He can bring this about. We are looking for more than just an experience, we are looking for genuine transformation.

Ultimately, it is the effortless bearing of the fruit of the Spirit that provides us with further tangible evidence of this transformation. It is when you begin noticing that you are spontaneously expressing love, joy, peace, patience, kindness, goodness, faithfulness and self-control (Galatians 5:22-23), that you can be assured His truth has been implanted in your heart. James said it clearly, "in humility receive the word <u>implanted</u>, which is able to save your souls" (James 1:21, emphasis added).

James uses the Greek word "émphytos" translated as "*to implant*" to make an important point. The word is descriptive of a seed planted in the ground for the purpose of germination. It also describes the process of engrafting a branch into a new rootstock. Both images express the idea of growth and life with the expected outcome of fruition.

When the Holy Spirit convinces our hearts of the truth, the expected outcome is "*fruit.*" If there is no fruit then "émphytos" has not occurred. Intellectual agreement with the truth is like holding the seeds in your hands. You hold the potential for a harvest, but unless the seeds are implanted in the soil, fruit will never be realized. We need the Holy Spirit to take the truths that we hold in our heads and implant them into the "*soil*" of our hearts.

In large part, this is why we no longer use what we formerly referred to as the "*peace test*" to check for transformation since neither the presence nor absence of pain is a valid indicator of transformation. You may seem to feel better, the same, or even worse after asking for the Lord's perspective. A wide assortment of things can impact how you feel, and as such, a change in emotion is not a reliable indicator of the Spirit's work. In fact, it is possible to feel worse after being convinced of the truth! This is often the case when you are persuaded of the truth regarding your *solution beliefs* (which will be discussed in a later chapter). The presence or absence of emotional pain is not a valid indication of the Holy Spirit's refining work.

This is not to say that when we are convinced of the truth that we will not feel peace, for indeed this is often the case. Feeling love, joy, peace, assurance, confidence, safety, security, and more are all potentially available when we believe the truth in our hearts. Even so, the true test for transformation is the change in belief that always follows our being persuaded by the Spirit to believe the truth.

Again, this is not to diminish any of what may occur before the TRANSFORMATION Box. We are merely stressing the importance of checking the right variable to determine if transformation has occurred. Many people have mistakenly been excited after experiencing what they believed to be transformation or an encounter with God, only to feel discouraged when the "fruit" didn't seem to last or show up at all. In TPM, we always verify if the Holy Spirit was involved. We do so by checking for a change in belief.

If you hear what you believe to be God's voice, and it results in a change in belief, the Holy Spirit was at work. If an image or visual comes to mind, and it results in the lie no longer feeling true, then the Holy Spirit was at work. If you sense a comforting presence and feel better because of it, ask yourself, "*Does the lie still feel true?*" If not, then it is evidence of the Holy Spirit's work.

What follows are examples of what this might look like in a TPM session:

Ask Yourself: *"Not that it is true, but does it feel or seem true that I am a defect?" (BELIEF Box)*

Your Response: *"...Yes, that feels true."*

Ask God: *"Lord, what do you want me to know?" (TRUTH Box)*

Your Thought: *"...It seems like I hear Him reminding me that I am fearfully and wonderfully made."*

Ask Yourself: *"Does it still feel or seem true that I am a defect?" (TRANSFORMATION Box)*

Your Response: *"No, that no longer seems true."*

Another example;

Your Thought: *"It definitely feels true that I am alone!" (BELIEF Box)*

Ask God: *"Lord, what do you want me to know?" (TRUTH Box)*

Your Thought: *"I can sense Him with me. It is as though His hands are on my shoulders. It is very comforting."*

Ask Yourself: *"But does it still feel true that I am alone?" (TRANSFORMATION Box)*

Your Response: *"No. It doesn't feel true that I am alone. He is with me!"*

Or, if you are applying the TPM Process with a Mentor:

Mentor: *"Not that it is true, but does it feel or seem true that you are stupid?" (BELIEF Box)*

Mentee: *"I logically know that's not true, but it sure feels true."*

Mentor: *"Lord, what do you want (Mentee's Name) to know?" (TRUTH Box)*

Mentee: *"I see Jesus dressed-up like a school teacher. He is pointing to a chalkboard that has the words "If you are reading this, you are not stupid" written in big, bold letters."*

Mentor: *"Does it still feel or seem true that you are stupid?" (TRANSFORMATION Box)*

Mentee: *"Ha, no. That just seems like a silly thought now."*

Another example:

Mentor: *"Not that it is true, but does it feel or seem true that you are worthless?" (BELIEF Box)*

Mentee: *"Yes, that feels true."*

Mentor: *"Lord, what do you want (Mentee's Name) to know?" (TRUTH Box)*

Mentee: *"I heard the words "I sacrificed my Son so that I could have you."*

Mentor: *"Does it still feel or seem true that you are worthless?" (TRANSFORMATION Box)*

Mentee: *"No. I am of great value to God. He paid the ultimate price for me!"*

In each of these examples, the protocol is the same: establish a baseline in the BELIEF Box, ask the Lord for perspective in the TRUTH Box, and then use the baseline as a point of comparison in the TRANSFORMATION Box. Own the lie, ask for truth, and then check for transformation.

CHECKING GOD'S WORK

Some may feel uncomfortable with the idea of challenging or testing the work of the Spirit, but checking the authenticity of God's work does not reduce its impact, power, or effectiveness. Testing the genuineness of His work only proves it and gives Him the glory He is due. His work will always hold up to any level of scrutiny. No matter how closely you look at it, the Spirit's work cannot be thwarted, threatened, or diminished. Because of this, it is safe to test it. In fact, He invites us to do so (1 John 4:1).

The TRANSFORMATION Box question (in conjunction with the baseline that is established in the BELIEF Box) enables us to evaluate what seems to have occurred in the TRUTH Box. It offers a practical means by which you can determine whether the Holy Spirit has actually persuaded you of the truth. Regardless of how spectacular or underwhelming your experience may have been after asking the Lord for truth, the only way to verify whether or not you "heard from God," is to check for a change in your belief.

As you learned from our discussion of the "Belief and Persuasion" Principle, unless the Holy Spirit convinces us to believe the truth in our hearts, the best we can hope for is an intellectual alignment with the truth. We can fully agree intellectually that the truth is true, and yet it may not feel true in our hearts. Unless the Spirit opens the eyes of our hearts (Ephesians 1:18) to know the truth we will not fully believe it.

Regardless of how you feel, if the lie still feels true, the Holy Spirit has not yet convinced you of the truth. Likewise, even if the thought or message that crosses your mind is perfectly in line with Scripture, but if it fails to produce a noticeable shift in your thinking, then it was not the Spirit's doing.

Remember, there are certain things that we can do without requiring God to do more than what He is already doing. You can continue breathing without having to constantly ask Him for air, and you can tell yourself the truth without involving Him. However, if He does not "implant" this truth in your heart, you will still not fully believe it (see James 1:21). In fact, you can remind yourself of the truths you have intellectually memorized with every waking moment of your life, but until the Spirit of Truth Himself persuades you to believe them, you will continue in your "double-mindedness" (See James 1:6-8).

In spite of this reality, it is common for people to quote Bible verses or declare the truth when in the TRUTH Box. But again, just because they are able to do this is not necessarily an indication that the Holy Spirit has persuaded them to believe. No matter what you experience after asking the Lord for truth, you should always *check for transformation* in the TRANSFORMATION Box.

It behooves us to bring the same measure of testing to other areas of church ministry that we are involved in. Too often we pour ourselves into service and ministry but never examine the outcome. Rather than solely focusing on the nobility of our goals and the amount of time and effort we pour into our work, we need to honestly evaluate what is being accomplished. When God is involved, there is <u>always</u> verifiable evidence of it. When He works, you will always be able to see the fruit of His labor.

A Noticeable Shift

When checking for transformation, you are simply searching for a shift in your thinking. This shift may be dramatic and obvious or subtle and seemingly gradual. Sometimes, after asking God for truth, the lie feels or seems as illogical and untrue as you intellectually knew it to be. Other times, it only seems "less true." In either case, a noticeable shift in your belief has occurred. That is all you are looking for: a noticeable shift.

As you have learned already, you cannot change what you have been persuaded to believe through effort, choice, willpower, or determination. You are convinced that what you believe is true because somewhere, someone or something persuaded you to believe it. Once you believe something to be true, you cannot willfully decide to stop believing it. You will continue to believe it until someone you trust, who holds a greater authority on the subject, persuades you of something else. Again, this is the essence of the "*Trust and Authority Principle.*"

If your belief has changed, it is because you have been persuaded to believe something other than what you believed before. In a TPM session, after you have acknowledged a lie-based belief that you are convinced is true, there is only One who can persuade you of the truth: the Holy Spirit! If you notice a shift in your thinking after asking for His perspective, even a subtle one, this is evidence of the fact that the Holy Spirit has convinced you of the truth, His "*peitho*" (Biblical Greek for "persuasion").

During your first few TPM sessions, your Mentor might offer some reminders and clarification when asking the TRANSFORMATION Box question. An example of this might be as follows:

Mentee: *"I think I just heard the Lord say that it was not my fault. I was an innocent little girl." (TRUTH Box)*

Mentor: *"Does it still feel true that your uncle's actions were your fault?" (TRANSFORMATION Box)*

Mentee: *"I am not sure what you mean." (needs clarification and orientation)*

Mentor: *"When the Holy Spirit persuades us of the truth, the lies we once believed will no longer feel true to us. Do you sense that this occurred? Did you notice a shift in your thinking? Does the belief that felt true a few moments ago still feel true now? You are not looking for a* *shift in emotion, but rather, a shift in belief. Does the lie you identified seem as true as it did before you asked the Lord for perspective, or has there been a shift?"*

Again, you are only looking for a noticeable shift in your belief. As we said, sometimes this shift is dramatic and life-changing, while at other times it is more subtle and subdued. In either case, if the lie no longer *seems* or *feels* as true as it did before asking the Lord for His perspective, then *mind-renewal* has occurred. This shift in your thinking indicates that the Holy Spirit has persuaded you to believe the truth. You may (and likely do) have other lie-based beliefs to identify, but if the lie you have already identified no longer feels true, this is cause to celebrate and give thanks to the "Spirit of Truth" (John 16:13).

HOW DO WE KNOW IT WAS THE SPIRIT?

Someone might say, "How do I know that the Holy Spirit caused the shift in my thinking? Could I not have simply chosen to stop believing the lie?" A simple test of this theory would be to *choose* to go back to believing the lie. If you no longer believe the lie because you chose to believe the truth, then you should be able to reverse the process. Try it! But do not be surprised if you cannot do it.

We encourage you to revisit the "Belief and Persuasion" Principle. We do not believe anything by choice. Our beliefs are the result of our being persuaded. Granted, in a TPM session, we choose to move in the direction of the Persuader, but the actual persuasion is completely out of our control.

Part Two

"What if the lie still feels true?"

If the lie that was confirmed in the BELIEF Box still feels or seems true in the TRANSFORMATION Box, then this is evidence that you have not yet been convinced of the truth. It also suggests that whatever happened in the TRUTH Box was not the Holy Spirit's doing. Someone might say, "But I heard the Bible verse *"I am with you always..."* It is in the Bible, so it is obviously true! Why does the thought that I am alone and abandoned still *feel* true to me?" Hearing a Bible verse in your head does not mean that you heard it from the Holy Spirit in your heart. If you have memorized a Bible verse, then you are capable of bringing that verse to mind. This is common in ministry sessions where people attempt to convince themselves of the truth that they already intellectually believe. We can (and should) memorize Scripture, but even after it is firmly established in our heads, we still need the Spirit to implant it in our hearts. The intellect is the front door to the heart, but unless the Spirit convinces us of His truth, it will not find its place in our hearts.

The following example demonstrates this possibility.

Mentor: *"Joe, let me ask you, "Not that it is true, but does it feel or seem true that you are a worthless loser?" (BELIEF Box)*

Mentee: *"Yes, that feels true."*

Mentor: *"Lord, what do you want Joe to know?" (TRUTH Box)*

Mentee: *"Oh wow! This is incredible. I see Jesus riding up to me on a great white horse. He seems delighted to see me. He is scooping me up and we are riding off together into the sunset. He is telling me that I am not a loser! He thinks that I am a winner! This is so wonderful! Thank you, Jesus!"*

Mentor: *"Does it still feel or seem true that you are a worthless loser?" (TRANSFORMATION Box)*

Mentee: *"...well...yeah...I guess that still feels true...But I know it's not true because Jesus said I am a winner! I just have to focus on Him and what He says about me, no matter what I feel!"*

As glorious and inspiring as Joe's report may sound, unless the lie no longer feels true (or at least less true), there has not been a change in belief, and he has not experienced mind-renewal. Some people have vivid imaginations and are capable of creating imagery and experiences that can appear to be spiritual and glorious. Even though a great imagination may distract us from what we feel for a time, it cannot bring about mind-renewal and genuine transformation. Later, we will discover that imagination and positive thinking is often used as a "solution behavior" that actually keeps people from shedding the lies they believe and embracing the truth with their hearts.

As we have said, there are many potential explanations for why the lie may still feel true after asking the Lord for His perspective. You may have simply gone to the BELIEF Box prematurely before rightly identifying a *lie-based heart belief* or *solution belief*. This is common when you have limited experience with TPM and are applying the TPM Process on your own. Or you might have mistakenly attempted to tell yourself the truth rather than receptively wait on the Lord. This is common with those of us who have committed ourselves to memorizing Scripture. New Mentees may immediately begin quoting applicable Bible verses to themselves after asking God for truth and perspective, but attempting to convince yourself of the truth at a heart level will likely prove to be fruitless.

You may also find that the lie-based belief still feels true when you have been convinced of a lie-based reason for not listening to God. For example, you may believe that asking the Lord for His perspective could have negative consequences. For example, what if the Lord doesn't show up? Or, what if he confirms the lie you believe and tells you that you are worthless, unlovable, or a reject? Looking to Jesus for His perspective may cause you to feel vulnerable and exposed. You may believe that you can protect yourself from being rejected by avoiding communicating with Him. When this is the case, it may result in your choosing not to listen– even if you consciously ask Him to speak. (This will be covered when we discuss solutions). You might also simply be angry at God without being consciously aware of it. This can make it hard to hear from Him about other beliefs (much like being forced into a conversation with someone with whom you are angry). No matter the reason you haven't heard from God, the next step is always the same.

What to Do After the TRANSFORMATION Box

After checking for a shift in your thinking, whether or not there has been one, your next step is to apply *"The Clock Principle."* You will see this posted on the side of the TPM Map located between the TRANSFORMATION Box and the EMOTION Box. This essentially means that you check to see if you have time to apply the TPM Process again. More time than you realize may have passed while you were focused on what you were doing. This point in the Process offers a convenient opportunity to "check the clock" to see if you have time to continue. If your allotted time has run out, this is a natural place to stop.

If you are applying the TPM Process by yourself, this is an easy principle to follow. If you have time to proceed just keep going. However, if you are working with a Mentor who has scheduled times with other Mentees, this is a principle that must be acknowledged. If you are out of time, then you are out of time. If you are with a Mentor and have a set time to meet, it is important to respect that restraint. Each of you may have responsibilities to get back to after the *TPM session.*

But if you are applying the Process of TPM on your own as a natural reaction to realizing that you are *"Triggered,"* your time restraints may differ dramatically. This is especially true considering that the amount of time required will likely decrease as you become more familiar with applying the TPM Process, and with the *"Principles"* it is built upon. This is yet another reason why TPM Mentors are focused on *equipping* and *mentoring.*

Whatever the context may be, if you are out of time, then you are out of time and can close the Session in prayer. But, if you have a few minutes remaining of your scheduled time together, we recommend that you use this time to discuss what happened with your Mentor, ask any questions you may have, and revisit portions of the TPM training. Remember, the primary goal of a TPM session is for you, the Mentee, to become more knowledgeable, experienced, and familiar with the Three Elements of TPM. Invest your time wisely.

Now, if you have time and want to apply the TPM Process again, move to the EMOTION Box. Your objectives are the same as the last time you were there. You are essentially working through the *TPM Process* again. Doing so affords you the opportunity to address another lie-based belief or figure out why there was no change in your belief (if that was the case in the TRANSFORMATION Box).

If you are applying the Process with a Mentor, after moving from the TRANSFORMATION Box to the EMOTION Box, they may reword the first question to be, *"What are you feeling now?"* This makes it more conversational and fitting for the context, but again, its purpose remains the same. You are simply checking to see if you are currently feeling any negative emotion.

Notice that the question is not, *"Are you feeling better now?"* or *"Do you still feel what you felt earlier?"* You are not looking for a change in emotion as this is unnecessary and potentially misleading. The first question in the EMOTION Box is not designed to see if you heard from the Lord or not. That was established in the TRANSFORMATION Box. Remember, a change in emotion is not the goal, nor is it an indication of transformation. The question is simply, *"What are you feeling now?"* This should remind you of your first objective while in the EMOTION Box: to connect to emotion.

You may realize that you are now feeling the peace of Christ. When we believe the truth in our hearts and are currently operating in it, we should feel what the truth feels like. Enjoy and walk in this newly found peace, security, and comfort! But do not be surprised if these positive emotions are occasionally overshadowed by the pain associated with other lie-based beliefs that have not yet been addressed. Remember, you feel whatever you believe. If you only believed the truth, you would only feel what the truth produces. But if any measure of your belief remains lie-based, then you will be faced with the consequences of that as well.

Although it is common for someone to report feeling peaceful, calm, assured, or relieved, after being persuaded of the truth from the Holy Spirit, the absence of these positive emotions does not indicate a lack of transformation. We know that we have been convinced of the truth by the Spirit when the lie no longer feels true. But even though the previously identified lie no longer feels true, and the truth is confirmed in our hearts, we may still feel bad. Our current emotional status is the outcome of the beliefs that are presently being accessed. When we think about the lie that no longer feels true, it will not produce the same negative emotion that it did before receiving the truth. However, if another lie is triggered while examining this transformation, we will feel the painful emotion that this lie-based belief produces. Again, we see that <u>feelings of peace and calm are **not** reliable indicators of whether transformation has occurred</u>! The only immediately available indicator of transformation is <u>a change in belief</u>.

As stated earlier, an absence of pain may be the result of any number of things. For example, a "pain-free" status may be the temporary outcome of successful suppression, inner distraction, or some form of self-medication, but only the Holy Spirit can convince you of the truth so that a lie no longer feels true. Therefore, if the lie in question no longer feels true, then transformation has occurred, and if you still feel negative emotions, there are simply other lies that are currently being triggered. This represents another opportunity to have your faith refined, your mind renewed, and your life transformed!

So then, you may experience a major shift in your belief but still feel bad due to other lie-based beliefs that are triggered. The following silly story may further illustrate this concept:

> Suppose a man enters the emergency room at the hospital with a large metal beaver trap clamped onto <u>both of his hands</u>. The attending doctor asks him, "What in the world happened?" The man replies, "I was in the swamp trapping beavers when I accidentally triggered my trap and got both of my hands stuck." "Oh, my!" the doctor says, "This is awful! Does it hurt?" The man screams, "Yes, it is excruciating! It is almost more than I can bear. Can you help me?" The doctor proceeds to loosen one side of the trap, <u>freeing the man's right hand</u>. The doctor, feeling good about this accomplishment, asks the man, "There you go, does your right hand feel better now? In desperation, the man cries out, "I suppose, but I really cannot tell because my other hand is still in a great deal of pain!"

The remaining pain in his other hand made it nearly impossible to appreciate the newly found relief in his freed hand. Likewise, when the Spirit persuades you of the truth regarding a portion of what you believe, your other "hand" may leave you feeling great discomfort. This does not mean transformation has not occurred, but rather that you simply believe additional lies and are in further need for His perspective.

In the illustration, the doctor was specific when he asked the beaver trapper, "Does the right hand that has been freed feel better?" But the trapper was unable to know for sure because the remaining pain overroad the relief he may have been feeling. Therefore, the trapper honestly answered, "I cannot tell because my other hand is still in a great deal of pain!" The pain coming from the trapped hand was overriding the relief in the freed hand. The trapper experienced genuine freedom in one hand but remained in pain because his other hand was still trapped.

Nevertheless, the pain in his one hand does not diminish the freedom in his other hand. We may experience the peace of Christ where the truth resides, but this peace can be difficult to appreciate when we are distracted by the pain coming from other lies that are triggered. The good doctor could have used a version of the TRANSFORMATION Box question and asked, "Does it still feel as though your right hand is caught in the trap?" This would allow the trapper to more closely examine his injured state and respond, "No, my right hand is free, but I am still in a whole lot of pain! Can you please work on getting my left hand free?"

So, if you find that you are still in pain, even after genuinely hearing from the Lord, do not be discouraged! Instead ask yourself, "Does the lie I identified earlier still feel true?" If there has been a shift in your belief, then the Lord has persuaded your heart of the truth. The pain that remains is evidence of additional beliefs that need to be addressed, offering you additional opportunities to have your faith refined, your mind renewed, and your life transformed!

If you find that you are not feeling any negative emotion when revisiting the EMOTION Box you may choose to call it a day. However, if you have time and desire to keep going, it may be helpful to trigger yourself by thinking about what you were focused on at the beginning of the ministry session or any memory that surfaced during the session. If you find that you feel bad or even worse than when you started, this is not a reason to be discouraged; it is an opportunity for refinement!

The Spirit is at work in your life replacing your lie-based heart belief with His perspective. This is a life-long journey of discovery and transformation. Remember, your overall goal is not to get over a hurdle, around some obstacle, or free of some measure of pain, but rather, it is to become more aware of God's work in your life and more proficient at cooperating with Him in it!

Exceptions to the Rule

Although the TPM Map directs you to the EMOTION Box after leaving the TRANSFORMATION Box, there are a couple "exceptions" to this rule that we should discuss. As you will discover in the next few chapters, if you feel angry at any point in a TPM session, you are to move to the ANGER Box. Likewise, if you ever notice a potential "*solution indicator*" (which will be explained later), you should immediately move to the SOLUTION Box. *Anger* and *solutions* can show up at any point in a TPM session, and as soon as they do, they become priority. HOWEVER, no matter what happens after asking the Lord for truth, you should always check for transformation (a shift in belief) in the TRANSFORMATION Box before doing anything else!

If you become angry or realize the fact that you might be engaged in a *solution behavior* immediately AFTER asking the Lord for truth, continue to the TRANSFORMATION Box, and check for a change in belief, BEFORE moving to the ANGER Box or SOLUTION Box. Essentially, the general "rule" that explains when to move to the ANGER Box and SOLUTION Box is overridden by the greater "rule" that requires you to check for transformation after asking the Lord for truth. Again, this will all make more sense after we have discussed the ANGER Box and SOLUTION Box protocols.

ERECTING STONES

In the Old Testament, God's people would erect monuments, stack up stones, or build an altar as a reminder of what God had done for them. They did this so that later, when they passed by these places, they would be reminded of their experiences with God. We can also "stack up stones" after having received truth from the Holy Spirit in a ministry session. By keeping a written record of what God does for us we can revisit milestones in our faith-refining journey.

We are not suggesting that you keep a record to ensure that you don't forget what the Holy Spirit said, for once He persuades you to believe the truth in your heart, you cannot and will not forget it. You may resist this idea and believe it is necessary to continually remind yourself of the truth. But how much effort did you invest in remembering the lies that you once believed? Did you have to continually remind yourself that you had no value or that you were alone and abandoned? Of course not! We don't forget our heart's beliefs whether they are the truth or lies.

We can't help but continue believing that which we currently believe. This doesn't change until we are persuaded to believe something else. We can try to suppress the lie-based beliefs and distract ourselves from the pain they produce, but the lies remain. We may not be able to consciously bring our heart belief to mind, but they still impact our every step. The good news is when we believe the truth in our hearts, we will be governed by it, and the *"peace of Christ will rule in our hearts"* (See Colossians 3:15) even when we are not consciously aware of it.

At the end of your TPM session, try writing down the lies that you identified and that felt true, as well as the truth that you received (the actual truth that produced a change in belief, of course). This record can be referenced in the days and weeks ahead so that, if you begin to feel discouraged when other lies are triggered, you can look back on your journey and realize that the mind-renewal and transformation are genuine and lasting. As you discover that the lies you once believed no longer *feel* or *seem* true, you will also likely feel encouraged to position yourself to receive even more.

Even after the Lord convinces you of many truths, your faith will never be 100% pure (on this side of Christ's return anyway). But if you look back at your faith-refining journey with Him and recognize the progress that you've made, you may find the strength and courage needed to press forward as additional lies are exposed. This journey is a marathon not a sprint!

CHAPTER 18

THE ANGER BOX

The Mentee's Objectives While in the ANGER Box

1) Determine if you are angry.
2) Identify who or what you feel angry towards.
3) Express a tentative reason for being angry.

The ANGER Box Questions:

"Is any portion of what you are feeling being felt towards any person or any thing?"

"Who or what do you feel angry towards?"

"Why do you feel angry towards _____?"

NOTICE: This chapter has been divided into four parts. The first part discusses several passages from Scripture that address anger. The second part summarizes some of the notable characteristics of anger. The third part presents many of the specific protocols that are involved in the ANGER Box. And the fourth part explains what it means to identify a tentative reason for why you are angry.

Part One

A Biblical View of Anger

There is an abundance of Bible passages that deal with anger. Rather than exploring all the verses mentioned in the Bible pertaining to anger, we will focus our attention on three primary passages. We can learn a great deal from these verses regarding anger: if we should feel it, for how long we should feel it, what we should do when we feel it, and more. The three specific passages are as follows:

"Be angry, and yet do not sin; do not let the sun go down on your anger, and do not give the devil an opportunity" (Ephesians 4:26-27).

"The anger of man does not achieve the righteousness of God" (James 1:20).

"Never take your own revenge, beloved, but leave room for the wrath of God, for it is written, 'Vengeance is mine, I will repay, says the Lord'" (Romans 12:19).

From these short passages, we can extract at least six helpful principles regarding anger that are applicable to TPM:

1. **We have been given permission to be angry.**
   "Be angry ..." (Ephesians 4:26-27)

Anger is fundamentally a God-created response to perceived injustice. God Himself is angered by the injustice that is present in the world. And when we witness or experience injustice, we are right to feel angry. In fact, much of the anger we feel was *initially* established in the context of injustice, such as abuse, cruelty or neglect. God has designed us to respond to such experiences in this way. It is unlikely that we will escape feeling some measure of anger when we face perceived injustice.

2. **It is possible to be angry without sinning.**
   "Be angry and <u>yet</u> do not sin ..." (Ephesians 4:26-27, emphasis added)

Anger is a powerful force that typically results in inappropriate action. Anger, in and of itself, is not sinful, but when we are angry, we must be careful how we react. Rather than behaving righteously when we are angry, we tend to engage in sinful behavior. God is the only person who can rightly act on His anger. If I act out my anger, I will *probably* sin. God's Word grants us permission to be angry, just don't sin if you are. Good luck with that one!

It is interesting to note how Paul links anger with behavior where he says, "rid yourselves of all such things as these: anger, rage, malice, slander, and filthy language from your lips" (Colossians 3:8 NIV). He first says to rid yourself of anger, rage, and malice but then follows with slander and filthy language. Paul recognized that we tend to open our mouths and release all manner of unpleasantries when we are angry.

3. **We should only be angry for a short period of time.**
   "Do not let the sun go down on your anger." (Ephesians 4:26-27)

We were designed to feel angry when faced with injustice or wrongdoings. The proper emotional response to an injustice is anger. However, if we hold on to our anger for very long, it will cease to be about the injustice and will become the fuel that motivates us to try to solve the problem that the injustice *seemed* to have created. This always leads to negative consequences.

4. **We afford the devil an "opportunity" when we are angry.**
   "... do not give the devil an opportunity ..." (Ephesians 4:26-27)

Satan desires to have the opportunity to provide us with lie-based reasons for holding on to our anger. If we decide to hold anger after the "sun has gone down," this indicates that we have been deceived by the enemy. If we are unwilling to let it go, or even resistant to the thought of giving it up, this is evidence that we are using it to solve a perceived problem.

We might believe such things as "My anger will protect me and keep me safe," "My anger holds the person who hurt me accountable and keeps them from getting away with what they did," "My anger helps me to control my situation," or "My anger punishes those who hurt me." As logical and rational as these thoughts may seem, none of them are actually true. By holding on to our anger, we have provided the devil with an "opportunity" to deceive us, and he takes full advantage of it, for he knows that if we remain angry, we will eventually sin.

5. **Our anger and revenge does not accomplish God's righteous purposes.**
   "Never take your own revenge, beloved, but leave room for the wrath of God, for it is written, 'Vengeance is mine, I will repay, says the Lord'" (Romans 12:19) for *"... the anger of man does not achieve the righteousness of God"* (James 1:20).

Even when our anger seems to be righteous indignation, it cannot accomplish God's righteous judgment. The Greek New Testament word found in James 1:20 that is translated "righteousness" is the word *"dikaiosunēn,"* which also means "righteous justice." Only God can bring about righteous justice for the wrongs inflicted upon the innocent. Even though my anger is a righteous response to an injustice, I cannot bring about the righteous judgment that such injustice demands.

Even though God has given us permission to be angry (Ephesians 4:26), He also tells us that it will not accomplish what He desires (see James 1:20). The psalmist understood this where he said, "Cease from anger and abandon wrath; Do not get upset; it leads only to evildoing" (Psalm 37:8). This is why God has said over and again, "vengeance is mine" (Hebrews 10:30, Romans 12:19). We cannot avenge with a righteous judgment; vengeance is God's alone. This being the case, it makes more sense to cast "...all your care upon Him ..." (1 Peter 5:7 KJV) realizing that anger will neither right the injustice nor accomplish God's will.

This does not mean that we are to do nothing in response to true injustice. We are to care for, support, and encourage those who have suffered injustice while viewing these injustices from a heavenly perspective knowing that God is at work in us amid anything that comes our way. The Scriptures are clear, "If God *is* for us, who *is* against us?" (Romans 8:31).

Most societies have some form of a criminal justice system in place designed to punish evildoers (see 1 Peter 2:13-14). Even so, after all this has been done, can we honestly say that justice has been served? Do those who have suffered injustice feel that all has been made right? Do those whose loved ones were unjustly taken from them feel like justice has been served because the evil person has been put in prison? Not at all! Nothing we do here on Earth can bring about true, righteous justice. Justice is coming, but it will not be found until He brings it! However, for the believer it still remains that "God causes ALL THINGS to work together for the good. . .to be conformed to the image of His Son" (Romans 8:28-29, emphasis added).

We should do what we can, but we must leave vengeance with God. Being angry may seem like our only recourse, but it will not accomplish the righteous purposes that we think it might. All our actions should be motivated by love since *the only thing that counts is faith expressing itself through love* (Galatians 5:6 NIV). Jesus taught us that the proper response to those who hurt us is a far cry from what we typically do. But remember, following these directions is humanly impossible unless the Holy Spirit convinces us of the truth in our hearts enabling us to view life from His perspective. Jesus said:

> You have heard that it was said, 'An eye for an eye and a tooth for a tooth.' But I say to you, Do not resist the one who is evil. But if anyone slaps you on the right cheek, turn to him the other also. And if anyone would sue you and take your tunic, let him have your cloak as well. And if anyone forces you to go one mile, go with him two miles. Give to the one who begs from you, and do not refuse the one who would borrow from you. You have heard that it was said, 'You shall love your neighbor and hate your enemy.' But I say to you, 'Love your enemies and pray for those who persecute you, so that you may be sons of your Father who is in heaven' (Matthew 5:38-45 ESV).

You cannot fulfill Jesus' instructions without first having the Holy Spirit persuade you of a Heavenly perspective. Only when we view our enemies as instruments in the hand of God as He brings about His perfect will in our lives can we ever "love" them and pray for them in this way.

Our Anger Always Falls Short of God's Righteous Judgment

Any behavior that is motivated by our anger will fall short of God's righteous judgment. If our actions are motivated by anger, they will always fall short of God's best, even if they appear to be "spiritual." As James said, "[our] anger does not bring about the righteousness of God" (James 1:20). The Scriptures are also clear that we are to confront injustice and evil by doing good (See Romans 12:17-21, Luke 6:33-35). If the *peace* of Christ is "ruling in our hearts," and we are genuinely motivated by *love*, then our behavior will be *good*.

As you will recall from our discussion of the "*Belief and Choice*" Principle, our outward behavior may appear to be just and righteous, but "God does not see as man sees, since man looks at the outward appearance, but the Lord looks at the heart" (1 Samuel 16:7, see also 1 Corinthians 4:5). If we hope to rightly evaluate our behavior, we must search where God is focused: our motives. If our actions are motivated by anger, then we are attempting to do God's job. But if we are truly motivated by God's love and the peace of Christ, we are fulfilling His call upon our life.

The Scriptures are clear, "Do not take revenge. . . but leave room for God's wrath, for it is written: "It is mine to avenge; I will repay," says the Lord" (Romans 12:19 NIV). Anytime we attempt to right wrongs, punish, take revenge, or bring about justice while we are angry, our actions will not fulfill God's righteous judgment. Some people call their acts of anger a "righteous indignation." However, James was clear when he said that our anger cannot accomplish a righteous outcome. Since this is so, even our best efforts in 'righteous indignation' still result in our trying to solve a problem that only God can righteously solve. It is God's job to bring about a righteous judgment; ours is to act in love.

Does this mean that we turn a blind eye to the evil injustices in our world? Not at all, for we are told to speak the truth in love (see Ephesians 4:15). Paul also reveals that God will use secular authority to punish evildoers where he wrote,

> [secular authority] is a servant of God to you for good. But if you do what is evil, be afraid; for it does not bear the sword for nothing; for it [secular authority] is a servant of God, an avenger who brings wrath on the one who practices evil (Romans 13:4, emphasis added).

When Paul said, "Be angry, and yet do not sin. . ." (Ephesians 4:26), he revealed that our initial reaction of anger was normal and expected. However, when he said, "just don't sin" he is stating just how far we should go in our anger. Since our anger cannot accomplish or bring about the righteousness of God, anything we do while angry will fall short and fit the definition of "sin" (see Romans 3:23).

So then, to paraphrase what Paul is saying: "feel what God feels (anger) when you witness an injustice, but don't react to the situation from this emotionally charged place. Leave vengeance up to God." Make room for God to do only what He can do. Our calling is to operate from a heart of love. Here is a sampling of what the Scriptures say should be our response in the face of injustice. These are all actions based upon a heart of love. If these verses seem to set too high a standard it is because we are not yet convinced in our hearts that they bear the truth:

> Blessed are you when others revile you and persecute you and utter all kinds of evil against you falsely on my account. Rejoice and be glad, for your reward is great in heaven (Matthew 5:11-12 ESV).

> Let all bitterness and wrath and anger and clamor and slander be put away from you, along with all malice. Be kind to one another, tenderhearted, forgiving one another, as God in Christ forgave you (Eph 4:31-32 ESV).

Repay no one evil for evil, but give thought to do what is honorable in the sight of all" (Romans 12:17 ESV).

Love your enemies and pray for those who persecute you (Matthew 5:44 ESV).

Bearing with one another and, if one has a complaint against another, forgiving each other; as the Lord has forgiven you, so you also must forgive (Col 3:13 ESV).

Do not be overcome by evil, but overcome evil with good (Romans 12:21 ESV).

Do not repay evil for evil or reviling for reviling, but on the contrary, bless, for to this you were called, that you may obtain a blessing (1 Peter 3:9 ESV).

Bless those who persecute you; bless and do not curse them (Romans 12:14 ESV).

If your enemy is hungry, feed him; if he is thirsty, give him something to drink; for by so doing you will heap burning coals on his head (Romans 12:20 ESV).

Again, each of us will feel angry at times. There is no avoiding it. And sometimes we are angry at what angers God, but it is for this very reason that we do not need to remain angry. God's wrath is sufficient! Our anger is ineffective and unnecessary. When we are able to see His wrath and righteous judgments, this revelation will extinguish our anger and cause us to give up our attempts at doing His job.

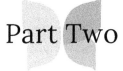

Part Two

Characteristics of Anger

When applying the Process of TPM, it is important to recognize when you are feeling angry, but this task can sometimes seem difficult to accomplish. Thankfully, understanding the characteristics and dynamics involved with anger can help you to distinguish it from other emotions, because some of these characteristics are unique to the members of the "Anger Family."

The "anger family" may include such feelings as revenge, hate, wrath, malice, rage, impatience, frustration, or feeling "ticked," "miffed," exasperated, flustered, aggravated, annoyed, irritated, resentful, and more. Even though each of these are described using different words, they all have common characteristics that secure their place in the anger family.

1. **We feel anger <u>towards</u> someone or something.**

The foremost characteristic that will help you determine when you are feeling angry is the direction anger typically flows. Most other negative emotions are felt <u>inwardly</u>, but we feel anger outwardly <u>towards</u> someone or something. For instance, I may feel angry "*at*" you, but I would not feel sad "*at*" you, scared "*at*" you, or worried "*at*" you. We feel angry *toward* other people, *toward* God, *toward* our situation, and even *toward* ourselves.

The direction that the emotion is flowing indicates whether or not it is a member of the "*anger family*." All forms of anger are felt outwardly, toward a person or thing. This unique characteristic is the basis for the ANGER Box question, "Is any portion of what you are feeling being felt *toward* any person or thing?" If what you feel is felt *towards* someone or something, then you are probably feeling some form of anger. People often ask us, "Is   (some particular emotion)   in the anger family?" We always answer their question with a question, "Is the emotion being felt *toward* someone or thing?" If so, then the answer is "yes." This is a crucial concept worth remembering.

Someone might say, "*I don't really think that I'm feeling angry at "So-and-So." I am just upset with what they did.*" Again, we would ask, "is any portion of your "upset" feelings being felt toward this person?" If the answer is "Yes," then you may not be raging, but you are angry. Someone else might protest saying, "*On a scale of one to ten, I am just barely a "one." Does this small measure constitute anger?*" It is not the intensity of our emotion that determines if we are angry or not. I would ask those who are mothers, were you ever only a little pregnant? Even if we are barely angry, we are angry.

2. We purposefully hold on to our anger because we believe it will accomplish something.

We hold onto anger because we believe it serves us in some manner or will help us "solve" a perceived problem. For example, we may believe that our anger keeps us safe and protects us, that it holds those who have hurt us accountable for their actions, or that our anger is a force for good as we fight for the innocent who are being mistreated. We may feel angry at ourselves as a form of punishment in hopes that we will change our poor behavior. Or it may seem as though being angry gives us a sense of empowerment or control. If we have been deceived into believing that there is a reason to hold on to our anger, we will feel compelled to do so no matter the consequence.

3. We cannot hold on to anger without suffering negative consequences.

Anger is too hot to handle for very long. Not only does anger lead to wrong decisions and sinful behavior, but it also takes a toll on us mentally, emotionally, and physically. Being angry burns up mental energy and causes us to be distracted. Remaining angry for an extended amount of time can lead to very real physical consequences. For example, we might develop ulcers, suffer from acid reflux, experience headaches, or even develop cancer. It is impossible to stay angry without paying a price.

4. When we are angry, we can have difficulty connecting with our other emotions.

If two parents were walking with their 3-year-old on the sidewalk near a busy street, and the child suddenly darts into oncoming traffic, what do you think they would immediately feel? Terrified! Out of control! Helpless! Powerless! But after the child is safely pulled away from the busy street, the parents' presenting emotion would likely change. At first, they may express relief, but they will probably also feel some measure of anger. They might feel angry at the child for his dangerous behavior. They may feel angry towards the drivers who sped past them. They may even feel angry at each other for allowing the child to escape their care. Whatever the case may be, their initial feelings of helplessness, powerlessness, and being out of control will be drowned out by their anger.

5. We usually choose not to listen to people we feel angry towards.

If I am angry at you, our ability to effectively communicate will be hindered. Little of what you say will make it through to me, and that which does will carry little weight. The same dynamic is at work in a TPM session when you are angry, especially when angry toward God. Anger is a common reason for not "hearing" from God during a ministry session. Until you address the reason you are angry at God and gain His perspective, you will likely be unwilling to hear from Him about much else. The belief that supports your decision to stay angry must be dealt with first.

6. **We often have reasons for not admitting that we are angry.**

Many of us struggle to admit that we feel angry. This is most often the case when we feel angry towards God. Being angry at God is typically viewed as sinful and unacceptable. Many of us have been led to believe we should stop being angry or, at the very least, deny and suppress our anger. This mindset can lead you to unknowingly ignore the fact that you are angry.

It is common to deny the fact that you feel angry, or claim to be feeling "nothing," even though you do feel angry. This can be for a myriad of reasons. Many cultures discourage expressing anger, as it is viewed as bad, sinful, inappropriate, and rude. We often encourage little children to "count to ten" and suppress their anger. Or worse yet, we console and comfort them if they feel scared, worried, or rejected but scold and punish them when they express anger.

These responses mistakenly communicate that some negative emotions are permissible while others are unwanted. And though these techniques may have seemed helpful and productive at the time, they likely had no impact on the reasons for why we are angry in the first place. We were not dealing with our anger; we were simply keeping ourselves from expressing it.

The fact of the matter is if you are angry, God already knows this. He is not interested in your attempts to deny your feelings. He wants you to acknowledge the fact that you are angry, take an honest look at the reason(s) for being angry, and come to Him for His perspective.

But if we have reasons for not admitting our anger, these *solution beliefs* must be addressed before we are able to deal with the anger itself. In these instances, we must first seek His perspective regarding our decision to deny our anger, and then we will be able to own and acknowledge the reasons we have for holding on to it. Attempting to address these kinds of *solution behaviors* out of order is usually not productive.

Part Three

A Preview of The ANGER Box

When you realize that you feel angry or that you are exhibiting any of the *characteristics of anger*, you are in the ANGER Box. This can occur at *nearly* any point in a TPM session no matter where you might be in the *Process* (the only exception being the time in between asking the Lord for truth and checking for transformation). While in the ANGER Box, your objectives are to determine if you feel an emotion that is in the *Anger Family*, and if so, identify who or what you feel it towards as well as a tentative reason for why you feel it. Once you have accomplished these objectives, you are ready to move to the SOLUTION Box.

Recognizing When You Are Angry

The first step in addressing your anger is to acknowledge it. Denying or suppressing it only makes it more difficult to address. And even if you are not consciously aware of when you feel angry, or are actively attempting to deny that you do, the mere presence of these emotions indicates your need for God's perspective and represents opportunities for truth and refinement. Realizing and acknowledging what you feel is one of the first steps towards what God has for you. Remember, God already knows when you are angry. He also knows why you are angry, and He is waiting patiently for you to acknowledge both so that He can offer His perspective.

The emotions that are members of the *Anger Family,* such as frustration, irritation, wrath, malice, aggravation, or being "ticked off" etc., share several notable characteristics. A specific characteristic that is especially relevant in the context of TPM is that these emotions are typically felt outwardly, *towards* someone or something. If you feel angry, you will find that you feel it *towards* yourself, *towards* someone else, or *towards* something specific.

If you think that you might be feeling angry but are unsure, you can go to the ANGER Box and ask yourself, "*Is any portion of what I am feeling, felt towards any person or thing?*" If so, then it is safe to assume that you are currently feeling a member of the *Anger Family.* As such, you should continue working through the Anger Box.

An example of this when working with a Mentor might be as follows:

The number indicates where you are on the corresponding "*Flowchart.*"

The following example begins in the MEMORY Box.

Mentee: "*I remember feeling a tightness in my chest when he said those words to me. He shouldn't have said that in front of everybody!*" (M1)

Mentor: "*How does that make you feel?*" (M3)

Mentee: "*...I'm not sure.*" (said while clenching his teeth and fists - suggesting that he might be angry) (A3)

Mentor: "*Well, is any portion of what you are feeling felt towards any person or any thing?*" (A4)

Mentee: "*Yes. I feel ticked-off at him!*" (A7) > (A10) > (A19) > (A20)

As you can see in the example above, if you simply haven't noticed or realized that you feel angry, examining the direction in which you feel what you feel can help you determine if any part of it is anger. Even though in this example the Mentee never used the word "anger" to describe what he felt, his acknowledgement that he felt it towards the other person revealed that he was indeed angry. This unique characteristic of the *Anger Family* can help us to determine if we are angry when we are otherwise unaware of it.

If a portion of what you are feeling is being felt *towards* someone or something, ask yourself, "*What am I feeling towards _____ ?*" If it is some form of anger, irritation, annoyance, hate, etc., then continue to your next objective in the ANGER Box.

Note: *If you notice that you are feeling an emotion towards yourself, another person, your situation, or at God but sense that you are having trouble acknowledging the specific emotion you feel, this is a potential indicator that you are engaged in a solution behavior. In other words, you may have a reason* *for not admitting that you feel some member of the Anger Family. When this is the case, move to the SOLUTION Box.*

"Who or what do you feel angry towards?"

After you have determined that you are angry, the next step is to identify who or what you feel angry towards. There will always be a subject or target of your anger. You are not just mad, but rather you are mad *at* someone or something. You might feel it towards another person or towards some specific circumstance. You might feel it towards yourself or even towards God. You are simply answering the question, *"Who or what do I feel angry towards?"* After you have done this, the next step is to determine a tentative reason for why you feel angry.

Note: It doesn't matter who or what we are angry with; all that matters is that we acknowledge the target of our anger. I recall a time when someone told me that they were justified in being angry because they were angry at the devil. This may have seemed reasonable, but it was not biblical. The Bible does not say that we are to "get rid of all bitterness, rage and anger, brawling and slander, along with every form of malice" (Ephesians 4:31 NIV) unless it is being felt toward the devil. The anger we might feel towards the devil will not "accomplish the righteousness of God." We are to resist the schemes of the devil, but we are not called to be angry at him.

WHAT ARE YOU FEELING?

Feeling and expressing anger is frowned upon in many cultures. It is viewed as being out of control, potentially harmful, and even sinful. Therefore, some people are slow to admit that they are feeling angry. They may be willing to admit that they feel "something" towards somebody and can even give a tentative reason for why they feel it but seem leery of admitting the fact that what they feel is anger. Their refusal to admit their anger can be due to a myriad of reasons, but generally speaking, they hesitate because they have a lie-based reason for not admitting what they feel.

If you are applying the TPM Process with a Mentor and fail to clearly acknowledge what you are feeling, you may be asked, "What are you feeling?" This is done to remind you of the importance of honestly admitting what you feel and gives you an opportunity to check for a potential solution behavior. If you notice any amount of resistance or hesitation when thinking about admitting what you feel, this indicates that you might be engaged in a solution behavior (which we will discuss, in detail, in the next chapter).

Part Four

A Tentative Reason for Why You Are Angry

Typically, when you acknowledge who or what you feel angry towards, you also express some reason for feeling that way. This is especially true when you are familiar with your objectives while in the ANGER Box. For example, rather than simply stating, "I feel angry at my sister," you would likely say, "I feel angry at my sister because of the way she treated me."

We describe this reason as *"tentative"* because, as you will discover in the next chapter, the reason for why you continue to feel angry after the initial offense is rarely what you believe it to be while in the ANGER Box. Your initial reasoning for feeling angry is usually based upon your perspective of what did or did not happen. For example, you might say, "I am angry because she lied to me," or "I am angry because he hurt me," or "I am angry because she did not protect me from him," or "I am angry because God did not keep that from happening."

These explanations describe what may have initially led you to feel angry, but they are not the reason you are still angry. As you will soon discover, you continue to feel angry not because of what happened, but because you believe that you can resolve a problem with your anger. Although it often seems that you are fully justified in feeling angry, and that your reaction was initially rooted in truth, more often than not, the true reason for why you _still_ feel angry is because you lack God's perspective.

You may have initially felt angry in response to a perceived injustice, but you remain angry because you have been deceived into believing that your anger will bring about a just result. This indicates that you have given the enemy "an opportunity," and he has deceived you into sinning with your anger.

This is not to say that your perspective is necessarily inaccurate or skewed (although this is often the case), but rather that there are elements of His eternal perspective of which you are not yet aware. There are additional pieces to the puzzle that you are currently missing. Because of this, your situation will likely seem unjust and problematic.

When we are confronted with a problem, such as a situation that we perceive to be unjust and are not yet convinced of *God's solution* to it, we typically attempt to solve the problem ourselves. After taking an honest look into why you feel what you feel, you may find that you are actually angry because you believe that it will protect you, or that it will hold someone accountable, or that it will motivate you to make better choices in the future.

Again, your initial flash point of anger may have seemed like righteous indignation over an injustice. You may have felt what God feels, but you are not equipped to bring about a righteous judgment. We may have rightly assessed the need for righteous judgment concerning the injustice that surrounds us all, but the reality is that we cannot bring about the justice we seek. Our anger is always insufficient. But if we believe that our anger keeps us safe, or empowers us, or holds others accountable, or punishes poor behavior, etc., then we will attempt to use our anger to accomplish the righteousness of God, which is something it simply cannot do (See James 1:20, Psalm 37:8).

Whatever the case may be, while in the ANGER Box, you are simply expressing a tentative reason for why you feel angry, knowing that it may not prove to be the actual reason. Having this tentative reason fresh in your mind will likely make accomplishing the objectives of the next *Box* much easier as these tentative reasons tend to describe the problem that we are attempting to solve by being angry. They usually allude to what we believe happened or should have happened which seems wrong, unfair, or unjust from our perspective. But the "sun has long gone down on our anger," and the actual reason we are angry is not about what happened (*we will discuss this concept in more detail in the next chapter*).

Examples of *tentative* reasons for being angry might include,

"She never acknowledged what she did!"

"He promised to be there, but he didn't show up!"

"They wouldn't stop even though I begged them!"

"God didn't keep that man from hurting me!"

"My mother simply cannot mind her own business!"

"He lied right to my face!"

"She refuses to drop it. She brings it up over and over again!"

"He acts like it didn't even happen!"

"I hate that I keep doing this! I know God expects more from me!"

"God allowed this to happen. He could have stopped it, but He didn't!"

"None of the kids listen. I can be screaming, and it's like I'm not even there!"

"It's like she keeps poking and poking me about it. She won't leave me alone!"

"It's like he refuses to open-up to me. He just puts a wall up between us!"

"They knew what was going on and did nothing about it!"

"They don't care about anybody but themselves!"

"He should have known that this would impact me and the kids!"

An example of what this might look like in a session where a person is working with a Mentor:

This scenario begins in the EMOTION Box...

Mentee: *"My wife always does that. I was just trying to ask her a simple question, and she jumped all over me!" (E1)*

Mentor: *"How does that make you feel?" (E2)*

Mentee: *"It makes me mad." (E5) > (E6) > (E7)...(A10) > (A15)*

Mentor: *"Who or what do you feel mad at?" (A16) (Notice that this reworded question uses "mad" as described by the Mentee rather than "angry" to better fit the context.)*

Mentee: *"At her, of course!" (A19) > (A20)*

Mentor: *"And why do you feel mad at her?" (A22)*

Mentee: *"Because she gets all defensive and accuses me of belittling her opinion, which is not even what I am doing. That ticks me off every single time!" (A21) > (A25)*

Another example:

Beginning in the MEMORY Box....

Mentee: *"After he was finished, my uncle told me not to tell anyone!" (M4) > (M6)*

Mentor: *"How does that make you feel?" (M3)*

Mentee: *"I feel really angry at him!" (M11)...(A10) > (A19) > (A20)*

Mentor: *"Why do you feel angry towards your uncle?" (A22)*

Mentee: *"Because what he did was wrong! I should have been able to trust him." (A21) > (A25)*

Another example:

Beginning in the MEMORY Box...

Mentee: *"I remember standing there as the other kids laughed at me." (M4) > (M6)*

Mentor: *"How does that make you feel?" (M3)*

Mentee: *"I feel rejected and embarrassed." (M1)*

Mentor: *"Why do you feel that way?" (M2)*

Mentee: *"Because I was immediately made fun of for what I had shared. I knew I shouldn't have said anything. I should have been more careful!" (M4) > (M6)*

Mentor: *"How does that make you feel?" (M3)*

Mentee: *"I guess I feel frustrated with myself." (M11)...(A10) > (A19) > (A20)*

Mentor: *"Why do you feel frustrated with yourself?" (A22)*

Mentee: *"Because it is my fault that the other kids know. I should have kept my big mouth shut!" (A21) > (A25)*

Final example:

Beginning in the MEMORY Box...

Mentee: *"While that man was hurting me, I remember begging God to make him stop." (M4) > (M6)*

Mentor: *"How does that make you feel?" (M3)*

Mentee: *"I am really angry with God." (M11)...(A10) > (A19) > (A20)*

Mentor: *"Why do you feel angry with God?" (A22)*

Mentee: *"Because it is His job to protect the vulnerable! I was just a little kid! And He let that man do what he did. God did not protect me!" (A21) > (A25)*

At this point in each of the previous examples, the Mentee has accomplished each of the objectives in the ANGER Box and is ready to move to the SOLUTION Box.

The ANGER Box in Review

If you notice that you feel angry or are showing signs that you might be angry, immediately go to the ANGER Box. Your objectives in the ANGER Box are simple: determine if you are angry, identify who or what you feel anger towards, and express a tentative reason for being angry. The questions found in the ANGER Box are designed to remind you of these objectives. The questions, "*Is any portion of what you are feeling being felt toward any person or any thing?*" and "*What are you feeling?*" are designed to help you recognize and acknowledge that you are feeling angry. The question, "*Who are you feeling angry toward?*" asks you to identify who you are specifically feeling angry toward. The last question, "*Why are you feeling angry?*" helps you to identify a tentative reason for being angry.

It is common for each of the ANGER Box questions to be answered before they are ever asked. For example, statements such as, "I am mad at my wife because she yelled at me," answers all of the questions. "I am mad. . . " reveals that I am feeling angry. "At my wife . . . " tells you who I am feeling angry toward. "Because she yelled at me" expresses the tentative reason I believe that I am currently angry.

Other similar statements might be, "I feel frustrated with myself because I can't seem to do anything right," "I am ticked off at my neighbor because of what he let his dog do in my lawn," or "I am angry with God because He let them hurt me." Each of these statements answers all of the ANGER Box questions and accomplishes all of the ANGER Box objectives.

Your Mentor will listen carefully to what you say while in the ANGER Box, for once you have accomplished these three objectives, there is nothing left to do in the ANGER Box. The next step is always to go to the SOLUTION Box.

The ANGER Box in Reality

You are essentially attempting to answer three simple questions while in the ANGER Box: (1) "Am I feeling angry?" (2) "Who or what am I angry at?" and tentatively, (3) "Why am I angry?" But, as simple and straight-forward as these objectives are, from time to time you may have trouble accomplishing them.

You may feel compelled to keep your anger hidden from others. You may feel reluctant to admit who you feel angry towards. You may even struggle to fully express why you believe that you are angry (this is common when we feel angry towards God). Each of these issues can be addressed using what you will learn in the next chapter.

When you have accomplished your objectives while in the ANGER Box, you are ready to move to the SOLUTION Box and begin your search for the _real_ reason why you are still feeling angry.

A CHANGE IN PROTOCOL: THE ANGER BOX

If you were familiar with the most recent version of the *TPM Process* before the publication of this book, then you have likely noticed many of the changes made to the *ANGER Box* as well as the omission of the "*anger towards God*" and "*anger towards anyone or anything other than God*" sections of the *Map*. These changes were made so that the Process would more accurately reflect the *TPM Principles* as we understand them today.

When the older training was released, we had already discovered that when people choose to stay angry at anything or anyone other than God, it very neatly fits the definition of a *solution behavior*. But the anger we felt towards God was viewed differently. We saw that there was a relationship between our perspective of God and the anger we felt towards Him. However, we did not clearly see a few important facets of that relationship.

Previously, it was taught that when we are angry at God, it is the result of our misunderstanding of Him. It was assumed that this lie-based perspective was the source of our anger. Although this understanding reflects a portion of the truth, we've since realized that our anger is not a <u>direct</u> result of our belief about God. When we are angry at God, we likely misunderstand Him, but we also have a lie-based reason to remain angry. It is important to understand that these two beliefs are distinct from one another.

Our inaccurate belief about God creates the *perceived problem* that we are seeking to solve by being angry at Him. For example, if you genuinely believed that God was cruel and untrustworthy, how would this make you feel? According to previous versions of the TPM training, the answer would be "angry." However, this assumption skips a few important steps.

If you really believed these falsehoods about God, they would likely first leave you feeling scared, nervous, on edge, uneasy, vulnerable, helpless, hopeless, or some other form of emotional pain. Just as with the negative emotions and the *perceived problems* that are produced by any other *lie-based heart beliefs*, you will likely respond to your lie-based perspective of God by doing something. Given enough time, you <u>will</u> engage in some form of *solution behavior*.

For instance, you may choose to deny what you believe or suppress what you feel or recite Bible verses until you "calm down," or you could get angry at God if you believe that it will help or accomplish something. Your anger is not a direct result of your misunderstanding of Him (as we previously taught). You are angry because you believe it will somehow help you to rightly respond to the lie-based perceived problem of God's cruelty and unfaithfulness. So, as with any other expression of anger, you are responding to a *perceived problem* and using your anger as a *solution*.

Essentially, the older version of the TPM training had mistakenly encouraged people to unknowingly attempt to work around their *solution behavior* and identify the lie-based *heart belief* that produced their *perceived problem*. Typically, they would initially blame their angry response on God's behavior, and the Mentor would then ask, "*Why does that make you feel angry at God?*" over and over until the person finally acknowledged their perspective of God Himself. This seemed to help people identify their lie-based belief about God, but it also proved to be a challenging point in many sessions for Mentors and Mentees alike.

We now understand why this older protocol seemed difficult and complicated. Essentially, we were unknowingly attempting to "skip steps" by attempting to address the *perceived problem* without first addressing the *solution behavior* that was presently engaged. In light of this, as with any other form of *solution behavior*, it is best to address our anger before moving on to the *heart beliefs* that are producing the *perceived problem* we are attempting to solve.

If we stay angry at anyone or anything (including God), it is because we are attempting to solve *perceived problems* with our anger. This concept helps to explain why a person could have difficulty identifying what they believe about God while being angry at Him, for they would be attempting to identify the belief that is producing their *perceived problem* while also actively attempting to solve that problem by being angry. It is simpler and more straight-forward for a person to address their heart belief after they have first addressed the *solution* they were employing in response to it. This is now reflected in the ANGER Box protocol.

This clarified concept also explains how a person can believe a lie about God (a lie-based State-of-being heart belief) but genuinely not feel angry in response. For example, if you believe that you are alone (which, if this were true, would mean that God isn't omnipresent) or that you are helpless (God is not your strength and help) or that your situation is out of control (God is not in control) or hopeless (God is not faithful), then you would feel some amount of negative or vulnerable emotions. But if you didn't believe that being angry at God would help solve any of these problems, you would not feel angry at Him. Rather, you would likely engage in some other *solution behavior* to cope with these *perceived problems*. One belief produces our *perceived problem,* while the other points us in the direction of a *solution behavior.*

What you have just read might seem overly complicated, but it will become clearer after we have worked through the next section concerning *solutions*. We use our anger in an attempt to solve some perceived problem whether it is focused on others, our situation, the devil, or God. Our tentative reason for being angry may seem to be a reasonable and logical course of action, but it is not the real reason we remain angry. Our anger is our vain attempt at accomplishing a "righteous judgment;" which is something we cannot do.

Much of the older protocol remains intact, though some parts have been moved around. For example, the second question that was asked when someone was angry at God, "*Why do you feel angry towards God?*" was retained, relocated, and repurposed. It was found to be helpful when asked about any occurrence of anger just before moving to the SOLUTION Box. This question asks you to express a tentative reason for being angry. Your response to it often reflects the *perceived problem* that you are attempting to solve by being angry. This can often lead to a smoother transition from the *ANGER Box* to the SOLUTION Box. As such, it is now to be asked regardless of who or what you feel your anger towards. This results in a simpler and more consistent ANGER Box that is more in line with existing *Principles* than what was found in previous iterations of the TPM training.

Hopefully, this brings some clarity as to *why* these changes have been made. Our goal is to present the most accurate information as possible and have the *Process* clearly reflect the *Principles* and *Purpose of TPM.*

CHAPTER 19

THE SOLUTION BOX

The Mentee's Objectives While in the SOLUTION Box

1) Determine if you are engaged in a *"solution behavior."*

2) Identify the *"perceived problem"* that you are attempting to solve.

3) Articulate a *"solution belief"* that explains your behavior.

The SOLUTION Box Questions:

"Do you sense any resistance or hesitancy at the thought of _____?"

"What do you believe would happen if you were to _____?"

"So then, the reason for (doing what you are doing) is what?" or
"What is the reason that you are _____?"

NOTICE: This chapter has been divided into six parts. The first part briefly introduces the three components of a "solution" and explains the concept we refer to as "solution indicators." The second part explains that solution indicators exist on a spectrum and expose our need for God's perspective. The third part explains how to determine if you are engaged in a "solution behavior." The fourth part illustrates how to effectively identify "perceived problems." The fifth part describes how to articulate "solution beliefs." And the sixth part offers examples of what it might look like to work though the protocols involved in the SOLUTION Box.

Part One

A Preview of The SOLUTION Box

As you will recall from our discussion of the TPM Principles, we use the term *solutions*, or *solution behaviors*, to refer to our attempts to solve *perceived problems*. We engage in solution behaviors throughout our daily life as well as during TPM sessions. And even when we are unaware of our own behavior, there are always observable indicators that let us know when we are engaged in a *solution*. We will either feel compelled to do something, feel resistant to do something, or feel as though our problems have been somehow alleviated after doing something.

When you notice any of these *solution indicators*, you should proceed to the SOLUTION Box (the only exception being the time in between asking the Lord for truth in the TRUTH Box and checking for transformation in the TRANSFORMATION Box). There you can identify both the *perceived problem* that you are attempting to solve and a belief that explains why you are doing what you are doing in response. After you have articulated this *solution belief*, you are ready to move to the BELIEF Box and continue following protocol.

Notice: Before our detailed discussion of your objectives in the SOLUTION Box, we will briefly examine each of The Components of a solution: *(1) solution behaviors, (2) perceived problems, and (3) solution beliefs.* We strongly encourage you to revisit the "Belief and Choice" Principle and review the sections that discuss "solutions" before reading further. Understanding these principles will be vitally important in the coming discussions.

A Preview of The Three Components of a Solution

As you will recall, our *truth-based problems* will appear to be unsolved and problematic if we fail to see God's purpose and involvement from an eternal perspective. Our genuine grief and sorrow will appear to be ours alone to carry, others who have hurt us will seem to get by with what they have done, or the regret and shame of our past sins will linger and hold us captive in irresolvable guilt. Even though God has already fully resolved each of these issues (or has promised to do so in the future), if we lack His greater perspective, we will likely view them as unresolved and attempt to address them ourselves.

Worse still, our lie-based and flawed perspectives cause us to *perceive* problems that do not even exist. Because we have been deceived, it can seem as though we are worthless, alone, or abandoned, or that our situation is hopeless and out of control when none of these things are true.

When we are faced with such *perceived problems* (either lie-based or truth-based), we will eventually search for ways to *solve* them. We may try to deny what we feel, blame those around us, hold onto our anger, or find a way to escape our current circumstances, but whatever we do in response, if it is done in an effort to "solve" these problems, it is a *solution behavior*.

We do what we do in response to our problems because we believe it will help. Each of us does what *seems* "best" from our current perspective. For instance, during a ministry session you may genuinely *want* to connect with your emotions, but if you *believe* that blocking them out keeps you safe, then you will feel compelled to do just that. As you learned from our discussion of the "Belief and Choice" Principle, we do what we believe. Every choice you make is based upon what you believe. You are motivated to do what you *believe* will work. The beliefs that support our use of *solution behaviors* are referred to as *"solution beliefs."*

As you will soon discover, you may find yourself engaging in a *solution behavior* at nearly any stage in the TPM Process. But it is also possible for you to make this discovery throughout your daily life. In the same way that your negative emotions indicate that you lack God's perspective, your *solution behaviors* can alert you to this need. We should learn to evaluate our motives and honestly answer the question, "Why am I REALLY doing this?"

Your familiarity with these three components (solution behaviors, perceived problems, and solution beliefs), as well as the dynamics associated with each, will largely determine how successful you will be in identifying them and responding appropriately. For that reason, it is important that you understand these concepts well. We will now look carefully at each concept.

Solution Indicators

Whenever you engage in a solution behavior, there are always signs or indications that this is so. *Solution indicators* expose the fact that you have specific reasons for doing what you are doing. There are three primary *solution indicators* to look for: "compelled behaviors," "alleviated problems," and "resistance/hesitancy." Let's take a few moments and explain each one of these in further detail.

Solution Indicator: "Compelled Behaviors"

When you have been persuaded to believe that a certain behavior will help you solve a *perceived problem*, you will be motivated to engage in that behavior for that purpose. You will feel driven or drawn in its direction. This is true *even* if you intellectually know that the *solution behavior* is unhelpful, destructive, or sinful. This explains why certain behaviors or "bad habits" are so difficult to break. If you let go of the behavior you are left with the "unresolved" problem that you were attempting to "solve" by engaging in the solution behavior.

You may genuinely desire to change what you are doing, but there is a great difference between your *"will"* and your *"desire."* Your desire is what you may *want* to do, but your *will* is expressed in what you are doing. Regardless, if at some level you are convinced that there is a good reason for engaging in a specific behavior, then you will feel yourself being pulled in its direction, and it will likely be your default reaction to certain *perceived problems.*

Examples of *compelled behavior* include (but are not limited to):

Feeling the need to "clean up your act" before attempting to talk to God,

Feeling drawn to search for explicit images online even though you know it is wrong,

Feeling compelled to lie about what you did to avoid facing the consequences of your actions,

Feeling driven to volunteer even though you know you are already overworked,

Feeling as though you must copy Jesus' behavior to earn God's approval,

Feeling compelled to wash your hands even though you know they are not dirty,

Feeling the need to eat even though you know you are not hungry,

Feeling compelled to stay angry at the one who hurt you,

Feeling the urge to position everything on your desk so that each item faces the same way,

Feeling the need to accomplish something notable to bring meaning to your life,

Feeling drawn to consume entertaining media rather than focusing on your work or other responsibilities,

Feeling the need to run away at the sight of a mouse, spider, snake, roach, etc.,

Feeling compelled to express your feelings of outrage or anger by posting your opinion on social media,

Feeling the need to share embarrassing gossip about somebody else,

Feeling as though you have to have the final word in a conversation.

The list can go on and on; there are as many "solutions" as there are "problems." But God desires that you look to Him alone as your solution for all your problems. He has already solved or has plans to solve every problem you encounter. His answer is that you gain His heavenly perspective and "trust in the LORD with all your heart and do not lean on your own understanding" (Proverbs 3:5).

Solution Indicator: "Alleviated Problems"

When you are actively engaged in a solution behavior, the negative emotional consequences of the problems you are attempting to solve will seem to be reduced. As a result, you may feel noticeably "better," safer, more comfortable, more in control, less fearful, less anxious, etc. It may seem that you have, in some measure, "alleviated" your problem, but the truth is that your real problem was not impacted at all. You have simply found a way to temporarily distract yourself from its symptoms.

Although our attempts to alleviate our pain do not solve the problem, they do make the problem seem more manageable. Though some behaviors may appear to be beneficial, good, or even biblical, if they are done to alleviate a *perceived problem*, they fall short of God's divine solutions and are still considered to be *solution behaviors*. And if you disengage from these behaviors, the problem will inevitably seem to regain its problematic nature and things will seem to get "worse." In other words, engaging in a *solution behavior* may result in a temporary change in emotion, but it will not result in a change in belief. And if you were to stop engaging in your *solution behavior*, the pain that is associated with the *perceived problem* would reemerge.

Examples of *alleviated problems* include (but are not limited to):

Feeling more empowered when angry,

Feeling safer when dissociated,

Feeling less alone while being the center of attention,

Feeling as though you have more control when suppressing your emotions,

Feeling less vulnerable when sitting with your back to a wall or while facing an exit,

Feeling safer while wearing certain clothes or accessories,

Feeling more secure and emboldened when surrounded by people who believe what you believe,

Feeling safer when publicly denying your true opinion,

Feeling less depressed by focusing on happier thoughts,

Feeling "happier" or more "desired" when engaged in an extramarital affair,

Feeling less angry after venting to a friend,

Feeling less stressed when reciting Bible verses,

Feeling less afraid after turning on the lights,

Feeling more accepted and appreciated at a bar than at home,

Feeling less anxious while listening to music, exercising, biting your nails, doing something productive, anointing something with oil, taking a smoke break, controlling your breathing, and so on.

Solution Indicator: "Resistance and/or Hesitancy"

When you are convinced that a certain "solution behavior" will help solve a particular problem, you will be *resistant* to the thought of not doing it and *hesitant* to the idea of trying anything else. For instance, if you were out in the cold, you would feel reluctant to take your coat off because you believe it keeps you warm. You would also hesitate exchanging it for a less insulated garment since you believe what you currently possess offers superior protection. In the same way, you will also resist the idea of letting your emotional guard down if you believe it protects you from harm.

If you considered choosing to do the opposite of your solution behavior (either taking your coat off or letting your guard down), it would cause you to recoil, pause, or push-back. Even if you genuinely desired to change your behavior, doing so would seem impossible or at the very least, require much effort, focus, or willpower. This is due to the fact that you would be attempting to act in opposition to what you believe to be true (*solution belief*).

For example, you may feel hesitant or resistant at the thought of letting go of the anger you feel toward someone who has hurt you because you believe that maintaining your anger is holding the person accountable (*solution belief*). According to this flawed logic, releasing your anger would let him get by with what he did (*perceived problem*). Even if you intellectually know that releasing the anger would be good, helpful, or moral, the resistance you feel indicates that you still believe there is a valid reason to hold onto what you feel.

Another example of this might be feeling hesitant or resistant at the thought of allowing yourself to remember some painful life experience. Even though you feel deep pain, no memory comes to your mind. If you believe that blocking out the memory keeps you from being overwhelmed by it (*solution belief*), then it would seem as though you are risking becoming overwhelmed if you choose to remember (*perceived problem*). You may logically understand that recalling memories is a step in the right direction, but your hesitation indicates that you believe blocking-out the past is preferred.

Other examples of *resistance/hesitancy* include (but are not limited to):

Resisting connecting with emotional pain,

Being hesitant at the thought of remembering an abusive experience,

Being unwilling to admit your own mistakes,

Struggling to forgive a debt,

Feeling resistant to the thought of going to your family reunion,

Hesitating when prompted to share your faith,

Being reluctant to fully accept that God's grace is sufficient for your sin problem,

Feeling hesitant at the thought of not being angry in response to a perceived injustice,

Struggling to admit your need for help,

Feeling hesitant at the thought of honestly acknowledging what you really believe,

Feeling reluctant to honestly acknowledge who you feel angry towards,

Feeling hesitant at the thought of letting your guard down,

Resisting hearing someone else's opinion if you believe it conflicts with your own,

Being reluctant to saying "no" when others ask you to serve,

Feeling as though you must put effort into staying focused while applying the TPM Process, etc.

Do not be surprised if you find that you feel resistant or hesitant to the thought of doing something that you genuinely want and desire to do. This simply indicates that you have reason to continue doing what you are currently doing even though you know you should do something else. It is common for someone who is new to this concept to claim to be "willing" to let go of their solution behavior because they know that it is the right thing to do. However, when asked if they feel any resistance or hesitation to do so, they are surprised at their dubiousness.

Part Two

Solution indicators exist on a spectrum.

When attempting to identify potential *solution indicators*, it is important to understand that they exist on a spectrum. It is not the magnitude of hesitation or resistance that determines whether or not a behavior is a solution. For even the slightest resistance to change your current behavior indicates that you have reason to continue doing what you are doing. For instance, when focusing on your feelings while in the EMOTION Box, you may notice a subtle tug pulling you away from the pain. Or you may encounter a strong resistance to the thought of embracing your emotions; so much so that it may seem utterly impossible to connect with any feelings whatsoever. Though there is an extreme difference here, both of these are forms of resistance.

Think of it this way: if you were to use your hand to stir a bucket of water, you would feel a small measure of resistance. If you added some concrete mix to the water and again attempted to stir the contents of the bucket with your hand, you would notice substantially more resistance. And if you waited for the concrete to harden and then attempted to stir it with your hand again, you would obviously be unable to move it at all. Each of these sensations is an example of the "resistance." Whether it is barely noticeable, impossible to move, or somewhere in between, it fits the definition of "resistance" and "hesitancy."

The other *solution indicators* we have discussed also exist on a spectrum. For instance, you would obviously feel an intense compulsion to escape a burning building, but the subtle urge to check your phone after hearing it make a sound is also an example of a *compelled behavior*. You would feel *compelled* to engage in both of these behaviors because you believe they are profitable courses of action to take.

This is just as true in a TPM session. If you feel drawn to engage in a particular behavior during the session, such as holding onto anger, blaming someone for your pain, being easily distracted by outside noises, persistently opening up your eyes, continually engaging your Mentor in conversation, or fidgeting in your chair, such things may be expressions of *compelled behavior*. They are done in hopes of solving perceived problems. This is true regardless of how *intensely* you feel the compulsion to do them.

If you feel noticeably "better" after engaging in a particular behavior, this is an example of an "alleviated problem." The degree to which the problem was alleviated is irrelevant. You may feel all of your anxiety and stress "leave you" as soon as you take your first bite of ice cream, or you may simply feel slightly more in control after shouting at your kids, but in either case, you are engaged in a *solution behavior*. When you are applying the TPM Process and you sense your emotional pain subside or diminish in some measure, this is usually an indication that you are engaged in a solution behavior. (*The obvious exception to this is when the Holy Spirit persuades your heart of the truth, and your emotions change to reflect the truth you believe in your heart.*)

When working on your first objective in the SOLUTION Box, your task is simply to determine whether or not you notice any *solution indicators*. The first question in the SOLUTION Box has been crafted to help you remember to do this. It is stated as, *"Do you sense any hesitation or resistance at the thought of _____?"* If you sense even a subtle resistance or hesitancy at the thought of disengaging from the behavior, then you have fulfilled your first objective of this box. If you sense any measure of compulsion to do what you are currently doing, then you have accomplished your first objective. If it feels as though it would be impossible to do the opposite of what you are currently doing, then you have accomplished your first objective. And if you feel even a little bit better after engaging in your *solution behavior*, then you have accomplished your first objective.

"Solution behaviors" indicate our need for God's perspective.

The presence of *solution indicators* suggests that you are currently engaged in a *solution behavior*. In other words, you are *potentially* doing what you are doing because you have been deceived into believing that it will help you solve a *perceived problem*. We believe that <u>being able to identify when you are engaged in a solution behavior will prove to be one of the most beneficial skills you will learn in TPM</u>. It is also a major time-saver when applying the *TPM Process* with a Mentor. Rather than waiting until you are seemingly unable to move forward, you can alert your Mentor, and go to the SOLUTION Box at the first sign of a *solution indicator*.

Not only does understanding these concepts aid in your application of the TPM Process, but it also enhances your ability to mentor others and further equips you to take advantage of the opportunities for refinement that God presents in your daily life. Just as our emotional pain indicates our need for His perspective, our behavior serves as another alarm system, indicating when something is wrong. For instance, feeling reluctant to engage others in conversation at a church function is not your problem, it indicates that you are attempting to *solve* a problem. If you find yourself always sitting in the back of the room or near an exit door, your behavior is not random, it is the way in which you are *solving* a problem. And if you stand in front of your refrigerator knowing that you are not hungry, you do not have an "eating problem," you have an "eating solution."

If we feel compelled to engage in any kind of solution behavior, we need God's perspective. When we feel hindered from doing the good works that God prepared for us, we need His perspective. If we feel less stressed, anxious, or angry after going somewhere, doing something, or talking with someone, we need to assess our own behavior. Opportunities for faith-refinement are all around us! But before we can intentionally take advantage of these opportunities, we must be able to spot them.

Understanding the concept of solution indicators will further equip you to see opportunities that you might otherwise miss.

WE ARE MOTIVATED BY OUR EMOTIONAL PAIN TO ENGAGE IN SOLUTION BEHAVIORS.

As you will recall from our discussion of the "Belief and Choice" Principle, our emotions motivate us to act. We are most driven to "do something" when we are in a heightened emotional state. And when we are faced with the painful emotional consequences of our heart belief, we <u>will</u> do something in response. This is by God's design. He wants us to respond to what we feel, but He also wants both our emotions and behaviors to reflect the truth.

For if you believe a lie in your heart, you will feel lie-based pain and be driven to do something about it. You will *likely* either attempt to make the pain go away or "solve" the perceived problem that you believe is causing you to feel what you feel. However, neither of these options will address the actual problem; you need God's perspective.

Even if you have a partial understanding of the truth in your heart, if you fail to see God's intimate and purposeful involvement, you will *likely* believe that your truth-based problems are not being adequately addressed. As a result, you will feel some measure of truth-based pain and be motivated to either alleviate the pain or "solve" the problem yourself. But, yet again, both of these strategies are futile and unnecessary.

What you need is God's perspective. You need the Holy Spirit to convince you of the truth regarding your hopeless attempt to meet your own needs as well as His perspective on the problem you are seeking to solve. Anything that you do in response to your emotional pain which does not result in a change in belief (mind-renewal) is essentially a *solution behavior*.

For example, what do you do when your emotions well up? Do you look for the television remote? Fill a bowl with ice cream? Call your mother? Study Scripture? Listen to music? Ignore your feelings? Lash-out on someone? Mix-up a margarita? Make a vow or promise to yourself? Regardless of what emotionally-charged behavior you choose, if it does not consistently result in you coming to believe the truth in your heart, you are forfeiting valuable opportunities for faith-refinement and need to try something different.

If you are ever in doubt regarding whether or not you are engaging in a *solution behavior*, check your emotional status. If you feel stressed, anxious, worried, afraid, angry, or some other negative emotion, then the answer is *probably*, "Yes!"

Part Three

Determining If You Are Engaged in a "solution behavior"

If it ever seems as though you are (or even *might* be) engaged in a solution behavior, you should stop what you are doing and move to the SOLUTION Box. For example, if you notice that you feel <u>compelled</u> to do something that you know you should not do (like eat an entire tub of ice cream, spew profanities at an out-of-control referee, or hold onto your anger long after the "sun" has gone down), then you are *probably* engaged in a *solution behavior*. If you notice that you feel "better" after engaging in a specific behavior (such as turning on your favorite show, "venting" to someone you believe will listen, or reciting Scripture to yourself), then you *might* be engaged in a *solution behavior*. And if you realize you feel resistant or hesitant at the thought of doing something (like admitting that you need help, letting go of your grief, or connecting to your emotions), then you *may* be engaged in a *solution*.

When you notice any of the dynamics associated with *solution indicators*, such as feeling compelled to hold onto your anger, feeling resistant to the thought of remembering a specific memory, or feeling less vulnerable when you open your eyes during a TPM session, then you are engaged in a *"solution behavior"* and have already accomplished your first objective in the *SOLUTION Box*.

If you are ever unsure about whether or not you are engaged in a *solution behavior*, the first question in the SOLUTION Box can help by reminding you of what you are looking for. The question related to this objective is: "Do you sense any resistance or hesitancy at the thought of _____?"

The resistance or hesitancy you feel when considering not doing some particular behavior (like not holding onto your anger) or conversely, choosing to do something (like remembering something that you don't want to remember), indicates that you are engaged in a solution behavior.

So, when you ask yourself the first SOLUTION Box question, *"Do I sense any resistance or hesitation at the thought of (letting my anger go, remembering something that I don't want to remember, allowing myself to feel emotional pain, keeping my eyes closed during the ministry session, etc.)?"* you are looking for any "push back" that may be present.

This question is not asking you to *start* or *stop* doing anything, nor is it asking if you *want* or are *willing* to do anything. Your focus must be on *sensing* for any resistance or hesitancy *at the thought of* doing or not doing something. Regardless of whether or not you genuinely *want* to take the next step in the TPM Process, if you sense any resistance or hesitancy (whatsoever) at the thought of moving forward, then, at some level, you believe there is a valid reason to stay where you are. This indicates that what you are doing is deliberate. You are actively attempting to "solve" a *perceived problem*.

What follows is an example of what it might look like to ask this question in a TPM session:

Mentee: *"When he said that to me, I knew I was in trouble." (E1)*

Mentor: *"How does that make you feel?" (E2)*

Mentee: *"Panicked!" (E5) > (E8)*

Mentor: *"What comes to mind as you focus on that?" (E10)*

Mentee: *"...I don't really notice anything happening. Nothing is coming to mind!" (E11) > (E12)*

Mentor: *"Do you sense any resistance or hesitancy at the thought of having something come to your mind?" (S1)*

Mentee: *"Yeah, actually...I know I should be remembering something, but a part of me feels reluctant to do that!" (S6)*

Just like any other question related to the TPM Process, it is important for you to understand both what this question is asking and the concepts it is designed to remind you of. Each question on the TPM MAP is a reminder of the objective or task at hand. For example, this first question is meant to remind you of how you can determine if you are engaged in a solution behavior by checking for solution indicators. It is not asking you to *do,* or even *try* to do, anything. It is not asking if you *want* or *desire* to do anything. It is not even asking if you are *willing* to do anything. This question only asks you to honestly assess what you are already doing by checking for *solution indicators*. This is an important concept that you must understand. Many Mentors and Mentees have stumbled here because they have failed to properly understand this objective.

Remember, the TPM Process is <u>not</u> a list of questions that are to be asked and answered but rather a series of objectives or tasks that are to be accomplished. The questions are included to remind you of your objectives at each step along the way. The "Objectives" version of the TPM Map should prove to be very helpful with this.

If you are working with a Mentor, they may offer a brief explanation before asking this question. They may say something like, *"The intent of the question I am about to ask you is not to have you try to do anything, let go of something, or try to make something happen. It is essentially a yes-or-no question that simply invites you to look for any resistance or hesitancy or any sense of push back or pause at the thought of doing the opposite of what you are currently doing."*

Becoming more familiar with the three *components of a solution*, as well as the primary *solution indicators*, will enable you to more readily identify when you are actively engaged in a *solution behavior*. You will learn to pay closer attention to why you are doing what you are doing. This will likely prove to be beneficial both in your TPM sessions and in your daily life.

Again, if you notice any of the dynamics associated with these *solution indicators* during your TPM session (which can happen at almost any point in the *TPM Process*), you are likely engaged in a *solution behavior* and have already accomplished the first objective in the SOLUTION Box.

WE ARE ONLY TROUBLED BY "PERCEIVED PROBLEMS."

We say "perceived problems" since *no problems exist from God's perspective. He has solved or will solve every legitimate concern we will ever have in His own way and in His own time. Every problem we encounter is only an issue because of our limited and flawed perspective.*

Either we are perceiving a problem that isn't real (flawed perspective) or we are failing to see God's solution to our genuine problem (limited perspective).

Peter reveals the proper response to perceived problems where he says,

Humble yourselves, therefore, under the mighty hand of God so that at the proper time He may exalt you. . . after you have suffered a little while, the God of all grace, who has called you to his eternal glory in Christ, will Himself restore, confirm, strengthen, and establish you (1 Peter 5:6,10 ESV).

Even with this promise given us, we are still prone to look to ourselves for solutions to the problems we perceive are before us. Whatever we do to resolve our perceived problems is our solution or solution behavior.

Again, we are not discounting the genuine suffering that may be required of us. We are simply suggesting that God has an eternal solution for any problem that we may face. Paul said it this way, "For our momentary, light affliction is producing for us an eternal weight of glory far beyond all comparison" (2 Corinthians 4:17).

Part Four

Identifying a perceived problem

Once you have determined that you are currently engaged in a *solution behavior*, your next objective is to identify the *perceived problem* that you are attempting to solve. As you will remember from our discussion of the TPM Principles, *perceived problems* are the issues you attempt to resolve, the situations you try to avoid, and the predicaments to which you react. They are the bad situations or unwanted outcomes that you are attempting to prevent, diminish, resolve, or escape from.

Since you are actively attempting to "solve" your *perceived problem*, you can more easily identify it by thinking about the hypothetical consequences of changing your current behavior. Your *perceived problem* is the problematic outcome that would seem to be unresolved if you stopped trying to solve it yourself. To illustrate this, imagine the problems that would arise if you stopped paying your bills, gave up brushing your teeth, or quit your job. The issues, consequences, and costs that would result from these decisions are the *perceived problems* that would be left unsolved if you stopped doing what you currently do.

With this in mind, after you have determined that you are engaged in a *solution behavior*, the second question in the SOLUTION Box can help you to identify the perceived problem you are attempting to solve. It has you examine what you believe might happen if you were to disengage your solution behavior. This undesirable outcome describes the problem you are attempting to solve with your solution behavior.

The question associated with this objective is: "What do you believe would happen if you were to _____?" When applying TPM on your own you would ask yourself, *"What do I believe would happen if I were to do the opposite of what I am doing or stop doing what I am currently doing?"* For example, if you noticed that you are struggling to connect with your emotions, you would ask yourself *"What do I believe would happen if I were to connect with my emotions or stopped suppressing the pain?"* Or, if you felt compelled to feel angry at your father, you would ask, *"What do I believe would happen if I were to let go of the anger I feel towards Dad?"*

In attempting to answer this question, you are looking for the potential outcome of this hypothetical change in your behavior which seems bad, sad, chaotic, unjust, dangerous, vulnerable, lonely, anxious, scary, depressing, regretful, or otherwise negative and unwanted.

The following sentences illustrate what you are attempting to articulate as you seek to determine your *perceived problem:*

"If I stop doing <u>this</u> (solution behavior), then I believe <u>that</u> (perceived problem) will happen."

"If I do the opposite of <u>this</u> (solution behavior), then it will result in <u>that</u> (perceived problem)."

"If I don't do <u>this</u> (solution behavior), then it will mean <u>that</u> (perceived problem)."

"If I give up on <u>this</u> (solution behavior), then it will seem like <u>that</u> (perceived problem)."

"If I choose to do <u>this</u> (Opposite of the solution behavior), then it feels as though <u>that</u> (perceived problem) will happen."

Some practical examples of this:

"If I connect with my emotions, <u>I will be overwhelmed by them</u>."

"If I remember what happened to me, <u>my life will be destroyed</u>."

"If I'm not angry, <u>my kids won't listen to me</u>."

"If I'm not angry at myself, <u>I will end up doing this again and again</u>."

"If I stay with her, <u>I will never be happy</u>."

"If I'm not hurting, <u>I will be ignored and forgotten</u>."

"If I don't eat this, <u>I'll stay antsy and anxious</u>."

"If I allow myself to feel, <u>it will consume me</u>, and <u>I will lose control</u>."

"If I admit what I did, <u>I will be rejected and alone</u>."

"If I let this go, <u>I won't have anything left to live for</u>."

"If I stop doing this to myself, <u>I will slip back into depression</u>."

"If I don't get her back, <u>I will never feel loved again</u>."

"If I let my anger go, <u>he will get away with what he did to me</u>."

"If I share my faith, <u>I will sound stupid and embarrass myself</u>."

"If I stop behaving this way, <u>I won't know who I am</u>."

"If I let go of this, <u>I will end up just like my mother</u>."

"If I decline from volunteering, <u>I will disappoint everyone</u>."

"If I ask the Lord for His perspective, <u>He will just confirm that I really am worthless</u>."

"If I don't maintain these boundaries, <u>they will walk all over me</u>."

"If I stop grieving, <u>it means that I didn't really love my son</u>."

"If I let my guard down, <u>it might happen again</u>."

"If I go there, <u>it will be more than I can stand</u>."

"If I am not upset about what happened, <u>it means that it was no big deal</u>."

"If I stop feeling bad about my sin, <u>God will distance Himself from me</u>."

"If I stop trying so hard, <u>I will never be good enough</u>."

Each of these hypothetical outcomes of choosing to do the opposite of what is currently being done would be considered the *perceived problem*. Each of them describes a potential negative outcome of abandoning the associated *solution behavior*. They represent the unsolved problem that needs to be addressed.

What You Are (And Are Not) Looking For

When attempting to identify the *perceived problem,* you are not aggressively trying to figure something out. Rather, take a more passive posture. Simply slow things down and take an honest assessment of what *seems*, *feels*, or *appears* to be true in response to the broad question, "What do I believe would happen if I were to stop doing what I am doing or attempt to do the opposite?" For example, "What do I believe would happen if I were to allow myself to feel?" or "What do I believe would happen if I let go of the anger I feel towards them?" or "What do I believe would happen if I were to allow myself to remember?"

Your initial, "knee-jerk" response to this question may seem illogical, childish, or even silly at first. But rather than quickly discounting or dismissing it, remember your goal; you are attempting to identify what you believe, even if that belief is obviously untrue. If it *seems* or *feels* true, then it reflects what you believe in your heart to be true.

Until you have a basic understanding of *perceived problems*, you may misunderstand what you are looking for and answer the second question in the SOLUTION Box with a positive or "spiritual" answer like, "...*I would be free*," "...*I would feel so much better*," or "*I would be able to move forward*," etc. Although these statements are likely true, they do not seem to describe the *perceived problem* or explain why you would need to engage in a *solution behavior*.

For example, if you answered the second question in the SOLUTION Box by saying, "If I let go of my anger, I will be free," this indicates that you do not rightly understand your current objective. For even though this answer may be the truth, it does not describe the theoretical problem you would face if you weren't angry, nor does it explain why you feel resistant or hesitant to letting your anger go. If anything, this type of response describes potential outcomes that would encourage you to change what you are doing rather than continue doing it.

Your goal is to determine the opposite. A *perceived problem* will motivate you to implement a *solution behavior*, not disengage from it. Consider the following belief statements and notice how each of them encourages you to hold on to your anger rather than release it:

"If I let go of my anger, the one who hurt me will get by with what he did."

"If I am not angry, I will get hurt again."

"Without my anger, I will be ignored."

"Unless I am angry at myself, I will make the same mistake again."

"If I am not angry, my grief will overwhelm me."

This part of the TPM Process is commonly misunderstood. When you are first starting out, it may feel more natural to answer the question, "*what do you believe would happen if ___?*" with something logical, positive, or obvious. But the actual answer is often illogical, negative, and unclear. You are looking for the problematic potential outcome of changing your current behavior. You are attempting to articulate that which *seems* or *feels* true, even though you are logically aware of the opposite. You may see the obvious fallacy in believing that you might die if you remember a specific memory, but if this is what you believe, then it is what you believe. And you must honestly take account of this to move forward.

As you remember from our discussion of the TPM Principles, we perceive and feel what we believe. So, when attempting to determine what we believe, we must pay close attention to what *seems* or *feels* true. If it *seems* as though you will be overwhelmed by your emotions if you connect to them, this is what you *believe* to be true. If you *feel* as though you will be rejected if you honestly admit what you did, this indicates what you really *believe*.

Some people temporarily augment this second question to better reflect its corresponding objective. They say it as, "What do you believe might happen if you were to [do the opposite of the solution behavior] that causes you to hesitate or resist [doing the opposite of the solution behavior]?" For instance, "what do you believe would happen if you were to connect with your emotion that would cause you to resist or hesitate the thought of connecting with your emotion?" This rewording may prove helpful, but once you understand your objectives in the SOLUTION Box, this rewording (and even the question itself) becomes unnecessary.

Part Five

Articulating a Solution Belief

After you have identified the *perceived problem*, your next objective in the SOLUTION Box is to express a "*solution belief*" that explains why your current behavior seems to be an appropriate response. This belief serves as the rationale or argument that supports the use of your *solution behavior*. In other words, your *perceived problem* explains *why* you must do *something*, but your *solution belief* explains *why* you are responding with that particular *solution behavior*. Your *solution beliefs* are the "reasons" for *why* you do what you do in response to your *perceived problems*. If it wasn't for these *solution beliefs,* you wouldn't attempt to "solve" your problems the way you currently do.

For instance, you would only retrieve a fire extinguisher in response to a kitchen fire because you *believe* it can be used to put out fires. You buckle your seatbelt while riding in a vehicle because you *believe* doing so will help you escape major injuries and unwanted fines. And because you *believe* that reducing your sugar intake will positively impact your health, you do your best to avoid it.

Consider the following simple example of this concept. If you have ever cared for plants (or any living thing), you probably know that they need water to survive. Because of this belief, you water them. If you don't, they will die. So, in this example, the three components of a solution are as follows: because you understand that your plants will die without water (perceived problem) and that you can keep them alive by watering them (solution belief), you water your plants (solution behavior).

To further illustrate the relationship between the three components of a solution, consider the following practical examples:

If you believe that your emotions might overwhelm you (perceived problem) but also believe that blocking them out will keep them from overwhelming you (solution belief), then you will likely block them out (solution behavior).

If you believe that remembering certain experiences will ruin your life (perceived problem) but also believe that suppressing them will keep your relationships and lifestyle intact (solution belief), then you will likely suppress what you remember (solution behavior).

If you believe that your uncle will try to hurt you again (perceived problem) but also believe that being angry helps to keep you safe (solution belief), then this will likely result in you being angry at him (solution behavior).

If you repeatedly make the same sinful mistakes (perceived problem) but also believe that you can motivate yourself to change through anger and punishment (solution belief), then you will likely get frustrated with yourself and feel self-guilt whenever you mess up (solution behavior).

If you believe that you are worthless (perceived problem) but also believe that performing well at your job will prove that you have value (solution belief), then you will likely contribute an enormous amount of your time and energy into your job performance (solution behavior).

If you believe that you are stupid (perceived problem) but also believe that you can hide this vulnerability by staying quiet (solution belief), then you will likely have a hard time sharing your honest opinion when prompted (solution behavior).

If it feels as though you are missing something in your life (perceived problem) but also believe that finding the "right" person will complete you (solution belief), then you will likely search far and wide for "love" and "connection" (solution behavior).

If you believe that you are on the path of becoming like your abusive father (perceived problem) but also believe that you can avoid this fate by vowing to be different (solution belief), then you will likely attempt to maintain this self-made promise (solution behavior).

If you struggle with some form of substance abuse and genuinely want to change it (perceived problem) but also believe that this can be accomplished through willpower and determination (solution belief), then you will likely be one of the most committed members of your accountability group (solution behavior).

And if you believe that a loved one died without knowing Christ (perceived problem) but also believe that your sadness and regret will motivate you to share your faith more often (solution belief), then you will likely attempt to bear that burden to save more souls (solution behavior).

Hopefully you see the distinction between each of the *components of a solution*. It is especially important to delineate between your *perceived problem* and your *solution belief*. The perceived problem describes the problematic circumstance that you are attempting to avoid, prevent, alleviate, or otherwise "solve," while your solution belief explains why a specific solution behavior would be an appropriate, effective, or otherwise beneficial response to that problem.

The third question in the SOLUTION Box should remind you of this distinction. It asks you to look for the logical (or sometimes illogical) connection between your current behavior and the problem you are attempting to solve. You are attempting to articulate the rationale, explanation, or reasoning behind why you are engaging in a specific *solution behavior.*

This is why the third SOLUTION Box question is worded, *"So then, the reason for (doing what you are doing) is what?"* or *"What is the reason that you are _____?"* For example, *"So then, the reason for suppressing your emotion is what?"* or *"So then, what is the reason for holding onto your anger?"* or simply put, *"How does doing what you are doing help to solve that problem?"*

In response to this question, you may say something like, *"It protects me,"* *"It prevents that from happening,"* *"It motivates me to change,"* *"It holds them accountable,"* *"It proves that I was right,"* *"It keeps me from becoming overwhelmed,"* etc. Each of these statements explains why engaging in the related *solution behavior* seems like a viable option. This flawed logic is the belief statement that you will take to the next *Box.*

After you have articulated a *solution belief,* you have accomplished your last objective in the SOLUTION Box and are ready to move to the *BELIEF Box.*

REWORDING THE QUESTIONS

Someone might think there are better ways to word the questions in the SOLUTION Box (or any of the questions included on the TPM MAP) so that the Mentee will have a better understanding of what he should do. Although the motive behind this desired change is good, the most efficient thing a Mentor can do is simply explain the objectives and the principles that support them.

Again, the purpose of the questions is to remind the Mentee of his objectives. When he hears the words, "So then, the reason for holding onto your anger is what?" he should be hearing, "You've acknowledged that you are purposely and deliberately angry in order to solve a perceived problem. You have also identified what that problem is, now you simply need to determine the specific way in which you believe your anger helps you solve that problem. You are looking for the lie-based rationale or thinking behind your decision to remain angry. How does your anger seem to be helping with that? What do you believe your anger is accomplishing?"

This is why we have stated, time and time again, that the Mentee's understanding of the TPM Principles, Purpose, and Process is paramount. When you understand what to do and how to do it, the questions and your Mentor's involvement becomes less and less necessary.

The SOLUTION Box in Review

As a general rule, no matter where you are in the *Process,* you should always go directly to the SOLU-TION Box as soon as you notice a potential *solution indicator* so that you can determine if you are currently engaged in a *solution behavior.* However, there are two exceptions to this protocol. First, if you have already asked the Lord for His perspective in the TRUTH Box, then your next move is ALWAYS to ask the TRANSFORMATION Box question no matter what is said or happens. And then no matter how you answer the TRANSFORMATION Box question, you will move to the EMOTION Box unless you are showing signs that you are engaged in some *solution behavior.* If this is so, then you are already in the SOLUTION Box. The second exception where you do not move directly to the SOLUTION Box is where there is the presence of anger. Even though all anger is a form of *solution behavior*, you will first move to the ANGER Box before moving on to the SOLUTION Box.

If you recognize that you are engaged in a solution behavior, then you have already accomplished your first objective in the SOLUTION Box. You are ready to identify the *perceived problem* that you are attempting to solve. The second question in the SOLUTION Box is designed to remind you of this objective. Lastly, you will need to articulate the *solution belief* that explains why you are doing what you are doing in response to that problem. The last question in the SOLUTION Box will remind you to do this, and finally, you take that belief to the BELIEF Box and continue following protocol.

The SOLUTION Box in Reality

Even when you intellectually understand your objectives in the SOLUTION Box and how to accomplish them, it may take a little while to get comfortable applying this part of the TPM Process. In many ways you are attempting to think, react, and process quite differently than the ways in which you have likely been accustomed. Rather than assuming you are reacting rightly to your situation and are justified in your position, you are encouraged to take an honest and thorough look into why you are doing what you are doing.

So often we lie to ourselves to justify our own behavior. We want to believe that our motives are pure, but if we are to move forward in a TPM session (and in life in general), we must honestly examine the beliefs that govern our behavior. Again, this is not a criticism of anyone, but rather, we want to encourage you to be honest with yourself and with God.

This is often trickiest when addressing behaviors that otherwise seem productive, beneficial, moral, or socially acceptable - such as helping others, attempting to emulate Jesus' behavior, "controlling" your temper (or some other form of suppression) etc. But you are not evaluating the morality or benefit of your behavior, but rather, you are simply taking a closer look into the reasoning and motive behind it. As we discussed in the "Belief and Choice" chapter, even behaviors that seem innocent, mundane, productive, or godly can be driven by motives that are less than pure. It is better to honestly evaluate your motive than it is to assume that it is pure. If your behavior is a result of His work in your life, then even the harshest scrutiny is no threat to your motives.

MENTORS ENGAGING IN SOLUTION BEHAVIORS

As we have discussed before, Mentors can and do occasionally become triggered during TPM sessions. When this happens, they feel the negative emotional consequences of their need for God's perspective. Many will immediately recognize this and respond appropriately. They will make mental note of the triggering, or jot it down on some paper, so that they can humbly cooperate with what God is trying to do in their lives at a more appropriate time.

However, this is not always the case. Instead, a Mentor might choose to engage in any number of solution behaviors in an attempt to "solve" their perceived problem. For instance, if the person they are mentoring seems to constantly get "stuck," this may trigger the Mentor's lie-based pain and cause them to feel anxious, worried, stressed, or out of control.

In response to this emotional pain, they may feel *compelled* to gently "encourage" the Mentee to stay focused, to try harder, to move forward. They may feel the need to "nudge" the Mentee in a certain direction. Some Mentors may even want to skip steps, reword questions, or take a more direct approach, and just tell the person what they think God wants them to know. They likely know better but will still feel *compelled* to engage in such behavior.

Or, rather than being compelled to do something, they may feel reluctant to do what they know they should do. This is most commonly seen in Mentors who struggle with the idea of pausing a Mentee's application of the TPM Process for the purpose of offering orientation. These Mentors are hesitant to share applicable Principles, explain the Process, and discuss TPM's intended Purpose. Whatever the reason, the fact that they are resistant or hesitant at the thought of offering adequate orientation throughout the TPM session indicates that they are engaged in a solution.

A Mentor may also engage in more subtle *solution behaviors*, but the *indicators* of this will still be present. For instance, some new Mentors feel a sense of relief when a Mentee claims to hear from the Lord and says that the lie no longer feels true. We obviously hope that the Mentee will be persuaded of the truth, but if this moment relieves any measure of the Mentor's negative emotion (such as anxiety, nervousness, stress, fear, etc.), then this fits the definition of "alleviated problems" and indicates that the Mentor was motivated by his or her own lie-based pain to "help" the Mentee. The Mentor should honestly assess his or her own behavior and seek out God's perspective.

If you ever find yourself doing any of these behaviors while mentoring others in TPM, take a moment to evaluate whether or not you feel any amount of anxiety, fear, anger, frustration, helplessness, etc. If you do, then you are triggered, and your need for God's perspective has been exposed. Do the best you can to not act out these impure motives, and purpose to address this with the Lord as soon as it is possible. Dismissing or excusing it will only guarantee that it will show up again!

The truth is this, we feel what we believe. No person, situation, or TPM session can cause us to feel something. If we feel any measure of negative emotion during a TPM session, it is always due to what we believe to be true. The session isn't stressful, slow-moving Mentees do not drive us crazy, and the relief we feel when God speaks to other people likely has nothing to do with mind-renewal; it is simply a *solution indicator*. But, again, becoming aware of our own triggers is not a bad thing. Each of these scenarios represents another opportunity to gain more and more of God's perspective!

Part Six

Brief Examples of Working Through the SOLUTION Box

What follows are several simple examples of what it might look like to work through the SOLUTION Box. These examples illustrate the *components of a solution* and your objectives while in the SOLUTION Box. Be sure to have your copy of the SOLUTION Box Flowchart with you as you read through the examples. (*As a reminder, the Maps and Flowcharts can be found in the back of your book.*)

A Very Important Note: The following scenarios are not a list of "difficult cases." In fact, we have found there are no difficult cases! There are essentially two possible explanations for every "difficulty," "issue," or "problem" that appears in a TPM Session: either (1) <u>the Mentee does not yet know what to do and how to do it</u>, or (2) <u>the Mentee is engaged in some form of *solution behavior*</u>. If you don't know how to apply the TPM Process, this will obviously be a hurdle for you. And if you have a lie-based reason not to do what you know you should do in a TPM session (*solution belief*), this will also obviously get in the way. Both problems can be addressed through the involvement of a knowledgeable Mentor, helpful orientation, ongoing training, and regular practice. For if you know what to do, you will do it. And if you have a lie-based reason not to do it, you will know how to address this issue (in the SOLUTION Box). In either case, as a Mentee, your understanding of the Three Elements of TPM is absolutely paramount!

Having Trouble Connecting with Emotion

Mentee: "I want to connect to the emotion, but I'm really struggling." (E3) > (E4)

Mentor: "Do you sense any resistance or hesitancy at the thought of connecting with your emotion?" (S1)

Mentee: "Yes. It seems like I would have to try really hard to stay connected." (S6)

Mentor: "What do you believe would happen if you were to stay connected to your emotions?" (S8)

Mentee: "I might be overwhelmed by them." (S12)

Mentor: "So then, the reason for not connecting with your emotions is what?" (S13)

Mentee: "It seems like choosing not to connect with my emotions keeps me from becoming overwhelmed by them." (S16) > (S17)

The Mentee would then go to the BELIEF Box with the belief, "*Choosing not to connect with my emotions keeps me from becoming overwhelmed by them*," and continue following protocol.

Nothing Coming to Mind While Focusing on Emotion

Mentee: "I still feel the emotion, but nothing is coming to mind." (E11) > (E12)

Mentor: "Do you sense any resistance or hesitancy at the thought of having something come to your mind or allowing yourself to remember something?" (S1)

Mentee: "I guess so. I can sense a little bit of hesitation." (S6)

Mentor: "What do you believe would happen if you were to have something come to your mind?" (S8)

Mentee: "I might remember something really bad; something that I don't want to remember." (S12)

Mentor: "So then, the reason for not allowing something to come to your mind is what?" (S13)

Mentee: "So that I don't have to remember anything bad!" (S16) > (S17)

The Mentee would then go to the BELIEF Box with the belief, "*By not allowing something to come to mind, I don't have to remember anything bad,*" and continue following protocol.

Claiming to Feel Angry

Mentee: "I still feel really mad at my neighbor because of what she did!" (A10) > (A19) > (A21) > (A25)

Mentor: "Do you sense any resistance or hesitancy at the thought of not being mad at her?" (S1)

Mentee: "Absolutely! What she did was wrong!" (S6)

Mentor: "What do you believe would happen if you weren't mad at her?" (S8)

Mentee: "There would be no consequences for her actions. She would get by with what she did!" (S12)

Mentor: "So then, the reason for staying mad at her is what?" (S13)

Mentee: "To hold her accountable!" (S16) > (S17)

The Mentee would then go to the BELIEF Box with the belief, "*Staying mad at my neighbor holds her accountable,*" and continue following protocol.

Truth-Based Problem in the MEMORY Box (Past Regrets)

Mentee: "I feel bad because I should have been there for my kids. They didn't get the dad they deserved because I acted irresponsibly, and that breaks my heart. It really makes me sad." (M12) > (M15) > (M16) > (M17)

Mentor: "Now, remember, I am not asking you to start or stop doing anything. I am simply reminding you of where you are in the TPM Process. What you are describing sounds like it may be the pain associated with a truth-based problem. But, like we've discussed in the past, we often choose to hold onto this type of pain because we believe that it will help us solve perceived problems. When this is so, we will feel compelled to hold onto it and resistant to the thought of letting it go. So, with that said, do you sense any resistance or hesitancy at the thought of not feeling sad about not being there for your kids?" (S1)

Mentee: "Yeah, I mean, what I did was wrong. I should have been there for them. And I should feel sad about what I've done." (S6)

Mentor: "What do you believe would happen if you were to let your sadness go and were no longer sad about not being there for your kids?" (S8)

Mentee: "It would mean that I don't regret my behavior...that I don't regret not being there for them." (S12)

Mentor: "So then, the reason for continuing to feel sad about it is what?" (S13)

Mentee: "Being sad proves that I am sorry for what I did." (S16) > (S17)

The Mentee would then go to the BELIEF Box with the belief, "*being sad proves that I am sorry for what I did*," and continue following protocol.

Truth-Based Problem in the MEMORY Box (Victimization)

Mentee: "I feel bad because I lost my childhood. That never should have happened to me!" (M12) > (M15) > (M16) > (M17)

Mentor: "Do you sense any resistance or hesitancy at the thought of not feeling bad about your lost childhood?" (S1)

Mentee: "I guess so. It seems as though if I didn't feel bad about it, I would somehow trivialize the abuse I suffered. It would mean that the loss of my childhood meant nothing to me." (S6) + (S12)

Mentor: "So then, the reason for holding onto these bad feelings is what?" (S13)

Mentee: "It seems as though my pain shows how much I lost and how the abuse affected me!" (S16) > (S17)

The Mentee would then go to the BELIEF Box with the belief, "*my pain shows how much I lost and how the abuse affected me*," and continue following protocol.

Truth-Based Problem in the MEMORY Box (Death of a Loved One)

Mentee: "I am sad because I loved my Grandmother, and even though I fully anticipated that she was going to die, it crushed me to see her suffer like that!" (M12) > (M15) > (M16) > (M17)

Mentor: "Do you sense any resistance or hesitancy at the thought of letting go of the sadness related to your Grandmother's death?" (S1)

Mentee: "Yes. Clearly, I am resisting letting it go. I have tried, but even after all these years, I still feel a deep sadness when I think about her laying in that hospital bed." (S6)

Mentor: "What do you believe would happen if you were to let that sadness go?" (S8)

Mentee: "It's as though, if I am not sad, then I didn't care about her pain or her passing. But I really did care. I loved her deeply and hated that she faced such a difficult end to her life." (S12)

Mentor: "So then, the reason for continuing to carry the sadness is what?" (S13)

Mentee: "I know this isn't true, but it seems like my grief and sadness offer me a way to express how much I cared for her. My pain proves that I loved her." (S16) > (S17)

The Mentee would then go to the BELIEF Box with the belief, "*My pain proves that I loved her*," and continue following protocol.

Verbalizing a Vow While in the MEMORY Box

Mentee: "In that moment, I swore I would never allow anyone to talk to me like that again!" (M4) > (M6)

Mentor: "How does that make you feel?" (M3)

Mentee: "Honestly, I feel a little better. It makes me feel empowered." (M7) (*solution indicator*: alleviated problems - feeling "better")

Mentor: "The decision you made to never let anyone talk to you in that way again was how you solved the perceived problem. This is why you feel "better" and somewhat empowered by doing so. If you feel some measure of negative emotion and then do something to make yourself feel better without addressing the belief that was producing the pain in the first place, then this behavior is considered a *solution behavior*. In a sense, you are doing what you are doing for the purpose of "solving" a *perceived problem*. And you can tell if your current behavior is a *solution behavior* by looking for *solution indicators*. For example, if you feel compelled to do what you are doing, it might be a *solution*. Or if you feel better after doing what you are doing, it might be a solution. And if you feel resistant or hesitant at the thought of disengaging from the behavior, it might be a solution." (S3)+(S7)

Mentee: "Oh, ok. That makes sense. It does feel like I need to maintain the promise I made to myself. I feel compelled, in a way, to ensure that no one gets by with talking to me in that rude, condescending tone. And I do feel noticeably better when I think about enforcing that vow. So, yeah, I guess this is one of those *solution behavior* things."

Mentor: "Great! I'm glad it's making sense to you. The better you understand all this, the better you'll be at applying it. So then, what do you believe would happen if you allowed someone to talk to you like that?" (S8)

Mentee: "Everyone would see me as weak and vulnerable. I would lose all respect!" (S12)

Mentor: "So then, the reason for never allowing that is what?" (S13)

Mentee: "Keeping people from talking to me like that ensures that I get the respect I deserve!" (S16) > (S17)

The Mentee would then go to the BELIEF Box with the belief, "*Keeping people from talking to me like that ensures that I get the respect I deserve*," and continue following protocol. There is never any need to renounce a vow, to ask Jesus to do anything with it, or pray against any demonic involvement. Vows are simply *solutions* to perceived problems. When you know the truth and have God's perspective, vows will no longer seem necessary or helpful because, in reality, they never are!

Reciting Bible Verses in the TRUTH Box

Mentor: "Not that it is true, but does it seem or feel true that you are all alone and by yourself?" (BELIEF Box)

Mentee: "I know that it is not true, but yes, it feels true."

Mentor: "May we present that belief to the Lord?" (TRUTH Box)

Mentee: "Of course. Let's approach His throne with boldness!"

Mentor: "Lord, what do you want Philip to know?" (TRUTH Box)

Mentee: "Yes, Lord, tell me your truth. Let me know that You are with me, just as you said in Matthew's gospel account, 'And lo, I am with you always, even unto the end of the world.' Lead my heart to believe the truth found in the book of Isaiah, "Fear thou not; for I am with thee..." Convince me that you are here just as you did your servant Jeremiah saying, "I am with you," over and over again. Speak Lord, for like Samuel, your servant is listening!"

Mentor: (taking note of the behavior) "Does it still feel true that you are all alone and by yourself?" (TRANSFORMATION Box)

Mentee: "Well, I know it's not true...but, yes, it still feels true. Maybe I'll ask the Lord to speak again..."

NOTE: Typically, after checking for a shift in belief while in the TRANSFORMATION Box, you move directly to the EMOTION Box. However, the Mentee has indicated that he does not yet fully understand what he should be doing at this point in the process. Because of this, the Mentor will take time to explain the objectives at hand. And since the Mentee has also indicated that he may be attempting to resolve his perceived problem with a solution behavior (telling himself the truth), his Mentor will ask the first SOLUTION Box question.

Mentor: "Hold on, before you ask God about it, can we take a moment to discuss something?"

Mentee: "Sure. What is it?"

Mentor: "If you'll recall from our previous meeting, when you are in the TRUTH Box, your goal is to focus on the belief you've identified, take a receptive mental posture, and be open to whatever God has for you. But, like last time, you keep praying out loud and reciting Scripture."

Mentee: "What's wrong with that? Are you saying I shouldn't pray or recall the truth found in Scripture?"

Mentor: "No, I am not suggesting that at all, for there is great value in doing both. However, if you feel *compelled* to do it every time you are at this stage of the *Process*, especially if it is to the point that it is compulsive and you are unable to be still and listen, you might want to examine the motivation behind your behavior. Like we've talked about, sometimes even our good, productive, and moral behaviors can be motivated and guided by the lies we believe. If you are trying to solve the problem yourself rather than listening for what the Lord has for you, then you will want to honestly acknowledge and address this. Remember how we have discussed that we cannot change our own heart belief, and that we need the Holy Spirit to bring this about?"

Mentee: "Yes. Ok. I guess I see your point. Tell me again, how am I supposed to know if this is one of those *solution behavior* things?"

NOTE: Since the Mentee has asked about the SOLUTION Box protocol and is obviously engaged in a solution behavior, the MENTOR proceeds to the SOLUTION Box.

Mentor: "You'll want to check for any *solution indicators* that we've discussed in the past: *compelled behavior*, *alleviated problems*, and *resistance/hesitancy*.

Mentor: "For example, do you sense any resistance or hesitancy at the thought of not reciting Bible verses after asking the Lord for His perspective?" (S1)

Mentee: "Yeah, I guess I feel both compelled to do it and resistant to the thought of not doing it." (S6)

Mentor: "What do you believe would happen if you chose *not* to recite Bible verses to yourself at this point in the TPM Process?" (S8)

Mentee: "As silly as it sounds, it seems hopeless...like I'll never really believe the truth." (S12)

Mentor: "So then, the reason for reciting Bible verses while in the TRUTH Box is what?" (S13)

Mentee: "It seems like reciting Bible verses gives me hope that I will someday believe the truth!" (S16) > (S17)

The Mentee would then go to the BELIEF Box with the belief, *"reciting Bible verses gives me hope that I will someday believe the truth,"* and continue following protocol.

Allowing Demonic Manifestations to Occur

Mentee: "I remember a sinking feeling coming over me when I saw my brother sitting next to me on my bed. He called me over to him. I knew what he was going to do! And then... wait...I...I don't...oh no!" (the Mentee's facial expression contorts and she begins speaking in a deep, guttural voice.) "GRRRRR...YOU CANNOT SPEAK WITH HER...SHE BELONGS TO US! LEAVE US ALONE!"

Mentor: "What's going on right now?" (LOST/UNSURE Box)

Mentee: "Please help me! I can't make this stop! I'm so scared! Please Help...It's a demon! GRRRRRR...LEAVE US ALONE YOU SILLY CHILD OF GOD! WE WANT NOTHING TO DO WITH YOU!"

The Mentor does not need to address the demon or command it to do anything, but rather, he needs to speak directly to the Mentee. Once he has the Mentee's attention, he should take a few moments to offer orientation and ask a few simple questions. These questions are not part of the TPM Process and are not found on the TPM Map. They are only asked to remind the Mentee of what they probably already know concerning what the Bible says about demons and the devil. They are used to bring clarity and intellectual understanding about what Satan can and cannot do. We will discuss demonization more fully in a later chapter, but, for now, let's continue the example:

Mentor: "Kaitlyn, I would like for you to please look at me while I ask you a few simple questions."

Mentee: "LEAVE US ALONE! WE WILL NOT ANSWER YOUR QUESTIONS! YOU HAVE NO POWER HERE!"

Mentor: "Kaitlyn, I was talking to you. Can we talk for a moment?"

Mentee: "...Ok...just please do something...this is really scary...I can't make it stop!"

Mentor: "You just did. You are talking to me. Just keep doing what you're doing."

Mentee: (remains silent)

Mentor: "Now, do you believe that a demon can violate your will or force you to do something that you do not choose to do? For instance, can a demon make you sin?"

Mentee: "No, it can't make me sin..."

Mentor: "Alright then, if a demon can't make you sin - which is exactly what it would try to make you do - what can it force you to do?"

Mentee: "...I guess it can't make me do anything."

Mentor: "Exactly! And if it can't make you do anything against your will, can you explain what was happening a few moments ago? Was it forcing you to do and say those things? Was it manifesting against your will?"

Mentee: "No, I guess not...I've never thought about it that way before."

Mentor: "So then, would you like to continue this session without allowing the demon to do that sort of thing?"

Mentee: "Yes."

Mentor: "Great! As you can see, if you simply resist, the demonic manifestation cannot continue. So, what are you feeling now?" (E1) (essentially resetting the Session)

Mentee: "I can still connect with the fear I was feeling earlier...but...no, no, no, no..."

Mentor: "What's going on?" (LOST/UNSURE Box)

Mentee: "It's the demons...they're back...I can sense them...it's like they're right behind me. I don't want them to manifest...I want to stay focused on what I'm doing...I want to move forward...but...I..."

Mentor: "Well, like we've talked about before, whenever it seems as though you are unable to do what you know you should do, this is an indication that you might be engaged in a solution behavior. You understand your current objective, but you have expressed the fact that you are struggling to move in that direction. Whenever this happens, you stop what you are doing and check to see if you are engaged in a solution behavior. So, do you sense any resistance or hesitancy at the thought of not allowing the demons to manifest?" (S1)

Mentee: "Of course I don't want them to manifest! I hate that!" (S2)

Mentor: "That's not really what I was asking. I wasn't asking if you *wanted* them to manifest. I was reminding you to look for *solution indicators*. For instance, when you think about choosing not to allow the demons to manifest, do you sense any amount of inner hesitation. Do you sense yourself resisting the thought of choosing to move forward without the demons? Do you feel compelled, at all, to allow them to do what they want to do?" (S3)+(S7)

Mentee: "Well…it feels wrong to admit it…but, yeah, I guess I sense some of that." (S6)

Mentor: "What do you believe would happen if you chose not to allow them to manifest?" (S8)

Mentee: "Strangely, I feel like I would be forced to remember and look at things that I really don't want to look at if the demons left me alone. It is as though they are distracting me so that I don't have to see what I don't want to see. This is a terrible thought, but I think that I might be doing this." (S12)

Mentor: "Alright, so then, the reason for allowing the demons to manifest is what?" (S13)

Mentee: "Having a demon problem keeps me from having to remember what I don't want to remember." (S16) > (S17)

The Mentee would then go to the BELIEF Box with the belief, "having a demon problem keeps me from having to remember what I don't want to remember," and continue following protocol.

Refusing to Hear from God in the TRUTH Box

Mentor: "Not that it is true, but does it feel true that you are a defect?" (BELIEF Box)

Mentee: "Yes. That feels true."

Mentor: "May we present that belief to the Lord?" (TRUTH Box)

Mentee: "I don't know…I mean, I will if you want me to, but I don't really see the point."

Mentor: "Well, I'm not asking you to do anything. You are applying the Process, not me. And, as you know, the next step is to ask the Lord for His perspective regarding the belief you just identified. But if you feel reluctant or hesitant at the thought of moving in that direction, this is important. It indicates that you might be engaged in a solution." (S3)+(S7)

Mentee: "Yeah, I know it's the next step, but I definitely don't feel excited about hearing what He has to say. I feel like there is something in my way…like I can't quite muster up the nerve to talk to Him." (S6)

Mentor: "What do you believe would happen if you were to talk to Him?" (S8)

Mentee: "Well, He would tell me the truth, and I would feel a lot better!" (S9)+(S11)

Mentor: "I would have to agree with you on that one. If God convinces you of the truth, there will be some measure of transformation. But this seems more like a reason *to talk* with Him rather than a reason *not to talk* to Him. At this point in the Process, you are looking to identify the *perceived problem* that you are attempting to solve by choosing not to talk to God. It is the perceived negative consequence of talking with God. What do you think that might be?" (S10)

Mentee: "I guess if I were to honestly ask Him for His thoughts, I might not like what He has to say. He might just confirm my fears and tell me that there really is something wrong with me." (S12)

Mentor: "So then, the reason for not talking with Him is what?" (S13)

Mentee: "As long as I don't ask for His perspective, I won't be disappointed by His answer." (S16) > (S17)

In this example, the Mentee indicated that he or she was hesitant or resistant to the thought of presenting the identified belief to the Lord. Since this occurred before asking the Lord for truth and perspective, they moved to the SOLUTION Box rather than continuing to the TRANSFORMATION Box. After working through the SOLUTION Box, the Mentee would then go to the BELIEF Box with the belief, "*As long as I don't ask for His perspective, I won't be disappointed by His answer,*" and continue following protocol.

Solutions on Top of Solutions

Occasionally, while working through the SOLUTION Box you may become aware that you are engaged in another *solution behavior* <u>in addition</u> to the one you are currently addressing. You might find yourself incredibly distracted while trying to articulate the *solution belief* that supports your decision to continue feeling angry. This "distraction" is a different *solution behavior* than your decision to hold onto your anger. And until you stop distracting yourself, you will not likely be able to attend to the *solution belief* that supports your *angry solution*. If this kind of scenario occurs while you are in the SOLUTION Box, simply focus your attention on the most recently exposed *solution*.

Although this may initially seem complicated or advanced, it is nothing unique or novel. Just as you would stop what you are doing and address that potential *solution* if it showed up while you were in the EMOTION Box or MEMORY Box, you do the same thing when one shows up while you are in the SOLUTION Box. The protocol is exactly the same. So, if you discover that you are potentially engaged in multiple *solution behaviors* at the same time, simply work on whichever potential *solution* showed up most recently.

Below is an illustration of what this might look like in the context of a TPM Session.

Mentor: "What comes to mind as you focus on that?" (E10)

Mentee: "Well...nothing really. I still feel panicked, but nothing is coming to mind." (E11) > (E12)

Mentor: "Do you sense any resistance or hesitancy at the thought of having something come to your mind?" (S1)

Mentee: "Yes, I guess so." (S6)

Mentor: "What do you believe would happen if something were to come to your mind?" (S8)

Mentee: "Well...I...I don't really know. I mean, I know I'm supposed to look for the 'bad thing' or consequence that might happen if I allow something to come to mind, but I can't seem to find the words to describe it." (S9)

At this point the Mentee has indicated that she is struggling to accomplish her current objective in the SOLUTION Box (identifying the *perceived problem* that she is attempting to solve by choosing not to allow a memory to come to her mind). This is potentially an example of a "solution on top of a solution." Her next step is to determine if her current struggle is actually another *solution behavior*. In essence, she is still in the SOLUTION Box, but is addressing a separate behavior.

Mentor: "Alright, do you sense any resistance or hesitancy at the thought of describing the *perceived problem* you are attempting to solve by choosing not to have something come to your mind?" (S1)

Mentee: "Yes I do." (S6)

Mentor: "What do you believe would happen if you were to describe that *perceived problem*?" (S8)

Mentee: "I know this sounds silly, but I feel like you would think less of me or think that I'm stupid if I acknowledge the *problem*." (S12)

Mentor: "So then, the reason for not acknowledging the *problem* is what?" (S13)

Mentee: "So that you won't think less of me." (S16) > (S17)

Mentor: "Not that it is true, but does it *feel* or *seem* true that the reason for not acknowledging the *perceived problem* is so that I won't think less of you?" (BELIEF Box)

Mentee: "Yes, that seems true."

Mentor: "Lord, what do you want Lillian to know?" (TRUTH Box)

Mentee: "He said that only His opinion matters, and He thinks highly of me!"

Mentor: "Does it still *feel* or *seem* true that the reason for not acknowledging the *perceived problem* is so that I won't think less of you?" (TRANSFORMATION Box)

Mentee: "No, that no longer seems true."

Mentor: (checks the clock) "So what are you feeling now?" (E2)

Mentee: "I still feel a little panicked." (E5) > (E8)

Mentor: "What comes to your mind as you focus on that?" (E10)

Mentee: "...I'm sorry...I still don't notice anything happening...nothing seems to be coming to mind!" (E11) > (12)

Mentor: "That's alright, do you sense any resistance or hesitancy at the thought of having something come to your mind?" (S1)

Mentee: "Yes, I still do." (S6)

Mentor: "What do you believe would happen if you were to have something come to your mind?" (S8)

Mentee: "...I think...I think I might be embarrassed by what I remember." (S12)

Mentor: "So then, the reason for not having something come to your mind is what?" (S13)

Mentee: "By blocking it out, I won't be embarrassed." (S16) > (17)

As you can see, the Mentee had to first address the solution of not admitting the *perceived problem* before she was able to address the solution of *not allowing something to come to her mind*.

The typical approach for addressing errant behavior in children is to focus on punishing unwanted behavior and offering incentives for positive behavior. Although this tactic can be helpful and appropriate, we would like to suggest that focusing primarily on a child's behavior is not always the best option. Like the rest of us, children do what they believe and are motivated by their emotions, and much of their problematic behavior consists of the *solutions* they employ in response to their *perceived problems*.

Children do not randomly lash out on their siblings, purposelessly disobey your rules, or aimlessly get angry. Again, like us, they do what they do on purpose (even if they are consciously unaware of those purposes). Because of this, rather than solely focusing on correcting poor behavior, parents can investigate the reasons (beliefs) for why their children are doing what they are doing.

For instance, rather than scolding or threatening to punish a child who is expressing anger, a parent could look into why they are angry and encourage them to talk to Jesus about it. If the child is only taught to "control" and suppress his anger, he will either discover that this solution does not work or, worse, employ it for the rest of his life. If a parent understood the principles that are outlined in this book, they could take a different approach.

What follows is a simple example of what applying these principles might look like:

Seven-year-old Jimmy screamed for his mother after the castle he built with blocks was destroyed by his little sister. Jimmy's mother ran into his room to find him sitting near the remnants of his block castle. He was extremely upset, red-faced, teeth clenched, and in tears. Mom asked, *"What happened here?"* Jimmy could hardly speak but eventually cried out, *"She ruined it! My castle is destroyed! I worked really hard on it! Punish her!"* Mom calmly replied. *"I am sorry that this happened, and I will deal with your sister in a moment. But first I want to talk with you. You seem pretty upset. What are you feeling?"* Jimmy quickly replied, *"I am mad! I didn't do anything to her! What she did was wrong!"* Mom replied, *"If what you are saying is true, then you are right. She should not have knocked down your castle. And, as I said before, I will deal with her. That is my job, and I will do it. However, do you think you are willing to forgive her and let go of your anger?"* Jimmy quickly responded, *"NO!* Mom asked, *"What do you believe might happen if you forgave her and let the anger go?"* Jimmy replied, *"She will just do it again! I want her to leave me alone!"* Mom said, *"Ok, so the reason for staying mad at her is what?"* Jimmy responded, *"To keep her out of my room so she won't do it again."* Mom replied, *"Does it seem true that staying mad at your sister will keep her out of your room and keep her from doing this again?"* Jimmy, *"Yeah."* Mom continued, *"I wonder what Jesus might want you to know about all of this. Would you like to sit quietly for a moment and listen with your heart to what He might want to say to you?"* Jimmy reluctantly replies, *"A little yes but a lot no."* Mom said, *"Well, would you be willing to listen a little?"* Jimmy responded, *"Okay."* Mom prayed, *"Jesus, Jimmy would like to hear what you have to say about all that happened here. He believes that staying mad at his little sister will keep her out of his room and keep her from bothering him. But what do you want him to know?"*

Jimmy was angry for the same reason you and I get angry; he was trying to solve a problem. Too often parents are more focused on trying to change what their child is feeling rather than identifying why they are feeling what they are feeling. But how often do we offer children "sweet treats" to calm them down or scold them for expressing the emotional pain they feel? Doing this simply teaches them to "solve" their emotional pain by distracting themselves with some form of "self-medication" or to block it out entirely. This isn't what God would have us do with our pain, and He doesn't want them to do it either. We should not teach the next generation to implement the futile solutions that have failed us time and time again. Just like adults, children need to be taught to look to Jesus when they realize they need His perspective!

CHAPTER 20

SATAN IS YOUR ENEMY, BUT HE IS NOT YOUR PROBLEM.

NOTICE: This chapter has been divided into nine parts. In the first part I encourage you to practice the TPM Process as it is taught and then summarize some of my background in spiritual warfare. The second part explains that Satan is the defeated "father of lies." The third part discusses the reality that Satan is crafty but utterly limited and managed by God. The fourth part investigates Satan's use of "fiery arrows" and short-sighted solutions. The fifth part explains the relationship between the roaring lion's evil schemes and our sinful behavior. The sixth part discusses the difference between "wrestling" with spiritual forces and standing firm in your faith. The seventh part explains how to effectively resist the devil without the use of force. The eighth part compares Satan to a bully and explains that he is never the problem even when he is genuinely involved in our lives. And the ninth part offers practical examples of potential demonic involvement both within the context of a TPM session and in our everyday lives.

Part One

An Important Note Concerning This Chapter

I fully recognize that many of you are not overly concerned about demons and devils, and the inclusion of this many pages concerning Satan might seem excessive and unnecessary. But we believe the information contained on these pages will prove to be crucial for those who have demons "interfering" in their ministry sessions. And although this chapter is substantially longer than many others, it is much, much shorter than it could be!

One of our biggest challenges with this specific topic was in deciding what to leave in and what to take out. I knew that by omitting certain information we would run the risk of leaving important questions unanswered, but the more we include, the more questions will potentially come up.

We probably all agree that something significant happened at the cross that put Satan in a different place. Probably most of us would agree that he was defeated. However, there are some of us who are waving the victory flag in one hand, but are still wielding a sword in the other. I believe doing this is a theological contradiction. I will briefly address this but I will likely not fully answer every question that you may have!

The good news is that we are currently working on an exhaustive investigation into Satan and his involvement in the life of the believer. This future work is a multi-volume series of books that are written from the post-resurrection viewpoint which considers Satan to be defeated and the believer securely sharing in Christ's victory. Each significant passage of Scripture that pertains to the devil will be examined and discussed. For now, I hope this discussion will motivate you to dive a little deeper into God's word and give you something to think about until the release of our future volumes!

Suffice it to say, if you follow the TPM Process as it is taught, you will never be sidetracked by demons. There are no special steps to take or questions to ask in response to demonic manifestations. In fact, there is never even a reason for a demon to manifest in a ministry session. For, as you will soon discover, demons and devils are not the *problem*, nor do they ever actually *interfere* with anyone's ministry session. If it ever *seems* as though they do, then you are *probably* in the SOLUTION Box.

Again, this chapter is <u>not</u> meant to be exhaustive or all-encompassing. Our intention in including this chapter is to briefly introduce a perspective of the devil that is rooted in the post-Resurrection Scriptures (the passages that describe events after Jesus exited the tomb) and our victory in Christ. We have intentionally attempted to limit the scope of this chapter to topics that are directly relevant to your application of the TPM Process. What you are about to read represents a <u>portion</u> of our beliefs regarding Satan, his capabilities, his evil schemes, and his involvement in a believer's life. Essentially, we want to present a synopsis of what we believe and explain the protocols we follow in our TPM sessions.

We obviously do not claim to have a perfect understanding of what Scripture says about the enemy, but we are genuinely committed to being as close to the truth as we can be. We believe our current perspective more closely aligns with God's word, as well as the *TPM Principles*, than any position we have previously held.

You may find that you initially question some of what is presented here, but please know that we are not somehow suggesting that *everyone* should agree with *everything* that we currently believe. The very existence of this updated book shows that we no longer agree with some of our previously held theological opinions. As the Lord refines our faith and expands our understanding of what He has already said in His Word, we will be the first to admit where we were mistaken and make the necessary corrections to the TPM Training.

That said, we encourage you to study God's word and seek His truth for yourself. As you do, be sure that you allow Scripture to say what it says instead of basing your interpretations upon your own personal experience and presuppositions. Remember, just because something *seems* or *feels* true doesn't mean that it is *actually* true; it only means that you *believe* it to be true!

Believe what you will but apply the TPM Process as it is taught.

We believe that something significant happened at the cross and our Savior's resurrection which requires us to deal with the devil differently from how he was addressed before his defeat. We have applied this "post-resurrection" perspective of the devil for many years and have found it to result in more productive and consistent TPM sessions, and the demon issues that used to be common have all but disappeared. Mentors from all around the globe are applying this same perspective and reporting great success! We believe that you will see similar results if you apply the concepts that are shared in this chapter. For that reason, we encourage you to test it for yourself!

You may not fully agree with all aspects of the Principles and Purpose of TPM or what we have said concerning Satan, but we ask that you apply the *TPM Process* <u>exactly</u> as it is taught. If you ever feel a need to add-to, take away from, or alter any portion of the *TPM Process* itself, we ask that you simply call what you are doing by a different name. For if you are not following the Process-related protocols outlined in this book, you are not applying the *TPM Process*.

A Retired "Demon Slayer"

I have a relatively extensive background in what is often referred to as "spiritual warfare." In the early years of TPM, I confronted demons and witnessed many, many examples of demonic manifestations and ministered to people who believed that they were held captive by the powers of darkness. During those grueling years of battle, I employed all kinds of spiritual warfare tactics and genuinely believed that I was fulfilling a biblical mandate and accomplishing something for the Kingdom of God.

Throughout these crusades I believed I was called to "fight the good fight" against Satan while simultaneously believing that he had been defeated at the cross. Because of this, *I wielded a sword in one hand and waved a victory flag in the other.* I eventually recognized that this was a glaring contradiction but did not know how to reconcile it.

I have learned a great deal from my fervent studies and the thousands of hours I have spent ministering to demonized people. Most notably, I have long since discovered that the *post-resurrection* Scriptures offer clear instructions on how to deal with the devil and the deceiving spirits in his company without the need for confrontation or "battle" of any kind. This approach is based upon the reality of both Satan's defeat and the triumphant victory we have been given in Christ Jesus.

For example, years ago I was praying with a man who began manifesting a demonic spirit before we had a chance to do anything else in the session. His eyes bulged out and saliva began spilling from his mouth. He yelled at me in a strained, guttural voice, "Leave us alone! This man belongs to us! You have no right to bother us! He will never be free! Grrrrr…"

In response to this demonic declaration, many would reach for their swords and anointing oil. And in the early years of this ministry, I would have done the same. However, I now had a different perspective. Instead of engaging the demon and trying to "take authority" over it or commanding it to do something or go somewhere, I calmly spoke directly to the man saying, "John, look at me." Immediately the demon began shouting, "We mean it! Go away! We will hurt him if you don't! Leave us alone! HE IS OURS!" But again, I simply repeated my request, "John, choose to look at me."

After a few moments the man's countenance changed from being angry and defiant to seemingly fearful and confused. He looked up at me and, in a weak and timid, almost childlike voice, he said, "Please, help me. I don't know what to do. I cannot make this stop!" I then looked him in the eyes and corrected him saying, "No John, you just did."

Whether he realized it or not, he had exercised his executive control by choosing to look up and talk to me. He was able to do this because, as we will soon discuss, the demons had to comply when the man exercised his free will. The demonic manifestations stopped when the man finally chose to resist them (see James 4:7).

After years of wrangling with the devil, my focus is no longer on him or his involvement but rather on the person he has deceived. Today, I realize that the person is always in executive control regardless of how chaotic or helpless their situation may appear. Today I better understand the important relationship between what we believe and what demons are able to do.

In those early years, I confronted demons because I genuinely thought that it was necessary. Like many others, I modeled my tactics after the behavior of Jesus and His disciples. However, there was a glaring issue with that strategy: every demon that Jesus and His disciples cast out was confronted before the cross, prior to Satan's defeat! To copy their pre-resurrection behavior is to ignore the victory that Christ has achieved and given to us (*more on this later*).

Not only did I need to view Satan in his proper context, but I also needed to honestly evaluate my motives. For I must admit that part of me found a strange fulfillment in fending-off these defeated foes. It felt good to exercise my authority over the demons that would manifest in those ministry sessions. I now realize that my own faulty thinking was to blame for much of what went on. I was like the seventy-two enthusiastic disciples who joyfully returned to Jesus saying, "Lord, even the demons are subject to us in Your name" (Luke 10:17). I too was distracted and had failed to see the more important truth. Today, I rest in the victory that Jesus has given us and am seeing much better results because of it.

I hope that you will remain open to what I am about to share, and I encourage you to consider the possibility that our victory is real and precludes our having to engage a defeated devil. You see, <u>Satan's defeat has more to do with what we gained at Calvary than it does with what he lost!</u> And in light of this, rather than attacking the devil, we are to "be of sober spirit, [and] be on the alert" (1 Peter 5:8, emphasis added) rather than "ignorant of his schemes" (2 Corinthians 2:11), and we should "resist [him and] his schemes" (James 4:7, emphasis added) and stand behind our "shield of faith" (Ephesians 6:16).

But before we discuss how to rightly stand in victory in response to Satan's defeat, we need to devote some time to clearly identifying and describing our enemy. There seems to be more confusion in the church today regarding the devil than many of us would care to admit. But until we rightly understand our defeated foe, we will not likely fully grasp the victory we have in Christ, nor will we be able to respond appropriately to the enemy's involvement in our lives and in the lives of those around us.

THE COMMON DENOMINATOR WITH DEMONIC MANIFESTATIONS

The main causes of demonic manifestations in ministry sessions are the presuppositions of the people involved. If those who are present believe that the demonized person is held captive by the devil and needs to be rescued and that the enemy needs to be confronted, then the stage is set for a predictable outcome.

All of this can be avoided with a proper understanding of who we are in Christ, the powerlessness of the devil and his demons, and the purpose they serve in God's greater plan (Romans 8:28-29). When we know and believe the truth, all manifestations simply go away or, better yet, never materialize at all.

If I honestly evaluate the years I spent confronting demons, the common denominator in every encounter was me. Others have admitted the same conclusion. It seems that the people who encounter the most demonic manifestations are the ones who are looking for them.

Sometimes the actions of an unwary Mentor can even encourage demon manifestations. For instance, if the Mentor misguidedly calls attention to demonic forces, prays "protective" prayers at the beginning of the session, or even commands a demon to reveal its presence, then he is setting the stage for a demon to show up. These individuals typically assume that the demon is the problem and feel compelled to address it.

This could be compared to having a "fly problem" after the neighbor's dog has left a present in your yard. Yes, there is a host of flies buzzing around, but they are not the problem, and swatting them away is not the solution. If a person has demons buzzing around them, this indicates that they have "pungent impurities" in their belief which need to be removed. When the source of the odor is removed, the annoying pests fly away.

Part Two

Know Thy Enemy

Before discussing our suggestions regarding how to respond to Satan and his involvement in our lives, it is important to understand the truth of who the devil is and what he can and can't do. I'm afraid that much of what is typically believed about the enemy is confused and baseless. Because of this, many members of the body of Christ maintain theological positions that are rooted in the misapplication of Scripture and engage in numerous unnecessary practices.

Thankfully, fears and distractions can both be eliminated by gaining a proper perspective of the enemy and the victory we have in Christ. Paul emphasized the importance of rightly understanding Satan when he wrote, "no advantage would be taken of us by Satan, for we are not ignorant of his schemes" (2 Corinthians 2:11).

Remember, the following discussion is not meant to be exhaustive or complete, but rather, we hope to offer a logical and scriptural basis for how we approach the topic of spiritual warfare in the context of TPM. If you discover that you would like to learn more, know that the concepts which are briefly presented here will be expanded and supplemented in a series of books that will be released in the future. Again, we do not need anyone to agree with us, but we hope that you will be open to what is said and thoughtfully consider what is discussed.

The Father of Lies

First and foremost, Satan is a liar. In fact, he is THE liar. According to Jesus, "[Satan] does not stand in the truth because there is no truth in him. Whenever he tells a lie, he speaks from his own nature, because he is a liar and the father of lies" (John 8:44). Birds fly, fish swim, and Satan lies. Deception is part of his nature. It is what drives his behavior, it defines his personality, and it is the means by which he carries out his will here on Earth.

From his very first interactions with humanity, Satan has lied to us. He tells us lies about God, about our situation, about ourselves, about him, and about what we should do moment by moment. If his ability to lie was somehow eliminated, then he would be paralyzed and rendered mute. Everything he says and does is rooted in deception. Even if he speaks some half-truth, it is for the purpose of manipulating and deceiving the hearer.

Satan does not want anyone to obey God or agree with God's perspective. He hates the truth and everyone who believes it. He desires to deceive the unbelieving masses so that they remain "children of disobedience" (Colossians 3:6, Ephesians 2:2) who are "asleep" (1 Thessalonians 5:6) in the "kingdom of darkness" (Colossians 1:13). And he is never more proud of his disobedient "children" than when they are deceived and carrying out his will.

But with the Apostle Paul we say, "thanks be to God, who gives us the victory through our Lord Jesus Christ" (1 Corinthians 15:57) and whose truth sets us free from the enemy's lies (John 8:32). When the Spirit of Truth persuades us of His perspective (John 16:13), we are able to stand firm in our faith with the belt of truth buckled around our waists (Ephesians 6:14).

A Defeated Foe

Prior to the Cross we were vulnerable to Satan in many ways. Because of God's perfect law, we were guilty, condemned to die, and under the curse of death. We were also by nature fallen children of wrath, the very sons of disobedience. We dwelt in darkness, followed the father of lies, and became lost in our sins and trespasses (Ephesians 2:2). Again, read what Paul said but in its fuller context.

> And you were dead in your offenses and sins, in which you _previously_ walked according to the course of this world, according to the prince of the power of the air, of the spirit that is now working in the sons of disobedience. Among them we too all _previously_ lived in the lusts of our flesh, indulging the desires of the flesh and of the mind, and _were_ by nature children of wrath, just as the rest (Ephesians 2:1-3, emphasis added).

Satan undoubtedly works in the lives of all fallen people. However, when Jesus obeyed His Father by going to the Cross, He took our sins upon Himself (2 Corinthians 5:21), condemned sin in the flesh (Romans 8:3), and fulfilled the requirements of the Law for us (Romans 8:1-2). And because we died with Christ (Colossians 3:3), we are no longer under the Law but are free from the power of sin (Romans 6:11), and sin no longer needs to be master over us (Romans 6:14). We now have a choice about whom we will obey (Romans 6:11-14). Since we have been raised up with Christ, our lives are now (presently) hidden with Christ in God (Colossians 3:1-3) and we are spiritually untouchable since the "evil one cannot touch [us]" (1 John 5:18, emphasis added). These things (and more) led the Apostle Paul to declare that we have become "more than conquerors" in Christ (Romans 8:37 NIV).

Despite Satan's best efforts to thwart God's plan for redemption, he was utterly defeated by Jesus' perfect sacrifice. As God promised through His prophet Isaiah, "He will swallow up death for all time, and the Lord GOD will wipe tears away from all faces, and He will remove the disgrace of His people from all the earth" (Isaiah 25:8). Christ freely gives this victory to those who believe in Him (see 1 Corinthians 15:57). Satan was not defeated as a result of what happened to him, but as a result of what has happened to us!

Satan's defeat had much more to do with _what we gained_ than it did about _what he lost._ Jesus did not come to curtail Satan's behavior but to destroy the "works of the devil" (See 1 John 3:8). The works that he did _before_ the cross were destroyed and have lost their effectiveness in the life of the believer. It is vital that we differentiate between Satan's behavior (what he is doing) and his "works" (the outcome of his actions).

For instance, the "works" of a carpenter are not his knowledge of how to build a house, the skills he employs, or even the act of constructing a house. Rather, the result of his labor (the house itself) is considered to be the carpenter's "works." The cross had little impact on Satan's actual behavior (his "carpenter skills"), but his "works" are no longer effective in the life of the believer. He is still doing the same things today that he did before the cross, but because of Jesus' death and resurrection the impact and effectiveness of his works are dramatically altered! John summed it all up when he wrote, "The evil one cannot touch us" (see 1 John 5:18).

For example, Satan can no longer effectively accuse believers of sin (Revelation 12:10) since "there is now no condemnation at all for those who are in Christ Jesus. For the law of the Spirit of life in Christ Jesus has set you free from the law of sin and of death" (Romans 8:1-2). He hopes that his accusations leave us feeling condemned, but his verbal attacks hold no weight before our Heavenly Father. For when we sin, "we have an Advocate with the Father, Jesus Christ the righteous; and He Himself is the propitiation for our sins; and not for ours only, but also for the sins of the whole world" (1 John 2:1-2). Satan can no longer effectively use his greatest weapon, the "law of sin and death," against those who are in Christ. With the Apostle Paul we can celebrate because,

> When this perishable puts on the imperishable, and this mortal puts on immortality, then will come about the saying that is written: "DEATH HAS BEEN SWALLOWED UP in victory. WHERE, O DEATH, IS YOUR VICTORY? WHERE, O DEATH, IS YOUR STING?" The sting of death is sin, and the power of sin is the Law; but thanks be to God, who gives us the victory through our Lord Jesus Christ (1 Corinthians 15:54-57).

Because of the all-encompassing victory that we have in Christ, everything the devil does, he does through deception and in defeat. He has lost already. God's plan cannot be thwarted! In fact, as we will soon discuss, even his evil motives and false accusations are used to accomplish good in our lives (see Romans 8:28). Christ's victory is absolute and has been given to those who have been born of God (see John 1:12-13). Jesus Christ is truly victorious, and we are victorious in Him!

Part Three

A Bad Dog on a Chain

Satan is evil and hates every one of us, but he is also completely under God's control and limited to what God allows him to do. The early protestant reformer Martin Luther understood this truth. And although I recognize that some have differing opinions of Luther's work, I believe that he has a good understanding of the limitations God placed upon the devil. He had this to say concerning our defeated enemy:

> Why should you fear? Why should you be afraid? Do you not know that the prince of this world has been judged? He is no lord, no prince anymore. You have a different, a stronger Lord, Christ, who has overcome and bound him. Therefore, let the prince and [so called] god of this world look sour, bare his teeth, make a great noise, threaten, and act in an unmannerly way; he can do no more than a bad dog on a chain, which may bark, run here and there, and tear at the chain. But because it is tied and you avoid it, it cannot bite you. So, the devil

acts toward every Christian (What Luther Says, Ewald Plass, St. Louis: Concordia Publishing House, 1959, emphasis added).

Again, I quote one of the most commonly overlooked passages of Scripture regarding Satan, "He who was born of God [Jesus] keeps [us], and the evil one does not touch [us]" (1 John. 5:18, emphasis added). The reason that he cannot touch us is "the Lord is faithful, and <u>He will</u> strengthen and protect you from the evil one" (2 Thessalonians 3:3, emphasis added). If you are in Christ (which also means He is in you) then you do not need to be rescued from the devil. "[God] has rescued us from the dominion of darkness and brought us into the kingdom of the Son'" (Colossians 1:13 NIV). Citizens of the Son's Kingdom do not need to be rescued. If they *seem* or *feel* as though they are captives, this is not a captivity problem; it is a belief and perception problem.

Satan may growl, bear his teeth, and bite *at* you, but you are outside of his reach. He can only do what God allows. He has been given strict limitations and does not act outside of these divinely designated parameters. We see this clearly demonstrated in the Job narrative. While Satan was given permission to do what he did with Job, this does not mean that Satan has free reign to do the same with us. Everything that Satan did to Job was by special permission from God. Satan was not without limits then, and he is not without limits today. God has always securely kept him on a short leash.

Satan can plot and scheme all he wants, but God's will still prevails. This is the promise that we have from Him; "If God is for us, who can be against us?" (Romans 8:31 NIV). Jesus said, "Do not be afraid of those who kill the body but are unable to kill the soul; but rather fear Him who is able to destroy both soul and body in hell (Matthew 10:28).

Even so, the question remains, "Why does God allow Satan (and other evil people) to commit such terrible acts?" We believe God is completely capable of accomplishing His perfect will in the context of evil. For an example of this, we need only to look to the Cross! Jesus was crucified by evil men who were deceived and guided by evil spirits, and yet, God's will was accomplished just as He had planned from the foundation of the world (See Ephesians 1:4, Isaiah 53). The same holds true for all those who are in Christ.

Those who killed Jesus were guilty of a grave injustice, but according to the prophet Isaiah, "the LORD was pleased to crush Him, putting Him to grief ..." (Isaiah 53:10). The NIV translates this same passage to say, "it was the Lord's will to crush him and cause him to suffer..." God uses "all things," regardless of the motivations behind said "things," to accomplish His perfect will in our lives (see Romans 8:28).

Again, Martin Luther understood this principle when he wrote,

> God uses the devil and the evil angels. They, of course, desire to ruin everything; but God blocks them, unless a well-earned scourging is in order. God allows pestilence, war, or some other plague to come, that we may humble ourselves before him, fear him, hold to him, and call upon him. When God has accomplished these purposes through the scourge, then the good angels come again to perform their office. They bid the devil stop the pestilence, war, and famine. <u>So the devil must serve us with the very thing with which he plans to injure us; for God is such a great Master that he is able to turn even the wickedness of the devil into good</u> (What Luther Says, Ewald Plass, St. Louis: Concordia Publishing House, 1959, underline added).

The writer of Proverbs said, "The king's heart is like channels of water in the hand of the LORD; He turns it wherever He pleases" (Proverbs 21:1). In the same way, God directs and limits what Satan does. Although the devil is evil and wishes to thwart God's plan, he is nevertheless slithering down a predetermined path that God has carved for him. No matter what he does or where he goes, the enemy is fully under the Lord's control. Satan is not running loose; he is held captive by the chain that God put upon him.

This reality should bring you great comfort and a sense of total security. Yes, God allows Satan to freely choose to do evil in this world, but our Heavenly Father is ultimately in control of what happens. God has complete foreknowledge of every choice Satan will make as well as the thoughts and motives behind those choices. Because of this, God can easily move the devil in any direction He chooses. The enemy is on a short, unbreakable leash, and his evil intentions are being worked together for our good (revisit Romans 8:28). Even darkness, disaster, and destruction are under His almighty control (see Isaiah 45:5-7, Amos 3:6).

A Finite Fighter

No matter how big, how strong, or how capable you may think Satan is, he is still finite. He is not all-powerful or all-knowing, nor can he be in all places at all times. He is a created being that exists within rigid limitations and parameters. God, on the other hand, is infinite and all-powerful. He had no beginning and will have no end. He is everywhere, all the time. He sees and knows everything and is in total control. He spoke the universe (including Satan) into existence.

Even if the devil was theoretically the most powerful, knowledgeable, and capable being in all of creation, he would still be nothing in comparison to God. Our Heavenly Father knows the enemy's every thought and has predicted his every action. And if God wanted to end the devil's existence, it would merely require a thought, nothing more.

Due to this immeasurable discrepancy, Satan cannot fight or even threaten God. Satan is subservient, while God is unstoppable. There is no competition or struggle going on between them. Satan may attempt to battle God, but God is not battling Satan. How could a finite being possibly wage war against the infinite God? It is comically impossible!

In spite of this, how often have you heard it said that there is a battle waging between the powers of good and evil? What are all the powers of evil in comparison to God? They can't even separate us from His love or pluck us from His hand (Romans 8:35-39, John 10:27-30). His plans cannot be thwarted (Job 42:2), He has a purpose behind everything that happens - including the evil acts of evil men who are guided by evil spirits (Proverbs 16:4) and works everything together for the good of those called according to His loving purpose (Romans 8:28). So, if God is for us, it doesn't matter who or what is against us (see Romans 8:31). Suffice it to say that God is not threatened by (or even concerned with) the devil!

A Crafty Serpent

Although we need not fear the devil, we must never discount or disregard him since he remains "more crafty than any beast of the field which the LORD God had made" (Genesis 3:1). He is also more crafty than any of us and can outwit us if we enter into dialogue with him. Our understanding is no match for his earthly "wisdom." This was the beginning of Eve's downfall. Without question, he hates us with a passion and is singularly focused on creating as much havoc as possible in God's created order, but he is sorely limited and can only accomplish his purposes through deception.

The enemy's behavior is not unique to him, for lies and deception have both plagued and been spread by humans ever since we were kicked out of the garden of Eden. But Satan mastered his craft long before we came on the scene, and he has devoted thousands of additional years to practice. He is the best at what he does. Thankfully, we are not called to a battle of wits with the enemy. All we must do is look to Jesus. John said,

> Beloved, <u>now</u> we are children of God, and it has not appeared as yet what we will be. We know that when He appears, we will be like Him, because we will see Him just as He is. And <u>everyone who has this hope set on Him</u> purifies himself, just as He is pure (1 John 3:2-3, emphasis added).

You will never win a debate with the devil. His understanding of human behavior is likely second only to God's infinite wisdom. It could be argued that Satan knows you better than you know yourself. He is not able to read your thoughts, but he also doesn't need to. For if a parent is able to watch their child and "know" what he is thinking, how much more capable is Satan of doing this very thing? As he observes humanity, it doesn't take him long to figure out what we are thinking and devise a deceptive scheme to use against us.

Although the evil one might outsmart us, he cannot touch us. And even if he is the craftiest of all creation, Satan is utterly stupid and blind when compared to his Creator. God is not threatened or impressed by the enemy's cunning plans and deceptive schemes. I often say, "the one most deceived is the deceiver himself."

John reminds us, "greater is He who is in you than he who is in the world" (1 John 4:4). Though we need to be aware of the enemy's capabilities, we need not fear or worry about him. We are now children of God, and our hope is fixed on Jesus who is purifying our faith by His Spirit.

God's Subjugated Servant

As strange as it may sound, Satan belongs to God and is serving a purpose in God's plan. He is a living creature who was created by God and for God just as the Scriptures declare,

> For in him <u>all things</u> were created: things in heaven and on earth, visible and invisible, whether thrones or powers or rulers or authorities; all things have been created through him and <u>for him</u> (Colossians 1:16 NIV, emphasis added).

The devil is God's possession and is by no means a threat to God's plan or purposes. In fact, he must ask for God's permission before he acts. Remember that God summoned Satan and gave him clear directions and limitations before releasing him to torment Job (Job 1:6-12). But this was not an example of Satan sneaking past God's omnipotence; rather, it was an example of God using the devil and his evil intentions to accomplish a good work in Job's life. For, as Job would experientially discover, "[God] can do all things; no purpose of [His] can be thwarted" (Job 42:2 NIV, emphasis added). Isaiah also knew of God's unstoppable purposes and plan when he said, "For the Lord Almighty has purposed, and who can thwart him? His hand is stretched out, and who can turn it back?" (Isaiah 14:27 NIV). No one, including the devil, can undermine God's plan!

Not only is Satan completely powerless against God's will, he has no choice but to be used by God to accomplish good. Again, there is no better example of this than the cross! Jesus' crucifixion was the most evil act that Satan has been involved in, and yet, it was used to accomplish God's perfect and loving plan of redemption (which is the last thing Satan wanted to do)! This should give you a sense of hope and security. No matter what the enemy does, he cannot escape the reality that he belongs to God and is inadvertently carrying out God's will for "those who are called according to [God's] purpose" (Romans 8:28, emphasis added).

Depending on which translation you read, the Scriptures say that on the night Jesus was arrested, He explained to His apostles, "Satan has <u>asked</u> to sift all of you as wheat" (Luke 22:31 NIV, emphasis added). Other translations have Jesus speaking directly to Peter. Whether Jesus was speaking to Peter alone, or all of the disciples, I think it is safe to say, all of them were "sifted" in the days that followed.

Notice <u>who</u> Satan asked for permission; He asked God. <u>Why</u> did Satan ask for permission? Because he belongs to God and is subjugated to the King of Kings. Satan was only able to "sift" the disciples because he asked God for permission, and God allowed him to do so.

This begs the question, "Why would God allow Satan to sift them as wheat?" To answer this question, we do not need to look further than Simon Peter's response. In typical fashion, Peter responded to Jesus' warning by boldly declaring, "Lord, I am ready to go with You both to prison and to death" (Luke 22:33)! But, as he would soon discover, this was not true. Peter did not yet fully believe the truth in his heart, and, because of this, he was unable to even associate himself with Jesus when pressure was applied, let alone die for Him. The Lord knew this and lovingly corrected Peter saying, "I tell you, Peter, the rooster will not crow today until you have denied three times that you know Me" (Luke 22:34). Jesus was not condemning or scolding Peter; He was pointing out Peter's problem. Peter did not yet fully believe the truth of who Jesus was and had been deceived into believing things that were untrue (as he would put on full display by swinging his sword in the garden of Gethsemane while the rooster was still fast asleep).

So, again, why did God allow Satan to sift Peter as wheat? To put it simply, Peter needed to be sifted! Wheat needs to be sifted so that the unwanted elements are removed from the grain. Peter needed to receive a similar "sifting." His faith was impure, and these impurities needed to be exposed. God wanted Peter to know the truth; Satan was simply volunteering to be used in the process of exposing the impurities in Peter's faith. Now, the enemy obviously hoped that Peter's faith would fail, but Jesus was praying for the opposite to occur (Luke 22:32). Here we see a loving God using "all things" for Peter's good (Romans 8:28). Satan may have hated Jesus' disciples, but this did not deter God from using him to "sift" out the impurities in their faith.

We have the same problem that Peter had: our faith needs to be "sifted." Because of this, God allows Satan to sift us as wheat. We must remember that this "sifting" is not a bad thing even though it can be very sorrowful (see Hebrews 12:11). Rather, it is the very thing we need! We need our impure faith to be exposed and refined. And when the devil is used to accomplish this task, it is no less loving and purposeful than when God uses any of the other tools that are at His disposal. Satan belongs to God and is part of the "all things" that are worked together for our good in this process of faith-refinement. The enemy hates you, but the One who owns him loves you deeply and uses Satan to accomplish good in your life! So, as Peter eventually learned, when you are suffering according to the will of God, you should entrust yourself to your faithful Creator (see 1 Peter 4:19).

The devil is our enemy, but he is not our problem. The enemy cannot touch you, but he can (and does) draw attention to that which needs to be exposed and addressed. Satan hates you and hopes that you will remain in deception and blame him for your pain and suffering. But all the while, the

Lord remains in control and is accomplishing His loving purpose even through His use of the devil's hateful behavior.

For more insight on this concept consider Jacob's son, Joseph. In the book of Genesis, we learn that Joseph was abused by his brothers and sold into captivity and forced labor. He was taken to a foreign land, far from home. Later, he was falsely accused of sexual assault and unjustly imprisoned. But all the while, God was with Joseph working all things together for his good. Years later, after reuniting with his family and realizing God's careful and loving plan, Joseph exclaimed this truth saying, "You meant evil against me, but God meant it for good in order to bring about this present result, to keep many people alive" (Genesis 50:20).

Just as those who wronged Joseph were fueled by hatred, jealousy, and revenge, Satan wants the worst for you. But even what the enemy means for evil, God means for good! No matter what Satan attempts to do to us, it is "for us" since "If God is for us, who is against us?" (Romans 8:31).

Part Four

Satan fires his fiery arrows at our deception.

In the sixth chapter of Ephesians, we learn that Satan launches "fiery arrows" in our direction (Ephesians 6:16). But it is important to understand both *what* the enemy is targeting and *why* his strategies are so effective. Contrary to popular opinion, the devil does not have *us* in his sights, for he cannot even touch us (see 1 John 5:18). Why would he waste his arrows by shooting at a target that he cannot hit? He is aiming for *what we believe*. Specifically, he shoots at the *lie-based impurities* in our faith.

The enemy understands that we feel what we believe, so he targets our impure faith hoping to stir up some emotional pain. In essence, he tries to *trigger* us with his fiery barrage. Now, these arrows are not some form of physical aerial missiles; they are simply lies. These deceptive darts are specifically tailored to your personal set of beliefs. He watches your behavior, assesses your beliefs, and targets the impurities in your faith with echoes of the deception that is already present in your heart.

Satan knows that each of these impurities represents a weak spot in your shield of faith (see Ephesians 6:16), and once he has his target, there is no reason for him to hold back. He will continue to launch his assault until either God tells him to stop or he sees that your "shield" has been mended. For when you know the truth in your heart, your "shield of faith" extinguishes the enemy's fiery arrows (see Ephesians 6:16). At that point, Satan realizes that he is wasting his time and moves to another target.

Someone might ask, "Why would the devil target our lie-based beliefs if he thinks we might look to God and have our shield strengthened?" The answer is found in the word, "might." He knows that we *might* look to God for truth, but we also *might* look to him for his shortsighted solution to the pain. For Satan, it seems that shooting arrows at our lies is worth the risk. For some of us, his risk is lower than for others. This is one of the primary goals of this training. We hope that by understanding this scheme of the devil, you will choose to resist him and look to your heavenly Father for truth.

Someone else might ask, "Why would God give Satan permission to shoot a "fiery arrow" in our direction if He thought we might be deceived and fall into sin?" God knows that we *might* look to Him for the truth. I believe rewards gained from receiving the Lord's perspective even once is worth the weight and cost of the thousand times we might fall for Satan's deceptive tricks. Sin and deception are temporal, but the Word of truth is eternal. As the Psalmist declared, "Your word, LORD, is eternal; it stands firm in the heavens" (Psalm 119:89). Every truth we are persuaded to believe becomes "implanted" (see James 1:21) and brings forth its eternal fruit. For this reason, being bombarded by fiery arrows is well worth it!

In spite of his ill intent, Satan plays the role of a "lie detector" as he targets and exposes the impurities in your faith. He does not shoot at the truth you believe in your heart, since he knows his arrows would immediately be extinguished. He only targets what is impure. He seeks to remind you of the lies you already believe.

Since this is true, we can infer that if one of the enemy's arrows makes it through our shield, it is a shield issue! For if our shield was built of a purified faith, it would protect us from the enemies onslaught, and the sizzle of his extinguished darts would prove the purity of our faith. So the fact that an arrow was able to pass through our defenses indicates a weakness in our armor. The enemy and his arrows are used to draw our attention to what needs to be addressed: our need for God's perspective. What Satan means for evil, God uses for our good (see Genesis 50:20, Romans 8:28).

Satan cannot make us feel anything; we feel what we believe.

In spite of what we have discussed here, there are some who protest saying, "You don't know what you are talking about! The devil has oppressed me all week long. I am worn out. I can feel the weight and pain of his oppression all the time!" Even though this may genuinely *feel* and *seem* true, it is not. You might feel oppressed and worn out, but the emotional pain you feel is not coming from Satan or his involvement in your life.

I used to view being *oppressed* by the devil as an indication that I was doing something right. I thought his "attacks" were targeting the good work I was doing. Today, I realize that he was aiming at my lie-based beliefs, not me or my behavior. Because of this, he was unwittingly playing a vital role in my sanctification. He was exposing what God wanted me to see so that I would humbly submit to His refining process.

The pain we feel as a result of the devil's volley is due to the beliefs that have been exposed, not the arrows that were used to expose them. The arrows only sting because we believe the lies that they strike. If you believe that you are worthless, you will feel bad when this lie-based belief is touched. Although Satan would love nothing more than for us to blame the "archer" for the pain that we feel and plan a counter attack, when our impure faith is exposed, we should attend to our shield, not the shooter.

Satan discovered that humans feel what they believe long before you and I did. This is likely, in part, why he is so focused on deceiving us. He knows that if we believe the lies he tells us, we will feel the emotional consequences and be motivated to look for a way to alleviate the pain. He is not responsible for our suffering, but he is more than happy to take the credit!

Sometimes it may seem as though you are growing tired from holding up your shield of faith, but this is simply not so. Bearing the shield of faith is effortless! But you may grow increasingly tired of feeling the consequences of your impure faith becoming exposed. Every time a fiery arrow finds its way past your defenses through one of the "holes" in your shield, you are faced with wearisome emotional pain. But again, this is not due to the arrows or the weight of your shield, and the pain itself is a good thing. The tiresome emotions you are forced to contend with were designed to motivate you to look in God's direction. They indicate that you need His perspective.

Someone may protest our current discussion by saying, "I have personal experience in this! I was tormented by the evil presence of demonic spirits. I felt oppressed and attacked. But when my Christian friends prayed over me and cast out the demons, I felt much better. The fear subsided and my anxiety decreased. I was delivered!" This testimony is both understandable and explainable, but it does not dispute any of what we are saying. We agree with the notion that you would feel better if Satan would simply leave you alone. If the "triggerer" is not triggering us, then we won't feel triggered. Even so, as long as there are lies to trigger and someone to trigger them, you will *likely* feel some measure of emotional pain from time to time. We may send the devil away, but it is just a matter of time before he will return to trigger us. God will see to it that he does! (And if the devil is not available to trigger us, God will find another "triggerer" in a spouse, work associate, overbearing boss, trying children, or the neighbor's barking dog.)

Consider the following fictitious example. If my wife continually triggered my lie-based pain through her constant criticism, I would likely feel better if I divorced her. By removing her from my daily life, things would seem to calm down. But "casting out" my spouse has no impact on what I believe, and the impurities in my faith would still be present. Because of this, it is only a matter of time before someone or something else will be used to expose the lies I still believe.

Likewise, "casting out" a demon may seem to bring some measure of relief, but this is nothing more than the removal of a trigger. If you send Satan away, he will be temporarily unable to send his fiery arrows in your direction, but their intended targets will still remain. In time, he will come back and again be used to expose the impurities in your faith. You may temporarily feel "better" after sending the evil spirits away, but this is not due to some manner of "healing," "release," or "freedom." Your lie-based pain is simply less exposed. Genuine and lasting freedom is not found by removing the devil; it is the result of acquiring the truth from the Holy Spirit (John 8:32).

Satan supplies short-sighted solutions.

Satan hates each of us and desires to lead as many people as possible into self-destruction. So, after he has exposed your impure faith with his fiery arrows, causing you to face your perceived problems and feel emotional pain, he then changes tactics. He knows that when you are in a heightened emotional state, you are more likely to explore his sinful solutions to your problems. His two-step strategy is simply: he first exposes a perceived "problem" and then offers "solutions," just as he did with Eve in the Garden (Genesis 3).

The devil wants us to remain in painful deception, so he offers distractions, recommends harmful behaviors, and suggests sinful solutions. For instance, after triggering a lie-based belief such as, "I am alone" or "I am a defect," the enemy suggests a sinful means by which you can make yourself feel better. He might encourage you to distract yourself with entertainment or food, he might suggest that you blame your feelings on those around you, or he may even argue that the only hope you have is to end your own life. (*This should all sound very familiar to our discussion of the SOLUTION Box.*)

In these moments, Satan is essentially accomplishing the same task as he did with his fiery arrows; he is exposing your need for God's perspective. For if you genuinely knew the truth regarding his sinful solutions, you would not be drawn to them. For each of these behaviors, "when it has run its course, brings forth death" (James 1:15). But since you have been deceived into believing that they might be helpful, you feel compelled to implement them. So, yet again, he is taking advantage of what is already there. He doesn't force you to sin, but he does his best to make the idea sound as enticing as possible.

The devil doesn't want you to notice his involvement and hopes that you claim his suggestions as your own thoughts. Rather than being forthright and saying "Hi there, it's me, your enemy. I really think you should try to alleviate your emotional pain by implementing a sinful solution," he veils his malicious marketing by putting it in the first person. So, when you suddenly have the thought, "I could really use a snack," even though you know you are not hungry, this thought may not be your own!

Some people may struggle with the idea that they are unknowingly accepting the devil's advice and following his suggestions, but this is a common reality that every believer faces on a day-to-day basis. Pay attention to the thoughts that immediately come to mind the next time you feel any measure of negative emotions. Notice how you are suddenly interested in eating something, taking a nap, entertaining yourself, gossiping about someone, expressing your anger, or finding some other distraction. Those thoughts may not be your own, and these pain-solving solutions may have been tailor-made just for you.

Next time you find yourself shopping when you don't need to buy anything, binging on TV reruns, logging onto social media to check your current number of "likes," rearranging your furniture for the fifteenth time, or typing an email that you know you should not send, realize that you *may* have just stepped into a snare of the devil. These behaviors may initially seem inconsequential or unimportant, but if they are done for the purpose of alleviating emotional discomfort, then the enemy is well pleased with your decisions!

Satan even offers his "services" during a TPM session by providing a distraction or way of escape from feeling painful emotion or remembering specific memories. For example, if the thought of remembering something stirs up in you some painful emotion, and you sense yourself resisting or hesitating to move forward, the devil may offer you a solution. He may create an illusion of an insurmountable wall between you and your memory that seemingly hinders you from moving forward. Rather than drawing your sword and confronting the enemy, slow things down and recognize that it is offering you a short-sighted way of escape. Instead of taking the bait, resist him and take responsibility for what has just been exposed: your lie-based belief. Remember, if you feel compelled to engage in Satan's suggested solutions, this is due to your lack of God's perspective, not the compelling arguments of the devil.

So we see again that the enemy is not the problem; rather, he is simply pointing it out. The fact that you are drawn and enticed to try out his solutions indicates that you lack God's perspective. For if you knew the truth regarding the enemy's offerings, they would not seem so enticing and you would not feel the urge to accept them. They only seem desirable because you have been deceived. Once the Holy Spirit convinces you of the truth, the allure of these sinful solutions will fade.

If you are aware of his intentions and schemes, you can responsibly respond to them by seeking God's perspective rather than submitting to his sinful suggestions. The very fact that he is offering you a solution indicates that you are believing a lie. Because this is so, the enemy's temptations (solution behaviors) are actually opportunities for refinement. If you respond to them by humbly admitting what you believe and prayerfully inviting the Holy Spirit to persuade you of the truth, then you will have cooperated with God and thwarted the devil's evil intentions.

Part Five

Satan cannot make us do anything; We do what we believe.

Some may argue that those who carry out Satan's will do so involuntarily, under duress. They seem to think that the devil and his deceiving spirits are able to force us to do things against our will. But do you believe that a demon can *make* you sin if you do not choose to? In other words, do you believe that the devil is somehow responsible for your sinful behavior and you are an innocent victim? Will you someday stand before God and say, "It was not my fault; the devil made me do it"? Although Satan would likely love to take credit for our waywardness, we are solely responsible for the choices we make. And if Satan can't make you sin, which is what he would do if he could, then what *can* he "make" you do?

If you can honestly acknowledge the fact that you are responsible for your own choices, we encourage you to continue this train of thought. If Satan is incapable of making you do something, then do you believe that he can somehow *keep you from* doing something? For example, can he keep you from praying, or sharing your faith, or serving at your local charity? If not, what can he keep you from doing?

Someone may challenge this notion by citing the biblical account of the demonized man who lived among the tombs (Matthew 8:28-34, Mark 5:1-20, Luke 8:26-39). Although it may initially seem as though the man was controlled by demons, a closer look at this Bible passage reveals a different explanation. Mark explains, "when [the man] saw Jesus afar off, he ran and worshiped him" (Mark 5:6 KJV). Now, if you were one of those demons, wouldn't you try to keep this man from running to Jesus? Of course! But this is exactly what the man did. He ran to Jesus because he chose to run to Jesus. Though filled with demons, the man was in executive control of his behavior. He did what he chose to do, and the demons could not hinder him.

We see this concept applied in the Garden of Eden as well. Satan did not force Adam and Eve to eat of the forbidden tree, and he does not force us to do what we do. He tricks us like he tricked them. He whispers lies into our ears, hoping to convince us to act inappropriately and implement his short-sighted *solutions*. He knows that if we believe things that are untrue, these beliefs will lead us down destructive, wasteful, and unfruitful paths, but he is not *making* you follow his instructions. If anything, it is our own lie-based thinking that "makes" us do what we do and hinders us from doing what we *want* to do. Satan is simply seeding falsehood and hoping for an abundant harvest.

To apply this concept further, consider the context of a TPM session. If you choose to look to Jesus, can Satan stop you? If you choose to connect with your emotions, is he able to keep you from feeling them? If you choose to remember, can he keep you from recalling past experiences? No matter how hard Satan tries to hinder you, whatever you choose to do, you will do.

As we have previously discussed, if it ever *seems* as though you "can't feel," "can't remember," "can't hear," it is because you are choosing not to. You may genuinely *want* and *desire* to take the next step, but the fact that you are not taking it indicates what you are *choosing* to do. In the same way, if a person is seemingly "unable" to make a demon stop manifesting through their body, what might we deduce from this? Either they do not know any better and are ignorant of the truth, or they have been deceived into believing that allowing the demon to manifest will help them *solve* a *perceived problem*.

You may be wondering, "why in the world would anyone *allow* a demon to manifest?" But this is no different than asking why someone would choose to cut themselves, or abuse medication, or cheat on their spouse. We do what we do because we believe it will help "solve" the problems that seem to stand in our way. And if a certain behavior *seems* as though it will help, we will be drawn to do it in spite of the consequences.

Allowing a demon to manifest through your body is obviously a terrible idea, but is it somehow more wrong, sinful, or destructive than carrying out any of its other evil suggestions? For instance, if the devil comes to you while you are feeling anxious and sneakily suggests that you should go browse through unsavory content on the internet, if you decide to comply, are you not submitting to his desires for you?

For this reason, we should not think more highly of ourselves than we do of those who acquiesce to the devil's request to allow him to manifest. They don't *want* the demons to manifest any more than you *want* to engage in your chosen sinful solution. If any of us were asked if we *want* to follow Satan's suggestions, we would say, "No! Of course not!" But regardless of our genuine *desires*, our will is displayed in the choices we make.

If you felt alone and genuinely believed that having a "demon issue" would ensure that you garner the compassionate attention of those around you, what would you do? If you believed that you were helpless and powerless and were going to be hurt again but also thought that keeping demonic company would ward off abusive relationships, what might you choose? If you believed that being the "victim" of the devil was better than having to acknowledge the painful experiences in your past, wouldn't you choose to beg for help rather than face the pain? Thankfully, once we have been convinced of the truth regarding our authority in Christ and the futility of our *solution behaviors*, we will make a different choice, and the manifestations will stop.

As you learned in our discussion of the "Belief and Choice" Principle, we do what we believe. Our behavior is a direct expression of what we believe to be true. So, if we are doing what Satan would have us do, then we either believe that we *must* (because we *seem* to have no other option) or believe that we *should* (because we have been deceived). In other words, we either do not know any better and are ignorant of the truth, or we have been deceived into believing that there is a valid reason for acting out Satan's will for our lives. Satan cannot push you off of a bridge, but he might convince you that jumping is your only viable option.

Again, notice the true source of the problem here. Is the demon the problem? No, it is simply a fly circling a dung pile. Is the person's choice to allow the demon to manifest the problem? No, this is the outcome of their belief. Is their lie-based belief the problem? No again. Their belief in a lie signifies that they have not yet been convinced of the truth. Their actual problem is that they lack God's perspective. So, here again, if it ever *seems* as though the devil is "making" you do something or "keeping" you from doing something, it is important to remember that he is not the problem; he is simply pointing it out for you.

A primary point to remember is that we are often quick to blame the devil for the seemingly bad things that happen in our world, but even the most evil acts that have ever been committed have human fingerprints all over them. For example, Satan played a part in the crucifixion of Jesus, but he did not arrest Him, whip Him, spit upon Him, or nail Him to the cross. Every physical act was carried out by people. Think of every known evil act ever accomplished throughout human history, and see how many were actually accomplished by the devil himself. The devil desires to thwart God's plan, but he needs willing participants to enact his evil schemes.

The Serpent in the Garden did not force the couple to eat the forbidden fruit. Eve had to pick it herself and put it into her own mouth. Adam accepted the fruit from Eve and willingly followed suit. The devil didn't make them do it; he had to trick them into doing it themselves. Sin came into the world through human choice, not demonic forces (see Genesis 3). This dynamic is just as true today! The devil does not make anyone do anything; but, at the same time, he also has no shortage of willful volunteers!

WHY DO WE FEEL TEMPTED BY THE TEMPTER'S TEMPTATIONS?

Fishing provides a great analogy to help us to understand why we are tempted by the devil. There is not a fish in the sea that desires to get its lip pierced. And yet, we have learned how to fool them into inflicting self-harm for our own satisfaction. But what makes our lures so alluring? There is nothing intrinsically tempting about a rubber worm on a metal hook, but if we can deceive the fish into believing that the worm will satisfy their hunger while concealing the violent potential of the sharpened barb, our deadly trap will seem desirable.

In this way, we play the role of "tempter." We cast our lines into the water hoping that the nearby fish are enticed to taste our treacherous treats. But, as every fisherman can attest, sometimes the fish just don't bite! And, assuming that our lures were seen by our prey, there are essentially two reasons why our fishing fails: (1) the fish aren't hungry, or (2) they know better than to bite. If either of these factors is in play, we will not make a catch.

In the same way, when we perceive problems due to our flawed and limited perspectives, we will feel "hungry" for solutions. James clearly writes that each of us is "drawn away and enticed by his own evil desires" (James 1:14 HCSB). The word translated as "desires" in James 1:14 is the Biblical Greek word "epithumia" which denotes a strong passion driven by an underlying emotion. This emotional passion sends us looking for solutions to our perceived problems or, at the very least, a way to alleviate their symptoms. The tempter may offer a "tempting" option, but we will only *feel* tempted if it coincides with our current beliefs and desires.

But we do not have to respond to this "hunger" by engaging in sinful solutions, for this emotional compulsion is simply indicating our need for God's perspective. Instead, we can respond appropriately to the "snares" that are placed in our path by looking to God and admitting our need for His intervention, not to help us keep from sinning but to grant us a change of thought (metanoia) "leading to the knowledge of the truth" (2 Timothy 2:25-26).

That said, there still exists the second reason why we take the tempter's bait: we fail to see the danger. Like an ignorant fish, if we fail to rightly perceive the true cost of using Satan's solutions, we will see no reason to look elsewhere. The enemy wants to direct your attention to all the potential "benefits" of solving your own problems. This has been one of his primary tactics since he crept up to Eve in the Garden (see Genesis 3). He knows that no one will be interested in following his lead, if they realize his final destination. Every path he presents leads to death (James 1:15)!

Like fish with scarred faces, we are marred by the consequences of our sinful choices. To our own astonishment and grief, we have taken the bait many times. And even though our Savior has protected us from the eternal punishment we deserve, the temporal cost and consequence of our foolish choices have riddled our experiences with disappointment and regret. But in spite of this, we continue to "do the very thing [we] hate" (Romans 7:15, emphasis added).

As you learned from our discussion of the "Belief and Choice" Principle, we repeatedly engage in self-defeating behaviors because we have been deceived into believing it will help. The tempter's offerings are only tempting because of the lies we believe. If we saw the deadly hook protruding through the bait, we would swim right past it in search for a better option. This is exactly what God wants us to do! The Holy Spirit desires to persuade us of the truth regarding our short-sighted, sinful behavior so that we will look to Him for a better solution.

Some experienced fishermen may protest saying, "You forgot a third reason for why fish don't bite. You may be using the wrong bait!" Although this is true (and plagues many amateur fishermen), notice the true source of the problem. The reason for why your choice of bait is so important has to do with the fish, not with the bait itself. Each fish is enticed by its own desires (see James 1:14). If you are using a lure that mimics what the fish already wants, then you have made the right selection. The fish bites because of its desires, not because of the lure. This is why a particular lure works well with one species but is useless when trying to catch another.

This illustrates why some people feel tempted by certain sins but not drawn to others. Whichever short-sighted solution seems most likely to meet our apparent needs will appear most enticing. We feel tempted by particular sinful behaviors because of what we believe about them. We are not "drawn and enticed" by the sin itself. We feel "tempted" to sin because we lack God's perspective. If we viewed our situation and available options through God's eyes, we would not be tempted to engage in Satan's short-sighted solutions.

When we feel tempted to sin, it is a belief problem, not a devil problem. Paul echoes this notion when he asks the rhetorical questions, "Are we to continue in sin so that grace may increase?" and "How shall we who died to sin still live in it?" (Romans 6:1-2) and then immediately points out the real problem by asking, "Or do you not know that all of us who have been baptized (immersed) into Christ Jesus have been baptized into His death?" (Romans 6:3, emphasis added). Paul clearly sees the real reason why a believer would be tempted to sin; they lack God's perspective!

So when the tempter tempts us to sin, he is simply exposing our lack of God's perspective. And though this encounter is not pleasant, but painful, "to those who have been trained by it, afterwards it yields the peaceful fruit of righteousness" (Hebrews 12:11). Instead of investing our energy into "not sinning," our goal should be to benefit from the experience by becoming trained by it. For there is something to be learned from every tempting encounter: we lack God's perspective.

Just as our emotional pain points out our need for truth, the pull we feel towards wayward behavior indicates that we do not yet fully believe the truth. Rather than simply fighting the temptation to sin, we should address the belief problem that it was used to expose. If we can learn to respond responsibly to Satan's temptations, then even his evil intentions can be used to accomplish good in us (Genesis 50:20, Romans 8:28).

The hardest fish to catch are the ones who aren't hungry. They will let food float by like a fleeting thought. But even if they are looking for something to eat, the fish who have learned the dangers of a fisherman's hook are less likely to take the bait than those who are ignorant of its intended purpose. In the same way, when we know the truth concerning Satan's short-sighted solutions, we will not feel tempted to try them. And once we are persuaded of the truth regarding who God is and who we are in Him, we will no longer look for "food" because we will be satisfied (see Matthew 5:6). (We encourage you to revisit the "Belief and Choice" Principle, the concept of "Solutions," and the last part of Chapter Four for more on this general topic.)

A Hungry Lion

Peter reveals both how the devil operates and how we are to respond to this scheming where he says,

> Be of sober spirit, be on the alert. Your adversary, the devil, prowls around like a roaring lion, seeking someone to devour. But resist him, firm in your faith, knowing that the same experiences of suffering are being accomplished by your brethren who are in the world. After you have suffered for a little while, the God of all grace, who called you to His eternal glory in Christ, will Himself perfect, confirm, strengthen, and establish you. To Him be dominion forever and ever (1 Peter 5:8–11).

Hungry lions prowl around looking for easy prey. They look for the weak, tired, and injured among the herd and target these vulnerable members. In the same way, Satan seeks to strike the weak spots in our "shield of faith." He looks for vulnerabilities and seeks to "devour" us by offering up short-sighted, sinful solutions to our perceived problems and emotional pain.

Peter did not encourage us to be "sober" and "alert" because the enemy might attack, oppress, or harm us. He wanted us to be aware of the devil's schemes and snares. Satan wants to deceive us, trigger our emotional pain, and offer us sinful solutions to our perceived problems. These are Satan's tactics. But since "we are not ignorant of his schemes" (2 Corinthians 2:11), we are less likely to fall into one of his traps and, instead, benefit from the faith-refining work that God is using the enemy to help accomplish.

The context of Peter's exhortation is a church that is suffering severe and unjust persecution. Like the scattered members of that first-century church, we feel emotional pain when our lack of God's perspective is exposed. In the context of this emotional upheaval, the "roaring lion" seeks out those interested in escaping their pain and offers them lie-based solutions.

Peter encourages his readers to be sober and alert to the fact that they have an enemy that wants to "devour" them. He understood that you must first recognize what Satan is doing before you can effectively resist him.

Satan is an opportunist who "prowls around" looking for easy prey. He seeks those who are either ignorant of the truth or already deceived. He roams about the earth seeking someone in emotional pain who is looking for a way of escape. If you are not currently "triggered," he will look for a weakness that he can exploit, not a weakness in you but a weakness in what you believe to be true.

He fires his flaming arrows hoping to hit a lie-based vulnerability. If you are hurting, he will sneakily suggest a solution. He attempts to deceive us into "solving" this problem through the use of food, sex, intoxicants, entertainment, religious performance, or by acting out our pain and hurting others.

Just as lions have mastered the ability to identify weak and vulnerable animals, Satan is highly skilled in locating the impurities in your faith. But this is not a bad thing! He does so by God's intent. Although we may not enjoy his involvement, our need for God's perspective must be exposed since we are unlikely to address it until the need is made evident. When the lies we believe are struck by one of his fiery arrows, and we feel their emotional consequences, we are motivated to do something about it. We must come to understand that God uses the "exposer" to give us opportunities for gaining a heavenly perspective.

There is no reason to fear this "roaring lion." He is on a short leash that is firmly grasped by One who is greater than him (1 John 4:4). Indeed, the enemy is seeking to expose and exploit the impurities in our faith, but those who are aware of his evil intentions and the role he plays in God's faith-refining process can learn to respond appropriately by resisting him and humbling themselves under the mighty hand of God, leading to the peaceful fruit of righteousness (James 4:7, 1 Peter 5:6, Hebrews 12:5-13).

DEMONS ARE ONLY PRESENT DUE TO DECEPTION.

Someone might misconstrue what we have said so far and assume that we are suggesting that demonic involvement in a TPM session is to be blamed on the Mentee or that little children who were traumatized are responsible for accepting Satan's solution of demonic manifestations. We fully acknowledge that demonization may have originally occurred in childhood when the person was in a very vulnerable state and trusted those who may not have been trustworthy. Children can be easily influenced and manipulated by evil perpetrators and led to believe lies while not realizing there are other options. However, the root cause for the demons' involvement remains the same; the child was deceived! The demons are not present because of a past traumatic or painful experience; they hang around because the person believes lies. And as long as the deception remains, so too will the demons.

So then, understanding how a demon may have found its way into a person's life is irrelevant. What is important is to identify why it is still present. If we assume that its entry point is a problem, then the practice of renouncing vows, breaking bonds, and curses, renouncing the sins of our forefathers, tearing down strongholds are viewed as a necessity and are often applied. Even though this is a frequent practice for some, it assumes that the devil is the problem, and the person is a victim. This misinformed approach lacks biblical support and stifles the TPM process.

Part Six

We can wrestle or stand, but we can't do both.

Throughout the *post-resurrection Scriptures*, we are given simple and straightforward instructions on how to respond to the devil. We are told to be "of sober spirit" and "on alert," not "ignorant of his schemes," and to "resist him" (James 4:7, Ephesians 6:13, 2 Corinthians 2:11, 1 Peter 5:8). We are to understand the enemy's evil intent, as well as God's loving and purposeful use of him, but we are not told to engage Satan in battle.

For an example of this, let's briefly examine the letter Paul wrote to the church in Ephesus to correct their misguided behavior. He explained, "We wrestle not against flesh and blood, but against principalities, against powers, against the rulers of the darkness of this world, against spiritual wickedness in high places" (Ephesians 6:12 KJV). Someone might interject, "See! Paul says that we are wrestling against a spiritual evil!" But notice that although Paul did say those involved were wrestling, he did not encourage them to continue this behavior. He was simply calling attention to what they were doing in hopes of correcting their flawed perspectives and fruitless behavior.

It appears that Paul is saying something akin to "Hey Ephesians! You have been deceived! You have fallen for one of Satan's schemes. He has tricked you into thinking that you are in conflict with each other (flesh and blood), when, in reality, you are wrestling with the forces of darkness. Stop it!" Notice that Paul compares their behavior to wrestling (which in those days was done mostly, if not entirely, unclothed). From Paul's perspective, they may as well have been naked! He was pointing out their exposed and vulnerable mental state.

The Ephesians needed to know what the Galatians had learned: that they were "clothed in Christ" (Galatians 3:27). Paul was encouraging them to stop their wrestling, put on the full armor of God, and stand (Ephesians 6:13). Again, he clearly states the purpose of wearing the armor of God. They needed to don their armor not so they would be better equipped to fight, but so they would be able to stand. Why shouldn't they use their weapons of war to engage the enemy? Because the war was over! They simply needed to stand in the finished work of Christ!

Like the Ephesians, we may wrestle with the forces of darkness (see Ephesians 6:12), but if we do, it is because we lack God's perspective. We are either not yet convinced of our victory in Christ or have been tricked into believing we need to fight this defeated foe. Satan obviously does not try to correct this misunderstanding and welcomes the invitation to wrestle! He knows that we will be unable to stand in the victory we have in Christ if we are distracted in our struggles against him, and he undoubtedly revels in reenacting the pre-calvary days!

As we have said before, victory and battle cannot co-exist. We have one or the other but not both. Satan is fully aware of his utter defeat, but he hopes that we are not. And he does his best to convince us that the battle is not over. If we feel the need to fight, we have the freedom to do so. We can challenge the enemy, and he is happy to go "toe-to-toe" with us, but our battle cries do little more than reveal our lack of confidence in the finished work of Jesus Christ.

Paul told us that "after having done all, to stand" (Ephesians 6:13 KJV). Wrestlers may begin their bout in a standing position, but in order to wrestle they must get down on the ground and grapple until one or the other pins his opponent to the ground. Paul is not calling us to do this with the enemy, though it may be the very thing that many of us are doing. He is encouraging us to get up off the ground, put on our clothes, and stand in the finished work of Christ. Paul intentionally uses two contrasting analogies: one, wallowing about naked on the ground and the other, a victorious soldier standing fully clothed in armor.

If we slow things down and take a moment to honestly evaluate what we are doing, the logical contradictions become obvious. How is it possible for us to wave a flag of victory in one hand while using the sword in the other to threaten Satan? How can we claim to have victory and yet continue to fight a defeated foe? This is an inexcusable discrepancy. Warfare and victory cannot coexist! No, they do not coexist! The battle is over! All that is left for us to do is stand firm in our faith and give thanks to God, "who gives us the victory through our Lord Jesus Christ" (1 Corinthians 16:13, 15:57)! When we rightly perceive God's authority, victory, and involvement, we will be bold, confident, and unafraid; not as we fight the devil, but as we stand in Christ's finished work!

MISAPPLYING SCRIPTURE TO JUSTIFY SPIRITUAL WARFARE

We are directed to "resist the devil" by "standing firm in the faith" (1 Peter 5:9), but many have misapplied various other passages of Scripture to justify their warfare tactics. I do not think ill of them for doing such things because I was unknowingly guilty of the same malpractice for many years (*though I hope to help others avoid making this same mistake*). Numerous Bible verses have commonly been misused in this manner. For example, in one of his letters to the church in Corinth, Paul writes the following:

"for the weapons of our warfare are not of the flesh, but divinely powerful for the destruction of fortresses. We are destroying arguments and all arrogance raised against the knowledge of God, and we are taking every thought captive to the obedience of Christ, and we are ready to punish all disobedience, whenever your obedience is complete" (2 Corinthians 10:4-6).

As much as some of us would like to use these verses to support our military campaign against the devil, doing so is a grave misuse of Scripture. This passage has absolutely nothing to do with Satan or our attempts to battle him. Without going into too much detail, Paul is actively defending himself against those who are spreading lies and challenging his apostleship. He is threatening to destroy the fortresses of deceptive arguments and arrogant ignorance that have been constructed in the Corinthian church. He is targeting the misinformation that is being spread by those who oppose his spiritual authority; he is not, however, threatening to strike down any demons or spiritual "strongholds."

Now, you may astutely respond by thinking, "But Satan was behind the scenes deceiving those who were falsely accusing Paul and encouraging them to spread lies about his apostleship." Quite true! In fact, Paul suggests this very thing in the following chapter where he says, "For such men are false apostles, deceitful workers, disguising themselves as apostles of Christ.

No wonder, for <u>even Satan disguises himself</u> as an angel of light. Therefore it is not surprising if <u>his servants also disguise themselves</u> as servants of righteousness, whose end will be according to their deeds" (2 Corinthians 11:13-15, emphasis added).

Paul obviously recognizes Satan's involvement, but his "weapons" are targeting the works of the deceptive "false apostles," not Satan himself. Paul concludes this portion of the passage by saying, "we are ready to punish all disobedience, whenever your obedience is complete" (2 Corinthians 10:6). This verse clarifies who Paul is talking about. He is not coming to discipline demons, he is targeting wayward members.

Another verse that is often misused to justify our use of force against the devil can be found in John's account of the gospel. In it Jesus says, "the thief comes only to steal and kill and destroy" (John 10:10). How many times have you heard this verse used to describe the enemy? But Jesus was not referring to Satan in this passage. If you read the fuller context of His words, the Lord is clearly comparing Himself (the "good Shepherd") to the religious leaders who were deceptive and thieving false shepherds. Jesus was using a parable to explain who He was, what He was sent to do, and the relationship He has with those He is bringing into His flock. But Jesus was not saying that Satan has come to steal, kill, and destroy.

There are other scriptural passages that have been misapplied to support the desire to fight the devil (which will be discussed in a separate book). But rather than misapplying these verses, we need to read and interpret them in their proper context. We must be careful not to attribute powers and abilities to the devil that he does not possess. He is an extremely capable adversary, but he does not have the authority to ever steal, kill, or destroy anything unless God directly grants him provisional authority to do so. But the truth is he doesn't need these abilities. Satan only needs to find someone who is open to deception because, when we believe his lies, we steal from, kill, and destroy each other! And in every case, we are the ones who are responsible for the theft, murder, and destruction, not Satan.

Another important principle to keep in mind is the chronology and context of passages that actually do pertain to Satan. For instance, some attempt to defend their military campaign against the enemy (who has been defeated for over two thousand years) by citing Jesus' interaction with demons while He was physically on Earth. But it is important to remember that each of these encounters occurred before His crucifixion and resurrection. Assuming this pre-calvary position ignores what was accomplished by our Savior on the cross. Things have changed drastically since then! To properly understand Satan and his role in our lives today, we must view him from a post-resurrection perspective. To do anything else is to deny Christ's finished work and decisive victory.

Standing Firm in the Faith

In spite of what we have discussed so far, some may still protest, saying, "I've been given a sword and a shield, and I am going to use them! Demons beware!" And we would support their fervent desire to use what God has given them, but we would also lovingly encourage them to use these items for the purpose God intended. He has not handed-out weaponry that is to be used in battle; we are equipped to showcase the victory that has already been secured for us. Just as He earned our salvation and freely gave it to us, He has also secured the battlefield by Himself and invited us to share in His glory by standing next to Him, adorned in the King's armor.

That said, I genuinely sympathize with those who struggle with the idea of not using our spiritual swords in battle. Years ago, I "battled" the devil by wielding my "sword" by quoting Bible verses at him. I based doing so on what I *thought* Jesus did in the wilderness when He was "led by the Spirit to be tempted by the devil" (Matthew 4:1). I now realize that Jesus was not warring with the devil but rather proving He was indeed the "Son of God" by not succumbing to any of the devil's temptations. When Jesus quoted the Old Testament passages in response to the devil's temptations, He was not fighting with the devil; He was affirming His identity as the Son of God. Notice how Satan began each temptation with, "If you are the Son of God then..." Jesus was led into the wilderness *by the Spirit* for this very purpose. He was not led there to fight but to stand, and stand He did.

There was no battle going on in the wilderness, and in fact, the Scriptures say that "when the devil had finished every temptation, he left Him until an opportune time" (Luke 4:13). Jesus used the "sword" but He did not use it for battle. He used it for verification. Our sword also has a purpose, but it is not so we might fight the devil.

A good practice to apply when seeking to interpret any particular Bible passage is to see if the same idea is taught or presented in other places in Scripture (this is what Bible scholars and teachers call "correlation"). By doing so you are letting Scripture interpret Scripture. Concerning the "sword" analogy used by Paul in Ephesians, the writer of Hebrews uses the same sword analogy but brings out what appears to be a different purpose for its use. He says,

> For the word of God is living and active, and sharper than any two-edged sword, even penetrating as far as the division of soul and spirit, of both joints and marrow, and <u>able to judge the thoughts and intentions of the heart</u>" (Hebrews 4:12, emphasis added).

> The New Living Translation reads, "...it exposes our innermost thoughts and desires (Hebrews 4:12 NLT).

First, there is no mention or suggestion that we should use this sword as a weapon of warfare nor is Satan mentioned or implied in this context. Rather, the Word of God is described as an extremely sharp blade that is meant to be used not only *by* us but used *on* us. Like a surgeon's scalpel, God's word cuts through every layer of performance, avoidance, and excuses to expose our motives and innermost thoughts. It is not a weapon of war but, rather, a surgical tool that was designed to cut through the outer layers of our spiritual chests and reveal what resides in our hearts. It is used to determine whether or not our faith (heart belief) is aligned with God's perspective.

Someone will surely point out the sword analogy used in Ephsians six. In this passage the "world forces of darkness" are addressed; nowhere does Paul suggest that we are to use our swords in an offensive manner against these forces. In fact, the "sword of the Spirit" [truth, the word of God] assists in the purification of our "shield of faith" by testing and judging the "thoughts and intentions of the heart," ensuring that we have what we need to extinguish the enemy's fiery arrows [lies, deception] (Ephesians 6:16-17, Hebrews 4:12).

Revisiting the passages where Jesus is in the wilderness with Satan, we saw that Jesus was not quoting the Old Testament to ward off the devil. Rather, He and Satan were both there to accomplish a purpose. Satan was there to tempt Jesus, and Jesus was there to prove that the "ruler of the world" had nothing on Him (John 14:30). Their encounter could not possibly be accurately described as a "battle." It was not a fight; it was a test. And the results of this test further proved that Jesus was the Son of God.

When the testing was complete, Jesus said, "Go away, Satan," and the tempter left. It is interesting that the devil did not retreat until the Lord resisted him and told him to leave. The devil was not scared away by the quoting of Scripture; he left because the job was done (Matthew 4:10). As it says in Luke's account, "When the devil had finished every temptation, he left Him until an opportune time" (Luke 4:13). Jesus had obeyed His Father (Matthew 4:1), and Satan had run out of things to do.

Satan did to Jesus what he does with each of us; he attempts to expose the impurities in our faith. He could not find any impurities in Jesus's faith, but there is plenty to target in ours! He looks for opportunities to expose the falsehood in our heart belief and then offers sinful solutions to our faith problem. But if we respond to this exposure by acknowledging what was hidden and seeking God's perspective, we cooperate with God as He works even Satan's evil intentions for our good (Romans 8:28).

Paul explains that we are able to "stand firm against the schemes of the devil" when we "put on the full armor of God" (Ephesians 6:11). The good news is that if you are in Christ, you have already done this! Someone might say, "But I feel naked and vulnerable to the devil's attack!" Indeed, you may feel this way since we always feel whatever we believe. Even so, the truth is still the truth regardless of what you believe (again, we encourage you to revisit the "Belief and Perspective" Principle). God's Word declares, "all of you who were baptized into Christ have <u>clothed</u> yourselves with Christ" (Galatians 3:27, emphasis added). And not only that, but you also "took off your former way of life, the old self that is corrupted by deceitful desires; you are being renewed in the spirit of your minds; you put on the new self, the one created according to God's likeness in righteousness and purity of the truth" (Ephesians 4:22-24 HCSB). If these truths do not feel true, then you need God to grant you "a spirit of wisdom and of revelation in the knowledge of Him" and for the Spirit of truth to "open the eyes of your heart" so that you might "know the hope of your calling" (see Ephesians 1:17-18).

These realities are presently true for every believer. If they don't *feel* or *seem* true, then we are simply not yet convinced that they *are* true. For whatever we *do* believe will *feel* or *seem* true to us. In a sense, our problem is not that we fail to stand *firm* in our faith; rather, the faith that we are standing in is not *firm*. The impurities of our enfeebled faith cause us to feel emotional pain and lead us to act in a manner unbecoming of saints (see Ephesians 5:1-5).

God loves you too much to sit back and watch you live your life from this limited and flawed perspective. He wants you to know the truth! But before He persuades you of His perspective, He exposes your need for it by drawing your attention to your impure faith. For instance, if you believe that you are dirty and shameful, He wants you to acknowledge this. If you believe that He is unfaithful, He wants you to admit it. And if you believe that suppressing your pain will keep you safe, that expressing your anger will hold others accountable, or that performing well at your job will prove you have value, then He wants these beliefs exposed as well.

With this in mind, reconsider the fiery arrows of the enemy. Regardless of the evil archer's intentions, what are his arrows accomplishing? Are they not exposing what God wants to expose? Your Heavenly Father wants you to honestly acknowledge what you *do* believe so that He can convince you of what you *should* believe. But until someone or something exposes your lack of God's perspective, it is unlikely that any of us will admit it.

In this way, Satan is used to expose what is lacking in our "shield of faith." A purified faith extinguishes every one of his fiery arrows. So, it stands to reason that if an arrow gets through our shield, the faith that is shielding us is not pure. The impurities in our faith permit the fiery arrows passage. Although it is painful when our spiritual defenses are breached, neither the "breach" nor the emotional pain we feel in response is a bad thing. On the contrary, they are good things! In fact, this is what God wants for us and what we would want for ourselves if only we saw clearly. They represent opportunities to gain God's perspective.

When we fully know who God is and who we are in Him, we can stand firm in the invincibility that we have in His righteousness and truth. Until then, God wants us to stand firm in the faith that we have and humble ourselves under His mighty hand as He exposes the impure vulnerabilities that remain in our shield of faith. As these impurities are exposed and removed, our faith becomes more and more purified, and we are better shielded from Satan's arrows. But notice that this enhanced security comes when we know the truth. It is not a result of battling the enemy or driving him away, but rather our protection is the outcome of a purified faith.

When we know the truth in our hearts, our spiritual shield will extinguish every flaming arrow that is sent our way, proving the genuineness of our faith (Ephesians 6:16, 1 Peter 1:7). Herein is the overall purpose that we should keep in our minds: a purified faith! Removing the enemy from the equation is not the goal. He is merely a means to an end. God uses Satan to expose our need for His refining work and then showcases the quality of that work in a steaming cloud of extinguished arrows!

Part Seven

Resisting the Devil

Someone might wonder why we are told to resist the devil if no battle is to be waged. Put simply, the purpose of resisting Satan is to silence him and have him leave the scene. There is no reason to allow him to continue talking after he has been used to point-out our lack of God's perspective. We are to immediately end the conversation, honestly acknowledge what he has exposed, and humbly invite God to persuade us of the truth that we do not yet have.

Many years ago, I would mistakenly engage demons, commanding them to leave, and their predictable outcry would be, "*We will not!*" I now realize that I was unknowingly being played. The demonic spirits obviously understood that they had to flee as soon as they were resisted, but my verbal commands indicated that I did not genuinely understand the authority I have in Christ. My actions were an invitation for them to do "battle" with me and further expose my lack of faith.

Since I was ignorant of their schemes, I would counter their protests by saying something like, "Oh yes you will! I take authority over you in the name of Jesus" or "I claim the blood of Christ," or I would attempt to control their behavior by saying, "I forbid you to speak!" All the while, the demons continued their charade and pretended to wrestle with me. And, because I didn't know any better, I viewed the many times I "successfully" drove the demons away as a victory, as though some battle had been won.

Having the devil flee is not the end goal but only one step in the process. Immediately after resisting him, we should attend to the reason he was there. You can swat away the flies that buzz around a dung pile, but if the pile remains, the annoying pests will return! In the same way, if we maintain the impure faith that initially drew the devil to us, he will simply "return at a more opportune time" (see Luke 4:13).

Just imagine how differently Eve's day would have gone if she would have followed these simple steps! Instead, she entered into conversation with the serpent and fell prey to his schemes. Today, the devil hopes we follow Eve's example. He wants us to engage him (in conversation or in battle). For as long as we are distracted by him, we will not acquire what we really need: the truth!

Rather than focusing on the "schemer," we need to acknowledge the "scheme," and instead of attacking the "snarer," we need to ask God for truth and perspective so that we can find freedom from the enemy's snare. It is vitally important that we come to understand that the "liar" is not our problem; we struggle because we believe what he is saying. If we knew the truth, all of his deceptive tactics would be done in vain.

Sadly, some wear their "oppression" as a badge of honor. They believe that they have Satan's attention because of their spiritual prowess or effectiveness in carrying out the Lord's work. They think to themselves, "I must be doing something right if the enemy has me in his sights," when, in actuality, they are not targeted because of the good things they might be doing; they are in Satan's sights because they believe lies. When celebrating the fact that they have been "oppressed" by the enemy, they are inadvertently boasting about their own deception. The frailty of their bragging becomes even more apparent when you consider the fact that the "oppression" would end as soon as the "oppressor" is genuinely resisted (see James 4:7) and the "oppressed" gains God's perspective.

We encourage the "oppressed" to more closely consider the context of the enemy's involvement. If a fiery arrow fails to fizzle-out, it is because our faith is impure. Regardless of Satan's intentions, we are only negatively impacted by his deception if we are already deceived. Again, he is only exploiting what is already there, and he does so with God's permission. Even the devil's evil intentions and tactics fit within the faith-refining process that God uses to conform us to the image of His Son.

Slowly reread Paul's words in this passage:

> And we know that God causes all things to work together for good to those who love God, to those who are called according to His purpose. For those whom He foreknew, He also predestined to become conformed to the image of His Son, so that He would be the first-born among many brothers and sisters; and these whom He predestined, He also called; and these whom He called, He also justified; and these whom He justified, He also glorified. What then shall we say to these things? If God is for us, who is against us? (Romans 8:28-31, emphasis added).

The evil intentions of those who are "against us" is utterly irrelevant because God is for us! He will use everything from "tribulation" to "persecution" to "famine" to "sword" or even the devil's fiery darts to refine our faith, renew our minds, and transform our lives so that they reflect the image of His Son (see Romans 8:35, 8:29). So even if Satan is against you, he is involuntarily for you!

Resisting Without Force

It is important to remember that we do not "resist the devil" by exerting force on him. We resist him by simply saying "no" to his schemes. If we say "no" and mean it, he will flee. Because of this, it stands to reason that there are only two possible explanations if he remains after we think we have resisted him. Either we have not actually resisted him or, when we did resist him, we didn't mean it. Both potential explanations suggest that we have a lie-based reason to not resist him (for more on this, revisit the concept of *solution beliefs*).

Remember, Satan has had thousands of years to study humans. He likely knows how we think and behave better than we do, and he can tell when we mean what we say. He knows what it looks like when a child of God is standing in his or her authority in Christ, but he is also keenly aware of when we doubt who we are and are not yet convinced of the victory we have. This lack of faith is exactly the kind of vulnerability that the "roaring lion" seeks to expose and exploit! In fact, this is one of the Creator's purposes for him: to identify and call attention to our need for God's perspective.

When the devil fulfills his purpose, driven by evil and cruel desires, your impure faith is left exposed. But he doesn't stop there! He wants you to attempt to *solve* your perceived problems yourself, so he offers alternatives to the one God has made available to us. Your Heavenly Father has sent His Spirit to lead you into the truth that you desperately need (John 16:13), but your enemy hopes that you explore other options. This is where we must resist the devil and his short-sighted solutions.

Again, the serpent did not force the forbidden fruit into Eve's mouth; she chose to implement the *solution* that he had offered to her. He lied to her, and she believed him. The moment that Eve was deceived, she was "carried away and enticed by [her] own lust" (James 1:14, emphasis added). It wasn't the devil's evil desires that compelled her to eat and disobey; it was her own. But she only wanted to take a bite because she lacked God's perspective. For if she had fully known the truth, would she ever have even considered disobeying God's command?

When Satan approaches us to expose our lack of faith and suggest his sinful solutions, will we follow in Adam and Eve's footsteps by agreeing with him and taking a bite, or will we say "no" to his *solutions*, acknowledge the impurities in our faith, and ask for our Father's perspective? If what we choose to do in response to the tempter's involvement does not result in our coming to believe the truth in our heads and in our hearts, then we have likely done exactly what he was hoping we would do.

Satan wants nothing more than for us to remain distracted and deceived. For as long as we believe falsehood, he has a soft target for his fiery arrows. He wants us to fight him. He wants us to take up our swords and go on the attack. When we do, he laughs at the "children of light" who act as though they are fighting in the "domain of darkness," unaware that they have been transferred out of it, and the "war" has been over for thousands of years (1 Thessalonians 5:5, Colossians 1:13). Satan hopes that we never realize our own deception and attempt to solve our problems ourselves rather than looking to our Heavenly Father for help.

We will not find victory through force, grit, or determination. Our victory has already been secured through Jesus and has been given to us (see 1 Corinthians 15:57). This victory can only be realized through faith. As John poignantly pointed out, "whoever has been born of God overcomes the world; and this is the victory that has overcome the world: our faith" (1 John 5:4). Peter affirmed this notion when he wrote, "Resist [the devil], standing firm in the faith" (1 Peter 5:9 BSB, emphasis added). If we are not experiencing victory, this is an issue of faith, not warfare! We need to *believe*, not *battle!*

In his letter to the Ephesians, Paul describes the authority we have because of the victory Christ has given to us. He writes:

> I pray that the eyes of your heart may be enlightened, so that you will know what is the hope of His calling, what are the riches of the glory of His inheritance in the saints, and what is the boundless greatness of His power toward us who believe. These are in accordance with the working of the strength of His might which He brought about in Christ, when He raised Him from the dead and seated Him at His right hand in the heavenly places, far above all rule and authority and power and dominion, and every name that is named, not only in this age but also in the one to come. And He put all things in subjection under His feet and made Him head over all things to the church, which is His body, the fullness of Him who fills all in all (Ephesians 1:18-23, emphasis added).

Read these verses again knowing that we (the church) are the "fullness of Him." We are seated with Him at the right hand of God (see Ephesians 2:6); we are presently "far above all rule and authority and power and dominion," and "all things" are "in subjection under [our] feet." The authority that was given to Jesus has been given to us all! Because of this, the evil one cannot touch us (see 1 John 5:18). Think about that for a minute.

The authority and victory that we have been given <u>do not</u> somehow empower us to fight the devil; rather, they are the reasons for why fighting is unnecessary! We do not need to battle the enemy because we already have authority over him, and we are presently victorious in Christ. It really is that simple!

Submitting to God's Use of Satan

Satan is your enemy, but he is not your problem. He is nothing more than a tool in the hand of God. His evil intentions are rendered irrelevant within the greater context of God's loving and redemptive plan. God will finish what He started using every means at His disposal, including Satan. The devil belongs to God, is contained within divinely set limitations, and is used by God to bring about the "good" intended for those "called according to His purpose." When our Heavenly Father is done using the enemy, He will cast Satan into the lake of fire (see Revelation 20:10). Until that day, we should humbly submit to God's loving, careful, and purposeful use of Satan's involvement to expose the impurities in our faith and conform us to the image of His Son (Romans 8:28-29).

If the devil triggers one of your lie-based beliefs, he has God's permission to do so. In fact, God may have even deliberately mentioned your name to Satan just as He did with Job (Job 1:8, 2:3). God uses the devil's predictable behavior to expose your need for truth and perspective. It is more important for us to come into the knowledge of who God is and who we are in Him than it is that we live our lives free from Satan's involvement. The devil's devious deeds are not a threat to God's plan; in fact, they are used to accomplish it! Your real problem is that you lack God's perspective; Satan is simply used to bring this need to your attention.

This role of "exposer" is also played by your spouse, boss, kids, and every life situation that you encounter. All of these can expose the impurities in your faith and cause your emotional pain to stir. We are not saying that your spouse is a demon, but rather, that God uses all available options to bring about this same refining purpose. Again, we must remember that "God causes ALL things to work together for the good..." (Romans 8:28, emphasis added). And "all things" includes the devil.

Based upon what you've read so far, when Satan's evil intent and involvement exposes your need for God's perspective, is this a good thing or a bad thing? We may not enjoy the experience of being exposed, but our faith needs to be refined! The faithful who came before would likely challenge and encourage us saying:

Job: "Shall we accept good from God but not accept adversity?" (see Job 2:10)

Joseph: "Does God not use what is meant for evil for good?" (see Genesis 50:20)

Paul: "Does God not use ALL things to accomplish His good purposes?" (see Romans 8:28)

Peter: "Are you really surprised at the fiery ordeal that has come upon you?" (see 1 Peter 4:12)

James: "Would you prefer that God let you remain immature and incomplete?" (see James 1:2-4)

Sadly, many have a backwards understanding of the enemy's "attacks." Yes, Satan's motives are evil and impure, but this does not negate God's purpose and use of the devil's barrage. Again, each missile is targeting that which <u>needs</u> to be exposed. We need the lie-based impurities that are present in our faith to be brought to the surface so that God can replace them with His truth. In light of this, we must realize that we do not need our "shield of faith" because of Satan's fiery arrows; rather, we need his fiery arrows because of the imperfect shield we carry!

Rather than viewing the devil as the problem and planning a counter attack, we need to realize that he is an integral part of God's faith-refining process. He is a created being that is serving a purpose in God's plan (as much as he would like to believe otherwise). He hopes that you will focus on him and give him the attention he craves, but if, instead, we respond to his involvement by turning our attention to the Spirit of Truth and seeking God's perspective, we cooperate with God and His refining work in our lives (see James 4:7).

SATAN'S DIVERSIONARY TACTICS

If you currently practice some kind of spiritual warfare or deliverance ministry, some of what I am presenting may be a stretch for you. I genuinely understand this. I was also highly invested in fighting the devil for many years, and I instructed others to pray against the devil, take authority over demons, break vows, lift generational curses, and confront any evil spirits that manifested during a TPM session. I genuinely believed that these practices were needed and helpful. Today, I realize that all of this is unnecessary.

I used to view demonized people as victims of the devil who needed the intervention of those who were more spiritually aware and mature. I mistakenly thought that these people needed to be rescued. I now realize that they were not in bondage. They did not need to be rescued from anything. They were simply deceived and in need of God's perspective. They were caught in the devil's snare (deception), but they were not held hostage by the devil himself.

Do you see the illogical nature of fighting a defeated foe? How can true victory and continual battle coexist? We must either give up the fight and embrace the victory we have in Christ or deny His finished work and muster the troops for battle. We cannot have it both ways!

By focusing on the devil, we inadvertently divert our attention away from the source of the problem and invest our time and energy into attacking the one who was used to expose it. This is exactly what Satan wants. He wants our attention to be focused on him so that we keep ourselves busy swatting flies away from the dung pile. As long as we are looking at him, we are unlikely to look to God and invite Him to clean up the mess.

Think about it! If wrestling with the enemy distracts us from the refining work that God is seeking to accomplish, who do you think supports our unnecessary use of force against Satan? And which shows more confidence in our God-given authority: waging war against a defeated foe or standing in the security that comes with knowing that God is fully in control and is actively working all things together for our good?

When we engage Satan in battle, we unknowingly fight both God's plan and purpose and deny the victory that He says He has won. Rather than focusing on the devil and delaying our own faith-refinement, we should humbly submit to the mighty hand that is holding the enemy (see 1 Peter 5:6) and invite God to do His refining work.

Part Eight

We find freedom from Satan's traps when the Holy Spirit persuades us of the truth.

Paul says it clearly: "no advantage would be taken of us by Satan, for we are not ignorant of his schemes" (2 Corinthians 2:11, emphasis added). If we invert what Paul is saying, the message becomes even clearer, "Satan can and will take advantage of us if we are ignorant of his schemes." A mouse who is ignorant of the trap will be tempted to take a bite of the bait. Similarly, if we are ignorant of Satan's schemes and the nature of his snares, we are destined for trouble.

In another letter, Paul wrote to Timothy regarding those who have succumbed to Satan's snare. He offered this advice, "With gentleness correcting those who are in opposition, if perhaps God may grant them repentance leading to the knowledge of the truth, and they may come to their senses and escape from the snare of the devil, having been held captive by him to do his will" (2 Timothy 2:25-26, emphasis added).

The word translated as "repentance" in this passage (and in most other passages where you find the English word repentance being used) is the Greek word *metanoia*. The literal meaning of this word is often *misunderstood* to mean "to turn from sin," but it actually means "to have a change in belief, thought, or mindset." Turning from sin is an expected outcome of *metanoia*, but the actual act of turning is not what this word means. This important distinction is tragically lost in many translations (usually because the translators look to the Latin definition rather than the Greek, but we digress).

Misunderstanding *metanoia* as "turning from sin" also mistakenly makes us responsible for this "turning." If "repentance" (*metanoia*) is rightly understood to be the act of having the Holy Spirit persuade our hearts of the truth, then *turning from sin* becomes an effortless and expected outcome of God's sanctifying work in those who believe.

In this particular passage from Paul's letter to Timothy, we see that it is God who grants "repentance" (change of belief) resulting in the person coming into the knowledge of the truth (epignósis - experiential knowing beyond intellect), thereby, coming to their senses (having mental clarity) and escaping the devil's snare (the lie they were deceived into believing).

Notice what frees the person from "the snare of the devil." Paul does not instruct Timothy to go on the attack, to anoint anything with oil, or pray against the devil. He recognized the true source of the problem. A person who is "held captive by [the devil] to do his will" needs to have their thinking changed. Only after God grants them "repentance leading to the knowledge of the truth" will they escape Satan's snare!

Here is where the "turning from sin" comes into play. When God grants a change in belief, the natural and expected outcome is that we will turn from sin or "escape the snare of the devil." Even so, turning from sin is <u>the outcome of</u> the "repentance" that God has granted, not repentance itself.

So, those who are caught in one of the devil's snares do not need someone to confront or pray against the "snarer;" they need God to grant them a change in thought" (*metanoia*). For when they know the truth, it will set them free (John 8:32)!

Viewing the Devil in His Proper Context

Understanding the victory and authority you have in Christ and the divinely appointed parameters that have been placed on Satan will equip you to view the devil in his proper context. Without this "post-resurrection" perspective, Satan may *seem* as though he is an enemy combatant that needs to be addressed or a threat that needs to be stopped. But, as you will recall, even Jesus did not attack or "wrestle" the enemy or even attempt to curtail the devil's evil behavior. Rather, Jesus destroyed the "works" of the devil. Since his works (the outcome of his behavior) were destroyed, his evil actions lost their effectiveness on all those who are in Christ (See 1 John 3:8)! Because of what Christ accomplished, His victory is presently (and eternally) ours! The battle is over; we only need to stand (see Ephesians 6:13).

The devil is our enemy, but he is not the problem. He is simply drawing attention to what is already there. His evil intentions and schemes are used to expose the impurities in our faith, giving us the opportunity to submit ourselves to God and receive His perspective. The evil archer aims for our shields of faith hoping to strike a vulnerability. But this is not a bad thing! The impurities in our faith need to be exposed so that the Refiner can perform His mighty work. The crafty serpent also seeks to seduce us with his short-sighted solutions. But they will only *seem* enticing if we believe that they will help us solve perceived problems; this, too, exposes our need for God's perspective!

An illustration may be helpful here: Picture Satan as an ill-mannered child who maliciously uses hateful words to manipulate his peers. He criticizes and belittles those around him hoping to evoke an emotional response. He gets in their faces and shouts, "You are a freak," "There is something wrong with you," "Nobody wants to be your friend," "You're an idiot," "You're so ugly that your mother doesn't even love you!" He does this hoping to strike a nerve, and when he sees that he has found his mark, he intensifies his verbal assault.

And once his targets are in an emotionally charged state, he challenges them to do something about it. He jeers at them saying, "Why don't you run home to your mommy?" "Are you going to tell the teacher about what I said, you little tattletale?" "What? Are you going to hit me? You wouldn't dare!" He mockingly suggests how they should respond knowing that if the other children follow his directions, he has further humiliated them.

But this bully can only continue pestering his peers so long as he is not "resisted," and his hateful rhetoric is only as harmful as it is believed. If the other children knew the truth in their hearts, his mockery would fall on deaf ears. He can't touch them; he can only make noise!

As hateful as he is, he does not cause them to feel what they feel nor does he make them do what they do. They each feel and do what they believe to be true. If his foul language leads to tears, it means the hearer believes what was said. Likewise, the taunted children will only follow his short-sighted suggestions if they believe doing so is their "best" option. In either case, the real issue is their lack of truth; they have been deceived.

Like this arrogant, malicious brat, Satan deserves to be punished (and he will be; see Revelation 20:10), but the most pressing problem is our lack of perspective, not the presence of the "bully." We need to hear the truth from our loving Father so that we can see ourselves the way He sees us. Once He persuades us of His perspective, the hateful noise will be drowned out by His glorious truth. Attending to the limited and flawed perspectives we have of ourselves (and of God) is more important than removing the "bully" from the "playground." For even if the little punk was kicked out, we would still not know the truth of who we are and who God is!

Think about it; would it be better if these hypothetical children were able to play on the playground without the bothersome involvement of the bully if it meant they went without genuinely knowing their true value, their identity, and the depth of their Father's love? What would you rather have: quiet and ignorant playtime or the peace and security that comes with knowing who you are in Christ, even if it means that you must endure "temporary, light affliction" (2 Corinthians 4:17)?

Rather than attempting to deal with the devil before his appointed time, we simply need to submit to God, resist Satan (as well as his short-sighted schemes), and attend to the belief problems that the enemy's fiery arrows expose. By doing so we stand in the victory that Christ has given *to us*, cooperate with the refining work that the Holy Spirit desires to do *in us*, and acknowledge the reality that our Heavenly Father works all things together *for us*. We encourage you to have this perspective in your TPM sessions.

Responsibly Responding to Demonic Involvement

When applying the TPM Process, your objectives remain the same, regardless of what (or who) made you aware of your need for God's perspective. For instance, upon discovering that you feel anxious, you are in the EMOTION Box and have already accomplished one of your objectives (being connected with your emotion). This is true whether you feel anxious in response to a coworker's poor behavior, the sight of your bank account balance, or being asked to help in the children's ministry at your local church.

But what should you do if you feel anxious in response to the devil's involvement? We suggest that you treat it as you would any other "trigger." Simply apply the TPM Process as usual. The words, "You are worthless," only evoke an emotional response if at some level you agree with their description of your value. This is true regardless of who says them. You feel what you believe. So, even if the devil is the one who exposes what you believe, the TPM Process is not impacted. Simply focus on what you feel and continue following protocol.

Similarly, if you find that you feel tempted to eat a large slice of chocolate cake even though you are not hungry, then you are in the SOLUTION Box and have already accomplished your first objective (determining that you are engaged in a *solution behavior*). This is true whether you feel this urge after watching a TV commercial, in reaction to finding out that you have been fired from your job, or after getting home from having dinner with your out-of-control mother-in-law.

But, if you feel this temptation in response to Satan subtly whispering, "I could really use some cake right now," what should you do? Again, we suggest that you treat this sneaky suggestion as you would any other *solution behavior*. Satan may be cunning and crafty, but he is no more capable of "forcing" you to do something than anyone else; *you do* what you believe. So, again, if the enemy is the one who offered this short-sighted solution, the TPM Process is not impacted. Simply work through the SOLUTION Box and seek out God's perspective.

If a random stranger walked up to you and said, "You belong to Satan," would this mean that you are now the devil's property? Of course not! What if Satan himself said this to you? Would his words hold any more authority than the words of the crazy stranger? Again, no. The truth is the truth regardless of what either one says. But if you believed these words, then your perception, emotional reaction, and subsequent behavior would *likely* be impacted. Here again, the issue is your belief, not the distorted message you received.

Because of this, if it ever *seems* or *feels* as though you are somehow possessed or oppressed by Satan, then you have a belief problem. You have been deceived into believing something that is not true and are viewing your situation from a flawed perspective. Rather than focusing on the deceptive messenger, turn your attention to identifying what you believe. Once the Holy Spirit has persuaded you of the truth, the words "you belong to Satan" will *seem* and *feel* as nonsensical as they truly are!

So, in every case, the devil's actions should be treated like the actions of anyone else because they are no different. Neither your spouse nor Satan can *make* you feel stupid. Neither your doctor nor the devil can *make* you feel anxious or fearful. Neither your boss nor the enemy of your soul can *make* you feel as though you are unwanted or rejected. You always feel what you believe. By focusing on your belief problem rather than on what (or who) exposed it, you respond responsibly to God's purposeful use of "all things" and humbly submit to His "mighty hand" (see Romans 8:28, 1 Peter 5:6).

Part Nine

Practical Examples of Demonic Involvement in TPM Sessions

Even when the devil is somehow involved in a troubling situation, he is never the problem. Now, some may still protest asking, "Then what are we to do about the devil? Are we just going to ignore him?" For the most part, yes. Apart from exposing our need for God's perspective, what can Satan do? He can't touch us. He can't make us feel anything. He can't make us do anything. He is only bringing attention to what is already there: our impure faith. Because of this, we encourage you to submit to God's use of the devil's actions as He refines your faith, renews your mind, and transforms your life.

To illustrate this concept further, consider the following scenarios:

Scenario One: "*Arthur's Temptations*"

Arthur feels overwhelmed. He is the first to come to work at his accounting office and the last to leave, but he is still unable to finish all that needs to be done. When he is especially stressed and overworked, he feels tempted to skip steps and smudge the numbers on forms. It is almost as though someone is whispering into his ear telling him that the only way for him to catch up is to cheat. He knows that doing so is wrong, and he genuinely does not *want* to do it, but he still feels compelled to cut corners.

It may be true that Arthur is overworked. It may also be true that these tempting thoughts are not his own; they may be demonic drivel. Even so, he feels what he feels because of what he believes and is only tempted to cheat at work because, to some degree, he has been led to believe that it is a valid and worthwhile option. He may effectively pray the demon away, but if he continues on without first gaining God's perspective, he is hardly better off.

Instead, Arthur should head to the SOLUTION Box. Since his compulsion to do what he should not do has already exposed the fact that he is engaged in a *solution behavior*, he should work on identifying the *perceived problem* that would seem to go unsolved if he chose not to cheat. Then, Arthur needs to articulate the lie-based *solution belief* that causes him to feel drawn to this particular behavior. And once he has gained God's perspective regarding this short-sighted solution, he should focus on the negative emotions that stir within him while thinking about work and continue processing through the EMOTION Box.

Scenario Two: "*Autumn's Oppression*"

Autumn believes that she is oppressed by the devil. She feels a constant heavy depression, and the memory of past sins repeatedly comes to mind throughout her day. Horrific images of those regretted experiences appear in her mind, and even though she knows that God has forgiven her of such things, she still feels dirty, beat-down, and ashamed. She is convinced that the devil is responsible for these hurtful, mental accusations. She doesn't know what to do, and she doesn't know how to make it stop.

Is the devil putting thoughts and pictures in Autumn's head? Maybe. Is the devil to blame for her emotional pain? No. These thoughts and images expose what she believes in her heart, and she feels dirty, ashamed, and depressed as a result. She feels what she believes. If the enemy is involved, he is only exposing what is already there. This is not a bad thing! Autumn's faith needs to be sifted, exposed, and refined. For once she knows the truth of who she is in Christ and the sufficiency of Jesus' sacrifice, she will no longer feel ashamed. The truth is that she has escaped condemnation; all that is left is for her to believe (See Romans 8:1)!

Rather than planning a counterattack or attempting to stop these fiery arrows from flying, Autumn should focus on what she feels in them and continue following protocol in the EMOTION Box. Her supposed oppression represents an opportunity for her faith to be refined. Once the Holy Spirit has persuaded her of the truth, she will find the rest and assurance she so desperately desires.

Scenario Three: *"Adam's Distractions"*

Adam is constantly distracted when applying the TPM Process. It seems like every time he closes his eyes and tries to focus on what he is doing, another seemingly random thought pops into his head. Phrases like, "I'll never be able to do this," "There is no hope for me," or "I may as well give up," appear to plague his mind and keep him distracted and discouraged. He has tried praying against the devil and asking God to help him focus. And even though he genuinely wants to stay focused and tries his best, the disruptive thoughts and distractions continue to pester him.

Are Adam's distractions caused by demons? Maybe. And if demons truly are responsible for the distractions, would they continue to interfere if Adam genuinely resisted them? No. Adam's problem is neither the *potentially* demonic involvement nor his distracted behavior. But both of these indicate what the actual problem is; he is attempting to solve a perceived problem by remaining distracted because he lacks God's perspective. He may genuinely *desire* to stay focused, but the fact that he is distracted indicates that he has a reason to remain distracted (*solution belief*). He might believe that staying distracted protects him from his pain, allows him to avoid remembering troubling events, or enables him to elicit sympathy from others. Whatever the case, the devil is not to blame. Adam simply needs to honestly admit *why* he is doing what he is doing and ask for God's perspective.

Adam needs to realize that he is in the SOLUTION Box, and he needs to identify the lie-based reasoning behind his current behavior. Even though he genuinely *desires* to stay focused, he is deliberately remaining distracted. Once he has identified the *solution belief* that has him distracting himself, he should move to the BELIEF Box and continue following protocol.

Scenario Four: *"Amber's Wall"*

As Amber focuses on her fear and anxiety while in the EMOTION Box, the only thing that comes to her mind is an image of a scary, black wall. She can't seem to see past it and feels "stuck" in her session. As she examines the mental picture more closely, it seems as though the wall is crawling with dark, menacing figures. The cruel shapes growl and spew curse words at her as she watches in terror. The imagery leaves her feeling more scared than she felt at the beginning of the session. As she focuses on the growing fear, nothing but the worrying image of the wall comes to her mind.

Is this imagery designed by demons? Possibly. Is the "wall" keeping Amber from remembering what she needs to remember? No. Nothing the enemy does or crafts can keep Amber from remembering what she chooses to remember. She may truly *want* to remember something, but the fact that she *seems* blocked by this dark wall indicates that she has a lie-based *reason* to not remember. In this case, the imagery of a wall indicates that she is engaged in a solution behavior. Until she is persuaded of the truth regarding the solution belief that has her choosing not to remember, the wall will likely remain, and she will continue not to remember. Amber's lie-based beliefs and misguided choices, not the demons or their wall, are what keep her from moving forward in the session. Yet again, the devil is not the problem; he is simply being used to point it out.

Amber needs to honestly acknowledge the beliefs that support her current behavior and seek out the Lord's perspective. She can do this by going to the SOLUTION Box and accomplishing her objectives there. She needs to honestly answer three simple questions: 1) "Does she sense any resistance or hesitancy at the thought of the wall being removed?" 2) "What does she believe would happen if the wall was removed?" and 3) "What is her reason for keeping the wall in place?" Once she has honestly answered these questions, she will have determined that she is engaged in a *solution behavior*, identified the *perceived problem* that she is attempting to solve, and articulated a *solution belief* that explains her current behavior. From there, she should move to the BELIEF Box and continue following protocol.

Scenario Five: *"Auston's Manifestation and Andrew's Impure Faith"*

As he waits to hear from the Lord in the TRUTH Box, Auston suddenly lifts his head and begins speaking in a guttural voice, "He belongs to us! He will never be free!" His TPM Mentor Andrew is shocked, as it is his first encounter with any form of demonic manifestation. Unsure of what to do, Andrew prays aloud, "Lord, please silence this evil spirit and remove it from our presence! We stand in your authority and ask you to deliver Auston from this tormenting demon!" Auston's face is filled with a grim grin as he laughs and then says, "Fool! You have no power here! This man belongs to us! We are not going anywhere!" Although Auston's Mentor feels very afraid and unsure of himself, he continues to argue with the demonic challenger saying, "Well...you have to leave! I take authority over you and resist you in the name of Jesus!" The exchange continues for longer than either Auston or Andrew cares to admit.

In this scenario, Auston is either unaware that he does not have to allow the demon to manifest in his body or he has been deceived into believing that submitting to the demon will solve or alleviate some other issue. In either case, he needs the truth. Auston is not held captive by the demon; he is simply in need of God's perspective. The demon will flee when it is resisted (see James 4:7).

But we also see that the demon's involvement exposed the impurities in Andrew's faith. The demon recognized that Andrew misunderstood the authority he possesses since it is entirely unnecessary to "take authority" over what is already under your authority! In attempting to "solve" the problematic situation by misapplying his authority, Andrew unknowingly expressed his lack of God's perspective. But, here again, this is a good thing because his need is more likely to be met after it has been exposed!

Even though he may not currently understand it, Auston has full executive control over what happens in the session. Andrew could illustrate this fact by asking Auston to look him in the eyes and choose to resist the manifestation. If Auston looks at Andrew, this clearly shows who is actually in charge of what is happening. But even if Auston does not immediately look up, Andrew should stay focused on him rather than diverting attention to the demon. Engaging the demonic spirit only further suggests that Auston is somehow out of control when this is not the case!

Andrew should pause the session and offer some basic orientation regarding the "Belief and Choice" Principle, the concept of *solutions*, and even explain some of what is shared in this chapter. Auston may simply be unaware of the fact that a demon cannot force him to allow it to manifest, use his voice, make facial expressions, etc. Andrew should focus on equipping Auston with knowledge and skill needed to apply the TPM Process as it is taught.

Remember, Auston is only allowing the demon to manifest because he either doesn't know any better or he has a lie-based reason to allow it to continue. Because this is true, if Auston's behavior does not change upon hearing his Mentor's explanations, this leaves only one possible explanation: he is engaged in a *solution behavior*. As such, he should move to the SOLUTION Box to determine *why* he is allowing the manifestations to continue.

Then, at a more appropriate time, Andrew should start his own TPM session in the EMOTION Box and focus on what he felt during the demonic ordeal. The fear that was present during the session had nothing to do with the demon. He felt what he believed. Andrew needs God's perspective just as much as Auston does!

As in each of the scenarios above, the devil is not our problem (even when he is genuinely involved in our situation). Our problem is our lack of God's perspective. If we knew the truth in our heads and in our hearts, we obviously would not also believe the lies that currently cause us to feel emotional pain and drive us to engage in harmful behaviors. Rather than focusing on the enemy who exposed our need for God's perspective, we should humbly ask for God to persuade us of the truth regarding the impurities in our faith.

Yes, Satan is the evil "father of lies" (John 8:44) who roams the Earth seeking someone to "devour" (1 Peter 5:8-11), and his evil schemes are designed by the craftiest being that was ever created (Genesis 3:1), but this is only a portion of the truth! The devil is God's property! He belongs to God, exists within the parameters that God set for him, and is used by God to accomplish a good and loving purpose in the life of the believer! Satan poses absolutely no threat to God or His plan. Satan is utterly defeated. He cannot even touch us (1 John 5:18)!

We encourage you to have this view of Satan in your TPM sessions. If he is ever involved, he is either acting as a "triggerer" or a "solution-provider." The devil is either exposing the lies we believe (just as our neighbors, coworkers, and family members do), or he is suggesting the use of *solution behaviors* (which we have already been deceived into implementing).

If Satan is *triggering* you, focus on what you feel and continue following protocol. If he is suggesting a sinful, short-sighted solution, head to the SOLUTION Box. And if it ever seems like he won't leave you alone, no matter how hard you resist him, honestly answer the question, "Do I sense any resistance or hesitancy at the thought of not allowing *this* to happen?" The devil's continued involvement is likely not "interference" but rather an expression of your currently employed *solution behavior*.

If the devil (or one of his demons) shows up in your ministry session, take heart! He also showed up in the wilderness with Jesus. And he is working to accomplish the same goal with you as he did with Jesus. He is testing to see if you are indeed "a son or daughter of God." He is only there because he believes some aspect of your faith is lacking, and his plan is to take advantage of the opportunity. He is not trying to help you; rather, he desires to "devour" you. But his intentions are utterly irrelevant since they are included in the "all things" that God is working together for our good!

Remember, if we were fully convinced of the truth, we would not implement Satan's short-sighted solutions, and his fiery arrows would be extinguished by our shield of faith (see Ephesians 6:16). For now, he is simply being used to expose what needs to be exposed: our impure faith. So, rather than focusing on the enemy, let's humbly cooperate with God and His use of the devil to refine our faith, renew our minds, and transform our lives!

"IF SATAN CAN'T MAKE YOU SIN, WHAT CAN HE MAKE YOU DO?"

When I pray with a Mentee who believes that they have a demon problem or even expresses some form of demonic manifestation, I focus on the person, not the demon. I first acquire the person's full attention by simply saying, "John, look at me." Even if the demon continues to manifest, I do not acknowledge it. I continue to ask the Mentee to give me his attention. The moment he does, he has exercised his free will and made evident that he is in executive control.

I then call his attention to the fact that <u>he</u> has stopped the manifestation by choosing to look at me and then offer some basic orientation in the form of questions that are based upon the information contained in this chapter. These questions are not a part of the TPM Process, but are designed to educate the Mentee in a biblical understanding of what the devil can and cannot do. The questions are as follows:

"What impact did Jesus's death and resurrection have on the devil?"

Almost always, the person will say that he was defeated. Once we have established that we are dealing with a defeated devil, I ask the second question:

"Do you believe that Satan can make you do something against your will? For example, can he make you sin?"

The person always answers by saying, "No." Then, I ask the person a follow up question:

"If he can't make you sin, what can he make you do?"

This usually causes a paradigm shift for the person. I ask the person what he wants to see happen in the ministry by asking a final question:

"Do you want a demon to manifest in this session today?"

If he says "No", then I agree with him that it will not happen. Since he has acknowledged Satan's defeat and the devil's inability to force his will on the person, any form of demonic manifestation would logically only occur if the person permits it to happen.

Ever since I began applying this protocol and the concepts that are discussed in this chapter, I haven't had any demonic manifestations in the ministry sessions, even with people who previously experienced extreme cases of demonization. Once the person has made the decision to not allow the demon to manifest, there should not be any further problem with any demon during the session. Now you can focus on the real problem at hand; belief. If a demon continues to manifest after doing what is proposed here, then you either are not dealing with a demon or you are in the SOLUTION Box.

CHAPTER 21

WHAT TPM IS NOT

Part One

Not Something New

God is the only Creator; nothing exists that He has not made (see Genesis 1:1, Isaiah 42:5, Isaiah 45, Colossians 1:16, Hebrews 11:3, Revelation 4:11). We can take various elements of what He has created and combine or rearrange them to form something different, but we cannot make something out of nothing. Science and industry have not created new things but rather have taken that which God has created and developed innovative ways to use different aspects of His creation. The same can be said of TPM. As you have learned, TPM is understood by three elements; the *Principles*, *Purpose* and *Process*. The *principles* and *purpose* of TPM are based upon what God has established and has been doing throughout the ages. Thus, these two aspects of TPM are not new. What might be considered to be some semblance of *new* is the defined ministry *process* where we seek to cooperate with what God is doing.

Even with the TPM Process we have taken existing concepts of reason and combined them together to form a series of questions that are based upon the principles that have been in place since the beginning of creation. So then, the TPM Process is only "new" in its specific protocols. However, the outcome is the same as has been experienced throughout the history of God's people as He has continually worked to refine their faith, renew their minds and transform their lives.

Someone may ask, "Why would God wait until now to reveal TPM?" Actually, He has not been waiting. He has been doing what He is doing all along the way. The TPM Principles and Purpose are not a new revelation, and the Process is merely an innovative way for cooperating with what God is doing. God's people have been looking to Him for the truth from the beginning. However, application of this effort has changed from generation to generation.

God has been inviting us to acknowledge what we believe and ask Him for perspective from the beginning. In the garden of Eden, He asked Adam and Eve, "Who told you that you were naked?" (Genesis 3:11). In other words, "How did you come to believe that you were naked?" God was inviting them to be honest about how they came to believe what they believed (which is also one of your objectives in the MEMORY Box). Later in the fourth chapter of Genesis, we see the same type of questioning of Cain where God asked, "Why are you angry?" (Genesis 4:6). God challenges Cain to look within, take responsibility, and honestly admit the true source of his anger (like we do in the ANGER and SOLUTION Boxes). Had Cain followed God's counsel and answered these questions correctly, the story might have had a different ending. Jesus asks similar questions of the disciples by saying, "Why are you afraid?" (Matthew 8:26), "Why do you doubt? (Matthew 14:31), "Where is your faith?" (Luke 8:25). Here again, these questions and those which are shown on the TPM Map are asked for a similar purpose.

The TPM Process provides a structure that may not have been previously practiced, but its application is reflective of what God has already been doing and our cooperating with Him in this work. TPM provides a teachable and transferable structure that can be easily incorporated into the Body of Christ. This ministry model affords a means to actively and intentionally engage in God's process of faith-refinement, mind-renewal, and transformation.

As we attempt to clarify what TPM is *not*, it is not our intent to criticize what other ministries may be doing. Our intention is to equip you with a proper perspective and accurate understanding of this ministry so that you will be able to distinguish it from other ministry models that you may encounter. Our purpose is not to criticize other ministries or elevate TPM above anything else, for God is not limited to any one ministry model, and He cares for His sheep in any fashion that He chooses. He is the Good Shepherd! We simply want to distinguish what is taught here from what is practiced elsewhere.

TPM is NOT A *Replacement for Other Biblical Practices*

TPM has a very narrow focus, and there are many aspects of the Christian walk that TPM does not attempt to do, nor was ever intended to. It does not replace biblical education or godly counsel and instruction (Proverbs 1:2-7; 1 Thessalonians 4:1-2; 2 Timothy 2:15, 3:16-17). It does not replace mission work and evangelism even though TPM could be applied in this context (Matthew 28:19-20). TPM does not focus directly upon sinful behavior or its consequences (Romans 6:13, Colossians 3:25). The Bible is clear in how to address each of these issues.

TPM focuses specifically upon our need for God's perspective and recognizes that the Holy Spirit is the only One who can convince our hearts of the truth. This does not mean that Bible study, preaching, and teaching are not vitally important in the Christian life. Each of these elements plays a key role in the Christian life; markedly, they inject the truth into a person's mind at the intellectual level. But none of these practices moves the truth from the mind to the heart. This is solely accomplished by the Holy Spirit (John 16:13-15). In TPM we learn to cooperate with the Spirit as He accomplishes this work within us.

TPM is Not the *"Troubled People's Ministry"*

People who seem to ineffectively manage their emotional pain or have difficulty performing "spiritually" at an acceptable level are often viewed as "emotionally wounded," "troubled," "broken," or "in bondage," while those who are able to suppress and manage their pain effectively and control their public behavior are viewed as more spiritual and healthy. But in reality, there is no real difference between any of us since we all need faith-refinement, mind-renewal, and transformation. Some of us are more successful at managing our emotional pain, but the manner in which we manage our emotions and spiritually perform is no indication of whether or not we are being transformed.

Labeling people as "emotionally wounded" is a faulty concept. As you have learned, our negative emotions are not wounds nor are they the result of difficult life experiences but rather, *accurate* expressions of what we believe. Regrettably, in the early years of this ministry I believed and taught that the focus of TPM should be upon helping the "emotionally wounded." People associated this ministry with those who could not manage their emotional pain in socially acceptable ways. The early training was mistakenly designed to equip those perceived to be "more spiritual" to help the needy and less spiritual.

Because of this flawed understanding, some people did not give much consideration to TPM since they did not view themselves "emotionally wounded" nor did they feel called to minister to those in that category. It was some time after TPM was established as a ministry that I came to realize TPM was not about "pain management" or "healing the past" (or healing anything for that matter), but rather its purpose related to faith-refinement, mind-renewal, and genuine transformation.

I am also embarrassed to say I helped others with this ministry for some time before realizing that I was in dire need of it myself! The appropriate context for TPM was not limited to the "wounded" who came to me for help. What I witnessed God doing in the lives of the hurting people who came to me for ministry was an example of what God desired to do in the lives of every believer, everywhere, every day!

With this realization I ceased to define TPM as "recovery ministry," "inner healing," or limited to emotionally troubled people. When TPM is understood to be a "Troubled People's Ministry," it is typically relegated to a recovery ministry and not considered by the general church membership. TPM is a ministry of faith-refinement and mind-renewal for all believers, with the end goal being genuine transformation.

Part Two

TPM is Not Inner Healing or the Healing of Memories

The Process of TPM is sometimes misunderstood to be associated with the "healing of memories." However, we do not believe that memories need to be healed of anything. They are not sick, damaged, wounded, or broken. Our memories are simply what we remember, but they are not a source of any emotional pain. Memories serve an important role in the TPM Process, and examining what we remember from past experiences can help us better understand how we came to believe what we currently believe, but our memories are not the focus and "healing" them is never the goal. In fact, it is not the goal of TPM to have anything "healed."

TPM is a means by which we may actively cooperate with God as He refines our faith, renews our minds, and transforms how we live. Those who have tried to fit TPM into the inner healing ministry, healing of memories, or other related categories have misunderstood TPM. The goal of TPM is not to heal anything but to experience renewal within the "spirit of the mind" (Ephesians 4:23, Romans 12:2) by having the Spirit convince our hearts of the truth. Not all people would say that they need to be "healed" of something, but we all need the Spirit to convince our hearts of the truth by renewing our minds "until we all attain to the unity of the faith, and of the knowledge of the Son of God, to a mature man, to the measure of the stature which belongs to the fullness of Christ" (see Ephesians 4:13).

To "heal" something means to take that which is sick, damaged, deformed, or broken, and restore it to its former or correct state of wholeness and health. True healing is valid in its proper context but that context is not TPM. Without question, physical healing is a valid gifting of the church, but healing of any kind is not the purpose of TPM. When God persuades our hearts of the truth, He is not restoring us to a former place or a position that we previously lost. He is not straightening out our "withered hand." He is renewing the "spirit of our minds" (see Ephesians 4:23). Mind-renewal is not the restoration or "healing" of what we believe, it is replacing what we believe with His perspective.

Even though physical healing is not a goal of TPM, people have reported that they have experienced spontaneous physical "healing" during a TPM session. How do we explain this? In comparison, if you were to cut your finger while peeling a potato and then after a few days the wound closes and a scar forms, would you say that you were healed? You would probably say that this is what the body does naturally. We believe that there is a natural mind and body relationship that can bring about "healing" when the lie-based beliefs are replaced with truth and the peace of Christ. Medical science has long known that there is an unmistakable connection between the mind and body. If the physical issues with which a person suffers are related to any lie-based belief they hold and the belief changes, they should expect that the body will adjust itself accordingly. Some of the physical problems we suffer can be traced back to our mental state. As we gain God's perspective and experience the peace of Christ, the body can be expected to naturally restore itself.

Our Heavenly Father is more concerned with our spiritual health than He is with our physical health. It is better to have a crippled body and a heavenly perspective than it is to be deceived in a well-built "tent" (see 2 Corinthians 5:1-17). God may allow and even orchestrate physical issues so that we may move in His direction and be persuaded of the truth. We are not saying that God cannot or will not heal a true physical ailment because He can and sometimes does. But we would also like to suggest that He uses physical ailments to accomplish good in our lives.

If, however, the physical symptoms we experience are due to the lies we believe, and God was to heal our bodies of the symptoms, this could potentially work against the mind-renewing work He seeks to accomplish.

Not A Form of Spiritual Warfare or Deliverance Ministry

As you learned in the previous chapter, we focused too much attention on Satan in the early years of TPM because we thought that he could somehow interfere or impact the ministry session. In the much older versions of the training, we referred to this as "demonic interference." We have since discovered that this assessment was very wrong. Without question, demonic spirits may show up in a ministry session, but, despite appearances, they do not have the power or ability to interfere with what is happening. We now understand that the only thing that can hinder your progress in a TPM session is your own belief and choice.

We approach Satan today from a post-resurrection perspective. We do not base what we do upon how Jesus or His disciples dealt with demonization, since every demon they cast out was prior to Satan's defeat at the cross (as we discussed the previous chapter). We operate in the victory that we now possess in Christ. Because of this, we no longer view him or his motley crew of demons as forcibly keeping anyone from the truth. We need to "be of sober spirit, be on the alert" since he is "like a roaring lion seeking someone to devour..." (1 Peter 5:8), but the greater truth remains: he has been defeated.

Satan cannot do anything by force and is totally limited to deception. Even so, when deception is believed, it can be devastating. We still fall for his evil strategies (lie-based solutions to our perceived problems) and get caught up in his snares (lies), but we can also find freedom from this captivity without ever directly engaging the devil. The "snare," not the "snarer," is holding us captive. When we embrace his deception, it becomes our own.

Again, Satan never accomplishes anything through force, power, or might. He can't, nor does he need to; He works through deception. Because of this, there is no reason to confront him with force since all deception is overcome with the truth. Therefore, TPM is not a form of deliverance or spiritual warfare since we do not attempt to engage the devil at all.

Peter did not direct us to fight the "roaring lion" or engage him in warfare. We are simply directed to resist him (his schemes) firmly in our faith (1 Peter 5:8). James said it succinctly and made it simple where he said, "resist the devil and he will flee" (James 4:7).

The devil is not a problem, but rather he is a defeated foe who belongs to God and serves God's purposes. As the Scriptures say, "For in him all things were created: things in heaven and on earth, visible and invisible, whether thrones or powers or rulers or authorities; all things have been created through him and for him" (Colossians 1:16 NIV, emphasis added).

God is not wringing His hands in concern about what to do about this menacing devil. In fact, Satan is not causing any trouble or concern for God even though he is influencing humans to wreak havoc throughout the world. How can this finite creature be any threat to his omnipotent Creator?

None of what we are saying diminishes the reality that Satan is evil. He hates each and every one of us and continuously searches for ways to trick us into believing things that are untrue, which often results in us doing things we really do not want to do. He is the enemy of our souls and only has evil planned for us. Even so, he is on a short leash and is limited in what he can do according to what God has determined.

We are not called to fight a defeated devil but are to "be of sober spirit, [and] on the alert" (1 Peter 5:8, emphasis added) concerning the schemes he wants to use against us. Paul revealed the answer to dealing with the devil where he said, "No advantage would be taken of us by Satan, for we are not ignorant of his schemes" (2 Corinthians 2:11). If you understand his strategies, you are in a better position to resist them.

Since the devil is God's property, he serves an important purpose in the grand scheme of things. Satan is not without limits and requires permission for all that he does. God didn't create him evil, but evil he is. How he became evil is a debated issue, but this discussion is not needed for this context. Even so, not only was he created by God, but he was created for God since "all things have been created through Him and for Him." Although Satan is an evil creature who always has evil motives, he is also part of God's created order and serves a purpose. As soon as God is through with him, Satan will be removed without any tussle, struggle, or fight. (Read the end of Satan's earthly stay in Revelation 20.)

Someone might say, "Yes, indeed, God created all things! Even so, if Satan was initially created for God, he rebelled and is now an enemy of God." This is true, and Satan does not view himself as being "for God." Satan is completely against God and has no desire to serve or please his Creator (which is also true for many people who have been used by God to accomplish His will). Even so, the truth remains that God created Satan for Himself (knowing full well that Satan would choose evil over good), and Satan is still being used by God to accomplish God's purposes whether the devil likes it or not. Satan is predictably evil in all that he does, and God easily uses him knowing in advance what he will do.

For example, was Satan involved in the crucifixion of Jesus? Do you think that Satan would have done what he did had he known that Jesus' death would offer redemption for anyone who believed? Had Satan known the outcome of his entering into Judas who betrayed Jesus, in his manipulating the religious rulers and stirring up the crowd that all led to the Lord's death, he surely would have devised a different strategy. He probably would have done all that he could to make sure that Jesus lived a long and uneventful life.

God used an evil devil who had nothing but evil intentions to accomplish His divine purpose and continues to do so to this day. For further clarification, look again at Colossians 1:16 that says all things were created by Him (Jesus), through Him (Jesus) and for Him (Jesus)! We do not need to focus our attention on the devil but on the work that Jesus is doing. Read the prayer of the early believers who saw how God used evil to bring about an eternal good where they prayed,

> In this city there were gathered together against Your holy servant Jesus, whom You anointed, both Herod and Pontius Pilate, along with the Gentiles and the peoples of Israel, to do whatever Your hand and purpose predestined to occur (Acts 4:27-28).

The Colossians 1:16 passage clearly says that God is the creator of all things. He did not create Satan evil, but He was not surprised that he chose to rebel and turn against his creator, just as all mankind did. Satan choosing evil also had no impact on the purposes and plans that God had and has for His people. God is still the Creator of all things and is fully in control of how everything turns out. God is working a perfect plan for His holy people that involves "all things," which includes His arch enemy, the devil. The believer can be confident that God will bring about His perfect will amid a fallen and evil world. Again, we hear Paul saying succinctly, "If God is for us, who is against us?" (Romans 8:31). In other words, anything that is brought against us —no matter the motive of its sender— becomes "for us."

TPM is Not Counseling or Therapy

TPM differs from protocols used for counseling or therapy and is *not* intended for the treatment of psychological disorders or addictions. Within the context of TPM, a Mentor does not offer advice, direction, counsel, life coaching, diagnosis of any kind, or even biblical instruction. Of course, each of these practices may offer good benefits in the proper context, but none of these things are needed or applicable during a TPM session.

The focus of a TPM session is two-fold. First, time and attention should be given to equipping the Mentee with the skills and understanding needed to properly understand and apply the TPM Process and make TPM a lifestyle. There should also be time spent helping the Mentee understand the principles and purpose of TPM. As the Mentee more fully understands the principles and the purpose of TPM he will more likely make the process a daily practice. The Mentor should make these things his or her goal and resist the desire to offer biblical instruction or counseling in the context of applying TPM. Again, in the proper context, doing this is needed, expected, and beneficial, but it is not the focus during a TPM session.

In the same way the treatment of mental disorders is NOT part of TPM, even though those who have been professionally diagnosed with such things can still benefit from the Spirit's refining work in the TPM Process.

If a Mentor also happens to be a qualified mental health professional, the protocols involved in a TPM session remain the same. There should be no psychological diagnosis, advice, counseling, or coaching during a TPM session. The Mentor's role is relegated solely to equipping the Mentee with a working knowledge of the Principles, Purpose, and Process of TPM.

Again, we are not suggesting that such practices do not have value and are appropriate in other contexts; we are simply saying that there is a time and place for all that we do. And when we are applying TPM, these other things should not be incorporated.

TPM is Not Guided Imagery or Directed Visualization

A TPM Mentor avoids all forms of guided imagery or directed visualization during a ministry session. A Mentee should never be asked to envision anything (such as looking for Jesus in your mind or memory), think about previous encounters with the Lord, imagine pictures, or ask Jesus to do anything (apart from offering truth and perspective at the appropriate moment). These practices are all subtle forms of guiding, directing, making suggestions, and potentially misleading by implanting ideas that did not originate from the Mentee. If the Mentor follows protocol, then none of these things will ever occur in a ministry session.

Sharing opinions, spiritual insight, prophetic words, speaking for God, or anything similar steps outside of the TPM protocols and process. None of these things plays any part in this prayer ministry model and may open the Mentee up for potential deception. While such practices may be well-intended, they are based upon the assumption that the Mentor knows what needs to happen in a ministry session when, in fact, he does not. These actions run the risk of suggesting information and direction to the Mentee.

A TPM Mentor should limit his or her questions to those that are specifically prescribed on the TPM Map. When the Mentor follows protocol the Mentee should have a genuine mind-renewal experience that is accomplished by their choosing and the involvement of the Holy Spirit, not one guided by the Mentor.

Part Three

TPM is Not for Authenticating Memories

In TPM we do not try to determine whether or not a Mentee's memory is accurate or complete. This may be important in other contexts but not in a TPM session. The reality is that rightly determining the accuracy of what a person reports in the context of a ministry session is not achievable. There is no way to determine if what the person reports is accurate or not in the context of a ministry setting. The Mentor should never assume that what the mentee reports is true no matter how convincing the mentee may be. The accuracy of what the Mentee remembers and reports is irrelevant when applying the TPM Process. The goal of the Process is to identify what the Mentee believes, not to determine whether or not their memory of past experiences is accurate. Anything reported is only what the mentee remembers and should be handled loosely until verified. The appropriate context for doing this is outside of a TPM session.

This authentication should be left with those who are professionally trained and in the proper context. The Mentor should view what the Mentee reports as what he or she remembers; never assume its accuracy. Memory is never the focus in a TPM session. In fact, *the Mentor does not need to know the content of a memory in order to follow the Mentee, ask appropriate questions, and offer orientation.*

There is NEVER any reason for the Mentor to ask for additional memory content or EVER offer suggestions regarding what may or may not have happened in the context of the remembered experience. If this occurs in any form, it should not be considered TPM. Again, when TPM protocol is followed as it is taught, these types of behaviors are not even possible.

NOTE: If a Mentee is a minor or elderly and reports some manner of abuse, then the Mentor should follow the legal guidelines as set by the laws of his local authorities. Doing this is not based upon whether the Mentor believes what has been reported but rather upon what the law requires. Every Mentor should know what is legally required of him concerning this.

TPM is Not Recovered Memory Therapy

Prior to the early 1970s, there was little discussion of child sexual abuse. Students preparing to work in the mental health professions had limited training in dealing with this issue and were led to believe it was a rarity. In the late 1970s and early 1980s, several new therapy techniques emerged, including what is now referred to as Recovered Memory Therapy (RMT). RMT appeared to have both beneficial and harmful results.

RMT helped expose the ugly reality of widespread sexual abuse in our society, pulling down the wall of denial that had kept it hidden for so long. Society was forced to acknowledge that child abuse and child sexual abuse were occurring in homes more than was ever suspected and had been occurring all along.

Today a common statistic reported by many different sources suggests that around 25% of all females have been sexually abused in some form. And the statistics for males being abused is nearly as high. Most victims report being abused by someone they know and should have been able to trust. These statistics are based upon *reported* cases and do not include all those who kept their abuse hidden. If the unreported cases could be added to the reported 25%, the number could be unimaginable.

But as often happens in such sensitive areas, the new information led to overreactions. This included a frenzy of assumptions and careless practices in therapy that resulted in innocent people being falsely accused, arraigned, and even jailed. And while allegations of abuse can undoubtedly be false, it is wrong to conclude that all memories of such abuses are invalid or false. There have been occasions when outside witnesses verified the truth of the abuse memories, the perpetrator confessed to the remembered abuse, or physical evidence was found to support the account. People should act responsibly by *neither* assuming that someone's report is absolute fact nor dismissing its authenticity simply because it cannot be corroborated by outside witnesses.

Again, when properly applying the protocols involved in TPM, a Mentor will NEVER make any suggestion regarding what might or might not have happened in someone else's past. The Mentor is not expected to *believe* or *not believe* anything that is shared in a TPM session. The Mentor's role is to equip the Mentee with the Three Elements of TPM. A Mentee's perspective or opinion of their past should only ever be their own.

Recovered memory therapists generally believe that dysfunctional symptoms are rooted in a repressed traumatic memory, which they propose can be uncovered using such techniques as symptom checklists, group dynamics, visualization, hypnosis, trance writing, dream interpretation, body massage, drugs, relaxation therapy, and spirit guides. Some therapists who use RMT believe that uncovering their client's repressed memories using these techniques will help resolve the symptoms. _None of these concepts or techniques are practiced in TPM._

Another clear distinction between TPM and RMT is in the way people's memories are accessed. In RMT people are sent looking for memories that the therapist believes are the cause of the person's troubles. Memory is important in TPM, but unlike RMT, it is not thought to be the reason people are in emotional pain. The focus of TPM is not on exploring the memory itself but rather on discovering the belief that was established in a life experience. Memory plays a role in TPM, but it has no bearing on the direction or outcome of the ministry session. The Mentee can even choose not to disclose any portion of what he or she remembers to the Mentor. The Mentor does not need memory content to fulfill his or her role in a TPM session.

In TPM, exposing lie-based beliefs, rather than memory content, is the focus. Again, validating memory content is occasionally needed for reasons outside of a ministry session, but it is not something that can or should be accomplished in a TPM session. For these reasons (and many more), TPM differs sharply from RMT.

IF A MEMORY IS EVER HIDDEN, THE ONE WHO HID IT IS IN THE ROOM.

How many times have you forgotten someone's name or gone to get something but forgotten what you were looking for when you got there? This form of forgetfulness is not deliberate, even at a subconscious level, but it is frustrating. And, for some of us, this exposes our age and faltering mental condition. Genuine forgetfulness is not deliberate but rather, some sort of brain glitch that we "elderly" experience from time to time. However, when memories are suppressed to avoid potentially negative consequences, this hindering of the association process is a deliberate, though often subconscious act.

I have prayed with many people through the years who were feeling strong negative emotions and yet had no related memory come to their minds. This was frustrating for them, and they often said things like, "I really *want* to remember, but nothing comes to my mind." Or, "My memory is hidden from me. I don't know where to look." People can suppress their memories, but the suppressed memory is not hidden from them or out of their reach. When the person is ready to recall what he has "hidden," he will. He is the one who hid it and knows where it is hidden. If remembering presents a problem, the Mentee simply does not want to look at the memory and subsequently is refusing to remember. His *desire* is to remember, but his *will* is not to remember.

In reality, Mentees are purposefully choosing not to recall a memory because, at some level, they believe that blocking out the memory will help them "solve" a problem. When this is the case, the person may *want* to remember (desire), but his *will* is to block it out and thwart association from working. Even though he is choosing not to recall a *memory*, he can choose to identify the *belief* that causes him to resist remembering. When the reason for not remembering is identified and acknowledged, he will be in the right position to have the Lord persuade his heart of the truth. And when he believes the truth, his resistance to remember will dissipate, and he should move forward unless there are additional reasons not to. Where this is the case, he simply needs more truth.

This might be compared to someone who purposefully conceals their car keys behind their back and says "Help me! I have hidden my car keys, and I don't know where to find them." If you purposefully hide them, then they are not lost. You can choose to retrieve them when you are ready to do so. But as long as you believe there will be undesirable consequences in remembering, the memory will remain "hidden." When you know the truth and view the consequence from God's perspective, the perceived threat will dissipate, and the process of mental association will re-engage.

Summary

TPM is unique and different from counseling, therapy, biblical instruction, and spiritual warfare and is clearly unrelated to Recovery Memory Therapy. The TPM Process is not guided or directed by a "minister;" rather it is part of the Mentee's personal journey with God. TPM does not try to fulfill many of the basic components of the Christian life but recognizes their vital importance in other contexts outside the ministry session.

TPM is <u>not</u> a "***Troubled People's Ministry***" or a "recovery ministry" (although it can be effectively applied in this context). There is no evidence that the "performer" is any further along in the mind-renewing journey than the so-called "emotionally wounded" who seems lost in his pain. Faith-refinement and mind-renewal is what God is doing in every believer's life, every day, as we cooperate with Him! TPM provides a frame of reference that views the trials of life as a refining fire under the supervision of a loving God who is determined to refine our faith, renew our minds, and transform our lives. This transformational work of the Spirit is the life purpose that God desires for all people.

The goal of TPM is not to heal memories, confront the devil, or diagnose mental issues. Rather, the goal is to experience the renewing of the *"spirit of the mind"* (Ephesians 4:23, Romans 12:2) by the intervention of the Holy Spirit, resulting in genuine transformation. The goal is to change belief rather than simply change behavior. It is not focused on resolving pain or offering pain management; rather, it offers a practical means of positioning ourselves to be persuaded of the truth within our hearts by the Spirit of Truth.

The Mentor and Mentee relationship is one of discipleship like the relationship between Jesus and His disciples. Even though Jesus went about teaching, healing, confronting demons, and even raising the dead, His primary focus concerning his disciples was on equipping them for what was to follow after His Resurrection. He invested into their lives knowing that they would continue the work of the Kingdom after He ascended.

Jesus could have just walked about healing the sick and raising the dead without spending much time with those chosen few, and the crowds would have still followed in amazement. Those who were personally touched by Jesus would have had lifelong benefit, but once Jesus was gone, the "fire" would have eventually gone out, and life would have returned to normal.

If you receive some measure of freedom as a result of submitting to a few ministry sessions but fail to understand the *Principles*, *Purpose* and *Process*, your gain will be a miniscule portion of what it could have been. It is our hope that you come to view TPM as a form of discipleship and make it part of your lifestyle, so that you benefit as much as possible, and so that God can continue using it to transform your life.

CONCLUSION

As TPM's founder, and after personally practicing TPM since the mid-nineties, I confess that I am nowhere near free of lies or emotional pain even after thousands of personal ministry sessions. In fact, the more freedom that I experience, the more I realize the impurity of my faith and the amount of work that God has yet to accomplish within me. Prior to this incredible journey with God, I was a stellar "spiritual" performer attempting to conform my life to the truth. I believed that I was doing well and felt that I was on course for a lofty finish, but I was sorely mistaken.

I am grateful that God convinced me of my need for His perspective and showed me that His intervention was my only hope of true success. Since I began practicing the TPM principles back in 1995, I have intentionally chosen to humble myself under His "mighty hand" and have been blessed as I have watched Him slowly and gradually transform me, little by little, with His truth. As Paul said, "Not that I have already obtained all this, or have already arrived at my goal, but I press on to take hold of that for which Christ Jesus took hold of me" (Philippians 3:12 NIV). Even though I have a long way to go, I am encouraged because I can see that I am far beyond where I was.

God gives me daily opportunities for faith-refinement, and though I still reject more than I accept, He is gracious and persistent. He is much more invested in this work than I am and for that I am grateful. I rejoice in the fact that I have found genuine and lasting freedom from so many lies and have come to know Christ in a deeper, more personal way.

Although TPM is obviously <u>not</u> the only way to identify the lies that we believe and to experience the freedom that God desires for us, it is the best means that I have applied for myself thus far. I rejoice with anyone who is consistently experiencing lasting freedom and effortless fruit-bearing while using other ministry models. I am always open to a better strategy.

As I have already said, God is not limited in what He does or how He does it, and TPM does not replace or add to what the Church has been called to do. Keep on teaching, preaching, instructing, correcting, reproving, encouraging, ministering, evangelizing, worshiping, "singing psalms and hymns and spiritual songs" and giving of your time and money to further Kingdom causes, but also identify any heart belief that you harbor that is inconsistent with the truth. Bring into the light the falsehoods that are producing negative emotions stealing your peace so that the "peace of Christ [may] rule in your hearts" (Colossians 3:15, emphasis added).

Faith-refinement is a life-long process.

The faith-refining work that God is doing is a lifelong process partly due to our resistance in taking ownership of what we believe, our unwillingness to humble ourselves so we might receive, as well as the volume of truths that He wants to persuade us of. Even so, God is committed to this refining and renewing task and is faithful to work all things for good in us as we choose to cooperate with what He is doing. We can either be a help or a hindrance along the way. I pray that we will cease our struggling against what He is doing and humble ourselves before Him so we may gain His Heavenly perspective.

I see much more work ahead, but I also see an abundance of good that has been accomplished from whence I have come. TPM has provided me with a way to purposefully attend to the lies I still believe as I submit to the refining work that the Spirit is bringing forth day-by-day in my belief and behavior. In the meantime, a day never passes in which God does not provide me with an opportunity for faith-refinement and mind-renewal. I choose to take ownership for what I feel and believe, and practice TPM as a lifestyle by positioning myself under His "mighty hand" as my personal spiritual discipline. I invite you to do the same.

Our Worldwide Vision

In the earlier years of this ministry, we had a lofty goal of equipping the entire Body of Christ with the purpose and principles of TPM. My hope was that pastors would equip their entire church membership with the knowledge of the *Purpose* and *Principles of TPM* so they may be motivated to apply the *TPM Process* naturally and spontaneously to their lives as a spiritual discipline. I had hoped that the basic teaching of TPM would become a part of the culture in the worldwide church and each member would choose to submit to God's faith-refining process (1 Peter 5:6), learn to be trained (Hebrews 12:11), have their minds renewed and experience genuine transformation (Romans 12:2). My heart's desire is to see my brothers and sisters in Christ taking advantage of the daily opportunities for growth, maturity, and transformation that God offers each of us everyday.

Even though we hoped that this vision might become a reality, the last twenty years have taught me that not all people are ready or even desire to apply the principles we are proposing. I have discovered that people have to be made ready (by God) before they will consider applying themselves to learn what is involved in applying this ministry model. The key factor in people investing time and energy to become equipped in TPM is *motivation*. It is basic human nature to take the path of least resistance and to avoid pain at all cost. But, as many of you know, moving in the direction of TPM requires that we address both pain and resistance.

I personally was on a path of least resistance and an avoidance of pain for the first twenty years of my Christian life. I blamed everyone else, my circumstance or the devil for my pain, and my solution was to be a victim and distract myself from what I did not want to feel. Neither approach was successful.

Today, I believe that TPM will find its place in the lives of many more people, but only with those who are motivated to be free. However, people will not seek freedom until they realize they need it. I did not realize I was caught up in the "snare of the devil" (2 Timothy 2:26) for a long time. I never made the connection between my negative emotions and my heart belief until TPM. I assumed that when bad things happen the natural reaction was to feel bad. The idea that the peace of Christ could actually "rule in my heart" was a verse that I had memorized but not something that I was experiencing. Until I realized my need, I was not seeking a way of escape.

Our focus today is not to reach everyone but rather to pour ourselves into all those who are genuinely seeking freedom. I have been amazed by the number of people who have shared testimony with me how they discovered TPM in a moment of crisis (motivation) and how God has used this ministry to move them in the direction of continual freedom. When the person who realizes that they need freedom incorporates the "Three Elements of TPM" into their daily walk, they can view life difficulties, personal conflicts, church-related issues, and all crises that may arise, NOT as something they must endure but as an opportunity for faith-refinement and mind-renewal (Romans 12:2).

Today, we envision a *portion* of the church in which TPM will become a fundamental part of its culture and DNA. Those believers who embrace these principles and purpose are afforded the opportunity to share the same basic frame of reference concerning life difficulties, speak the same ministry language, take personal responsibility for one's own faith-refining journey with the Lord, and where members naturally and spontaneously pray with each other for the purpose of attaining transformation and freedom. We can envision this happening within some measure of the global Body of Christ who will embrace these concepts and make TPM a lifestyle ministry. We do hope that you and your fellow believers will become a part of this group.

For a Time Such as This

As I write these final words an ominous storm seems to be on the horizon. Our world appears to be unraveling at the seams. Followers of Jesus are being viewed with ever increasing hostility all around the world. I cannot say with any level of certainty, but it appears that things are winding down as we are nearing the second coming of the Lord. Before that great day comes, I believe that a great refining fire will come upon the Church. God is preparing the Bride of the Lamb who will be found without "stain or wrinkle." Paul declared that,

> Christ loved the church and gave Himself up for her to sanctify her, cleansing her by the washing with water through *the Word*, and to present her to Himself as a glorious church, without stain or wrinkle or any such blemish, but holy and blameless (Ephesians 5:25-27 BSB, emphasis added).

It is important that we differentiate the "washing with water through the Word" from the cleansing of sin that occurs through the shed blood of Christ. The washing of the water through the Word is the sanctifying work of the Spirit as He refines our faith. Jesus' blood washed all our sins away. His Word, which is poured into our hearts, is sanctifying (making holy and pure) our belief, so that our heart belief matches the reality of our new selves. As our faith is cleansed by His Word, our thinking is brought into alignment with our newly created selves that "in the likeness of God has been created in righteousness and holiness of the truth" (Ephesians 4:24).

This purification is accomplished through the Spirit washing us with "water through the Word" that persuades our hearts of the truth. This purification is not about purifying the believer himself since the blood of Jesus has taken care of that. We were made holy and blameless through the work of Christ. This washing through the water of the Word is the purification of our faith so that our perceptions, emotions, and behaviors align with the finished work of Jesus in our inner man. This persuasion of truth will result in good works and Christlike living and as a "glorious church, without stain or wrinkle or any such blemish."

There is a storm coming which will expose what we truly believe. Our response to this storm will be an accurate reflection of what we believe in our hearts. Some will cry out in fear and pain, feeling abandoned by God and forsaken. We believe TPM will become most effective *in a time such as this*. God has raised up people from all corners of the world who are learning how to position themselves to be "washed" by the water of the Word of the Spirit. Not all believers will be distressed by the storm. Some will "rejoice in [their] afflictions" (Romans 5:3, HCSB, emphasis added) and will "consider it all joy when they encounter various trials" (James 1:2-3) because they will know that the testing/refining of their faith produces the "peaceful fruit of righteousness" (Hebrews 12:11).

Our prayer is that more believers will learn to cooperate with what God is doing in their lives and will take advantage of this ministry while the "fire" is not too hot. We hope that they will utilize the day-to-day difficulties as an opportunity to have a portion of their faith refined. A greater fire is coming; we need not be caught off guard or be surprised by the fiery ordeal that has come upon us (1 Peter 4:12), but rather we can take advantage of the opportunity that it brings!

Because you are reading these words, we assume that you are preparing yourself for the storm on the horizon. Train well, position yourself under His mighty hand at every opportunity, receive His truth, and expect to bear His fruit! And if God calls you to encourage and mentor others in this ministry model, do so with grace, humility, and an honest testimony of God's work in you!

We are very grateful for those of you who have felt led to financially support this ministry.

We never ask people to support this ministry, but we do give thanks for all those who do. We don't do fundraisers or matching gift champions, but rather assume that God will prompt those He chooses. We want you to give according to what you have purposed in your heart so you might give cheerfully and not under any compulsion. If God has prompted you to give, we say thank you!

Donate Online:

www.transformationprayer.org

or www.tpm.kindful.com

Donate by Mail:

Transformation Prayer Ministry

PO BOX 80056

Simpsonville, SC 29680-9998

GLOSSARY OF TERMS

We have included a numbering system that enables you to find expanded discussions of each of the terms included in this glossary. The first number indicates the "Chapter," and the second number indicates the "Part." Example: (Chapter.Part)

For instance, a notable usage of the term *Heart Belief* can be found in the second part of chapter five, and this is indicated next to its glossary entry by the following notation: (5.2). We have also underlined the notations that represent the most informative instance of that particular word (when applicable).

If you find a set of parentheses containing only one number, this either means that the cited chapter is not divided into multiple parts or that the associated term is discussed throughout the entirety of that chapter. For example, the term "anger" is obviously discussed throughout chapter 18, and next to its glossary entry you will find the following notation: (18).

We have used the same numbering system for the list of "Notable Illustrations, Topics, and Examples," which immediately follows the Glossary of Terms.

Alleviated Problems (solution indicator):

If after engaging in a particular behavior, your *"perceived problems"* seem to be reduced or your negative emotions subside and you feel noticeably "better," safer, more comfortable, more in control, less fearful, less anxious, etc., this indicates that you are likely engaged in a *"solution behavior."* This is especially true when you attempt to stop or refrain from doing the solution behavior, and the perceived problem seems to regain its problematic nature, and things will seem to get "worse." (<u>19.1</u>), (19.6)

Anger:

an emotion that is often believed to offer a false sense of empowerment, control, and protection and is felt outwardly (towards others, our circumstances, or even ourselves). Remaining angry about something is a common "solution behavior." Which is why we say, if you stay angry about something, you are attempting to solve something. See *"anger solutions."* (5.1), (6.2), (6.4), (13.1), (17.2), (<u>18</u>), (<u>19</u>)

Anger Family:

a category of emotions that we feel outwardly, *towards* someone or something. Examples include anger, frustration, hate, wrath, malice, aggravation, etc. They have several of the *"characteristics of anger"* in common. (<u>18.2</u>), (18.3)

Anger Solutions:

If we stay angry, we are attempting to solve something:

If you continue to feel angry about something, it is because you believe that you are faced with an unsolved problem, and that the proper response to it involves staying angry. As long as the *"perceived problem"* remains unsolved and you remain convinced that your *"solution behavior"* of being angry is effective, you will remain angry. (18), (<u>19</u>)

Association:

a God-created mental process of remembering by way of connecting one thing with another. For example, if you think of the word "birthday," you will quickly remember some life experience that had to do with a birthday. This effortless mental function is utilized to accomplish several "*Objectives*" in the "*TPM Process*." (5.1), (5.7), (12.4), (13.1), (13.2), (21.3)

Baseline:

a term used to describe what happens when in the BELIEF Box during the TPM Process. The BELIEF Box question is designed to determine if the lie-based belief identified in the MEMORY Box feels true. If it does *feel* true to the Mentee, then it will serve as the "baseline" later in the TRANSFORMATION Box. After the TRUTH Box, and while in the TRANSFORMATION Box, the Mentee determines if there has been a shift in his thinking by reflecting on the belief that felt true in the BELIEF Box to see if it still *feels* or *seems* true. The former belief is the "baseline" by which he determines if there has been a change in his belief. (15), (17.1)

Boxes on the TPM Process MAP:

The stages, or steps, that make up the "*Process of TPM*." They include the "*EMOTION Box*," the "*MEMORY Box*," the "*BELIEF Box*," the "*TRUTH Box*," the "*TRANSFORMATION Box*," the "*ANGER Box*," and the "*SOLUTION Box*." (12)

Clock Principle:

states that if you have time for another "*TPM Session*" after checking for transformation in the "*TRANSFORMATION Box*," then you can continue by moving to the "*EMOTION Box*." It also reminds "*Mentors*" not to have a "*Mentee*" continue applying the Process if they only have a few minutes left in the scheduled time allotment. (17.2)

Compelled Behavior (solution indicator):

When you have been persuaded to believe that a certain behavior will help you solve a "*perceived problem*," you will be motivated to engage in that behavior for that purpose. You will feel driven or drawn in its direction. This is true even if you intellectually know that the "*solution behavior*" is unhelpful, destructive, or sinful. It will also likely be your default reaction to certain perceived problems. (6.1), (6.2), (6.3), 6.4), (6.7), (19.1), (19.2), (19.3), (19.6), (20.4)

Components of a Solution:

include the "**solution behavior**," the "*perceived problem*," and the "*solution belief*." (19.1)

Confession:

The New Testament Greek word typically translated as "confession" is "**homologeó**" which means "to say the same thing" or "to come to the same conclusion and agree with someone." Unfortunately, when this word is used in the church, it is almost exclusively understood to be the act of admitting sinful behavior to others or to God. The primary Bible passage that supports this church doctrine is the single verse found in 1 John 1:9. This passage has been debated by theologians as to whether the first chapter of 1 John was written to believers or whether it was an invitation for those who believed that they were "without sin" to "agree with" God that they indeed were sinners.

The doctrine of confession is usually focused on confessing each sin as it is committed and is a practiced discipline of many believers. In the context of TPM, confession has a broader application. We view confession as *agreeing with* God about what we believe by bringing such lies into His light so that He may reveal His perspective to our hearts. (4.5), (10), (15)

Controlled Behavior / Conformity:

an attempt to self-govern one's behavior for the purpose of achieving conformity. It is foundational to all world religions and is practiced in some measure by everyone. Christianity, on the other hand, is based upon the work of Christ. In Christianity, the Spirit's fruit of self-control is a natural outcome of believing the truth in our hearts that calms us and allows us to rest in God during trying situations. Controlled behavior is accomplished through self-effort and strong willpower to do what is proper or expected. The fruit of self-control is spiritual and accomplished by God, whereas controlled behavior is what all humans do to some degree all of the time. (11.2)

Deception:

This is like lying, but with a different focus. Deception is when someone shares untrue or even true information for the purpose of misleading us so that we arrive at a false conclusion. It is important to note that such misleading doesn't necessarily involve lying, someone can deceive another with the truth or half-truths (as seen in the Garden with Adam and Eve and the serpent).

Deeds of the Flesh:

Galatians 5:19-21 provides a sample list of deplorable deeds of the flesh as "sexual immorality, impurity, indecent behavior, idolatry, witchcraft, hostilities, strife, jealousy, outbursts of anger, selfish ambition, dissensions, factions, envy, drunkenness, carousing, and things like these." Deeds of the flesh are not just the immoral and wicked things one might do but also include what might appear as good and noble. Anything that we do that is not *Christ living His life in and through us* (Galatians 2:20) is a deed of the flesh. Deeds of the flesh can appear good, but the impure motive behind them contaminates their value with God. God desires that we do good works that express His transformation and fruit. A way to distinguish between fleshly deeds that look good and genuine fruit is in the effort required to experience them. So, God's fruit is His fruit and requires no effort from us to bear it. Whereas deeds of the flesh that resemble fruit require effort to perform. (9.1), (11)

Demon:

a God-created, spiritual being that has chosen to be a part of the "world forces of darkness" under the leadership of Satan. (20)

Demonic Manifestation:

when a demon utilizes the physical body of a human to express itself. This might present itself through using the person's voice, body, facial expression, or even through some mental imagery. (19), (20), (21.2)

Demonic Possession:

a misunderstanding of the Greek word "daimonizomai" which suggests that demons can overpower and control a person. This is never the case. Demons cannot violate a person's will. A better understanding of this Greek term would describe someone as being "demonized" or someone who is willfully complying with a demon's wishes because he has been deceived into believing a "***solution*** *belief."* As hard as it may be to accept this understanding, demons only do what they are permitted to do. They cannot force anyone to do anything. (19), (20), (21.2)

Devil (Satan):

a generic term or name given to Satan which is also sometimes applied to a demon. (19), (20), (21.2)

Discipline:

There are basic personal disciplines practiced by Christians that include Bible study, Bible memorization, meditation on the Scriptures, fasting, worship, etc. Such disciplines are a vital part of living the Christian life, but why we do them varies from person to person. In this book, we have suggested that personal disciplines will not bring about transformation, but they can help us to position ourselves so that God might do this work within us. If our motive for applying personal discipline is to bring about transformation or to become more holy, then we will not succeed. Our most sincere effort in personal discipline will not add one measure to our holiness, nor will it bring about transformation. (11.2)

Dissociation:

is the act of distracting yourself from a thought, memory, or experience that you do not want to face, acknowledge, or connect with. This is done in response to *"perceived problems"* and is an example of a *"solution behavior."* (19)

Dysfunction:

not functioning, operating, or behaving according to the intended design. We are all dysfunctional in some manner and to some degree. We are dysfunctional because of the lies we believe and the sin we practice, and we sin because we lack God's perspective.

Faith:

all that we believe with the heart. It motivates our actions and produces our emotions. Some of our faith is not based upon the truth and needs to be refined (replaced with the truth). Purified faith reflects the truth. (9)

Faith-refinement:

God orchestrates our lives, allowing difficulties, tribulations, and injustices to befall us in order to expose our lie-based beliefs and purify our faith. Like a refiner's fire that purifies gold, God exposes the falsehood in our faith and renews our minds with His truth. The outcome is a refined faith, a renewed mind, and a transformed life. (8), (9)

Flesh:

The New Testament word translated as "flesh" is *sarx*. The Bible uses this term in several different ways. Sometimes it merely describes the physical flesh in which we dwell while on this earth. However, it is also used to describe attempting to live holy apart from the inner working of Christ within us (Romans 8:3-4). This would describe what some refer to as a works sanctification. The New Testament also uses this term to describe all that remains from our former manner of life prior to our co-crucifixion and co-resurrection with Jesus (see Galatians 2:20). This includes all that has fallen within our physical bodies, the lusts of the "flesh," wanton passions, and desires. The flesh also includes all the lie-based beliefs we still hold in our hearts. The flesh is <u>not</u> the same as the old self. The old self was crucified with Christ and is dead, whereas the flesh is alive and pertains to our physical "body of death" and our unrenewed minds. Paul said it clearly where he said, "our old self <u>was</u> cruci-fied with Him, *in order that* our <u>body of sin</u> might be done away with" (Romans 6:6, emphasis added). (9.1), (9.4), (11.2)

<u>Flowcharts</u> (The TPM Flowcharts):

offer visual illustrations of the protocols described in this book. The various Flowcharts can be found at the back of this book as well as on the TPM website. In the example scenarios that are found throughout this book, the "*EMOTION Box*" is indicated by an (E), the "*MEMORY Box*" with an (M), the "*ANGER Box*" with an (A) and the "*SOLUTION Box*" with an (S). (12.1), (12.2)

<u>Forgiveness</u>:

is the natural and expected outcome of genuine compassion which is the result of viewing those who have hurt you and their offenses the way that God sees them from an eternal perspective. This is an effortless and automatic response to having the "*Holy Spirit*" persuade ("*<u>peitho</u>*") you of the truth. The Greek New Testament word most often translated as "to forgive" is *aphiémi* which means to cut off, sever, let go, cast away, or dissolve. When God forgives, He forgives us our sin and not us (see 1 John 1:9-10). He cuts off our sin but does not cast us away. When we forgive others, we are not "forgiving" *them* but rather releasing them from their *debt*. Forgiveness is a natural and expected outcome of releasing someone from the debt they owe us when we have genuine compassion for them. Compassion arises from our hearts when we can view those who have hurt us along with their offenses through the eyes of truth from God's perspective. When this is so, it will be effortless. If forgiving is a struggle or difficult, then we harbor a lie-based reason for not letting go. In the Gospel narrative where Jesus taught about forgiveness, He described a king forgiving his servant of an enormous debt. Jesus said that the king "had compassion on him, forgave his debt, and released him" (Matthew 18:27). It was because he felt compassion that he forgave his debt, and then released him. (19) (See the book titled <u>Effortless Forgiveness.</u>)

<u>Fruit of the Spirit</u>:

the God-produced characteristics, emotions, and behaviors that we were destined to bear and ex-press because we possess the Holy Spirit and have His perspective. (11), (17)

<u>Glory</u>:

Though the word "glory" is commonly used by believers, most would probably have difficulty defin-ing what it means. Of course, it is impossible to begin to define glory outside of the context in which it is used. In the Scriptures, God's glory is often understood to be the outward expression of His perfect magnificence. The stars and moon express His glory; the evening sunset, the snow top mountains, and the vastness of the oceans all exclaim His glory. It is the nonverbal communication God exhibits when He, in a sense, walks into the room. It is His splendor, wonder, holiness, and magnitude that exude from Him without His even saying a word. We have been promised to share in His glory (John 17:22). When we effortlessly express the fruit of the Spirit in our life, we're, in a sense, sharing in His glory, by displaying a reflection of His character. We are like the moon that reflects the light of the sun as it shares in the sun's glory, shining brightly in the darkness of the night. When we bear the fruit of the Spirit, we're displaying the reflection of His nature and glory.

<u>God's Perspective</u>:

the truth. God has a perfect and complete understanding and point of view. He knows and is the truth. Anything that accurately reflects God's perspective is true, while anything that contradicts it, is untrue.

God's Solutions:

the methods God has used to solve our "*truth-based problems.*" Both our "*lie-based problems*" and our "*truth-based problems*" will seem resolved when we are convinced of the truth. For He has already solved (or promised to solve) all of our "*truth-based problems;*" the only thing left is for us to see His involvement and trust in His solutions. They only seem problematic because we do not yet know the truth. You are not in need of His solutions (for He has already offered them freely to you), rather, you need to be persuaded of this reality, which will lead you to trust in what He has done on your behalf. And since our "*lie-based problems*" are not real, we need to be persuaded of the truth regarding the fact that they are imaginary For instance, since you <u>are not</u> worthless, you do not need God to "solve" your worthlessness; you need Him to convince you of your worth. (4.3), (4.4), (<u>4.5</u>), (5.5), (5.6), (5.7), (7), (10)

Greater Truth:

We use this term when we are dealing with emotional pain resulting from believing some particular truth. For example, when someone we love dies, we will feel grieved. Our grief is based upon the truth that a person is no longer with us, and we will not see them again until eternity. However, there are "greater truths" that can lift our grief and sorrow once we are persuaded of them in our hearts. For example, if we genuinely believe that they are with Jesus and enjoying His presence, this greater truth will cause us to rejoice even though we miss them. It is also a greater truth that Jesus is bearing all of our grief and sorrow (Isaiah 53:4). (5.5), (5.6)

Another example of a greater truth is the fact that we all have sinned and fallen short of the glory of God. Because we have sinned, we are destined for eternal damnation. Because this is the truth, there is cause for much despair. However, there is a greater truth that brings us hope. Because of the death of Jesus and His resurrection, we have been offered grace, mercy, and forgiveness of our sins and the hope of an eternal place with God. (4.3), (5.5), (5.6)

Hagios:

The Greek New Testament word often translated as "holy." Its root meaning is to set apart for special use or to be particularly different. In Paul's letters, he often addresses his readers as *hagios,* or holy ones, those set apart. Most translations, unfortunately, translate *hagios* in these places as "Saints," which is a non-descript term that has little meaning in our current English language. (9.4), (11)

"Happy Places" and Guided Imagery:

Some well meaning ministry models encourage the one being prayed with to imagine some pleasant place in their minds where they feel safe or "happy." It is assumed that it is helpful to stir up "happy" emotions before choosing to remember "unhappy" memories. TPM does not practice this and views this as a form of suggested or guided imagery. (12), (13), (14), (21.2), (21.3)

Head:

what we use to think, perceive, understand, and reason. This is, in part, the definition of the Biblical Greek word "nous." In more current terms, that which we believe with our "nous" is believed in our "heads." Although the information stored in our "heads" may be useful and even reflect the truth, it is not the only place where we believe things, nor is it the source for what we feel. Our emotions appear to come from somewhere else. We feel what we feel because of what we believe in our "*hearts.*" (5.2)

Heart:

derived from the Greek word *"kardia"* which means *"the fountain and seat of the thoughts, passions, desires, appetites, affections, purposes, endeavors...the heart, inner man, etc."* (Strong's Concordance - 2588). Our feelings and motivations flow from our *"kardia,"* our "hearts." More specifically, we feel what we feel because of what we believe in our "hearts." The beliefs that are stored in our "hearts" are referred to as *"heart beliefs."* (Preface), (1), (4.5), (5.2), (5.7), (6.5), (7.2), (7.4), (8), (9.1), (9.4), (14.3)

Heart Belief:

All that you believe with your heart. It is the essence of your faith and produces what you feel. This type of belief is the primary source of your *"perceived problems."* The two primary categories of heart belief are *"self-identity"* and *"state of being."* Some of your heart's belief accurately reflects the truth; the rest is considered lie-based. TPM draws a distinction between intellectual belief and heart belief. Intellectual belief can increase our knowledge of something and make us smarter, whereas believing the truth in our hearts will transform us. The Scriptures are clear that salvation occurs through heart belief (Romans 10:10). The intellect is the front door to the heart, but until the Spirit persuades us of the truth within our hearts, we will not believe and be transformed by it. (5.2), (9.1), (14.3), (14.4)

Holiness:

Our holiness is derived from who we are in Christ. It is maintained and sustained by the faithfulness of Christ, and nothing we do can make us more holy or take away from what Jesus has already accomplished. If our holiness is determined and maintained by our behavior, then we are only one sin away from being unholy. That which is holy is also pure and free of all contaminants. Jesus' death and resurrection made us pure. Unlike the Old Covenant of daily sacrifices, the blood of Jesus was not a temporary covering of our sins, but rather, His death took our sins away once and for all times. Jesus' cousin, John the Baptist, made this declaration one day as Jesus was passing by, "Behold, the Lamb of God who takes away the sin of the world!" (John 1:29). Because all our sins have been taken away, our holiness remains. According to the Scriptures, everything that pertains to Jesus and all that He contains is also true for us since we are the "fullness of Him" (Ephesians 1:23). We are holy children of God, "partakers of the divine nature" (2 Peter 1:4). It is because we are now holy that we can "come boldly to the throne of grace" (Hebrews 4:16 NKJV). (1), (4.4), (7.5)

Homologeo:

a Biblical Greek word that is typically translated into English as "to confess." It means "to agree with and openly acknowledge something," or even more literally it means to come into alignment with another and share the same perspective (see *"confession"*). (4.5), (10), (15)

Identity in Christ:

who God has declared us to be since we have believed the truth of the Gospel message. (4.2), (8), (11.1), (14.3)

Illumination:

what the Spirit does when He shines His light of truth into our hearts.

Impure Faith vs Pure Faith:

The Bible describes two different kinds of faith. There is a "pure faith" that originates and proceeds from God, and there is an "impure faith" that consists of all that we hold in our hearts that is false. Every true believer (people who possess the Holy Spirit) has both a pure faith and a measure of faith that needs to be purified. Everything that we believe in our hearts is our faith, and we are walking in all of it. The faith that God has given is a pure faith that transforms us and is made evident by the effortless expression of the fruit of His Spirit. When we operate from an *impure* faith, we will act according to it and will be robbed of His peace and, in turn, feel anxious, fearful, overwhelmed, stressed, and more. (8), (9.1), (9.3), (10), (20.3)

Imparted/Imputed Holiness:

When we received the Holy Spirit, we were joined with Christ and became the "fullness of Christ" (Ephesians 1:23). Being the fullness of Christ means that whatever Christ is, we are as well, and whatever is true for Him is true for us since we are partakers of His divine nature and share in His holiness. Being holy does not mean that we will always act holy; but our behavior does not determine our holiness. Our holiness is based upon our spiritual birth (John 3:4-6, Titus 3:5, Ezekiel 36:25-27) According to the Scriptures, we are *hagios,* or holy ones, set apart by God for special use. We should rejoice that we are holy, not by works but only by faith. It is by faith that we should "pursue peace with all people, and the holiness without which no one will see the Lord" (Hebrews 12:14). None of us want to stand before God on our own merit because unless we are holy, we will not have a place with Him.

Inner Healing:

A term used to describe many ministry models that view people as emotionally wounded, who carry painful memories that are in need of "healing." This is not taught or practiced in TPM. (21)

Inner Man / Inner Person:

A person's true identity; who and what they really are. Before a person is in *Christ* this same inner person is considered dead and separated from God. In this state it is referred to as the old self or man. This same inner person is crucified with *Christ* and is *raised* to life as the new self or new man. (5.2), (8), (9.4), (11.1)

Intellectual Belief:

that which we believe with our heads rather than our hearts (see "mind," "head"). (5.2), (7.4)

Interpretations:

are conclusions and perspectives which are based upon what you believe to have happened and why you believe it happened. This is largely reflective of your *"heart belief."* (4)

Lie-based Thinking:

thoughts, ideas, assumptions, and conclusions that we believe are true even though they are not.

"Looping" Question:

the third question in the "*MEMORY Box*" which is labeled "(M8)" on the MEMORY Box "*Flowchart.*" It is asked when the Mentee's belief-related responses to the other questions begin to "loop" or repeat. (14.2), (14.3), (14.4), (14.5)

MAP (The TPM Map):

illustrates many of the protocols included in the TPM Process. The various forms of the TPM Map can be found at the back of this book as well as on the TPM website. There are seven possible locations a Mentee might be during a ministry session. When the Mentee knows what he is expected to do at each step or location on the MAP, the session should flow freely and without much difficulty. (12)

Members of Our Physical Body:

all aspects of our physical bodies, where sin dwells (see Romans 7:23).

Memory:

the mental record of our past experiences. This term includes all that we remember, what we believe we have seen, heard, felt, or otherwise experienced.

Mentee:

the person who is applying the "*TPM Process*" in a "*TPM Session.*" He or she may be mentored by a "*Mentor.*" The Mentee is the one who accomplishes the "*objectives*" in each of "*The Boxes.*" (Preface), (1), (2), (3), (8), (12), (21)

Mentor:

the person who observes the "*Mentee*" apply the "*TPM Process.*" He or she follows the Mentee during the "*TPM Session,*" asking the appropriate questions and offering orientation where needed. (Preface), (1), (2), (3), (8), (12), (21)

Metanoia:

a Biblical Greek word that is typically translated into English as "repentance." It literally means "a change of mind, a change in thought, a change in the inner man, an afterthought." We experience this "change of thought" when the Holy Spirit persuades us of the truth. We go from believing a lie to believing the truth. This is what we look for in the TRANSFORMATION Box. (4.5), (5.5), (6.4), (16), (20.5), (20.8)

Mind:

the mental interpreter that gathers input from our senses and interprets what it means through the lens of our beliefs (prioritizing our "heart beliefs"). We then perceive, feel, and respond based upon this interpretation of our experience. (4.1), (5), (6)

Mind-renewal:

occurs when the "*Holy Spirit*" convinces us of the truth regarding the impurities in our faith which become exposed through His process of "*faith-refinement.*" When genuine mind-renewal occurs, the lie we once believed no longer feels or seems true, and the truth feels or seems true from our new perspective. (10)

Ministry Facilitator:

a discontinued term that was used in the past to inaccurately define the Mentor's role. This person was believed to be the one who applied the TPM Process on someone else. It has since been discovered that this is not true. (Preface), (12.3)

Nature of Man:

the spiritual essence of who we are, our spirit person or self.

New Nature/ New Self:

When a person is persuaded of the truth of the Gospel and confesses Jesus as Lord, he or she is made right with God and is saved (Romans 10:10). However, there is also a spiritual transformation of the inner person that takes place as well. The Bible calls this transformation "born again." It is the emergence of a new person or new creation. At salvation, we share in the death and resurrection of Jesus and become new creations. The Scriptures are not completely clear as to all that this means, but certainly, our old self (our state of being apart from God) dies with Jesus, and our new self is raised up with Him. Our inner person, or spiritual self, is the unique person that God brought into existence at our physical conception. This is the self that was separated from God before Christ, but it is also the same self that is brought to life as a new creation. Our heart's original spirit/inner person did not cease to exist at the cross, but rather, we died with Him and we were brought to life, transformed, and made holy in Christ. We are a new creation, but we are also the same person. (4.2), (5.2), (5.7), (6.7), (8), (9.4), (11.1), (14.3)

Obedience:

The willful choice to submit to and carry out the wishes of those we serve. According to the Scriptures, obedience to God should not be burdensome or difficult (see 1 John 5:3). Our obedience to God should be motivated by our love and, therefore, an expression of the fruit of the Spirit. When obeying God is difficult, something is wrong. The trouble will be found in our impure faith, which is our lie-based heart belief. (See the "*Belief and Choice*" Principle and the "*Ice Cream*" illustration for more.) (6.1)

Old Nature/ Old Self:

We are each created with a unique self or personhood. This self is who we are. At some point in early childhood, every person knowingly and willfully chooses to sin. This willful choice results in spiritual death or separation from God. Some people refer to this initial act of willful sin as the start of the "age of accountability." When this occurs, we become a dead self that is cut off from the life of God. Every person is destined to fall in this manner due to their relationship with Adam. People identify this state of being in different ways, such as our dead self, old man, old nature, the Adamic nature, or fallen nature. An important aspect of this fallen self is that the original self we were created to be is the same self that becomes the fallen or dead self. It is also the same self that becomes the "new self" or new nature, created in righteousness and truth. When a person becomes a partaker of God's divine nature at salvation, they become a "new self" created from the "original" self. So then, the old self and the new self are the same "self," just at different points in time. My "old self" is who I was <u>before</u> I died and was raised with Christ. My "new self" is the new creation that I am today. We are the same person that we were at conception, but we have a new heart that is pure and righteous. (4.2), (5.2), (5.7), (6.7), (8), (9.4), (11.1), (14.3)

Objectives (of "The Boxes"):

These tasks are the responsibility of the "*Mentee*." Each of "*The Boxes*" has its own set of objectives that are to be accomplished when the Mentee is at that stage of the "*TPM Process*." It is imperative that the Mentee understands each of these objectives and how to accomplish them. A "*Mentor's*" primary responsibility is to help the Mentee understand these concepts. (12)

Pain:

The ability to feel pain was created by God to alert us when something is wrong. Physical pain and emotional pain are similar in that both alert us to a problem, move us in the direction of the problem, and motivate us to do something to resolve the problem. Emotional pain warns us when we lack God's perspective. (5), (6.5), (7.1), (9.1), (9.2), (13), (14)

Paradigm Shift:

A major change in a long-held belief.

[The] "Peace" Test (TRANSFORMATION Box):

a discontinued approach for "*Testing for Transformation*" that was practiced in the earlier years of TPM, which was based upon the mistaken notion that your current emotional state indicates whether or not you have recently heard from the Lord. Today we recognize that feeling better is not a reliable indication of transformation. We now look for a change in belief rather than a change in emotion. (17)

Peitho (Greek – "Persuade"):

is a Greek word found in Scripture which means "to persuade or to be persuaded and have confidence in what is trustworthy." It is the result of the "*Holy Spirit's*" persuasion and leads us to effortless obedience. (9.1), (10), (11.2), (16), (17.1)

Perceived Problems:

the issues, challenges, difficulties, burdens, and pain that we believe to be problematic because they appear to be unsolved. After the "*Holy Spirit*" persuades us of the truth and we gain His perspective, we will find freedom from our "*lie-based problems*" and find rest and satisfaction in His solutions to our "*truth-based problems.*" (4), (6.3), (6.4), (19.1)

Performance/Performance-based Spirituality:

an attempt to live rightly and do what Jesus would do through controlling our behavior and conforming ourselves to the truth. By definition, this is considered to be a "solution behavior." This is the effort to perform the fruit of the Spirit or behave and mimic the life of Jesus. God has called us to be transformed into the image of Jesus rather than attempting to act like Him. (6.5), (6.6), (6.7), (11)

Persuade / Persuasion:

the act that results in a change of belief. If we have been persuaded to believe something, we will be convinced that it is true. A primary goal of TPM is to have the "*Holy Spirit*" persuade our hearts to believe the truth. The Greek term for this is "*Peitho.*" (7)

Positioning Prayer:

a term used to classify TPM. It is the act of positioning yourself to receive truth and perspective from the "Holy Spirit." (12.1), (21)

Post-resurrection:

anything that occurred after Jesus was resurrected from death.

Post-Resurrection Deliverance:

how the early Church dealt with demonization, exorcism, and spiritual warfare, and the model we should follow as opposed to a pre-Calvary perspective. (20), (21.2)

Prayer Partner:

a Mentee in training who participates in the TPM Process as an intercessor.

Pre-Calvary:

Anything that occurred before Jesus was crucified on the cross at Calvary.

Pre-Calvary Deliverance:

how Jesus and His disciples dealt with demonization and exorcism before Satan was defeated at the cross. (20), (21.2)

Principles of TPM:

the concepts, ideas, perspectives, and explanations that support the protocols included in "*The Process of TPM*" and explain the importance and impact of "*The Purpose of TPM*." (2), (3)

Process of TPM:

a practical and systematic approach for applying the "*Principles of TPM*" in order to accomplish the "*Purpose of TPM.*" It consists of the *Mentee's* "*Objectives*" and how he or she is to accomplish them while applying the *Process*. The Process is illustrated in the "*TPM Map*" and "*TPM Flowcharts.*" (2), (12)

Propitiation:

atoning sacrifice for the purpose of reconciling us to God by the atonement, the paying for sin by a sin-offering. Biblical Greek: "hilasmos" (1 John 2:2, 4:10) (4.5), (20.2)

Purified Faith / Refined Faith

heart-belief that has been established through having been persuaded of the truth by the Holy Spirit. (9.1)

Purpose of Pain:

to alert us to the fact that something is amiss, to motivate us to do something in response, and to help us locate its source. (5.4)

Purpose of TPM:

to provide a frame of reference that views life's difficulties from a heavenly perspective so we might intentionally and purposefully cooperate with what God is doing as He refines our faith, renews our minds, and transforms our lives. (2), (8)

Recipient / Ministry Recipient:

a discontinued term that was used in the past to inaccurately define the Mentee's role. (Preface), (1), (12.3), (21)

Repentance:

Typically, repentance is thought to be the act of turning away from sin and turning toward God. Even though this is a popular understanding, it is riddled with theological concerns. First, the Greek meaning of the word does not mean to turn from anything but rather denotes a change in belief. The Greek NT word typically translated as "repentance" is *metanoia*. The word means to have a change of thinking or belief. Once there is a true change in our heart belief, we will turn from sin. However, the act of turning is not repentance but rather the outcome of a change in belief.

Repentance (change of belief) is granted by God through the persuasion of the Holy Spirit, "leading to the knowledge of the truth" that causes us to "come to [our] senses, having escaped from the snare of the devil," resulting in a change in direction, behavior, and attitude. All of this is accomplished naturally and effortlessly and made evident by the presence of the fruit of the Spirit. (See 2 Timothy 2:25-26 for a great explanation of this entire process.)

Being persuaded of the truth and having a change in belief is a work of God's Spirit in the heart of the believer. Willful turning requires self-effort and personal discipline, whereas the Spirit accomplishes a change of heart belief, and turning from sin is an expected outcome. Unbelievers can turn from sin and hold their position for a time if they choose to (just as we sometimes try to do), whereas a genuine change of thinking is the work of God that is followed by transformation and spiritual fruit.

If repentance is understood as the Spirit changing our heart belief, which results in us moving in God's direction, then this perspective fits nicely into the fuller understanding of salvation being "grace through faith" and not of works. It is all about God and nothing about us. (4.5), (5.5), (6.4), (16), (20.5), (20.8)

Repression:

the outcome of suppressing a thought, idea, emotion, or memory to the point that it becomes unconscious. This term is somewhat distinct from "*suppression*" which is accomplished by a conscious process. Although, in a "*TPM Session*," both are understood to be "*solutions*" and are addressed the same way.

Resistance / Hesitancy (solution indicator):

When you are actively engaged in a "*solution behavior*," you will often feel a level of resistance or hesitancy at the thought of doing anything else. This is especially true if you contemplate acting in total opposition to your "*solution belief*." (19.1), (19.2), (19.3), (19.6)

Righteousness:

to be right or be in right standing. Our right standing is made possible through the death and resurrection of Jesus. We are righteous in Him and not of ourselves.

Salvation:

the result of "confess[ing] with your mouth Jesus as Lord and believ[ing] in your heart that God raised Him from the dead...for with the heart a person believes, resulting in righteousness, and with the mouth he confesses, resulting in salvation" (Romans 10:9-10, emphasis added).

Sanctify:

setting something or someone apart for a holy and special purpose. It is also declaring something to be holy or pure. This is the designation that Paul gives the early Christians when he addresses them as saints. The Greek word translated as "*saint*" is *hagios*, which means holy.

Sanctification:

the ongoing work of the *"Holy Spirit"* in the life of the *"believer."* It consists of the purification of our faith and the renewing of our minds that results in the transformation of our belief. This sanctification is not a process of becoming something that we are not but one of discovery in who our *"New Selves"* are in Christ. Rather than becoming like Jesus, we are discovering who we are and have been since we first believed (1 Corinthians 13:12). It is a work of His Spirit brought about as we "humble [ourselves] under the mighty hand of God" (1 Peter 5:6, emphasis added). (8), (9), (10), (11)

Sarx:

The New Testament Greek word translated as "flesh". (See flesh above.)

Satan:

The name or term designating the Serpent, the former "Ruler of the earth." It is the chief fallen creature that is the leader over the "world forces of darkness." (20), (21.2)

Self-Control:

As one of the "fruits" listed in Galatians 5:23, self-control is different from controlled behavior. Controlled behavior is a human trait that can be practiced in some measure by anyone who chooses to do so. Whereas the Spirit's fruit of self-control is an effortless outcome of having been persuaded of the truth within the heart by the Spirit. It is being controlled by the Spirit as opposed to attempting to control how we behave. (11)

Self-Identity Belief:

a *"heart belief"* that reflects the perception we have of ourselves. (Ex. *"I am unlovable," "I am stupid," "I am worthless," "I am a defect,"* etc.) (4.4), (5.2), (14.2), (14.3)

Session (A TPM Session):

is essentially an allotted time devoted to a person's application of the *"TPM Process."* This can occur with or without the supervision of a *"Mentor."* (2), (12)

Solutions:

a term used to refer to the general dynamics of how we tend to respond to *"perceived problems"* through the use of *"solution behaviors"* because we have been persuaded to believe *"solution beliefs."* The term *"solution"* is often used when speaking more generally about *"solution behaviors."* (6), (19)

Solution Behavior:

anything done in response to a *"perceived problem"* that you believe will help solve or alleviate it. The use of every solution behavior is supported by a *"solution belief."* (6), (19)

Solution Beliefs:

the belief that explains why a particular *"solution behavior"* was chosen as a *"solution"* to a specific *"perceived problem."* It serves as the lie-based rationale for why you are choosing to do what you are doing (ex. suppressing emotion, blocking out memory, holding onto anger, etc.). It is the rationale or thinking that supports the actions and behavior engaged (solution behavior) to resolve a perceived problem. For example, if I remember what happened to me, I will be overwhelmed by it (the problem), so then, by not remembering and blocking out the past (solution behavior), I will keep me from being overwhelmed (solution belief). (6), (19)

Solution Indicators:

consist of the signs and indicators that can help you determine if, and when, you are engaged in a "*solution behavior*" (which is your first objective while in the SOLUTION Box). Common solution indicators include "*compelled behavior*," "*alleviated problems*," and "*resistance/hesitancy*." (19.1)

Spirit of the Mind:

The apostle Paul uses this phrase to describe the renewing of the mind (Ephesians 4:23). The fact that he says the "spirit of the mind" seems to indicate that it is more than gaining intellectual knowledge.

Spirit Person:

the uniquely created person who we are and who we will eternally be. It is the inner person who dwells in a body of flesh while upon this earth and, for those who are in Christ, in a new glorified body after Jesus returns (also see "nature of man").

Spiritual Warfare:

the idea that we are in a spiritual battle with the world forces of darkness even though the Scriptures declare that Satan has been defeated, and we have already been given our victory in Christ. Engaging the spirit world in battle makes no logical or theological sense. Standing in our present victory while having put on Christ (the armor) is more consistent with what the Bible teaches. (20), (21.2)

State of Being Belief:

a "***heart belief***" that reflects our understanding of God and/or describes our perceived surroundings, environment, and status. (Lie-based examples include, "*I am alone*," "*I am out of control*," "*I am trapped*," "*God can't be trusted*," "*God is cruel*," etc.). How we view our state of being is also how we understand God's involvement in our life. (4.4), (5.2), (14.2), (14.3)

Suffering:

In the context of the Scriptures, suffering includes everything that comes our way that is painful, trying or difficult, whether it be physical torture for our faith or "normal," stressful life situations. Suffering is a primary means that God uses to expose our need for His perspective so that we might position ourselves to have Him refine our faith, renew our minds, and transform our lives. (8), (9), (10), (11)

Suppression:

the act of consciously choosing to resist unwanted ideas, thoughts, emotions, or memories. This term is somewhat distinct from "*Repression*" which is accomplished as a subconscious process. Although, in a "*TPM Session*," both are understood to be "*solutions*" and are addressed the same way.

Test for Transformation (TRANSFORMATION Box):

the Mentee's objective while in the TRANSFORMATION Box. The Mentee checks for a shift in his or her thinking. If the lie-based belief that was identified no longer feels or seems true, this indicates that "*mind-renewal*" has occurred. This is how we check to see if the Holy Spirit has persuaded someone of the truth. (17)

Three Elements of TPM:

consist of "*The Purpose of TPM*," "*The Principles of TPM*," and "*The Process of TPM*." (2)

Time for Weeping *(truth-based problems)*:

the period of time after you have become aware of a "*truth-based problem*" during which you likely feel "*truth-based pain*" and have not yet been convinced of "*God's solutions*" to the problem. If you remain in this state for longer than necessary, you run the risk of being deceived into believing that you have a valid reason for continuing to carry the burden of "*truth-based pain*." If this happens, your "weeping" will likely become a "*solution behavior*." (Examples: staying angry, continuing to grieve, remaining regretful, etc.) The phrase "*time for weeping*" was taken from Ecclesiastes 3:4. (5.5), (5.6), (14.5)

Transformation:

consists of the effortless and permanent changes in our perspective, feelings, and behavior which are the expected outcomes of "*mind-renewal*."

Trigger / Triggered / Triggering:

the state of being when your need for "*God's perspective*" is exposed and made evident. This occurs when we are faced with the consequences of our lie-based beliefs. An example of being "triggered" would be feeling worried or anxious before, during, or after opening a medical bill. (5.7), (6.2), (12.1), (12.4), (13.1)

The Trust and Authority Principle:

Everything that we believe, we came to believe because we were persuaded to believe it. No one just decides to believe one thing or the other. Even our belief that resulted in our salvation was the outcome of being persuaded by the Holy Spirit concerning the truth of the Gospel. This persuasion is contingent upon two basic elements. First, we must have trust in the source of the information, and second, we must believe that the source holds more authority and understanding of the information than we do ourselves. Therefore, we are persuaded to believe something when we trust the source and perceive that it knows more about the information than we do ourselves. (7.4), (7.5)

Truth:

All that God says is so, objective reality. It is that which accurately reflects "*God's Perspective*."

Truth-based Pain:

the painful emotions associated with the "*truth-based problems*" which seem to be unsolved. Until we are convinced of the existence and effectiveness of "*God's solutions*" to our "truth-based problems," we will continue our attempts at carrying the burden of "*truth-based pain*" associated with these "*perceived problems*." (4.3), (4.5), (5.5), (5.6), (14.5)

Truth-based Problems:

the "*perceived problems*" that are real, actual, and in need of "*God's solutions*" to them. Problems such as our sinful state-of-being, the loss of a loved one, and the injustice that we have experienced throughout life are all real, and unless we are convinced of "*God's solutions*" to these problems, they will appear to remain unsolved and problematic. When these "*perceived problems*" seem to be un-

h-based pain" associated with them. ([4.3](#)), (4.5), (5.5), (5.6),

_s made (usually to ourselves or to God) to do something or refrain from doing _vs are made and upheld for the purpose of accomplishing something and are therefore _u to be "_solution behaviors_." Since vows are a form of solution behavior, the vow itself has _al power, nor is it demonic or even spiritual. And casting out demons or renouncing the vow will not have any real impact. Vows are resolved when the lie-based belief on which they are resting is identified and replaced with God's perspective. When a vow is encountered you are in the SOLUTION Box. (19.2)

We believe what we are persuaded to believe:

The "_Belief and Persuasion_" Principle. (7)

We do what we believe:

The "_Belief and Choice_" Principle. (6)

We feel what we believe:

The "_Belief and Emotion_" Principle. (5)

We perceive what we believe:

The "_Belief and Perception_" Principle. (4)

"Will vs. Desire" (the difference between them):

We may genuinely _want_ and _desire_ to follow God's promptings, but our "_will_" is expressed in what we do. Our "desire" is what we _want_ to do, but our "will" is what we _choose to do_. Our default behaviors frequently contradict what we genuinely _want_ and _desire_ to do. (6.1)

NOTABLE ILLUSTRATIONS, TOPICS, AND EXAMPLES

The list below can help you find a specific illustration that was used in this book. This way you can locate an illustration without having to remember where the illustration was used or even the concept that it was used to explain. Each entry includes several descriptive words to help you in your search. As with the terms in the Glossary, each illustration offers the chapter and part in which it can be found.

Again, the first number indicates the "Chapter," and the second number indicates the "Part." Example: (Chapter.Part) For instance, the illustration of "stepping on a thorn" can be found in the fourth part of chapter 5, and this is indicated by the following notation: (5.4).

2 + 2 = 5 / Choosing to Believe: (7.2)

Abortion / Regret / Disappointment / Truth-based Pain: (5.5)

Airplanes / Airport / Flying:

> *Airport / Scream / Help / Warning / Perception: (4.1)*
>
> *Flying in Turbulence / Fear / We feel what we believe: (5.7)*
>
> *Oxygen Masks / Secure Yours / Assisting Others / Mentors: (6.2)*

Association:

> *Christmas / Childhood Memory: (13.2)*
>
> *God doesn't "take us" to our memories / Holy Spirit: (13.2)*
>
> *Smoke / Barbeque / Grilling / EMOTION Box: (13.1)*
>
> *Word Search / Online / EMOTION Box: (13.1)*

Bigfoot / Camping / Friend / Persuasion: (7.3)

Boxer / Fight / Gang / Muggers / Perception / Purpose / Context: (9.2)

Bucket / Water / Concrete / Stirring / Resistance / Hesitancy: (19.2)

Burden / Traveling Merchant / Cart / Wagon: (5.6)

Bully / Satan / Playground / "You're a freak!" / "Tattletale!" / The Father's Love: (20.8)

Brownies / Chocolate Chips / Raisins / Impure faith: (9.1)

Car / Vehicle / Driving:

> *Car Accident / Daughter was Killed / Truth-based Pain: (5.5)*
>
> *Ed and Joshua / Learning to Drive / Mentoring / The Process: (12.3)*
>
> *Road Trip / Wrong Way / Our Perceptions Seem True: (4.2)*
>
> *Wrong Car / Parking Lot / Ed / Boys / Our Perceptions Seem True: (4.2)*

a of God / Born of the Spirit / Born Again / Identity:

    Fullness of Him / The Church / Beloved / Children of God: (9.4)

    God Loves You / Eyes of Your Heart / The Helper: (7.5)

    Heart Belief / Knowing Your Identity / Chosen / Holy / Beloved:(5.2)

    Heretical Hypothetical / Was Jesus the Son of God / You are a Child of God: (4.4)

    What Is Being Transformed / New Creation / Born Again / Child of God: (11.1)

Child / Children:

    Abortion / Regret / Disappointment / Truth-based Pain: (5.5)

    Blame-Shifting / "He pulled my hair!" / "She kicked me!"/ Disobedience: (6.1)

    Bully / Satan / Playground / "You're a freak!" / The Father's Love: (20.8)

    Car Accident / Daughter was Killed / Truth-based Pain: (5.5)

    Castle / Blocks / "She ruined it!" / "Listen a little?" / Parenting with TPM: (19.6)

    Child Abuse / Teacher / "He didn't mean to do it" / Truth-based Pain: (5.5)

    Cleaning Up / Four Children / Daily Routine / Powerless / Out of Control: (5.7)

    College Student / Losing Faith / Liberal Professor / Persuasion: (7.5)

    Electric Fence / Joshua Shocks Himself (our emotions motivate us to act): (6.2)

    "Elijah pulled Penelope's hair" / "Penelope kicked Elijah" / Blame-Shifting (6.1)

    Frog / Poison / Knowing the Dangers of Sin: (6.4)

    Hairbrush / Tangles / Faith-refinement: (9.2)

    Ice Cream / Obedience / Without Struggle: (6.1)

    Jelly on Hands / Child / Our Solutions / Causing Problems: (6.3)

    Little Suzie / Johnny / "He took my toy!" / Blame-shifting: (5.1)

    "Papa, Did I do a good job?" / Impure Motives / Good Things: (6.6)

    Sarah's Death / Ed and Sharon's Firstborn / Truth-based Problems: (5.6)

    "She just hit me" / "He's not sharing" / "They won't let me play" / Partial Truth: (4.3)

    Spider / Small Child / Observing Her Mother / Scared of Spiders: (7.3)

    Swing / Zipline / Big Picture / "Trust me Ruby." (5.6)

    Look Them in The Eyes / Hold Their Hands / I Love You / Important: (7.5)

Christmas / Childhood Memory / Association: (13.2)

College Student / Losing Faith / Liberal Professor / Persuasion: (7.5)

Compassion / Pain of Others / Feeling Your Own Pain: (6.6)

Crucifixion / Jesus' Death:

    Jesus Perceived the Truth / Eternal Perspective / The Father's Will: (5.3)

    Lamb Led to Slaughter / Isaiah 53 / Calm / Trusting (5.3)

> God Loves You / Sent His Son / Brutal Punishment / Truth is Truth: (7.1)
>
> Grieved Over Christ's Death / Disciples / Bit Picture / Greater Truth: (5.6)
>
> Father Forgive Them / God's Perspective / Limited Perspective / Short-Sighted: (6.4)
>
> Joy / Set Before Him / Endured the Cross / Perspective / Suffering: (9.3)
>
> Weight of His Father's Request / Grieved / Blood Like Sweat: (5.3)

David / Goliath / Psalms:

> God's Instruction / God's Commands / Great Reward: (6.1)
>
> Limited Perspective / David Saw the Greater Truth / Truth-based Problems: (4.3)

Demons / Devil / Satan / Demonic / Evil Spirits:

> Anger / Afford the Devil an Opportunity / Sin: (18.1)
>
> Bully / Playground / "You're a freak!" / "Tattletale!" / The Father's Love: (20.8)
>
> Demonic Manifestation / TPM Session Example / Grrrrrr: (19.6)
>
> Eating Fruit to Solve Problems / Solution Behavior: (6.4)
>
> Oppressed / Heaviness / Depression / Impure Thoughts / Temptation: (5.7)

Dog

> Burglar / Dog / Trash / Emotion: (5.1)
>
> On a Chain / Satan / Martin Luther: (20.3)
>
> Poop on the Floor (choosing not to feel): (5.4)

Dentist / Numb the Pain / Purpose of Pain: (5.4)

Electric Fence / Joshua Shocks Himself (our emotions motivate us to act): (6.2)

Emmaus / Traveling with Jesus (we feel what we believe in our hearts): (5.2)

Endurance / Hypomone / Holding Us Under / Held Back / Submissive: (9.1)

Ed's Counseling Years / Early TPM / First TPM Sessions:

> Double-minded / Head / Heart / We Feel What We Believe: (5.2)
>
> Emotional Pain / Not a Result of Their Abuse: (5.1)
>
> FACTS / Choose to Believe / Memorize the Truth / Intellectual: (7.2)
>
> History / TPM's Origin / "It wasn't my fault!" / First Session: (1)
>
> Persuasion / Trust / Authority / Could not convince: (7.5)

Eyeglasses:

> On Ed's Head / Unaware / Truth-based Problems: (4.3)
>
> Wrong Pair / Right Pair / We need God's perspective: (7.1)

Fear Not / Do Not Be Afraid / Take Courage / God's Perspective: (5.4)

Finances / Giving / Spending / Money:

> Credit Card Bill / Paycheck to Paycheck / God Supplying / Philippians 4:19: (5.7)

Generous Giver / Compelled / Pressured / Recognition / Appreciation: (6.6)

Scammer / Reverend Zimbolo / Give Money / Online Forum / Persuasion: (7.4)

Fire / Flame:

House Fire / Unaware of the Truth / Truth-Based Pain: (5.5)

Home on Fire / Kidnapping / Kicked-in Door / Motives: (6.5)

Office / Interrupted Conference Call / Orange Glow in Hallway / Persuasion: (7.4)

Refiner's Fire / Gold / Impurities / True Selves Revealed / New Creation / Glory: (9.4)

Refiner's Fire / Image of Jesus / Revealed in Us / Praise / Honor / Glory: (9.2)

Refiner's Fire / Physical Pain / Why We Hurt / Emotional Pain: (9.2)

Refiner's Fire / Refining Fire / Precious Metal / The Refinement of Our Faith: (9)

Refiner's Fire / What Is Being Refined / Not Us / Our Belief / Faith: (9.4)

Fish / Fishing:

Fish Bowl / Online Shopping / Reviews / Persuasion: (7.4)

Lures / Bait / Temptation: (20.5)

Teach Others to "Fish" / Hungry Neighbors / Mentoring Others: (2)

Food in Commercials / Fake Food / The Truth About Our Solutions: (6.4)

Frog / Poison / Knowing the Dangers of Sin: (6.4)

Garden of Eden / Adam and Eve / The Serpent:

Blame-Shifting / Disobedience / "It was the woman!" (6.1)

Eating Fruit to Solve Problems / Solution Behavior: (6.4)

Satan's Short-Sighted Solutions / Perceived Problems / Satan's Tactics: (20.4)

Satan didn't force them to eat / Desperate Recruiter / Tricked Them: (20.5)

"Why are you naked?" / Adam and Eve / TPM Not New: (21.1)

Garden of Gethsemane / Jesus is Arrested / Peter's Sword / Ear:

Weight of His Father's Request / Grieved / Blood Like Sweat: (5.3)

Peter / Sword / Big Picture: (5.6)

Peter / Problem Solver / Sword / Solution Behavior: (6.3)

Gift Card / $500 / Stolen Gift: (6.5)

Gold / Impurities / Refinement:

Faith-Refinement / Precious Metal / Melting Point / Impurities: (9.1)

Proves Authenticity / Pure / Fire Does Not Change the Gold: (9.2)

Impurities Not Part of the Gold / Fire Exposes / The Refiner's Reflection: (9.4)

Hairbrush / Tangles / Faith-refinement: (9.2)

Hand Caught In Trap / Doctor / Pain / TRANSFORMATION Box: (17.2)

Heretical Hypothetical / What If Jesus Didn't Know / What If Jesus Believed Lies: (4.4)

Holy Spirit:

> *Following the Spirit / Leading / Persuading: (12.4)*
>
> *God doesn't "take us" to our memories / Holy Spirit / Association: (13.2)*
>
> *Helper / Spirit of Truth / Taught / Reminded / Convicted / Led: (7.5)*

Home Invasion:

> *Burglar / Dog / Trash / Emotion: (5.1)*
>
> *Kidnapping / House on Fire / Motives: (6.5)*

Ice Cream / Obedience / Without Struggle: (6.1)

Interpreter / Smelly Drink / Miscommunication / Your Mind's Role as an Interpreter: (4.1)

Island / Tropical / Map: (12.2)

Israelites / Exodus out of Egypt (trusting God's solutions): (4.3)

Jelly on Hands / Child / Our Solutions / Causing Problems: (6.3)

Jesus:

> *God doesn't "take us" to our memories / Holy Spirit / Association: (13.2)*
>
> *Holy Spirit / Helper / Spirit of Truth / Taught / Reminded / Convicted / Led: (7.5)*
>
> *Misinterpreted / Differing Opinions of Christ / Son of God / Commotion: (4.1)*
>
> *Refiner's Fire / Image of Jesus / Revealed in Us / Praise / Honor / Glory: (9.2)*
>
> *Storm / Boat / Disciples / Reaction / Peace / Normal: (6.2)*

Judge / Trial / Evidence / Persuasion: (7.4)

Justice / Criminal / Law / God's Righteous Purpose / Anger: (18.1)

Keys / Hidden / "Help me, I can't find them!" / Memories / Suppressed: (21.3)

Mary and Martha:

> *God is not looking for more "Marthas" / Hard Work / Performance / Discipline: (6.7)*
>
> *Positioned at Jesus' Feet / Receiving from God / The Process of TPM: (12.1)*

Marriage / Spouse / Family / Conflict / Difficulty:

> *Working Overtime / No Phone Call / "Where were you?" / Lie-based Pain: (5.7)*

Matchstick / Fire / Carbon / Transformation: (11.1)

Ministry / Church / Pastoring / Worship:

> *Compassion / The Pain of Others / Feeling Your Own Pain: (6.6)*
>
> *"Just Do It" Mentality / Discipline / Obedience / Transformation / Fruit: (11.2)*
>
> *Pastor / Highly Organized / Schedule / In Order / Anxiety: (6.6)*
>
> *Prayer / Fasting / Bible Study / Discipline / Will Not Transform Us: (11.2)*
>
> *Prayer Minister / Emotionally Wounded / Draining / Compassionate: (6.6)*

Thorn in Your Foot / The Purpose of Pain: (5.4), (5.7)

Trap / Hand / Doctor / Pain / TRANSFORMATION Box: (17.2)

TV Game Show / Choose a Door / $10,000 / Ants: (6.1)

Volunteering / Serving / Giving / Motives:

    Difficulty Saying No / Nursery / Feeds Hungry / Sings in Choir: (6.6)

    Generous Giver / Compelled / Pressured / Recognition / Appreciation: (6.6)

    Pastor / Highly Organized / Schedule / In Order / Anxiety: (6.6)

    Spread Too Thin / Crisis Pregnancy / Planning Committee / Greeter: (5.7)

Word Search / Online / Association / EMOTION Box: (13.1)

Worship Music / Praise Music / Listening to Music / Solution Behaviors: (6.7)

TPM Process Map - "Mentee"

THE CLOCK PRINCIPLE

EMOTION BOX
- How does that make me feel?
- What comes to mind as I focus on that?

MEMORY BOX
- How does that make me feel?
- Why do I feel that way?
- Why does believing _____ make me feel _____?

BELIEF BOX
- Not that it is true, but does it feel or seem true that _____? (THE LIE-BASED "HEART BELIEF" OR "SOLUTION BELIEF")

TRUTH BOX
- Lord, what do you want me to know?

TRANSFORMATION BOX
- Does it still feel true that (THE LIE-BASED BELIEF) THAT WAS ACKNOWLEDGED IN THE BELIEF BOX)?

ANGER BOX
- Is any portion of what I am feeling being felt towards any person or any thing?
- Who or what do I feel angry towards?
- Why do I feel angry towards _____?

SOLUTION BOX
- Do I sense any resistance or hesitancy at the thought of (DOING THE OPPOSITE OF THE BEHAVIOUR)?
- What do I believe would happen if I were to (STOP ENGAGING IN THE SOLUTION BEHAVIOR)?
- So then, the reason for (ENGAGING IN THE SOLUTION BEHAVIOR) is what?

Summarized Instructions:

The "TPM Map" is a training tool that illustrates the "TPM Process." It portrays each of the seven "Boxes," the questions contained in each box, and the typical path a Mentee takes when transitioning from one box to another. The "TPM Map" and the "TPM Flowcharts" are designed to help you more efficiently learn, practice, and apply the Process of TPM.

Detailed instructions on how to use the "TPM Map" can be found in the TPM training material.

TPM Process Map - "Mentor"

THE CLOCK PRINCIPLE

EMOTION BOX

- How does that make you feel?
- What comes to mind as you focus on that?

MEMORY BOX

- How does that make you feel?
- Why do you feel that way?
- Why does believing _____ make you feel _____?

BELIEF BOX

- Not that it is true, but does it feel or seem true that _____ (THE LIE-BASED "HEART BELIEF" OR "SOLUTION BELIEF")?

TRUTH BOX

- May we present that belief to the Lord?
- Lord, what do you want _____ (THE MENTEE) to know?

TRANSFORMATION BOX

- Does it still feel true that _____ (THE LIE-BASED BELIEF THAT WAS ACKNOWLEDGED IN THE BELIEF BOX)?

ANGER BOX

- Is any portion of what you are feeling being felt towards any person or any thing?
- Who or what do you feel angry towards?
- Why do you feel angry towards _____?

SOLUTION BOX

- Do you sense any resistance or hesitancy at the thought of _____ (DOING THE OPPOSITE OF THE BEHAVIOUR)?
- What do you believe would happen if you were to _____ (STOP ENGAGING IN THE SOLUTION BEHAVIOR)?
- So then, the reason for _____ (ENGAGING IN THE SOLUTION BEHAVIOR) is what?

LOST OR UNSURE

- What's going on right now?

Summarized Instructions:

The "TPM Map" is a training tool that illustrates the "TPM Process." It portrays each of the seven "Boxes," the questions contained in each box, and the typical path a Mentee takes when transitioning from one box to another. The "TPM Map" and the "TPM Flowcharts" are designed to help you more efficiently learn, practice, and apply the Process of TPM. *Detailed instructions on how to use the "TPM Map" can be found in the TPM training material.*

TPM Process Map - "Objectives"

THE CLOCK PRINCIPLE

EMOTION BOX

1) Connect with your emotion.
2) Focus on what you feel until a memory comes to mind.
3) Repeat the first two objectives until the same memory comes to mind twice or no other memory comes to mind.

MEMORY BOX

1) Stay connected with your emotion.
2) Determine why you feel what you feel (belief).
3) Determine why you believe what you believe (experience).

BELIEF BOX

1) Determine if you currently believe the lie-based belief that you identified in the previous "Box."

TRUTH BOX

1) Invite the Holy Spirit to persuade you of the truth.
2) Be willing to receive what He has for you.

TRANSFORMATION BOX

1) Determine if the Holy Spirit has persuaded you of the truth.

SOLUTION BOX

1) Determine if you are engaged in a "Solution Behavior."
2) Identify the "Perceived Problem" that you are attempting to solve by engaging in your behavior.
3) Articulate a "Solution Belief" that explains your behavior.

ANGER BOX

1) Determine if you are angry.
2) Identify who or what you feel angry towards.
3) Express a tentative reason for being angry.

Summarized Instructions:

The "TPM Map" is a training tool that illustrates the "TPM Process." This version portrays each of the seven "Boxes," the Mentee's objectives in each box, and the typical path a Mentee takes when transitioning from one box to another. The "TPM Map" and the "TPM Flowcharts" are designed to help you more efficiently learn, practice, and apply the Process of TPM.

Detailed instructions on how to use the "TPM Map" can be found in the TPM training material.

THE EMOTION BOX
("FLOWCHART")

Mentee's Perspective - First Person Perspective

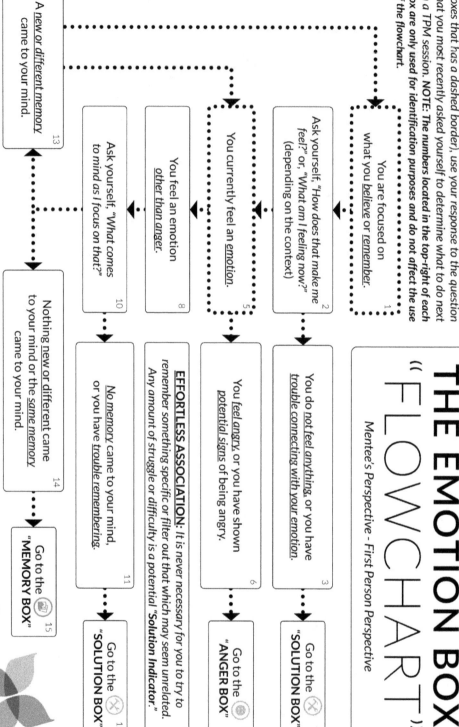

Summarized Instructions:

Beginning at the top-left of the flowchart (typically, in one of the boxes that has a dashed border), use your response to the question that you most recently asked yourself to determine what to do next in a TPM session. **NOTE: The numbers located in the top-right of each box are only used for identification purposes and do not affect the use of the flowchart.**

1 — You are focused on what you *believe* or *remember*.

2 — Ask yourself, "How does that make me feel?" or, "What am I feeling now?" (depending on the context)

3 — You do *not* feel anything, or you have *trouble connecting with your emotion*.

4 — Go to the "SOLUTION BOX"

5 — You currently feel an *emotion*.

6 — You *feel angry*, or you have shown *potential signs* of being angry.

7 — Go to the "ANGER BOX"

8 — You feel an emotion *other than anger*.

9 — **EFFORTLESS ASSOCIATION:** *It is never necessary for you to try to remember something specific or filter out that which may seem unrelated. Any amount of struggle or difficulty is a potential "Solution Indicator."*

10 — Ask yourself, "What comes to mind as I focus on that?"

11 — *No memory* came to your mind, or you have *trouble remembering*.

12 — Go to the "SOLUTION BOX"

13 — A *new or different memory* came to your mind.

14 — Nothing new or different came to your mind or the *same memory* came to your mind.

15 — Go to the "MEMORY BOX"

16 — **REPEAT UNTIL THE SAME MEMORY OR NOTHING NEW COMES TO MIND TWICE:** *As you focus on what you feel, thoughts and memories should naturally begin coming to mind. Continue this pattern of focusing on what you feel and allowing an associated memory to come to mind until the same memory comes to mind twice or until nothing new or different comes to mind. When this happens, you have accomplished your goals in the EMOTION Box and are ready to move to the "Memory Box."*

Chart Ver: ME5132022
TransformationPrayer.Org

tpm
Transformation
Prayer Ministry

382

THE EMOTION BOX
"FLOWCHART"

Mentor's Perspective - Third Person Perspective

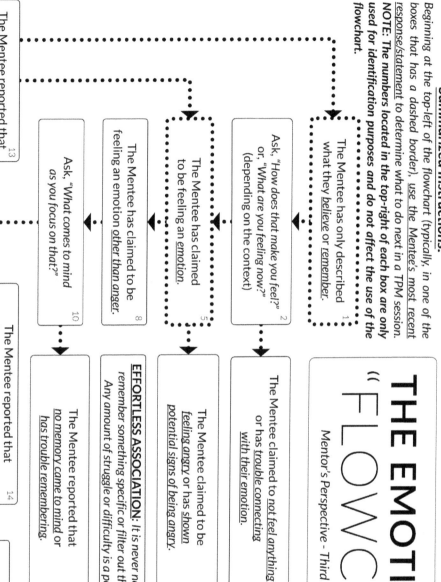

Summarized Instructions:

Beginning at the top-left of the flowchart (typically, in one of the boxes that has a dashed border), use the Mentee's most recent response/statement to determine what to do next in a TPM session.

NOTE: The numbers located in the top-right of each box are only used for identification purposes and do not affect the use of the flowchart.

1 — The Mentee has only described what they *believe* or *remember.*

2 — Ask, *"How does that make you feel?"* or, *"What are you feeling now?"* (depending on the context)

3 — The Mentee claimed to not feel *anything* or has *trouble connecting* with their emotion.

4 — Go to the ⊗ "SOLUTION BOX"

5 — The Mentee has claimed to be feeling an *emotion.*

6 — The Mentee claimed to be *feeling angry* or has *shown potential signs of being angry.*

7 — Go to the ⊙ "ANGER BOX"

8 — The Mentee has claimed to be feeling an emotion *other than anger.*

9 — **EFFORTLESS ASSOCIATION:** *It is never necessary for the Mentee to try to remember something specific or filter out that which may seem unrelated. Any amount of struggle or difficulty is a potential "Solution Indicator"*

10 — Ask, *"What comes to mind as you focus on that?"*

11 — The Mentee reported that *no memory came to mind* or *has trouble remembering.*

12 — Go to the ⊗ "SOLUTION BOX"

13 — The Mentee reported that *a new or different memory* came to mind.

14 — The Mentee reported that *nothing new or different* came to mind or that the *same memory* came to mind.

15 — Go to the "MEMORY BOX"

16 — **REPEAT UNTIL THE SAME MEMORY OR NOTHING NEW COMES TO MIND:**

As the Mentee focuses on what is felt, thoughts and memories should naturally begin coming to their mind. They should continue this pattern of focusing on emotion and allowing an associated memory to come to mind until nothing new or different comes to mind twice or until the same memory comes to mind. When this happens, they have accomplished their goals in the EMOTION Box.

Chart Ver: MR5132022
TransformationPrayer.Org

tpm
Transformation
Prayer Ministry

THE MEMORY BOX
("FLOWCHART")

Mentee's Perspective - First Person Perspective

Summarized Instructions:

Beginning at the top-left corner of the flowchart (typically, in one of the boxes that has a dashed border), use your response to the question that you most recently asked yourself to determine what to do next in a TPM session. NOTE: The numbers located in the top-right of each box are only used for identification purposes and do not affect the use of the flowchart.

1. Your most recent statement was a description of how you *currently feel.*

2. Ask yourself, *"Why do I feel this way?"*

3. Ask yourself, *"How does this make me feel?"*

4. Your most recent statement was a description of what you believe or remember.

5. Your responses are now repetitive.

6. Your responses are *not yet* repetitive.

7. **POTENTIAL SOLUTIONS IN THE MEMORY BOX**
If you seem to have trouble accomplishing your *"Goals"* in this *"Box,"* you may need additional orientation on what to do, or you might be engaged in a *"Solution Behavior."*

8. Ask yourself the *"Looping Question."* *"Why does believing _____ make me feel _____?"*

9. You responded with something new or different.

10. Stay in the *"MEMORY BOX"*

11. **FEELING ANGRY IN THE MEMORY BOX**
If at any point you feel angry or show signs that you are potentially feeling angry, any of the members of the *"Anger Family,"* go to the *"ANGER Box."*

12. You responded with the same repetitive response.

13. Your repetitive response fits the definition of a lie-based *"Heart Belief."* (Self-Identity or State of Being)

14. Go to the *"BELIEF BOX"*

15. Your repetitive response *potentially* fits the definition of a *"Truth-based Problem."*

16. You are potentially attempting to "solve" or "alleviate" this problem.

17. Go to the *"SOLUTION BOX"*

18. Your repetitive response *does not* fit the definition of a lie-based *"Heart Belief,"* or a *"Truth-based Problem."*

19. This typically means you need more training and practice, or that you are engaged in some form of *"Solution Behavior."* If this is the first time it has happened, stay in the *"MEMORY BOX."*

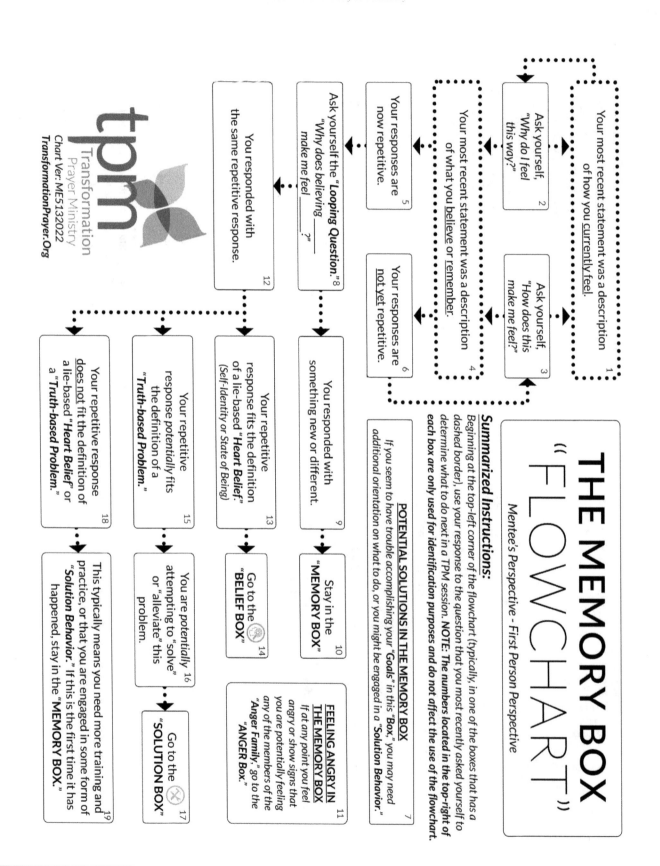

tpm
Transformation
Prayer Ministry
Chart Ver: ME5132022
TransformationPrayer.Org

THE MEMORY BOX ("FLOWCHART")

Mentor's Perspective - Third Person Perspective

Summarized Instructions:

Beginning at the top-left corner of the flowchart (typically, in one of the boxes that has a dashed border), use the Mentee's response to the most recently asked question to determine what to do next in a TPM session. NOTE: The numbers located in the top-right of each box are only used for identification purposes and do not affect the use of the flowchart.

POTENTIAL SOLUTIONS IN THE MEMORY BOX

If the Mentee seems to have trouble accomplishing their "Goals" in this "Box," they may need additional orientation on what to do or they might be engaged in a "Solution." [7]

FEELING ANGRY IN THE MEMORY BOX [11]

If at any point the Mentee claims to be feeling angry or shows signs that they are potentially feeling any of the members of the "Anger Family," go to the "ANGER Box."

1. The Mentee's most recent statement was a description of how they currently feel.

2. Ask, "Why do you feel that way?"

3. Ask, "How does that make you feel?"

4. The Mentee's most recent statement was a description of what they believe or remember.

5. The Mentee's responses are now repetitive.

6. The Mentee's responses are not yet repetitive.

8. Ask the "Looping Question." "Why does believing _____ make you feel _____?"

9. The Mentee responded with a different or new response.

10. Stay in the "MEMORY BOX"

11. (see above)

12. The Mentee responded with the same repetitive response.

13. The mentee's repetitive response fits the definition of a lie-based "Heart Belief." (Self-Identity or State of Being)

14. Go to the "BELIEF BOX"

15. The Mentee's repetitive response potentially fits the definition of a "Truth-based Problem."

16. The Mentee is potentially attempting to "solve" or "alleviate" this problem.

17. Go to the "SOLUTION BOX"

18. The Mentee's repetitive response does not fit the definition of a lie-based "Heart Belief" or a "Truth-based Problem."

19. This is typically due to the Mentee's limited understanding of the TPM Process or some form of "Solution Behavior." If this is the first time it has happened, stay in the "MEMORY BOX."

tpm
Transformation
Prayer Ministry
Chart Ver: MR5132022
TransformationPrayer.Org

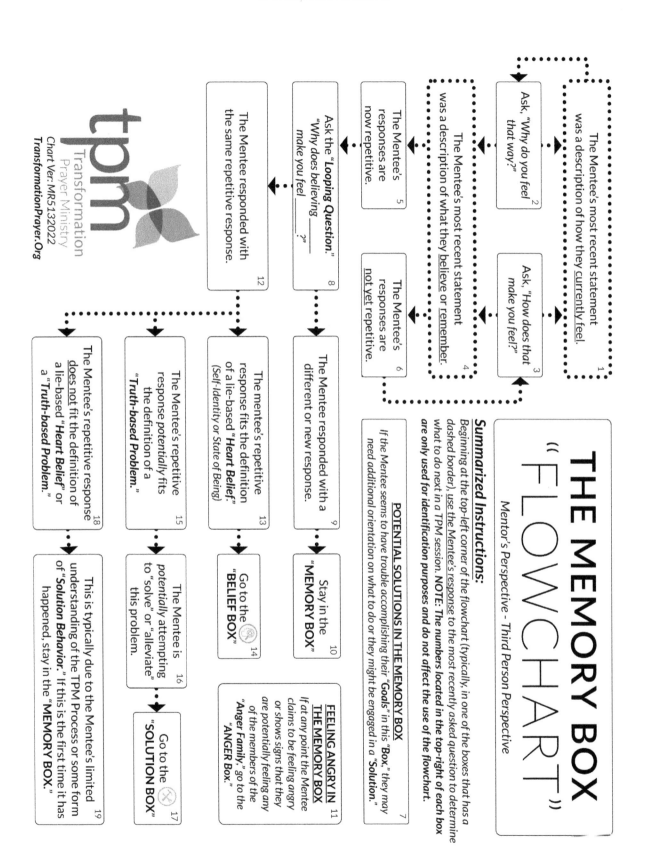

THE ANGER BOX
"FLOWCHART"

Mentee's Perspective - First Person Perspective

Summarized Instructions:

Beginning in the top-left corner of the flowchart (typically, in one of the boxes that has a dashed border), use your response to the question that you most recently asked yourself to determine what to do next in a TPM session. NOTE: The numbers located in the top-right of each box are only used for identification purposes and do not affect the use of the flowchart.

WHEN YOU STRUGGLE TO MOVE FORWARD:

If you understand your goals while in the ANGER Box but have trouble acknowledging what is felt, or identifying who or what you feel it towards, or expressing a tentative reason for why you are angry, etc., this indicates that you might be engaged in a "**Solution Behavior**." Go to the "SOLUTION Box."

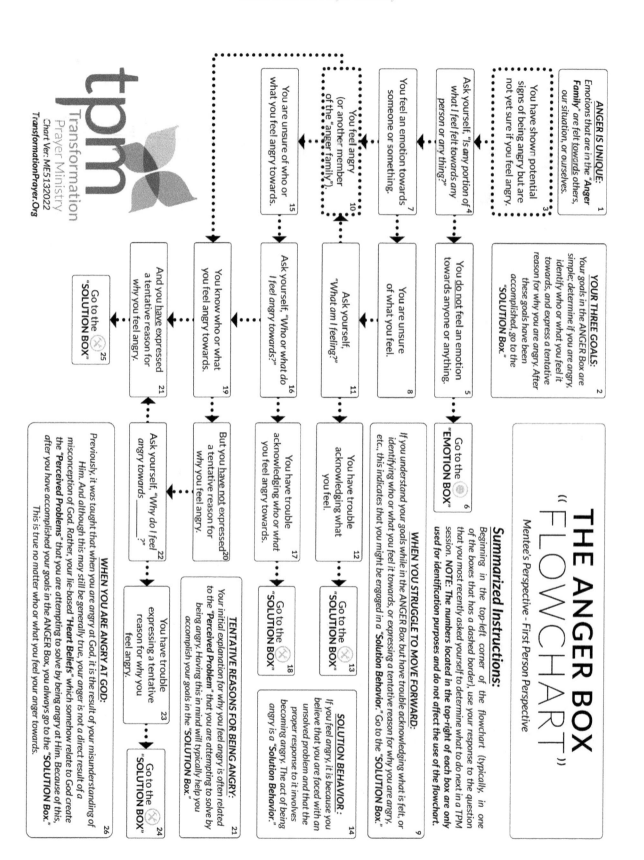

1 — **ANGER IS UNIQUE:** Emotions that are in the "Anger *Family*" are felt towards others, our situation, or ourselves.

3 — You have shown potential signs of being angry but are not yet sure if you feel angry.

4 — Ask yourself, "Is *any portion of* what I feel felt towards any person or any thing?"

7 — You feel an emotion towards someone or something.

10 — You feel angry (or another member of the "anger family").

15 — You are unsure of who or what you feel angry towards.

2 — **YOUR THREE GOALS:** Your goals in the ANGER Box are simple; determine if you are angry, identify who or what you feel it towards, and express a tentative reason for why you are angry. After these goals have been accomplished, go to the "SOLUTION Box."

5 — You do not feel an emotion towards anyone or anything.

8 — You are unsure of what you feel.

11 — Ask yourself, "What am I feeling?"

16 — Ask yourself, "Who or what do I feel angry towards?"

19 — You know who or what you feel angry towards.

21 — And you have expressed a tentative reason for why you feel angry.

25 — Go to the "SOLUTION BOX"

6 — Go to the "EMOTION BOX"

12 — You have trouble acknowledging what you feel.

13 — Go to the "SOLUTION BOX"

17 — You have trouble acknowledging who or what you feel angry towards.

18 — Go to the "SOLUTION BOX"

20 — But you have not expressed a tentative reason for why you feel angry.

22 — Ask yourself, "Why do I feel angry towards _____?"

23 — You have trouble expressing a tentative reason for why you feel angry.

24 — Go to the "SOLUTION BOX"

9 — **SOLUTION BEHAVIOR:** If you feel angry, it is because you believe that you are faced with an unsolved problem and that the proper response to it involves becoming angry. The act of being angry is a "**Solution Behavior**."

14 — **TENTATIVE REASONS FOR BEING ANGRY:** Your initial explanation for why you feel angry is often related to the "**Perceived Problem**" that you are attempting to solve by being angry. Having this in mind will typically help you accomplish your goals in the "SOLUTION Box."

26 — **WHEN YOU ARE ANGRY AT GOD:** Previously, it was taught that when you are angry at God, it is the result of your misunderstanding of Him. And although this may still be generally true, your anger is not a direct result of a misconception of God. Rather, your lie-based "**Heart Beliefs**" which somehow relate to God create the "**Perceived Problems**" that you are attempting to solve by being angry at Him. Because of this, after you have accomplished your goals in the ANGER Box, you always go to the "SOLUTION Box." This is true no matter who or what you feel your anger towards.

tpm
Transformation
Prayer Ministry
Chart Ver: ME5132022
TransformationPrayer.Org

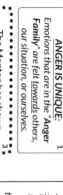

tpm
Transformation
Prayer Ministry
Chart Ver: MR5132022
TransformationPrayer.Org

THE ANGER BOX
("FLOWCHART")

Mentor's Perspective - Third Person Perspective

1. ANGER IS UNIQUE:
Emotions that are in the "**Anger Family**" are felt towards others, our situation, or ourselves.

3. The Mentee has shown potential signs of being angry but has not yet verbally claimed to be feeling angry.

4. Ask, "Is any portion of what you are feeling felt towards any person or any thing?"

7. The Mentee determined that this was the case. ("Yes")

10. The Mentee has verbally claimed to be feeling angry.

15. The Mentee has not stated who or what the anger is being felt towards.

2. THE MENTEE'S THREE GOALS:
The Mentee's goals in the ANGER Box are simple; determine if they are angry, identify who or what they feel it towards, and express a tentative reason for why they are angry. After these goals have been accomplished, the Mentee should go to the "**SOLUTION Box.**"

5. The Mentee determined that this was not the case. ("No")

6. Go to the "**EMOTION BOX**"

8. The Mentee has not verbally claimed to be feeling angry.

11. Ask, "What are you feeling?"

16. Ask, "Who or what do you feel angry towards?"

19. The Mentee has stated who or what the anger is being felt towards.

21. And they have stated a tentative reason for why they feel angry.

25. Go to the ⊗ "**SOLUTION BOX**"

Summarized Instructions:

Beginning in the top-left corner of the flowchart (typically, in one of the boxes that has a dashed border), use the Mentee's most recent response to determine what to do next in a TPM session. **NOTE: The numbers located in the top-right of each box are only used for identification purposes and do not affect the use of the flowchart.**

WHEN THE MENTEE STRUGGLES TO MOVE FORWARD:
If the Mentee understands their goals while in the ANGER Box but has trouble acknowledging what s felt, or identifying who or what they feel it towards, or expressing a tentative reason for being angry, etc., this indicates that they may be engaged in a "*Solution Behavior.*" Go to the "**SOLUTION Box.**"

9.

12. The Mentee has trouble acknowledging what is felt.

13. Go to the ⊗ "**SOLUTION BOX**"

14. SOLUTION BEHAVIOR:
If the Mentee feels angry, it is because they believe that they are faced with an unsolved prob em and that the proper response to it involves becoming angry. The act of being angry is a "*Solution Behavior.*"

17. The Mentee has trouble acknowledging who or what their anger is felt towards.

18. Go to the ⊗ "**SOLUTION BOX**"

20. But they have not stated a tentative reason for why they feel angry.

22. Ask, "Why do you feel angry towards ___?"

23. The mentee has trouble expressing a tentative reason for why they feel angry.

24. Go to the ⊗ "**SOLUTION BOX**"

TENTATIVE REASONS FOR BEING ANGRY:
The Mentee's initial explanation for why they feel angry is often related to the "**Perceived Problem**" that they are attempting to solve by being angry. Having this in mind typically helps them accomplish their goals in the "**SOLUTION Box.**"

26. WHEN THE MENTEE IS ANGRY AT GOD:
Previously, it was taught that when the Mentee is angry at God, it is the result of their misunderstanding of Him. And although this may still be generally true, their anger is not a direct result of a misconception of God. Rather, their lie-based "**Heart Beliefs**" which somehow relate to God create the "**Perceived Problems**" that the Mentee is attempting to solve by being angry at Him. Because of this, after the Mentee accomplishes their goals in the ANGER Box, they always go to the "**SOLUTION Box.**" This is true no matter who or what they feel their anger towards.

THE SOLUTION BOX
"FLOWCHART"

Mentee's Perspective - First Person Perspective

Summarized Instructions:

Beginning in the top-left corner of the flowchart, use your response to the question that you most recently asked yourself to determine what to do next in a TPM session. **NOTE: The numbers located in the top-right of each box are only used for identification purposes and do not affect the use of the flowchart.**

1 — Ask yourself, "Do I sense any resistance or hesitancy at the thought of (doing the opposite of the behavior)?"

2 — You do not sense any resistance or hesitancy.

3 — Revisit "*Solution Indicators*" in the training material and ask yourself again.

4 — You still don't notice any potential "*Solution Indicators*".

5 — Go to the "EMOTION BOX"

6 — You have noticed a potential "*Solution Indicator*".

7 — NOTICING SOLUTION INDICATORS:
These are the effects and characteristics that appear when you are actively engaged in a "Solution Behavior". Examples include, "Compelled Behaviors," "Alleviated Problems," and "Resistance/Hesitancy."

8 — Ask yourself, "What do I believe would happen if I were to (stop engaging in the Solution Behavior)?"

9 — Your response does not fit the definition of a "*Perceived Problem*."

10 — Revisit "*Perceived Problems*" in the training material and ask yourself again.

11 — IDENTIFYING PERCEIVED PROBLEMS:
If your response to the second question in the SOLUTION Box is basically true, or describes something positive or hopeful, then it likely does not fit the definition of a "*Perceived Problem*."
Your response should describe something unwanted, bad, unjust, vulnerable, or otherwise negative. And it may seem illogical or obviously untrue to you at first. After revisiting this topic in the training material, ask yourself, "What do I believe would happen if I were to (stop engaging in the Solution Behavior) that would cause me to resist or hesitate doing so?"

12 — You have identified a "*Perceived Problem*."

13 — Ask yourself, "So then, the reason for (engaging in the Solution Behavior) is what?"

14 — Your response does not fit the definition of a "*Solution Belief*."

15 — Revisit "*Solution Beliefs*" in the training material and ask yourself again.

16 — You have articulated a "*Solution Belief*."

17 — Go to the "BELIEF BOX"

18 — ARTICULATING A SOLUTION BELIEF:
A "*Solution Belief*" is the expressed logic or rationale that explains why you are engaged in this specific "*Solution Behavior*" in response to the "*Perceived Problem*."
(Examples: "It protects me," or "It holds them accountable.")

tpm
Transformation
Prayer Ministry

Chart Ver: ME5132022
TransformationPrayer.Org

THE SOLUTION BOX
((FLOWCHART))

Mentor's Perspective - Third Person Perspective

Summarized Instructions:

Beginning in the top-left corner of the flowchart, use the Mentee's most recent response to determine what to do next in a TPM session.

NOTE: *The numbers located in the top-right of each box are only used for identification purposes and do not affect the use of the flowchart.*

1 — Ask, "Do you sense any resistance or hesitancy at the thought of (doing the opposite of the behavior)?"

2 — The Mentee <u>does not</u> sense any resistance or hesitancy.

3 — Offer orientation regarding "**Solution Indicators**," and ask the question again.

4 — The Mentee claims to not be engaged in a "**Solution Behavior**."

5 — Go to the  "**EMOTION BOX**"

6 — The Mentee has noticed a potential "**Solution Indicator**."

7 — **NOTICING SOLUTION INDICATORS:**
These are the effects and characteristics that appear when someone is actively engaged in a "Solution Behavior." Examples include, "Compelled Behaviors," "Alleviated Problems," and "Resistance/Hesitancy."

8 — Ask, "What do you believe would happen if you were to (stop engaging in the Solution Behavior)?"

9 — The Mentee's response <u>does not</u> fit the definition of a "**Perceived Problem**."

10 — Offer orientation regarding "**Perceived Problems**," and ask the question again.

11 — **IDENTIFYING PERCEIVED PROBLEMS:**
*If the Mentee's response to the second question in the SOLUTION Box is basically true, or describes something positive or hopeful, then it likely does not fit the definition of a "**Perceived Problem**." Their response should describe something unwanted, bad, unjust, vulnerable, or otherwise negative. And it may seem illogical or obviously untrue to them at first. After offering orientation regarding this topic, ask, "What do you believe would happen if you were to (stop engaging in the Solution Behavior) that would cause you to resist or hesitate doing so?"*

12 — The Mentee has identified a "**Perceived Problem**."

13 — Ask, "So then, the reason for (engaging in the Solution Behavior) is what?"

14 — The Mentee's response <u>does not</u> fit the definition of a "**Solution Belief**."

15 — Offer orientation regarding "**Solution Beliefs**," and ask the question again.

16 — The Mentee has articulated a "**Solution Belief**."

17 — Go to the "**BELIEF BOX**"

18 — **ARTICULATING A SOLUTION BELIEF:**
*A "**Solution Belief**" is the expressed logic or rationale that explains why the Mentee is engaged in this specific "**Solution Behavior**" in response to the "**Perceived Problem**." (Examples: "It protects me," or "It holds them accountable.")*

tpm
Transformation
Prayer Ministry

Chart Ver: MR5132022
TransformationPrayer.Org

ABOUT THE AUTHORS

Ed Smith is the developer of Transformation Prayer Ministry. He holds a master's degree in education (focus in marriage and family counseling) from Southwestern Baptist Theological Seminary in Fort Worth, TX and a Doctorate of Ministry from Midwestern Baptist Theological Seminary in Kansas City, MO. He also completed most of his work toward his Doctorate of Education in marriage and family counseling (Ed.D.) from Southwestern Baptist Theological Seminary in Ft. Worth, Texas.

Smith's ministry career includes 17 years of service to local Southern Baptist churches prior to developing TPM in 1996 as a pastoral counselor. He and his wife, Sharon (45+ years married), also have led Marriage Enrichment conferences across the country (The Basic Ingredients for a Happy Marriage). He has authored many articles for Christian magazines, authored, Beyond Tolerable Recovery, The Trouble Shooter's Guide for TPM, Healing Life's Hurts Through Theophostic Prayer, developed both the Basic and Advanced Training programs for TPM, presented at many national conferences to include the American Association of Christian Counselors (AACC), Christian Association for Psychological Studies (CAPS), and the National Leader's Conference for Catholic Renewal.

Ed's son, Joshua, is the co-author of the new TPM training. Joshua has shadowed his father's journey since the founding of TPM (he was 8 years old at the time). Around the time he graduated from Liberty University in 2009 (majoring in English, Phycology, and Christian Counseling), Joshua sensed that he was called by God to participate in what He was doing in this ministry. He traveled alongside his father as they hosted and presented training seminars around the globe. The combination of his education, skills, and calling has brought a great measure of refinement and clarity to this ministry. In addition to the book that you are currently reading, Joshua has co-authored much of the recent TPM material including Effortless Forgiveness, The Essentials of TPM, The Process of TPM. He also served a pivotal role in the development of the training aids referred to as "The TPM Maps" and "TPM Flowcharts" along with several other resources. Joshua and his wife, Kaitlyn, are happily married with three children. They apply the biblical principles that are taught in TPM both in their marriage and parenting.

Ed and Joshua hold a traditional conservative protestant theology. And this ministry focuses upon faith refinement, mind renewal, and transformation for all members of the Body of Christ. Since its beginning in 1995, TPM has touched lives in over 150 countries worldwide. TPM training material is freely available at TransformationPrayer.Org.

At the time of this writing, Ed and Joshua also host a LIVE video broadcast where they expound on the topics discussed in this book and field questions that are submitted by the viewing audience. These video broadcasts are a valuable resource to anyone who has questions regarding TPM.

Printed in the USA
CPSIA information can be obtained
at www.ICGtesting.com
LVHW080323111123
763485LV00009B/352

9 781915 930507